VIOLENT
DEMOCRATIZATION

VIOLENT DEMOCRATIZATION

Social Movements, Elites, and Politics in Colombia's Rural War Zones, 1984–2008

LEAH ANNE CARROLL

University of Notre Dame Press
Notre Dame, Indiana

Manufactured in the United States of America

Library of Congress Cataloging-in-Publication Data

Carroll, Leah Anne.
    Violent democratization : social movements, elites, and politics in
Colombia's rural war zones, 1984/2008 / by Leah Anne Carroll.
        p.   cm. — (From the Helen Kellogg Institute for International Studies)
    Includes bibliographical references and index.
    ISBN-13: 978-0-268-02303-4 (pbk. : alk. paper)
    ISBN-10: 0-268-02303-4 (pbk. : alk. paper)
    1. Democratization—Colombia.   2. Violence—Colombia.
3. Political violence—Colombia.   4. Social movements—Colombia.
5. Elite (Social sciences)—Political activity—Colombia.   6. Colombia—
Rural conditions.   7. Colombia—Politics and government—1974–   I. Title.
    JL2881.C37   2011
    986.106'35—dc22
                                                                                2010033409

 This book is printed on recycled paper.

CONTENTS

FIGURES

TABLES

ANAPO. Alianza Nacional Popular (National Popular Alliance), a Conservative/populist political movement, modeled on Peronismo, founded by General Gustavo Rojas Pinilla in the late 1950s.

ANUC. Asociación Nacional de Usuarios Campesinos (National Peasant Association). Initially created by Colombian President Alfonso Lleras, it became and remains an independent peasant advocacy organization, with most activity focused on the local level.

AUC. Autodefensas Unidas de Colombia (United Colombian Self-Defense Committees). The national association of right-wing paramilitary groups founded in the late 1990s.

CAC. Communal Action Committee (Junta de Acción Comunal). Neighborhood organization with official standing; in these case studies, in both rural areas and urban squatters' neighborhoods, these are often the basic "cells" of social movements.

CGSB. Coordinadora Guerrillera Simón Bolívar (Simon Bolívar Guerrilla Coordinating Committee), an umbrella group consisting of FARC, ELN, EPL, and M-19 and two smaller groups from 1987 through the early 1990s.

ELN. Ejército de Liberación Nacional (National Liberation Army), the pro-Cuba, second-largest guerrilla group in Colombia.

EPL. Ejército Popular de Liberación (Popular Army of Liberation), the third-largest guerrilla group in Colombia throughout the late 1980s. Originally espoused a Maoist ideology.

EPL dissidence. In 1991 this group broke away from the majority of the EPL, which had demobilized, and returned to armed struggle.

Esperanza, Paz y Libertad. Hope, Peace, and Liberty party. In 1991 the majority of the EPL demobilized and took this name.

FARC. Fuerzas Armadas Revolucionarias de Colombia (Armed Revolutionary Forces of Colombia), the largest guerrilla group in Colombia. Ideologically associated with the PCC (see below).

Fensuagro. Federación Nacional Sindical Unitaria Agropecuaria (National Agrarian Unified Union Federation). A national peasant and rural worker association, historically influenced by the Colombian Communist Party.

FP. Frente Popular (Popular Front), the electoral front associated with the PCML and the EPL during the late 1980s.

IDEMA. Instituto de Mercadeo Agropecuario (Institute for Agrarian Marketing). For fifty years, this Colombian government entity facilitated the purchase of rural products and the sale of basic necessities to Colombian peasants. It was liquidated in 1997.

INCORA. Instituto Colombiano de Reforma Agraria (Colombian Agrarian Reform Institute), the Colombian government agency in charge of titling land claims in frontier zones as well as redistributing underutilized latifundios to landless peasants who occupied these landholdings.

INDERENA. Institututo Nacional de Recursos Naturales (National Institute for Natural Resources). The entity of the national government in charge of managing Colombia's natural resources. Its functions were taken over by the Ministry of the Environment in 1993.

M-19. Movimiento 19 de abril (19th of April Movement), a guerrilla group of Left-populist ideology, founded after General Gustavo Rojas Pinilla, presidential candidate for the ANAPO, was allegedly robbed of victory by fraud on April 19, 1970.

PCC. Partido Comunista Colombiano (Colombian Communist Party), a Soviet-line party founded in the 1930s.

PCML. Partido Comunista Marxista-Leninista (Marxist Leninist Communist Party). The Maoist party associated with the EPL, founded during the Sino-Soviet split in the late 1960s.

UP. Unión Patriótica (Patriotic Union), the electoral front founded as a by-product of FARC-government peace negotiations in 1985.

A C K N O W L E D G M E N T S

Many more people than can be named here have contributed in essential ways to the completion of this project, the product of many years of arduous effort. No one has sacrificed more for this project than my husband, Gustavo Rojas, who accompanied me to Urabá and the Caguán, performing the triple function of bodyguard, research assistant, and companion and also helping me with Bogotá archival data collection. Later he spent countless hours caring lovingly for our daughters while I turned my dissertation into this book. My daughters deserve my deep thanks for putting up with my absences and helping me keep my work in perspective. My mother has supported me in every way through the long years. My father, were he still alive, would be proud.

Peter Evans and Laura Enríquez gave essential intellectual feedback on the dissertation that became this book, offering enthusiastic encouragement to publish it and helping me discover my voice as a social scientist. The anonymous outside reviewers and the staff at the University of Notre Dame Press provided direction for the major revision of the dissertation, and the Press staff attended to every detail throughout the production process. Of course, errors and weaknesses that remain are the exclusive responsibility of the author.

My affiliation with the Instituto de Estudios Políticos y Relaciones Internacionales at the National University of Colombia opened many doors for me in 1992 and beyond. It provided me with an office, ever-supportive staff members such as Gloria Inés Muñoz, and helpful colleagues such as Gonzalo Sánchez, Alejandro Reyes Posada, and Javier Guerrero.

At the Kellogg Institute for International Studies, University of Notre Dame, I spent an academic year (1994–95) with full financial support and a remarkable institutional infrastructure with friendly and helpful staff. I received helpful feedback and support at the difficult moment of formulating my central argument for the reform period from Notre Dame faculty members Guillermo O'Donnell, Scott Mainwaring, Robert Fishman, and Mary Ann Mahony and my visiting fellow colleagues Carlos Acuña, Kevin Healy, and Paulo Sergio Pinheiro.

Friends from the University of California, Berkeley, graduate sociology program and St. Lawrence University provided support and advice throughout the many phases of the writing process. My workmates at UC Berkeley's Office of Undergraduate Research and Undergraduate and Interdisciplinary Studies, especially Terry Strathman, offered not only flexibility with my work obligations but also full and enthusiastic support of the book project; I can't think of a better place to work.

I received generous financial support from many sources. At UC Berkeley, I received a Tinker Foundation travel grant, administered through the Center for Latin American Studies; a Simpson Fellowship from the Institute for International Studies; and assistance from the Provost's Research Fund. I also received an Oberlin College Alumni Fellowship and a National Science Foundation Doctoral Dissertation Improvement Grant. Especially crucial was a Fulbright Hays (DDRA) fellowship, which provided generously, both financially and logistically, for my fieldwork year and connected me to a vibrant network of Colombianist scholars and peers.

I am indebted to those in Bogotá who facilitated access to invaluable archival records: Sandra Marín at the Registraduría Nacional del Estado Civil; Francisco Gutiérrez at the Instituto de Estudios Políticos y Relaciones Internacionales, who kindly sent me a customized version of the lethal political violence database he had compiled; and the Comité Permanente por la Defensa de los Derechos Humanos, Congregación Intercongregacional de Justicia y Paz (CIJP), the CINEP news clippings archive, and the *Noche y Niebla* team at CINEP. This book is written in the hope that their essential but very dangerous work may carry on.

I have received dedicated research assistance from Germán Hislén Giraldo, who accompanied me to San Alberto and Arauca in 1993; Raquel Viña Rojas and Ruth Bastidas Castro, who helped me gather archival data in Bogotá; Mónica Hurtado, who assisted in data analysis at Kellogg Institute; and my daughter, Irene Rojas-Carroll, who compiled the political violence database for 1993–2006. Undergraduate cartographers Emily Busch and Aaron Lui created clear, complete maps with the utmost professionalism. Finally, copy editor Kathleen Babbitt meticulously plowed through hundreds of pages of text and references to ferret out errors.

My fieldwork would have been impossible without the crucial help of individuals and organizations that facilitated my access to regional activists and later provided comments on drafts, chief among them Boris Alberto Cabrera Silva. Most of these people must remain anonymous, as they are among my interviewees, but I am deeply grateful that they were willing to share their contacts so generously. Similarly, my case study hosts and my many interviewees trusted in me and generously gave of their time to explain the political intricacies of each region. I am grateful to every one of them and hope the result comes close to justifying their faith in me.

INTRODUCTION

THE CENTRAL QUESTIONS AND
THEIR IMPLICATIONS

The implementation of democratic reforms has usually been examined in urban areas, in parts of the world with stronger states, or in contexts where social movements of subordinate groups lack strength or autonomy. This study examines the implementation of democratic and decentralizing reforms,[1] and the subsequent violent backlash[2] and counterreform,[3] in rural regions with weak states, strong social movements,[4] and armed leftist insurgencies. My focus is on those reforms that allow the direct election and increased fiscal autonomy of county executives *(alcaldes)* and governors,[5] as well as the peace process with guerrilla groups, and other reforms that are meant to weaken clientelist practices and increase the ability of civilians to rein in abuses of the state.

Theorists and political actors alike have often assumed that democratizing and decentralizing reforms would permit a peaceful resolution of formerly violent social conflicts. They reason that reforms that allow the institutional political process to represent previously excluded subordinate groups and agreements that facilitate the disarming of rebel guerrilla groups and rechanneling of their participation into electoral politics and legal social movements would encourage these constituencies to realize their substantive and political goals through peaceful, institutional means rather than through violence. In some contexts reforms have indeed facilitated substantive and political social movement gains and a marked reduction in levels of violence. The outcomes of the peace processes in El Salvador and Guatemala would seem to fall into this category. Peaceful democratization has also occurred in contexts where the opposition social movements had largely been defeated during the authoritarian era before democratizing reforms took place: Chile and Argentina come to mind as examples of this pattern. However, in these latter cases, social movements have largely accepted material setbacks as a trade-off for political gains.

On the other hand, the experiences of several democratizing countries have shown that under certain circumstances reform can also bring higher levels of conflict. In these countries democratization, promoted by reformist national elites, allows powerful rural social movements (and in some cases the armed insurgencies linked to these social movements) to make real political and substantive gains. These gains, however, provoke violent backlash from antireformist rural elites and military sectors, and the weakness of the judicial system allows these violent acts to go unpunished. Examples of postdemocratization peasant/worker mobilization followed by violent elite backlash include the post-Marcos Philippines and rural Brazil in the late 1980s. Eventually, in some cases, the elite backlash encourages previously nonviolent movements to take up arms or demobilized guerrillas to revert to violent tactics. Examples of new guerrilla movements or resurgence of old ones in the wake of democratization include Peru in the 1980s, rural southern Mexico since the mid-1990s, and Colombia after 1984. In some of these cases, the guerrilla (re)mobilization is enough to provoke a de jure reversal of reforms, as occurred in both Colombia and Peru after 1992.

Ideally, new political solutions in cases where reform leads to escalated violence would bring social movement gains to create the foundations of a more just society, without provoking the escalation of elite and then guerrilla violence. Such intensified violent conflict not only causes tremendous human suffering in and of itself but also ultimately can contribute to a counterreform that blocks further progress toward redistributive goals through peaceful means. The design and implementation of such solutions, however, requires a deeper understanding and more complete theorization of the phenomenon of violent democratization.

Specifically, I hope to contribute to theories of democratization/ decentralization, social movements and transnational activism, armed insurgencies, and political violence. Three overarching questions guided my inquiry:

1) How do democratization, decentralization, and globalization (trends over time) affect the state and elites (the view from above)? How do they affect social movements, the electoral Left, and armed insurgencies (the view from below)?
2) What are the overarching principles determining social movement gains, in revolutionary-type situations and in contexts where only incremental social movement gains are possible?
3) Within a single national case, what political/economic and geographic factors can explain contrasting regional social movement types, elite responses to social movements, and outcomes?

By addressing these questions, I hope to add a regional political economy component to analyses of democratization processes that have frequently focused exclusively on the national level; a focus on center/ periphery conflicts and inequalities to a decentralization literature that has often assumed a "win-win" scenario; an element of institutional change to cross-sectional comparisons of regional political economies and the rural social conflicts they generate; and a systematic comparison of successful and failed instances of transnational solidarity to a literature that to date has drawn overwhelmingly on successful examples.

Beyond these theoretical goals, which are addressed in detail in the concluding chapter, the central empirical objectives of this study are to explain which specific mechanisms provoke escalated violence in contexts of violent democratization; under what exceptional conditions reform brings peace; and which factors and social movement strategies might maximize substantive and political social movement gains, both during the reform period and during periods of counterreform.

COLOMBIA AS A NATIONAL CASE

Colombia provides an excellent case of violent democratization in a weak state context both as it evolves over time, on the national level, and as the regional variations on the theme diverge from the overall pattern. Although

Colombia has long qualified as one of Latin America's most stable democracies, its democracy has traditionally been described as restrictive, elite, and violent. But Colombia's democracy made clear moves toward a less restrictive and centralized model from 1982 to 1992, as government-guerrilla peace negotiations coincided with and spurred reforms allowing local autonomy and a broader democratic participation for groups previously excluded from the electoral process. By 1987 elite backlash, fueled by the boom of the drug economy, introduced simultaneous but contradictory trends toward counterreform. In the 1990s and especially after 2002, the government reemphasized a military solution to the armed insurgency and selectively recentralized local government in areas where successful leftist electoral parties and armed insurgencies coincided.

The discussion that follows identifies the historical sources of Colombia's paradoxical combination of violence and democracy and describes the major phases of the reform process. In analyzing the reform and its aftermath, I introduce the central national political actors that figure in the regional case histories constituting subsequent chapters.

Before the Reform Period

There is near-universal agreement that Colombia's government constitutes a "weak state." Social science analyses that have attempted to classify states as strong or weak have generally focused on two major characteristics: state autonomy and state capacity. Colombia, by almost all measures, ranks quite low on both. Without a full labor incorporation period, a populist phase, or a history of radical land reform, Colombia has not even experienced moments of temporary autonomy from national elites—such as that experienced by the Peruvian state in 1968, when elite interests were sacrificed in the name of development or modernization—much less permanent autonomy from elites.[6] Although Colombia's relatively diverse economy has meant that no single sectoral elite has completely captured the state and although the Colombian state has often driven a hard bargain with foreign investors, in the elements of state policy related to the protection of the political and human rights of labor, peasant movements, and leftist parties, the Colombian state can clearly be considered an elite-captured rather than autonomous state.

The Colombian state can also be considered weak in terms of almost any definition of state capacity.[7] In defining strong state capacities, Migdal focuses especially on the state's ability to be the predominant agent of social control, without competing vertical systems such as clans, religious leaders, families, or local strongmen.[8] But the Colombian government not only faces powerful competing vertical systems of social control in long-settled regions in the form of regional *gamonales* (political bosses/strongmen) and paramilitary groups.[9] It also faces an important armed challenge from below, especially in frontier regions. Guerrilla groups were said to have a presence in 61 percent of Colombian municipalities in 1995.[10] Thus Migdal would classify Colombia in the 1980–2006 period as anarchic: characterized by both a weak state (not the sole vertical agent of social control) and a weak society (social control not fully imposed by elites within civil society either). He would probably argue that such state weakness contributed to Colombia's high levels of violence while also facilitating the formation of pockets of resistance that evolved first into strong regional opposition groups and then into armed insurgencies.

Such competing vertical systems of control in Colombia, in the form of long-standing interelite competition between the Liberal and Conservative parties, reinforced three seemingly contradictory characteristics of Colombian political history: stable electoral institutions, political institutions largely co-opted by factional elite interests rather than acting in the public interest, and constant war. During the nineteenth century Colombia had a total of nine civil wars between pro–free trade, anticlerical Liberals and protectionist, church-allied Conservatives, each with its legions of vertically organized peasant clients. Due to the persisting stalemate between the two elite-led forces, the last Liberal-Conservative conflicts occurred unusually late by Latin American standards: at the end of the nineteenth century *(la guerra de los mil dias)* and, in a somewhat different type of conflict, in the middle of the twentieth century (La Violencia).[11]

By the end of this last conflict (1948–57), which was especially intense in the Andean peasant regions and in which nearly 200,000 were killed, each town tended to be clearly dominated by one or the other political tendency, and institutional resources became viewed as war booty.[12] Once institutions such as the church, the judiciary, the police, and the army lost their claim to be acting in the public interest, those who might have appealed to them to mediate disputes instead took matters into their own hands. This led to rampant vigilantism, armed self-defense groups, and high levels of violent conflict. In order to end the conflict a political pact called the National Front was formed. By guaranteeing each traditional party access to power, the pact halted the interelite competition and violence but also further excluded nonelite interests from political power.[13]

Colombia's government restricted participation by both (national) nonelite interests and interests from the peripheral regions. Although formally democratic, with presidential elections regularly observed every four years, Colombia had highly centralized institutional arrangements. These derived from a long history of governmental attempts to squelch the centrifugal forces of regionalist separatism in this weakly unified nation— separatism reinforced by the rugged Andean geography that created formidable barriers to interregional trade and communication.[14] Although interregional communication and integration improved with the advent of railroads in the late nineteenth century and highways subsequently, the centralized institutions remained. These guaranteed that the two dominant parties, the Liberals and the Conservatives, would virtually monopolize political power, chiefly through clientelistic means. Presidents appointed governors; governors appointed county executives based on their ability to get out the vote for Departmental (provincial) Assembly members of the same line.[15] The Left was thus in effect excluded from local power and, furthermore, lacked sufficient national influence to elect a critical mass of senators or representatives.

Colombian political institutions were elite dominated as well as centralized, even before the National Front. In Argentina, Brazil, Chile, Peru, and Mexico labor incorporation in the 1930s and 1940s—when the state's response to labor conflict shifted from repression to some form of institutionalized mediation—dramatically increased labor's political influence. In contrast, in Colombia, even after incorporation, organized labor was generally weak, used as a mere electoral tool for one or the other of the oligarchy-led traditional parties.[16] As labor received few benefits from Colombia's limited labor incorporation of the 1930s and 1940s it is not surprising that the Left gained a foothold in the Colombian labor movement by the 1980s. And with workers afforded little institutional recourse in cases of labor conflict—and with a weak state, chronic violence, and long-standing armed insurgencies as a backdrop in rural areas—it is unsurprising that leftist guerrillas at times intervened in labor disputes on behalf of rural workers in a phenomenon called "armed trade unionism."[17]

Colombian peasants, meanwhile, were left nearly unincorporated.[18] Here I will not attempt a thorough explanation of Colombia's complex and contradictory agrarian history of the twentieth century. Suffice it to say that while state mediation mechanisms for agrarian conflicts were created and land reforms did occur, in the 1930s and again in the 1960s, these policies had as their primary objective the stimulation of capitalist production in the countryside rather than redistributive justice or peasant political incorporation. In the wake of significant moments of peasant mobilization focused on land in the 1930s and 1970s, Colombian peasants were often promised land and occasionally given it. However, even where this occurred, such as in the frontier zones, where peasants were given 11 million hectares of state lands between 1937 and 1971, insufficient credit, infrastructure, and technical support often doomed peasant beneficiaries to a precarious existence or repossession, radicalizing them.[19] This fact, together with continuing illegal eviction of peasants from land by large landholders and concentration of land via economic means, led to a bottom line of a land tenure distribution that was judged to be average in Latin America in the late 1980s and has worsened considerably since then, as documented by Richani.[20] It is not surprising that insurgencies have arisen in frontier zones where a precarious peasant economy coincides with especially weak state institutions, strong social movements, and weak elite social control.[21]

Such insurgencies first emerged in Colombia in the early 1960s, not long after the National Front went into effect. Although their emergence corresponded to the aftermath of the Cuban Revolution and other external factors, it was primarily a response to the political exclusion imposed by the National Front and the continuing weakness and politicization of the Colombian state, especially in rural areas. Colombia's is now the oldest, largest, and most active guerrilla movement in Latin America.

The first group founded, the Ejército Nacional de Liberación (ELN), in 1964, was inspired by the Cuban Revolution and the radical church. It had about four hundred fighters in the early 1980s, and its influence was mainly in Santander near the Magdalena River.[22] After the mid-1980s, with a new base in the frontier region of Arauca, a new focus on the demand of nationalizing oil, and the new tactic of blowing up the oil pipeline from Arauca to Barranquilla (and then extorting funds from contractors hired to fix it), the ELN experienced remarkable growth, becoming the second-largest guerrilla group.[23] In the 1980s and 1990s the ELN had particular influence among frontier region rural settlers, or *colonos,* peasant squatters in regions of traditional latifundio, the teachers' union, various rural unions, and the powerful oil workers' union. The ELN did not have a political party or electoral front until the late 1980s.

The largest guerrilla group (about two thousand fighters in the early 1980s), founded in 1966, was the Fuerzas Armadas Revolucionarias de Colombia (FARC). It was linked ideologically to the Colombian Communist Party (Soviet line), which had been founded in the 1930s and had long-standing connections with the radical peasant movements of the Andes. However, the FARC had its earliest origin among the rural Liberal guerrillas of La Violencia in areas where the Communist Party had had peasant strongholds. These were in essence self-defense forces to protect smallholder peasants from the Conservative-controlled police and army. Later, as these persecuted Liberal peasants fled long-settled regions in the Andes to establish new settlements in the eastern plains of Colombia, they were accompanied by the armed radical peasant self-defense groups that would eventually become the FARC, in what Molano has called "armed colonization."[24] This history explains the near-nonexistence of the Conservative Party throughout Colombian Amazonia and Orinoquia (where the Middle and Lower Caguán and Arauca, respectively, are located), with political conflict limited to Left versus Liberals. It also explains why the Communist Party and the FARC tend to be especially influential in newly settled peasant regions, or *zonas de colonización*.[25]

The Maoist Ejercito Popular de Liberación (EPL), associated with the Colombian Communist Party Marxist-Leninist (PCC-ML), with about four hundred fighters in the early 1980s, was founded in the late 1960s when Mao broke with the Soviet Union.[26] This ideological orientation was especially influential in the departments of Antioquia, Córdoba, and Cesar, within the banana workers' movement of Urabá, the teachers' union, and the movement of peasant squatters attempting to break up latifundio in these regions.[27] Its presence in the rest of the country was relatively limited.

In contrast, the Movimiento 19 de abril (M-19), founded in 1972, had its strongest constituency among urban students. Although it had a military presence in the countryside, it generally did not have a solid organizational base. Its populist ideological origins and penchant for media-friendly actions (stealing Bolívar's sword, for example, or high-profile kidnappings) were also quite different from the other guerrilla groups.[28] In the early 1980s the M-19 had about one thousand fighters.

Thus, on the eve of the reform period, the Colombian Left consisted of four major ideological tendencies, each with armed wings as well as some type of social movement base. Of these four tendencies, only the

PCC had engaged in occasional electoral contests, and even then they had often been forced by electoral rules to disguise themselves as Liberals.[29]

Tables 1.1 and 1.2 summarize the evolution of these guerrilla groups/ political tendencies during the reform and counterreform periods. Figure 1.1 identifies the location of the regional strongholds for each guerrilla group in the late 1980s.

The Reform Period: 1982 to Late 1992

Two separate categories of major political reforms occurred between 1984 and 1992, each with a major impact on the Left: reforms allowing broader democratic participation for groups previously excluded from the electoral process, including decentralizing reforms, and government-guerrilla peace negotiations. A process of economic opening began after 1990 as well, and throughout the 1980s the cocaine economy was growing quickly. The latter two trends tended to have contradictory effects, depending on the regional context and the moment in time: sometimes they strengthened the Left, sometimes the Left's elite adversaries. The decade may be further subdivided into four main periods: a first euphoric moment of reform (1982–86); a period of mixed signals, when further democratizing reforms coincided with a retrenchment of the guerrilla-army war and increased political violence (1986–90); and a period of bifurcation of both the Left and elites (1990–92).

Colombia's democratic reform period began in late 1982, when the newly inaugurated Betancur administration (August 1982–August 1986) initiated peace negotiations with guerrilla groups, putting democratizing reforms on the table and also demonstrating a new willingness to concede material gains to peasants and workers in war zones.[30] This first round of the peace process succeeded in achieving truces of two to three years in duration with three of the four guerrilla groups (all but the ELN) but no permanent demobilizations. The agreement with the M-19 lasted from late 1982 through mid-1985; that of the EPL, from March 1984 through June 1985; and that of the FARC, from March 1984 through mid-1987.[31] In addition, about eight hundred FARC guerrillas accepted amnesty to become political activists in the new Patriotic Union party that they had founded.[32] While only the FARC openly endorsed a new electoral option in conjunction with its peace process and the ELN did not participate in

Table 1.1. Main Guerrilla Groups and Associated Parties in Colombia, Reform Period

Guerrilla Group or Party/Electoral Front	Founded	Main Region(s) of Influence	Main Social Sectors	Approx. Size Early 1980s	Response to Reform, 1984–88	Response to Reform/ Dirty War, 1988–92
Guerrilla group FARC (Party/electoral front PCC, founded 1930s)	1966	Meta, Caquetá, Arauca, and bordering Andean regions; Urabá	Peasant settlers	2,000	Truce/amnesty, 1984–87; 1985 formation of Patriotic Union, stronger links to social movements	Intensified combat
Guerrilla group ELN (No party/national electoral front; clandestine)	1964	Santanderes, Arauca, Cesar	Rural squatters, peasant settlers, oil workers, teachers' union	400	1984 forms A Luchar to promote links to social movements	Greatly intensified combat
Guerrilla group EPL (Party PC-ML, founded late 1960s)	late 1960s	Antioquia, esp. Urabá; Córdoba	Rural squatters; Urabá banana union; school-teachers	400	Cease-fire 3/84–6/85; forms mass org./ electoral front Frente Popular	Most of group demobilizes for 1991 Constitutional Assembly, becomes legal party Esperanza, Paz y Libertad
						1991 part of group remains an armed insurgency, thereafter known as the EPL dissidence; intensified combat
Guerrilla group M-19	1972	Atlantic coast, Valle del Cauca, Cauca, Bogotá	Students; few workers—weak social base	1,000	Cease-fire 11/82–6/85	Demobilizes and becomes legal party (Alianza Democrática M-19), late 1989. Wins 27% of vote for 1991 Constitutional Assembly

Table 1.2. Main Guerrilla Groups and Associated Parties in Colombia, Counterreform Period

Guerrilla Group or Party/Electoral Front	Counterreform, Paramilitary and Coca Expansion, 1992–98	Pastrana Peace Efforts, 1998–2002	No. of Fighters ca. 2000	Uribe War, U.S. Military Aid, 2002–5	Paramilitary Demobilization, Growing Criticism of Uribe, 2005–8
Guerrilla group FARC (Party/electoral front: PCC, UP)	Military expansion, turn against institutional norms and electoral participation. UP: no senators in 1998	Despeje in Upper Caguán; negotiations unfruitful	17,500	FARC flouts human rights norms; takes territory lost by ELN	Weakened by Uribe: 9,000 fighters in 2008
Guerrilla group ELN (semiclandestine electoral front: Saravena Liberals in Arauca)	Military expansion, turn against institutional norms and electoral participation	Paramilitary-organized protests prevent despeje for ELN	4,500	Flouts institutional norms, weakens	Negotiations 2005–7; 2,200–3,000 fighters
Esperanza, Paz y Libertad (demobilized guerrilla group/political party)	Becomes openly Right-aligned; electoral growth in Urabá but loses national electoral representation				Becomes more oppositional, loses favored status with elites
EPL dissidence	Ceases to exist in 1994 (defeated)[a]				
Alianza Democrática (AD) M-19 (demobilized guerrilla group/political party)	By 1998 drops to 0.3% of national vote[b]			Polo Democrático founded with AD M-19, labor, ANAPO	UP remnants and other movements also join Polo; wins 22% of national vote in 2006

[a] After the leader of the EPL dissidence was imprisoned in 1994, virtually no combat actions were recorded for the group in my regions. United Nations, Working Group on Arbitrary Detention, "Civil and Political Rights, Including the Questions of Torture and Detention," 78.
[b] Pizarro, "Las terceras fuerzas en Colombia hoy," 313.

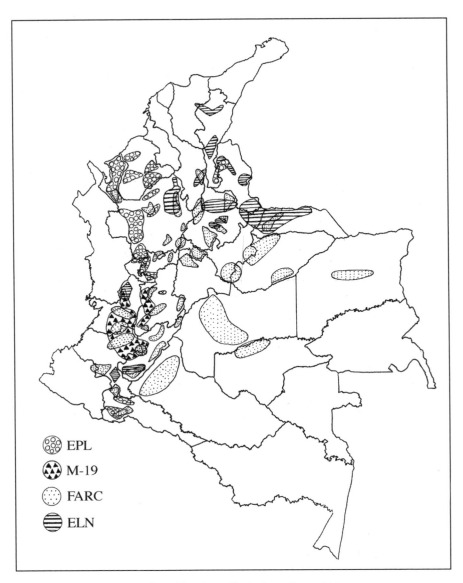

Figure 1.1. Regions Affected by Guerrilla Actions, Late 1980s

Source: Reyes Posada and Bejarano, "Conflictos agrarios y luchas armadas en la Colombia contemporánea," foldout between pp. 24 and 25. Redrawn with permission from the publisher by Aaron Lui.

this round of negotiations, all four guerrilla groups made moves toward declandestinization during this period. This strengthened their links to social movements and contributed to a burst of mobilizations in areas of guerrilla influence.[33]

Despite the progress made in this first round of government-guerrilla negotiations, it was ultimately doomed to failure. As the process continued and guerrilla groups not only refrained from turning in their arms but sometimes violated the truce as well, President Belisario Betancur increasingly found his peace policies bitterly and publicly opposed by many elite groups and much of the military. At the same time, the dirty war of illegal assassinations against amnestied guerrillas and other leftist activists began to escalate in 1987. Impunity for these crimes undermined guerrillas' support for the peace process.[34] The Andean cocaine economy contributed to this trend by creating, virtually overnight, a new class of wealthy narco-landowners who purchased land in areas bordering frontier zones, where guerrillas had influence.[35] Death squad violence was generally their tactic of choice to "clean" the zone of leftist influence so that they could (re)claim the zone politically.[36]

In other ways, though, the expanding cocaine economy benefited guerrillas, peasant social movements, and the electoral Left. In particular, the expansion of coca cultivation in some frontier zones of the Amazon and Orinoco watershed—near zones where the Communist Party and the FARC were already quite strong due to the presence of precarious frontier zone settlers from the 1960s—brought a new flood of peasant settlers to more remote areas of these regions. These settlers were followed by the FARC, which became the de facto state in these unsettled regions, deriving both new supporters and new sources of revenue from this role.[37] This fact, in combination with the political closing that for some demonstrated the futility of nonviolent social change, fueled the rapid expansion of the armed insurgencies,[38] which grew from a total of about 4,000 in the early 1980s to a total of about 12,000 by 1990.[39]

In this context, President Virgilio Barco (August 1986–August 1990) took a harder line with the guerrillas, using the stick as much as the carrot. When negotiating, he insisted on guerrilla demobilization as an end goal, offering material incentives for individual fighters who complied but cutting off material concessions to war zone social movements.[40] However, at the same time, he continued to promote and implement a key decentralizing reform demanded by the FARC in the peace process (as well as supported by some elite groups), the direct election of county executives.[41] The terms of office of county executives would get progressively longer: elections for this office have been held in 1988, 1990, 1992, 1994, 1997, 2000, 2003, and 2007. With this reform's implementation in 1988, Colombia was transformed from one of Latin America's most centralized countries to one of its most decentralized.[42]

Decentralization created real opportunities for increased political representation of previously excluded Left-influenced constituencies such as peasant settlers, rural labor unions, and small town urban squatters in the case study regions. In 1986 President Barco facilitated the appointment of the first leftist county executives, and in 1988, 18 of Colombia's 1,025-odd counties elected leftist county executives—all in rural areas with a FARC presence.[43] These new elected officials were able to advocate for their constituencies in unprecedented ways, especially in counties blessed with abundant fiscal resources.

However, as the Left gained politically from the democratic reforms, the backlash from national military leaders and regional (rural) elites intensified, especially where there were strong social movements and/or guerrilla presence and where newly wealthy drug traffickers were acquiring territories.[44] The number of political assassinations rose precipitously.[45] Most of these were social movement activists killed by elite-led death squads (many of them narco-landowner led), usually with military complicity, although in guerrilla-dominated combat zones repression against peasants was often carried out directly by army personnel or police.

In either case, nearly all the crimes went unpunished, notwithstanding the period from 1989 to 1993 when the government, having been provoked by the assassination of a leading Liberal presidential candidate and other prominent public figures by groups associated with the Medellín drug cartel, pursued some of the cartel's members.[46] For example, an October 1992 report by the Defensoría del Pueblo (National Ombudsman Office) stated that of 717 murders of Patriotic Union activists that took place between the party's founding in 1985 and September 1992 (306 carried out by paramilitary and 129 by state forces), only 10 cases had reached the sentencing stage, with only 4 convictions.[47] In response to the rampant impunity, guerrillas began to carry out *ajusticiamientos,* or assassinations of elites allegedly financing paramilitary activity, although the "solution" only intensified violence against the noncombatant Left.[48]

In the first half of President César Gaviria's administration (August 1990–August 1994), the era of mixed signals yielded to the era of division. Bold reform initiatives bifurcated the guerrilla movement, which then reinforced a bifurcated state policy toward the two halves. Gaviria continued the peace initiatives begun by Barco, offering material incentives and political representation in the Constitutional Assembly to guerrilla groups that would demobilize but, again, no material concessions to war zone social movements. In December 1990 elections of representatives to the Constitutional Assembly (held February–July 1991), the fully demobilized guerrilla group M-19, in alliance with three other demobilized guerrilla groups (most of the EPL and two much smaller guerrilla groups, the indigenous Quintín Lame and the Partido Revolucionario de los Trabajadores, or PRT), won nearly one-third of the seats.[49] A host of additional democratic and anticlientelist initiatives were passed, among them the direct election of governors (after 1991 elected on the same schedule as county executives), the election of senators by national proportional representation rather than two per department (province), due process protections for citizens in war zones, and a new ballot meant to impede vote buying by rural political bosses.[50]

Although the four smallest guerrilla groups, the "good guerrillas," had demobilized for the Constitutional Assembly and had become legal parties, the two largest guerrilla groups and part of a smaller one—the FARC, the ELN, and the EPL dissidence—had not demobilized. State policy toward these "bad guerrillas" now became much more belligerent. On December 9, 1990, precisely the day when the coalition led by the M-19 was winning nearly a third of the national vote for the Constitutional Assembly, the army bombed the FARC's national headquarters, Casa Verde, where several rounds of peace talks had once been held with the insurgency. As the possibilities for a negotiated peace with the bad guerrillas became more remote, the number of combatants in these organizations stayed constant at about twelve thousand through 1992. Furthermore, the intensity of guerrilla-army combat rose considerably during the same period.[51]

By 1992 many urban intellectuals once sympathetic to armed struggle became harshly critical of the still-active insurgencies.[52] Furthermore, following Colombian National Front customs, based on the M-19's success in the May 1990 presidential elections despite the assassination of its original candidate, President Gaviria offered the new political party the administration of the Ministry of Health. By accepting, the M-19 cemented its "good guerrilla" status and reduced the risk of assassination for its remaining leaders but lost its autonomy and credibility as an oppositional voice.[53] Gaviria seized on this moment to turn the tide definitively toward counter-reform.

The Counterreform Period: Late 1992 to 2008

In late 1992, confronted by army representatives who condemned the new civil liberties protections and democratic reforms for allowing guerrillas access to state resources, and openly admiring the apparent success of President Alberto Fujimori's anti–Sendero Luminoso crackdown in Peru, President Gaviria moved toward counterreform. All peace negotiations with guerrillas were broken off, and "Comprehensive War" was declared on guerrillas. Defense expenditures more than doubled from 1990 levels, which were twice 1980 levels. The armed insurgencies responded in kind with escalated attacks, and of course civilian casualties increased as well.[54]

Soon Gaviria had also suspended broad areas of the new Constitution by declaring several consecutive ninety-day "States of Internal Commotion," with some provisions later signed into permanent law. Among other exceptional powers, the declarations permitted the president to issue decrees without legislative approval and remove governors and mayors who were deemed to be aiding guerrillas. The new measures also restricted the media, mandated special audits of territorial entities to prevent diversion of funds to guerrillas or drug traffickers, and provided incentives for informers against guerrillas.[55] Also instituted, largely at the insistence of the United States as part of its War on Drugs, was a new system of "faceless justice." Although intended to protect judicial personnel against drug trafficker retaliation, in fact, the "faceless" judges—and witnesses—were frequently used against leftist elected officials and social movement activists, who were then denied due process for their own defense against accusations of being guerrilla auxiliaries.[56]

Finally, Gaviria also favored export producers by quickly removing protective tariffs on domestic production, devaluing the currency, and moving toward an export-led economic development model.[57] Despite the protests of producers for the domestic market, the economic opening was largely left in place by Gaviria's successors, causing a major crisis in regions dependent on domestic crops. Rural areas were disproportionately affected; in fifteen years the gap between urban and rural incomes doubled.[58]

By 1994 many Colombians favored a changed direction. President
Ernesto Samper (1994–98) was elected on a platform to restart guerrilla
negotiations and to slow the pace of economic opening.[59] However, his
administration is now remembered primarily for its paralysis, resulting
from his refusal to resign in the face of overwhelming accusations—from
within Colombia and from the U.S. government—of links to the Cali
drug cartel.[60] The Colombian economy, which had experienced steady
growth through 1995, contracted dramatically.[61] The mid-1990s also
witnessed an explosion of paramilitary violence, with well-documented
collusion from military forces that received U.S. military training and
support.[62] Paramilitary forces first organized regionally, with Córdoba
(near Urabá) and the Magdalena Medio as focal points, then nationally,
as the Autodefensas Unidas de Colombia (AUC). Samper's creation of the
Convivir security cooperatives were seen by illegal paramilitary groups
as a symbolic green light. They doubled their number of fighters, from
about 2,000 to more than 4,000, during Samper's administration. Paramilitary assassinations of political activists increased from about 1,000 to
about 1,800.[63]

Coca crops also expanded significantly during this period, from about
50,000 to 100,000 hectares.[64] The number of guerrilla fighters rose from
12,000 to 15,000,[65] and they seemed to be taking the upper hand. In one of
quite a few dramatic and unprecedented attacks between 1996 and 1998,
for example, 1,000 guerillas in the Caguán killed 62 soldiers and took
43 hostages.[66] Concern within U.S. government circles that the FARC
could topple Colombia's government spurred discussion of an increase in
military aid, which had already tripled from $28.5 million in 1995 to
nearly $100 million in 1997.[67] Meanwhile, the electoral Left had nearly
disappeared by 1994, and it lost further ground in 1998.[68] In the rural war
zones, as guerrillas focused on demonstrating their military might, they no
longer supported the electoral process. To the contrary, they often actively
sabotaged county executive elections to try to create an ungovernable situation.[69] Any war zone activists who, despite the new guerrilla approach,
had persisted in pursuing electoral or social movement activism had been
virtually exterminated by paramilitary violence or had reclandestinized.
The moderate urban Left, meanwhile, had succumbed to co-optation, internal divisions, and demoralization.[70] Only new indigenous political parties appeared to thrive, riding a tide of popularity with nonindigenous
urban voters.[71]

In 1998 Andrés Pastrana took office, staking his presidency on the peace process. In 1998 he demilitarized five contiguous counties straddling the border of Caquetá and Meta, near Cartagena del Chairá, to facilitate negotiations with the FARC. In 2000 he attempted to set up a similar demilitarized zone in the southern tip of Bolívar Department to negotiate peace with the ELN. But, as during the Betancur presidency, tensions mounted on both sides. The FARC accused the Pastrana government of failing to halt the rising paramilitary tide, among other truce violations.[72] Indeed, between 1998 and 2000 the numbers of paramilitary fighters doubled again, from 4,000 to 8,000, and assassinations by paramilitary forces increased from 1,800 to 2,800 per year.[73] The government, meanwhile, accused the FARC of crimes against prominent politicians, as well as of expanding its manpower from an estimated 16,000 in 1998 to a high point of almost 18,000 in 2000. Kidnappings were said to increase from about 3,000 per year to almost 3,800 per year in the same time frame; and, fueling both sides of the conflict, national coca cultivation rose from 102,000 hectares in 1998 to its high point of 163,289 hectares in 2000.[74]

Unsurprisingly, the AUC was adamantly opposed to the proposed demilitarized zone for the ELN and mobilized hundreds of peasant protesters to oppose it, forcing Pastrana to capitulate and withdraw it.[75] Furthermore, military expenditures as a percentage of gross domestic product (GDP) rose quickly, from 2.16 percent in 1996 to 3.5 percent in 1999.[76] Adding more weight to the forces pulling Pastrana toward the right, President Bill Clinton proposed, and the U.S. Congress passed (albeit with some human rights preconditions), a $1.3 million package of mostly military aid to Colombia in June 2000, with the plan to spend $4.4 billion in five years. This made Colombia the third most important U.S. military aid recipient in the world.[77] By early 2002 Pastrana had abandoned peace initiatives; he adopted a hard-line approach to counterinsurgency and bombed the FARC demilitarized zone.[78]

This trend carried over into the presidential elections of May 2002. Alvaro Uribe, an enthusiastic proponent of Samper's Convivir security cooperatives as governor of Antioquia, easily swept into the presidency on a platform promising to defeat the guerrillas militarily.[79] As part of his strategy to accomplish this goal, one of his first acts on taking office was to decree the restriction of constitutional citizen protections and political rights—not just the usual Colombian de facto arrangement but de jure—in order to carry out unimpeded counterinsurgency in Colombia's war zones. Thus Uribe declared a ninety-day State of Internal Commotion in September 2002 and renewed it twice (the maximum permitted by law). Among other late 2002 Uribe decrees granting extraordinary powers to the military was that establishing Zones of Rehabilitation and Consolidation (ZRCs) in Arauca and another oil-producing region on the Atlantic coast. Within these zones the population's civil rights were restricted, foreign journalists were forbidden from visiting without permission from the Ministry of the Interior, and the central government was allowed to overrule and remove from office directly elected county and departmental officials.[80]

By 2003, however, a reaction to the excesses of 2002 on the part of regional social movements, the Supreme Court, the Procuraduría (attorney general), international human rights organizations, and even the human rights certification process required for the issuance of U.S. military aid reined in the most extreme abuses against ordinary civilians and violations of constitutional and political rights in the ZRCs.[81] Furthermore, from early 2004 through late 2005, although "destroying the FARC" remained a top priority—the other two priorities were to negotiate the demobilization of paramilitary groups and the ELN—Uribe refocused on the southern Amazon watershed coca-growing regions, in a massive new U.S.-supported military operation, Plan Patriota.[82] Unlike the wave of leftist presidents taking office in other nations in Latin America, Uribe alone was "forcefully pro-Bush."[83] Bush demonstrated his appreciation by visiting Colombia, continuing the massive military aid infusions of almost $1 billion per year,[84] and increasing the number of U.S. advisers in Colombia from 400 to 800.[85] But Plan Patriota was costly in terms of citizen abuses and soldiers' lives and left coca acreage unchanged by 2006; coca cultivation simply moved to other regions.[86] After being reelected in May 2006, Uribe's counterinsurgency strategy reemphasized combat in Arauca, creating material incentives for guerrilla desertion, and using intelligence and infiltration to capture top leadership.[87]

Without a doubt, by late 2008 Uribe accomplished much that he set out to do. A paramilitary cease-fire was declared in 2002, negotiations began in July 2003, and Uribe declared that the last AUC contingent had demobilized in July 2006, about 30,000 fighters total.[88] Even Uribe's implacable critic, Human Rights Watch, notes in its in-depth 2008 report on the paramilitary demobilization effort that on Uribe's watch, through the post-2004 "Justice and Peace" process of taking confessions from demobilized paramilitary leaders and prosecuting those complicit with paramilitary forces, "Colombia's institutions of justice have made historic gains against paramilitary power."[89] Furthermore, between 2002 and late 2008 kidnappings declined by 75 percent, homicides declined by 40 percent, and urban areas became much safer.[90] Most notably, although by late 2008 Uribe had defeated neither the FARC nor the ELN and negotiations with the ELN from late 2005 through 2007 ultimately failed, both organizations were weakened considerably. The Council on Foreign Relations estimated in March 2008 that the FARC's numbers, calculated at nearly 18,000 in 2000, had declined to 9,000, and the ELN's numbers, once estimated at 4,500, had declined to 2,200 to 3,000.[91] Since that date the FARC has been further weakened by the loss of several top leaders and the infiltration of its communication networks, facilitating the spectacular bloodless rescue of the high-profile hostage Ingrid Betancourt in mid-2008.[92] These accomplishments help to explain why Uribe's approval ratings frequently hovered around 80 percent.[93]

However, Uribe also experienced serious setbacks in his second term. Most important, Colombia's human rights situation is viewed as dire by much of the international community. Impunity for crimes perpetrated by military or paramilitary forces remains almost absolute.[94] The UNHCR states that Colombia has three million internal refugees,[95] a number that is already the second highest in the world but is quickly climbing due to new right-wing groups (termed "emerging groups" by the Uribe administration) that have filled the vacuum in rural areas left by the demobilized paramilitary forces and in late 2008 had as many as ten thousand fighters.[96] To the extent that the "Justice and Peace" process has yielded important revelations about military, elite, and politician complicity with paramilitary forces, it has been due to international pressure and to the Supreme Court's amendments of the process made despite Uribe's objections.[97] Furthermore, in a related scandal unfolding since the fall of 2006, sixty of Uribe's political allies, including his vice president and his minister of defense, have been accused of *"parapolítica."*[98]

With a Democrat-dominated U.S. Congress since late 2006 and the election of a Democratic U.S. president in 2008, these human rights issues have cost Uribe dearly: a free trade agreement between Colombia and the United States negotiated by Bush and Uribe in 2006 remained unratified in mid-2009, with then President-elect Barack Obama citing Colombia's abysmal record of impunity for murdered labor leaders (of the nearly 500 union slayings during Uribe's presidency, only 14 perpetrators had been brought to justice as of late 2008) as his reason for opposing it.[99] Furthermore, the late 2008 "false positives" scandal, in which military forces were shown to have executed many innocent civilians who were then presented as guerrillas killed in battle, had as of late 2008 caused the removal of 27 officers, including army Commanding General Mario Montoya; the investigation of 2,742 other officers;[100] and the decertification for U.S. military aid to three army units (the second such decertification during the Uribe years).[101] Meanwhile, given the U.S. economic crisis and the fact that coca acreage actually rose 15 percent from 2000 to 2008, despite the U.S. expenditure of nearly $6 billion on Plan Colombia, U.S. military aid to Colombia peaked in 2004 and was set to decline further in late 2009.[102] Uribe's efforts to reverse that trend by offering the United States the use of seven bases in Colombia greatly worsened already tense relations with his Left-led Latin American neighbors in mid-2009.[103] Yet within Colombia, in late 2009 Uribe's popularity ratings continued to be as high as 78 percent.[104]

Even in Uribe's first administration, as his successes delighted his supporters, his excesses solidified—and strengthened—the opposition: regional, national, and international. The visibility and questionable constitutionality of de jure restrictions of citizens' rights intensified outrage among Colombian anti-Uribistas and international public opinion, focusing action on especially offensive (and ultimately overturned) policies such as the Rehabilitation and Consolidation Zones.[105] There have been some important victories. As one example, having sued the Colombian government in the Interamerican Human Rights Court in 1993 for genocide against the Patriotic Union—almost 1,300 murders or disappearances were documented of the 2,500 total said to have occurred—the Colombian nongovernmental organizations (NGOs) Corporación Reiniciar and Comisión Colombiana de Juristas have won reparations for many surviving family members, as well as the reopening of 294 cases that had been abandoned.[106]

In this context the Left has gained breadth, unity, strength—and international allies,[107] proving to be a crucial resource for rural human rights activists. Starting with the bifurcation of the Left in 1990, the electoral Left in Colombia has become increasingly critical of the FARC and the ELN guerrilla groups as these have more frequently and flagrantly violated international humanitarian law.[108] This fact, together with the extreme nature of Uribe's policies, has helped cement the Left's commitment to the democratic process. The Polo Democrático, founded in 2002, originally combined the Alianza Democrática (AD) M-19, the Left-populist Alianza Nacional Popular (ANAPO), most of the labor movement, and many independent human rights figures and intellectuals. It received 6 percent of the presidential vote in 2002 and won the Bogotá mayoral elections in both 2003 and 2007, its administration relatively well received. In 2006, joined by the remnants of the Patriotic Union, indigenous groups, and others, the Polo Democrático Alternativo won 10 percent of the vote in the March 2006 legislative elections and 22 percent of the vote in the May 2006 presidential elections.[109] Furthermore, the Polo's senators, especially the former M-19 guerrilla Gustavo Petro, have been major protagonists in the unveiling of the parapolítica scandal.[110] Despite these positive trends for the electoral Left, a cautious prognosis is in order. Uribe met Petro's parapolítica accusations with "Farcpolítica" accusations against some top Polo leaders based on findings from a FARC commander's laptop.[111] More generally, the Polo Democrático Alternativo covers a broad political spectrum. Its unity is fragile at best, and considerable political skill, commitment, and luck will be required to maintain it.

SITUATING THE CASE STUDY REGIONS IN THE NATIONAL CONTEXT

The case study regions must be situated geographically as well as historically, since they were chosen not because they are typical rural counties in Colombia but, to the contrary, because they represent an ideal type in the Weberian sense: an extreme example of social movement strength and leftist electoral influence accompanied by armed insurgency. The following figures illustrate just how exceptional these regions are. Of 1,041 Colombian counties that existed in 1988, the midpoint of the reform period, about 1,000 had a clear rural majority.[112] Of these 1,000, only 105 elected one or more leftist county council members in 1988; the Left won 20 percent or more of the county council vote in only 36 counties. Leftist candidates actually won the county executive's office in only 16 counties.[113] Two other counties that had not elected leftist candidates in 1988 did so in the 1990 local elections. One of them, San Alberto, Cesar, elected a county executive from the newly demobilized M-19.[114] Thus the total number of counties where candidates from leftist parties won either 20 percent or more of the county council vote in 1988 or the county executive's office in 1990 was 38.

Choosing cases that were anomalies rather than typical rural counties allowed me to focus precisely on the phenomenon that is the subject of this study: the implementation of democratic reforms in rural regions with weak states, strong social movements, and armed insurgencies. The case study regions include counties where the Left won postreform local elections most overwhelmingly, due to the unusual strength of the social movements that form its base, and therefore where institutional political change could be expected to provoke the most dramatic changes and reactions. The reforms unleashed the social movements' substantial latent electoral potential, quickly displacing local elite factions that had long held sway. And due to the weakness of state institutions in these regions as well as collusion on the part of central elites, elite backlash occurred with almost total impunity.

What geographic, historical, and social factors help explain why the history of these counties diverged from the rest? First and foremost, all the counties had strong and well-organized social movements. All had peasant movements; a few had labor movements and/or urban squatters' movements as well. While all of them also had guerrilla presence, the social movements were the strongest predictor of leftist electoral success. After all, in 1988, 275 to 285 counties were reported to have had at least one guerrilla-army confrontation, but only 38 counties had more than 20 percent leftist electoral strength in 1988 or a leftist mayor in 1990.[115] What, then, is the root of this social movement strength that provides the basis for the electoral Left? Figure 1.2 illustrates the discussion that follows.

For three of the thirty-eight counties, the origins of social movement strength can be found in the peasant land struggles of the 1930s in the coffee-growing region of Sumapaz—as documented by LeGrand, Marulanda, and Bergquist, among others—or the aftermath of the legislation that these struggles won.[116] With massive mobilization that was essential to forcing national land reform legislation, coffee-growing peasants managed to consolidate a peasant economy under the leadership of the Communist Party (among other leftist political forces). Since then the Communist Party has outlived other leftist parties and has maintained its historic following as it continues to defend smallholder interests (promoting infrastructure, organizing producer and inputs cooperatives, etc.).[117] This

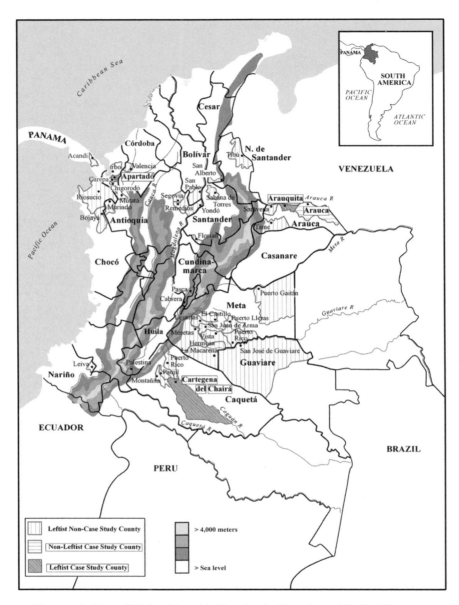

Figure 1.2. Map of Colombia, with Case Study Counties and Leftist Counties, 1988–1990

Sources: Marulanda, *Colonización y conflicto,* map, p. 19; DANE, *Colombia Estadística,* 1989, vol. 2: *Municipal,* 16–78; Registraduría Nacional del Estado Civil, *Estadísticas electorales 1988: Asambleas, Consejos Intendenciales, Consejos Comisariales, Concejos Municipales, Alcaldías* [marzo 13 de 1988]; Registraduría Nacional del Estado Civil, *Estadísticas electorales 1990: Senado-Cámara, Asambleas, Consejos Intendenciales, Consejos Comisariales, Concejos Municipales, Alcaldes, Consulta Popular* [marzo 11 de 1990]. Redrawn with permission from Marulanda and IEPRI by Emily Busch, revised by Aaron Lui.

region is located where the departments of Meta, Cundinamarca, and Huila meet and the towns of Pasca and Cabrera are located. On the southern tip of Huila is Palestina, a coffee-growing area founded in 1936 and made a county in 1948, likely due to new colonization spurred by the 1936 land reform bill.[118]

In the 1950s, when La Violencia broke out, it was most likely to be resisted in a collective way in these highly organized regions. First, Liberal guerrillas formed as self-defense groups. When these did not succeed in keeping the Conservative forces at bay, in the regions with highly organized peasantries the Liberal guerrillas became the forerunners of the FARC. They led peasants from the Sumapaz region over the Cordillera Oriental toward the east, to settle in the Piedmont regions of Meta and Caquetá, while similar refugees in Huila fled to Caquetá.[119] Four of the counties with over 20 percent leftist electoral strength followed this pattern: Mesetas and Lejanías in Meta and La Montañita and El Paujil in Caquetá.

As can be seen in figures 1.2 and 1.3, the largest and newest colonization zone in Colombia extends along the entire eastern flank of the Cordillera Oriental, from the Venezuelan border to the Ecuadoran border. The other major areas of post-1950 settlement are the Magdalena Medio (along both banks of the mid-Magdalena River); the area centered on Norte de Santander Department, including the areas around Bucaramanga and Cúcuta; the Urabá region on the border with Panamá and around the Patía River valley in Cauca/Nariño.[120] After the initial wave of Liberal and Communist refugees from La Violencia subsided, a new wave of colonization was spurred in these areas by deliberate state intent as the Instituto Colombiano de Reforma Agraria (INCORA) tried to respond to the growing demands of the peasant movement in the 1960s and 1970s.[121]

While land recipients were initially pacified by the frontier zone land titles, the almost total lack of transportation infrastructure, credit, and technical support made their holdings precarious, radicalizing their struggles against the state and creating sympathy for the Left.[122] Furthermore, they needed to be highly organized and collectively oriented just to survive on the frontier. Collective work brigades known as *mingas* were the norm. When guerrilla groups, especially the FARC, later moved into these regions, they helped rural settlers organize further and were able to gain a foothold as an alternative state due to the sparse social, judicial, and police services; the trees that concealed guerrillas' presence; and the lack of elite presence, at least initially. Conflict intensified if and when

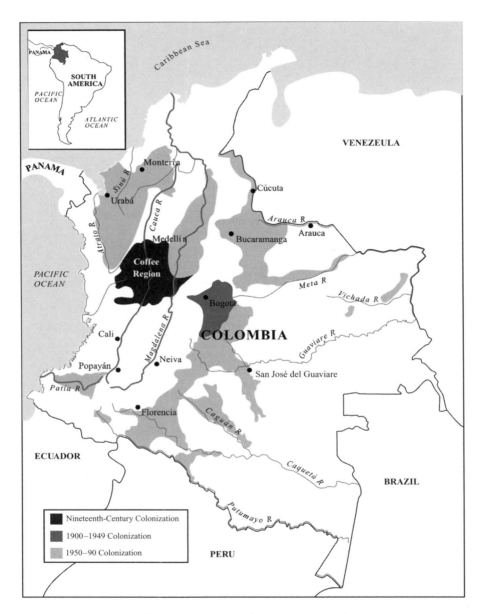

Figure 1.3. Phases of Colonization in Colombia, Nineteenth Century to 1990s

Source: Marulanda, *Colonización y conflicto,* map, p. 28. Redrawn with permission from the author and IEPRI by Emily Busch.

lucrative economic activities began to draw elites into the zones who then began to force out the homesteaders, often by violent means. As LeGrand writes, "This enclosure process led to social conflict over public lands between peasant settlers and . . . speculators. . . . This is the major form of rural conflict in Colombia historically, and it is the major form today."[123] Of the thirty-eight counties with strong leftist tendencies in 1988–90, sixteen, including the case study county Arauquita, had peasant settlers' movements launched by 1960s colonization processes as the main impetus of the electoral Left.[124]

A final wave of colonization occurred as a direct result of the coca boom of the late 1970s and early 1980s. The areas affected were located in the same watersheds of Orinoquía and Amazonía (and the Valley of the Patía) as the wave of the 1960s but farther out toward unsettled or sparsely settled areas, often those officially designated as wildlife preserves or indigenous reservations. Eight of the thirty-eight counties with strong leftist tendencies in 1988–90 fall into this category. In most of these the FARC had effective military control at the time and acted as the state: taxing production, resolving property line disputes, organizing peasant protests and work brigades, and acting as a police force. Peasant movements in these regions, like those in the INCORA regions, made demands for infrastructure, credit, and technical assistance. However, the illegality of both their holdings and their livelihood made their status even more precarious, vulnerable to fumigation/eradication and forced eviction as well as insolvency. Thus they also demanded land titles and an end to coca eradication, and they drew benefits from guerrilla presence more clearly than the INCORA-zone settlers. Despite this stronger link to the FARC, this coca-colonization route was the least dependable of all the routes to leftist electoral strength. While most of the counties with strong electoral presence in 1988 retained this strength in 1990 and 1992, in those with coca leftist electoral influence was severely diminished by 1990, reflecting the relative instability of peasant organization and the larger influence of the FARC and its political whims in these regions.[125] The case study county Cartagena del Chairá (Middle and Lower Caguán, Caquetá) exemplifies this pattern.[126]

For eight more of these thirty-eight counties, leftist electoral success derived primarily from the strength and leftist affiliation of organized rural worker organizations. However, the location of these counties in or very near settler zones contributed to their radicalization by facilitating contact with armed insurgencies as well as alliances with radical peasant organizations, increasing their potential autonomy from elite political forces. Colombian workers in general are not highly unionized, as Collier and Collier have documented.[127] To the contrary, in 1980 less than four thousand unions existed in the entire country.[128] Thus the strength and political autonomy of these labor movements are indeed exceptional. Four of these counties (Turbo, Carepa, Chigorodó, and the case study county Apartadó in Urabá) have banana plantations; two (Segovia and Remedios, near the Middle Magdalena colonization zone) have gold mines; one (San Alberto, near both the Norte de Santander and Middle Magdalena colonization zones) has a palm oil plantation; and one (Sabana de Torres, Santander, in the Middle Magdalena region) has both oil and palm oil workers.[129] Oil palms and bananas are continuous-harvest crops; as Paige notes, the resulting stability of employment facilitates unionization.[130]

Different nonleftist regions may be contrasted directly with each of the categories named above. Most of the coffee-growing regions of Colombia have been settled since the nineteenth century.[131] Colonization of these areas was led and initiated by commercial elites rather than by peasants themselves. As a result, if peasant smallholders are organized at all (and the ones on the Central Cordillera are much less likely to be organized than those of Sumapaz) they are not radical.[132] To the contrary; as Zamosc documents, for most of the period studied peasants of the Andes aimed to consolidate an already relatively stable peasant economy through the improvement of existing services and credits.[133] When the National Peasant Association (ANUC) split in the early 1970s, the Andean peasants were quite clearly on the moderate side of the divide, leaving the more radicalized peasant factions—the precarious peasants of the colonization zones and the landless peasants of the Atlantic coast—to bear the brunt of state repression. Furthermore, at least until the coffee crisis of the late 1980s, the Federación Nacional de Cafeteros performed an important parastate role by funding schools, infrastructure, and social services, as well as stabilizing prices paid to smallholder coffee farmers.[134]

Other regions characterized by the scant presence of the Left have been settled since before the nineteenth century and thus have very well established elites and clientelist systems and little political space for the development of leftist social movements. The lack of leftist electoral presence is noteworthy on the Atlantic coast: Atlántico, Sucre, Guajira, and Magdalena are all characterized by latifundio and semifeudal relations. The exceptions—inland areas of Córdoba, Bolívar, and Cesar discussed above—are all colonization zones. While landless peasants in these coastal departments and in Córdoba mobilized to force land redistribution in the 1970s and again emerged in the 1980s, they were overwhelmed and defeated both times by the strength of elite organization and repression.[135] The exceptions to the rule—San Alberto (Cesar), nearby Aguachica (Cesar), which had an M-19 county executive in 1994, and two counties in Magdalena, all of which developed a strong electoral Left presence after 1988—have strong worker movements, based on palm oil and bananas, respectively. And although the department of Boyacá, located high on the Cordillera Oriental, is typified by smallholding and cold-weather subsistence crops like potatoes and beans, it also had powerful clientelist organizations. With 122 counties, Boyacá had not one leftist county councilor in 1988. Before 1988 one county in Boyacá had a leftist presence: Puerto Boyacá, located in the Middle Magdalena colonization zone. However, the Left was decimated there by the first narco-landowner–sponsored death squads of the 1980s.[136]

Thus the counties that I chose to study differ from the norm in rural Colombia in clear ways: all had much more powerful social movements than are normally found, due to autonomous worker organization of an organizable commodity such as gold mining or continuous-harvest agricultural crops or to the location in or proximity to colonization zones, or both. They also had a weaker state, with fewer state or parastate mediation mechanisms, than most of rural Colombia.

METHODOLOGICAL ISSUES

Research Design

Within the anomalous class of counties with strong electoral presence of the Left, I selected cases—Apartadó, Arauca/Arauquita, and Cartagena del Chairá—and incorporated time periods—1982–92 and 1993–2008— that typified the following variations expected to affect the outcome: regional political economy (export plantation, peasant settler–produced coca, and oil production in a peasant settler context); social movement types (plantation labor, urban neighborhood, peasant settler, and human rights movements seeking outside allies); degree of social movement unity (monolithic leftist tendency, dual but coordinated tendencies, and warring tendencies); social movement target (plantation owners and national, departmental, and/or county government); repressor (military/"public" and paramilitary/"private"); and county administrations (traditional party, leftist, and right-wing labor based). The cases also exemplified different outcomes. In the reform period, I sought to explain two separate outcomes: increased/decreased violence and social movement gains/failure. In the counterreform period, the central outcome I sought to explain was social movement success or failure in mobilizing transnational alliances to influence national policies or judicial outcomes.

These contrasting regional conditions, processes, and outcomes provide an ideal means to pinpoint those factors, in the larger context of violent democratization, that might contribute to variations in outcome. The intent is to go beyond a cross-sectional snapshot of contrasting variables and outcomes, to follow the changing experience and actions of key actors in each region over time—before and as the reform period unfolds, reaches its apex, degenerates, and is reversed—in order to understand fully the political economy–linked *mechanisms* that underlie the different results of violent democratization. To accomplish this, I gathered data for each region on the above central variables from 1982 to 2008.

Data Gathering

Across the three case study regions, procedures for gathering data were consistent and focused on the above-named independent and dependent variables, as well as key intervening mechanisms: level of social movement activity and strength of social movement organizations, and electoral success of the different political tendencies in each region. However, for theoretical and practical reasons, data gathering for the reform period focused more heavily on the actions of the local government, whereas my emphasis in the postreform period shifted to the actions of national and international actors in each regional conflict. First, regional autonomy was maximized during the reform period, in turn maximizing the impact of each county executive's actions. In contrast, national and international alliances became much more determinant of each region's outcome once counterreform had severely curtailed this regional autonomy. Second, systematic information on county executive actions was available only through interviews. I had conducted such interviews toward the end of the reform period, when it was still (relatively) safe to travel to each region, but the escalation of violence after 1994 made it impossible to return to these counties for follow-up interviews. The later period, therefore, is based on written and Internet sources only, with the exception of a few interviews carried out in Bogotá or by telephone.

I collected information on four main forms of political violence: (a) violent repression—especially assassinations—against social movement activists, presumably sponsored by elites and/or the military; (b) guerrilla violence against noncombatant elite individuals; (c) guerrilla violence against noncombatants of the Left (Left-on-Left violence); and (d) guerrilla-army combat itself. The term *repression* is derived from the social movements literature, which conceptualizes it as an elite and state response to social movement actions, carried out with the intent of dissuading social movement participants or potential participants from further acts of protest. In this study *repression* is defined as incidents of elite- or military-perpetrated political violence against noncombatant (i.e., unarmed) leftist party or social movement activists that took place within each county's limits. Overwhelmingly, recorded incidents of violence were assassinations. However, with the exception of counterreform period Urabá (addressed below), I also tabulated incidents of assassination attempts, torture, detention, and death threats that were documented by the sources. In order to compare trends in violence across counties or especially over time within a single county, I quantified "repression," with higher values assigned to forms of violence more likely to deter activism: assassinations were counted as one unit, assassination attempts and torture as 0.25, and detentions/threats as 0.1. Guerrilla violence against noncombatant elites or noncombatant leftists was quantified using the same formula.

I also documented social movement activity (including national and international alliances) and success, as measured by concrete gains wrested by the movement from the social movement target. Regional economic trends were judged by volume of production and prices for each major regional product. Finally, I documented the political: the relative electoral strength of different political sectors and changing coalitions for all elections during the period of study, paying especially close attention to county- and departmental-level electoral processes. For the reform period,

I also documented the actions of the local/departmental government, especially interventions in social movement/elite conflicts, geographic/political patterns in public spending, and patterns in political appointments.

Before traveling to each region (in 1992–93) I generated some initial hypotheses to explain repressive violence and social movement success using a combination of secondary literature and consultation with individuals in Bogotá familiar with the region. Secondary literature was especially relevant for Urabá in both periods and the Lower and Middle Caguán in the reform period. My consultations with academics, political activists, and human rights activists in Bogotá who were familiar with the region were especially essential for Arauca in the reform period, but in the counterreform period I was able to draw on many human rights and media reports. My next step in 1992–93 was to gather as much information as possible from archival sources in Bogotá and then establish a regional sponsor/host and dates for my trip to the region. On arriving in the region, I gathered additional information using archival sources before completing extensive interviews with direct participants in each region's conflicts.

Table 1.3 shows the sources for the different forms of political violence against noncombatants and the way in which I combined them into a single database covering political violence against noncombatants in the four counties. These are the most complete and credible sources of information on specific incidents of political violence against noncombatants in Colombia during these dates. Nonetheless, some biases are inherent. While the *Permanent Committee for Human Rights Bulletin* and both the written and on-line database versions of *Noche y Niebla* are well-respected sources, they drew data primarily from denunciations by regional human rights committees, tending to underreport guerrilla violence against elites and report mainly on anti-Left violence. Also, regions with stronger social movements denounced violations more thoroughly than those with weaker movements. Press-based sources (CINEP archives, *Justicia y Paz*, IEPRI) aimed to achieve regional and ideological balance in their selection of different sources, but some regions, such as Caquetá, and some ideologies, such as leftist sectors with no connections to the Colombian Communist Party (whose well-established weekly newspaper is indexed by all of these sources), receive scant coverage. Further, mainstream press accounts (ElTiempo.com, Semana.com) tend to draw disproportionately on military sources and can thus be expected to underreport military abuses. As most

Table 1.3. Sources for Databases of Political Violence against Noncombatants

	1984	1984–87	January–June 1988	July 1988–June 1990	July 1990–1992	1993–June 1996	July 1996–2000	2001–4	2005–6	2007–8
Apartadó	CPDH, CINEP	CPDH	CPDH, JyP	CPDH, JyP	JyP	IEPRI	IEPRI	IEPRI	NyNDB	NyNDB
Cartagena del Chairá	CPDH, CINEP	CPDH	CPDH, JyP	CPDH, JyP	JyP	JyP, IEPRI	NyN, IEPRI	NyNDB, IEPRI	NyNDB	ET. C S. C
Arauquita and Arauca	CPDH, CINEP	CPDH	CPDH, JyP	CPDH, JyP	JyP	JyP, IEPRI	NyN, IEPRI	NyNDB, IEPRI	NyNDB	NyNDB

Abbreviations

CINEP = Press archive of the Bogotá-based Jesuit progressive think tank Centro de Investigación y Educación Popular, which draws from major Colombian newspapers from different regions and political perspectives.

CPDH= Comité Permanente por la Defensa de los Derechos Humanos, *Boletín de Prensa* (1984–88). Main section, "Hechos de violencia: Asesinatos, desapariciones, detenciones, y torturas."

JyP = *Justicia y Paz*, quarterly bulletin produced by the Left-leaning Conferencia de Religiosos de Colombia, Comisión Intercongregacional de Justicia y Paz (CIJP), vols. 1–9, January 1988–June 1996. Main section, on incidents of political violence, organized by type and date.

IEPRI = Database of lethal political violence, "Violencia política letal en Colombia: 1930–1949 y 1957–2004," elaborated by Francisco Gutiérrez of the Instituto de Estudios Políticos y Relaciones Internacionales at the National University of Colombia (Bogotá). Files covering the four counties of this study, as well as Carepa and San Alberto (Cesar), for the years 1974–2004 were sent to me as Excel files by Francisco Gutiérrez.

NyN = *Noche y Niebla: Panorama de derechos humanos y violencia política en Colombia*, quarterly bulletin produced by the CINEP and Justicia y Paz Banco de Datos and published by these same entities in Bogotá, starting in July 1996 (taking over from *Justicia y Paz*). Information from major newspapers as well as denunciations sent by social movement organizations.

NyNDB = Noche y Niebla searchable on-line database, available at www.nocheyniebla.org/, drawn primarily from social movement denunciations but including more extensive descriptive information about each incident.

ET. C, S. C = On-line archives of *El Tiempo*, Colombia's most important and largest circulation newspaper, usually center-right in its orientation, and *Semana*, Colombia's largest news magazine, center-left in its political orientation.

of these incidents of violence constitute uninvestigated crimes, complete information on perpetrators may never be available. Finally, all the sources chosen would tend to undercount victims who do not hold specific positions in social movement organizations or political parties, as the murders of these relatively anonymous individuals would be difficult to distinguish from Colombia's rampant common crimes and might go unreported. Thus figures for violence that I have compiled based on these sources are a rough estimate of actual repression, but in each case they reveal the very clear overall longitudinal trends in violence in each region, verified by interviews and human rights reports.

Because incidents of political violence in Urabá numbered in the hundreds per year in the postreform period when nonlethal violence was included, it was impractical to use the same sources and method for Apartadó as I had for the other cases. Instead, for the years 1993–2004 for Apartadó, I relied exclusively on the IEPRI lethal political violence database. As only assassinations were included in this database, it revealed a smaller total number of incidents, yet included the most important ones and showed the trends over time just as clearly. A weeks-long server crash of the Noche y Niebla on-line database while I was completing the update for the Cartagena del Chairá chapter led to substituting ElTiempo.com and Semana.com for this source for the years 2007 and 2008.

Guerrilla-army combat itself was also documented and measured, drawing on some of the same sources when possible. In all regions the main source for combat data for 1985–91 was a database drawn from figures from the Consejería de Paz, or President's Peace Advisory Board, and compiled and given to me by Alejandro Reyes Posada, formerly of IEPRI at the National University of Colombia. For the period 1992–June 1996 the main source for combat incidents was *Justicia y Paz*; for July 1996–December 2000, it was *Noche y Niebla,* followed by the Noche y Niebla on-line database for 2001 to 2005. After 2006, when this on-line database stopped reporting on combat incidents, I drew combat data from ElTiempo.com and Semana.com, the on-line archives of the daily newspaper and weekly news magazine, respectively.

Information on social movement activity and success for both the reform and postreform periods was drawn from CINEP's press archive. This information was quite complete for Urabá, which is closely linked to the well-established Medellín newspapers, but was more scant for Arauca and nearly nonexistent for Cartagena del Chairá. Regional archival research was especially essential in these regions to establish a precise and detailed chronology of social movement events and outcomes: this was based on documents from the archives of leftist parties, peasant organizations, and, for Urabá only, local newspapers. Other information regarding social movement conflicts and outcomes was derived from documents regarding titling and selling of homesteads (or squatters' plots) and granting of credit. In Arauca and Cartagena del Chairá, these documents revealed trends in government aid to settlers, the chronology and geographic patterns of settlement, and land concentration. These were gathered from INCORA, whose officials I also interviewed in all three regions to get exact data on size, dates, and status of land invasions (squatters' attempts to force land redistribution through illegal occupation).

Although I could neither conduct interviews nor collect archival documents in the regions during the counterreform period, I was able to use an abundance of Internet resources to study state actions vis-à-vis social movements as well as social movement activity, including actions of national and international allies. LexisNexis Academic provided access to articles in many world newspapers, for example, and Colombian news magazines such as *Semana* and newspapers such as *El Tiempo* have very complete archives of articles. Furthermore, after about 2000, Web sites were developed by many social movement organizations such as the San José de Apartadó Peace Community (www.cdpsanjose.org/), Araucan social movement organizations (www.organizacionessociales.org/), Amazon Watch (for the U'Wa struggle), and social movement–affiliated media Web projects such as Prensa Rural (http://prensarural.org/spip/). Many human rights reports on these regions were also posted to the Internet by Amnesty International, Human Rights Watch, European human rights organizations, and others.

Another category of archival research documented the electoral trends of each region. For county council elections held before 1988, the Registraduría Nacional del Estado Civil in Bogotá had electoral data, in book form, that included names of all elected county council members and votes received by each party. However, after the democratic reforms began in 1988, the number of elected offices and parties multiplied geometrically, and the standard "book" election results format became much less detailed, especially for county council and county executive elections. Finding the full list of candidates' names and the votes received by each in county council and county executive elections then required consultation of "Actas

electorales"—printouts from unpublished databases at the Bogotá Registraduría (1992, 1994, 1997, 2000) or often handwritten records at each
county's registrar of voters itself (1988 and 1990). To further clarify the
party affiliation of candidates listed as "coalition," "other," "civic movement," and so on, I conducted interviews with political activists in the case
study counties. After 2002–3, the names and party affiliations of all candidates, with the number of votes obtained by each, even for county elections, became available on-line at www.registraduria.gov.co (in 2002–3
some but not all local and departmental election results were available at
this site).

Consequently, during the initial archival stage of fieldwork in each
region, a visit to the local or departmental electoral office (Registraduría
Municipal del Estado Civil) was essential for tracking the electoral strength
and history of coalitions of Left and elite parties and factions. Electoral
results by precinct, also gathered from the Registraduría Municipal, further
revealed the geographic patterns in these trends, especially for rural voters,
suggesting the presence of social movement or elite territorial strongholds. In conjunction with such geographic electoral data, it was also essential to gather a detailed county map identifying the *inspecciones de policía*
(precincts) and *veredas* (rural neighborhoods) and an urban map showing
the different neighborhoods. These documents allowed a more thorough
understanding of, and thus more astute interview questioning, regarding
social movement and electoral patterns over time and space. In combination with the annual approved county budget for the reform period years,
these maps revealed the geographic trends in county public spending and
thus the county executive's fiscal intervention in social conflicts.

I also aimed to document trends in the prosperity of each region's
main economic sectors. Extensive data were available on trends in prices
and national and regional production for bananas, which has a well-
established trade group, AUGURA, with detailed annual reports; much
of these statistics were available on AUGURA's Web site after 2000. The
cattle ranchers' association publication was less helpful in documenting
regional production trends, but like AUGURA's publications, it was very
helpful in documenting the group's (far Right) political positions. Trade
group publications share a tendency to exaggerate the dire nature of their
plights at any given moment and the need for government support. As
trends in coca production were subject to intense speculation, I drew on

three major sources for the purposes of "triangulation"—UN Office on Drugs and Crime, U.S. State Department, and Dirección Nacional de Estupefacientes—and also tried to verify alleged coca production via references to this activity in human rights and social movement sources, interviews, and press articles. Because oil production figures for Arauca were difficult to measure directly, my estimates were drawn from royalties received by county and departmental governments (reform period) and the Occidental Petroleum Web site (counterreform period). Prices were drawn from the *Monthly Energy Review,* a publication of the U.S. government Energy Information Administration.

After completing basic background research and establishing a list of categories of information to be gathered, I arranged a trip to the region to conduct regional archival research and interviews. After my first trip—to Arauca in August–September 1992—was less productive than it might have been due to insufficient contacts and exhaustion, I revised my fieldwork protocol: I traveled to the rest of the regions (and returned to Arauca in 1993) with a full array of recommendation letters from across the political spectrum but especially emphasizing human rights, leftist party, and social movement references; accompanied by my husband or a male Colombian research assistant (fewer than ten of my interviewees were female; sexual harassment was an issue); and having established a central contact in the town, a well-respected social movement or Left party leader connected with my Bogotá academic/human rights/party activists contacts who would arrange my lodging and personally introduce me to interviewees. I then arranged the dates for my time in each region—two to three weeks in each case—directly with that host, to assure that he would be available and that travel to the region would be (relatively) safe at that moment in time.

I conducted key informant interviews, with individuals chosen based on their knowledge about specific events and trends. My sponsor and letter technique in some senses introduced biases: it meant that my leftist interviewees far outnumbered those of the Right, for example, and that leftist interviewees tended to be more forthcoming than those of the Right. It may have led to an undercount of incidents of antielite guerrilla violence, or a less than complete understanding of elite motivations for entering pacts with the Left. Furthermore, within the Left I had greater access to activists sympathetic to the political tendency of the host—in Arauca, the UP more than the "Saravena Liberals"; in Apartadó, the UP more than the

"Esperanzados." (In Cartagena del Chairá there was just one leftist political tendency.) However, the new protocol greatly enhanced my safety; indeed, many of the interviews I conducted and even my travel to these regions would have been impossible without such a procedure. In carrying out field research in small towns, asking about events of the recent past, and in the context of near–civil war, full access to both sides is impossible, as the researcher's original chain of contacts soon becomes common knowledge in the town and determines which side the researcher is perceived to be on. Given my central interest in the effects of democratization and violence on social movements, privileging access to the Left over access to the Right made sense. Furthermore, as many practitioners of "history from below" have noted, elites leave a much more extensive paper trail than do social movements and the Left. They are much more frequently interviewed and covered in press accounts, they have well-established trade and political publications, and, more recently, sophisticated Web sites. Thus interviews are a less essential source for understanding elite actions and perspectives than for understanding those of social movements and the Left.

A final concession to conducting research in war zones was the length of my stay in each region. Ideally, I would have engaged in a classic fieldwork procedure typical of anthropology, remaining in each region at least for several months. However, I was often cautioned by people in the region that my visit in 1992–93 was occurring during a rare *calma chicha,* or calm before the storm—an interpretation that was ominously prescient, given the bloodbath that would occur in 1994–96 in Urabá, killing my fieldwork host from my December 1992 interview visit in early 1993.[137] Thus I was forced to interview very intensively—typically twelve to fourteen hours a day, seven days a week—for relatively short two- to three-week periods. This limited my ability to conduct second interviews for the purpose of clarification, or to compare two versions of the same event. However, as the level of detail in my accounts attests, I was able to gather an extraordinary amount of information in a very short time. The host system guaranteed that I spent a minimum amount of time seeking interviews and a maximum amount of time actually interviewing. Furthermore, interviewees of all political tendencies felt the documentation of their histories and perspectives was a task of great consequence. Each spent at least an hour with me; some, several hours.

DEFINITIONS AND CONCEPTS

Before introducing the book's argument, it is necessary to define central terms and identify the key social movement and elite actors in the regional case studies. Table 1.4 presents a summary of the discussion that follows.

The *Left*, as a whole, is understood as the set of political and social movement organizations that represent subordinate groups, share a radical ideology, and were excluded from institutional representation before democratization. It is composed of three main parts that are autonomous, yet associated by virtue of sharing the same territories, constituencies, and, sometimes, ideologies: social movements, guerrilla groups, and leftist electoral parties. Although all these groups are autonomous, the guerrillas are especially so, as they are able to act without consulting the other parts and have sometimes acted coercively to force certain actions from social movement leaders or leftist elected officials.

Social movement is understood here as organized subordinate constituencies that confront a *target*—concession-sponsoring elites or the state—in order to gain material or political concessions. In each region during the reform period, the electoral stability of each sector of the Left depended primarily on the stability of the social movements to which it was linked.

In Arauca and the Middle and Lower Caguán region (Cartagena del Chairá), the main group that formed the basis of the Left is the *peasant settlers movement*. This is a movement comprising organizations of smallholders occupying untitled lands or recently granted land titles to previously state-held lands. Their main demands, targeted at the national or departmental state, focused during the reform period on titles and improved credit and transportation infrastructure in order to stabilize the peasant economy. Success was determined by the fiscal prosperity of the targeted state sector and/or political opportunity at the appropriate level of government. In the postreform period, these organizations refocused their demands on human rights: the prosecution of especially egregious past incidents of human rights violations or the cessation of ongoing abuses against the general population.

In the more urbanized region of Urabá, the *plantation labor movement* formed the base of the electoral Left during the reform period. It

Table 1.4. Actors and Tactics in Three Regions in the Reform Period

| Region | Social Movement | Left | | Elites + State Sectors |
		Guerrilla Groups	Electoral Participation	Repression Sponsor
Urabá	*Movement 1* Banana workers *Target:* plantation owners	FARC, EPL, ELN	Unión Patriótica Frente Popular 1992: Esperanza	• "Guerrista" banana plantation owners • Narco cattle ranchers
	Movement 2 Urban squatters/civic movement *Target:* county and departmental government			Military as accomplice of elite-initiated death squads
Cartagena del Chairá	Coca-growing peasant settlers *Target:* national government	FARC	Unión Patriótica	• "Turbayista" large cattle ranchers from near departmental capital • Repression carried out directly by army
Arauca	Peasant settlers (small cattle ranchers) from piedmont *Target:* national government (1984–87); departmental government (1987–92)	FARC, ELN	Unión Patriótica Saravena Liberals	• "LaTorrista" large cattle ranchers from plains • Repression carried out directly by army

confronted the relevant concession-sponsoring private elite—plantation owners and managers—to seek improved wages, working conditions, and guarantees of employment. The success of this movement was determined not only by the economic prosperity of the concession-sponsoring elite but also by political opening, which influenced the nature of state intervention in the conflict.

As the workers live in urban areas, there are strong links and membership overlaps between the labor movement and the *urban civic movement/ urban squatters movement.* The latter typically demanded legalization of occupied urban lots, infrastructure improvements, and basic public services (water, sewers, electricity, etc.) from the county government itself or, for larger public works or larger land disputes, from the departmental government. Success was determined by the fiscal prosperity of the target and/or political opportunity for the political party sponsoring the squatters' neighborhood.

In the counterreform period, once most regional social movements shifted to *human rights demands* (justice for assassinated leaders, a halt to civil rights abuses by the army, etc.) targeting the Colombian national government, support from *transnational advocacy networks* such as Amnesty International, Amazon Watch, or Peace Brigades International became crucial to social movement success.

In all the cases, *guerrilla movements* arrived in the region after the social movement was already established, forging links with the movement on its arrival. The guerrillas' main tactic in all regions was armed attacks on army units. However, guerrillas also engaged in political violence and kidnapping against private sector elites and, increasingly in the counterreform period, against nonelite individuals suspected of siding with paramilitary and/or opposing leftist groups. Early in the reform period, they intervened in social movement–target conflicts on behalf of the former, although this practice grew more rare as the dirty war against social movement activists intensified.

All tendencies within the *electoral Left,* in all regions, participated in the local electoral process during the reform period. While some openly identified themselves as leftist parties of particular tendencies, others participated clandestinely by using factions of the traditional parties as electoral fronts. In contrast to traditional parties, which used clientelistic means (vote buying, votes in exchange for employment, services, etc.) to build an electoral base, leftist parties drew votes directly from politically affiliated social movement organizations (e.g., specific labor unions, squatter neighborhoods, peasant organizations). Leftist county executives' actions on election—such as advocacy or mediation in conflicts and targeted public works—tended to further strengthen the social movement.

In contrast to the Left, *elites* are those economically and politically privileged groups within civil society that are the Left's main economic, military, and political antagonists. *Concession-granting elites* and *concession-granting state sectors* are those that have the power to grant concessions to social movements and determine the movement's success or failure; they are the main targets of the movement's economic demands. For the labor movement studied (in Urabá), these were private elites, whereas for the urban movements and the peasant movements studied, the concession sponsor was the county, departmental, or national government.

Local/regional repression-sponsoring elites, on the other hand, are those that are most threatened politically by the Left's electoral success and that therefore take the most initiative in organizing repression against the Left (during the reform period). They are the faction that dominated the region politically before reforms were implemented. In Urabá the banana growers were both concession sponsor and repression sponsor. Generally, they have regional economic and political interests only and can acquire national political power only from a regional electoral base; thus the loss of political control of the region is a serious one for them. In the counter-reform period, *supra-regional elites* in the form of *nationally linked paramilitary groups* take the initiative in repression in areas with local elites, motivated largely by the desire to control certain geopolitically and economically strategic areas in order to consolidate power. Dominating a certain locality is seen as a step toward a larger geopolitical-military goal.

Where a repression-sponsoring private elite—either local or supra-regional—has taken the main initiative for repression in a region, with most repressive incidents carried out by *"private"* actors (hit men, paramilitary groups, etc.), frequently the *Colombian Armed Forces* support this elite's actions in indirect ways. However, the army does the main repressive work in areas without important local elites to sponsor the initial repressive effort, such as relatively newly settled colonization zones and areas with strong guerrilla presence. These regions are typified by *"public"* repression, which generally is less lethal than private repression but can negatively affect larger numbers of people through checkpoint harassment, preventive mass detention, and other abuses of war zone civilians. In these localities the armed forces' actions are often supported behind the scenes by the repression-sponsoring elite from the larger regional area but outside the immediate locality.

In the postreform period, *U.S. military aid* has become a major factor in the national conflict as well as in regional conflicts with mostly public repression. It has boosted the size of the Colombian Armed Forces and has redirected its actions toward certain regions—in particular, those in the south of the country, where the FARC is strongest—and away from others. The magnitude of the increased aid has also brought the armed forces and the Colombian government under greater U.S. scrutiny and increased its vulnerability to U.S. directives.

THE ARGUMENT IN BRIEF

The argument for the reform period is summarized in figure 1.4. Before reform all three regions, like all of Colombia's rural counties with strong electoral leftist presence, were characterized by powerful social movements and weak states, where local elite factions had long dominated local political institutions. In all three regions, reform led to Left/social movement gains, which then provoked violent backlash. This was sponsored and largely carried out by politically displaced elites where these had a local presence (Urabá, Arauca County), with military support; or by the military in counties with very weak elites (Cartagena del Chairá, Arauquita), but with the support of displaced elites from the larger departmental setting.

During the reform period, when both leftist electoral success and regional political autonomy were maximized, contrasting regional outcomes were determined by the regional balance of power. Specifically, lower levels of violence and greater social movement gains resulted from a balance of power favoring the Left, since an electoral Left that was strong relative to elites could force displaced elites to negotiate electoral alliances in return for continued access to local or departmental state resources. A corollary of such alliances was decreased elite-sponsored repression against the Left.

There were two major sources of leftist leverage: unity and electoral success. Leftist unity meant either only one leftist tendency present in the region or more than one leftist tendency present but all responding to

Figure 1.4. Determinants of Regional Variation in Balance of Power, Reform Period

Pre-reform, all regions are characterized by powerful social movements and weak states, where local elite factions have dominated local political institutions. In all regions, reform leads to Left/social movement gains, which leads to violent backlash. This is sponsored by politically displaced elites in most regions but by the military in regions with very weak elites.
Regional outcome is determined by regional balance of power: lower levels of violence and greater social movement gains result from a balance of power favoring the Left.

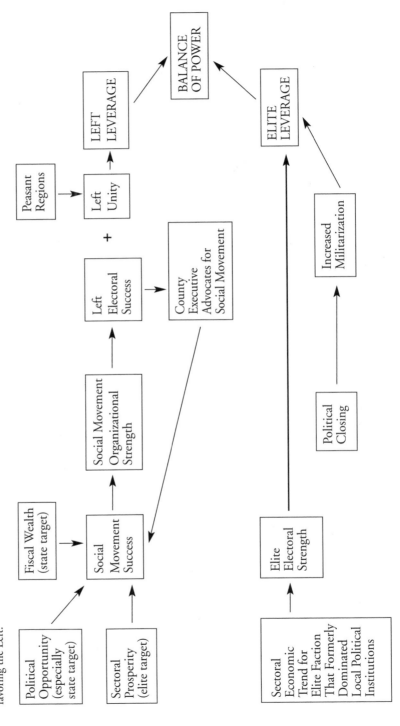

government peace initiatives similarly (either all rejecting or all accepting such initiatives). It contributed to leftist leverage, and thus pacted peace agreements, because it prevented one leftist sector from sabotaging another's agreement with elites. For reasons explained in greater detail in the conclusion, the peasant regions presented greater unity than did the worker region, Urabá.

Leftist electoral success both derived from and reinforced social movement success. Leftist county executives could aid social movements with specific actions: advocacy vis-à-vis social movement targets or repressors, public spending in social movement strongholds, and appointment of social movement leaders to key county posts. Social movement success, by reinforcing the organizational strength of a movement (number of members, stability of the organization, etc.), created a stronger electoral constituency for associated leftist parties. Social movement success, meanwhile, could stem from the increasing fiscal wealth of a state target or the growing prosperity of a private target. Political opportunity could benefit either state-targeting movements or labor movements targeting the private sector. Such opportunities derived from a conjunctural political shift, that is, a momentary coincidence of several propitious factors, that made it more politically beneficial, or less politically costly, for the state to grant social movement demands or pressure other actors to grant them. As an example, in all three regions, the 1984–87 peace process and political opening was crucial to boosting the success of social movements.

On the other side of the equation, elite leverage derived primarily from elite electoral success. However, in contrast to leftist parties, elite parties derived electoral success not from social movement strength but from economic strength, both absolute and relative to other elite sectors. Such economic strength translated into votes via various clientelistic means (vote buying, votes in exchange for employment, provision of services, recommendations for employment, etc.). As political opening enhanced Left electoral success, it undermined elite electoral success. Conversely, elite electoral parties benefited from political closing both because it weakened Left-affiliated social movements and thus the electoral Left and because it once again made elites more useful to the central government.

The argument for the counterreform period is summarized in figure 1.5. In all regions, after 1992 counterreform measures decreased regional political autonomy, destroying the possibility for pro–social movement actions in regions where pacted peace agreements existed. The new period also brought the largest waves of repressive violence ever experienced in these regions, whether carried out by private or public forces. Leftist social movement and electoral strength were reduced significantly by these changes. Faced with failure of the reform period strategies (bread-and-butter demands such as roads, schools, health clinics) in the changed context, social movement demands shifted to human rights. Both the counter-reform and the coca boom of the 1990s contributed to a massive guerrilla military buildup and increasing insurgent human rights violations. As U.S. military aid increased, social movements recognized that regional outcomes were determined largely by actors outside the region, and they increasingly sought outside allies. Their success in this endeavor derived from their ability to attract outside allies. There were two major components to this ability: the strength of social movement as and after the major repressive wave took place and the set of movement and target characteristics that determined the cause's attractiveness to outside supporters.

Some of the factors that contributed to social movement ability to garner outside support and attain success were the same as those in the reform period. Fiscal or economic prosperity of the concession sponsor and (now rare) political opportunity continued to facilitate greater social movement success, for example, and public (army-perpetrated) repression was still less destructive to the movements than paramilitary violence. But the timing of the wave of violence in each region now became a crucial factor in movement survival. Later waves of repression not only allowed activists to implement new strategies derived from the rare successes and many failures of the regions repressed earlier; it also allowed them to benefit from the strengthened urban moderate Left of the later period. Furthermore, earlier waves of repression, taking place in the mid-1990s rather than the early 2000s, were also more private and thus more lethal and difficult to prosecute. These focused on areas with a critical mass of local elites (as opposed to new colonization zones), especially in the northern half of Colombia.

If it survived this massive counterreform period wave of repression, a movement was more likely to attract outside allies if it had certain characteristics. First, it needed to be strong enough to present itself as viable and to have the time and resources to cultivate new alliances. Second, it needed to have a target that was vulnerable to political pressure or bad publicity. In these cases, somewhat ironically, U.S.-based corporations were more vulnerable than Colombian elites, as they could be prosecuted in U.S.

Figure 1.5. Determinants of Variations in Regional Outcome, Counterreform Period

In all regions, after 1992 counterreform measures decreased regional political autonomy, especially in regions with greater fiscal wealth and Left institutional representation, and spurred increased repressive violence. Leftist social movement and electoral strength were reduced significantly, and social movement demands shifted to human rights. Both the counterreform and the coca boom of the 1990s contributed to a guerrilla military buildup and increasing insurgent human rights violations. As U.S. military aid increased, social movements recognized that regional outcomes were determined largely by actors outside the region, and they increasingly sought outside allies. Their success in this endeavor derived from the below factors.

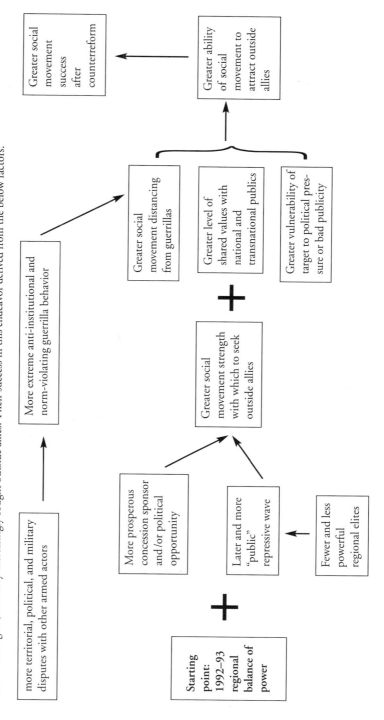

courts; U.S. mandated military operations were both more easily criticized as imperialist and more susceptible to the U.S. human rights certification process than ones responding to Colombian government initiatives; and the Colombian military was similarly more vulnerable than paramilitary forces, as they were more identifiable and could be threatened with a reduction of U.S. aid. Also ironically, more dire regional humanitarian crises and more extreme and overt restrictions of civil and political rights made the Colombian government more vulnerable by drawing the attention and presence of international relief agencies and human rights advocacy groups to the zone, creating bad press.

Third, the movement had to have the ability to reframe its demands in terms of values shared with the new allies. Demands emphasizing human rights, peace, democracy, an honest livelihood (i.e., untainted by coca cultivation), environmentalism, indigenous rights, and an internal decision-making process and organizational culture typified by New Left democratic practices all facilitated alliances with transnational publics, as did leadership with a relatively high educational level, as this appeared to increase credibility with (largely middle-class) solidarity activists in industrialized countries. "Shared values" in the case of a right-wing movement could also include a virulent anti-FARC ideology, which could facilitate alliances with military, paramilitary, and elite leaders. National and international alliances then greatly facilitated social movement success, as social movements could ask allies in Bogotá, or Europe, or Washington, D.C., to help them pressure the Colombian government.

Distancing itself from guerrillas may facilitate a social movement's national and international alliances, especially for U.S.-based transnational advocacy networks, but social movements in zones of guerrilla influence may still be deriving some benefits from guerrilla presence, and/or guerrillas may be willing to attack those who openly denounce them. Which consideration predominates depends on guerrilla behavior, itself a result of political/historical and economic factors. Social movement distancing from guerrillas is more likely where guerrillas have engaged in a greater number of human rights violations, such as killing alleged informers or elected officials, planting mines, or setting off bombs that kill civilians. Guerrillas, in turn, are more likely to carry out such acts when one of two conditions is in effect: there are political divisions between guerilla groups (e.g., one is negotiating with the government and one is in all-out war), or the guerrilla group is competing for control of the population and territory with other armed actors (guerrilla groups, paramilitary forces, or both), which maximizes the possibility that peasants will be asked to help both groups and will be seen as traitors by each.

In sum, political and economic opportunity, in conjunction with a later and more public repressive wave, lead to a movement that is stronger after the massive wave of counterreform period repression. This is especially the case if the movement ended the reform period strong. This strength allows the movement to dedicate personnel and resources to the mammoth task of cultivating alliances beyond the region. If this strength is combined with factors that facilitate the existence and effectiveness of transnational alliances, then the movement will have a greater likelihood of recruiting outside allies. Consequently, it will be more successful, as the outside allies help pressure the Colombian government to change policies.

STRUCTURE OF THIS BOOK

This book is presented in the form of three regional case studies, each divided into an analysis of the reform and counterreform periods, followed by a comparison and conclusion. The cases are presented in descending order of the level of elite-sponsored violence against social movement activists during the reform period.

Chapter 2 examines the experience of Urabá during the reform period, where the continued success of the banana workers' union, based on the prosperity of the banana sector, maintained leftist electoral stability. However, the continued economic strength of the banana sector (which was the repression-sponsoring as well as the concession-sponsoring elite) and the extreme divisiveness of the Left undermined the banana workers' and the Left's ability to negotiate a lasting regional pacted agreement. Violence thus escalated continuously in this region, even as workers made steady gains.

Chapter 3 addresses Urabá in the counterreform period. The period opened with several years of bloody FARC guerrilla attacks on the activists of a former leftist guerrilla group that demobilized to become a paramilitary-linked and government-endorsed party called Esperanza, Paz y Libertad (Hope, Peace, and Liberty). Then, in the mid-1990s, a paramilitary-led wave of repression wiped out the Patriotic Union in the banana sector, leaving only the San José Peace Community as survivors. The community explicitly prohibited both army and FARC presence, despite its history as a Communist Party stronghold, and has garnered considerable international attention, support, and success. Despite "Esperanza's" staunch military allegiance to the Right, it was both autonomous and successful in labor negotiations as well as the electoral arena. Its star began to fade with the paramilitary negotiation process, however, as its paramilitary alliances became liabilities.

Chapter 4, which examines the experience of Cartagena del Chairá in the Middle and Lower Caguán region during the reform period, shows an intermediate outcome in a peasant region where the state was both concession sponsor and repression sponsor. The unity of the movement was absolute, with only one political tendency represented in the Left. However, although the peasant settlers' movement in the region was tremendously successful and virtually unrepressed from 1984 through 1987, reflecting national political opening, it then collapsed and suffered a wave of repressive violence in the late reform period. The electoral strength of the Left quickly waned immediately afterward in response to political closing.

Chapter 5 discusses the 1993–2008 period in Cartagena del Chairá, when a new coca boom fueled—and counterreform inspired—a rapidly expanded and much more belligerent FARC and a near-total absence of social movements and the electoral Left. After three years of peace, from 1998 to 2001, while the president attempted negotiations with the FARC in the contiguous demilitarized zone, the Caguán reverted to the political closing pattern. Targeted by the U.S.-endorsed and funded Plan Patriota in 2004, it was subjected to intense military operations. Although this was the latest and most public wave of repression of the three regions, social movements there were weak. Attempts at peasant antimilitary mobilizations in 2005 were cross-regional and drew on allies in Bogotá, but the coca link and lack of explicit movement distancing from the FARC inhibited international alliances. In contrast, an Italian priest who ran a crop substitution program vastly expanded his Europe-funded project and received a great deal of attention in the press.

Chapter 6 presents the most favorable reform period outcome for the Left: Arauca. There the peasant settler movement, which targeted the departmental government, was tremendously successful, reflecting both the oil boom—enhanced fiscal wealth of the target and departmental political opening. It was also relatively unified, with only two guerrilla groups in the region, both refusing to demobilize despite reform initiatives. The resulting electorally successful Left confronted a cattle-ranching sector that had long undergirded the formerly dominant faction of the Liberal Party. Not only was oil rapidly eclipsing ranching as the mainstay of the region, weakening the ranchers' control of the political process, but direct election of county executives also divided the traditional party faction. Thus the leverage of the Left was maximized, and the displaced elites that had once sponsored repression were forced to establish a pact with leftist legislators in order to retain access to the abundant fiscal resources of the department. As a result, repression against the noncombatant Left virtually ceased, despite the continuing strength, activity, and success of the peasant movement.

Chapter 7 shows the continuing success of Araucan social movements in the counterreform period. Launched from a strong starting point in 1992, Araucan social movements benefited further from a late and relatively public wave of repression. This allowed movements to begin building outside alliances around new human rights demands in the mid-1990s and the electoral Left to retain its majority in the region through 1997. By the time the worst paramilitary violence and the most extreme selective recentralization measures hit, Araucan social movements were strong and connected nationally and internationally. Further, the targets of the Araucan social movements—Occidental Petroleum and the Colombian army—were well defined and vulnerable. When the FARC/ELN/paramilitary territorial conflicts intensified after 2001, FARC abuses against civilians skyrocketed, and social movements distanced themselves from the group, boosting their legitimacy with international allies. Araucan social movements have won several historic prosecutions of human rights cases by mobilizing allies in other regions or countries to pressure the Colombian government.

In Chapter 8 the case studies are systematically compared and explanations advanced for the outcomes found during both the reform and the counterreform period. The findings are used to extend existing theories of democratization/decentralization, social movements and the state, transnational activism, peasant and rural labor movements, guerrilla movements, and elite-organized political violence. An attempt is made to generalize these findings to similar social contexts and draw out the implications of my findings for social movement strategies.

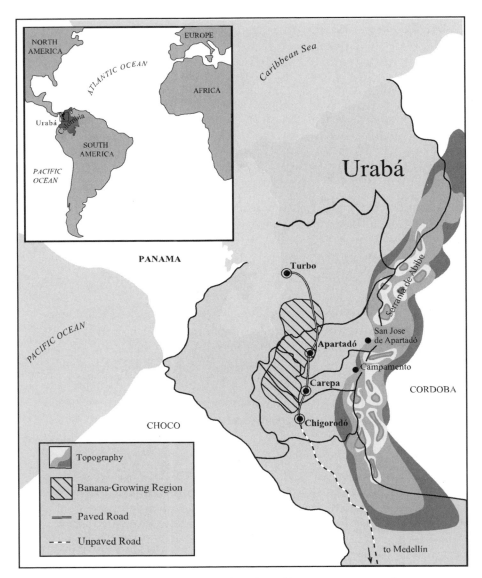

Figure 2.1. Urabá in Regional, National, and World Context, 1980s and 1990s

Sources: O'Connors, "El Mercado Común Europeo y la regulación del mercado del banano después de 1992," 60; Corpourabá, "Plan de desarrollo económico y social de Urabá," 12; DANE, *Colombia Estadística,* 1989, vol. 2: *Municipal,* 16; Instituto Geográfico Agustín Codazzi, *Atlas de Colombia,* 26. Map drawn by Emily Busch.

URABÁ IN THE REFORM PERIOD

Social Movement Gains with High Violence

Reform brought stalemate in Urabá, notwithstanding a brief negotiated peace in 1990–91: there were gains for the Left but with high levels of elite-sponsored violence. The electoral Left was strong and stable throughout the period of study, based on the continuous success of the banana workers' union. However, the increased economic influence of the banana plantation owners and large cattle ranchers gave these two elite sectors both the will and the way to seek to reverse, through violence, the material concessions and institutional political power won by the Left over the course of the decade. The deepening divisions between the different political tendencies of the Left in the late reform period made this macabre task that much easier.

On the one hand, a series of coinciding circumstances strengthened the Left. Previous attempts to make labor gains by organizing the banana workers had failed due to lack of state mediation. However, the peace process between the government and both of Urabá's main armed insurgencies allowed the declandestinization and reactivation of the sector's labor movement, which became highly militant and, by the mid-1980s, powerful, successful, and legal. The growth or stability of the banana sector, in the context of such militancy, made concessions to labor the most feasible choice—at least economic concessions, if not ones involving labor's political rights. Once democratic reforms allowed the translation of this labor strength into electoral strength and then local political power, such power then further benefited the labor movement as well as the corollary urban neighborhood and peasant movements.

On the other hand, the Left's rapid gains in the banana workers' union and institutional politics provoked an equally rapid, violent, and sustained reaction on the part of elites who had been displaced politically from an important regional stronghold. The same economic stability of the banana sector that had maintained labor and Left electoral success also fueled continuously high levels of repression throughout the reform period, with only the briefest interruptions. The coffee crisis and the move to an export-oriented national development model further boosted national *bananero* (banana producer) influence relative to other elite sectors, allowing them to increase militarization of their region. Finally, the rapid late 1980s expansion of large narco cattle ranchers—elites who had become wealthy from the cocaine economy and then purchased large cattle ranches in the north of Urabá—created a new regional ally for the banana plantation owners. That the labor movement and its political representatives were able to withstand this onslaught and the Left was able to sustain its electoral strength through 1992 is itself remarkable and in a context of weakening elites might have led to a regional peace. But as elites sensed that perhaps their war to roll back the Left's political and material gains was winnable in the long run, they were disinclined to negotiate a lasting regional peace with the Left.

Finally, the disunity of the Left, which had its roots in disparate reactions of different guerrilla groups to government peace offers, further sabotaged a brief negotiated peace. There were rare, relatively unified moments when the FARC and the EPL guerrilla groups shared similar positions vis-à-vis the peace process (before 1984, 1984–85, late 1987–early 1990, and 1991), and these moments correlated with the greatest labor and political gains for Urabá's banana workers. But at moments of disunity— 1985 through early 1987 and especially after mid-1991, after the EPL's demobilization—the divisions between the two sectors became bitter and violent. The still-active insurgencies accused the demobilized sector of the EPL of becoming an accomplice to the right-wing repressors; and the latter's need for protection against attacks from the still active insurgencies led them in some cases to fulfill the prophecy, ending the brief regional negotiated peace. Thus, although Urabá represents a clear case of Left electoral success and social movement strength, sustained despite intense repression, it also shows that such sustained success is not sufficient to win a regional pacted or negotiated solution if elites are strong or the Left is divided.

The chronological narrative below highlights the evolution of mobilization, Left electoral success, repression, and especially county executive actions in Apartadó. The major urban center of the banana axis, Apartadó is a workers' stronghold, and thus had leftist county governments from 1986 through 1992 that openly intervened in favor of leftist social movements—workers, workers' neighborhood movements, and Left-associated peasant movements—as well as high levels of repression. In the 1950s and 1960s, land was settled by colonos and banana plantations were established. From the mid-1960s through the early 1980s, two leftist tendencies arrived in the zone, establishing footholds in the banana worker, peasant, and urban neighborhood movements. However, lack of state mediation doomed these early efforts to limited success, despite rapid sectoral growth. From 1984 to 1987, the peace process, to which the two leftist tendencies responded similarly at first, allowed the banana workers' movement to make its first major gains despite slower sectoral growth, but violence increased as well. Between 1987 and 1989, maximum gains were made, supported again by political opening, leftist unity, and sectoral stability. Both leftist tendencies responded to the reform allowing the direct election of county executives by running candidates for local office successfully and in coalition and by creating a single unified banana workers' union, but elite-organized violence spiked in response to this success. From late 1990 to late 1991, a negotiated peace between banana plantation owners, paramilitary groups, and Esperanza, respected while the FARC was still negotiating with the government, briefly reduced violence against social movements in Urabá even while promoting labor success. But the peace came to a violent end after late 1991 due to deep intra-Left animosity and increased elite strength and influence in the region.

WHY APARTADÓ?

The Urabá region is located near the Colombian border with Panamá in close proximity to the Gulf of Urabá, giving it a port on the Caribbean Sea and easy access to the Panama Canal. Urabá is divided into three subregions: the north, along the Atlantic coast, where cattle ranching is the

predominant economic activity; the banana axis, composed of the flatlands sections of the counties of Turbo, Apartadó, Carepa, and Chigorodó;
and the south, where peasant settlers predominate and sustain themselves
with subsistence agriculture (see fig. 2.1). Urabá is in the department of
Antioquia, one of Colombia's wealthiest and most developed departments. Antioquia's capital, Medellín, is Colombia's second city and an industrial center for the textile industry, among others.[1]

As in the other banana axis counties, in Apartadó's sparsely populated,
mountainous, and largely roadless east, relatively recent peasant settlers
(most having arrived in the 1970s) held titles to an average of twenty hectares per family, using the land to grow cocoa, subsistence crops, plantains,
and food for the banana sector employees. Many belonged to the cocoa producers' cooperative, in operation from the late 1970s through at least the
early 1990s, located in mountainous San José de Apartadó.[2]

The urban center of Apartadó, populated by workers, professionals,
and merchants, is located on the central highway, in the flatlands, halfway
between the mountains and the Gulf of Urabá (see fig. 2.1). It was flanked
by banana plantations, some with camps for housing workers and their
families, mostly on the gulf side of the highway. One step farther out from
the urban center, adjacent to the banana plantations, small farmers grew
plantains to sell to export companies. Especially in Carepa and Turbo, these
sometimes took advantage of their buyers' monopoly to exert clientelistic
(Guerrista Liberal faction) control over the farmers. However, in Apartadó
between 1984 and 1992, most sympathized with the political tendencies
that evolved from the PCC-ML and the PCC.[3]

In Apartadó as in the rest of the banana axis, the main social antagonism was between banana plantation owners—generally represented by
Liberals of the Guerrista faction or occasionally Conservatives—and banana workers, usually represented by the Leftist tendencies. Large cattle
ranchers and their clients were also prominent among Guerrista Liberals,
while the Left represented peasant settlers, rural squatters, and urban squatters, as well as banana workers. The urban population—in particular, the
commercial sector and professionals—sometimes voted for Guerrista Liberals, sometimes for the Left, or sometimes for any of several more reformist Liberal factions, which were almost exclusively urban.[4]

However, this central social antagonism between banana workers
and plantation owners was especially sharp in Apartadó, making it the best
case study of violent democratization in the region. Apartadó was the un-

disputed capital of the banana-producing region, with most of the region's banks and commerce, as well as about 30 percent of the plantations, a good tax base that led to a respectable budget for the county executive to control.[5] Furthermore, its population is the second largest (48,969 as compared to 79,883, 25,815, and 13,329 for Turbo, Chigorodó, and Carepa, respectively, in 1985) and one of the two most urban (two-thirds of the population of both Apartadó and Chigorodó was urban; Carepa and Turbo were both about one-third urban) of all the banana axis counties. These characteristics made control of Apartadó's political institutions especially strategic.[6]

In addition, both the Left and the Right were especially well organized in Apartadó. The Apartadó unions were the first to organize after the peace process, and almost half the region's banana workers' union members belonged to Apartadó locals during this period, as shown in table 2.1. Furthermore, Apartadó became the residential center for non–work camp laborers as early as the 1970s, including those who worked on plantations in other banana axis counties. As these workers gained housing mostly by means of Left-organized squatters' invasions, at least four large urban squatter neighborhoods in Apartadó became leftist strongholds. All the labor, urban squatter, and peasant organizations were headquartered in Apartadó, as were the main leftist parties of the region. Even the Carepa and Turbo locals of the banana workers' unions had their offices in urban Apartadó. Apartadó thus was the banana axis county with the greatest Left electoral strength and the only one where leftist county executives were elected during the 1980s.[7] At the same time, Apartadó plantation owners were well represented within AUGURA. Also, from 1984 to 1990 the Guerrista faction of the Liberal Party clearly predominated over reformist Liberal factions in Apartadó county council elections by a ratio of about 3:1, making elite-Left political relations especially polarized.[8]

CHRONOLOGY OF CHANGE IN URABÁ

1950s–1964: Plantation Owners versus Workers and Settlers

Before the 1950s Urabá was sparsely settled, primarily by peasants from the neighboring departments of Chocó and Córdoba. They dedicated themselves in the north of Urabá to small-scale cattle ranching and in the

Table 2.1. Chronology of Membership in Main Banana Workers' Unions of Urabá

	Apartadó[a]				Urabá[b]		
	Sintagro /FP/Esp.	Sintraba- nano/UP	Not Unionized	Total	Sintagro /FP/Esp.	Sintraba- nano/UP	Total Unionized in Urabá
1984	3,300 (57%)	1,500 (26%)	1,000 (17%)	5,800	3,000	2,000	5,000
1985	3,800 (57%)	2,200 (33%)	700 (10%)	6,700	8,000	2,000	10,000
1986	4,000 (57%)	2,330 (33%)	750 (11%)	7,080	9,000	4,000	13,000
1987	4,000 (57%)	2,600 (37%)	400 (6%)	7,000	10,000	4,000	14,000
1988	4,000 (57%)	2,600 (37%)	400 (6%)	7,000	10,000	4,000	14,000
1989[c]	3,000 (56%)	2,000 (37%)	400 (7%)	5,400	10,000	4,000	14,000
1990	3,000 (56%)	2,000 (37%)	400 (7%)	5,400	10,000	4,000	14,000
1991	3,000 (55%)	2,060 (38%)	400 (7%)	5,460	10,000	4,000	14,000
1992	3,180 (56%)	2,180 (38%)	400 (7%)	5,680			14,500

Sources:
[a] Apartadó data from interview 44.
[b] Urabá data: 1984–91, interview 43. For the years 1984–87, discrepancies between the data from interviews 43 and 44 may reflect whether interviewee was providing figures from the beginning or the end of the year.
[c] In 1989, 1,600 workers were transferred from the Apartadó local to the Turbo local. Also in 1989, Sintagro, Sintrabanano, and tiny Sindejornaleros combined to become Sintrainagro.

south of Urabá and what would become the banana axis to subsistence farming. In the late 1940s and early 1950s Liberal refugees began to arrive from the mountainous, long-settled coffee-producing regions of Antioquia, fleeing La Violencia and persecution by Conservatives. These political refugees would further reinforce an already existing key trait of politics in Urabá that continues to this day: the virtual nonexistence of the Conservative Party and the presence of dissident and populist factions of the Liberal Party. In the mid-1950s a major new incentive for the settlement of the region was provided by the construction of a road from Medellín to the port of Turbo, allowing highlands Antioquia to take advantage of Urabá's strategic geographic location and encouraging further settlement by *antioqueño* peasants.[9]

In 1957 a blight devastated Colombia's traditional banana-growing region in the department of Magdalena, on the Atlantic coast. This, on top of the devastating effects of four hurricanes in the space of a decade and the exhaustion of the soil after forty years of cultivation, led the United Fruit Company to abandon its former center of operations in the zone of Santa Marta (Magdalena) and look toward Urabá. The hot, wet climate, soil type, flat piedmont topography, cheap land and labor, and location near an Atlantic seaport and a highway to the interior made the new location ideal for the cultivation and export of bananas.

Although when it was located in the Santa Marta banana zone, the United Fruit Company (or more correctly, its Colombian affiliate, Frutera de Sevilla) had owned the land directly, it decided to try a new strategy in Urabá. It would provide easy credit and technical assistance to Colombian plantation owners and monopolize the most lucrative part of the banana business, commercialization. And it would avoid the risks of natural disasters, labor conflicts, price fluctuations, and expropriation by not owning the land directly. Despite the risks, the Compañía Frutera de Sevilla had many takers for its offer. Primarily urban business owners (although with businesses of different sizes) and mostly from Medellín, the entrepreneurs obtained land with titles, generally at below-market prices, from the often uneducated peasants that had settled the area demarcated by Frutera de Sevilla as most suitable for banana cultivation. Often deception and coercion were used to facilitate the transfer of land from settlers to banana entrepreneurs. Despite these conflicts, production soon began, and the first shipment of bananas from Urabá took place in 1964. A total of 1,276,000 boxes of 55 pounds each, Urabá's production for that year represented 14 percent of the national total.[10]

The initiation of banana production introduced a labor market that attracted thousands of migrants. Drawn primarily from neighboring, very poor regions, especially Chocó and Córdoba, the new residents altered the demographic, cultural, and racial makeup of Urabá. Between 1951 and 1964 the population of Urabá increased by a factor of five, from 15,700 to 77,000, with three of four new residents being migrants from other regions. Most of this growth was concentrated in the banana axis.[11]

The Antioquian peasant settlers from the 1940s and 1950s, as well as the 22 percent of the banana workers who came from the highlands coffee region and the mostly Antioquian banana plantation owners, were generally white or mestizos prone to attitudes of racial superiority. The Chocoanos, who by 1979 constituted almost half of all banana workers, were Afro-Colombian; and the Cordobeses and natives of Urabá that made up another 20 percent of the banana proletariat were generally mulattos. The stage was set for future confrontations in which race and political affiliations further inflamed land and class conflicts.[12]

1964–1983: Left and Elite Political Consolidation but Limited Labor Success

Urabá's banana sector grew rapidly between 1964 and 1983. Production expanded from 1.3 million boxes per year in 1964 to 39.0 million in 1983; Urabá's share of national production rose from 14 percent to 93 percent; banana plantations occupied 6,000 hectares in 1964 as compared to almost 20,000 in 1983; and productivity rose from 3.9 tons per hectare to 35.5 tons per hectare during the same period. Banana exports, constituting about 2.7 percent of Colombia's export earnings in 1976, provided 4.5 percent of Colombia's hard currency earnings by 1981–82.[13]

Almost all conditions in Urabá favored worker organization. Because bananas are harvested continuously throughout the year by a permanent workforce and because shop size on banana plantations is fairly large (over fifty workers per plantation), banana plantation workers, as a rule, are said to be relatively unionizable.[14] Furthermore, workers in Urabá were physically concentrated in a relatively small space, on their work site (an estimated 80 percent lived in the work camps during this period), which generally facilitates meeting attendance and rank-and-file activism. There was relatively little internal economic stratification among them,[15] and the sector was growing rapidly. However, two mutually reinforcing factors created nearly insurmountable obstacles to successful unionization before 1984: (1) the high level of organization of Urabá's banana plantation owners, which increased their national political influence and thus facilitated their efforts to obtain antilabor government intervention in Urabá's labor conflicts; and (2) the lack of preexisting Colombian government labor institutions to protect labor's interests.

During their first decade of operation (1964–74), the plantation owners of Urabá became very well organized. In Medellín on December 13, 1963, the Colombian banana plantation owners formed a trade association, Association of Banana Plantation Owners and Farmers of Urabá (AUGURA).[16] AUGURA's central purpose was to represent the interests of Colombian plantation owners vis-à-vis the multinational Frutera de Sevilla and in the long run nationalize and vertically integrate the banana industry in Urabá. Thus it facilitated the establishment of the first Colombian commercialization company, UNIBAN, which by 1969 broke Frutera de Sevilla's monopoly over this lucrative activity. By 1970 UNIBAN created a U.S-based subsidiary to market bananas directly in the consumer countries.[17] As the president of UNIBAN's board of directors immodestly but accurately claimed in 1990, "The risky and courageous decision to counter the pressures of Frutera de Sevilla and plunge into the complex international world of direct banana marketing was without a doubt the motor of growth and consolidation of the banana industry of Urabá."[18] By 1976 UNIBAN was marketing 42.5 percent of the total volume of banana exports from Urabá.[19]

With the addition of the Urabá-based Colombian marketing entities Proban and Banacol and the withdrawal of Frutera de Sevilla and Standard Fruit from the zone, by late 1983 Urabá's banana industry was virtually 100 percent national in terms of landownership and the first stage of marketing and 80 percent national in terms of the final stage of marketing in consumer countries.[20] At the same time, a clear process of land concentration was occurring, with the largest plantations (from 90.1 to over 150 hectares) representing 6 percent of all Urabá plantations in 1977 but 15 percent by 1986.[21] AUGURA was becoming an economic power to contend with.

This economic success was echoed by the banana industry's growing political power. By the early 1980s the banana plantation owners of Urabá had become a central constituency of the Guerrista faction of the Liberal Party in Antioquia. (The Guerristas were led by Senator Bernardo Guerra, a staunch anticommunist opposed to most reform measures). In fact, the 1982 Guerrista candidate for the House of Representatives was a plantation owner and UNIBAN board member. That year, the Guerristas were Antioquia's most successful political faction, winning both House seats and Senate seats in the national parliament for the period 1982–86, as well as eight of thirty seats in the 1984–86 Departmental Assembly. This political representation, together with the growing economic clout of the Urabá bananeros, no doubt facilitated the militarization of the region and of labor conflicts in particular.[22]

AUGURA pressed the national and departmental governments to provide basic transportation infrastructure and public services (especially malaria eradication) and increase military presence in the zone, winning both demands.[23] But at any rate, military solutions to social conflicts were the norm under the government of President Turbay Ayala (1978–82), who, in the words of two mainstream Colombian journalists, showed "a marked inclination toward the repression of political alternatives through persecution, coercion, intimidation, and generalized application of torture."[24] His Statute of Security increased the army's judicial powers and restricted citizen rights,[25] keeping the labor and peasant movements in Urabá weak throughout this period.

The years between 1964 and 1983 witnessed several attempts to organize the large, new labor force of the banana plantations. However, the employers reacted to these attempts with a series of effective antiunion strategies: discriminatory hirings and firings, bribes, use of subcontractors, detentions, and, when none of these worked, outright violence. Workers who tried to denounce any of these illegal labor practices through the normal institutional means were sure to be discouraged by the gross inadequacy of government mediating mechanisms. For the entire region there was only one labor court to resolve grievances, and it was located at a substantial distance from the banana axis in the county seat of Turbo (on the Gulf of Urabá). As the employer was allowed to miss the first two court dates, workers had little incentive to resolve conflicts by this means. Furthermore, the national government was quite willing to either tolerate or actively support these illegal strategies as well as to militarize the plantation or the region.[26] Not surprisingly, the early attempts to unionize overwhelmingly met with failure.

Sintrabanano was the first to attempt unionization. Founded in 1964, it was affiliated with the Communist Party's labor federation (see table 2.2). By 1970 it had 1,500 to 1,600 members but then faced a wave of repression. Between 1974 and 1975, 543 unionized workers from Sintrabanano were fired by six plantations.[27] By December 1977 its membership was only 350 to 400. After a year or two of inactivity, Sintrabanano attempted to regroup but was again foiled by increasingly violent repression. In 1979 Sintrabanano union representatives presented a list of demands to the management of a plantation it was trying to organize. The plantation was militarized, and workers were forced to sign a "collective pact" (employer-imposed contract). In another example, after a union representative presented a list of demands, the plantation owner offered him a bribe of $50,000 Colombian pesos (about U.S.$1,000) to desist and to facilitate the signing of a collective pact. The labor leader refused; five days later he was found dead. Workers held a protest strike the next day, but the plantation was militarized, forcing workers to resume their activities. Three days later a member of the Sintrabanano Board of Directors was detained for twelve days, accused of fomenting all the disturbances on the plantation.[28]

The second main union in Urabá, Sintagro, was founded and given a legal charter in 1972. At first it was affiliated with the Conservative Party labor confederation, the UTC, and focused on organizing the palm workers of the Dutch firm Coldesa. However, when it presented its first list of demands to be negotiated in a strike in 1976, not only was the plantation militarized and the union officials threatened, but military county executives were appointed for Turbo, Apartadó, Chigorodó, and Mutatá and reappointed in 1980.[29] As a reaction to the failure of this strike, guerrillas from the EPL (see table 2.2), in their first labor-linked action, killed the director of industrial relations at Coldesa, on the grounds that he betrayed the working class of Urabá and persecuted organized labor.[30] From then on, Sintagro would be ideologically associated with the PCC-ML, a Maoist tendency, and the similarly associated EPL. The new affiliation did nothing to boost the union's success: the strike failed. After the president and fiscal officer of the union were exiled from the region, the union lapsed into inactivity.[31]

Like Sintrabanano, Sintagro tried to reactivate its organization in 1979. It presented a list of demands, but the only response obtained from employers was the firing of the union's board of directors. At that point the union decided to carry out future activities clandestinely. In 1983 another attempt was made to resuscitate the union, but once again the board of directors was fired. Furthermore, a board member of one of the locals was killed, and the treasurer from the same local was left paralyzed after an assassination attempt.[32]

Table 2.2. Main Political, Military, and Mass Organizations of the Left in Urabá, 1964–1992

	1964–75	1976–84	1984–88	1989–July 1990	July 1990–November 1992
Political party	PCC	PCC	PCC	PCC	PCC
Guerrilla group		FARC; arrives mid-1970s	FARC: Cease-fire 1984–85 (unity with EPL) Cease-fire 1985–86 (disunity with EPL) End cease-fire 1987–88 (unity with EPL)	FARC: No new peace accords (unity with EPL)	FARC: Respects Esperanza's pact through the end of 1991, then growing tensions with Esperanza.
Banana workers' union	Sintrabanano (weak)	Sintrabanano	Sintrabanano grows quickly, declandestinizes	Stable membership; joins Sintagro to form Sintrainagro.	Sintrainagro has stable membership. Labor peace through late 1991, then growing tensions within union.
Electoral Front	Via traditional parties	UNO (1976–82); Frente Democrático (1982–84)	UP wins 48 percent of country vote in Apartadó in 1986; stable in 1988	UP electoral strength stable in Urabá	UP maintains or increases electoral strength in counties of Urabá.
Political party	PCML	PCML	PCML	PCML	Majority faction of the PCML becomes Esperanza, Paz y Libertad. Minority sides with EPL's dissident faction after most of EPL demobilizes.
Guerrilla group	EPL arrives 1970–72	EPL	EPL: Cease-fire 1984–85 (unity with FARC) No cease-fire 1985–86 (disunity with FARC) No cease-fire 1987–88 (unity with FARC)	EPL: No new peace accords (unity with FARC)	Most of EPL demobilizes, becomes party, Esperanza, Paz y Libertad. A dissident faction remains an armed insurgency, thereafter called EPL dissidence.
Banana workers' union		1980: Sintagro becomes PCML-affiliated but clandestine	Sintagro grows quickly, declandestinizes	Stable membership; joins Sintabanano to form Sintrainagro.	Sintrainagro has stable membership. Labor and intra-Left peace through late 1991, then growing intraunion tensions.
Electoral/social movement front	None	None	Frente Popular: first participates electorally in 1988, wins 11 percent of Apartadó county vote.	Frente Popular wins 16 percent of Apartadó county vote.	Esperanza, Paz y Libertad wins 19% of Apartadó county vote.

Another smaller union, Sintraexpoban—which, far from being leftist, was affiliated with the Conservative Party labor federation UTC—faced equally severe repression during this prereform period. In September 1982, after the union had presented a list of demands, the union representative for a plantation was killed. Only fifteen days later the treasurer was killed and the president of the union wounded. The rest of the members of the board of directors decided not to continue to press their demands, the union local's office was closed for weeks, and approximately 250 members withdrew from the union.[33]

Only one small union, Sindejornaleros, survived this period to become the strongest banana workers' union at the end of the 1970s. It was influenced by a leftist party, Movimiento Obrero Independiente Revolucionario (Revolutionary Independent Workers Movement; MOIR), which had no armed expression. However, the apparent strength of Sindejornaleros at the end of the 1970s may say more about the weakness of the labor movement as a whole. By 1979 it was estimated that only 46 percent of plantations had labor agreements, and of these, 77 percent were employer imposed. In other words, only 11 percent of plantations had collective bargaining agreements negotiated between unionized workers and management.[34]

Working conditions, as a result, were abysmal. Labor relations were characterized by piecework and day labor, the total absence of benefits, the employers' use of subcontractors to evade their legal obligations to their workers, failure to pay overtime for workdays over eight hours, and, in general, the near-total disregard of labor regulations by employers, often with the complicity of the Ministry of Labor. By AUGURA's own admission, while the plantation owners "could enjoy the results of their businesses . . . the rest of Urabá's society [including the banana workers] lacked even minimal conditions for health, education, and housing."[35] A University of Antioquia survey of Urabá banana plantations revealed that even as late as 1979, only 6.6 percent of work camp dwellings had running water, only about one-third had latrines, and only half had electricity. As a result, one union reported, in 1971, 25 percent of workers had tuberculosis.[36]

Thus, despite the rapid expansion, nationalization, and vertical integration of the banana sector and the supposed unionizability of banana workers, the project of organizing banana workers in Urabá progressed little during this period. The intransigence of plantation owners, manifested in the use of illegal union-busting measures with the national government's complicity, would block the progress of banana workers through 1983. This lack of progress created the opportunity for the armed insurgencies of the region to attempt to forge links with the banana workers' unions. Not until 1984, when the two guerrilla groups in the region entered peace negotiations with the Executive, could leftist labor activists organize openly and the main banana workers' unions build truly powerful organizations.

Repression was also an impediment to peasant organizing. However, the very fact that progress through nonviolent means for these constituencies had been blocked by repression and elite intransigence helped to create an opening for the entrance of guerrilla groups into the region. Some nonviolent oppositional efforts did succeed: urban squatter invasions became common and even successful in the region, helping to establish the basis for the Left's first electoral expressions.

The guerrilla movement, in its two main expressions, the Maoist EPL and the FARC, associated with the Communist Party (Soviet Line), entered Urabá during this period. Founded in 1967 in the neighboring coastal department of Córdoba, the EPL had its first documented confrontation with the armed forces in Urabá in early 1970. The FARC had been created one year earlier than the EPL but had its strongest regional presence in the Cordillera Oriental and eastern plains among constituencies that had been intensely affected by La Violencia: its first documented actions in Urabá occurred in early 1972.[37]

The primary focus of both insurgent groups during this period was the problematic situation of peasants and peasant settlers in the region, especially those in the mountainous sectors just east of the banana axis (Serranía del Abibe; see fig. 2.1). The FARC focused on settlers in the banana axis and the south of Urabá, while the EPL's strongest presence was in the north. One fruit of these early organizing efforts of settlers, with the possible participation of the FARC, was the cocoa cooperative in San José de Apartadó, founded in 1976.[38]

According to one study cited by Botero, the FARC also worked with small peasants in the flatlands to organize land invasions of underutilized large landholdings, although much of the rural squatters' movement was autonomous of leftist or guerrilla influence. A wave of this type of invasions occurred in Urabá in the first half of the 1970s, with squatters at times defying army-led eviction efforts to occupy large landholdings in banana axis counties in December 1970, October 1971, and May 1973.

These were organized by the Asociación Nacional de Usuarios Campesinos (ANUC), the central association leading a powerful national movement of landless peasants.[39] However, an important peasant leader was assassinated in 1973, the movement in general was subject to military harassment, and it was also stymied by the four military county executives appointed in 1976 and again in 1980, producing a hiatus of a few years in both peasant and labor mobilization. On the other hand, a joint peasant-labor movement public denouncement of repression distributed during this time also illustrates the growing links between the movements, which would serve them well in the future.[40]

Finally, urban neighborhood movements met with partial success during this period. At first, these were not overtly led by the Left. In 1964 and 1968 two invasions were organized by the Movimiento Revolucionario Liberal (Liberal Revolutionary Movement; MRL)—a Liberal Party faction also used by the Colombian Communist Party as an electoral front during these years—taking over vacant lots in the urban center of Apartadó. Although repressed, they eventually were able to legalize their claims. Similarly, in 1972, a priest in Apartadó organized a third invasion, with three hundred families participating. As the priest had previously negotiated with the owner, there was no repression, and the priest became more powerful politically.[41]

After 1973, as it saw that squatter invasions could be politically useful and tolerated, the Left became openly active in the urban squatter movement. Between 1973 and 1985 the population in the banana axis counties had nearly doubled, from 83,383 to 150,463; in Apartadó about half the county's population was urban by 1983. The burgeoning population had inflated land prices until they were out of reach of those banana workers, usually those with families, who sought to leave the work camps. Thus the banana economy indirectly spawned the first in a long series of politically sponsored squatters' invasions in Urabá's urban centers. In 1983 the Communist Party's housing organization, together with activists from the MOIR, initiated an invasion of lands belonging to a powerful banana plantation owner and Liberal politician. It was Apartadó's largest urban invasion to date, but the squatters managed to resist eviction despite intense repression, creating two stable neighborhoods that would become Communist Party strongholds (the MOIR soon disappeared from the region).[42]

The urban squatters were not only well organized internally, but they were also linked to the banana workers' movement formally through the

Communist Party—influenced Sintrabanano union as well as informally due to the fact that many in the neighborhood were banana workers. Demonstrating the neighborhood activists' importance within the party was the Frente Democrático's (the Communist Party's electoral front in 1982 and 1984) choice of county council candidates, elected in March 1984: one labor leader and one neighborhood leader.[43]

Another legacy of this initial period of mobilization was the Left's incipient participation in electoral politics. Uribe (1992) makes references to leftist county council members in Apartadó and Turbo as early as 1972, principally from the Communist Party's different electoral fronts, since the PCC-ML (the Maoist party that sympathized with the EPL) was unwaveringly abstentionist. While the Communist Party had participated in Urabá's electoral politics even before 1972, it had tended to express itself through the MRL, led by Alfonso López Michelsen (president 1974–78).[44]

By 1983 the electoral Left had gained a critical mass of the electorate in Apartadó. In the 1982 county council elections, the Frente Democrático won 20 percent of the vote and the MOIR 9 percent. Despite this foothold, the Left lacked any real power over county institutions since the county executive was appointed by the governor and was almost invariably a Guerrista Liberal (when not a military man). This antireformist faction, which represented banana plantation owners, held a comfortable majority of about 64 percent of the county council vote in Apartadó.[45]

In summary, between 1964 and 1983, despite numerous attempts and a booming banana economy, banana workers' unionization efforts were impeded by illegal repression carried out with the complicity of the national government. The peasant movement was similarly stymied by repression. Nevertheless, some foundations were established for a more powerful Left in the years to come: the urban squatters' movement was relatively successful and growing, both the peasant movement and the urban squatters' movement had forged essential links with labor, the electoral Left had won a critical mass of the vote in Apartadó, and the guerrillas who had arrived in the region were poised to declandestinize.

1984–1987: The First Peace Process

The period 1964–83 had been characterized by extremely rapid growth of the banana sector but without improved wages, working conditions, or collective bargaining conditions for banana workers. In contrast, although banana sector growth was slower between 1984 and 1992, government-guerrilla peace processes indirectly facilitated rapid improvements in the level of unionization, wages, working conditions, negotiating conditions, and especially the electoral representation of the region's banana workers through leftist parties. Once elected, leftist county executives strengthened the hand of the banana workers' union and aided the urban squatter and peasant movements as well. However, elites reacted violently to these clear gains, unleashing an escalating wave of repression. A slight decrease in repression in 1985–86 during the peace process failed to develop into a full-blown pact due to intra-Left divisions, growing elite strength in both the banana and cattle sectors, and concomitant increased militarization.

After more than two decades of rapid expansion, the banana economy of Urabá settled down to stability in production and a slow rate of expansion in hectares cultivated from 1984 through 1992. The number of boxes of bananas exported in 1984 was 46.6 million; in 1992, 44.0 million. Colombia's share of world banana production stabilized at about 12 percent, after a bumper crop year in 1984 when it reached 14 percent; and the banana sector's contribution to Colombia's export earnings remained stable at around 4.5 percent, notwithstanding a peak in 1988 of 6 percent. Productivity per hectare also stabilized at around 33 to 38 tons per hectare, aside from a peak in the rainy year of 1984 and a low point in 1990 (table 2.3). The proportion of commercialization carried out by Colombian firms also held steady at 78 to 79 percent. Only the number of banana hectares in Urabá would show slow but steady expansion, from 20,100 hectares in 1984 to 23,850 hectares by 1992.[46]

While the stable economy formed a backdrop for the labor gains that occurred during this period, the main factor that made these possible was President Betancur's peace process, which allowed more open union organizing and encouraged the national government to adopt a more neutral stance with regard to labor conflicts in the region. Betancur's negotiations produced successful cease-fires with both the FARC (May 14, 1984) and the EPL (August 24, 1984). Soon after, in 1984–85, both organizations founded new, nonclandestine electoral/mass organization fronts. That associated with the FARC, founded in 1985, was called the Unión Patriótica (Patriotic Union, UP); that associated with the EPL, the Frente Popular.[47] The two organizations' similar relations with the presidency and the peace process facilitated some steps toward unity in 1984 and 1985.

Table 2.3. Urabá Banana Production in National and World Context, 1963–1992 (selected years)

Year	Area Planted, in Hectares[a]	Productivity, Tons/Hectares[b]	No. of Boxes Exported (1,000s)[c]	Urabá Production as % of Colombian Production[d]	Colombian Production as % of World Production[e]
1964	6,000	3.9	1,276	14%	3.8%
1966	14,450	16.0	12,694	74%	5.8%
1968	16,730	20.1	18,530	84%	7.0%
1969	18,950	15.5	16,148	88%	5.7%
1971	15,385	13.9	11,792	94%	3.5%
1972	11,498	16.7	10,549	90%	3.2%
1974	13,725	21.3	16,110	87%	5.0%
1976	15,300	26.5	22,319	89%	7.1%
1978	16,789	32.2	29,706	92%	8.2%
1980	17,365	39.2	37,406	94%	10.6%
1982	19,300	35.2	37,428	91%	10.8%
1984	20,100	42.1	46,591	93%	13.9%
1985	20,300	34.2	38,183	90%	10.9%
1986	19,700	38.5	41,772	87%	11.9%
1987	20,400	39.0	43,711	87%	12.2%
1988	20,000	37.3	40,993	81%	NA
1989	20,400	NA	NA	NA	NA
1990	21,400	35.4	41,638	74%	NA
1991	21,600	42.9	51,000	73%	12.0%
1992	27,570	33.0	50,033	67%	NA

[a] 1984–82: Ramírez G., "Consolidación de la actividad bananera de Urabá," 89; 1984–91: Ministerio de Agricultura, *Anuario estadístico del sector agropecuario 1991*, 13; 1992: AUGURA, "Urabá: Area sembrada en banano."

[b] 1964–82: Ramírez G., "Consolidación de la actividad bananera de Urabá," 89; 1984–91: Rey de Marulanda and Córdoba Garcés, *El sector bananero de Urabá*, 17; 1992: AUGURA, "Coyuntura bananera colombiana: Primer semestre de 2001," 31. Figure was derived by converting boxes to metric tons (55 boxes = 1 ton) and then dividing by hectares.

[c] 1964–82: Ramírez G., "Consolidación de la actividad bananera de Urabá," 78; 1984–88: Rey de Marulanda and Córdoba Garcés, *El sector bananero de Urabá*, 17; 1990–92: AUGURA, "Coyuntura bananera colombiana: Primer semestre de 2001," 31.

[d] 1964–82: Ramírez G., "Consolidación de la actividad bananera de Urabá," 78; 1984–88: Rey de Marulanda and Córdoba Garcés, *El sector bananero de Urabá*, 17; 1990–92: AUGURA, "Coyuntura bananera colombiana: Primer semestre de 2001," 31.

[e] 1964–82: Ramírez G., "Consolidación de la actividad bananera de Urabá," 78; 1984–87: Rey de Marulanda and Córdoba Garcés, *El sector bananero de Urabá*, 21; 1991: AUGURA, "Mensaje del Presidente de la República," 28–29.

Virtually all sources discuss the role of the EPL and the FARC in Urabá's labor movement, which began in the late 1970s, with most concluding that such an association intensified repression against banana workers. However, it is also important to explore why guerrilla movements were able to gain influence within the banana workers' movement in the first place. I argue that labor support for guerrillas in Urabá was a response to the banana sector's unusually harsh combination of extreme repression, management intransigence, and especially the total lack of government mediation of labor conflict, especially in the years before 1984.[48] And while the guerrilla-labor link certainly intensified repression later on, during the peace process it allowed the now-declandestinized guerrilla movement to organize openly, eventually inducing plantation owners to negotiate for the first time. A former EPL guerrilla reported that the EPL first began to work with Sintagro (the PCC-ML–associated labor union) and urban groups in 1980, ending the banana sector's "first stage of labor history." According to him, the four stages are as follows: (1) The law of the jungle prevailed (plantation owners did whatever they wanted); (2) the guerrillas arrived; (3) the banana workers' union became very strong; and (4) paramilitary groups arrived. He argued that at first the EPL guerrillas played an essential role in organizing Sintagro, protecting it against repression, and pressuring plantation owners to negotiate.[49] While Sintrabanano had a longer history and was somewhat better established than Sintagro by 1980, presumably the FARC's role in Sintrabanano fulfilled the same functions at this stage.

But the guerrilla-labor link did not weaken once reform began. To the contrary. Botero suggests that this involvement became more noteworthy after 1984, when the democratic opening facilitated contact between the previously clandestine guerrilla groups and banana workers,[50] ushering in a period of unprecedented labor militancy. Both Sintrabanano and Sintagro especially were highly militant during 1985. Furthermore, as the EPL and the FARC both had peace agreements with the government, the labor movement was quite unified. At this stage most strikes involved one or several plantations. For example, in 1985 one strike in Apartadó involved twelve plantations and a total of 1,100 workers. In all of Urabá, a total of 166 lists of demands were presented in 1985. Leaders from both major tendencies agreed that 1985 was a major turning point, the first time the two unions had coordinated their actions. On July 19–20, 1985, for

example, the two labor organizations—along with the smaller Sindejornaleros (by then associated with another leftist tendency, A Luchar; see
table 1.1)—led a joint regional strike. At first the Apartadó-based mobilization was confronted with the arrests of several labor leaders and anti-
strike radio spots orchestrated by Apartadó's military county executive.
However, after a second day of massive protest and unwavering labor support for the strike, he apparently perceived that the path of least resistance lay elsewhere and requested that AUGURA meet with the labor
negotiators.[51]

In late 1985, however, the EPL broke off peace negotiations with the
government while the FARC's efforts to seek a peace agreement continued. Consequently, a serious rift developed between the labor organizations associated with each political tendency. Nevertheless, the high level
of militancy continued in 1985. Sintagro was especially active, organizing
a strike on November 25, 1985, that affected 33 percent of the banana-
growing area and demanding the reactivation of their legal charter (suspended after the joint Sintagro-Sintrabanano strike in July 1985). Another
Sintrago-led strike involved only one plantation in Carepa but lasted thirty-
five days; it was successful in winning 85 percent of its demands. Without
distinguishing which union led the protests, Botero also mentions strikes
on December 5, 1985 (100 percent of Apartadó's workers participated,
as did 80 percent of workers in the other banana axis counties); April 30,
1986 (workers at 120 plantations struck to demand protection against
violence); December 13, 1986 (when 1,500 workers went on strike); and
February 20, 1987 (when about 8,000 workers stopped work to protest
the assassination/disappearance of four workers).[52]

As a result of this wave of militancy and the declandestinization
launched by the peace process, the two unions grew rapidly in size and
organizational strength. In Urabá, Sintagro grew from 300 members in
August 1984 to 3,000 in December of the same year and 10,000 by the
end of 1987 (table 2.1).[53] In Apartadó, Sintagro membership increased
from 3,300 to 4,000 between 1984 and 1987. Sintrabanano remained
the smaller of the two organizations, representing about one-third of the
unionized banana workers, but it grew at a similar rate. Between early
1984 and 1987 Sintrabanano grew from 100 to 4,000 members in the banana axis and from 1,500 to 2,600 members in Apartadó. By 1985 plantations organized by Sintagro and Sintrabanano covered 49.5 percent

and 8.9 percent respectively of the total banana acreage in Urabá. In all, by 1985, 73.9 percent of Urabá's banana land was tended by unionized workers.[54]

The militancy of this period not only solidified the organizations involved but also contributed to the unions' first major successes, among them the eight-hour workday. Furthermore, reflecting the changed government role in Urabá's labor conflicts in the wake of the peace process, at the end of 1985 two more labor courts were added in the banana axis—one in Apartadó and one in Chigorodó. Gains were made in terms of wages and other demands as well. Sintagro's eighteen-day, twelve-plantation strike in Apartadó in 1985 was arbitrated by the Ministry of Labor. The union had asked for a 70 percent raise and received 26 percent, but this was still a substantial improvement over the earlier era of labor relations. Meanwhile, in a joint Sintagro-Sintrabanano strike at two plantations in Carepa in 1985, workers held out for fifteen days and were rewarded when 80 percent of their demands were met. Most tellingly, while banana workers' real wages had remained stagnant from 1978 to 1981, at the level of 3,700 to 3,850 pesos per month in 1978 pesos (approximately U.S.$77/month), in 1984 real wages rose substantially to 5,931 pesos per month (in 1978 pesos) and increased significantly again in 1987 to 7,762 pesos per month (in 1978 pesos), double the 1978 wage in real terms.[55]

The 1984–87 peace process, in addition to strengthening labor, greatly enhanced the standing of the electoral Left in Urabá. This is not only because it strengthened Sintrabanano, which along with urban squatters and peasant settlers would become a key constituency for the Communist Party's latest electoral front in 1986, but also because it stimulated the FARC to participate more actively in the electoral process via the Patriotic Union. Although the peace process also spurred the EPL's creation of a similar mass organization/electoral front, the Frente Popular, this group would not participate in electoral activity until 1988, focusing instead on building mass organizations like Sintagro.[56]

The creation of the Patriotic Union greatly increased PCC-associated electoral success. In 1984 the Frente Democrático (the previous Communist Party electoral front) won 23 percent of the county council vote in Apartadó, but in 1986 the UP won more than twice that, 48 percent. The UP's success was also manifest in the other banana axis counties of Urabá, winning 17 percent, 30 percent, and 32 percent of the 1986 county council vote in Carepa, Chigorodó, and Turbo respectively and a whopping 89 percent in Mutatá, a settler zone just south of Chigorodó. Apartadó's UP county council members were clearly linked to social movements. Candidates in 1986 included a national leader of the Communist Party; the president of Sintrabanano; a peasant leader from San José de Apartadó, where the peasant settler cocoa cooperative was located; and a leader from one of the squatter neighborhoods that had been established by organizers associated with the Frente Democrático in 1983.[57]

The first direct election of county executives did not occur until 1988. However, by decree of President Barco, in order to further the peace process, in counties where the Patriotic Union won more county council votes than any other party the governor would appoint a county executive from the UP in 1986. By virtue of this provision, Apartadó's first leftist county executive was appointed and took office on November 1, 1986—no small prize, given Apartadó's respectable fiscal resources and regional political importance.[58] With this institutional power, the Apartadó's UP-led 1986–88 county administration used county resources to benefit its worker, squatter, and peasant constituencies. It legalized (i.e., arranged to provide property titles for) one of the earlier and larger squatter neighborhoods, an UP stronghold where residents had lived on plots without titles since 1968.[59]

Also demonstrating its "class content," Apartadó's leftist county administration was the first to risk offending bananeros in the interest of boosting fiscal revenue. In 1986, given the necessity to respond to the county's needs and the reality of a property tax long made meaningless by obsolete appraisals of banana plantations and other rural properties, Apartadó's UP-led county administration passed a tax on the production of the banana packing plants located in the county.[60] This unprecedented act caused alarm, then extreme anger, among some of the most powerful plantation owners. They later sued Apartadó to reverse the tax and refused to pay it, perceiving it as an omen of future attacks on capital, an extension of guerrilla warfare as well as the labor movement.[61] Jaime Henríquez Gallo, a plantation owner, key figure in UNIBAN, and a newly reelected member of the House of Representatives for the Guerrista Liberals, unleashed a telling diatribe against the UP-led county administration of Apartadó in a presentation at an AUGURA congress in November 1986:

In the county council of Apartadó, it is painful to see how, recently, a tax on the packing plants was approved with defiance and fury. This tax implies a strategy against the economic system in which we live. . . . When there are forces of anarchy interested in undermining the system and the regime, there will be a cascade of taxes through property appraisals. . . . They do not understand solidarity with those who produce and work. Rather, they understand that it is a clear-cut class struggle like that which has been unleashed against us in the zone.[62]

Interestingly, as one UP county executive of Apartadó wryly noted in 1989, the Liberal-dominated Chigorodó and Carepa had passed similar taxes by 1988, which the bananeros paid willingly.[63] Thus it became clear that it was not the tax itself but the fact that the resources would be controlled by the Left that the plantation owners found disturbing.

At the root of the bananeros' anger over the new tax was Guerrista Liberal alarm at their political displacement from local political institutions by the Left. The banana interest group had maintained its representation at the national level. Henríquez Gallo was reelected to a four-year term in the House of Representatives with 26 percent of the vote, more votes than any other candidate from Antioquia; and Senator Guerra was similarly reelected for the same period with more votes than any other candidate in the department. However, they had indeed lost significant ground to the Left at the county level. The proportion of votes for Guerrista Liberals in county council elections in Apartadó had been reduced from 44 percent to 33 percent between 1984 and 1986, and the proportion of votes for all traditional parties had been reduced from 69 percent to 51 percent.[64]

Henríquez Gallo clearly aimed to amplify this sense of Liberal alarm, drum up anticommunist sentiments, and mobilize Liberals to take back Apartadó:

The county is the basic cell of political life. . . . In the case of Apartadó, the apathy of the agricultural and banana sectors has allowed the Liberal and Conservative parties . . . to weaken to such an extent that they lost [the county elections] to anarchic forces that have been gaining ground rapidly and dangerously; today they control the administration of the most important county in Urabá. If we do not become aware of the urgent and unpostponable need to participate, the county of Apartadó will not have a Communist county executive appointed by the governor (and removable by him) but one directly elected for a period of two years [and] . . . not subject to any kind of supervision. These men [the elected officials of the UP] have to proceed in accordance with a philosophy, a doctrine, and a discipline which is dictated to them from a place far from Urabá. . . . The orders and the philosophy of the Communist Party are dictated . . . in Moscow or Peking.[65]

Henríquez Gallo proposed a two-pronged solution to the problem of political displacement by the Left. On the one hand, he urged the banana plantation owners to lobby hard for militarization of the region: "Security, which we request daily from the government, which we demand from the Armed Forces of the Republic, which we cry for from every trade organization, is something . . . that we must make the government aware of at every opportunity." On the other hand, while they waited for the government to respond, Henríquez Gallo issued a thinly veiled apology for paramilitary violence against the Left: "As long as [the president, the ministers, the governor, and the armed forces] give us slow, late, solutions that make us despair, we must form our own strategies." Furthermore, he constantly referred to the activists and elected officials of the UP, a legally sanctioned party, as subversives and anarchists, indistinguishable from armed insurgents: "What is of concern is not the fact that the subversives have 15,000 or 20,000 men in arms or that they have taken some county councils . . . ." Such an equation of armed insurgency with electoral activity was used to justify violent paramilitary actions against these noncombatants and contributed to impunity for their assassins.[66]

Just as Henríquez Gallo's diatribe had denounced the UP's electoral success rather than the material gains of the banana workers' movement, repression in 1986—more than in 1984 or 1985—was focused mostly on leaders from the UP and Sintrabanano and not on Sintagro or the Frente Popular. This occurred despite the fact that Sintagro was far more influential within the labor movement—Sintagro had organized about 70 percent of Urabá's workers and had initiated 63 percent of all negotiations in 1985 as compared to Sintrabanano's 20 percent—and that the EPL had abandoned the peace process while the FARC had not.[67] In Apartadó in 1984–85, attacks on the Frente Democrático, UP, Communist Party, and

Sintrabanano measured 1.3 on the total repression index of 12.0, or 11 percent, but in 1986 this increased to 3.55 out of 4.4 on the repression index, or 81 percent.[68] This sudden emphasis on UP-associated sectors among victims of political violence in 1986, as well as the fact that all the incidents of violent repression occurred after the March 1986 elections, indicates that Urabá's repressors found leftist political power even more offensive than organized labor power and also explains the apparent anomaly that violence was greater against the political tendencies closest to negotiating peace.[69]

Had circumstances been slightly more favorable to the Left, however, the bananeros might have been forced to coexist with their new sworn enemies via a "pacted peace," that is, an agreement between two opposing electoral forces to form an electoral alliance and cease violent attacks against each other. After all, in many ways 1984–87 was an optimal moment for the Left in Urabá, with impressive organizational and material gains by the banana workers' union, greatly increased Left electoral strength, and reduced repression as a result of the peace process. However, the desire of regional elites to reverse Left electoral gains, in the context of the continuing stability of banana elites, led to the increased militarization of the region. The deepening division between the two sectors of the Left further reduced the Left's ability to force a pacted solution to the regional confrontation with the bananero elites.

Reflecting the still-valid FARC-government peace agreement in 1985–86, levels of repression fell slightly in Apartadó. In 1984, 1985, and 1986 in Apartadó, the repression indexes were 7.3, 4.7, and 4.4 respectively (see fig. 2.2 and table 2.4). However, the *potential* for violent repression had increased. Although Henríquez Gallo complained that the banana plantation owners' demands for militarization had fallen on deaf ears, in fact the number of troops in the region had risen considerably. In 1984 the military presence was significantly increased in Urabá when troops from the IV Brigade were fortified by the establishment of the Batallón Voltígeros (a battalion usually has about 800 soldiers), headquartered at the military base in Carepa.[70] The increasing availability of state military forces, together with the plantation owners' economic stability, provided a disincentive for negotiation with the Left.

Furthermore, disunity prevented the two main tendencies of the Left from negotiating as a unified bloc. On November 30, 1985, due to the assassination of EPL political spokesperson Oscar William Calvo, this organization declared the end of its cease-fire with the government while

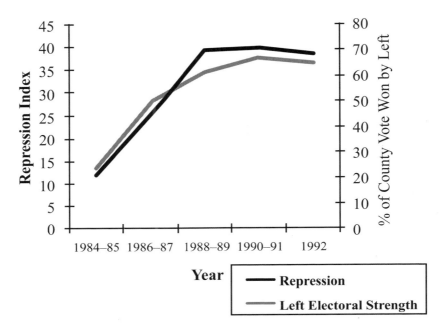

Figure 2.2. Repression and Left Electoral Success in Apartadó, 1984–1992

the FARC continued to pursue the peace process.[71] This turn of events brought a sudden halt to the tentative unity of the labor movement, souring relations between the FARC and the EPL, the UP and the Frente Popular, Sintrabanano and Sintagro. Conflict was manifested not only in the lack of coordinated actions between the two unions during this period but also in mutual denouncements of treachery. According to sources cited by Botero, Sintrabanano accused Sintagro of being anarchist, ignoring the possibilities for conciliation and dialogue, and creating obstacles to labor unity, and the UP accused Sintagro of being manipulated by the EPL. Meanwhile, Sintagro accused the FARC of acting as a fifth column and even of killing some of its activists. The political conjuncture had exacerbated long-standing underlying causes of disunity: the historical ideological antagonisms between the two groups and the underlying rivalry to control the labor movement.[72]

Table 2.4. Evolution of Conflict in Apartadó

Year	Repression Index	Left Electoral Success (percent)[a]	Number of Guerrilla-Army Combats
1984	7.3	24	No data
1985	4.7	—	2 with EPL
1984 + 1985	12.0	—	—
1986	4.4	50	1 with EPL
1987	20.75	—	2 with EPL
1986 + 1987	25.15	—	—
1988	23.25	61	15 with EPL; 3 with FARC
1989	16.1	—	4 with EPL
1988 + 1989	39.35	—	—
1990	32.75	67	1 with EPL; 4 with FARC
1991	7.0	—	4 with FARC; 1 with ELN
1990 + 1991	39.75	—	—
1992	19.25 doubled = 38.50	65	1 with EPL; 1 with FARC; 1 with ELN

Note: The repression index for 1992 is doubled to make it comparable to the figures for 1984–85, 1986–87, and 1988–89 without extending the analysis to the counterreform period. For additional explanation, operationalization, and sources for these data, see the methods section of chapter 1.

[a] Of those votes deposited for candidates who were elected to office, the percent that went to leftist candidates; data are recorded only for even-numbered years because no elections occurred in odd-numbered years.

This last factor had grown in importance after mid-1985, as the number of unorganized plantations rapidly dwindled and competition to control the remaining ones intensified. For example, one former plantation manager reported that in 1986 Sintrabanano had just finished signing a contract for the plantation when it became apparent that several of the workers belonged to Sintagro. This led to a struggle that ended in the death of two workers affiliated with Sintagro and the control of the plantation by Sintrabanano. The former plantation manager said this type of struggle had at times led to the massive resignations of workers. Figure 2.3 shows that while the FARC clearly controlled peasant zones from Apartadó south and the EPL just as clearly controlled peasant zones from Apartadó north, the "worker zones" in the banana axis—plantations and urban areas— were claimed (i.e., permanently contested) by the two groups. While each

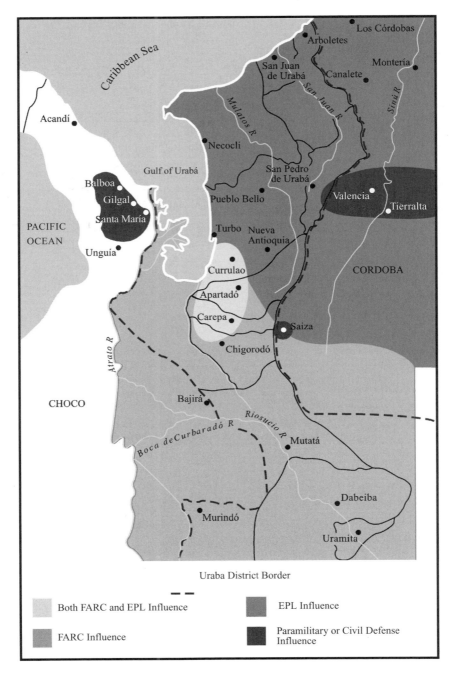

Figure 2.3. Armed Groups in Urabá as of 1991

Source: Uribe de Hincapié, *Urabá: ¿Región o territorio?,* map 7. With permission from Corpourabá and INER; redrawn by Emily Busch.

plantation eventually became affiliated with one or the other union, there was no geographic pattern to the affiliations: Sintagro and Sintrabanano (and other union) plantations were intermixed like a patchwork quilt, intensifying competition and antagonisms between the groups.[73]

The labor movement and the Left made tremendous gains between 1984 and 1987. The peace process with both the FARC and the EPL initiated a rapid process of declandestinization, with the most immediate result of greatly strengthening both banana workers' unions, boosting their militancy, and winning impressive gains for the workers. A slightly longer-term result was the greatly increased electoral representation of the Left, which helped to strengthen the Left's social movement base with the aid of the new leftist county executive. But these material gains and especially the political gains were highly threatening to the Guerrista banana elite, who called for increased militarization of the region and hinted at future paramilitary action to retake political institutions. The ongoing peace process in 1985–86 briefly interrupted the trend toward escalating violence. However, a full negotiated or pacted peace was prevented by the stability of the banana sector, the increased militarization of the region, and the division of the Left.

Early 1987–July 1990: Parallel Consolidation in the Left and among Elites

Between 1987 and 1990 the Left and the elites in Urabá solidified their respective positions, maintaining a regional stalemate that became increasingly violent as each side grew stronger and the conflict grew more polarized. The breakdown of the FARC-government peace process ironically facilitated intra-Left reunification, reflected in the labor movement as well as the electoral arena. Despite escalating repression, the continued success of the banana workers' union bolstered both social movement militancy and Left electoral success. Meanwhile, the first direct election of county executives in 1988 permitted the Left to retain control of Apartadó's local political institutions—now without fear of being removed from office by the governor—and advocate in favor of their social movement constituencies.

However, by 1990 Apartadó's elites were also considerably stronger than they had been in early 1987. Banana plantation owners in Urabá continued to maintain their departmental political influence and economic strength. Meanwhile, their regional political and military might was reinforced by the growth of the narco cattle ranching sector and its paramilitary forces. Military presence in the zone also increased considerably, and the three prongs of the antileftist project in Urabá—bananeros, narco cattle ranchers, and the military—increasingly coordinated their actions. By the end of the period, therefore, despite the remarkable strength and momentary unity of the Left, the concomitant strengthening of the rightist project continued to prevent a negotiated peace.

The View from Below

By the end of 1987 the FARC-government cease-fire had clearly broken down, ending a year of steadily worsening relations between that armed insurgency and the Executive. This development undeniably contributed to the sharp escalation of repression in 1987–90, but it also facilitated unprecedented steps toward leftist unity in Urabá, as the positions of the FARC and the EPL vis-à-vis the peace process became very similar. Both armed insurgencies were at war with the government, and both were intensifying their actions nationally and in Urabá, but both also made occasional attempts at dialogue. Both supported social movement activity, and by 1988 both engaged in electoral participation, as the Frente Popular became an electoral front.[74]

Within the labor movement, the strides toward unionization of the workforce were maintained, and militancy reached its highest point, with greater unity and greater success in winning bread-and-butter union demands. Joint negotiations were held in April 1987: Sintagro and Sintrabanano presented a unified list of demands and negotiated with AUGURA in Bogotá rather than with individual plantation owners in Urabá. Historic agreements were made to respect the minimum wage, the eight-hour workday (and forty-eight-hour week), housing, and other benefits, and additional provisions guaranteed job security and severely limited subcontracting. More strikes followed in 1987 to force individual plantation owners to respect the regional contract. In June the Apartadó local of Sintagro led a strike involving 400 workers. Another strike involved 70 workers and lasted eight days; and yet another involved 80 workers and lasted three days. Meanwhile, Sintrabanano had sixty-three plantations and 4,000 workers in negotiations and on strike alert for seventy-five days, but eventually negotiations were successful.

Just as the bananero elites had found labor and the Left's increased political power more threatening than labor's improved wages per se, however, the banana workers found it harder to win demands related to political citizenship than to win improved wages. For example, a regional mobilization held in September 1987, part of a national day of protest, demanded the elimination of the despised Statute of Security, a late 1970s presidential decree limiting freedom of organization for workers. Despite the UP-appointed Apartadó district attorney's support for the striking banana workers, a worker was killed during the strike, and the statute remained firmly in place. During this period, short work stoppages to protest human rights violations against labor became increasingly common: in 1987 three such strikes occurred, two of them involving almost all of Urabá's plantations. This showed not only that political demands were becoming the primary concern of workers but also that in this context of growing labor strength and unity, repression, instead of intimidating the labor movement into quiescence, made it even more militant.[75]

In 1988 the same pattern occurred: militancy continued, succeeding when the demands were strictly economic but failing when they were related to workers' political rights. Two small strikes with economic demands succeeded in Carepa, for example, both led by Sintagro. In the first, forty-five workers were on strike for fifteen days, winning 90 percent of their demands. In the second, thirty-five workers fought to defend previous wage, benefit, and organizing gains against the plantation owner's attempts to reverse them. Ultimately, workers not only maintained their previous gains, but even managed to advance a little. At the same time, however, the trend toward increased numbers of mostly unsuccessful strikes with political and human rights demands continued. In 1988 there were six strikes to protest assassinations and/or to demand the "right to live" *(derecho a la vida),* two peasant exoduses, and a peasant march.[76]

But the major social movement event of 1988 was the military ID card strike in September. In March a notorious massacre of more than twenty banana workers—in which members of the army were later found to be complicit—had taken place in Currulao (a subdivision of Turbo next to Apartadó). Four more massacres occurred by September, with some evidence of bananero complicity as well. In April President Barco had created a new Urabá Military Headquarters (Jefatura Militar) as part of a military solution to the region's crisis. Given the military's role in the year's massacres, workers were outraged when the new military chief for Urabá, General Arias Cabrales, ordered all banana workers to inform the battalion about their movements and to carry special ID cards that would include personal data about the worker and his or her family. Labor leaders argued that the ID cards would facilitate selective assassinations and demanded the withdrawal of the proposal, as well as Arias's resignation. General Arias countered by citing the need to prevent access of nonemployees (read: guerrillas or political organizers) to plantation work areas; plantation owners supported his proposal.[77]

The strike broke out on September 15. Led by both Sintrabanano and Sintagro, it quickly spread to involve virtually all workers in the region. Both a mainstream weekly magazine and an alternative Left-leaning publication stated that 26,000 workers participated and used the term *insurrection* to describe the strike. A week later the strike became a massive general protest that paralyzed commerce and transportation in the four banana axis urban centers, coinciding with the exodus of five thousand peasants to the urban center of Apartadó and some acts of sabotage by the guerrillas against packing plants and electric infrastructure. By the end of the strike AUGURA estimated that plantation owners had lost more than U.S.$1.5 million.[78] Eventually, though, a compromise emerged. General Arias was forced to withdraw his proposal, but the union and AUGURA agreed to a campaign to provide workers with ID cards furnished by their employers—already the status quo on many plantations. However, General Arias remained in his post, and many plantation owners began to call for the cancellation of the legal charters of Sintagro and Sintrabanano.[79]

Soon they got their way. But the repressive measure did not have the intended effect. The two main unions, as well as the tiny Sindejornaleros, which was ideologically affiliated with the ELN, promoted and then participated in a national day of protest on October 27, 1988, which had been declared illegal by the Ministry of Labor; the national government responded by canceling the legal charters of the three unions, preventing them from engaging in collective bargaining. Ironically, however, this repressive act was the key to cementing labor unity in the region. Workers responded to the measure by disaffiliating from Sintagro, Sintrabanano, and Sindejornaleros and reaffiliating with Sintrainagro, a national union of agroindustrial workers with few members but with a charter that had been legal since 1974. Thus the three unions became one, and Sintrainagro was recognized as the legal bargaining agent for the banana workers by the Ministry of Labor.[80]

In 1989 the wave of militancy continued, and the success of the labor movement was enhanced by its new unity. In addition to four small strikes that protested incidents of political violence,[81] Sintrainagro had its first regional strike. In June 1989 Sintrainagro presented a unified list of demands, covering 186 plantations, to AUGURA. The top priority was to negotiate the parameters for collective bargaining, with Sintrainagro pushing for agreements to be negotiated with AUGURA, in Bogotá, then ratified plantation by plantation, and AUGURA arguing for a continuation of the plantation-by-plantation, union versus individual plantation owners status quo. One month later, however, the union won—from AUGURA, after negotiations in Bogotá—almost all its demands regarding social benefits: health, housing, education, and transportation subsidies.[82]

But winning the remaining demands would require a struggle. In late August negotiations continued, focusing on salary, bonuses, and legal conditions for organizing: closed shops, leave to perform union duties, and the all-important right to live for banana workers, in particular, their leaders, making it the plantation owners' responsibility to protect their workers.[83] One by one, the stages of legal arbitration were exhausted. Meanwhile, on October 21, two members of the union's negotiating committee were assassinated. This was the last straw: on November 5 the workers voted to strike. On November 7 the strike became a general protest. In Turbo 1,400 peasants took over the county administration building, and similar protests occurred in Necoclí and Apartadó. Workers set up tents in the plaza in front of the county administration buildings, where they remained for thirty-three days.[84]

By November 20 conversations were reinitiated in Medellín, and by the end of November an agreement was finally reached that gave workers 70 percent of their demands, including a salary increase of 30 percent (slightly larger than the rate of inflation), a 27 percent increase in bonuses, leave for union duties, and wage increases tied to productivity—but again, no "right to live" guarantees. While this was a very successful strike in terms of material concessions, the more significant result was the profound alteration of the pattern of labor conflict and negotiations in Urabá. Negotiations plantation by plantation would become a thing of the past; the new norm would be negotiations between AUGURA and Sintrainagro, at two-year intervals, in Bogotá. This change not only brought a new era of relative labor peace to the region; it reduced the direct influence of armed actors in the negotiation process.[85] In other words, a major step toward institutionalization of class conflict mediation had occurred.

As evidence of this new pattern, in 1990 there were neither regional nor plantation-wide labor conflicts, although there were two one-day work stoppages to protest repressive violence: one to protest the Pueblo Bello massacre of more than twenty banana workers on January 14 and the other to protest the assassination of the UP county executive of Apartadó.[86]

The wave of unified militancy between 1987 and 1990 led to a further strengthening of the labor organization as well as significant improvements in wages and working conditions. The total number of workers affiliated with Sintagro and Sintrabanano (or those tendencies within Sintrainagro) remained stable in Urabá and Apartadó (see table 2.1). By 1991 an AUGURA-commissioned publication reported that more than 85 percent of the banana labor force was unionized, one of the highest unionization rates in the country.[87]

However, plantation owners in Urabá began to vote with their feet, responding to the success of Urabá's labor movement by investing in new banana plantations in Santa Marta rather than in Urabá. After representing 93 percent of national banana production in 1981, Urabá's share of national banana exports dropped to 74 percent by 1990 as Santa Marta's production increased (see table 2.3 for sources and full series). However, organizers of the banana workers' union were not far behind: a new local of Sintrainagro was founded in Santa Marta in 1991.[88]

The increased militancy, unity, and success of the labor movement allowed the electoral Left to advance markedly by March 1988, when the first direct election of county executives was held. In Apartadó the worst fears of Henríquez Gallo, the Guerrista political representative of the banana plantation owners, were realized: not only had the UP repeated its electoral showing of 1986, with 46 percent of the vote, but it had also formed a coalition with the now electorally active Frente Popular, which had contributed another 11 percent of the vote.[89] And despite the continuing high level of repression against the Left between 1988 and 1990, both the UP and the Frente Popular maintained their electoral strength within local politics two years later. In addition, the two continued to be electoral allies, forming coalitions to successfully elect a representative to the House and a Departmental Assembly member in 1990. In Apartadó the UP, again in coalition with the Frente Popular, won the 1990 county executive race.[90] The UP's share of the county council vote shrank slightly to 44 percent in 1990, but since the Frente Popular's share of the vote increased from 11 percent to 16 percent, total Left electoral strength increased from 57 percent to 60 percent between 1988 and 1990.[91] Given the intensity of repression, this small electoral gain is remarkable and can be attributed to the banana workers' union's remarkable success: activists who were killed or intimidated into quiescence were replaced by others willing to fight for the labor concessions still to be won.

While both the UP and the Frente Popular were successful electorally, the above figures demonstrate that the Patriotic Union was much more so, even though Sintagro's membership was three times that of Sintrabanano at that point in time (about 60 percent of all unionized banana workers, as compared to about 20 to 30 percent).[92] According to interviewees from both political tendencies, as well as precinct-level voting results, this phenomenon is due to two factors. First, the Patriotic Union had many more years of electoral experience than did the Frente Popular. The Communist Party, the largest of the groups that coalesced to become the UP, had been electorally active since its founding in the 1930s, whereas the Frente Popular first participated in elections in 1988, inspired by the direct election of county executives. Second, the UP/Communist Party had organized more and larger urban squatters' neighborhoods than the Frente Popular, especially in Apartadó, and therefore had more influence in urban areas. In contrast, those that sympathized with the Frente Popular were more likely to live in the work camps.[93]

All interviewees agreed that workers who lived in urban areas were more likely to vote than those who lived in work camps. Urban residents had to wrest any infrastructural improvements of their neighborhoods (extension of water and electrical lines, street pavement and drainage, etc.) from city hall, whereas work camp residents had to win these improvements directly from the banana plantation owner via the collective bargaining process, a process in which county politics was nearly irrelevant. In late 1990, perhaps realizing the electoral advantages of an urban rather than work camp–based electorate, the Frente Popular began to sponsor squatter invasions, especially in Apartadó.[94]

If social movement influence translated into votes, it was also true that electoral strength further strengthened the base movements of workers, urban worker neighborhoods, and peasant settlers. Pro-urban neighborhood public works during the 1988–90 period, when Apartadó's directly elected UP county executive presided, included the purchase of land for and legalization of two urban squatters' neighborhoods invaded by the Frente Democrático in 1983, the provision of basic urban infrastructure in the urban workers' neighborhoods (street drainage, pavement, street lights, running water, electricity, etc.), the establishment of a new cobblestone-making community enterprise in one of these UP urban strongholds, and the establishment of a fund to subsidize workers' housing and home improvement loans. However, it seems the UP's control of city hall also forced a reevaluation of strategy by the Communist Party's housing organization in Apartadó. From 1989 on, the housing organization no longer promoted invasions but rather acted as intermediary for collective purchases of land. In this way they avoided repression as well as the politically awkward dilemma of forcing a county executive from the UP to sign a legally mandated eviction order against UP-organized squatters. Regardless, urban squatters continued to be a central constituency of the UP in Apartadó, as two of the UP's six 1990–92 county council members were associated with this movement. Peasant areas, meanwhile, especially benefited from another major public works category: the construction of schools, the hiring of teachers, and the opening of school cafeterias.[95]

Workers were especially favored by leftist county executives' intervention in strikes on behalf of labor (or as pro-labor mediators), the provision of meeting spaces and demonstration permits, and pro-union public declarations. For example, in the late 1980s Apartadó's county administration helped promote a union-initiated boycott of Colombian bananas through the Colombia solidarity organizations in Europe and hosted international human rights delegations that came to visit the region.[96] Similarly, during the 1988 military ID strike, Apartadó's county executive mediated by arranging meetings between army, union, and AUGURA officials, and his actions were central to the compromise that eventually emerged.[97] Then in October 1988, shortly before the national day of protest that had been declared illegal, the county executive met with the army to try to minimize repression.[98] And in November 1989, when Sintrainagro's negotiations with AUGURA had reached an impasse and workers had camped out in each county's central plaza for thirty-three days, Apartadó's UP county executive worked to improve the physical conditions for the protesters (providing food, water, sanitary measures, etc.). She also intervened to prevent the army from evicting the strikers from the plaza in Apartadó, allowing the protesters to stay and minimizing army harassment. Further, she went to Medellín to advance negotiations, a step judged by the labor leaders I interviewed to be crucial to the eventual successful resolution (from labor's point of view) of the five-month conflict.[99]

The UP county executives of Apartadó also acted as human rights advocates for their constituents before authorities and served as liaisons to international solidarity movements. In early 1989 Apartadó's county executive negotiated directly with the local military commanders regarding harassment of the population, persuading him to switch from a "drain the sea" strategy to a "hearts and minds" strategy typified by civic-military acts—a decided improvement. Furthermore, leftist elected officials in Apartadó gave social movements new political resources, legitimacy, and connections with national and international allies. As soon as a human rights violation occurred in the banana-producing county, the fax machine in the county administration building sent off the labor movement's account of the incident to political allies and human rights organizations locally, in department capitals, in Bogotá, and even in international solidarity and human rights groups.[100]

By early 1990, then, repressive measures such as suspension of charters, labor's inability to win human rights and political demands without unity, and the similar position of the EPL and the FARC with regard to the peace process facilitated unity. This greatly strengthened the labor movement, which led to continued success in extracting concessions from the banana plantation owners as well as a more institutionalized model of labor relations by the end of the period. Labor success, in combination with the direct election of county executives, which stimulated the Frente Popular's first electoral participation, translated into increased electoral success for the Left, especially the UP. Finally, the increased leftist representation in local political institutions allowed leftist elected officials to offer strategic aid to their social movement base.

The View from Above

While the Left advanced, the elite side of the local balance of power matched them stride for stride. Banana plantation owners, the military, and especially paramilitary groups backed by narco cattle ranchers each gained in absolute strength and also became more closely linked as they cooperated to repress the Left. With the breakdown of FARC-government negotiations as a backdrop, repression against the noncombatant Left sharply escalated.

Despite their loss of the Apartadó county administration to the Left (the Guerrista county council lists garnered only 24 percent and 19 percent of the vote, respectively, in 1988 and 1990, even though the 1988 list was headed by Henríquez Gallo himself), the Guerrista Liberals continued to be well represented at the departmental level. Guerra Serna, the faction's leader, was the most successful departmental assembly candidate in 1988, winning 26 percent of the vote. Also elected on his slate was Diego Miguel Sierra Botero, executive director of AUGURA in 1986. In March 1990 Sierra was elected senator with 27 percent of the departmental vote, and in the same election Henríquez Gallo was reelected to the House of Representatives with 23 percent of the departmental vote.[101] Furthermore, with the sharp reduction of coffee prices that occurred after 1986, the relative and strategic importance of bananas as an agricultural export increased. Whereas in 1988 the value of banana exports was 18 percent that of coffee exports, by 1990 that proportion had increased to 23 percent.[102]

The militarization of Urabá also increased markedly during this period, reflecting the importance of the region for the president as well as the breakdown of the peace process. Whereas in 1984 there was only the Voltígeros Battalion in Carepa, in 1987 the XI Brigade was created in Montería (the capital of the contiguous department, Córdoba); by decision of the national Ministry of Defense, its jurisdiction included Urabá. At the insistence of AUGURA, in April 1988 the Military Headquarters of Urabá was created and was maintained through July 1990. Although General Arias, the regional military chief, had failed in his attempt to impose the military ID card, in other ways the military's project had prospered. With the creation of the Jefatura Militar, Urabá became the region with the greatest number of troops per square kilometer. As part of the changes in 1988, the X Brigade was also created in Carepa, and in 1989 yet another battalion was added: the Batallón Francisco Paula de Vélez in Chigorodó. This brought the total number of soldiers in the banana axis alone to about 1,600 by 1989.[103]

The third element in the strengthening of the Right in Urabá during this period was perhaps the most deadly: the growth of narco paramilitary groups, death squads sponsored by the beneficiaries of the cocaine boom of the mid- to late 1980s. These drug lords invested their gains in enormous landholdings (usually cattle ranches, due to the liquidity of this activity relative to other agricultural endeavors) in regions with guerrilla presence. Having done so, they became violently anticommunist, attempting to "clean" their regions of guerrillas not by attacking the insurgents themselves but by killing those perceived as guerrilla sympathizers. One 1988 estimate placed the number of hectares purchased by drug traffickers at one million in the nation, with 46 percent of that total in the environs of Urabá—300,000 hectares in Córdoba and 160,000 in the north of Antioquia, including Urabá. In 1989–90 the Colombian Institute for Agrarian Reform confiscated some of these narco landholdings: ten in Urabá, four in Córdoban counties contiguous to Urabá, and three more on the Gulf of Urabá in Chocó (see fig. 2.1).[104]

Activists identified one narco cattle rancher as especially central to the region's paramilitary groups: Fidel Castaño. Rabidly anticommunist, Castaño designated two of his many ranches in Córdoba as his center of operations. He had close ties to the Medellín cartel during its heyday (1986–90) and was considered a key part of its military wing, especially after 1989. His own paramilitary force consisted of three hundred men who were strictly accountable to him and had a well-developed and well-financed communication and transportation infrastructure.[105] Through connections to a vast network of local rancher-sponsored self-defense groups, Castaño's paramilitary infrastructure extended its radius of action to the south of Córdoba and the north of Urabá. By 1990 the police listed paramilitary bases in all of the banana axis counties of Urabá, as well as Arboletes and Necoclí in the north of Urabá. In the same year several mass graves were discovered on Castaño's properties in Urabá, and a deserter from his organization reported that between January 1989 and April 1990 he had witnessed ninety-five executions.[106]

A number of notorious examples indicate that Castaño's paramilitary infrastructure was tolerated and even aided by the armed forces, but the organizational links between the narco paramilitary apparatus, the army, and the banana plantation owners were revealed most clearly by a series of massacres carried out during this period.[107] The first occurred on March 4, 1988, on two plantations in Currulao, the banana axis subdivision of Turbo immediately contiguous to Apartadó. Twenty-eight workers affiliated with Sintagro were murdered in this incident. According to an investigation by DAS (the Colombian equivalent of the FBI), in the weeks before the massacre a captured EPL guerrilla had accompanied army personnel to identify members of the EPL's support network on the two plantations. The massacre itself may well have been carried out directly by army personnel, the DAS report concluded, but with the important financial support of banana plantation owners. Castaño's organization was linked to this massacre as well.[108] A subsequent judicial report implicated three military officials, a police lieutenant, the county executive of Puerto Boyacá, and eleven civilians. The report presented evidence that an army major from the Voltígeros Battalion in Carepa had contracted with assassins from Puerto Boyacá, the paramilitary stronghold in the Magdalena Medio region, and lodged them in Medellín prior to the massacre.[109]

The examples of narco-military complicity became more frequent. Just two days after the March 4, 1988, massacre in Currulao, an activist in the organization Juventud Trabajadora Colombiana (JTC) was killed; his assassin fled into the police station. Between August 1988 and June 1989 a series of five collective assassinations occurred in the banana axis. In each incident the killers had exact information about the victims and left the site of the massacres without hurrying, encountering resistance, or being detected at military checkpoints. On January 14, 1990, forty-two peasants were "disappeared" from Pueblo Bello, a Frente Popular stronghold in Turbo. The bodies of seven of them were discovered on Fidel Castaño's properties in Córdoba. In Apartadó massacres occurred on March 13 and 28, 1990.[110]

Overall, due to the strengthening of the Right (banana plantation owners, the military, and the narco paramilitary apparatus), the level of repression rose markedly between the end of 1986 and mid-1990. This occurred despite clear trends toward the institutionalization of labor conflict and the reduction in number of strikes after 1989. For the entire region of Urabá, Botero notes that the average number of assassinations per month increased from 13.58 in 1986 to 24.75 in 1987 and 45.75 in 1988.[111] Similarly, in 1986 the repression index in Apartadó was 4.4, but in 1987 it nearly quintupled, to 20.75, and rose again in 1988 to 23.25. It fell slightly in 1989 to 16.1 (probably because 1989 was not an election year) and then rose even further to 32.75 in 1990.[112]

In contrast to 1986, when the UP was clearly the main target of repression, during this period—January 1987 through the end of July 1990—

most of the victims sympathized with the Frente Popular. The three major massacres in Turbo (March 4, 1988; May 11, 1988; January 14, 1990) and another notorious massacre of twenty-eight people that occurred in central Córdoba on April 3, 1988, were all aimed at Frente Popular sympathizers, as were most repressive incidents in Apartadó and Carepa. This changed repressive strategy may be due to two main factors. First, the Frente Popular became electorally active in 1988 and signed a preliminary peace accord with the government in late July 1990.[113] If the repressors' preference for the UP in the previous period was a reaction to their success in the peace process and the electoral arena, the Frente Popular had now become a serious contender as well. Second, Fidel Castaño's paramilitary apparatus was especially strong in EPL-influenced areas (Córdoba, north of Urabá; see fig. 2.3). Thus the EPL and its perceived collaborators were his natural enemies.[114]

In conclusion, despite the considerable progress made by the Left in unifying and strengthening its labor and electoral organizations during these years, the Left was not able to increase its overall leverage relative to elites in the region. Even as the Left became stronger, so did the Right, with banana plantations economically stable, narco cattle ranchers and their paramilitary apparatus in rapid expansion, greatly increased militarization of the region, and considerable coordination between the three groups. Thus elites had few incentives to negotiate with the Left; rather, they had reason to believe the Left could be defeated by means of repressive violence.

July 1990 to November 1991: A Brief Regional and Labor Negotiated Peace

By mid-1990 the stalemate began to resolve in favor of elite military dominance. By the time the EPL negotiated its preliminary peace accord in July 1990, the group had been severely weakened by the narco paramilitary attacks—especially those led by Fidel Castaño—against its peasant base in Córdoba and Urabá.[115] Given this history, the EPL hoped to negotiate nonaggression agreements to prevent the wave of post–peace agreement violence that had plagued the Patriotic Union. Leaders of the EPL initiated contacts with Ariel Otero, a paramilitary leader from the Magdalena Medio, and also with Fidel Castaño himself. In fact, Castaño went as far as to turn 10,000 hectares of his land in Córdoba into a foundation for peasants. According to a consultant to a national Esperanza leader, much of this land was given to demobilized EPL guerrillas in early 1991.[116]

The government's conciliatory gesture of July 1990 was to grant one of the labor movement's central demands since early 1988: the withdrawal from the region of the Jefatura Militar. The peace process with the EPL culminated on March 1, 1991, when the group disarmed and became Esperanza, Paz y Libertad, projecting a peaceful image while keeping the same acronym. Its demobilization agreement granted Esperanza two representatives in the February–July 1991 Constitutional Assembly. By December 1991 a total of 2,149 EPL guerrillas had demobilized, soliciting access to government programs for *reinsertados*.[117]

In contrast to the EPL's weak position in relation to the paramilitary groups, Esperanza sympathizers negotiated from a position of strength in Urabá's banana industry labor relations. Esperanza-line workers and union leaders continued to make up 71 percent of Sintrainagro in Urabá, and the union had maintained the same number of workers as in 1989, even gaining two hundred members in Carepa and sixty in Apartadó between 1990 and 1991. The new institutionalized model of labor relations established in 1989 continued to hold, creating precedent for less conflictive labor relations. AUGURA thus had significant incentive to make the government-EPL peace agreement work by cultivating good relations with Esperanza as the 1991 contract negotiations approached.[118]

Conversely, soured AUGURA-Esperanza relations could easily induce some demobilized guerrillas to return to the armed struggle. While all of the EPL in Urabá had demobilized in March 1991 and in general Esperanza-line Sintrainagro leaders remained committed to the peace process, in Córdoba in late 1990 the dissident EPL commander Francisco Caraballo had broken from the rest of the EPL to continue the armed struggle, and his faction was growing quickly. AUGURA members were anxious to prevent its spread to the banana axis.[119]

Consequently, both AUGURA and Esperanza engaged in unprecedented conciliatory actions and rhetoric. In July 1991, for the first time ever, representatives of the union were invited to the Banana Congress (held in Cartagena). Esperanza's message opened, "We have come to this important Banana Congress by the very kind invitation of AUGURA . . . because we believe our modest contribution here can serve to strengthen the good labor relations that today predominate in Urabá."[120] Furthermore, in conjunction with the department of Antioquia, AUGURA had donated $23 million pesos (approximately U.S.$33,000) to a special peace fund to facilitate the former insurgents' economic reinsertion into society. AUGURA, Esperanza, and the regional diocese also collaborated to design a social pact to address the basic needs of the population. In return, Esperanza activists would promote increased productivity.[121]

An unprecedented labor peace reigned in Urabá during 1991. There were no small strikes in Apartadó, and for the first time ever, in November 1991, significant concessions were gained by the union without a strike and without assassinations of the negotiating committee members during the negotiations (although some would occur later). Both parties compromised: workers asked for a 55 percent raise but accepted 30 percent and asked for a 50 percent improvement in benefits but accepted 31 percent. They also got about 40 percent of what they had requested in terms of improved organizing conditions. But as one organizer put it, "The people were satisfied." Esperanza delivered on its promise to improve productivity. In 1991 the number of boxes of bananas exported from Urabá and the number of tons per hectare reached all-time highs of 51,000 and 42.9, respectively.[122] Thus the EPL's demobilization contributed to a regional negotiated peace from mid-1990 through the end of 1991 by placating paramilitary forces through a virtual capitulation, yet at the same time inspiring the bananeros to seek Esperanza's continued acquiescence by granting concessions to a labor organization at the height of its strength.

In contrast to the EPL, the FARC was far from being militarily defeated in 1990 and had rejected the terms of demobilization proposed by President Gaviria—demobilize first, then negotiate—when the EPL had accepted them.[123] However, for several reasons, Esperanza's conciliatory gestures toward the government, the paramilitary forces, and AUGURA were tolerated by the FARC and even emulated to some extent by UP-line Sintrainagro leaders and the UP itself through late 1991. First, after reaching a point of maximum mutual hostility after the December 1990 attack on FARC headquarters, FARC-government relations began to thaw, and the FARC, EPL dissidence, and the ELN reengaged in peace dialogues from April 1991 through March 1992. Although ultimately unsuccessful, the negotiation process did prevent an escalation of the armed conflict in Urabá and elsewhere. In Apartadó, for example, there was no change in the number of armed confrontations between 1990 and 1991.[124]

UP-line Sintrainagro leaders were not entirely satisfied with Esperanza's new cordial relations with management. Many felt Esperanza should press harder, given the stable banana economy and impressive labor strength at that moment. Yet the UP union delegates "tagged along" with Esperanza's initiatives rather than breaking ranks because Esperanza was the majority force in Sintrainagro and because the UP could derive most of the benefits from Esperanza's good relations with AUGURA—no strike, satisfactory concessions, social spending in the region—without acquiring the same implicit commitments to unconditional support of demobilization of armed insurgencies.[125]

The UP county executive of Apartadó from 1990 to 1992 went further, actively initiating parallel conciliation efforts. He pursued improved relations with the military and the regional diocese (which in the past had been typical of Colombia's church hierarchy as a whole in its sympathy to elite interests). He also hoped to win new constituencies for the UP—the urban middle class and especially downtown merchants—through public works focused on public urban areas and wealthier urban residents. These included the new marketplace, a transportation terminal to decongest the downtown, the long overdue paving and beautification of the main street through town, and the crowd-pleasing giant satellite dish mounted on top of the county administration building, which functioned as a repeater and allowed all owners of TV sets in Apartadó to receive international cable TV, with perfect reception, at no charge.[126]

A key benefit of the Esperanza-AUGURA Social Pact was a dramatic reduction in repression during 1991 in Apartadó. This began earlier in larger Urabá, as Uribe argues, due to both the EPL demobilization and the termination of the military headquarters in Carepa in July 1990 (although the two battalions and the X Brigade remained). In Apartadó 1991 was the least violent year since 1986: the repression index dropped from 32.75 in 1990 to 7.0 in 1991. A military source concurred that this was a regional trend, estimating that violence in all of Urabá in 1991 was a third of the 1990 level.[127]

Immediately after the EPL's first negotiations, only that political tendency was protected from violence. Whereas the Frente Popular had been the main focus of repression from early 1987 to July 1990, from July to December 1990 the UP was disproportionately targeted. Of the victims with known political affiliations in Apartadó during this period, eight were from the UP and none from the Frente Popular.[128] Once the FARC and other guerrilla groups recommenced peace negotiations in 1991, however, Esperanza and the UP were equally protected (or targeted). Of the four victims in Apartadó in 1991 with known political affiliations, two were from the UP and two were from Esperanza.[129]

Despite the conciliatory rhetoric that predominated, the relative peace of 1991 was perceived as a green light by the region's social movements, which escalated their activities. A 12,000-person mobilization, led by the UP in May 1991, protested the establishment of a free trade zone in Urabá. Furthermore, a virtual explosion of urban squatter invasions had followed the closure of work camps after 1989, itself an indirect result of the labor movement's success in winning improved wages and working conditions. In Apartadó the UP's housing organization facilitated the collective purchase of one neighborhood for seventy families, and Esperanza activists carried out their first urban land invasion in Apartadó. UP sources said the "La Paz" invasion involved fifteen hundred families who squatted on land owned by a banana plantation owner. The (UP) county executive, again seeking conciliation and unity with Esperanza (and vice versa), purchased land in another part of the city, and most of the squatters moved to the new site. An Esperanza source claimed the archdiocese, not the county executive, took the initiative for the solution, and the governor was also involved in the negotiation.[130] Given the size and frequency of these invasions, it is noteworthy that they did not provoke incidents of repression, due to the region's negotiated peace at that moment.

A broader geographic view of Esperanza's experience, however, revealed problems on the horizon. Esperanza's activists were not nearly as protected from paramilitary violence as their pacts with paramilitary leaders had led them to expect. By July 1991 eight "Esperanzados" (lit., "Hopeful Ones") had been killed in Urabá, primarily in Turbo and San Pedro de Urabá, and by October the group would announce that more than forty of its activists had been killed nationally. That the overwhelming majority of these incidents were attributed to paramilitary groups or the armed forces had crucial implications. In 1991 it strengthened the cause of the EPL dissidence—those EPL guerrillas who had returned to armed struggle— leading to the establishment of a new front in Urabá;[131] provided a rationale for the FARC's and the ELN's return to a more bellicose position; and later inspired Esperanza's renewed attempts at rapprochement with paramilitary forces.

Late 1991 to Late 1992: The Negotiated Peace Unravels

Although in many ways social movements and the electoral Left in Urabá were stronger, more active, and more effective than ever, a number of factors undermined the negotiated regional peace of late 1990–91. First and foremost, the government's termination of peace negotiations hardened the position of the still-active insurgencies. Guerrilla activity escalated and intra-Left relations disintegrated into violence, with these tensions reflected in social movement and electoral activity as well. Meanwhile, the new national emphasis on neoliberal reforms and exports gave banana exporters unprecedented access to the Executive, which they used to obtain the further militarization of the region. These factors, together with the intensification of paramilitary activity in the north of Urabá, caused a new escalation of rightist violence in 1992.

Intra-Left unity in Urabá was dealt a serious blow in late 1991, when the EPL dissidence began to assassinate demobilized Esperanzados, accusing them of sharing military secrets with Castaño's organization and the armed forces. The first such assassination in Urabá occurred in November 1991, and at least two, possibly as many as ten, took place in Apartadó in the first half of 1992. *Justicia y Paz* figures reveal that between October 1991 and late April 1992, nearly fifty Esperanzados had been killed nationally, mostly by the EPL dissidence, Esperanza sources claimed, but also by paramilitary groups.[132] By the end of 1992, *Justicia y Paz* reported, nine Esperanzados were killed in Apartadó, presumably by the dissidence but possibly by paramilitary groups acting under cover of the dissidence's onslaught.[133]

The demobilized EPL guerrillas, or Esperanzados, appealed to the state for protection, and by mid-1992 they were allowed to have armed escorts and to form a new militia group called the Comandos Populares, which reportedly received support from the army and its intelligence agency, the SIJIN. Needless to say, this made the Esperanzados even more suspect in the eyes of their rivals—not just their former comrades in the EPL dissidence but now the FARC and the UP as well.[134]

During the dialogues of 1991 and early 1992, the FARC had made some attempts to restrain the EPL dissidence's attacks on Esperanza. As the dialogues were ending (April–May 1992), Esperanza leaders, recognizing the potential for escalated attacks on its members, met formally with the Simón Bolívar national guerrilla coordinating committee (CGSB, composed primarily of the FARC, the ELN, and the EPL dissidence) to try to obtain the FARC's continued support in this regard. However, these efforts were in vain. The FARC's role in reining in the EPL dissidence ended abruptly once the CGSB-government negotiations broke down, radicalizing the actions and philosophies of CGSB members and widening the already existing gulf between them and the now state-protected Esperanzados.[135]

Shortly thereafter, guerrilla-army combat increased dramatically over 1991 levels, and EPL dissidence military presence expanded rapidly. Whereas in 1991 there was only one incidence of combat in Urabá involving this group, in 1992 there were twenty-two, almost all after June 1.[136] Given the vastly superior force of the FARC in the region, it seems this EPL dissidence expansion was at the very least tolerated by the FARC. Thus, by the end of 1992, the FARC was viewed as complicit in the dissidence attacks, at least by omission. What had once been a powerful unity was quickly on its way to becoming warring factions only nominally united by the banana workers' cause.

The FARC's increasingly complicit role vis-à-vis the anti-Esperanza violence perpetrated by the EPL dissidence after late 1991 and the increasingly close relation of the Comandos Populares with the army during this same period were the central issues dividing the Esperanzados and the UP activists within the union and in regional politics. However, conflicts in other areas—labor, squatter movements, and the electoral arena—both reflected and exacerbated this central conflict.

In late 1992, when I asked union leaders to retroactively evaluate the 1991 round of contract negotiations, Esperanza-aligned union leaders attributed the negotiations' success to the demobilization of the EPL, which they said made AUGURA more willing to invest in the region. Furthermore, they claimed that the UP-aligned union leaders had attempted to provoke a strike by pressing for too many concessions, too quickly, instead of following Esperanza's more prudent and moderate approach. One UP interviewee countered by referring to the Esperanzados in the union as *concertacionistas,* that is, individuals who preserved harmonious relations with the employer at the expense of worker interests.[137]

The emerging 1992 banana crisis accentuated the difference in approaches. That year, the European Economic Community (EEC), the destination of half of Urabá's banana exports, decided to favor bananas from its former colonies, through quotas and differential tariffs, starting in 1993.

Prices for all Latin American bananas soon dropped by as much as 28 percent in U.S. and European markets. When it became clear in 1992 that AUGURA would ask the union for givebacks and layoffs, UP-aligned leaders denounced the proposal, argued that AUGURA was exaggerating its dire straits, and called for continued real improvements in wages and working conditions. In contrast, Esperanza-line union leaders argued that the sector's crisis should be taken into consideration and demands reduced accordingly. This division weakened the overall bargaining position of the union, even though membership continued to be stable or even increase through 1992. At the regional level, Sintrainagro membership rose from 14,000 to 14,500, and in Apartadó it increased from 5,060 to 5,280.[138]

The explosive growth of the urban squatters' movement, though highly successful, greatly exacerbated UP-Esperanza tensions in Apartadó. After the success of the 1991 urban squatters' invasion in Apartadó, in early 1992 Esperanza confronted the UP county executive with two more squatters' invasions—apparently timed to boost Esperanza's electoral showing in the March 1992 county elections. UP county administrators viewed these actions as attempts to sabotage the planning process in a rapidly growing urban area and to discredit the Patriotic Union. The first invasion consisted of forty or fifty families who invaded a county-owned lot. While the squatters were not evicted, neither were the plots legalized immediately, revealing the UP's hardening position toward Esperanza.

And in an action that would irreversibly embitter relations between the two tendencies, in February 1992 Esperanza housing organizers challenged Apartadó's UP county executive with one of the world's largest squatter invasions: five thousand families squatted on 106 hectares belonging to a powerful and politically well-connected banana plantation owner, Guillermo Gaviria. Initially, Gaviria refused to negotiate with the squatters, calling for their eviction by force. Eventually, however, the county administration, the national government, the county priest, and county council members negotiated a multipartite solution for what would become known as the "La Chinita" invasion, later Barrio Obrero: the squatters would abandon 56 of the 106 hectares and consolidate on 50 hectares. Of the remaining 56 hectares, the department of Antioquia would buy 30 hectares, which the squatters would then buy in installments; AUGURA would similarly buy 6 hectares to resell to the squatters and the county 14 hectares. However, by late 1992 UP sources claimed more squatters had arrived, and the old ones had not consolidated on 50 hectares per the agreement, causing additional resentment of the UP toward Esperanza. An Esperanza source concurred that the original agreement fell apart but blamed it on self-aggrandizing gestures on the part of the UP.[139]

As always, both the changed peace process configuration and the squatters' invasions had immediate ramifications in the electoral arena. The Frente Popular had been the UP's coalition-mate in 1988 and 1990, but now Esperanza was an outright competitor—and an increasingly strong one. In Apartadó in 1988 and 1990 the Frente Popular had won 11 percent and 16 percent of the county council vote, respectively, but in 1992 Esperanza won 19 percent. In the 1992 county executive contest, Esperanza's candidate led a coalition against the UP that won 27 percent of the vote. With perhaps some extra effort to get out the vote, the UP slightly increased its share of the county council vote from 44 percent to 46 percent between 1990 and 1992 and once again won the county executive race, despite running alone.[140]

Finally, the peasant movement also experienced a moment of heightened activity. Although this did not exacerbate intra-Left antagonisms as other (shared between tendencies) movements had, it does demonstrate significant peasant social movement strength, which was especially threatening to elites. In December 1991 ten thousand peasant settlers from the mountainous cocoa-growing regions demanded restitution for army bombardments of their communities, with partial success. In July 1992, similarly, one thousand peasants mobilized again to demand the fulfillment of the government's commitments from the previous mobilization.[141]

In summary, the increasingly deep divisions within the Left, originating with the late 1991 EPL dissidence attacks on the Esperanzados and exacerbated by the end of the peace process with the CGSB-member armed insurgencies, were quickly reflected in the powerful but now bitterly divided labor movement, squatter movement, and electoral arena. Thus elites could now consider responding to the burgeoning social movement and Left electoral activity with a "divide and conquer" strategy.

Elites must have felt some urgency to respond, as this burst of social movement activity was coupled with a continued loss of electoral ground. The Guerrista Liberals' proportion of the county council vote continued to atrophy in Apartadó, from 45 percent in 1984 to 15 percent by 1992.

Apparently this trend was echoed elsewhere in the department of Antioquia as the Constitutional Assembly enacted new anticlientelist measures and new political forces entered the electoral fray. When a special new congressional election was held in October 1991, neither Jaime Henríquez Gallo nor Bernardo Guerra Serna nor any other plantation owner was elected to either the Senate or the House of Representatives. And although Guillermo Gaviria (owner of "La Chinita") was elected to Antioquia's Departmental Assembly for the 1992–94 period, he won only 3 percent of the votes.[142]

But local elites more than compensated for this electoral loss through rapid regional land concentration and increased national political influence. Due to the Gaviria administration's neoliberal economic approach prioritizing export sectors, AUGURA now enjoyed unprecedented access to the Executive. For example, in July 1991, for the first time, the minister of government attended and spoke at the annual Banana Congress, and the president of the republic himself sent a message of greeting, congratulating the plantation owners of Urabá on their spectacular growth and international competitiveness. AUGURA used this new access to lobby—successfully—for diplomatic support with respect to their struggle with the EEC. On August 17, 1992, Colombia's minister of foreign commerce convened a meeting of the banana-producing countries of Latin America to formalize a collective document rejecting the protectionist measures of the EEC.[143]

AUGURA also called for increased militarization, hoping to minimize or even eliminate concessions to the union in the upcoming contract negotiations due to the banana crisis and also neutralize the security threats of escalating guerrilla activity. Granting this request, in 1992, a new Operational Command was added to the army base in Carepa.[144] Filling the gap created when the military headquarters left in July 1990, the new militarization marked a symbolic end to the era of negotiated conciliation. The trend was reinforced by the national counterreform and State of Internal Commotion that was implemented in November 1992 and renewed three times, for three months each, before key provisions would be written into permanent law in late 1993.[145]

Meanwhile, by 1992 land conflicts in the north of Urabá intensified, as large cattle ranchers carried out an "agrarian counterreform," usurping peasant lands by means of paramilitary violence. Peasants—some sympathetic to the EPL dissidence—sought to resist them. In earlier periods paramilitary activity (the 1988 Curralao massacre, for example) had typically been organized from afar, with Fidel Castaño (headquartered in Córdoba) implicated. By 1992, however, the paramilitary and self-defense groups were actually based in the north of Urabá, in particular, Necoclí and San Juan de Urabá.[146] As the Comisión Verificadora, charged with carrying out a thorough investigation of Urabá's violence, noted, the fact that these paramilitary groups had never engaged in combat with the army— and to the contrary had been known to carry out joint actions with the armed forces—shows the continuing linkages between them.[147] As a result of all these conditions, rightist violence increased significantly in Apartadó, from a level of 7.0 in 1991 to 19.25 in 1992, about the same level as in 1987.[148]

The fragile negotiated peace that had held during 1991 broke down in 1992 for two main reasons. First, the division of the Left derived from the EPL dissidence attacks on the Esperanzados and the end of the peace process with the CGSB, bringing the escalation of combat, intramovement violence, and an end to the UP's (grudgingly) shared discourse of conciliation within the labor movement. Second, increased bananero access to the Executive, renewed militarization of the zone, and the growth of an autonomous, Urabá-based paramilitary infrastructure greatly strengthened the hand of elites in the regional balance of power. All these things further weakened the Left's bargaining leverage with respect to the Right, making the 1991 accord tragically brief.

CONCLUSION

In Urabá the economic stability of the banana sector, in combination with reform, created a strong and continuously successful banana workers' union. This labor success fostered other linked social movements and favored the construction of a stable and electorally strong Left, further reinforcing social movement strength. However, this strength was not enough to win a lasting regional negotiated peace with elites. Continuous expansion of elite economic and military power, as well as influence with the Executive Branch, gave regional elites both the will and the way to keep fighting to eliminate the Left. They were aided in their aims by the Left's bitter divisions, rooted in different postures with respect to the peace process as well as the inherent competitiveness of a labor-based (less territorial), rather than peasant-based, Left.

The peace process and democratic reform, in the context of a growing or stable banana economy, were crucial to the ability of the Left to construct powerful and effective labor organizations. Despite a booming banana economy from 1964 to 1983, labor progress had been blocked by the dearth of state mediating institutions. Reform made possible first the open and legal organization of banana workers in 1984, then by 1986–88 the electoral expression of worker, peasant, and urban squatter movements— including formerly abstentionist leftist and other nontraditional parties. Apartadó's newly elected leftist county executives were then able to use their newfound institutional political resources to benefit their worker, urban squatter, and peasant constituencies, intervening on their behalf in labor and other social conflicts and focusing public works expenditures on worker and peasant districts. After 1989, when the major unions of the region became one, the reform process bore fruit in the form of more formalized state mediation and negotiation procedures, resulting in lower levels of militancy but continued success, a clear-cut example of democratization leading (indirectly) to new conflict mediation institutions.

But the Left's gains were experienced as absolute losses by regional elites, who were adversely affected by both the peace process and democratic reforms. First, both plantation owners and large cattle ranchers were electorally displaced by the Left, losing access to both local and departmental political offices and resources as a result. This grievance clearly contributed to elite violence against the Left, perhaps even more than labor's economic gains. Not only was elite violence focused disproportionately on those sectors perceived to represent the greatest electoral threat; labor's economic gains were also won far more easily than their political demands such as human rights protections.

The steadily increasing electoral and mobilizational strength of the Left throughout the reform period—remarkable in its stability, despite high levels of repression, due to the continuous success of the banana workers' movement in wresting concessions from its employers—created incentives for negotiation as well as reaction on the part of regional elites. However, a regional peace was successful only briefly, from July 1990 through the end of 1991. During that period, AUGURA's efforts to maintain cordial relations with Esperanza were respected by the FARC, which was engaged in peace negotiations with the government and which in addition derived some indirect benefits from the Esperanza-AUGURA pact. However, by 1992 the negotiated peace failed, for two main reasons.

First, by late 1991 the Urabaense Right was growing in economic and political influence. Although no longer engaged in rapid economic expansion, the banana sector was enjoying increased national political influence due to the newly adopted neoliberal model, which favored export producers. Their access to the Executive facilitated the further militarization of the region in early 1992. The large cattle ranchers of northern Urabá, many linked to the drug economy, were also expanding both economically and geographically and were interested in expelling the Left—armed, elected, or organized—from the region. Weaker elites in other regions were forced to tolerate the Left's increased political and economic power after reform, but Urabá's elites, with a growing sense of efficacy and tripartite coordination (bananeros, narco cattle ranchers, and the military), continuously sponsored attempts to further militarize (and paramilitarize) the region to reverse the gains of the electoral Left and the labor movement through violence.

Second, the inherent division of the labor-based Left was accentuated by different insurgencies' disparate reactions to the peace process. In contrast to peasant regions where different guerrilla groups had distinct territories, with few overlapping jurisdictions, within Urabá's banana axis there was no clear geographic pattern to the influence by one tendency or another; rather, any unorganized plantations would be considered up for grabs. In addition, the isolation of the Esperanzados from the rest of Urabá's Left after the EPL's demobilization made the co-optation of the moderates that much more likely. Their peace-making attempts with elites were soon perceived by the armed Left as treachery; and Esperanza's resulting vulnerability to violence from still-active insurgencies led them to seek protection from the elites with whom they had pacted. Thus, in the context of overwhelmingly powerful regional elites and the violent division of the Left, one sector's attempt at peace-making induced the different sectors of the Left to turn against each other violently, later facilitating the attempts of the Right to retake Urabá.

THE COUNTERREFORM PERIOD IN URABÁ

Decimation of the Left, Right-Wing Unionism,
and Transnational Human Rights Alliances

In a neoliberal economic climate characterized by union givebacks and paramilitary scorched earth tactics against labor and peasant movements, the Esperanza-led banana workers of Urabá were exceptional in surviving the counterreform period with steady and even increased wages and benefits while becoming the leading electoral force of the region as well. They accomplished this by realigning with the Right and participating, at least by omission, in the violent destruction of the non-Esperanza Left. Some of the survivors of this paramilitary assault succeeded in transforming their strategy, successfully mobilizing transnational activism in their support. Meanwhile, by the end of the period, it seemed the Right-Esperanza alliance was weakening, with Esperanza showing both growing signs of independence from elites and internal dissension.

CHRONOLOGY OF CHANGE

1993–1997: Decimation of the UP and Solidification of Links between Esperanza, AUGURA, and the Military

By early 1993 the FARC's passive tolerance of the EPL dissidence's violent attacks on Esperanza had become active participation. The FARC

was implicated in the assassination of Alirio Guevara, president of Sintrainagro and Esperanza activist, on January 29, 1993. In revenge, on February 28 Esperanza's militia, the Comandos Populares, killed the general
secretary of Sintrainagro, a member of the Communist Party Central
Committee.[1] Many more examples of political assassinations committed
by the EPL dissidence and the FARC against Esperanza or by the Comandos Populares against the UP followed.

In 1993–94, as tensions between the FARC-EPL dissidence and Esperanza worsened, there was a sharp escalation of violence of the EPL
dissidence and the FARC against the Esperanzados, especially in Apartadó.
When the EPL dissidence virtually ceased to exist with the June 1994 imprisonment of its leader, Francisco Caraballo, the FARC continued the attacks on the Esperanzados.[2] These actions were rationalized, in the eyes of
the assassins, by Esperanza's increasing closeness to paramilitary and military leaders but served, in the eyes of the Esperanzados, to further justify
the necessity of that alliance. The political violence index against Esperanza members rose from 9.0 in 1992 to 25.75 in 1993 and 37.25 in 1994
(fig. 3.1)—the latter figure mostly from a single massacre in April by the
FARC in the Esperanza-organized squatter invasion of La Chinita. FARC
combat levels also increased: four armed confrontation in 1993 and five in
1994, compared to three in 1992.[3]

The FARC's turn against pursuing goals through the democratic process was further evidenced when it prohibited *any* party from proposing a
candidate for county executive of Apartadó. In this context, only two
days before election day in October 1994, the Catholic Church brought
together twelve political organizations, including Esperanza and the UP,
urging them to take part in the democratic process and not to give in to
the threat of arms. Gloria Cuartas emerged as the consensus candidate
by default. She knew the region and its people, had leftist sympathies,
especially for the Perestroikos branch of the UP, which had distanced itself from the FARC, but she was neither a member of a traditional political party nor an activist in any armed group. The county council over
which she presided was not clearly dominated by any one group: four
councilors from the UP; four from Esperanza; three Liberals; one Movimiento Fuerza Progresista, a Liberal offshoot; and one each from two evangelical Christian parties. After her unanimous election, she made valiant
efforts to bring peace to Apartadó, gaining national and international
recognition and defying numerous death threats and attempts on her life.

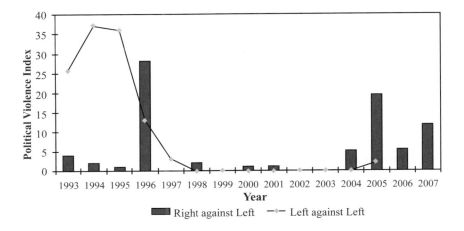

Figure 3.1. Political Violence in Apartadó, 1993–2007

Note: For explanation, operationalization, and sources for these data, see the methods section of chapter 1.

She spoke to all the armed actors to try to decrease the level of conflict in the zone.[4]

Cuartas succeeded to a certain extent for a short time. Between August 1994 and March 1995, according to the IEPRI lethal political violence database, the repression index by the FARC against the Esperanzados was 2.0 in Apartadó, and there were no combats in 1995. However, this effort at a new negotiated solution was purely regional in scope. Whereas it might have met with success in the earlier reform era, now supraregional interests stepped in to override and reverse the steps toward peace made by Cuartas and the architects of "the Consensus." The first of these was the newly formalized Autodefensas Campesinas de Córdoba y Urabá, which was rapidly expanding its sphere of action into Urabá (ACCU), led by the same Fidel Castaño who had earlier created alliances with Esperanza, Paz y Libertad. By 1995 it would force more than one thousand families to abandon their lands in the northern Urabá county of Necoclí.

The second, Alvaro Uribe, was the governor of Antioquia Department at the time. Although at first he seemed open to the suggestions of the Consensus and its supporters among human rights organizations, by

1996 he clearly opted to heed the urgings of AUGURA and military leaders and focus on strengthening the military presence in Urabá, called Plan Return to Urabá. Furthermore, when a group of county executives from Urabá went to Bogotá to plead for permission to carry out regional peace dialogues, they were refused in no uncertain terms. The central government representative stated, "The national government will not endorse a direct dialogue between the representatives of Urabá society with members of paramilitary groups and guerrillas for an eventual pacification of the region. . . . [A] direct dialogue with paramilitary leaders and guerrillas would imply dividing that territory between the FARC and Fidel Castaño."[5]

The result was the highest level of violence ever witnessed in Urabá—a region where even in less violent times the local homicide rate was predictably at least seven times the Colombian national rate, itself one of the highest in the world.[6] First, in 1995 the violence against the Esperanzados by the FARC in Apartadó escalated dramatically, reaching its highest point, 36, including one September massacre in which twenty-six people were killed, presumably by the FARC. The number of FARC-army combats also returned to preconsensus levels: 3 in 1996 and 4 in 1997. The following year the paramilitary responded by decimating the Patriotic Union and Communist Party representation in local politics, the banana workers' union, and the neighborhood organizations. The total "Right against Left" political violence index surged to 28 in Apartadó in 1996, according to the more stringent IEPRI database. Among those killed were some of the most central activists for the UP's local political power, including three county council members in Apartadó—one a longtime Sintrainagro leader, another the president of the county council, and the third a peasant settler activist. Two members of Gloria Cuartas's municipal administration were also killed, as were the central leaders of the Coca-Cola Bottling Plant union in Carepa. Organized less than a decade before, the union was completely dissolved as a result of the repression.[7]

The general secretary of Urabá's Communist Party, who by the end of 1996 had become clandestine, had survived an assassination attempt and accused, by name, an Esperanzado of carrying out the attack directly. Asked by a journalist from the Communist Party newspaper if the UP's majority influence over the region was a thing of the past, he confirmed emphatically that it was. He then enumerated the victims of the double assault on the party: the selective recentralization measures initiated by Gaviria as part of the State of Internal Commotion declared in late 1992 had resulted in the imprisonment of many elected representatives from the UP, and the paramilitary assault on the region had killed the others. Of twenty county council members whom the UP had elected in the banana axis in 1994, all had been killed, imprisoned, or exiled. The UP-supported county executives of Turbo and Chigorodó had been imprisoned, and the one in Mutatá (directly south of Chigorodó) was in exile. Apartadó's county executives from the 1990–92 and 1992–94 periods were imprisoned. The two from the 1986–88 and 1988–90 periods had been killed. "There is not a single leader from the earlier generation who is alive and free," the general secretary said.[8] By February 1997 the surviving UP county councilors from Urabá held a press conference in Bogotá to announce their permanent withdrawal from the region.[9] Not only UP leaders were leaving the zone: the Communist Party–organized Bernardo Jaramillo neighborhood in Apartadó, where 8,000 people had resided in the early 1990s, had 1,000 empty houses by 1997.[10] Following this turning point, violence against Esperanza and of the Right against the few remnants of the UP dropped considerably until the mid-2000s.[11]

1997–2008: From the UP's Remnants, a New Model of
Transnational Human Rights Activism

In this context one more experiment in neutrality was born, in the former UP stronghold of the cocoa-growing peasant settler hamlet, San José de Apartadó. In February 1997 members of the agricultural cooperative originally organized by the UP were murdered. Control of the road from San José down to Apartadó was taken over by paramilitary groups, but the FARC continued to be present in the hills. The settlers were truly between a rock and a hard place. Inspired by Monseñor Isaías Duarte (later killed), a major force behind the Cuartas "Consenso" experiment, the San José de Apartadó Peace Community had fourteen hundred members at its beginning in March 1997 and was a radical experiment in nonviolent neutrality: no one was allowed to carry a gun, and no armed actors—neither the FARC nor the army—were allowed to enter the zone. Economic activity and public services were organized communally. The tactic, though seemingly quixotic, captured the imagination and support of nonviolence organizations in Colombia and worldwide, including many religious organizations.[12]

The governor and later president, Alvaro Uribe, was hostile to the idea of the community, however. He insisted on military presence in San José and environs, despite the community's pleas that this invited the FARC to retaliate against them. After 2004 and through late 2008, political violence escalated (see fig. 3.1), with almost all incidents occurring around San José de Apartadó. Combat also spiked around the same time: in 1998–2004 there were 0, 1, 1, 0, 0, 0, and 1 combats; in 2005, 4. The number of combats then dropped to 0 in 2006, 2 in 2007, and 0 in 2008, as the FARC weakened nationally and a regional commander turned herself in in 2008. By early 2008 more than two hundred community members had been killed. Although a September 2006 *Los Angeles Times* article estimated that 20 percent of the Peace Community deaths to that point had been at the hands of guerrillas, since late 2005 all the deaths reported in the Noche y Niebla database have been at the hands of rightist forces.[13]

The deaths included a widely publicized early 2005 massacre of eight members of the family of a community leader, with considerable evidence pointing to a counterinsurgency battalion as the culprit. With the Jesuit priest and national human rights activist Javier Giraldo at the forefront of efforts to punish those responsible, heavy pressure was placed on the Colombian government. In 2005 U.S. Senator Patrick Leahy's (D-Vt.) testimony citing the case succeeded in holding up military aid to Colombia for a few months; by 2007 Leahy was joined by fifty-eight other members of Congress with the same demand and citing the same case.[14] In early 2007 sixty-nine members of the military implicated in the massacre were called to be investigated by the Fiscalía. *Semana* magazine called it "the most serious accusation in the history of the Armed Forces."[15] Fifteen of them were detained in March 2008, a sign that the massacre may be a rare exception to Colombia's rule of impunity. Furthermore, Father Giraldo, with Gloria Cuartas, the Consensus county executive of Apartadó, led efforts to bring to justice the 1995–97 Urabá military commander, Rito Alejo del Río, for ties with paramilitary forces. Del Río's trial was ongoing as of late 2008.[16]

The San José de Apartadó Peace Community is also highly successful by other measures. In a region where exodus from paramilitary-influenced rural areas is the rule, the community miraculously has retained its fifteen hundred members. Furthermore, after 2002 organizations such as Peace Brigades International and Fellowship of Reconciliation sent a constant stream of volunteers to accompany community leaders to prevent their assassination.[17] Press coverage has been substantial and overwhelmingly sympathetic: a search for "San José de Apartadó" in the *El Tiempo* archive shows an average of 547 articles per year from 1997 to 2008, with 710 in 2008, and in-depth stories have also appeared in the *Toronto Star* and the *Los Angeles Times*. At least three documentary films have been made about the social experiment, one with EEC funding, as well as a prize-winning photo essay in *El Tiempo*.[18] In 2007 the community won the Testimony *[sic]* de Pace Prize in Italy and the Aquisgran Prize in Germany and was nominated by the American Friends Service Committee for the Nobel Peace Prize. In 1997 Father Giraldo and his Intercongregational Peace and Justice Commission won the Humphrey Prize from the Montreal-based International Centre for Human Rights and Democratic Development, and in 2008 Gloria Cuartas was awarded the Nantes Prize for defense of human rights by the Third World Forum for Human Rights in France.[19]

The surrounding region provides other examples of the effectiveness of international human rights activism—especially when U.S.-linked elites were the "target." U.S.-based activists took up the cause of prosecuting Coca-Cola for the 1995–97 murders of the union leadership at its subsidiary's Carepa bottling plant, filing a claim in a Miami court under the Alien Tort Claims Act in 2001. Although no settlement had been reached as of late 2008, the suit brought about considerable negative publicity for Coca-Cola in the press and at shareholders' meetings in 2006 and has inspired twenty U.S. universities to boycott Coke in response to student activism.[20] The case of Chiquita Banana is more dramatic: in March 2007 an investigation by the U.S. Securities and Exchange Commission found Chiquita Banana's Colombian subsidiary, Banadex, guilty of having contributed U.S.$1.7 million to paramilitary groups between 1997 and 2004, as well as contributing crucial logistical support to paramilitary arms importing operations. Chiquita was fined U.S.$25 million. As the high-ranking paramilitary leader "H. H." confessed in his Justice and Peace trial, not only Chiquita, but all banana plantation owners financed the paramilitary groups, yet only U.S.-owned Chiquita was prosecuted.[21] Undoubtedly inspired by the success of the first anti-Chiquita sanction, lawyers from International Rights Advocates in July 2007 filed a civil suit in U.S. courts against Chiquita seeking reparations on behalf of the families of 173 victims of the paramilitary forces in Urabá and Santa Marta.[22]

1992–2008: The Rise and Decline of Esperanza's Rightist Labor Political Project

As the UP was being exterminated and survivors transitioned to a new model of organizing, Esperanza-Sintrainagro's labor and electoral strength grew steadily from 1992 through 2000 but then declined. In the context of an expanding and consolidating paramilitary project tolerated by the national government, Esperanza's paramilitary links were an asset. In the context of an expanding banana economy, it used both effective labor mobilization and its role as staunch opponent of the FARC to wrest an unusual level of labor concessions and political tolerance from AUGURA and the national government. However, the banana economy's post-2000 stagnation brought conflict with AUGURA, and a weakened FARC and President Uribe's post-2003 prosecution of those with paramilitary links made Esperanza's continuing paramilitary ties a liability. Esperanza's rhetoric became both more divided and more oppositional as its electoral strength eroded, yet AUGURA retained its influence with the presidency.

The Autodefensas Unidas de Colombia were created in 1997 near Urabá, worked in conjunction with the state-sponsored Convivir in Urabá in the late 1990s, and then consolidated and expanded its national political and military project significantly. Paramilitary troops rose from fewer than a thousand to more than eight thousand between 1992 and 2000,[23] with little interference from the national government. However, in July 2003, in response to growing criticism of the paramilitary forces, President Uribe began pressing the AUC to demobilize its fighters. In Urabá 358 members of the Bloque Bananero of the AUC demobilized in late 2004, but not until 2006, on two different dates, would 1,531 members of the Elmer Cárdenas Bloc demobilize. This foot-dragging, along with the attempts of the United States to extradite at least eight of the top AUC leaders beginning in late 2004 created incentives for Uribe to prosecute those with paramilitary links.[24] Although demobilization in Urabá officially concluded in 2006, a new violent surge of "reemerging bands" occurred in 2007–8. Specifically, the Black Eagles and the Autodefensas

Gaitanistas, led by "don Mario," were struggling to control the region's valuable trafficking routes.[25]

The Esperanzados announced their affinity for the pro-military, pro-paramilitary, and anti-FARC project in Urabá—and distanced themselves from the rest of the Left—increasingly publicly and frequently from 1992 through 2003. In October 1997, as Esperanza prepared to participate in its first local elections without competition from the Patriotic Union for the banana worker vote, Sintrainagro's president Guillermo Rivera gloated, "The electoral event will take place in complete peace . . . not because the guerrillas have decided not to sabotage the elections, kidnap candidates, or kill candidates . . . but thanks to the presence of the army and the police."[26] In March 1999 Mario Agudelo, an Esperanza deputy in the Antioquian Assembly, was present and Guillermo Rivera was a speaker alongside the 1994–97 governor of Antioquia, Alvaro Uribe, at an event to honor two army generals, one of whom, Rito Alejo del Río, had overseen the 1995–96 Plan Return to Urabá (and in late 2008 was on trial for his paramilitary links). The event was organized by AUGURA and the Antioquian governor's office, among others, to protest the removal of the two generals from their posts by the president due to accusations of close paramilitary ties.[27] Not surprisingly, Sintrainagro also endorsed Alvaro Uribe's 2002 presidential bid, even while the rest of the labor movement overwhelmingly supported the Polo Democrático Independiente's candidate, Lucho Garzón.[28] And even though Esperanza-Sintrainagro adopted a more oppositional stance toward AUGURA and President Uribe after 2002, some signs of paramilitary links still remained. A high-level Black Eagles paramilitary leader captured in 2008 had belonged to the Comandos Populares in the 1990s, for example, and also in 2008 the president of the Chigorodó local of Sintrainagro was found to have lent his DAS armored car to two paramilitary henchmen.[29]

Prosecution of Esperanza leaders for their paramilitary links began after 1999, creating tensions between Sintrainagro-Esperanza and AUGURA. In early February 2000 Sintrainagro leader, La Chinita neighborhood committee president, two-term Apartadó county council member, and 2000 Apartadó county executive candidate Jairo Suárez was accused and detained—together with Apartadó's 1997–2000 Esperanzado mayor—for allegedly forcing a banana worker's family member to engage in arms trafficking for paramilitary groups.[30] Sintrainagro immediately called a

strike, and Sintrainagro's president labeled the accusation "political persecution" against "the labor organization which has helped consolidate peace
in Urabá." AUGURA officials were unmoved by the appeal, however. They
denounced the strike as illegal, discounted the days not worked, and reported that plantation owners were "disconcerted" by the action.[31] Mario
Agudelo, the Antioquian departmental assembly deputy from Esperanza,
Paz y Libertad from 1994 to 1997, was also imprisoned in 2005 on similar
accusations.[32]

Earlier, however, Sintrainagro's political allegiance to AUGURA and
the military had been crucial in winning the union's continued material
gains despite a now-stagnating banana industry. As shown in table 2.3, in
Urabá banana acreage, productivity, and production had expanded quickly
in the 1960s and more slowly in the 1970s. It was only slightly more than
stable in the 1980s, but growth picked up again in the 1990s. Between
1992 and 1999 banana-cultivated area increased from 27,570 hectares to
30,696 hectares, volume of production increased from 50 million boxes
to almost 68 million boxes, and productivity (thousands of boxes/hectare)
increased from 1.81 to 2.29.[33] After 1999, however, stagnation occurred.
Cultivated area rose just 2,000 hectares, to 32,387 by the end of 2007;
volume fell to 64.1 million boxes, and productivity as measured in thousands of boxes per hectare fell slightly, from 2.11 to 1.98.[34] The devalu-
ation of the dollar relative to the peso after 2007 was another challenge
for the banana industry. Meanwhile, as the biofuels revolution accelerated a boom in palm oil production in Colombia—2003 production was
140 percent of 1999 production, making Colombia the world's fifth palm
oil producer by 2006—some Urabá plantations began to convert banana
land to African palm.[35]

During both the expanding 1990s and the stagnating 2000s, Sintrainagro was quite successful in maintaining and in many cases improving
wages and benefits, at least partly because they were also successful in
lobbying for national subsidies of the banana industry.[36] In 1996 the
19.46 percent raise accorded was just below the cost of living (COL) increase of 20.2 percent.[37] In 1998 the pacted 20.95 percent wage hike was
slightly above the 20.3 percent COL increase.[38] In 2002 the 9 percent wage
increase for the first year considerably exceeded the COL increase (5.8 percent), while the second year of the contract specified a wage increase to
match the COL increase.[39] And in May 2006 the outcome of negotiations

was a raise of 6.5 percent for the first year (the COL increase was 4 percent) and 1.5 points above the cost of living for the second year. Furthermore, union membership had expanded, from 14,500 in 1992 to 20,000 in 2008. An exhaustive search revealed no evidence of regionwide negotiations in 2008, although there was a one-plantation strike.[40]

However, as time went on, Sintrainagro had to fight harder for its continued success. There were no strikes between 1989 and 1996, which AUGURA attributed to its own "timely intervention" as well as the "maturity of the union leaders."[41] Sintrainagro also carried out sectoral advocacy with AUGURA's blessing, such as pleading the Colombian banana industry's case before the EEC, aiding in the organization of a bloc of Latin American banana-producing nations, seeking greater banana industry subsidies from the national government, and negotiating the dollar/peso exchange rate with the Bank of the Republic.[42] But Sintrainagro increasingly carried out class advocacy as well. The 1996 contract required a (never-realized) strike threat, which moved AUGURA from their initial offer of no wage increase to a second offer of 10 percent to the final offer of 19.46 percent.[43] The May 2002 strike lasted twenty-four hours and required dramatic intervention by the minister of labor to resolve, and the May 2006 accord required fifty days of intense negotiation.[44]

Along with the trend toward banana sector labor negotiations that took longer and were more bitter to achieve continued improvements in wages and benefits came a trend toward more polarized rhetoric. In its 1997 annual report AUGURA had spoken of the "maturity" of banana union labor leaders, but just two years later AUGURA officials complained of the union's "lack of mature positions."[45] By the April 2000 strike the union's president angrily denounced AUGURA's tactics: "It's always the union that compromises and never the plantation owners; you can't negotiate that way."[46] By June 2007 decorum had broken down entirely: a Sintrainagro press release denounced an AUGURA leader's "serious and systematic violations of labor law" and "sickening hatred of organized labor" and threatened to promote an international boycott of Colombian bananas.[47]

Union statements in 2008 similarly denounced widespread contract violations but also for the first time alluded to internal dissension in the banana workers' union (also evidenced by the one-plantation strike in 2008). Banana sector layoffs and the expanding (and less labor intensive, un-unionized) production of palm oil lent a certain resignation to the tone, as it began to appear that Urabá's banana sector was headed inexorably toward contraction. Nonetheless, the statement angrily denounced "divide and conquer" tactics that aimed to separate "bad" union leaders from "good" ones, putting the ones labeled "destabilizing agents" at great physical risk. In fact, there was evidence that some Sintrainagro members were once again becoming targets of the Right: two union leaders denounced paramilitary threats in late 2006; another was killed, apparently by paramilitary forces, in early 2007; and the Esperanza-line Apartadó County executive in late 2008 called for state intervention to curb the paramilitary upsurge.[48]

Reflecting the growing oppositional voice of Sintrainagro, as well as some internal dissension, one of the locals of Sintrainagro and two Sintrainagro members who belonged to the Confederación Unitaria de Trabajadores (CUT) national labor federation leadership defied the national organization by supporting Polo Democrático Alternativo candidate Carlos Gaviria rather than Alvaro Uribe in the May 2006 presidential elections.[49] Furthermore, Sintrainagro's leadership declared itself firmly and publicly against President Uribe's highest-priority agenda item for the U.S. Congress: the Free Trade Agreement.[50]

Esperanza's electoral success rose and fell with the warmth of its relationship with AUGURA and the national government. At first it was quite successful in the electoral arena, especially at the local level, drawing on both the banana worker electorate and its new urban neighborhood electorate, obtained via the La Chinita/Barrio Obrero invasion and other moves into the urban arena. These local elected officials in turn were directly helpful to the labor movement in much the same ways that the UP administrations had been to their constituencies, such as providing infrastructure, public services, and health and education projects and creating county enterprises in worker neighborhoods.[51] In 1994 Esperanza held four of fourteen seats on Apartadó's county council.[52] Also, that same year, Mario Agudelo, who in 1999 spoke at the homage to the two generals, was elected to the Antioquian Departmental Assembly. In 1997 Esperanza won the county executive elections in Apartadó and increased its number of county council seats from four to six.[53] In 2000 the results were roughly equivalent: Esperanza retained the county executive post in Apartadó and also won in Turbo, a position occupied by one of Esperanza's 1991–94 senators, Aníbal Palacio. County council seats held by Esperanza in Apartadó slipped slightly in 2000, from six to five.[54]

But Esperanza had lost its national electoral clout in 1994, with no more senators or representatives to the house elected after that year.[55] By 2003 it became clear that Esperanza was slipping electorally at the local level as well, despite the fact that its labor and neighborhood organizations continued to be robust and successful.[56] In Apartadó, even though the county executive candidate was a longtime high-ranking Sintrainagro leader, Oswaldo Cuadrado, he obtained only 26 percent of the votes for candidates and was edged out by a Liberal who garnered 43 percent of the vote. In 2007 the same candidate, with almost the same percentage of the vote (29 percent of votes for candidates), emerged victorious as a result of the highly fragmented electorate. Nevertheless, that his electoral vehicle of the moment, the Convergencia Ciudadana, won just 17 percent of the county council vote for candidates reveals that the Sintrainagro leader owed much of his victory to allies' votes rather than to his own constituency.[57]

While Esperanza's electoral strength and influence diminished, AUGURA's link to departmental and national power seemed quite secure. The April 2006 strike had been mediated by both the governor of Antioquia, Alvaro Uribe, and the minister of labor, and one of the results was that banana exporters received an increased national government subsidy through May 2006.[58] Furthermore, the governor of Antioquia from 2000 to 2003 was none other than Guillermo Gaviria, former owner of the La Chinita plantation that had become the Esperanza urban neighborhood stronghold in Apartadó (although he was killed by the FARC in May 2003).[59] In 2002–6 and again in 2006–10, Uribe, AUGURA's staunch ally from the Plan Return to Urabá days, was president of Colombia. In more ways than one, AUGURA did not need Sintrainagro and Esperanza anymore.

CONCLUSION

In the years after 1992, factors outside the region—regional paramilitary groups, the president's direct intervention in the labor conflicts, and transnational activism—had a much larger impact than in the reform era. With this in mind, Urabá had a unique outcome in the postreform period.

Most war zone social movements, associated in the military mind with active insurgencies, had been devastated, and the UP in Urabá was hardly an exception. However, Urabá's Esperanza-led labor and neighborhood movements were not only intact, but thriving, and their electoral expression was impressive as well. This was due first to Esperanza's strategic alliance with AUGURA, the military, and the paramilitary around the shared agenda of defeating their mutual enemy, the FARC and the UP, itself a result of the FARC's policy of assassinating the Esperanzados in the early to mid-1990s. It was also due, however, to Esperanza's and Sintrainagro's continued organizing and labor militancy, which strangely coexisted with their otherwise right-wing ideology. After 2000 the tensions inherent in this contradictory alliance became more prominent, as the defeat of the UP made Esperanza less useful to the plantation owners, as AUGURA's protection of Esperanza became more costly to its economic solvency in a stagnant sectoral economy, and as Esperanza's ties to paramilitary forces became a greater liability in the changing national political climate.

Meanwhile, the remnants of the non-Esperanza Left, long the victims of supraregional forces aligned with the Right, learned to use forces outside the region in their favor. The San José de Apartadó Peace Community, the Coca-Cola workers, and the families of victims of Chiquita-sponsored paramilitary groups have all used national and international support for their causes to make significant steps toward survival, prosecutions of human rights violators, or even reparations.

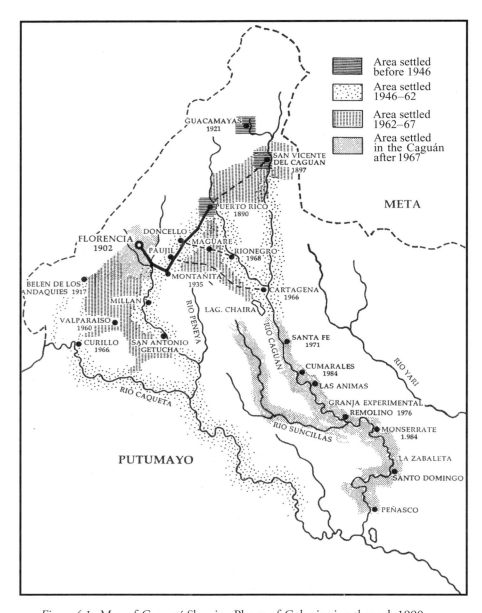

Area settled
before 1946

Area settled
1946–62

Area settled
1962–67

Area settled
in the Caguán
after 1967

META

GUACAMAYAS
1921

SAN VICENTE
DEL CAGUAN
1897

PUERTO RICO
1890

DONCELLO

FLORENCIA
1902

PAUJIL

MAGUARE

RIONEGRO
1968

MONTAÑITA
1935

BELEN DE LOS
ANDAQUIES 1917

CARTAGENA
1966

MILLAN

LAG. CHAIRA

RIO PENEYA

VALPARAISO
1960

CURILLO
1966

SAN ANTONIO
GETUCHA

SANTA FE
1971

RIO CAGUAN

RIO YARI

CUMARALES
1984

LAS ANIMAS

GRANJA EXPERIMENTAL
REMOLINO 1976

RÍO CAQUETÁ

RÍO SUNCILLAS

MONSERRATE
1.984

PUTUMAYO

LA ZABALETA

SANTO DOMINGO

PEÑASCO

Figure 4.1. Map of Caquetá Showing Phases of Colonization through 1990

Source: Jaramillo, Mora, and Cubides, *Colonización, coca y guerrilla,* map 1. Redrawn with permission
from Cubides and publisher by Aaron Lui.

THE CAGUÁN IN THE REFORM PERIOD

Negotiated Peace and Social Movement Gains,
Followed by Defeat of the Left

Caquetá's Middle and Lower Caguán Valley had not one but two out-comes in the reform period: first, in the most euphoric moments, a peace with significant social movement gains negotiated with the national government (not pacted with repression-sponsoring elites); then Left defeat, as the impacts of national political closing and a changing political economy swung the regional balance of power back to its starting point, favoring the Turbayista Liberal cattle ranchers who had provided much of the impetus for repression. No pacted peace with regional elites therefore occurred in Cartagena del Chairá.

The late-twentieth-century history of the department of Caquetá was one of constant conflicts between peasant settlers and large landowners for land itself, as well as for the state resources needed to establish a stable peasant economy. Frontier zone settlers, many of whom after the late 1970s were coca growers, were traditionally represented by different sectors of the Left. The settlers' struggle was expressed through different means—institutional electoral participation, peasant social movements, or guerrilla violence—depending on the political moment: political opening encouraged increased emphasis on the first two forms of political participation; political closing encouraged a return to armed struggle.

The large cattle ranchers, meanwhile, were most faithfully represented by the Turbayista faction of the Liberal Party, which dominated departmental politics from the late 1960s until the mid-1990s (table 4.1). Traditionally, this faction had a mutually supportive relationship with the military, the main actor carrying out repression against the Left in the Middle and Lower Caguán during the period studied, because of the relative weakness of landed elites there. That repression has been almost entirely "public" in this region, that is, carried out by the army, is an important reason for the *relatively* low levels of repression (as compared to other regions with powerful homegrown paramilitary groups), even during repressive waves. Since Caquetá, like Arauca, is a relatively small department, with only fifteen counties (Antioquia, where Urabá is located, has more than 120), politics at the departmental level have a major effect on politics at the local level. As political confrontation focuses on the department level, any pacted peace would also have needed to be departmental.

During the reform period, the peasant movement came closest to achieving material success (state concessions) and freedom from repression—the most desirable outcome from the movement's point of view—at moments when it was strongest relative to the Turbayistas on the departmental level. The relative power of the peasant movement and its electoral expression derived from four factors: (1) its unity; (2) national-level reforms that enhanced social movement and Left electoral success, pressured the Turbayistas to support the reform process, and decreased military attacks on guerrilla-controlled areas; (3) coca booms that brought new settlers to already Left-dominated regions; and (4) expansion of the areas under control by the guerrillas. Conversely, the relative power and electoral strength of the Turbayistas was strengthened by political closing on the national level, with the accompanying militarization this implied; a process of land concentration and cattle economy expansion that both weakened settler unity and allowed the emergence of a Turbayista political machine on the local level; and military initiatives that reduced the amount of territory under guerrilla control. Each of these factors—leftist and peasant unity, national-level reforms, trends in political economy and population flows, and trends in geographic territory held by the guerrillas or military—changed several times over the course of the late 1970s through 1992, causing the relative influence of the peasant movement to wax and wane.

In the years before 1984 the electoral Left, the peasant movement, and the armed insurgency were created and then expanded based on the

Table 4.1. Turbayista Liberal Political Power, 1980–1992

Year	Turbayista Departmental Electoral Strength in Caquetá[a]	Political Positions Held or Controlled
1980	NA[b]	Military/Turbayista *intendente,* June 1980–September 1992[c]
1982	18%	1 representative to the House 1 senator: Hernando Turbay Turbay Turbayista governor, September 1983–April 1985
1984	33%	Turbayista governor, April 1985–August 1986
1986	29%	1 representative to the House: Rodrigo Turbay Cote 1 senator: Hernando Turbay Turbay Turbayista governor, August 1986–January 1988
1988	42%	Military governor, January 1988–August 1990
1990	38%	1 representative: Rodrigo Turbay Cote 1 senator: Hernando Turbay Turbay Turbayista governor, August 1990–January 1992
1991	—	1 representative: Rodrigo Turbay Cote (Turbayismo lost senator and governor)
1992	21%	

Sources: Political affiliation and terms of appointed governors from Gobernación del Caquetá, Secretaría de Planeación Departamental, División Estudios Regionales, *Anuario estadístico Caquetá 1989,* 43; Artunduaga, *Historia general del Caquetá,* 182; interview 22; Jaramillo, Mora, and Cubides, *Colonización, coca y guerrilla,* 213–15; Pedraza, "Departamento nacional de planeación. El proceso de paz en el Caquetá (caso del Caguán)," 20, 30, 37. Electoral results are from Registraduría Nacional del Estado Civil, *Estadísticas electorales, marzo 1980: Asambleas Departamentales, Consejos Intendenciales, Consejos Comisariales,* 1980 (for 1980 Departmental Assembly); *Estadísticas electorales, marzo 1982: Senado-Cámara, Asambleas Departamentales, Consejos Intendenciales, Consejos Comisariales,* 1982 (for 1982 Departmental Assembly, House, and Senate); *Estadísticas electorales: Asambleas Departamentales, Consejos Intendenciales, Consejos Comisariales, Concejos Municipales, marzo 11 de 1984* (for 1984 Departmental Assembly); *Estadísticas electorales: Senado-Cámara, Concejos Municipales, Consejos Comisariales, Consejos Intendenciales, Asambleas Departamentales, marzo 9 de 1986* (for 1986 Departmental Assembly, House, and Senate); *Estadísticas electorales 1988: Asambleas, Consejos Intendenciales, Consejos Comisariales, Concejos Municipales, Alcaldías* [marzo 13 de 1988] (for 1988 Departmental Assembly); *Estadísticas electorales 1990: Concejos Municipales, Alcaldes, Consulta Popular* [marzo 11 de 1990] (for 1990 Departmental Assembly, House, and Senate); *Estadísticas electorales: Elecciones del 27 de octubre de 1991,* vol. 1, *Senadores, Representantes, Gobernadores,* 1991 (for 1991 governor); *Estadísticas electorales: Elecciones del 8 de marzo de 1992,* vol. 1, *Alcaldes, Concejales, Diputados, Ediles* (for 1992 Departmental Assembly).

[a] Of votes for those candidates who were elected to departmental assembly, percent won by Turbayista Liberals.
[b] No data available on which Liberals were Turbayistas.
[c] Before Caquetá was made a full-fledged department, it was an intendencia, and the equivalent of the office of governor was referred to as an *intendente.*

arrival of many new settlers in Caquetá, drawn by the boom in coca culti-vation in its frontier zones. There was a rapid expansion of territory under guerrilla control. However, the Left's electoral progress and leverage were limited by disunity, a closed political system, and a steady expansion of the cattle economy and large landowner wealth that would continue through-out the reform period.

Between 1984 and 1987 the Left achieved peace, with social movement gains as a by-product of the national government's peace negotiations with the FARC. With the amnesty or defeat of the armed insurgencies that had once competed with the FARC for territorial control in Caquetá, the Left became monolithic, with only one political tendency represented for the remainder of the reform period and beyond. Important reforms at the na-tional level allowed guerrillas to express their strength electorally, winning an unprecedented proportion of the departmental vote and (slightly and temporarily) reducing the electoral strength of the Turbayistas. The same reforms made the guerrilla-influenced peasant movement of coca growers much more successful and less repressed, reinforcing this new electoral strength and, together with solid coca prices, drawing new migrants to guerrilla-controlled zones. Between 1987 and 1992, although democratic reforms such as the direct election of county executives were implemented, with the UP victorious in the first county executive election, this reform benefited the peasant movement in fiscally impoverished Cartagena del Chairá very little. Meanwhile, the collapse of FARC-government peace negotiations induced the national government to retract the "carrot" it had offered to the peasant movement in the previous period (state resources) and replace it with the "stick" of violent repression. Guerrilla territory was eroded as well, and each of these changes—reinforced by an exodus from guerrilla-controlled regions speeded by a coca price crash—reduced left-ist electoral strength considerably. The continuing process of land con-centration both outside and within guerrilla-controlled zones simultane-ously undermined the unity of the peasant movement while allowing local Turbayista political figures to become more powerful. Thus the local Turbayistas regained a local electoral majority by 1990 while easily regain-ing the small amount of departmental electoral ground lost in the previ-ous period.

Although in the previous period the Turbayistas had been pressured by the government to respect the negotiated peace and had done so, they were now free of such pressure. Without a lasting electoral displacement by the Left, they had no need or incentive to form a pacted peace with the Left either. They reverted to their previous antagonistic relationship with the Left, and the FARC echoed this response by abandoning its support of electoral action and escalating combat activities.

CHRONOLOGY OF CHANGE IN CARTAGENA DEL CHAIRÁ

Before May 1984: Conflict between Settlers and *Latifundistas*

The history of the recently founded (1982) department of Caquetá is one of successive waves of colonization and rapid population growth since the turn of the century (fig. 4.1). Cut off from the rest of Colombia by the massive Cordillera Oriental (which runs along the Huila-Caquetá border), with poor soil, and connected by river only with the rest of the Amazon watershed (see fig. 1.2), it remained virtually unpopulated for most of Colombia's history. However, at the turn of the century the rubber boom brought the first wave of colonization. The second wave of colonization occurred in the 1930s and 1940s as Colombia encouraged settlement to strengthen its hand in the border war against Peru. And the third and largest wave of settlers arrived as political refugees in the wake of La Violencia. Their numbers were augmented by Colombia's agrarian reform efforts of the 1960s, which sought to give untitled lands *(baldíos),* mostly in the Cordillera foothills, to landless peasants to ease land pressures in more densely populated regions. All in all, from the 1930s through 1984, the region's population has multiplied more than twentyfold, reaching 380,000.[1]

Although the new settlers were given land with titles, the poor soil required expensive fertilizers to produce anything other than pasture for cattle. In addition, credit, technical assistance, and transportation infrastructure were insufficient to build a stable peasant economy. As a result, the new settlers' failure rate was quite high, and land tenure concentrated rapidly in the hands of the largest landowners. Some of the more notorious of these landed elites, such as the Lara family, used illegal and violent means to amass exorbitant amounts of land and wealth in short periods while the local and national state turned a blind eye. Between the mid-1960s and the mid-1970s the brewing conflict began to polarize. The Left, which was split between several different ideological factions, began to organize peasant struggles as well as to express itself electorally. However, it was hindered in this goal by waves of brutal repression against the most organized peasant regions, the illegality of the Communist Party at the time, and the fact that both regional and local government executives were appointed rather than elected. These positions were usually chosen in consultation with the department's senator—after 1978 usually belonging to the Turbayista faction of the Liberal Party.[2]

By the early 1960s the Turbay family patriarch, Hernando Turbay Turbay, had consolidated his position as regional political strongman, winning appointment as an *intendente* (governor of an *intendencia,* one step short of a department) from 1962 to 1965, then using his perennial congressional post and family connections to key Liberal Party leaders to faithfully represent cattle rancher and *latifundista* interests in Caquetá after 1968. His faction of the Liberal Party would dominate regional politics throughout the entire reform period (see table 4.1). It would be perceived by the Left as the primary obstacle to peace, social reform, and increased political influence for peasant interests and the primary motor behind the successive waves of repression against the Left.[3]

By the mid-1970s the rural Left had grown considerably stronger and more militant, with several massive peasant protests occurring. Furthermore, the Left now had a strong foothold among the urban squatters of the capital, Florencia, as well as the teachers' union. But the major development of the mid-1970s was the initiation of armed struggle in Caquetá, led by three guerrilla groups: the EPL, the FARC, and the M-19. The state responded quickly and violently. Between 1979 and 1981, as part of a national policy of increased repression and militarization headed by President Turbay Ayala (related to the Turbays of Caquetá), a massive repressive wave attacked peasants in guerrilla-influenced rural areas of Caquetá, with many egregious human rights violations committed by the military. A huge new military headquarters, Comando Operative No. 12, with seven battalions and more than six thousand soldiers, was inaugurated in January 1981. It would become a permanent fixture in Caquetá politics by 1985, nearly always intervening against reform initiatives, in concert with Turbayista politicians.[4]

Between late 1981 and 1984, however, with Belisario Betancur's campaign and presidency, some reform initiatives took place. These were the creation of the first peace commission, under outgoing President Turbay Ayala, in October 1981; an army cease-fire in February 1982 to facilitate the acceptance of amnesty by guerrillas; the creation of a national peace commission under President Betancur in September 1982; the congressional approval of a second (and more successful) amnesty law for guerrillas in November 1982; and finally the signing and implementation of a cease-fire and peace agreement with the FARC in March and May 1984, respectively.[5]

On the departmental level these moves toward reform had two main effects. Much of the M-19 in the department accepted amnesty and demobilized, and the remainder, along with the much smaller EPL, was defeated militarily and had virtually no presence in the department after 1985. This created a near-monolithic Left in Caquetá, as the FARC was the only guerrilla group, the Communist Party the only leftist party, and the FARC- and CP-influenced peasant organization Sinpeproagrica the only major peasant organization. Furthermore, the level of violence—both guerrilla-army combat and rightist repression against peasants—dropped considerably, creating an opening for the Left's most successful and peaceful era in Caquetá.[6]

From each wave of colonization mentioned above, the Middle and Lower Caguán (since 1985 the county of Cartagena del Chairá) received the spillover. During the first wave inspired by the turn-of-the-century rubber boom, rubber extractors based in San Vicente or Puerto Rico would come down the Guayas or Caguán River to fell trees in the Middle and Lower Caguán. Between the 1920s and the 1960s, after the rubber economy crashed, adventurers based upriver continued to extract natural resources from the downriver regions, but these now consisted mostly of illegally poached wild animal pelts (ocelot, jaguar, capibara, etc.), timber, and turtle eggs.

It was not until the mid-1960s that some permanent settlements began to be established in the future county, mostly by settlers from the Caquetá foothills who had been radicalized by their indebtedness and the consequent loss of their original land stakes. Below Santa Fe del Caguán, the land could not be titled because it had been declared a wildlife reserve in 1959; consequently, most settlement was above that point. The jurisdiction's population grew rapidly, with a corresponding increased political importance: the town of Cartagena del Chairá was founded in 1966, it became an official subdivision (subcounty seat) of Puerto Rico in 1967, and by 1974 it had become a departmental *corregimiento,* one step below a county.[7]

At first the new settlers grew food for themselves and continued to hunt for food and for pelts to sell. A boom for pelts occurred between the mid-1960s and the mid-1970s, followed by an ephemeral marijuana boom from 1972 to 1976. Although each of these bonanzas drew new settlers to the region, their effects were dwarfed by the coca boom from about 1978–79 through 1981. With prices as high as U.S.$16,000–$20,000 per kilo of coca paste, the population of the corregimiento rapidly rose to an estimated 22,000 by 1982, including both settlers (colonos), who intended to settle on land permanently to grow coca, and transient coca harvesters *(raspadores),* young single men who floated in and out of the region. Although prices since 1982 have never been higher than U.S.$5,000 per kilo (and have often been lower than U.S.$1,000 per kilo), coca has remained the region's primary economic activity since the late 1970s.[8]

Drawn by the wave of new settlers and fleeing the intense military operation of 1979–81 in the Caqueteño Piedmont regions that had previously been the guerrilla group's stronghold, the FARC arrived in the Middle and Lower Caguán in the late 1970s. It quickly established effective military control throughout the county and even slightly beyond its borders, due to the scant police presence and absence of any military base in urban Cartagena del Chairá; the lack of transportation infrastructure other than the Caguán and Guayas Rivers (the Paujil-Cartagena road shown in fig. 4.1 was not constructed until 1988); and the concentration of population on the riverbanks. The FARC's territory from 1978 to 1979 through 1983–84 extended from Rionegro (on the Guayas River) and about halfway between San Vicente del Caguán and Cartagena, on the Caguán, through the union of the Caguán and Caquetá Rivers (see fig. 4.1).[9]

The meager police presence and extreme distance of municipal administrative services (available in Puerto Rico only, accessible via very expensive river travel) meant that settlers in the Middle and Lower Caguán lived in a virtually stateless society—a vacuum quickly filled by the FARC. The FARC adopted basic policing functions—both directly and through organizations it later created for that purpose—punishing robbery and other criminal actions as well as patroling the discotheques on Saturday nights to prevent violence. Given the large number of bars, the plentiful supply of beer and money, and the large floating population of migrant worker–adventurers, incidents of personal violence flared up easily, making this an important function. The guerrillas also took on the role of the judiciary branch, mediating property line conflicts between landholders (no land within the wildlife reserve could be legally titled at this time) and enforcing the unwritten rights of the migrant harvesters vis-à-vis the growers and those of the growers vis-à-vis the much wealthier intermediaries, especially when prices crashed.

The FARC also encouraged the establishment and strengthening of already existing Communal Action Committees (CACs), a traditional and legally recognized form of peasant organization in Colombia, and coordinated volunteer work assignments (mingas) in order to build small-scale public works such as footpaths, bridges over creeks, and construction of schoolhouses. Some of these projects were financed by the taxes the guerrillas imposed on the coca intermediaries, usually a flat rate charged per kilo purchased, which since 1992 has averaged about 4 percent of the total. Finally, there is the obvious utility, to coca growers and raspadores, of a strong guerrilla force: protection of the crops from fumigation and the growers from military harassment. Both the pseudostate and defensive functions helped the FARC to create a base of support among the population's most vulnerable members, as well as to build a political-military organization strong enough to establish a clear set of incentives for supporting the Left politically, even for otherwise disinclined wealthy landowners and coca intermediaries in the county's northern half.[10]

Yet there were some state functions that the FARC simply could not fulfill. The lands within the wildlife reserve were untitled and untitleable without a change in their legal status. For successful crop diversification—essential to the creation of a stable regional economy—agricultural credits and technical assistance were also needed. There were real political disadvantages to guerrilla mediation of conflicts, as the "guerrillas as enforcer" role inevitably conflicted with the guerrillas' need to maintain popular support. Thus, especially after 1988, the FARC increasingly sought to delegate its judicial functions to actual state institutions. In a zone with some of the nation's highest rates of malaria infection, infant mortality, anemia, hepatitis, and parasites, health and sanitation investment and services were desperately needed. Only twenty-two schools served the entire region in 1984, for a total population estimated at 33,000, and there was no vocational training for adults. Finally, all transportation was via the rivers, raising transportation costs considerably.[11] All these needs for increased state presence and investment became the focus of settler-state struggles in the next period.

The Backdrop: The Political Economy of Coca

An understanding of the workings of the coca economy is essential for making sense of the political evolution of the Middle and Lower Caguán. Like any other commodity chain, the cocaine economy may be understood as a pyramid: raw materials producers on the bottom, intermediaries in the middle, and marketers and distributors at the top, reaping the main profits. However, this commodity's illegality alters the usual political alliances associated with each layer of the pyramid. Raw materials producers can in turn be divided between landowners and migrant laborers. The laborers, known in Colombia as *raspadores,* or scrapers, because they strip the leaves off the coca bushes, are hired by settlers for a week or so once every three months, rotating throughout the region rather than in the permanent employ of any one settler. Although the settlers are certainly wealthier than the raspadores, they are not latifundistas, nor are their holdings plantations. Rather, Cartagena del Chairá's coca growers are almost invariably peasant settlers who have only recently occupied (usually without title) relatively small amounts of land devoid of any transportation or social infrastructure, and they have done so only after failing to acquire land in long-settled regions of their countries. Because of the crop's illegality, its price fluctuates wildly. It must be grown in remote areas where malaria is endemic, and it is vulnerable to confiscation and crop fumigation (with herbicides) by authorities. Thus direct production is unattractive for elites.

Nonetheless, it is attractive for poor peasants because coca prices are higher than those for legal smallholder crops and because the intermediaries, unlike most for legal crops, offer seeds and credit. In the 1980s almost all coca-growing occurred in Bolivia and Peru; Colombia's coca-growing regions played a supplemental role only. Although prices were very high when the coca economy first began, they plummeted by the late 1980s as the market became glutted.[12]

The coca-growing peasants process their own harvested coca leaves into a paste in primitive laboratories, usually using gasoline as a solvent. They then sell this paste to an intermediary from outside the region who represents a major marketing cartel. In the 1980s the Medellín cartel of Colombia was clearly dominant for the entire Andean cocaine industry, but after Pablo Escobar's death in the early 1990s, the Cali cartel grew quickly. The intermediaries also arrange the processing of the paste into cocaine, which requires imported chemicals such as ether and greater capital investment. The product's illegality means the gap between the top of the coca commodity chain and the bottom is far larger than that for legal agricultural crops.[13]

Coca's illegality also creates unique political alliances. First, the coca economy creates a symbiotic relationship between peasants and guerrillas. As peasants are vulnerable to (U.S.-encouraged and U.S.-financed) crop destruction and the usual vicissitudes of price booms and busts and as guerrillas can help protect coca growers against both threats, peasants have clear incentives for supporting the insurgents. Guerrillas find the coca regions attractive because this natural support base, along with the remoteness of the regions and their lack of established elites, facilitates the creation of a guerrilla military and political stronghold and because taxing coca production can be a lucrative source of financing. Thus both Colombia's and Peru's coca-growing regions had a strong guerrilla presence in the 1980s.[14]

In Colombia typically the political interests of the coca economy elites have evolved over time. Emergent coca elites may perceive a strategic alliance with the guerrillas who are protecting the growing zones. However, as the coca elites became major landowners, as occurred in the case of the Medellín cartel, they aspired to gain control over the local political institutions in regions where they have established footholds—often peripheral regions with guerrilla presence. (In Colombia they usually invested in low-risk, easily liquidated cattle ranches.) To do so, they needed to "clean" the zones of guerrillas, leftists, and all other political competition, a goal that put them in alliance with the army and the Right. This alliance occurred quite frequently in rural Antioquia, the department where Medellín and Urabá are located, but top elites of the Medellín cartel did not buy land in Caquetá, according to my interviewees and other sources. Thus there was no direct political antagonism between cartel elites and the peasants of the Lower Caguán during the reform period.[15]

In contrast, there was clearly a direct political antagonism between the army and the Lower Caguán's peasant coca producers. The army, charged by Colombian elites with counterinsurgency and charged by the

United States with fighting drugs, could kill two birds with one stone by attacking the FARC or its perceived sympathizers in the coca-producing region.

May 1984–June 1987: High Point of the Peace Process

From 1984 through 1987 most factors favored the advancement of the Left—especially the institutional Left—in the Lower Caguán. A government-guerrilla peace agreement brought not only a reduced level of combat and repression to the zone but also increased state investment and services. This change from the stick to the carrot (along with a slight recovery in coca prices) encouraged new immigration to the zone, which further reinforced the much-increased level of peasant mobilization and Left electoral success. Although the area under guerrilla control decreased, the full impact of this change would not be felt until the 1987–92 period.

Between late 1982 and May 1984 the early peace initiatives of Betancur became more definite, encouraging a tentative declandestinization of the FARC in Cartagena del Chairá. This brought a more explicit linking of this insurgency with peasant organization and mobilization and exerted some pressure on recalcitrant departmental authorities to negotiate. Thus the first massive peasant mobilizations, consisting of five thousand to six thousand participants, to Florencia from the Caguán occurred in May and December 1983 and early 1984, with peasant leaders managing to wrest a written agreement regarding credit, technical assistance, and human rights demands from the Turbay-dominated departmental government.[16] The FARC-government peace process was also reflected in the overwhelming success of the Communist Party's electoral front: in 1984 the Frente Democrático won more than 80 percent of the vote in Cartagena del Chairá for the Departmental Assembly (table 4.2).[17] The FARC had contributed to this result by actively campaigning for the Frente Democrático and encouraging speedboat owners to provide free transportation for voters (with gasoline reimbursement collected and provided by the region's Communist Party cells) in a region with prohibitively expensive river transportation.[18]

Yet before May 1984 the peace was not yet full-fledged. In particular, there was a guerrilla attack on the military in mid-1983 near Cartagena del Chairá. In retaliation and also in response to the peasant movement's increased militance and the growing regional political and military power

Table 4.2. County Electoral Trends in Cartagena del Chairá, 1982–1992

	Percent Vote for UP/PCC Electoral Front, County Executives Elected	Percent vote for Turbayista Liberals, County Executives Elected
1982		
House	88%	6%[a] (Not yet a county)
1984		
Departmental Assembly	81%	5%
County executives		4 Turbayista county executives, 1984–86
1986		
County council	84%	6%
City executives		4 Turbayista county executives 1 military county executive, April–June 1988
1988		
County council	82%	18%
City executives	2 UP county executives, June 1988–June 1990	
1990		
County council	29%	58%
City executives		1 Liberal Turbayista county executive, June 1990–June 1992
1992		
County council	37%	47%
City executives		1 Liberal Turbayista county executive, June 1992–January 1995

Sources: For election results for House of Representatives 1982, Departmental Assembly 1984, county executive 1988–1992, and county council 1982–92, Registraduría Nacional del Estado Civil, sources for appropriate elections. Names of elected county council members for 1986 and 1994 from unpublished printouts at the Registraduriá Nacional del Estado Civil. For names and parties of elected county council members for 1988, 1990, and 1992, unpublished Actas Electorales at the Registraduría Municipal del Estado Civil de Cartagena del Chairá. For dates of taking office of pre-county (pre-1985) *corregidores* and political affiliation of all county executives, interview 17. For dates of taking office after Cartagena del Chairá became a county, consultations with clerks at the Cartagena del Chairá county courthouse. County council results represent votes won by this political party as proportion of votes for *elected* county council members only.

[a] Remainder of votes were for neither UP/PCC electoral fronts nor Turbayista Liberals.

Table 4.3. Evolution of Conflict in Cartagena del Chairá, 1984–1992

Year	Repression Index	Left Electoral Success (percent)[a]	Number of Guerrilla-Army Combats
1984	6.65	81	No data
1985	2.0	—	0
1984 + 1985	8.65	—	—
1986	0	84	0
1987	0	—	1 with FARC
1986 + 1987	0	—	—
1988	6.75	82	1 with FARC
1989	0	—	0
1988+1989	6.75	—	—
1990	0	29	0
1991	0	—	1 with FARC
1990+1991	0	—	—
1992	0 doubled = 0	37	2 with FARC

Note: The repression index for 1992 is doubled to make it comparable to the figures for 1984–85, 1986–87, and 1988–89 without extending the analysis to the counterreform period. For additional explanation, operationalization, and sources for these data, see the methods section of chapter 1.

[a] Of those votes deposited for county council candidates who were elected to office, percent that went to leftist candidates; data are recorded only for even-numbered years because no elections occurred in odd-numbered years.

of the FARC, intensive military operations took place in the Middle and Lower Caguán from late 1983 through August 1984. With three peasants dead, twenty-four detained arbitrarily, and five tortured—all directly by army personnel—this was one of the three great waves of repression that occurred in the region during the reform period (table 4.3 and fig. 4.2). The military operation inspired two other protests—one in December 1983 and the other in May 1984—but it also reduced significantly the territory under the hegemony of the FARC. After a new military base was established in urban Cartagena in 1984, the FARC's presence north of that point became sporadic at best, with permanent presence from Cartagena del Chairá south (downriver) only.[19]

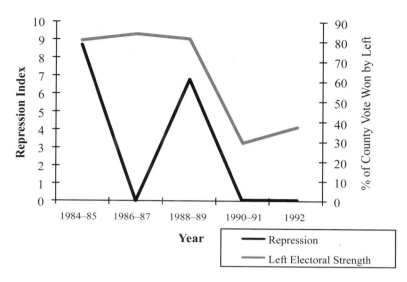

Figure 4.2. Repression and Left Electoral Success in Cartagena del Chairá

Note: For explanation, operationalization, and sources for these data, see the methods section of chapter 1.

From May 1984 through June 1987, however, the peace process solidified. On May 28, 1984, a FARC-government cease-fire took effect, with the agreement including provisions for guerrilla amnesty, national democratization, and state resources to peasants in war zones.[20] From that point through late 1985 the peace process achieved its maximum adherence by the guerrillas and its maximum level of support from elite groups both nationally and at the department level. There were only eleven guerrilla-army confrontations in all of Caquetá in 1985 and 1986, none of them in the Middle and Lower Caguán. Repression also decreased markedly, with a total of two assassinations between August 1984 and the end of 1986. Both the army commander for the entire department of Caquetá and the army commander for the Cartagena base were seen as being sympathetic to the peace process during late 1984 and 1985.[21]

The sudden peace and possibilities for development of the region drew a flood of new settlers and workers to the region. Contributing to this trend was the slight recovery of coca prices that occurred between 1982 and early 1986 (from a 1982 low of US$1,300/kilo to a 1984 high of

U.S.$5,000/kilo, with a slow descent to about $2,000/kilo by mid-1986). By one estimate the population increased from 22,000 to 35,000 between 1982 and 1986. Since these new residents disproportionately settled in the downriver portions of the corregimiento—where coca was grown and where guerrillas effectively exercised state power—their arrival strengthened the peasant movement and, by implication, the electoral strength of the Left as well.[22]

In response to this unprecedented moment of political opening, the FARC increasingly emphasized legal and peaceful means to political power over violent actions. And in the changed political context these new tactics were remarkably successful. By mid-1984 the first concrete benefit of the peace agreement became evident, as a "store-boat" run by a national agency (IDEMA) began to cruise the waters of the Caguán, buying (legal) peasant produce and selling supplies to peasants, drastically reducing their transport costs.

Encouraged, the FARC and the Association of Communal Action Committees organized the First Communal Forum of the Caguán in Santa Fe in August 1984. Attended by delegations from thirty-nine CACs and three state entities as well as key political leaders from the FARC, the assembly resolved that withdrawing the 367,500 hectares (808,500 acres) below Santa Fe from the wildlife reserve was of the highest priority. This would allow land to be titled, facilitating access to credit and the diversification of the local economy. The Colonization Committee was thus created to negotiate this withdrawal with the state natural resources agency, INDERENA (one of the attendees).[23]

In the next year and a half, a frenzy of organizational activity occurred in the Caguán, with FARC initiatives answered by support from state entities and independent intellectuals alike. In August 1984 the Inter-Institutional Committee was formed by six state agencies based in Caquetá's capital, Florencia, in order to support the peace process and rural development in the Caguán. In late 1984 and then in January 1985, the second and third forums were organized by the Caguán Colonization Committee and the FARC, with four state entities attending each instead of the three present at the August forum. Meanwhile, in December 1984, the first Artists' Peace Action had brought nationally known performance artists to the remote Lower Caguán outpost of Remolino, many of them personal acquaintances of one of the FARC's most charismatic leaders,

"El Abuelo" (the Grandfather). This was a grassroots initiative of intellectuals, based mostly in the nation's capital, who saw the region as a "Laboratory of Peace"—an essential "pilot project" in which to prove the viability of peace and reform in Colombia.[24]

The moment of heady optimism continued in early 1985, as eight hundred FARC guerrillas demobilized in order to create a new political movement, the Patriotic Union. It would include the Communist Party, demobilized FARC guerrillas, and disaffected members of traditional parties. By April things had advanced so far that one public statement in support of the peace process was signed by three political leaders from the FARC and members of the Communist Party, as well as non-Turbayista traditional party leaders and the new leader of Turbayismo himself, Rodrigo Turbay Cote.[25]

The apex of the process occurred between June and November 1985. At the fourth forum in June delegations of directors from eighteen state entities were in attendance, all promising to offer services in the region. In addition, representatives of forty-eight CACs were there, as well as leaders from the Association of CACs, the Colonization Committee, and the regional fronts of the FARC. After long and difficult negotiations between INDERENA and the Colonization Committee regarding the conditions for canceling the wildlife reserve, an accord was signed in September 1985 permitting the titling of the lands—an enormous victory.[26]

Also at the fourth forum, a new committee, the Committee for the Investigation and Transfer of Technology to Support the Colonization of the Middle and Lower Caguán and Sunciya (or simply the Transfer Committee), was formed. Made up of twenty state agencies as well as the Association of Communal Action Committees, the Colonization Committee, and the FARC, its main purpose was to bring resources into the region to support the peace process, and its accomplishments were considerable. In just one year it managed to bring more resources into the region than had been seen since it was first settled, facilitate important research on the zone, and effectively advocate on behalf of the Caguán settlers. Concretely, new state resources included the construction of a vocational training center, a day care center, twenty-three rural schoolhouses, and a weather station; the purchase of a 200-hectare plot to become an experimental farm and the planting of 50 hectares of rubber plants on it; the establishment of a thirteen-family community agricultural enterprise (La Zabaleta); and

plans for an aqueduct in Remolino. The Transfer Committee also wrote
two separate regional development plans, supported three major social
and scientific research projects, and met with both President Betancur
and a regional military commander to advocate on behalf of the Caguán
settlers.[27]

Additional evidence of the high-level official support received by
the Caguán movement in mid-1985 is provided by two events. A second
Artists' Peace Action occurred in late June, this time with the president
of the republic lending an airplane to transport the sixty artists. And on
September 28 the Transfer Committee met with the president himself.
In a meeting slated for fifteen minutes but extended to an hour and a
half, Betancur expressed enthusiastic support for the efforts of the committee and scolded the Turbayista departmental administration for not
supporting the Caguán experiment more actively. In response, the governor actually attended his first Lower Caguán event (the fifth forum) on
November 2, formally pledging his support and reinforcing the tremendous optimism that permeated the gathering.[28]

By March 1986 the Colonization Committee elaborated an ambitious new plan to further strengthen the peasant organizations of the
Caguán and develop the region; Cartagena del Chairá was declared a full-
fledged county with a right to its own county council; the FARC and the
government signed an agreement to prolong the cease-fire;[29] and the
Patriotic Union won an unprecedented electoral success for the Left in
Caquetá: 5 of 6 county council members in Cartagena del Chairá; 28 of
68 county council members in the department; 5 of 15 departmental assembly members (the previous high point had been 3 of 15); and, for the
first time ever, a representative in Congress from the Communist Party,
with his alternate one of the most active political leaders in the FARC,
Luciano Marín (alias Iván Márquez), both from the UP. Furthermore,
the UP had also participated in the coalition that elected a non-Turbay
Liberal to the Senate, thus gaining essential access to both legislative bodies (see tables 4.2 and 4.4).

The UP's electoral triumph, however, did very little to dilute the political strength of the Turbayistas, the Caquetá political force most strongly
opposed to the peace process in Caquetá. While the proportion of Departmental Assembly votes for Turbayista candidates had dropped slightly
between 1984 and 1986 (from 35 percent to 29 percent), this official

Table 4.4. Leftist Electoral Strength and Alliances in Caquetá, 1980–1992

Year	Leftist Electoral Strength When Running Alone[a]	Electoral Strength of Leftist Forces When Running with Elite Allies	Alliances with Elite Parties	Alliances for Which Political Office	Left-Led or Elite-Led Coalition
1980	22	—	None	None	None
1982	—	21	PCC/New Liberals	Departmental Assembly	Left-led
1984	17	—	None	None	None
1986	—	35	UP/New Liberals/ Independent Liberals	Assembly	Left-led
			UP/Non-Turbay Liberals	House	Left-led
			Non-Turbay Liberals/ UP/Conservative	Senate	Elite-led
1988	16	—	None	None	None
1990	13	—	UP/Non-Turbay Liberals/ Conservatives	House	Left-led
			Non-Turbay Liberals/ UP/Conservatives	Senate	Elite-led
1991	NA[a]	NA[a]	M-19/Non-Turbay Liberals/ Conservatives/UP	Governor	Left-led (by M-19, not UP)
1992	11	—	None	None	None

Sources: For alliances and faction for Liberal candidates, Delgado, *Luchas sociales en el Caquetá*, 168; interview 22. For electoral results, Registraduría Nacional del Estado Civil sources cited in table 4.1.

[a] Of all votes deposited for candidates elected to Departmental Assembly, percent that went to leftist parties; no assembly election in 1991.

faction of the Liberal Party still held one of two Senate seats and one of two House seats for Caquetá, as in 1982 (see table 4.1). In other words, the traditional party sectors displaced by the UP were not those most closely associated with militarist policies but rather the most reformist sectors, creating an important disincentive for the Turbayistas to seek regional pacted peace.

By mid-1986 it was clear that the height of the peace process had passed. In May a new president, Virgilio Barco, was elected, with a reversal of Betancur's policies widely anticipated. The government dialogues with the FARC had stalled, and the echoes of this change were soon felt in the Lower Caguán. At a late May 1986 event, few of the expected state agencies invited by the Transfer Committee appeared, and there was a strong sense of disillusionment among the Caguán settlers due to government betrayal and broken promises. Although the Transfer Committee organized a regional planning meeting in July 1986 and the Colonization Committee organized a massive public event in late March 1987, the visits of state officials to the region had virtually ceased, and activity around the ambitious organizing campaign initiated in January 1986 had come to a halt.[30]

In retrospect, there had been signs of trouble even during the most euphoric moments of the peace process under the Betancur administration, with actors from both the Right and the Left expressing doubts as to the viability of the peace agreement. In January 1984 the minister of defense openly declared the armed forces' refusal to carry out the president's peace plan. He was removed from his post, but his replacement continued to make similar public statements through late 1984. Similarly, the regional directors of several state agencies invited to participate in the Caguán's peace process had been forbidden by their national directors from doing so because of the danger of being branded guerrilla auxiliaries.[31]

Regional elites and military commanders had been similarly disinclined to support the president's peace policies. The Turbayista governor of Caquetá from September 1983 to April 1985 openly stated to a Transfer Committee leader in August 1984 that to support the peace process in the Caguán was to play into the hands of the guerrillas. Her successor participated briefly and unenthusiastically in the Caguán's process in late 1985 only after the specific exhortation by the President to do so—the exhortation itself a response to the Transfer Committee's denunciations of sabotage of the process by Turbayistas and high military commanders in Caquetá. Furthermore, departmental state entities had been the least likely to invest or offer services in the Caguán.[32]

Similarly, after a brief moment in 1984–85 when regional and local military commanders were open to the peace process, each was replaced by a more bellicose colleague. In October 1985—less than a month after President Betancur's visit to Caquetá and his scolding of the bellicose Turbayistas—it took the specific intervention of the Transfer Committee to cancel an army fumigation operation of the Lower Caguán planned for early 1986. In addition, even at the high point of the process, there had been frequent incidents of military harassment of amnestied guerrillas as well as of individuals from state entities who were participating actively in the process.[33]

As a result, doubts regarding the peace process were not limited to the Right. By the end of 1984 human rights groups, leftist parties, and the FARC protested army violations of the cease-fire, the proliferation of paramilitary groups, and the escalating dirty war: by November 1985, just half a year after the UP's founding, seventy activists from the UP had been killed. The FARC's withdrawal of the charismatic guerrilla leader El Abuelo from the region at the end of 1985 probably reflected a reshuffling of priorities, away from political work and toward war.[34]

Thus the time between President Barco's inauguration in 1986 and the final rupture of the cease-fire in June 1987 was typified by escalating tensions on both sides, countered by the desperate last attempts on the part of the activists of the Caguán to keep the Laboratory of Peace alive. Soon after Barco's inauguration, the new presidential councilor for peace disauthorized any further official participation by state entities in the Transfer Committee (which included representatives of the FARC but no representatives of traditional parties or the church). Instead, participation would have to be channeled through the new Rehabilitation Councils—in which traditional parties and the church must participate but guerrillas could not. This undermined peasant movement success, weakened the settler movement's links with the FARC, and reclandestinized the insurgency.[35]

Following this cue, the new governor of Caquetá (appointed by Barco) and the regional army commanders stepped up their hostile propaganda campaign to discredit the Caguán experiment. At a meeting of all governors with the president in October, three governors, including Caquetá's, complained bitterly of FARC violations of the cease-fire. From there, the fragile consensus in favor of the cease-fire began to deteriorate quickly.

By March 1987 Congressman Rodrigo Turbay denounced the political assassination of fourteen of the local leaders of the main faction of the Liberal Party in Caquetá by the FARC. In addition, the army, which was building the road from Paujil to Cartagena del Chairá, denounced several skirmishes and dynamite attacks by the FARC against the road and its builders.[36]

The FARC and the population of the Lower and Middle Caguán, meanwhile, viewed the road's construction as part of a larger military strategy to advance on the region, establish a larger military presence, and forcefully evict the FARC, in clear violation of the spirit of the accords. In another grievance in late 1986, the UP had accused the president of reneging, in Caquetá only, on his promise to appoint county executives from the Patriotic Union wherever this party had won a plurality in the March 1986 county council elections. According to the decree, the UP had a right to four county administrations in Caquetá: Puerto Rico, Paujil, Cartagena del Chairá, and Montañita. However, it was offered only the two with the smallest budgets, Cartagena and Montañita. In protest, the UP refused to accept any county administrations in Caquetá that year.[37]

Sensing the extreme danger posed to the peace process by these hostilities, and in a last-ditch attempt to avoid a rupture of the truce, representatives of the Caguán settlers traveled to Bogotá to invite the presidential councilor for peace to the Caguán. When he came to the region around April 1987, no holds were barred in encouraging the maximum possible attendance at his public appearances. As one former raspador who attended the speech testified, everyone—without exception—*had* to go to Remolino to hear the councilor, and attendance was enforced by the guerrillas. Transportation was free, although speedboat owners' gasoline expenditures were reimbursed by the CACs. By all estimates, the organizational efforts were wildly successful: at least five thousand people were present, and the event was covered extensively and sympathetically in the press.[38]

However, the councilor's visit ultimately failed to accomplish its main goal to deactivate the hostile political climate. Although he received an elaborate $2.5 billion peso (about $8.1 million) development proposal from the Caguán activists, which he promised to give careful consideration, by August 1987 a mass peasant protest would denounce lack of funding for the proposal. And although he met with the two regional FARC fronts to discuss ways to avoid further military confrontations, when the accorded mechanisms were presented to the commander of the XII Army Brigade in Florencia, he reaffirmed his intention to advance down the Caguán, and the military operations continued. By then more than four hundred UP activists had been killed nationally.[39]

A FARC ambush on an army convoy in the county of Puerto Rico on June 16, 1987, was the last nail in the coffin of the truce. With twenty-seven soldiers dead and forty-three wounded, the dynamite attack sent shock waves throughout the military and political establishment. One week later President Barco declared the truce null and void, and the Tur-bayistas of Caquetá were quick to suggest excluding Left-influenced regions from *all* material benefits of the new National Rehabilitation Plan. The Laboratory of Peace era had ended.[40]

June 1987–September 1992: Strengthening of the Right and Weakening of the Left Despite Decentralizing Reforms

June 1987 to September 1992 was a contradictory period, when moves toward reform and counterreform occurred simultaneously, with equally contradictory results. In the county of Cartagena del Chairá in particular, remaining trends toward (or vestiges of) reform brought the movement a directly elected UP county executive in 1988–1990 and a last attempt at a cease-fire in 1989 and 1990. Vestigial pro-reform sentiments (or perhaps simple inertia) also kept some state entities in the Lower Caguán through about 1990, all of which helped the peasant movement stay alive and sustained some hopes of change through peaceful means.

But especially after 1990 these trends favoring social movements and the Left were far outweighed by trends that weakened them, strengthened the Right, and induced the FARC to reemphasize armed struggle. In mid-1988, as FARC-government relations became increasingly bitter, an intensive military operation was unleashed on the Middle and Lower Caguán. It permanently reduced the FARC's territory and, together with a coca price crash, provoked an exodus from the region. As state entities abandoned the region and stratification among settlers undermined unity, peasant organizations were severely weakened. Meanwhile, the same political and military trends, along with a cattle boom and increased land concentration in upriver zones, strengthened the local and departmental economic basis for a Liberal clientelist machine. The FARC reacted to the changed context first by reducing their support for electoral action and then by escalating combat. As a result, both locally and departmentally, leftist electoral strength plummeted and Turbayista Liberals became the dominant electoral force (see tables 4.1, 4.2, and 4.4).

The years between 1987 and 1990 witnessed the last vestiges of reform. Even after President Barco ended the truce in late June 1987, the UP held out some hope for reviving the peace process and promoting economic development of the Lower Caguán. On August 18, 1987, an estimated four thousand settlers from the Middle and Lower Caguán (as well as other regions of Caquetá), all affiliated with the UP-influenced peasant organization of Caquetá, marched on Florencia. They demanded funding for the U.S.$8.1 million development plan presented to the presidential councilor during his late March 1987 visit to the Caguán and denounced the increased militarization of the zone since the rupture of the truce. Neither of these points was addressed in the final negotiated agreement from the protest;[41] however, the mere fact that so many mobilized reveals the continuing (albeit diminished) viability of the Caguán's peasant movement at this point in time.

Furthermore, though the flow of new state resources to the Middle and Lower Caguán had stopped around mid-1986, the exodus of state entities already established there had not yet begun. The Instituto Colombiano para la Reforma Agraria (Colombian Institute for Agrarian Reform, INCORA) and the National Rehabilitation Plan both offered relatively good levels of credit, with good conditions, from 1986 through 1989 and from 1987 through 1988, respectively. Furthermore, the store-boat that had traveled the river to buy non-coca crops continued to operate regularly through about 1990. Finally, a new resource entered the region in late 1987: an Italian priest, Father Jacinto, established Remolino's first parish, built the rectory and church with donations from Europe, and began to make plans for establishing a crop substitution program for the Lower Caguán. Like the malaria prevention workers, the priest was viewed sympathetically by all parties — FARC guerrillas, settlers, and the army — although due to his location he worked more closely and amicably with the first two.[42]

Another last-ditch effort to revive the institutional option occurred in early 1988. To alleviate the rising tensions between the UP and Turbayistas, the FARC proffered a very brief unilateral cease-fire (February 27–March 14, 1988) on the eve of the first direct election of county executives. The settlers of the Caguán, for their part, believed that a strong vote for the UP would help to avoid the military attack on the region that was rumored to be imminent.[43] As a result, the local showing of the UP in the March 13 county elections was nearly as strong as in 1986: 82 percent of the vote (compared to 84 percent in 1986) won the party six of seven county council seats, as well as the county executive's post (see table 4.2).

In many ways the direct election of county executives in general and the UP's election of Cartagena del Chairá's county executive in particular were major advances. The budget for county executives had been increased nationwide, so this county executive had nearly twice the budget as his predecessor in 1986–87. Also, for the first time this budget was devoted to the newest and politically most isolated settlers (since they were in areas of continuous FARC control), those in the Lower Caguán. Whereas the appointed Liberal county executive who had held office from November 1986 to April 1987 had devoted only 11 percent of the budget to the residents of the former wildlife reserve, the two UP county executives who shared the June 1988–June 1990 term devoted 26 percent and 55 percent of the budget to this constituency, respectively. In addition, the first of the two UP county executives especially was quite active and effective in obtaining funding for local projects from the National Rehabilitation Plan, such as the waterworks and sewer for the Middle Caguán population of Santa Fe and the waterworks for urban Cartagena del Chairá.[44]

Nonetheless, because of the meager local budget of Cartagena del Chairá (an average of U.S.$70,250/year for the UP's term, the price for just 117 kilos of coca at 1990 prices), the county executive was severely limited in his ability to stimulate economic development through the county's own public investment. Thus the main option available to increase public investment was to solicit funding from departmental and national entities. However, success in this endeavor depended on a favorable political moment, which was increasingly rare after 1988. Several sources, for example, specifically denounced a departmental embargo against county executives from the UP. That Cartagena's subsequent two (Turbayista Liberal) county executives had considerably larger budgets than their UP predecessor appeared to bolster this claim.[45]

One other vestige of reform during this period bears mentioning: from February 1989 through December 1990 the FARC declared a cease-fire on the national level. Although this agreement did not come close to replicating the level of euphoria or hope produced by the 1984–86 accord, it lowered the intensity of combat significantly in Caquetá in 1989 and 1990. The Presidential Council for Peace reports the following numbers of armed confrontations (FARC vs. the army) in Caquetá: 29 in 1987; 34 in 1988; 8 in 1989; 15 in 1990. Similarly, in Cartagena del Chairá, in contrast to 1988, when a major military operation and guerrilla ambush occurred, no confrontations took place in either 1989 or 1990.[46]

Despite these last gestures of reform, overall this period's political closing and trend toward land concentration weakened the Left and strengthened the Right. After the breakdown of the FARC-government truce in June 1987, mutual accusations of political violence flew between the UP and the Turbayistas in Caquetá, escalating the climate of hostility. In the national press in the days before the county executive election, the Turbayistas claimed that thirty-five party cadres had been killed by the FARC, including Turbay's alternate and the county executive candidate for Florencia. (Sources sympathetic to the FARC, meanwhile, countered that the assassinations of Turbayistas were attempts to dismantle emerging paramilitary groups.) In the national press the Turbayistas waged a fierce propaganda campaign against the UP in general and its peasant sympathizers in the Lower Caguán in particular with headlines such as "Caquetá: Pilot Project of Subversion." Whereas just three years earlier President Betancur had rebuked the Turbayistas for obstructing peace, Barco now viewed them as martyrs. In response to their clamor, he appointed a military governor for Caquetá in late January 1988.[47] Not surprisingly, the dirty war against the UP escalated sharply as the rhetoric became more heated: in Caquetá alone, the UP claimed twenty-two victims in late 1987 and early 1988.[48]

Although the county's residents had overwhelmingly voted for the UP in March 1988 in the hope of prolonging the peace process and staving off military operations, they soon discovered that the UP's local electoral victory had just the opposite effect. Soon after the elections the County Voter Registration office was bombed, claiming the lives of two peasants. Then, on April 1, the military governor appointed by Barco appointed a military county executive for Cartagena del Chairá who held office until the UP county executive's inauguration on June 1, 1988. But the most dramatic punishment inflicted on the Caguán settlers for having voted UP — and the settlers and their political representatives saw it exactly in these terms — was a massive military operation from July 7, 1988, through February 15, 1989, aimed at retaking the Caguán by force.[49]

Operation Alfa Justiciero established, for the duration of the operation, effective military control from Cartagena down to the union of the
Caguán and Caquetá Rivers, as guerrillas had evacuated this zone just prior
to the operation to avoid confrontations. Temporary bases were established
in the most important hamlets in Panamá and below (see fig. 4.1), and in
these hamlets in particular the army perpetrated numerous human rights
violations on the civilian population. This second wave of repression
slightly surpassed that of 1983–84 in its magnitude, with two people
killed, nineteen tortured, two others arbitrarily detained, and one wounded
by the army (see table 4.3). Highlighting the fact that the institutional Left
was viewed as highly threatening rather than as part of the power structure,
the repression especially targeted those individuals who had been most active in "institutionalizing" the Left: two county council members for the
UP, including the treasurer of La Zabaleta Community Enterprise, one of
the most solid accomplishments of the Laboratory of Peace era. The other
UP county council member was saved from death only by Father Jacinto's
intervention.[50]

The military operation, together with the completion of the Paujil-
Cartagena road (which destroyed the FARC's previous ability to control
all access routes to the region), permanently reduced the areas under guerrilla influence. From the late 1970s through the 1983–84 military operation, the guerrillas had controlled the area from Rionegro on the Guayas,
and the equivalent latitude on the Caguán River, through the union of the
Caguán and Caquetá Rivers (see fig. 4.1). Between mid-1984 and Alfa Justiciero in 1988–89, they had effectively controlled the area from Cartagena south, with sporadic presence above Cartagena. But after Alfa Justiciero the FARC was able to reestablish effective state control only from
Santa Fe south, with sporadic presence from Santa Fe to Cartagena and
even less frequent presence above Cartagena. During the same period, military presence had increased steadily. During 1979–82 military presence in
the Middle and Lower Caguán had been sporadic, with a small police
force in Cartagena only. In 1984–85 a small military base with about 200
to 250 soldiers was established in the county seat, but the police force left.
And after 1989–90, the police force returned and the number of troops
increased to about 400.[51]

This shift in military control instantly reversed the incentives for participating in the leftist political project in those zones that had changed

hands. According to several activists from both the UP and the Liberal Party, before Alfa Justiciero the wealthier landowners above Cartagena had voted UP and even made campaign contributions to the party to avoid "ruffling feathers" *(para no desairar)*. After July 1988, however, they could, and did, cease to do so, facilitating the first steps toward building a Liberal clientelist machine.[52] Conversely, given the escalating dirty war against the UP, even the most devoted sympathizers of the party in the upper third of the county now controlled by the army might think twice about voting their conscience.

Beyond the simple loss of guerrilla territory, however, the military operation, in combination with the lowest regional coca prices since 1979, provoked a virtual exodus from the region, primarily from the downriver coca-growing zones that had supported the settler movement and the electoral Left. While coca prices from 1979 to 1981 were in the range of US$18,000 to $22,000 per kilo and while they had varied from about U.S.$900 to $1,300 per kilo between 1982 and 1986, between 1987 and 1991 they hovered between U.S.$400 and $700 per kilo, experiencing a slight recovery to about $U.S.1,100 per kilo only toward the final months of 1992. The population was reduced from a high of 35,000 during the most euphoric moments of the peace process in 1986 to 25,000 to 26,000 by the end of 1988 (after the military operation) and to a low of 23,638 by 1992.[53]

The price crash also accelerated the ongoing process of stratification of coca-growing peasant settlers, undermining peasant movement unity and also reducing support for the FARC. The rapid differentiation associated with this crop—much more rapid than for subsistence crops because of the higher rate of accumulation—inevitably created tensions between the haves and have-nots of the zone. Despite retaining military control of the coca-growing zones, the FARC was not able to prevent this process of land concentration, as it occurred through generous purchases by insiders to the zone, previously supportive of the Left, rather than through usurpation by rightist outsiders. Although the cultivation of an illicit crop had initially created incentives for the *entire* coca-growing population to support the FARC, now the wealthier settlers increasingly resented the FARC's taxes (especially during price crashes), the obligations imposed by the CAC, such as to participate in work assignments and contribute to community and mobilization expenses, and the pressure to vote for the UP.[54]

The same process of land concentration that hindered the Left helped the Right. Even before 1979 more land concentration had occurred in the upper third of the county than in the lower two-thirds, because of the northern zone's earlier settlement and because its greater proximity to the capital brought higher land values. The coca boom accelerated this process. These new large landowners had not accumulated their wealth *directly* from the coca trade; they were neither coca cultivators (who lived downriver) nor intermediaries (who were outsiders representing the national cartels). Rather, the new owners of the county's most valuable plots of land were urban merchants who had become very wealthy overnight selling beer or gasoline or running hotels or brothels for their coca-grower and raspador clientele.[55]

The completion of the Paujil-Cartagena road accelerated the already rapid process of land concentration above Cartagena led by these elites, establishing the economic foundation for a Liberal clientelist machine. Almost immediately after the road was completed, lowering transportation costs, the areas of the county above Cartagena (on the Caguán and Guayas Rivers and on the road) converted from coca production to cattle production, especially dairy cattle. The cattle funds (trade association entities that lend to cattle ranchers and provide technical assistance) facilitated this conversion by providing credits for this activity after 1989, but only to those ranchers with land along the road, that is, the wealthiest ones. Soon the original settlers of the zone above Santa Fe, many of whom had arrived in the mid-1960s, were forced to sell their land to avoid foreclosure as they could not compete with the larger cattle ranchers. Most chose to move farther downriver to plant coca. Their original upriver plots became the third or fourth plot belonging to landed elites such as the two best known of Cartagena's large landholders, whose deeds I found in the departmental capital. Of a random sample I took of every tenth title granted to a settler by the INCORA since 1979 ($N = 75$), 17 percent had been resold, all of these above Santa Fe and most above Cartagena. Meanwhile, interviewees could name at least nine wealthy landowners who had emerged since 1988 with at least 500 hectares each, all of them quite active in the Turbayista faction of the Liberal Party.[56]

While the coca economy crashed, provoking an exodus of the population from leftist strongholds in Cartagena del Chairá and other Caquetá counties, the cattle-ranching sector, with which most Caquetá Turbayista *gamonales* (strongmen) were associated, was doing just fine. The cattle economy in Caquetá had expanded very rapidly in the 1970s: from 366,000 to 625,000 head between 1971 and 1975. It grew at a slower pace after that and doubled again, from 692,000 to 1,553,000 between 1976 and 1987.[57] For the period after 1987, national data show a stable volume of beef cattle slaughtered between 1981 and 1992, with very rapid growth for the dairy cattle and milk production—most prevalent in Cartagena del Chairá. Milk production more than doubled between 1978 and 1992, with Colombia attaining self-sufficiency and even surplus production by 1994.[58] If Cartagena del Chairá and Caquetá followed these national trends, which seems likely, then this cattle sector growth would have aided Turbayista efforts to continue financing their established clientelist system of vote buying and politically conditioned allotment of state spending, services, and employment throughout the period studied.[59]

An additional factor weakening the electoral Left and the social movement that formed its base was the movement's rapidly declining ability to obtain state resources, a reflection of the national government's abandonment of the carrot in favor of the stick, evidenced by several events and trends. First, the August 1987 march mentioned above obtained no concrete concessions *except* for the Paujil-Cartagena road, which had never been a high priority for the peasant movement and directly antagonized the FARC.[60] Second, between 1989 and 1991 even the accomplishments of the Laboratory of Peace era began to erode as first the state natural resource agency and then the agrarian reform agency closed its Remolino branch. By 1990 the state-subsidized agricultural production credits had been reduced to one-sixteenth of their 1986–89 amounts, and the National Rehabilitation Plan credits of 1987–88 had run out as well. Even the store-boat, one of the first and most stalwart of the peace era accomplishments, had become undependable by 1990, and La Zabaleta Communal Enterprise had disintegrated by 1992. Third, a proposal for a crop substitution program to be presented to the United Nations (via the governor) was elaborated in October 1990 by the Colonization Committee with the participation of the local branch of only one state entity (the agrarian reform agency). By the end of 1992, although other (non-UP-influenced) counties in the department had received funding from this source, Cartagena del Chairá had not.[61]

Meanwhile, those state investments and services that remained in the Middle and Lower Caguán were not seen as fruits of the peasant movement's struggles and therefore did not arrest the decline of the movement. The public investments of the National Rehabilitation Plan and the military, for example, were deliberately designed to weaken the guerrillas and the Left politically and tended to do so. While the National Rehabilitation Plan funding continued through 1992 at a fairly steady rate of about U.S.$70,000 per year, input as to where and how it would be disbursed explicitly excluded the FARC and mandated the inclusion of the traditional parties. The military's public works—the Paujil-Cartagena road, storm sewers and paving in Santa Fe, a small gasoline generator for Remolino— were part of a "hearts and minds" strategy to boost popular sympathy for the armed forces. A somewhat different phenomenon was presented by Father Jacinto's crop substitution project in Remolino. While the priest did not set out to sabotage the Lower Caguán peasant movement, the similarity of his services to those the movement had demanded unsuccessfully from the state and his control over the same amount of resources as the county meant his organization, with sixty to seventy members in 1992, in effect lured these members away from the peasant movement after 1989. A noteworthy example was the former president of the Colonization Committee, who no longer participated in the UP-influenced peasant organizations after 1989 but was active in the priest's program.[62]

As a result of the movement's declining success rate, compounded by the reduction of FARC-controlled territory, the population exodus, and the rising gap (and tensions) between the wealthier and poorer settlers of the zone, the peasant organizations of the Middle and Lower Caguán weakened quickly between 1987 and 1992. In April 1988, even before the military operation, a third assembly of the Colonization Committee had convened under the telling motto, "For the Recuperation of our organization: unity and culture." Only thirty CACs attended, and only two state entities were represented, by employees with no decision-making capacity. A mood of demoralization, atomization, and disillusionment with both the government and the peasant organizations prevailed. In 1989 and 1991 not a single meeting of the peasant organizations was held; in 1990 and 1992 there were only a few activities aimed at reviving the organization, with mixed results. In 1990 a brief protest demanded the presence of the long-overdue store-boat; a general assembly took place (with forty people attending), a few meetings between the peasant organization and Father Jacinto were held, and the crop substitution program for the UN was elaborated. A revival appeared again to be under way in 1992. The steering committee met several times a month throughout the year, and three business meetings were held. However, in mid-September 1992, even though preparations were under way for an October 1992 protest, virtually all the steering committee members expressed great frustration with the lack of response by the Caguán settlers.[63]

Further tipping the electoral balance away from the UP and toward Liberals, as the state withdrew the carrot and offered the stick, the FARC embraced armed struggle again while moving away from support of electoral action. Combat climbed sharply. Although there had been only eight FARC-government confrontations in Caquetá in 1989 and fifteen in 1990, in 1991 there were thirty-five. In Cartagena the increase was less dramatic but still important: there were no confrontations in 1989–90, but there was one in 1991 and two in 1992.[64]

More damaging for the UP's electoral prospects was the FARC's ambivalence about the electoral project in 1990 and after. The FARC was not only disillusioned with the government as a result of truce violations and the dirty war against UP activists. It was also disenchanted with the UP itself due to party divisions between *mamertos* (a derogatory term for Communist Party members, roughly equivalent to "Stalinist") and *perestroikos,* or soft-liners. While the former refrained from public criticism of the FARC's post-1987 increasingly bellicose stance, the latter openly criticized the FARC and were given extensive and favorable coverage in the mainstream press. Not surprisingly, this dampened the FARC's support for the UP. The former FARC guerrilla who had been elected as an alternate to Congress for the UP, Iván Márquez/Luciano Marín (1986–90) by 1989 had returned to arms. And in the March 1990 and March 1992 elections in Cartagena del Chairá—in marked contrast to all the elections in the region since 1978—the FARC did *not* actively campaign for the UP, nor did it encourage speedboat owners to provide free transportation for voters (with gasoline reimbursement collected and provided by the region's party cells). The FARC's marginalization from the politics of reform was reinforced by the government's bombing of the FARC's national directorate in December 1990 and its exclusion from the February–July 1991 Constitutional Assembly due to its refusal to lay down arms prior to negotiating.[65]

While the FARC distanced themselves from electoral tactics, the Turbayista Liberals—favored by the increased military-controlled territory, the emergence of wealthy landowners, and a growing cattle economy—

embraced electoral action. Vote buying by Cartagena del Chairá's Turbayistas became a common practice beginning with the 1990 elections, accounting for the dramatic electoral strengthening of this faction. Whereas in 1988 they had won only 18 percent of the county council vote, they garnered 58 percent by 1990 and 47 percent in 1992, as well as the county executive post in each of the latter two elections. As vote buying was especially prevalent in the areas that were now under effective, permanent military influence and that had experienced land concentration and conversion to cattle—urban Cartagena del Chairá and the rural areas north of the county seat along the Caguán and Guayas Rivers and on the Paujil-Cartagena road—these areas quickly became the new Liberal strongholds.[66]

An analysis of precinct-level voting results for elections held in March 1988, October 1991, and March 1992 shows that almost all the votes taken by Liberals from the UP after March 1988 were deposited in the county seat (although an overwhelming proportion of all votes, 75 to 100 percent, were deposited in urban Cartagena del Chairá in every election, with 25 percent deposited in the two rural precincts, Santa Fe and Remolino). In the county seat the UP garnered 82 percent of votes in the March 1988 election (before the military operation) but only 24 percent and 28 percent, respectively, of these votes in the October 1991 and March 1992 elections. The UP's loss of electoral influence was less dramatic in Santa Fe, two hours downriver from the county seat and the post-July 1988 line of demarcation between military and guerrilla control, with votes for the UP declining from 67 percent of all votes cast in Santa Fe in 1988 to 43 percent in 1991 and 49 percent in 1992. And in Remolino del Caguán, four hours downriver from the county seat and well within guerrilla-controlled territory both before and after the military operation, there was virtually no change in political influence, with the UP winning 89 percent of the Remolino vote in 1988, 83 percent in 1991, and 91 percent in 1992.[67]

In other regions of Colombia, the combination of economic strength and political ambition had fueled the creation of rightist landowner- or political boss–sponsored paramilitary groups. However, this did not occur in Cartagena del Chairá. The county's most powerful landed elites were certainly beginning to express their autonomy from the Left in electoral terms. However, they continued to maintain relatively cordial relationships with the FARC and the UP and had not been suspected of paramilitary leanings as of 1992. This fact accounts for the low level of repression against the noncombatant Left in Cartagena del Chairá relative to other leftist strongholds in Colombia, as well as the decidedly public nature of repression there (nearly all incidents were attributed directly to the army rather than to privately hired gunmen, or *sicarios*). In effect, between military operations—such as from February 1989 through the end of 1992—there was no repression at all.[68]

As a result of the preceding factors, the UP's local electoral influence plummeted in March 1990. The UP had swept local elections in March 1988 with 81 percent of the vote, but two years later their electoral strength had shrunk to just 31 percent, giving them the right to just three of nine county council seats. Similar results were obtained in March 1992 (37 percent of the vote; three of nine county council seats). The Turbayista Liberal administrators elected in 1990 and 1992 reduced public works investment in the middle and lower segments of the county (where the UP still maintained influenced) and increased it in their strongholds: the county seat and rural areas north of Cartagena. Similar trends prevailed on the departmental level, with the UP's proportion of votes for Departmental Assembly shrinking from 16 percent in 1988 (down from 35 percent in 1986) to 13 percent in 1990 to 11 percent in 1992. The UP also had reduced access to Congress. Whereas in 1986 it had supported one of the two winning Senate candidates (in coalition with non-Turbay traditional parties) and had independently won a House seat, in 1990 it retained only the House seat. The UP lost even this congressional foothold in the special election of 1991 after the Constitutional Assembly, never to regain it.[69]

As the UP's electoral strength melted away, the Turbayistas easily regained lost ground. Within the departmental assembly, their proportion of votes rose from 29 percent in 1986 to 42 percent in 1988, declining only slightly to 38 percent in 1990. Meanwhile, in 1990 as in 1986 Hernando Turbay held one of the two Senate seats, and his son Rodrigo Turbay held one of the two House seats allotted to Caquetá. Rodrigo continued to hold this seat in the 1991–94 special congressional period (after the Constitutional Assembly).[70]

Only three exceptions interrupted this triumphant scenario for the Turbayista Liberals from 1987 to 1992. First, the UP participated in a successful, non-Turbayista-led coalition in the first direct election of governors in 1991. (As governors had previously been appointed by the president, usually in consultation with the department's senators, this in effect had meant mostly Turbayista governors for Caquetá since the late 1960s.) The victory gave the UP unprecedented access to the governor from early 1992 through the end of 1994. Second, the momentary electoral boom of the M-19 reduced Turbayista electoral influence in 1992 to 22 percent of the Departmental Assembly; and in 1991 no Turbay family member was elected senator, due to the switch from departmental to national proportional election for this legislative body.[71]

Despite this brief electoral setback in 1991–92, however, the Turbayistas became no more inclined to negotiate any kind of peace and public works pact with the UP via the electoral system than they had been in earlier years, since (1) the UP's electoral capital was shrinking even more rapidly than the Turbayistas, and its peasant movement had faded away; and (2) with the M-19 upsurge fading, the Turbayistas could reasonably anticipate a full electoral comeback by 1994. In sum, the Turbayistas had absolutely no incentive during this period to seek to placate the UP, its peasant constituency, or the FARC through increased public spending in UP-influenced areas or reduced paramilitary repression in those parts of Caquetá where it was present.

CONCLUSION: OUTCOME OF THE REFORM PERIOD

Although the Middle and Lower Caguán experienced several very distinct phases of political development—one quite favorable to social movements and the Left—leftist representatives of the settlers' movement were never able to cement with repression-sponsoring regional elites the type of pacted peace with social gains that had prevailed in other regions. There was a brief moment of peace and peasant settler gains, imposed on regional elites and military commanders by President Betancur at an unusually favorable national political conjuncture (late 1984 to 1987). And there were other moments, from 1978 to 1983 and from 1989 to 1992, when the de facto guerrilla control of the Middle and Lower Caguán was tolerated by the national government and there was little repression. However, these were due not to a successful peace but to neglect; that is, they reflected the region's low national priority at that moment and the lack of repression-sponsoring elites at the county level. During this time the peasant settlers were starved of state resources, and at any moment they could be punished by a massive wave of repression associated with military attempts to retake guerrilla territory by force, as occurred in 1983–84 and again in 1988.

The Caguán settlers did experience peace with social movement gains during the Laboratory of Peace period, when an enthusiastically supportive president in effect ordered his underlings—the Turbayista Liberals of Caquetá, the military commanders of the region, and other state entities—to uphold the peace process in the Middle and Lower Caguán. The rhetoric of peace and the flow of resources to peasant communities boosted the electoral and organizational strength of the Left enormously. The monolithic nature of the Left in Caquetá in the mid- to late 1980s, with only one political tendency, further enhanced the UP's bargaining power. Had the peace policies continued, it is possible the UP's electoral success would have continued to grow, facilitating its electoral displacement of the Turbayistas and encouraging a regional pacted peace via the electoral system such as occurred in other regions.

But the national peace policies did not last. Even at the high point of the Laboratory of Peace, those actors forced against their will into a show of support for the peace process often dragged their feet or even actively sabotaged peace efforts, reflecting the lack of national consensus. Among the guerrillas there were also doubters, due to the escalating dirty war against the UP on the national level. Once the naysayers became the dominant voice (after mid-1986), the process quickly disintegrated. State resources stopped flowing to the settlers in Cartagena del Chairá, repression and military operations increased, and with coca prices at a ten-year low settlers flowed out of the Middle and Lower Caguán. As a result the electoral Left was severely weakened, and the chances for a peace pacted with regional repression-sponsoring elites via the electoral process withered away as well.

Not only was the Left severely weakened after 1986 and especially after 1988, but its Turbayista antagonists, who were never really weakened, grew even stronger after 1987. Because of their links with a steady beef cattle economy and a rapidly growing dairy cattle economy and the reversal of government peace policies after 1987, the Turbayistas were never really displaced. Their departmental assembly strength had dropped only slightly and momentarily in 1986, and they retained two seats in Congress through 1991 (by which time the UP was an insignificant electoral force on the department level). Thus the process that had preceded other regional pacted peaces in Colombia—leftist electoral displacement of repression-sponsoring elites following economic contraction in that elite's main economic sector or loss in regional economic influence—never occurred in Caquetá.

Although the Left did in fact displace some elite sectors electorally (non-Turbayista Liberals and Conservatives) and did form electoral alliances with such elites, these were neither the main sponsors of repression nor the main political force controlling departmental resources. Thus making agreements with these non-Turbayista elites, while beneficial in strictly electoral terms, did not lead to a pacted peace with social movement gains.

FIVE

THE COUNTERREFORM PERIOD
IN THE CAGUÁN

FARC Belligerence, Renewed Military Attacks,
and a Revived Settlers' Movement

Like the reform period, the counterreform period in Cartagena del Chairá can be seen as having several outcomes. From 1992 to 1998, while counterreform weakened an already failing settlers' movement and its electoral expression, coca expansion brought new population to the area and strengthened the FARC, which increasingly responded to counterreform by rejecting and sabotaging electoral institutions and norms and escalating attacks on the military. This provoked a major—but relatively late and public—repressive wave in 1998.

From 1998 to 2002 a new FARC-government agreement brought peace to the region but without the social movement mobilization and success or the FARC rapprochement with institutional politics that had characterized the Laboratory of Peace era. After the failure of the *zona del despeje* (demilitarized zone), President Uribe implemented the U.S.-supported Plan Patriota, which aimed to defeat the FARC militarily and eradicate coca from southern Colombia's FARC-influenced coca-growing zones such as Cartagena del Chairá. Plan Patriota reversed many of the previous period's trends—coca production and population plummeted to a fraction of their former levels, and FARC presence in the zone was reduced—for a time.

But military abuses revived the flagging Caguán settlers' movement. The open U.S. role in their suffering helped the Caguán settlers gain national allies and caused widespread questioning of Uribe's strategy. The Caguán settlers, however, received no international monetary or political support until the regional humanitarian crisis grew severe in 2008, whereas Father Jacinto's crop substitution program received such support starting in the reform period as a result of his international connections and his greater distancing from the FARC and the coca economy.

CHRONOLOGY OF CHANGE

November 1992–August 1998: Rapid Growth of the FARC
and Escalation of Armed Confrontations

This stage witnessed a return to a situation much like the period before reform. As before 1984, there was a full-scale armed confrontation between the military and the guerrillas, with few peace initiatives and few opportunities for the Left to make gains through either peasant mobilization or electoral participation. And as in 1979–83, there was an expansion of the coca economy, of the population within coca-producing zones, and of guerrilla military power. Finally, as prior to the FARC peace process in 1984–87, the Caguán became an especially strategic territory for both sides because of its status as a FARC stronghold.

The major contrast between the period before reform and the 1992–98 period is that in the latter the FARC was much more powerful both in terms of its absolute numbers and because it was the only guerrilla group in Caquetá. As a result of this strength and the end of opportunities for negotiating via institutional means, the FARC increasingly used forms of violent coercion and military attack as its primary bargaining tool. This tactic intensified army repression of peasant communities, but it also managed to wring some concessions from the FARC's elite antagonists.

The definitive end of the reform period was announced with a major guerrilla offensive and a national wave of peasant mobilizations in early

October 1992, timed to commemorate the five hundredth anniversary of Columbus's arrival in the Americas. One of these protests, a departmental mobilization in Florencia, gathered 2,500 settlers from the Lower Caguán. But the national mobilization was widely described by government sources as being promoted by subversives; none of the Florencia protest's demands were met. By November 8 President Gaviria (1990–94) had suspended broad areas of the new Constitution by declaring a State of Internal Commotion and many of its provisions were written into permanent law in October 1993.[1] Little progress toward peace was made on President Ernesto Samper's (1994–98) watch: his administration became engulfed in a political crisis, and his launching of the Convivir state-sanctioned paramilitary groups undermined his credibility.[2]

As these events unfolded, the national coca boom that was occurring was especially noteworthy in Caquetá, where coca hectares nearly quintupled, from 8,400 in 1992 to 39,400 in 1998.[3] This probably led to increased population in the county's guerrilla-controlled areas, as had occurred with every coca acreage increase in the past.

The FARC responded to the combination of political closing and the coca boom with a rapid military buildup, from about 12,000 fighters in 1992 to about 16,000 nationally in 1998,[4] and a series of impressive military feats. In Cartagena del Chairá in 1993, fifty FARC guerrillas attacked the police station in urban Cartagena del Chairá, destroying the town's electric plant, killing five policemen, wounding four others, and taking six prisoners.[5] In 1994 the FARC ambushed a patrol. There were two armed confrontations in 1995 and one each in 1996 and 1997 (fig. 5.1).

The escalating series of actions was meant to force the government to negotiate, and at first it seemed to accomplish just that. For example, the FARC kidnapped Caquetá's perennial Turbayista congressman, Rodrigo Turbay Cote, in Paujil and took him toward Cartagena del Chairá. As early as September 1995, directly as a result of Turbay's kidnapping, the Official (Turbayista) Liberals of Caquetá surprisingly favored a controversial regional dialogue with the guerrillas. In a later communiqué the FARC explained that the condition for Turbay's release was the completion of the Florencia-Suaza (Huila) road. In essence, the FARC intended to use the kidnapping to accomplish precisely what could no longer be won through electoral action and peasant mobilization. However, due to circumstances that remain unclear, when the Turbayista governor went to meet the FARC

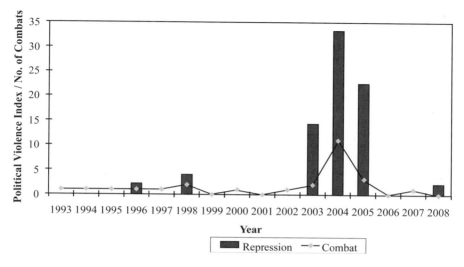

Figure 5.1. Political Violence in Cartagena del Chairá, 1993–2008

Sources: For explanation, operationalization, and sources for these data, see the methods section of chapter 1. The following sources supplemented the Noche y Niebla database and the Gutiérrez database for the years 2003, 2005, and 2006–8. For 2003: "La gran redada"; Emanuelsson, "Militares norteamericanos encabezan 20 mil soldados colombianos en operativo militar contra la guerrilla"; Cortés, "Capturas masivas." For 2005: "Daba plata oficial a la guerrilla"; "Concejales de Caquetá se salvaron otra vez." For 2007: "Farc vuelan lancha en Cartagena del Chairá"; "Detenido dirigente agrario en el Caquetá"; "Detenciones masivas en Caquetá."

in mid-1996 to reclaim the hostage, the governor was assassinated. The kidnapped Turbay was later found drowned in the Caguán River.[6]

The situation quickly descended into a contest of brute force between the army and the FARC, with the latter increasingly gaining the upper hand, especially in Colombia's Amazon and Orinoco watersheds.[7] In August 1996 FARC guerrillas in Putumayo routed the army, taking sixty soldiers hostage and killing thirty others. These hostages and several others were held in the Lower Caguán. After months of tense and unproductive negotiations, the army agreed to withdraw temporarily from a five-thousand-square-mile area around Remolino in exchange for the release of the hostages. In an emotional ceremony on June 15, 1997, in Cartagena del Chairá—decked out with FARC slogans for the occasion—the seventy soldiers were released to their family members while bands played both the Colombian and the FARC anthem. The case captured national news for months, humiliating the military. One presidential representative said, "It's humiliating, it's denigrating to have to take orders from these guerrillas."[8]

Finally, in early 1998, as part of an offensive to block the March legislative elections, the guerrillas overwhelmed the army in the hamlet of El Billar, Lower Caguán, in what the Colombian army called the worst single defeat in thirty years: Colombia's largest-circulation daily newspaper, *El Tiempo,* gave figures of 83 soldiers dead, 30 wounded, and 43 taken prisoner. Not surprisingly, violence by the army against the Caguán's peasants increased markedly. Although no incidents of violence against the peasant population are recorded between 1992 and 1995, in 1996, as a military and antinarcotics operation unfolded, five people were wounded and one was arbitrarily detained. In 1997, with the conclusion of the military operation and the army's mid-1997 abandonment of the county and concomitant closure of the base in downtown Cartagena del Chairá, there were once again no incidents of violence. However, in 1998, in response to the FARC's March ambush of the army, bombings in "extensive areas of the Lower Caguán" killed four civilians.[9]

The intensified combat silenced social movement activity. From the unsuccessful October 1992 protest until the despeje, or demilitarization, in 1998, social movement actions were infrequent. A January 1995 article quotes FARC guerrillas as saying the Caguán peasants were ready at a moment's notice to protest if fumigation occurred, but a military operation that claimed to destroy forty artisanal coca laboratories took place in late 1996 and early 1997 without a protest recorded.[10] Only when the national government declared Caquetá a "special public order zone" and restricted the sale of cement and gasoline in the department, tripling gasoline prices from $2,000 pesos per gallon to $6,000 to $8,000 per gallon and paralyzing river transportation, was there a reaction: merchants in the county seat spearheaded a countywide protest but with no mention of downriver peasant settler participation.[11]

On the other hand, two factors favored the local electoral Left in 1994. First, the expansion of the local coca economy brought more people to the downriver parts of the county. Second, the closing of institutional avenues had driven the soft-line UP perestroikos, those critical of the FARC, from the county's rural outposts, making the FARC less ambivalent about supporting the UP's county executive candidates in 1994.[12] As a result, the UP actually recovered in 1994, taking back the county executive's office in

Cartagena del Chairá in October 1994 with 47 percent of the vote (and 43 percent of the county council vote,[13] as opposed to 37 percent in March 1992). Similarly, at the departmental level, the UP's electoral strength held steady or even grew between 1992 and 1994. The UP had won 11 percent of the vote in the 1992 Departmental Assembly elections but in 1994 won 2 of 13, or 15 percent, of Departmental Assembly seats and 11 percent of the vote for the House of Representatives.[14]

Although the UP recovered the Cartagena del Chairá county executive's office, the 1994–97 administration was limited in its actions not just by the fiscal poverty of the county but now also by President Gaviria's "selective recentralization" measures, which not only prevented elected officials from carrying out their programs but also stigmatized the party as a whole. Specifically, a leading Communist Party official who had served several terms as county council member of Cartagena del Chairá and parts of terms as acting county executive was detained during this period and later released.[15]

By 1997, however, it seemed the FARC no longer intended to have county executives chosen via the electoral process at all. Thus, in August 1997 the FARC obligated all three candidates to the county executive's office and all twelve candidates to the county council to withdraw their candidacy, *including* the UP and PCC candidates.[16] No candidates ran in subsequent attempts to hold elections in October or December 1997. Finally, in March 1998, a Liberal candidate ran for county executive and won, but he was promptly kidnapped by the FARC. The county executive's seat remained empty through August 1998.[17]

Departmental electoral trends similarly reflected the disappearance of the electoral Left. By 1997 the UP won no seats in the departmental assembly. In March 1998 there was no UP candidate for Caquetá's House of Representatives, and the Communist Party Senate candidate won a total of 103 votes for the entire department. In the May 1998 presidential elections only 209 voters in Caquetá voted for the M-19 candidate, the only leftist on the ballot.[18]

Meanwhile, as the national (and presumably the Caquetá) cattle economy continued to prosper[19] and the Turbayistas benefited from the growing anti-FARC backlash, the Turbayistas regained the ground they had lost in the wake of the Constitutional Assembly. Although they failed to regain a senator from Caquetá, they retook the governor's office in 1994, and they retained, as always, a seat in the House (occupied by Rodrigo Turbay until his kidnapping). Another Turbay, Diego Turbay Cote, became one of Caquetá's two representatives in 1998.[20]

By 1998 it had long been clear that neither electoral participation nor peasant mobilization could inspire the governing Turbayistas to negotiate, for peace or for state resources. Therefore, amid a backdrop of national and regional guerrilla expansion, the FARC's moves away from institutional expressions and toward violence as its primary negotiating tool were not surprising. The FARC's new military might forced the government to negotiate regarding the hostages in 1997 and soon created incentives for a larger national negotiation.

1998–2002: The Zona del Despeje Brings Peace but No Other Gains

During this period, a renewed peace process took place, with President Andrés Pastrana (1998–2000) designating a five-county demilitarized zone that did not include Cartagena del Chairá. As during the 1984–87 peace, Cartagena del Chairá benefited from a dramatically lowered level of repression. But in contrast to the earlier peace, levels of mobilization were very low, no material resources flowed to Cartagena del Chairá's peasant movement, and the FARC's rejection of electoral politics was not reversed. By 2002 a national backlash against the expanding FARC, backed by the United States, had gained momentum, ending the peace.

President-elect Pastrana had met with the FARC's high commander, Manuel Marulanda, even before taking office and declared on taking office that he would stake his presidency on making peace with the organization. By November 7, 1998, he ordered the military to leave five contiguous counties to the FARC in return for peace negotiations.[21] These were, in Meta, the counties of Vista Hermosa, La Uribe, La Macarena, and Mesetas (shown as leftist non–case study counties in figure 1.2), and in Caquetá, San Vicente del Caguán, upriver of Cartagena del Chairá. Although the FARC argued strenuously for Cartagena del Chairá to be included as a sixth county in the demilitarized zone and proposed a detailed (and expensive) crop substitution plan to benefit the county, the government declined, probably on the grounds that giving the FARC full formal control of Cartagena del Chairá would give it too much of a strategic advantage.[22]

As a result Cartagena del Chairá benefited only partially from the peace process. On the one hand, the general reduction of tensions lowered the level of conflict in the county considerably during the despeje period. Although aerial fumigations took place in 2000–2, only one clear-cut incident of Right-on-Left violence is recorded between 1998 and 2002: a threat against a Cartagena del Chairá UP activist who was a departmental assembly candidate.[23] After the March 1998 confrontations, the military abandoned the downriver parts of the county for the entire period of the demilitarized zone, maintaining a minimal presence in the county seat only.[24] On the other hand, Cartagena del Chairá received none of the resources destined for the zona del despeje.

Possibly because of this dearth of resources, the FARC's attempts at mobilizing the community to choose a county executive, while representing a token return to institutional participation, paled in comparison to the Laboratory of Peace era. The process to select local officials starting in August 1998 began auspiciously enough. The election procedure was, according to one source, "designed by the guerrillas but supported by the state." Candidates were chosen via community assemblies *(cabildos populares)* rather than through a voting process organized by the Registraduría Nacional del Estado Civil. All were from a single movement, the Integral Democratic Movement for Life and Peace; candidates were not allowed to be affiliated with specific parties. There was a great sense of optimism, relatively high levels of citizen participation, and considerable press coverage on election day.[25] Nevertheless, in the long run the activists I interviewed judged that the elections brought neither noteworthy gains for the peasant population nor even much enthusiasm on the part of peasant activists for those who were elected, because, they said, politicians had "broken their promises." Peasant activists insisted that, like before, each CAC had to raise its own funds and carry out its own public works.[26] Moreover, in October 2001, as the zona del despeje era was coming to a close, one of these county executives was killed, along with four other people with whom he was traveling to Montañita, most likely by the FARC.[27]

Along with the lack of peasant mobilization and the scant and short-lived guerrilla and peasant movement support for institutional action, another key contrast between this peace and that of 1984–87 was the much shorter "honeymoon." In January 1999, when talks had just begun, there were mutual recriminations: among other grievances, the FARC accused the government of failing to crack down on the AUC, while the military high brass demanded the abandonment of the peace process after the FARC killed representative to the House, Diego Turbay, and his mother, Inés Cote de Turbay, along with four others in December 2000.[28] In a statement to the press, although they did not explicitly admit to the act, the insurgents appeared to justify it by stating that the Turbay family had long sponsored paramilitary groups responsible for persecuting the Democratic Front and the Patriotic Union in Caquetá.[29] Tensions were increased by the continued rapid expansion of kidnappings and the FARC's manpower, from an estimated 16,000 in 1998 to a high point of almost 17,500 in 2000.[30] One of these kidnappings occurred in Cartagena del Chairá in 1999, when a judge was kidnapped by the FARC.[31]

Meanwhile, although the United States initially supported Pastrana's peace process, by late 2000 the White House drug policy director General Barry McCaffrey termed the creation of the zona del despeje "a naive mistake on the part of the government." Plan Colombia—representing $4.4 billion in aid to be spent over five years—was passed by the U.S. Congress in September 2000 to end cocaine production and defeat the guerrillas.[32] The new policy succeeded in reducing coca cultivation from its high point of 163,789 hectares in 2000 to 102,071 hectares nationally in 2002 and from 26,603 to 8,412 hectares in Caquetá.[33] However, the U.S. presence and intervention further provoked the guerrillas. Commander Iván Ruiz of the FARC's high command said, "The gringos want to intervene in Colombia, and we're ready for them."[34]

On February 20, 2002, after three years of stop-and-start negotiations and mutual recriminations, Pastrana ended the peace process. He demanded that the FARC leave the demilitarized zone in early 2002, ordering bombings of the FARC-held zone the next day. Soon, hard-liner President Uribe won in a landslide victory, although in Cartagena del Chairá 67 percent of voters registered their strong protest by voting for Polo presidential candidate Lucho Garzón.[35]

After great expectations of material gains, the residents of Cartagena del Chairá derived little from the Pastrana-FARC peace process beyond a respite from violence. They ended the period more demobilized than they had begun. However, the next assault would force them to revive their social movement organizations.

August 2002–Late 2008: The Uribe Years—Increased Repression,
Some Revival of the Movement

Uribe's government, with the U.S.-backed Plan Patriota, brought the worst
ever wave of repression to the Lower Caguán in late 2003 through late
2005. Although at first coca cultivation was reduced and the FARC's presence made more sporadic, by 2008 it became clear that the FARC was still
powerful and willing to kill opposing politicians in the zone. Furthermore,
Plan Patriota unwittingly helped to revitalize the Lower Caguán's languish-
ing peasant social movements with new demands and alliances. Even so,
the settlers' movement was less successful than Father Jacinto's crop substitution project in capturing urban sympathies and international resources.
However, Father Jacinto's departure from the zone in mid-2008 interrupted this social experiment, highlighting the vulnerability of a movement so dependent on a single leader.

 Although its early phase began in late 2003, Plan Patriota's major push
officially began on January 1, 2004. The Colombian government's big-
gest campaign ever against the FARC sent more than 17,000 troops to
the southern coca-growing regions of Colombia—with the Caguán Valley high on the list because of its importance to the FARC.[36] The operation, which stepped up aerial fumigations in the county as well as combat
against the guerrillas, reduced coca cultivation significantly in Cartagena
del Chairá according to mid-2005 interviews with Lower Caguán residents and late 2006 statistics from the State Department, Office of National Drug Control Policy, and the UN Office on Drugs and Crime cited
in the *New York Times*.[37] The army also claimed to have compromised the
FARC's coca-dependent finances, dismantled important FARC camps, and
confiscated six hundred tons of food and 500,000 arms.[38]

 In 2006 Cartagena del Chairá was Uribe's poster child for the success
of Plan Patriota. It was reported that the FARC had moved its top national
commanders to other regions, that cattle ranching was the new economic
base of the county, and that the army controlled the Caguán River.[39] In
December 2006 the defense minister even made a speech in Cartagena del
Chairá—where, *El Tiempo* reported, "the FARC had a strong influence in
the 1990s"[40]—celebrating the year's counterinsurgency accomplishments.
A year later he and the minister of mines gave another speech in the town
to celebrate the long-awaited arrival of twenty-four-hour electricity.[41]

But in fact the FARC was far from defeated in Cartagena del Chairá. During Plan Patriota combat increased considerably. Between 1993 and 2003 only one to two guerrilla confrontations are recorded for each year, but eleven are recorded for 2004 and three for 2005.[42] FARC threats in 2004 forced the county executive to carry out his duties from the safety of Florencia,[43] and Lower Caguán residents reported daily battles throughout the region in mid-2005.[44]

No combat was reported in any of the major media outlets consulted for 2006, but there was irrefutable evidence that the FARC had regained regional power in 2007 and 2008, with no softening of their anti-institutional stance. In 2007 the FARC killed two mainstream county executive candidates and a departmental assembly candidate; threatened a county council member, who left the region; dynamited an army boat, leaving one soldier dead and eight wounded; and kidnapped three policemen. In 2008 the FARC killed a longtime Turbayista Liberal county council member and possibly perpetrated an attempt on another mainstream county council member's life. As a result, all twelve county council members and the county attorney *(personero)* went to Bogotá to demand better protection: the only public forces in the town were twenty-eight policemen, fourteen of them rookies, who had told the council members they could protect them only if they remained within a hundred-meter "security ring" around the police station.[45]

Not only were the government's gains in the region fleeting; they were made at the considerable expense of the civilian population. Although most of the repression was not lethal, a very wide swath of the population was negatively affected, fueling deep resentment. In 2003 the total repression index of 14.2 was derived from 4 civilians killed, 6 wounded or tortured, and 87 detained—accused by a paid informer of being "guerrilla auxiliaries."[46] But 2004 was the most violent ever: the repression index of 33.2 was derived from 5 people killed; 69 tortured or wounded; 132 arbitrarily detained, threatened, or who had their possessions damaged or stolen; and two instances of a school in session being used as a "human shield."[47]

In 2005 the abuses continued, on an only slightly smaller scale. The total repression index was of 22.5, composed of 5 assassinations or disappearances; 40 tortured or wounded; and 75 arrested, threatened, or whose material possessions were damaged or stolen. In addition, a much larger group of people were affected by a different category of abuses: on June 30, 2005, all food, medicine, and other consumer goods coming down the river were blocked, and in October at a checkpoint maintained for three days in Remolino, men, women, and children traveling up or down the river were made to strip naked.[48]

The operation ended in October 2005; no incidents of army violence against the Lower Caguán's civilian population were recorded for 2006.[49] In 2007–8, however, repression began again, following a "selective recentralization" pattern: the Polo candidate for county executive of Cartagena del Chairá was arrested days before the October 2007 election, and in May 2008 twenty-one agrarian activists from the Lower Caguán, especially but not exclusively leaders in Father Jacinto's Chocaguán (Chocolate del Caguán) project, were arrested and accused of "rebellion" in what they described as a crude effort to frame them. They condemned continuing military harassment and restriction of the flow of foodstuffs and medicine downriver. Even Father Jacinto was indirectly accused of "rebellion," although these charges were dropped after a timely intervention by the Italian embassy.[50]

Not surprisingly, many residents of Santa Fe and points downriver—the focus of the military's operation—left the region. In fact, by April 2008 the International Red Cross Committee listed Cartagena del Chairá as one of the ten Colombian counties with the greatest absolute number of displaced people, especially noteworthy since the county's total 2005 population was only 20,219. Even the important downriver population of Peñas Coloradas, which had as many as 2,000 residents before Plan Patriota, was reported to have only 230 in April 2007.[51]

Yet not everyone left. The government's actions had unwittingly succeeded in uniting the remaining activists and remobilizing the long-inactive Caguán settlers' movement. This time, however, demands focused on judicial action and changing national political policies rather than material resources, and the main form of action was not protests per se but forums to create alliances, garner media attention, and force government concessions.

Shortly after the first mass arrests in conjunction with Plan Patriota, in December 2003, a forum was held in Cartagena del Chairá to plan a response. Initiated by Cartagena del Chairá's CACs and attended by three hundred people, including representatives of local government and more than ten NGOs from Bogotá, it denounced the U.S. role in Plan Patriota and aimed to create connections with other, similarly affected regions in Colombia, promote alternative policies within the Colombian Congress, and arrange a visit from the attorney general's office *(fiscalía)* to record peasants' testimonies of abuses against them.[52] A year later, at the height of Plan Patriota, the First Forum for Human Rights, a Dignified Life, the Right to Work, and Peace with Social Justice was held in Remolino. Attended by two thousand people from the region, including Father Jacinto, it provided an opportunity for victims of human rights violations to denounce the perpetrators and be heard. Also in attendance were representatives of Colombia's leading human rights organizations, as well as thirty outsiders including journalists, some of them from the United States and Europe. The outsiders were welcomed by FARC guerrillas as their boats made their way downriver.[53]

In July 2005 this alliance-building project bore fruit in a two-day, three-city event protesting the abuses of Plan Patriota and the U.S. role in promoting this military operation. Spearheaded by Cartagena del Chairá's 179 CACs, it was sponsored by eleven prominent national human rights NGOs. Participants came from all of Colombia's Plan Patriota regions — Meta, Guaviare, Putumayo, Caquetá, and Cauca — who gathered simultaneously in Florencia, Cartagena del Chairá, and Bogotá. At the Bogotá press conference, which I attended, a sophisticated twenty-minute documentary made by Cartagena del Chairá's CACs explained the context and also echoed the Rodney King case by having captured live on film some of the abuses. Other regions had also produced slide shows and films. The impressive display of cross-regional organization generated several detailed news articles for national and international sources.[54] A follow-up event, to invite outsiders to witness conditions in Remolino and other Plan Patriota zones in Meta and Guaviare, was planned for December 2005 and was endorsed by ten national human rights NGOs.[55]

The series of events may have contributed to growing criticisms of Plan Patriota. Increasingly it was recognized that not only did such tactics alienate the population, but the FARC was still strong, one-third of the troops sent to fight the FARC in Colombia's Amazon watershed became ill with tropical diseases, and just in the first half of 2004, 226 soldiers had died throughout the country.[56] Furthermore, coca cultivation in late 2005 had recovered to its 2000 levels — although it was now located mostly in paramilitary-controlled zones.[57]

But it appears the movement slowed down from late 2005 through mid-2008, following the usual Caguán boom-and-bust mobilization pattern. There was no report on the December 2005 event. Instead, starting in March 2005, representatives of Caguán began to participate in a cross-regional initiative, the so-called Peasant University. Led by the San José de Apartadó Peace Community, the idea was to bring together several rural communities suffering from conflict, in different corners of the country, with courses given alternately in different rural settings. However, the last evidence of Cartagena del Chairá's participation was in late November 2006.[58] Furthermore, not surprisingly given the exodus from the lower regions of the county and the many massive arrests, the proportion of Cartagena del Chairá's votes that went to the Polo in the presidential elections decreased considerably, from 67 percent in 2002 to 50 percent in 2006. In the October 2007 county elections, the Polo's county executive candidate (arrested days before the election) won just 15 percent of votes for candidates; Polo county council candidates similarly won just 20 percent of votes for candidates.[59]

Movement activity rose again in late 2008, when the visit to Colombia of the UN's High Commissioner for Refugees coincided with the re-escalation of Cartagena del Chairá's armed conflict, increased army harassment of the population, and worsening humanitarian crisis. A unique opportunity for successful movement pressuring of the Colombian government presented itself with the October 2008 visit to the region of a humanitarian mission composed of UNHCR representatives, the Swiss embassy, the Red Cross, the Defensoría del Pueblo, and Bogotá-based human rights organizations. After hearing testimonies of abuses in locally organized events, the Humanitarian Mission demanded that the army cease its harassment of the civilian population and committed to writing and disseminating a report on the region as well as initiating an "accompaniment" project (like the Fellowship of Reconciliation's project in San José de Apartadó) to ensure that the army followed through on agreements. The Caguán peasant movement was at last receiving its first taste of transnational solidarity.[60]

In Remolino, Father Jacinto's crop substitution program, long a recipient of international support, especially from the padre's native Italy, was gaining in influence and renown and was described with great enthusiasm by the Remolino CAC's president in 2005. Rubber had failed, but cacao had succeeded. The Remolino cacao growers had launched their own brand, Chocaguán, which Father Jacinto planned to have certified organic to market nationally and internationally. His efforts had captured the imagination of national leaders and the mainstream press. In 2004, from among hundreds of candidates, he was awarded the National Peace Prize, sponsored by the UN Development Programme; national media outlets *El Tiempo, El Colombiano,* Caracol Radio, Caracol Televisión, and *Semana* magazine; and the Friedrich Ebert Stiftung Foundation in Colombia (Fescol). In addition, two long-planned works, the Remolino aqueduct and the boarding high school for local students, were under construction, with public funds as well as with international funds that Father Jacinto had raised.[61]

By March 2007 the Remolino factory processed 15,000 pounds of cacao per month and involved 75 families and more than 100 hectares in the Lower Caguán, as well as single mothers who made the packaging in Bogotá. The arrival of Chocaguán products on Bogotá supermarket shelves—and the intention to market internationally, starting in Italy— was announced with a flurry of publicity.[62] The project had also been officially endorsed and advertised by the UN Office against Drug and Crime (UNODC), with one of the main goals "transferring technology" to the region to facilitate the planting and marketing of legal crops. The use of this phrase made it appear that the long-sought-after UN grant proposal from the Laboratory of Peace era had finally been funded—but under the auspices of Father Jacinto Franzoi rather than the UP/PCC-influenced Caguán settlers' movement.[63]

Notably, the region's longer-term and more stable example of significant international support for a grassroots initiative was clearly pacifist, neutral, church- and intellectual-led, and explicitly against coca cultivation. Although Father Jacinto was vocally opposed to aerial spraying of coca crops, his pacifist leanings created tension with the FARC.[64] He thus attained and maintained a rare bilateral tolerance in the region. However, Father Jacinto was the first to recognize the fragility of the enterprise, admitting even at this moment of success in 2007 that "the peasant platform is very weak and can be destroyed by the drug economy. . . . The key will be to consolidate the [peasant cacao-growers'] committee so it can advance by itself and can begin exporting."[65] It is possible his fears have been realized: Father Jacinto returned to Italy, for good, in mid-2008 due to heart problems.[66] It remains to be seen if the project can continue without its crucial intellectual spokesperson and international liaison.

In contrast to Father Jacinto, the Caguán settlers' movement was historically closely associated with the FARC and did not explicitly distance itself from the insurgency. At the July 2005 anti–Plan Patriota mobilizations, denunciations against the FARC were not part of the main brochures or statements at the events, although a supplemental handout documenting human rights violations attributed 10 of 294 infractions against International Humanitarian Law to the insurgent organization.[67] It seemed that despite the FARC's abuses, it still had some noteworthy support. One Caquetá military commander lamented in mid-2005 that in the Middle and Lower Caguán "there were deep ties of affection between the population and the guerrillas" that would not quickly be broken.[68] This fact and the Caguán peasant population's remaining ties to the coca economy have probably hampered the movement's efforts to gain international allies. Apparently recognizing these symbolic liabilities, an activist at the July 2005 Bogotá event confessed to a journalist that he anticipated lack of national solidarity and further directed her, "Don't call us coca growers, because we're not!"[69]

How can the population's (relative) support of the FARC be explained? The FARC in Cartagena del Chairá has carried out political assassinations and threats against mainstream politicians. Clearly, the relationship between the FARC and the civilian population has also become more coercive over time as the FARC's authority in the region has become contested. For example, in 2003–4 the FARC stole a pickup truck from a rural resident, made death threats on a census worker and a teacher, and gave a woman an ultimatum to leave the county or be killed because two of her sons had performed military service.[70] However, this level of human rights violations, while still reprehensible, was considerably lower and more targeted than that carried out by guerrillas in other regions or even the contiguous counties, San Vicente del Caguán or Puerto Rico.[71] It was also much lower than that inflicted by the public forces. And to the extent that coca still existed in the region, it created some incentives for support of armed actors to protect the crops and provide "state" services.

Uribe's efforts to defeat the FARC in southern Colombia dealt some heavy blows but ultimately fell short of both its military and its social goals. The FARC returned to the region, and the population, which bore the brunt of the military operations, mobilized against the president's policies after long years of inactivity. While the peasant social movement, with a new human rights–focused strategy, succeeded in mobilizing national allies in Bogotá as well as rural allies in other regions in 2005, only in 2008 did it receive effective transnational advocacy. In contrast, the explicitly neutral, pacifist, and anti-coca Italian priest was able to garner international support for his coca substitution project starting in the late 1980s. Now that he is gone, however, his centrality to the project may in the long run prove a detriment.

CONCLUSION: OUTCOME OF
THE COUNTERREFORM PERIOD

Counterreform had the effect of reducing the success of and therefore greatly weakening the Caguán's social movements. At the same time, it spurred the FARC to reject and even sabotage institutional action, deemphasize support of social movement actions, and turn its attention toward building a more powerful and belligerent military organization.

Like other frontier peasant regions in southern Colombia without well-established local repression-sponsoring elites, Cartagena del Chairá experienced, and was benefited by, a relatively late (1998, 2004–5) and almost entirely public (army-initiated) wave of repression in the counterreform period. This allowed for a relatively lower level of repression, with most incidents nonlethal, and also allowed the 2005 anti–Plan Patriota movement to build off of an already existing infrastructure of human rights NGOs in Bogotá. The presence of only one guerrilla group in Cartagena del Chairá also meant no intra-Left territorial conflict and therefore a lower level of guerrilla violence against peasants.

Like other regions' peasant movements, the anti–Plan Patriota movement astutely switched from the failed strategy of protests aiming to extract material resources from the national government to forums for building national and interregional alliances to change government policies—although it did so much later than other regions, as movement weakness impeded a quick transition to a new set of strategies and alliances. Ironically, Plan Patriota created these interregional alliances by its direct targeting of southern coca-growing regions for similar treatment. The movements experienced some success, as demonstrated by the critical evaluation of Plan Patriota excesses and failures in the mainstream press.

However, the Caguán settlers' movement faced several key disadvantages. First, coca as a basis of the local political economy continued to create dramatic ebbs and flows of the population, which undermined organizational stability, especially in the wake of large-scale aerial fumigation campaigns. Second, in contrast to the reform period, the FARC's presence and relationship with Caguán settlers no longer presented the advantages it had once offered. If the region's status as a FARC stronghold had once given the state reason to prioritize aid to the Caguán settlers over aid to settlers from less strategic coca regions, now it gave the state reason to prioritize the Caguán for military attack and harassment of the population.

Third, and compounding this problem, to win powerful international allies required some distancing of the movement both from guerrillas, who were increasingly disrespectful of international norms, and from the coca economy itself. Yet this caused a dilemma, as other factors created disincentives to condemning the FARC. The FARC's coercive power, the region's continuing dependence on coca as a livelihood, the FARC's monolithic control and thus *relative* respect for the civilian population in this zone in comparison with others, and the army's flagrant lack of such respect— all created continuing incentives for tolerating the FARC as a defender of illicit crops and as a parallel state. Only the extreme nature of the humanitarian crisis in 2008 allowed the Caguán peasant movement to overcome this disadvantage and finally obtain an international airing of their grievances and advocacy on their behalf.

The relative ease with which Father Jacinto's Chocaguán crop substitution project gathered foreign resources, when contrasted with the Caguán settler movement's frustrating experience in this regard, amply demonstrates both the importance of international alliances in these war zones and the centrality of embracing international norms in building these alliances. On the other hand, the centrality of Father Jacinto's role as spokesperson and fund-raiser to the success of his project made for a more difficult transition after he returned to Italy.

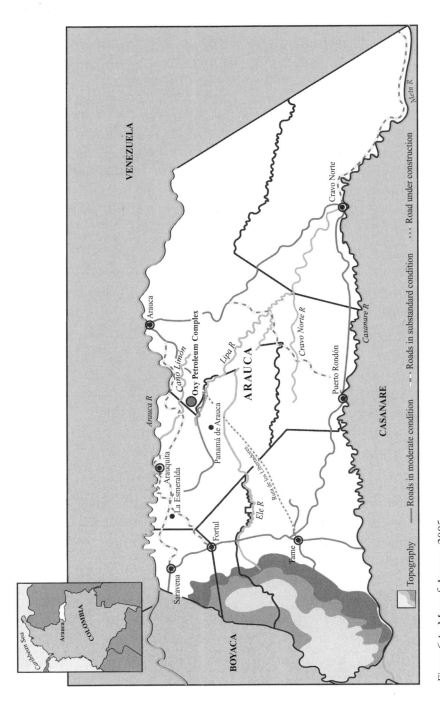

Figure 6.1. Map of Arauca, 2005

Sources: Instituto Geográfico Agustín Codazzi, *Atlas de Colombia* (Santafé de Bogotá: Instituto Geográfico Agustín Codazzi, 2002), 36; location of Caño Limón oil complex from interview 60.

CHAPTER

SIX

ARAUCA IN THE REFORM PERIOD

Pacted Peace and Social Movement Gains

In Arauca a relatively unified, strong, and stable peasant movement and electoral Left, combined with a repression-sponsoring elite faction declining in economic influence and dividing, facilitated the most exceptional outcome of the four cases: a regional pacted peace with clear gains for social movements. Oil and the direct election of county executives in 1988 (as well as the direct election of governors in 1991) were fundamental to creating both of the essential ingredients of the pacted peace.

The discovery of oil in Arauca in 1986, and the subsequent injection of fiscal resources into previously impoverished regional and county governments, strengthened the peasant movement and the leftist parties based on it, as peasant settler mobilizations demanding public works in recently settled areas became both more frequent and more successful in terms of concessions.[1] This success allowed the electoral Left to remain successful despite repression. The direct election of county executives stimulated the electoral participation of the Left, which between the two leftist parties won nearly half the vote in departmental elections after 1986. This first democratizing reform, and later the direct election of governors, strengthened the peasant movement by facilitating for the first time the election of county and departmental executives willing to intervene politically in

177

favor of peasant interests, during mobilizations as well as during the formulation of their respective public works budgets.

By the same token, both the new importance of oil as a source of abundant fiscal revenues and the direct election of county executives seriously weakened the regional influence of the main elite sponsors of repression: the large cattle ranchers represented by Senator Alfonso LaTorre. The advent in 1987 of county and departmental budgets ten to twenty times larger than before oil was discovered immediately made government and government-contractor employment, rather than employment on cattle ranches, the crucial resource to control in order to maintain political power.

Once the direct election of county executives was implemented in 1988, LaTorre's protégé could establish and control his own large clientele of grateful constituents, public servants, and contractors, later breaking away from his former patron. With LaTorrismo thus in an electoral minority and cattle ranching nearly irrelevant economically to the post–oil boom Araucan political process, LaTorre's best option for political survival after 1990 became an electoral alliance with one of the two leftist electoral fronts, the Patriotic Union, which held nearly one-third of the departmental vote. A corollary of this informal pact was an end to the paramilitary violence that had been sponsored by the largest LaTorrista cattle ranchers against peasants and activists associated with the Left before 1989.

By 1990 the other major leftist electoral front, the Saravena Liberals,[2] had followed suit, arranging their own pacted peace–electoral coalition with a new petrocrat faction. The direct election of county executives in 1988 and then the direct election of governors in 1991 played a key part in facilitating these conjunctural peace agreements, that is, agreements depending on a special combination of political circumstances. It did so not only by creating clear electoral incentives for Left-elite alliances but also by allowing Araucan political actors the autonomy from the central government to enact them.

I divide the evolution of the Araucan political process into four major periods. Before 1970 the piedmont half of the department was virtually uninhabited, and wealthy Liberal cattle ranchers from the flatlands half of the department dominated the region both politically and economically. Then demographic expansion and growing peasant social movement strength in the piedmont led to the initial wave of elite-sponsored repression against the peasant movement and the Left in 1984, through which the large plains cattle ranchers sought to prevent their imminent political displacement by the Left. Between 1984 and 1988 both oil production and democratic reforms continuously strengthened the peasant movement and the Left, causing an escalation in elite-sponsored repression. Arauquita's peasant movement was able to resist this onslaught, but the urban sympathizers of the Left in the department capital were not. During the fourth period, 1989–92, the latent divisions of the Liberal Party became manifest. These divisions eventually led to elite-Left electoral alliances that dramatically lessened repression against the Left despite—and largely because of—the continued strength and stability of the peasant movement.

The regional events in each period are explained below, highlighting comparisons between the two contiguous counties on which my analysis is centered, leftist Arauquita and Liberal Arauca. The most salient of the shared characteristics is the unusual pattern of violent repression against the Left, which from 1984 to 1988 increases, along with the Left's electoral strength and peasant mobilization, but after mid-1989 suddenly drops off despite continued Left electoral strength in Arauquita and at the departmental level. The contrasts between the two counties relate to the greater strength of the Left and the social movements on which it is based in Arauquita. Arauquita's Left is both more repressed and more resilient to repression because of its greater social movement success. Furthermore, Arauquita's leftist county executives did more to aid the peasant movement than did Arauca's Liberal county executives, although directly elected Liberal county executives in Arauca County and directly elected Liberal governors were clearly much more responsive to pressures from below than their appointed predecessors had been.

EVENTS LEADING TO PACTED PEACE

Arauca before 1970: Domination of the Piedmont by
the Plains Demographically and Politically

Since their first settlement in colonial times the Araucan plains, located in the Orinoco River watershed (the Orinoco is Venezuela's largest river system) and separated from the most populated parts of Colombia by the

Andes, had been connected more closely with Venezuela than Colombia (see fig. 1.2). Smaller twin Venezuelan cities are located across the Arauca River from each Araucan town, with close links between each pair based on significant trade, both legitimate and illicit. Only the direction of this trade varies with time and relative exchange rates. Many residents have dual citizenship, and there is considerable intermarriage between Venezuelans and Colombians. In the flatlands and along the abundant rivers and creeks in both the piedmont and the flatlands, flooding is an annual certainty and an important focus of requests for state aid, given rainfall patterns, the flatness of the terrain, and the proximity of much of the population to the Arauca River.[3]

Although these characteristics unite the entire region, the intendency of Arauca was divided historically into two major subregions: the plains and the piedmont (fig. 6.1),[4] each consisting of only a few counties as the region was sparsely populated. The plains counties, to the east, are Arauca, the eastern half of Tame, Cravo Norte, and Puerto Rondón. The piedmont counties, to the west, are Saravena, the western half of Tame, Arauquita, and Fortul. The plains have sandy soil and flood annually; the piedmont counties, which are slightly sloped and at a higher elevation, flood less (except along riverbanks) and have higher soil quality. Because the department of Arauca is composed of only seven counties, departmental politics have a far greater effect on individual counties than in the departments where the other case study counties are located.

Before the 1970s most of the intendency's population resided in the plains subregion. However, the intendency as a whole was still sparsely populated, with a population of only about 80,000, and this dearth of population dictated the region's status as an intendency rather than a department before 1991. The floods and poor soil quality in the plains made this region suitable only for land-intensive cattle ranching, which had been the mainstay of the economy for centuries. Because the flooding made it necessary to move cattle constantly, the plains were characterized by unfenced ranges, with the cattle branded to identify ownership. The flooding and the fact that the first settlement of the plains dated to the colonial era also caused a peculiarity in plains land titles: holdings tend to be very large— holdings of up to 1,000 hectares are quite common, and some approach 100,000 hectares—and their owners wealthy and powerful, but frequently without formal and universally recognized titles. Instead, the large cattle rancher would have a right of possession (*derecho de posesión,* a legal figure dating from colonial times and recognized by some Colombian courts but not by the Colombian Institute for Agrarian Reform, INCORA).[5] The legal precariousness of the right to possession probably contributed to the vehemence with which the wealthiest ranchers later reacted to the emergence of the peasant settler–based Left.

The poorer residents of the plains were Colombians and Venezuelans who had trickled into Arauca from more densely populated areas. Because they tended to arrive with insufficient capital to buy cattle, they farmed small subsistence plots—some of it with ambiguous ownership—and worked for wages for the large cattle ranchers to supplement their incomes. Their dependent relationship with their much wealthier employers or landlords led to the development of clientelistic ties that became the electoral foundation of the Liberal Party in Arauca (the Conservative Party has a rather weak presence in almost the entire eastern plains region of Colombia, since migrants came almost exclusively from Liberal regions). Thus political representatives of the department of Arauca before the reform era generally were plains large landowners or those dependent on them.[6]

1970–1978: Arrival of Peasant Settlers in the Piedmont but Continued Plains Political Hegemony

During the late 1960s and early 1970s INCORA, pressed by a strong peasant movement on the national level, began to promote an effort to settle the piedmont counties. By the end of the decade the balance of population in the department had reversed, with almost three-fourths of its 78,000-odd residents living in the piedmont.[7] These peasant settlers usually had legally titled holdings of 50 to 100 hectares each and worked their own land. Most raised beef cattle, but cocoa was cultivated in Arauquita along the banks of the Arauca River, downriver from the county seat (see fig. 6.1).[8]

A number of factors helped lay the foundations for a strong and stable peasant settler movement. First, INCORA had explicitly encouraged peasants in regions with land conflicts (especially neighboring Santander and Boyacá) to settle land in Arauca. Thus from the outset Arauquita's peasant settlers had more experience with successful peasant mobilization than the average Colombian peasant. Furthermore, the steady if not lucrative cattle ranching and cocoa economy of the Araucan piedmont offered the peasant settlers economic stability rather than quick money (and quick stratification). A survey of piedmont settlers later showed that those who came to the Araucan piedmont were attracted by the possibility of having enough land and credit to sustain themselves comfortably and permanently as small cattle ranchers.[9] Those settlers who sought quick money went elsewhere. Another indication of their intention to remain permanently was the fact that many settled in clusters according to their region of origin and family relationships.[10]

Stability was realized through the end of the reform period: land tenure in Arauquita and the rest of the Araucan piedmont was extraordinarily stable, with very little turnover or concentration of landownership.[11] The previous mobilization experience of Arauquita's peasant settlers as well as the stability of landownership and lack of stratification facilitated the establishment of tight organizational networks. An additional incentive for organization was provided by the context. On arrival, at INCORA's suggestion, the settlers organized in community groups, called Communal Action Committees *(juntas de acción comunal)*, in order to establish through community work brigades basic physical infrastructure such as footbridges and paths.[12]

With a basic organizational infrastructure already in place, the settlers' shared grievances vis-à-vis the departmental and national governments gave their community organizations one more reason for being. Although settlers had land titles and minimal access to credit through the INCORA-sponsored Caja Agraria (Agrarian Bank), the transportation infrastructure to get cattle and other products to market was woefully inadequate. Before 1984, when the first road connecting the county seats of Arauca and Arauquita (via the Caño Limón oil field) was opened, river transportation was the only option available, and it was prohibitively expensive: US$12.50 at the exchange rate of that time for each passenger. Furthermore, until 1986 the condition of the unpaved road from the piedmont counties over the Cordillera to the mountainous Colombian departments of Boyacá or Santander was so deplorable that the trip could take a week. The road was completed only in 1974, with questionable technical specifications, according to one Araucan author. And although it was quite easy to transport products across the river to Venezuela, Araucan agricultural products faced tariff barriers when the Colombian currency was weaker than the Venezuelan bolívar or serious competitive disadvantages when the Colombian currency was stronger. The peasants themselves sometimes faced harassment by Venezuelan authorities, a reflection of tensions between the two countries.[13]

Peasant settler demands also focused on improving the inadequate social infrastructure of the rural piedmont, especially the construction of one-room rural elementary schoolhouses (which in frontier zones doubled as neighborhood meeting halls) and hospitals. Demands for improved credit, transportation, and social infrastructure became central to the emerging peasant movement. The first major mobilization, a civil strike in 1972, concentrated five thousand protesters in Saravena and succeeded not only in bringing national authorities to the negotiating table but also in reactivating INCORA's loan and expenditure programs, which were in danger of being curtailed.[14]

Despite the piedmont settlers' success in wresting concessions from the national government and despite the fact that they had doubled the region's population and greatly increased its agricultural and ranching production, their interests were largely ignored by the dominant plains politicians, who continued to monopolize political power and to direct state resources toward the flatlands. The settlers, after all, were not easily converted into clients of the plains elites. They were not beholden to them or to the politicians that represented them in any way; instead, they derived benefits directly from INCORA. In contrast to the plains electorate, which tended to request from elites and politicians personal favors such as grants or jobs in the regional administration, most of the settlers' petitions demanded resources far beyond those controlled by a senator or intendential councilor.[15] Consequently, the piedmont settlers were uninterested in and uninteresting to the plains clientelist Liberal establishment.

After 1966 that Liberal establishment was controlled largely by the faction led by representative (1962–66), then senator (1966–70, 1974–90) Alfonso LaTorre Gómez. Senator LaTorre's link to the presidency ensured that he would be the first consulted by the Executive regarding the appointment of intendents (governors of intendencies). An intendent thus appointed would owe LaTorre a favor, appointing LaTorrista county executives as well. The appointed officials in turn would require of employees recommendation letters from LaTorre or prominent LaTorristas. The discretionary funds *(auxilios)* associated with LaTorre's post in the Senate allowed him to finance campaigns for county council and other elected posts, as well as to offer other favors, further ensuring the adherence of the intendency's aspiring Liberal candidates, civil service employees, and other strategic individuals to LaTorrismo. This was especially true in the pre-oil years, before 1985–86, when LaTorre's auxilios, along with campaign contributions from the region's most powerful elites, were virtually the only source of campaign funds.[16]

Late 1970s–1984: Arrival of Guerrillas and Leftist Confrontation of LaTorrismo

From the late 1970s two guerrilla groups had established themselves in the Araucan piedmont: the ELN, which was recovering from near-decimation of its ranks, and the FARC, which was in a position of strength and expansion. The FARC initiated its first military action in Fortul in 1980; the ELN's first attack on the army occurred in 1981 in the small settlement in Tame County called Betoyes (near the border with Fortul).[17] Both groups were clearly based on peasant settlers in the foothill counties of Saravena, Arauquita, Fortul—part of Tame until 1990—and the piedmont half of Tame. Although the two groups shared the same demographic constituency of peasant settlers, the geographic boundaries between the two groups were relatively clear-cut. The FARC had its strongest influence in rural Arauquita, Fortul, and the parts of Saravena bordering Arauquita but not on the banks of the Arauca River. The ELN, in contrast, had its major stronghold in Saravena, with some influence along the banks of the Arauca River in Arauquita County but upriver of the county seat.[18] That these boundaries were relatively static and clear to all residents is characteristic of guerrilla presence in frontier zones in general and a strong disincentive for the entrance of new guerrilla movements. This political territoriality helps explain why there are only two guerrilla groups in the Araucan piedmont, a factor that would later contribute to the electoral Left's relative unity and impressive bargaining power.

As the piedmont peasant movement was already highly organized and increasingly radicalized before the armed insurgencies arrived, it was a relatively small step for the guerrillas to gain the sympathies of some organizers within the established peasant organizations. Eventually the Asociación

Nacional de Usuarios Campesinos (ANUC) and the Federación Nacional Sindical Unitaria Agropecuaria (Fensuagro)—the Araucan chapters of two national organizations—came to have zones of influence that roughly paralleled those of the ELN and the FARC, respectively. A leading peasant organizer from Arauquita identified Saravena as the county with the largest number of ANUC members and Arauquita as that with the largest number of Fensuagro members. Although interviewees were hesitant to elaborate the exact ways in which the guerrillas influenced peasant mobilizations, it was clear that they encouraged participation through a system of incentives (e.g., each peasant should either participate or contribute money to the effort) and also had some influence over the choice of demands.[19]

By the early 1980 civic strikes became the main weapon of the peasant settlers. A large number of protesters would gather in a strategic, visible place, refusing to leave until the governor had met with their leaders to negotiate their demands. In 1982, for example, ten thousand protesters camped out on the runway in Saravena for twenty days, effectively preventing oil executives and engineers from completing tasks necessary to build the oil pipeline. In other cases protesters camped out in the main plaza of the department capital for up to a month, receiving considerable press attention, even from national newspapers. Almost all these protests were aimed at the departmental government, although those in support of an interdepartmental highway were aimed at INCORA or the national government as well.[20] Although the peasant movement's impressive level of organization would seem to create tremendous electoral potential for the Left in the early 1980s, the Left abstained from any electoral participation until 1984.

In 1984 the incipient political fronts associated with the Fensuagro (table 6.1), and to a much lesser extent the ANUC (which was loosely linked to the ELN and would eventually become the Saravena Liberals), made their first attempts to elect their own "political representatives" to the Intendential Council and garnered 22 percent and 6 percent of the vote, respectively. The candidates for the leftist political movements were identified rather vaguely in the case of the Fensuagro/PCC (Communities of the Piedmont) or somewhat deceptively in the case of the ANUC (Conservative).[21] Nevertheless, since these peasant settler constituents had contributed votes to the list, the movements received some auxilios for piedmont public works. The Fensuagro and the Conservatives made similar

Table 6.1. Araucan Leftist Organizations, 1984–1992

	1984	*1985–1987*	*1988–1992*
Party	PCC	PCC	PCC
Political movement/ electoral front	PCC candidates ran as part of coalitions led by traditional parties.	UP	UP
Guerrilla group from which derived	FARC	FARC	FARC
Peasant organization sympathetic to this "line"	Fensuagro	Fensuagro	Fensuagro
Guerrilla group	ELN	ELN	ELN
Electoral front sympathetic to this "line" and based in same geographic area	Ran candidates as part of coalitions led by traditional parties	Ran candidates as part of coalitions led by traditional parties	Saravena Liberals (they led their own list)
Peasant organization sympathetic to this "line" and based in same geographic area	ANUC	ANUC	ANUC

arrangements for Arauquita's county council elections of 1984, when the peasant movement's votes contributed to the Conservative victory with 58 percent of the vote.[22]

But the first wave of repression against the piedmont-based Left had not waited for this first manifestation of the Left's electoral influence. It had begun even before the 1984 elections, and by 1984 repression in Arauquita had reached its first peak of 16.25 (90 percent of the reform period maximum in 1988).[23] Similarly, in Arauca County repression had reached the highest point that it would attain during the entire period, 6.0. Unified and well-organized LaTorrista cattle ranchers from Arauca County—in particular, the largest of them, according to UP activists—had reacted to the electoral threat of the Left while it was still incipient.[24]

Although repression first peaked in both Arauca and Arauquita in 1984, there was considerably more repression in Arauquita. Despite the similar population figures for the two counties—Arauca County's population grew from 20,334 to 40,518 between 1984 and 1991; Arauquita's, from 21,643 to 43,127 during the same period[25]—the absolute level of repression was much higher in Arauquita, due to its much stronger peasant settler movement and Left. Only a small corner of Arauca County, bordering Arauquita, was populated by peasant settlers. Although they voted faithfully for the Patriotic Union and participated in peasant mobilizations, there were very few of them. Most (78 percent) of Arauca County's population was urban, and most of its rural residents had ties to plains elites through clientelism. In contrast, Arauquita was mostly populated by peasant settlers who participated actively in the peasant settler movement, and its population was at least half rural.[26] Thus there was more to repress in Arauquita in 1984 than in Arauca.

1985–1987: Success of the Peasant Movement and
a Decrease in Repression

The period 1985–87 was a turning point for the Araucan peasant movement and the Left. First, as a result of the FARC-government peace process, repression declined, the UP was founded and was electorally successful, and UP county executives who could aid the peasant movement were appointed. Second, after oil production began in Arauca, the direct expenditures of the oil sector as well as the department's new fiscal wealth facilitated peasant movement gains.

Political opening benefited the peasant movement and the Left in two ways. First, the initial escalation of repression against the peasant movement in 1983–84 was interrupted by a national truce between the FARC and the Colombian government. The decline in repression was especially noteworthy in those areas, such as Arauquita and rural Arauca, where the FARC was the dominant guerrilla group. In both counties repression declined in 1985 to a fraction of the 1984 level (see figs. 6.2 and 6.3), despite

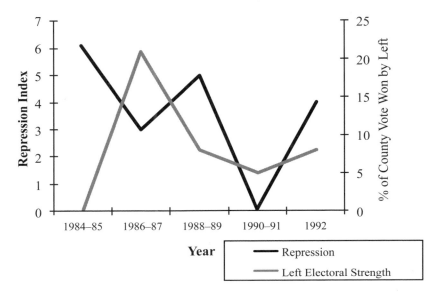

Figure 6.2. Repression and Left Electoral Success in Arauca County, 1984–1992

Note: For additional explanation, operationalization, and sources for these data, see the methods section of chapter 1 and table 6.2.

the fact that the level of regional peasant mobilization increased substantially from 1985 to 1987, as did Left electoral success between 1984 and 1986. In fact, all these changes resulted from the same root cause: national political opening.

Along with the truce, the 1984–85 government-FARC negotiations led to the reassignment of about eight hundred guerrillas from armed struggle to civilian political life and the formation of the Patriotic Union. In addition to Communist Party members, those who joined the UP included many (non-LaTorrista) traditional party leaders from the piedmont in Arauca County who had long been frustrated with the lack of responsiveness of the plains politicians to the interests of their constituents.[27] By the March 1986 elections the UP was in a powerful position in Arauca, drawing electoral influence not only from the growing strength of the piedmont peasant movement but also from an impressive "transition effect." The FARC, as the largest guerrilla group and the first to turn fighters into

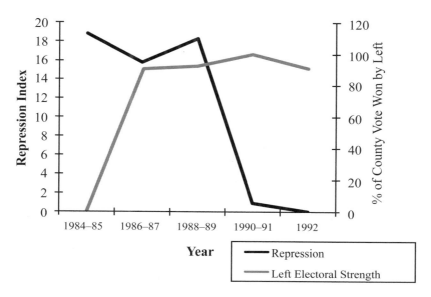

Figure 6.3. Repression and Left Electoral Success in Arauquita, 1984–1992

Note: For additional explanation, operationalization, and sources for these data, see the methods section of chapter 1 and table 6.3.

politicians, and the UP, as the fruit of this peace process, enjoyed tremendous legitimacy, inspiring hope for the peace process and democratic reforms in general.

An example of this honeymoon between authorities, the FARC, and the FARC-founded UP, which had no counterpart in elite relations with the ELN at that moment, was a regional forum held in the city of Arauca in August 1986, the First Forum for Peace and Development in Arauca. It was attended by the usual representatives of Araucan elites: the president of the chamber of commerce, the bishop and another parish leader, the commander of the regional army battalion, and the president of the Cattle Ranchers' Association. No representatives of the ANUC were present, but six activists from the Patriotic Union attended, four of them county officials and one the president of the Departmental Assembly. Most notably, alongside the regional military commander and the large cattle ranchers, a FARC representative was also present and participating in the debate.[28]

Indeed, overnight the UP had become Arauca's most influential political party, largely displacing the long-dominant plains Liberals and nearly erasing the Conservatives. While Senator LaTorre managed to retain his Senate seat in March 1986, the UP elected the other senator for the jurisdiction—with 1,285 more votes than LaTorre received (41,391 to 40,106). In fact, had the jurisdiction for the election been Arauca alone, rather than Arauca and Meta, LaTorre would have lost his position altogether, as the two top vote winners for the Senate in Arauca were the UP (7,563) and the also mostly piedmont-based Independent Liberals (4,056).

The vote for Arauca's lone representative to the House was more decisive. The candidate for the coalition UP–Independent Liberals garnered 8,335 votes of a total of less than 17,000—more than 4,000 more than either the non-LaTorrista Liberal candidate or the LaTorrista. Similarly, in the Intendential Council, the Patriotic Union–Independent Liberal coalition (which was labeled exactly that way) had garnered 47 percent of the vote, electing four of nine deputies. Meanwhile, the ANUC continued its more clandestine electoral participation, electing one deputy, who was second on a traditional Liberal list, to the Intendential Council.[29]

At the county level the UP's piedmont electoral success was even more clear. The UP swept the county council elections in Arauquita with 84 percent of the vote, won a majority in Tame with 56 percent of the vote, and won more than any other party in Saravena as well, with 45 percent of the vote. (The Saravena Liberals at that point were electorally active at the departmental level only, not at the municipal level.) According to President Barco's directive,[30] intended as a gesture of goodwill to encourage the peace process, the UP would have the right to choose the (appointed) county executive in those counties where the new political movement had won more votes than any other political force. Therefore, the UP's county-level success in March 1986 entitled them to have county executives in Arauquita, Tame, and Saravena. They took office in September 1986, just as the oil sector was beginning to have a regional impact. Although the UP did not win enough votes in Arauca County to take the county executive's office, they did win an impressive 21 percent of the county vote, again reflecting the unique window of opportunity presented by this political conjuncture.[31]

The Araucan peasant settler movement was doubly blessed in the period between 1985 and 1987. Not only did the national political opening facilitate electoral representation and increased and more open mobilization, but the oil boom also greatly increased the movement's chances for success, further strengthening the peasant settler organizations.

There had been rumors of an oil bonanza that significantly predated its realization. On July 1, 1980, Occidental Petroleum signed a contract of association with Ecopetrol, the Colombian state oil enterprise, specifying the conditions for oil exploration in Arauca. In July 1983, after a long and arduous exploratory process and a $70 million investment, Occidental discovered oil, in Caño Limón (see fig. 6.1). By November tests had confirmed that the find—reserves of up to one billion barrels—was one of the world's most important in the previous fifteen years. It would double Colombia's oil production from about 265,000 to 480,000 barrels per day, transforming the Latin American nation from an oil importer, which it had been since 1974, to an exporter once again by 1986. First, though, a massive work of infrastructure had to be built: the Caño Limón–Coveñas oil pipeline, which extended 800 kilometers from the Araucan oil field over the Cordillera Central to Colombia's Atlantic port of Barranquilla. This and other necessary infrastructure was completed in a record two years, and the first oil production began in December 1985.[32]

By fiscal year 1987 (March 1987–March 1988) oil royalties began flooding the coffers of Arauca's intendential government as well as the two counties in which the oil field was located: 90 percent of the wells were in Arauca County, with the other 10 percent in Arauquita, making the plains county nine times as wealthy per capita as the piedmont county but still making Arauquita much wealthier than most colonization zone counties. Between 1986 and 1987 the intendency's budget had increased twentyfold, and Arauca County's had increased by a factor of twenty-seven. In Arauquita the increase was more modest: the budget in FY 1987 grew by a factor of about three over the previous years.[33]

One of the first indirect effects of Occidental's activities in Arauca was, ironically, the strengthening of the ELN guerrilla group, which had ended the 1970s in a position of weakness. In particular, the ELN assaulted four times the installations of the German-based multinational Mannesman Corporation, with which Occidental had contracted for the rapid building of the pipeline between mid-1983 and late 1985, and kidnapped four of its employees. Although Occidental representatives and Mannesman deny that any ransom was paid, a near-consensus in the Colombian press estimates ransom payments anywhere from U.S.$3 million to

$50 million. Furthermore, no sooner was the oil pipeline built than the ELN began bombing it, later extorting a "tax" from the contractors that came to repair it.[34]

These resources allowed for the rapid reconstruction of the ELN's military organization. The ELN then took advantage of the space left open by the FARC's cease-fire with the government to try to gain territorial military control within the intendency and especially within the FARC's strongholds. Thus, in contrast to 1985, when there had been only one guerrilla action in Arauquita, carried out by the FARC, in 1986 there were fourteen, all carried out by the ELN, and in 1987 thirteen, four involving the FARC and nine involving the ELN. The difference in tactics between the two groups during this period (1985–87) caused tensions between the two armed organizations that at times spilled over to the peasant movement.[35]

While the oil boom strengthened the ELN and probably the FARC as well, it did not create a strong or radical oil workers' union. The oil workers' union, Sindicato de Trabajadores de Occidental (SintraOxy), headquartered in the city of Arauca, had almost a thousand members in 1992. However, as the union president lamented, the rank and file were highly stratified, were mostly white-collar engineers or near-engineers (due to the high-tech nature of the Caño Limón oil field, the capital-intensive pipeline transportation system, and the absence of refineries), and in general were quite privileged. Thus militant and radical activism rarely occurred.[36]

The peasant movement grew tremendously in militancy and success between 1984 and 1987. The peace process and direct oil sector investments contributed to the success of the mobilizations in 1984–85; the UP's electoral success and the actions of leftist county executives further aided the mobilizations in 1986; and in 1987 all these factors as well as the huge increase in oil-derived fiscal revenues brought peasant social movement success to an all-time high.

Before 1986, however, peasants did not receive support from county executives. In 1984 thirty-five protesters had marched from the capital of the intendency to Bogotá to demand from the national government the construction of a road along the same southern route through Tame and the department of Casanare along which they had marched. In early 1985 a more massive protest was held, as two thousand peasant protesters marched through Arauquita on their way to neighboring Saravena, again demanding from the national government a land route connection between Arauca and the rest of Colombia. This time the focus was on the northern route, connecting Arauca to Arauquita, Arauquita to Saravena, and Saravena to the department of Norte de Santander.[37]

Both protests had been stimulated in part by the fall of the Venezuelan currency, the *bolívar*, in February 1983. While Venezuelans had long found Araucan agricultural products and livestock cheap because of the weaker Colombian currency, after the fall of the bolívar Colombian products became prohibitively expensive to Venezuelans. Suddenly, then, it became much more urgent for Araucan peasants to be able to market their products in Andean Colombia, and thus the need for a road. Furthermore, the oil economy, incipient as it was, had already created real costs to peasant settlers by seriously inflating local prices for transportation.[38]

Fortunately, the oil economy also brought some benefits. What the national government at that pre-cease-fire moment was unwilling or unable to grant, Occidental did. Since Occidental itself had massive transportation needs in order to bring in construction materials, it had by 1984–85 completed the construction of the road that connected Arauca City to the Caño Limón oil complex and Caño Limón to Arauquita. Furthermore, by 1986–87 it had improved the road from Saravena to Norte de Santander substantially, so that the trip that had once taken three days now took less than twenty-four hours.[39]

Lack of support from county executives, however, hampered the success of these two protests. In 1985 all Araucan county executives continued to be LaTorre appointees (most of them appointed in 1984), as were most of the governors, who had short terms of appointment. And notwithstanding the recently initiated honeymoon with the FARC and the UP, the instructions given to county executives by their LaTorrista patrons were clear: the peasant movement was to be repressed and politically excluded.[40] The first protest thus received no aid at all, from any county executive. In the case of the second protest, a sympathetic Liberal appointee in Arauquita, Elsa Rojas, tried vainly to support the cause, despite her political debt to her LaTorrista appointer. Her pro-settler leanings were based on her residence in Arauquita and her consequent sympathies for the piedmont peasant settlers' demands for regional development—and possibly on her consideration, even then, of becoming one of the piedmont Liberals turned UP. (She became the successful UP–Independent Liberal candidate to the House of Representatives in March 1986.)[41]

When the two thousand peasant protesters, on their way to neighboring Saravena, camped in Arauquita for three days, the governor, a La-Torre appointee, ordered doña Elsa to declare and enforce a curfew for the duration of the protest. Instead, doña Elsa not only refused to establish the curfew but also declared her support for the protesters' demands. She was thereupon summarily dismissed, replaced by a police lieutenant considerably more obedient to the governor. The president also appointed a military governor in response to the protest.[42]

In 1986, however, the appointment of leftist county executives shifted the context in the peasant movement's favor, allowing it to receive full county executive support for the first time. In September 1986, in response to a massacre of eleven fishermen by the Venezuelan army, the Fensuagro (aligned with the UP) and the ANUC (aligned with the Saravena Liberals) together organized a protest in which 3,500 peasants camped in Arauca City's main square for thirteen days. The central demands made of the departmental government were the investigation of the specific incidents of violence, as well as running water and electricity in the piedmont county seats and health clinics in all the major piedmont settlements. This time the protest could count on the appointed UP county executives in Arauquita, Tame, and Saravena as allies. They supported the protesters by making public declarations, soliciting donations from local merchants, and preventing military harassment of the settlers as they boarded buses for the capital. In contrast, Arauca County's appointed Liberal county executive did not intervene in any way, although his mediation between the peasants camped out in his central square and the intendent who had appointed him would have been logical and justified.[43]

A protest held in November 1986 made the usual demands related to rural development (transportation infrastructure, waterworks, human rights, electricity for the piedmont county seats, health clinics, and schools). Five thousand peasants participated, camping out in the central plazas of Arauquita and Saravena for more than a week while they awaited the arrival of the intendent to negotiate their demands. This protest, however, was organized solely by the ANUC, exemplifying the tensions that were beginning to surface between the two peasant organizations as a reflection of the increasingly divergent paths chosen by the FARC and the ELN with respect to the peace process. The UP county executives in the two towns served as intermediaries, convoking the leaders in order to solicit the list of demands and the presence of intendential authorities. However, they hesitated to offer overt support of the protest, since it was sponsored by the ANUC partly to discredit the more moderate UP in the eyes of its settler constituents.[44]

Neither of the protests of 1986 was very successful at wresting concessions directly from their primary target, the intendential government, largely because this entity had yet to receive its first round of oil royalties. In the first case, the central demand—an investigation of the incidents of violence—was virtually ignored, although a few roads were repaired and maintained. In the second case, many promises were made by the departmental government but not kept. However, as in the case of the 1984–85 protests, some public works were carried out directly by Occidental's Community Action Programs office during the first year of oil production (1986). In an effort to maintain good public relations with their piedmont settler neighbors (as Occidental's regional management maintained) or under threat of violence from the ELN or civic strikes by the peasant movement (as other sources claimed), Occidental built ninety-seven schoolhouses in the department, offered health services to those peasants who lived closest to the oil field, and greatly improved the route from Saravena to La Esmeralda (a settlement midway between Saravena and Arauquita).[45]

Fiscal prosperity in the form of oil royalties and improved leftist unity further increased peasant protest success in 1987. The first of 1987's two major protests was held in February to force the national government to fulfill the promises it had made during the November 1986 rural development protest. However, in contrast to the previous protest, this civic strike was organized and fully supported by both peasant organizations. Now that the FARC peace agreement with the government was beginning to falter, the FARC and the ELN were back on equal footing, facilitating the unity of the two groups and their linked organizations. In this first protest, demanding that the intendential and national governments negotiate their lengthy and carefully elaborated list of demands, three thousand peasants camped out in the central plaza of the department capital, Arauca City, for nineteen days. As this protest was fully supported by their organization and as the ends of their terms were approaching at any rate, the UP county executives were bolder in their support of this protest than of the previous one, helping to organize it and making many public statements in favor of it. In contrast, the Liberal county executive from

Arauca acted as an elite advocate, requesting that the police evict the protesters from the town's central square.[46]

The agreement that resulted from this follow-up protest, along with the original list of demands, was printed in a twenty-seven-page booklet that enumerated each concession that was to be granted and which entity would carry it out. By any standard, this was a well-organized and successful protest, building on the two previous ones and benefiting from a conjuncture in which the aid of leftist county executives, leftist unity, and the oil economy's salutary effect on departmental fiscal revenues all favored the peasant movement. Accordingly, eight entities of the national government were represented in the final negotiating meeting. These promised to open a new branch of the Caja Agraria (which gave subsidized credit to settlers in coordination with the INCORA) in Fortul; expand the role of the IDEMA, the entity that bought agricultural and livestock products directly from the piedmont settlers and their cooperatives; construct more footpaths connecting the veredas, or hamlets; and through the Institute to Defend Natural Resources (INDERENA) induce Occidental to build a tree nursery to facilitate the reforestation of the more mountainous and eroded areas of the piedmont. Furthermore, the Ministry of Health, in conjunction with INCORA, would build hospitals in Fortul, Cravo Norte, and Puerto Rondón and construct twelve health clinics in the smaller settlements of the piedmont.[47]

This protest was also timed perfectly to coincide with the intendential budget deliberations for the 1987 fiscal year (March 1, 1987–April 30, 1988), the first hugely oil-expanded intendential budget. As a result of the protest, the following items were included in the intendential public works budget: the purchase of heavy machinery for road construction and maintenance; grants to piedmont peasant cooperatives for a total of 140 million pesos (about U.S.$450,000); completion of the construction of the Saravena Hospital by August 1987 and of the hospital in Tame by January 1988; 40 million pesos (about U.S.$130,000) for the construction of schools in the piedmont and the same amount for the purchase of educational materials; the purchase and delivery of fifteen hundred desks each for Arauquita, Saravena, and Tame; a slaughterhouse and park in the settlement of Panamá in Arauquita; containment walls to reinforce the banks of the Arauca River in the piedmont; and many other smaller projects. The agreement was signed by the intendent himself, representatives of the Liberal and Conservative Parties, the Araucan Cattle Ranchers'

Committee, the Cattle Ranchers' Bank, and the Araucan Cattle Ranchers' Fund (all of which represented the largest ranchers).[48] Never before had an Araucan peasant protest won so many concessions from the departmental government.

The second protest of 1987 was part of a larger seminational peasant protest, the Civic Strike of the Northeast (participating regions included Arauca, Norte de Santander, part of Santander, and southern Cesar). A total of twelve thousand peasants participated in Arauca in June 1987, camping out for twenty-two days in the central plazas of the piedmont counties of Arauquita, Tame, and Saravena. Once again, the demands focused on regional development. Amos Ríos, the second appointed UP county executive of Arauquita (the first had been replaced as part of a routine changing of the guard by the newly appointed intendent) was much bolder than his predecessor in terms of supporting the peasant marches, perhaps because the tripling of his county's budget increased his autonomy from the intendent. Not only did he organize and lead a march in solidarity with the protesters, whose progress along the road to Arauquita had been blocked by the military; he also donated county gasoline to the protesters, as well as food and the use of one of the county's few radio-telephones.[49]

This protest was also quite successful. The government's peace process—linked National Rehabilitation Plan agreed to the appointment of more teachers in the piedmont and the extension of national television coverage, the Caja Agraria agreed to forgive part of the settlers' debts,[50] and the intendential government pledged to equip the hospitals of the piedmont and pave a road between Fortul and Tame. Following the pattern of the three previous civic strikes, the real fruits of this protest, in terms of concessions made, would not become manifest until the next civic strike, in May 1988.[51]

In summary, between 1985 and 1987 all factors favored the growth and success of the peasant movement and the electoral Left. The oil economy stimulated mobilization and increased concessions to the peasant movement both through Occidental's direct public works in the piedmont and through expanding the intendential and county budgets. The "bigger pie" enabled intendential political leaders to spend more on piedmont public works while maintaining or increasing spending levels in the plains. The government-FARC peace process also favored the peasant movement by decreasing the level of repression, legitimating the peasant movement's cause through the UP's electoral success, enabling the appointment of pro-settler

UP county executives, and creating incentives for the national government to make concessions to the UP's peasant base to rescue the faltering (by 1987) peace process.

1987–1989: Setting the Stage for a Regional Pacted Peace

Before 1970 the plains elites had ruled the intendency of Arauca, uncontested either demographically or politically. Between 1970 and 1983 the LaTorrista Liberals were challenged by the rapidly expanding population of the piedmont peasant settlers as well as by their increasing militancy. It was not until 1984–87 that this challenge from the piedmont became an electoral and political one as well, and the LaTorrista large cattle ranchers unleashed a major wave of repression interrupted only briefly by the peace process of 1985–86 before resuming in 1987 and 1988. Despite this, at the end of 1987 the two major political forces were nearly evenly matched in regional influence. Between 1987 and 1989, however, various factors combined to maintain the strength of the Left and further unify the two factions even while dividing, weakening, and eclipsing the LaTorrista Liberal elites that were the main sponsors of repression, ultimately favoring the Left in the regional balance of power.

Three factors explain the strengthening and unification of the Left. First, the continuing success of the piedmont peasant movement, which now wrested concessions from the wealthy intendential government, meant that leftist electoral success was maintained despite increased repression in the wake of the collapse of FARC-government peace talks. Second, after 1988 directly elected leftist county executives in the piedmont aided the peasant movement and provided additional material incentives to support leftist electoral fronts. Third, the oil economy had strengthened the two regional guerrilla groups, and the end of the peace process with the FARC placed both guerrilla groups in similar positions vis-à-vis the government (non-negotiating), facilitating leftist unity.

At the same time oil and the direct election of county executives combined to divide and weaken the long-dominant LaTorrista faction of the Liberal Party in Arauca. Arauca County's abundant oil revenues gave the new incumbent Liberal faction the means with which to create a new and much more powerful clientele than cattle ranching had ever created for the old LaTorristas, eclipsing the old guard. The direct election of county executives provided the incentive and the means for the first directly elected county executive of Arauca County to break away from his LaTorrista mentor, and this he did.

The first ingredient of the pacted peace was established when the electoral Left maintained its strength despite increased repression. At the end of 1987 the FARC-government truce broke down, and the dirty war against the UP was unleashed again full force. The Left now represented much more of a threat to elites than in 1984, before the peace process began. Not only had the peasant movement grown in mobilizational strength and success, but it had also gained unprecedented electoral strength, controlling substantial oil-enhanced budgets in three piedmont counties and threatening to displace traditional parties from regional political institutions altogether. With the post–peace process reversion of the FARC to the same outlaw status as the ELN, the repression-sponsoring elites viewed the Fensuagro, UP, and all peasants who lived in their strongholds and even urban sympathizers in the capital city as guerrilla auxiliaries.

Thus, in late 1987 and early 1988, repression increased markedly in Arauca County, rising to levels close to that of 1984 (table 6.2 and fig. 6.2). In Arauca County repression rose to levels close to that of 1984. In 1984 there had been six political assassinations of leftists in Arauca County. In 1985, 1986, and the first half of 1987 there had been a respite, with only one assassination. Then between July 1, 1987, and mid-March 1988, when the first direct election of county executives took place, five people were assassinated by rightist gunmen. After the elections repression continued to increase, with five political assassinations in 1988 and early 1989. In addition, public rhetoric against the UP changed from conciliatory to very threatening during this period. In contrast to 1986, when FARC guerrillas had been welcomed at public forums, now even the fully legal UP and its various mass organizations were under attack as subversives. During the county executive campaign of March 1988, for example, when the UP, the Conservative Party, and a non-LaTorrista Liberal faction had formed a coalition to elect a candidate from the latter group, a vicious smear campaign by the LaTorre camp labeled even the elite members of the coalition as subversives.[52]

Repression also increased markedly in Arauquita (and presumably in the rest of the piedmont). In 1984 the repression index had been 16.25, and in 1986 it was lowered to 11.45. In the nonelection years of 1985 and 1987 it had been lowered further, however, to 2.5 and 4.35, respectively. But from March through December 1988—apparently in response

Table 6.2. Evolution of Conflict in Arauca County, 1984–1992

Year	Repression Index	Left Electoral Success (percent)[a]	Number of Guerrilla-Army Combats
1984	6	0	No data
1985	0	—	4 with ELN
1984 + 1985	6	—	—
1986	1	21	1 with FARC, 1 with ELN
1987	2	—	2 with FARC, 3 with ELN
1986 + 1987	3	—	—
1988	3	8	4 with ELN
1989	2	—	1 with ELN
1988+1989	5	—	—
1990	0	5	1 with FARC, 5 with ELN
1991	0	—	2 with FARC, 5 with ELN, 2 with CGSB[b]
1990 + 1991	0	—	—
1992	2 doubled = 4	8	4 with ELN, 2 unidentified

Note: The repression index for 1992 is doubled to make it comparable to the figures for 1984–85, 1986–87, and 1988–89 without extending the analysis to the counterreform period. For additional explanation, operationalization, and sources for these data, see the methods section of chapter 1.

[a] Of those votes deposited for candidates who were elected to office, percent that went to leftist candidates; data are recorded only for even-numbered years because no elections occurred in odd-numbered years.
[b] National Guerrilla Coordinating Committee.

to the Left's sustained electoral success in March 1988, as well as the end of the truce—the repression index was 18.2, the highest level of repression during the entire reform period (table 6.3 and fig. 6.3).

Both Arauca and Arauquita experienced escalated repression immediately preceding the March 1988 county executive elections. However, only the electoral Left in Arauca County was adversely affected. There the electoral strength of the UP dropped substantially between 1986 and 1988, from 21 percent of the votes for elected county council representatives to

Table 6.3. Evolution of Conflict in Arauquita, 1984–1992

Year	Repression Index	Left Electoral Success (percent)[a]	Number of Guerrilla-Army Combats
1984	16.25	0	No data
1985	2.5	—	1 with FARC
1984 + 1985	18.75	—	—
1986	11.45	90	14 with ELN
1987	4.35	—	4 with FARC, 9 with ELN
1986 + 1987	15.8	—	—
1988	18.2	92	1 with FARC, 16 with ELN
1989	0	—	8 with ELN
1988 + 1989	18.2	—	—
1990	0	100	3 with FARC, 12 with ELN
1991	1	—	12 with ELN, 2 with CGSB
1990 + 1991	1	—	—
1992	0 doubled = 0	91	4 with ELN, 1 with FARC, 1 with CGSB

Note: The repression index for 1992 is doubled to make it comparable to the figures for 1984–85, 1986–87, and 1988–89 without extending the analysis to the counterreform period. For additional explanation, operationalization, and sources for these data, see the methods section of chapter 1.

[a] Of those votes deposited for candidates who were elected to office, percent that went to leftist candidates; data are recorded only for even-numbered years because no elections occurred in odd-numbered years.

only 8 percent. In contrast, in Arauquita the electoral strength of the Left had actually increased slightly between 1986 and 1988: in 1986 the UP alone had won 90 percent of the votes for elected city council candidates; and in 1988, while the share of the UP shrank to 69 percent due to the entrance of the Saravena Liberals into the electoral contest, the Left as a whole won 92 percent of the vote. I attribute this difference to the greater strength and especially the greater success of the base of the electoral Left in Arauquita (peasant settlers) relative to that of Arauca County (a small group of peasant settlers, plus a loosely organized urban squatter neighborhood and some unorganized sympathizers).

In Arauca County, the propaganda and the political assassinations were effective in achieving the goal of weakening the Arauca County Left electorally. The votes lost were not those of the small peasant settler area in Arauca: they remained steadfast supporters. An examination of electoral results for 1990 and 1992, when the UP obtained about the same percentage of votes it had in 1988, reveals that the overwhelming majority of the UP's votes (70 percent in 1990; 81 percent in 1992) came from the two rural county subdivisions on the border with Arauquita, populated by peasant settlers who participated actively in all the regional civic strikes.[53]

Rather, the UP votes lost between 1986 and 1988 were those from the county's urban center. These fell into two categories: unorganized urban sympathizers and precariously organized urban squatters. (While the regional teachers' union, Asociación de Educadores de Arauca, or ASEDAR, is both Left associated and militant in the piedmont counties, plains rank and file tend to work through strikes and vote for Liberals, despite leadership encouragement to emulate their piedmont brethren.)[54] The unorganized sympathizers in Arauca County had voted for the UP in March 1986, when the FARC was fully participating in a cease-fire agreement, the UP had the "peacemaker" aura, and supporting the UP was a nearly risk-free way to express dissent. Furthermore, these sympathizers lacked ties to a successful mass organization, which might have made them more resistant to repression by allowing them to share the fruits of mobilization and solidarity. Without such ties, when repression increased these unorganized urban UP supporters were the first to abandon ship.

Perhaps anticipating this defection of fairweather friends, the UP had tried to consolidate and organize its urban constituency by founding a squatters' neighborhood in Arauca County. In mid-1986 intendential councilors from the UP had obtained some intendential resources and bought a piece of marginal urban land near the river. In early 1987 residents for the neighborhood were sought via radio announcements, which stated that the only requirements were that potential residents must have children, must not own a house, and must join Provivienda, the Communist Party's housing organization. Virtually all the sixty families that responded ("99.9 percent," according to the UP neighborhood organizer I interviewed) had previously voted for the Liberal Party—in stark contrast to the piedmont settlers, who even before their arrival in Arauca were radicalized peasant activists. By mid-1987 topographic studies were carried out, the lots were raffled off, and then the anti-UP campaign began full force. Alleging that the neighborhood was organized by FARC guerrillas,[55] the propaganda succeeded in frightening off all sixty of the would-be residents, whose ties to the Left were incipient and tenuous, to say the least.[56] Thus the plan to make up for the shortfall in the sympathizer vote by creating a new organized constituency failed.

Eventually—around December 1988, well after the elections—the UP was able to lure most of the original families back. But then they faced another obstacle to the building of a solid UP constituency: the astute and very successful preemption efforts on the part of wealthy Liberal county administrations (discussed below),[57] which created loyalties to their own political cause by establishing basic infrastructure in the neighborhood such as landfill, electricity, and running water.[58] Consequently, even though repression in the department and in Arauca County virtually ceased after 1989, the UP suffered yet another electoral loss between 1988 and 1990, as the party's share of the county electorate dropped from 8 percent to 5 percent.[59]

In contrast to Arauca County, in Arauquita the UP's constituency was solidly rural peasant settlers. Electoral results by voting precinct for 1988, 1990, and 1992 showed UP strongholds in the rural areas farthest from the urban center and Saravena Liberal strongholds in some of the veredas (rural subdivisions) closest to the urban center. As the Saravena Liberals in Arauquita were also closely tied to the peasant movement through the ANUC, their considerable electoral stability and even growth—they won 23 percent of the county council vote in 1988 and 28 percent in 1992, abstaining in 1990—can be explained by the same factors that explain the Left's electoral stability in general.[60]

In sum, as a result of their lack of connection to the successful peasant movement, the urban voters of Arauca County were easily intimidated by (relatively) low levels of repression. In contrast, Arauca County's rural voters for the UP—like the peasant movement–affiliated voters in Arauquita—continued to vote for the Left, despite the renewal of repression in late 1987 and early 1988, due to a high level of organization within the successful peasant movement.

If steady electoral success depended on continual movement success, the continuing strength and success of the peasant movement was in turn due to two main factors: the success of the peasant movement in wresting concessions from its targets up until the moment of the March 1988 elections and its prospects for continued future success, *despite* the suddenly hostile attitude of the national government toward the movement.

In many other peasant settler regions where the UP had influence, peasant movements had received concessions exclusively from national government agencies during the cease-fire; therefore, when the cease-fire ended, concessions to the peasant movement ended as well. In contrast, the Araucan peasant movement had received concessions both from national government agencies and from the now-wealthy intendential government. Consequently, even after the national government's rhetoric regarding the Araucan peasant movement became blatantly hostile, the movement could expect continued concessions and success. In this sense, the fact that Arauca was both an oil-producing region and one with some autonomy from the national government at this moment made the peasant movement, and thus the peasant-based electoral Left, much more stable and resistant to repression than the peasant movement in other regions.

The peasant mobilization of May 1988 confirmed this expectation of continued success. For twenty-one days, fifteen thousand peasants camped out in the central plazas of Saravena, Arauquita, Tame, and Arauca, again demanding public investment from both the national and intendential governments. Demands on national government agencies included more subsidized loans from the Caja Agraria, more branches of the IDEMA to buy agricultural products from peasants, completion of the health clinics in the larger rural settlements of the piedmont, and the demilitarization of rural areas and investigation of specific incidents of repression. Demands on the intendential government included pavement of the most heavily traveled intermunicipal piedmont routes, electricity for piedmont county seats, reinforcement of the banks of the Arauca River to prevent its annual changes of course, indemnization of those who had suffered property damage or loss resulting from the annual floods, an intendential education program, and most important, funding for a proposal called the "Sowing of Oil." This program would set aside a percentage of annual intendential oil royalties to establish loan funds for the cooperative sector, for small businesses, for educational loans, and for small farmers.[61]

Although representatives of both the national and intendential governments met with peasant leaders to negotiate the list of demands, virtually all the concessions granted came from the intendency's budget. The national government declared the mobilization illegal. Furthermore, rather than investigate previous incidents of violence, the army perpetrated more violence during the protest, wounding three protesters and even striking doña Elsa Rojas, who by then was Arauca's representative to the House for the UP. In contrast, the intendential government reimbursed those affected by flood damage, agreed to reimburse those who built their own containment walls on the riverbanks, and, most important, established the Sowing of Oil loan program more or less as proposed by the peasant movement.[62] Finally, during 1988 a joint investment made by the Cravo Norte Association (Occidental's public works branch) and Arauca County gradually brought electricity to the county seats of Arauca and Arauquita, using energy generated directly by the oil from Caño Limón. Arauquita's appointed UP county executive, Amos Ríos (who was to be replaced on June 1, 1988), was again bold in his support of the protest. Ríos prevented the military from intervening against the protesters in Arauquita's town square and also provided protesters with first aid, medicine, and food. Doña Elsa, in her position as congresswoman, and the four UP Intendential Council deputies were also crucial in pressuring the intendential and national governments to negotiate with the protesters. In contrast, the last appointed Liberal county executive of Arauca had called out the police to disperse the protesters camped in his city's central plaza.[63]

Thus, despite the turn in national politics against the Patriotic Union and despite the instability of the urban Left in Arauca city, the fiscal wealth of the intendential government facilitated the peasant settler movement's continued success and the Left's regional electoral strength. Therefore, in the Araucan context the UP in particular and the Left in general was in a

very powerful and stable position as the first directly elected county executives took office on June 1, 1988.

The elections of March 1988 had three major consequences for the
Araucan political process. First, the Left's continuing electoral success demonstrated to elites that repression would not easily diminish their strength.
Second, it stimulated the first full-fledged electoral participation of the
ANUC's electoral front, centered on its stronghold in Saravena. Third,
the leftist county executives, now elected rather than appointed, had greatly
increased autonomy to continue supporting the peasant movement and
were no longer beholden to LaTorrista political forces in any way. This allowed the Left to formally evict from the piedmont the last vestiges of La-
Torrista power and to instead solidify its own political strongholds.

On March 13, 1988, three leftist county executives were elected in
Arauca of six in the intendency. In Arauquita and contiguous Tame, UP
candidates won the county executive elections with 69 percent and 50 percent of the vote, respectively, while a Saravena Liberal was elected county
executive of Saravena, with 67 percent of the vote.[64] The opportunity to
have its own county executive stimulated the ANUC, via its recently created electoral front, to participate directly in elections, running its own
candidates rather than including them in lists headed by traditional politicians. Nevertheless, the ANUC's electoral participation was still nominally clandestine: their candidates appeared on the ballot as Liberals, but
"real" Liberals (i.e., Liberals from the plains counties) understood that
these were Saravena Liberals, occasionally referring to them disdainfully
as *Liberales elenizados,* or "ELNized" Liberals.[65]

In addition to their success at the county level, the two leftist electoral fronts continued their strong showing at the departmental level. The
change of national mood and the loss of the loosely organized sympathizers in urban Arauca County had decreased the UP's share of the departmental vote by twelve points between 1986 and 1988 and the Saravena
Liberals' share by two points. Nonetheless, the UP still commanded an impressive 38 percent of the region's votes, and the Left as a whole won 46 percent of the departmental vote. From 1988 to 1992 the Left's total share of
the departmental vote would remain steady at 46 to 50 percent, with the
Saravena Liberals winning 8 percent, 15 percent, and 20 percent of the vote
in 1988, 1990, and 1992, respectively, while the UP garnered 38 percent,
36 percent, and 29 percent during the same years.[66] (See table 6.4.) The

Table 6.4. Left Electoral Strength in Arauca's Intendential Council /
Departmental Assembly, 1984 –1992

Year	Saravena Liberals	Patriotic Union	Combined
1984	6	22	28
1986	10	50[a]	60
1988	8	38	46
1990	15	36	51
1992	20	29	48

Sources: For number of votes won by each candidate and names of all elected councilors/assembly members, Registraduría Nacional del Estado Civil for appropriate intendential council or departmental assembly election. For identifying which councilors/assembly members represented leftist political forces, interviews 15, 53, 56, 70, and 71. These interviews were especially crucial for identifying votes for the Saravena Liberals, and for the UP when these forces ran as a part of coalitions (1984).

Note: Left Electoral Strength = of votes for those candidates elected to office, percent that went to leftist candidates.

[a] UP ran in elections for the first time in 1986. Previously the same political forces used a different electoral front.

two halves of the Left in Arauca, despite some tactical disagreements, occasional territorial conflicts, and now intensified electoral competition, had continued to maintain a basic working unity in which a series of mutual goals were recognized and competition usually stopped short of bloodshed. That they were now in the same position vis-à-vis government peace negotiations (i.e., neither was actively seeking demobilization) helped solidify this tactical unity.

The direct election of county executives not only confirmed the resistance of the peasant movement to repression and stimulated the county-level electoral participation of the ANUC. It also gave the peasant movement new, more autonomous allies in the form of sympathetic directly elected county executives who were able to make greater contributions to peasant movement success.

The peasant movement was moving to a new, more institutionalized model of mobilization that was both a sign of its success and recognition on the part of organizers of the considerable costs of mobilization. In contrast to the impressive numbers of peasant mobilizations between 1986 and 1988, the peasant movement had only one mobilization between 1988 and 1990. This shift seems to have been a national trend due to protester burnout: the month-long protests were frequently accompanied by hepatitis A and cholera outbreaks, as well as loss of livestock and crops abandoned during the course of the protest, as activists told me.[67] Furthermore, the end of the FARC-government peace process, which brought with it an end to national government concessions, also put a damper on cross-regional protests such as the June 1987 Paro del Nororiente referred to above. This reduced the overall frequency of protest in Arauca and elsewhere, but uniquely in Arauca, it also correlated with the increased overall effectiveness of the protests.

The one protest of the period involved only the county of Arauquita and took place in November 1988. However, the first directly elected county executive of Arauquita, the UP's Amparo López, was instrumental in supporting it. Two teenagers had been assassinated in the neighboring department of Casanare, reportedly having been accused of being guerrillas simply because their citizen identification cards were from Arauquita.[68] In response to a general mobilization in protest, Amparo López not only had the county assume all the costs of transporting and burying the bodies but also made numerous public declarations denouncing the human rights violation. She also negotiated with the local military commander, who during 1988 had been harassing the town's population, broadcasting his daily harangue against subversives over the urban loudspeaker system each morning at five o'clock. After López met with him, he agreed to stop. UP activists whom I interviewed spoke admiringly of her willingness to risk her life by confronting him.[69]

Arauquita's first directly elected county executive also directed the county's oil-enhanced fiscal resources toward peasant settlers—although her choice of her fiancé as one of the major contractors raised some eyebrows and hackles. She carried out a total of 103 projects that year, 73 percent of them in rural areas (60 percent benefiting the UP's constituency among the more remote rural settlers and 13 percent benefiting the Saravena Liberals' constituency in rural areas closest to the county seat).[70] The rural population was the neediest, hence the fiscal preference for peasant settlers was certainly justifiable in moral and regional development terms. However, these spending patterns were also useful as a means to solidify the UP's incipient political stronghold. Wresting from the plains Liberals two key links in the clientelist chain—county employment and county public works spending—the UP's county executive used them to strengthen the peasant cause.

Also contributing to the electoral Left's leverage with respect to the plains Liberals was the fact that Arauca's two guerrilla groups, especially the ELN, had continued to grow rapidly in strength, drawing resources indirectly from the oil sector. By 1988 there was an all-time high of seventeen guerrilla attacks in Arauquita, all but one of them involving the ELN rather than the FARC. By the late 1980s, according to my interviewees, the guerrillas were clearly in a position of military superiority in the piedmont. On several occasions, for example, guerrillas attacked the military base in Arauquita, and an examination of the chronology of combat in Arauca reveals that many guerrilla actions, especially those aimed at sabotaging the oil pipeline (a tactic used to extort money from the oil sector), went virtually unpunished by retaliatory military operations.[71] The guerrillas' military dominance in the piedmont probably presented serious obstacles to plains Liberal efforts to gain new followers there and facilitated attempts to build an electoral base for the Left, given guerrilla support for electoral participation at the time.

Thus the electoral strength of the Left had been maintained, despite repression, due to the continuing success of the piedmont peasant settler movement. The successful election of three leftist county executives in the piedmont counties then further solidified the peasant movement. Together with the guerrillas' military control of the piedmont, this organizational strength gave the Araucan Left tremendous leverage. Combined with the division and weakening of the Liberals from the plains counties, this leftist leverage would allow the formation of the pacted peace in 1989.

Oil and the direct election of county executives were the two fundamental changes that divided LaTorrismo. The first large oil-based county budgets created a new major interest group within Araucan LaTorrismo, state employees and contractors, dividing LaTorrismo and threatening the status of the LaTorrista cattle rancher old guard. The new guard/old guard gap grew wider in 1988 as the direct election of county executives facilitated the oil-linked officials' autonomy from their Senate sponsors. Table 6.5 summarizes the divisions that took place between 1989 and 1992.

Since 1986 oil had eclipsed cattle ranching as the region's most important economic activity and since 1987 as a source of fiscal revenue in

Table 6.5. Liberal Party Factions and Coalitions in Arauca, 1984–1992

	1984–1987	March 1988 First Direct Election of County Exectives	May 1989 Col. F. González Muñoz Appointed Intendent by President	March 1990 Second Direct Election of County Executives	August 1990 New Coalitions within the Intendential Council	October 1991 First Direct Election of Governors	March 1992 Election of County Executives, Departmental Assembly
LaTorrismo (led by Sen. Alfonso LaTorre Gómez)	LaTorrismo is monolithic.	LaTorre chooses Julio Acosta as county executive candidate for Arauca County. He wins.		LaTorre supports Marcos Ataya as county executive candidate for Arauca County. He loses. LaTorre loses Senate seat held since 1974.	LaTorrista (1) allies with UP (4), Saravena Liberals (1), Conservatives (1), and independent Liberals (1) to form the "group of eight" in the Intendential Council.	LaTorrista/UP candidate wins 38% of vote.	1 LaTorrista assemblyman is united with 3 UP colleagues in the opposition coalition of the Departmental Assembly, representing 35% of the vote.
Faction led by Julio Acosta			González's appointments strengthen Acosta's position vis-à-vis LaTorre.	Julio Acosta supports Goyo González, who wins. Acosta also supports winning Senatorial candidate Elías Matus.	Acosta's 3 councilors are left isolated on the Intendential Council.	Acosta wins 13% of vote; not elected.	Acosta wins 13% of dept. vote but forms part of governing coalition in the Departmental Assembly.
Faction led by Gregorio "Goyo" González and Gov. Alfredo Colmenares						Goyo sponsors his own candidate, who, with support of the Saravena Liberals wins 39% of the vote and the governor's office.	Goyo's candidate wins Arauca county executive race. Goyo governor line wins 4 of 11 assembly seats. Governing coalition also includes Acosta, 1 Saravena Liberal, and 1 evangelical Christian.

Arauca County and the department. Oil revenues had increased both the county budget and the department budget more than twentyfold.[72] Immediately this reduced the dependence of the county government on the cattle-ranching sector as a source of revenue—and therefore that sector's leverage over the political process. In the 1986–87 fiscal year fully 45 percent of revenue had derived from property taxes, whereas by 1987–88 that figure had been reduced to a mere 3 percent. Meanwhile, oil royalties from 1987 through 1992 represented an average of 88 percent of fiscal revenue.[73]

The sudden flood of resources entering into a backwater political bureaucracy with few checks and balances led, predictably enough, to frequent examples of corruption, in particular, the use of state funds for political campaign financing for the elections in 1988 and thereafter.[74] The reliance on oil royalties as a source of fiscal revenue, however, did not give Occidental Petroleum direct influence over the Araucan political process. Whether or not they approved of the incumbent politicians, Occidental was obligated by law to pay oil royalties to all counties and departments/intendencies in which extraction was taking place. Thus the economic underpinnings of political power were not transferred from large cattle ranchers to Occidental but rather to incumbent politicians.

Increasingly, as the fortunes of incumbent Liberal petrocrats soared, the status and influence of the LaTorrista old guard waned. A close inspection of the leaders of the Cattle Ranchers' Committee reveals that virtually all of them—the LaTorre, Ataya, Guerrero, Loyo, and LoMonaco families in particular—were firm LaTorristas. The LoMonaco family was especially well represented in the Cattle Ranchers' Committee by Francisco, Mario, and Otorino LoMonaco.[75] Probably Arauca's most powerful family, they owned 94,000 hectares of ranchland in Arauca alone, with more across the river in Venezuela. They were reputed by all my leftist interviewees to be the family most active in sponsoring paramilitary groups such as the newly formed and notorious Grupo Cívico Armado de Arauca (Armed Civic Group of Arauca), known as Gruciarar, which had carried out the wave of repression in 1988.[76]

Although the new rising faction of petrocrats may have also had their earliest origins in cattle—for example, Arauca's first directly elected county executive, Julio Acosta, was from a cattle ranching family—their cattle ranching wealth was not of the magnitude of the leading LaTorristas.[77]

The oil boom allowed these state administrators and contractors to become powerful (and wealthy) through their access to the state. In contrast, in the old model wealthy members of civil society gained easy access to the state through their extensive properties.

The cattle ranchers were clearly feeling the threat to their status by early 1989, as documented in an article published in *ASPAVisión,* the magazine of the Araucan Professionals' Association. There, cattle ranchers lamented the new state of affairs:

> Before, the cattle rancher of our intendency had no complaints and caused no problems; he was content as long as they called him rich or wealthy. The poor government invited him to events, accompanied him, and even defended him. After the discovery of the famous Black Gold, he was displaced and with him went his image. . . . He became the hole-filler forced into that role by the abandonment of his government. . . . He didn't ask for help, either because of his characteristic pride or because he knew the government did not want to help him. . . . As a clear and concrete proposal, we [the Cattle Ranchers' Committee] ask to be given greater participation in decision making in the rural production issues of the intendency. . . . We also want it to be clear to all the sectors that make up our society that Arauca will be left without oil but never without cattle.[78]

The shift in the Liberal Party's class basis from cattle ranchers to petrocrats, however, did not immediately manifest itself in political divisions within LaTorrismo. Senator LaTorre had been reelected in March 1986 (for a term extending through June 1990), before oil royalties had entered Arauca's county and departmental coffers. He had presumably been elected the old way, that is, using his senatorial discretionary funds and contributions from his wealthiest supporters among the large cattle ranchers to ensure reelection, according to Colombian political custom. On taking office, he controlled the appointment and removal from office of Araucan county executives and intendents. From 1986 through late 1988, three LaTorrista intendents were appointed. Furthermore, two LaTorrista county executives of Arauca were appointed between LaTorre's reelection in 1986 and the direct election of county executives in March 1988.[79]

Given their desire for future appointments and Senate funds, these appointed officials had considerable incentive to use state revenues to strengthen the political party faction that had appointed them. Even the LaTorre–appointed county executives and intendents of the oil boom era, therefore, were careful to appoint other LaTorristas to their cabinet, spend public works money in LaTorrista strongholds, hire LaTorrista contractors (perhaps at inflated prices), and so on.

For the first direct election of county executives in March 1988, the LaTorrista machinery was put to work to elect Julio Acosta in Arauca County. Born into a relatively wealthy cattle ranching family in the plains county of Puerto Rondón, Acosta had begun his political career in the early 1980s as the supervisor of education for the intendency. Loyal to the LaTorrista cause, he had risen to the post of secretary of government for the intendency in 1986. Winning the 1988 county executive elections in Arauca easily, with 62 percent of the vote, Acosta at first rigorously followed the rules of clientelism, appointing LaTorristas to his cabinet for the full two-year period.[80] Thus Acosta's election appeared to prove that the direct election of county executives would change nothing in LaTorre's plains strongholds.

In fact, however, the direct election of county executives, in the context of the oil-enriched Arauca County government, had fundamentally altered the basic equation of clientelism in Arauca. Demonstrations of loyalty to one's clientelist sponsor, once an asset to a county executive's political future, could now be a political liability, for he was now accountable directly to his or her voters and constituency, which demanded strategically focused public works (and sometimes padded contracts). An elected county executive who could successfully build his or her own following in this way would have little incentive to continue toeing the line of a party boss. The temptation to break away would be great indeed.

Acosta's efforts to build his own constituency were facilitated by an unprecedented public works budget based on advance oil royalties as well as additional loans. Hundreds of county employees were hired. An explosion of public works spending followed, bringing waste, exorbitance, and corruption (and well-satisfied contractors), as well as many real and necessary improvements in previously ignored neighborhoods and rural hamlets. All effective opposition—from the UP, Afro-Colombian urban neighborhoods, evangelical Christians, or other unrepresented groups—was preempted through strategic spending and political maneuvers.[81]

Acosta had an enormous budget to start with: 3.1 billion pesos, or about U.S.$8.1 million[82] for a population of 31,000. In 1990 Arauca

County had by far the highest per capita fiscal revenue—406,905 pesos—
of the 953 Colombian counties with populations of under 50,000.[83]
Furthermore, he spent considerably beyond his already substantial budget, multiplying the county's debt more than tenfold, to leave an accumulated debt of 1.5 billion pesos for his successor. Before taking out the
loans, he had induced the county council to pass a new fiscal code that
minimized checks and balances and maximized county executive discre-
tion over spending.[84]

Acosta thus had the ability to spend exorbitantly, and he did. Func-
tioning expenses (mostly salaries) were increased by a factor of seven, so
that salaries now took up 9 percent of the total budget as compared to
1 percent in the 1987–88 fiscal year. This increase was due to greater numbers of employees (read: more clients) rather than higher salaries. Most important, however, Acosta spent on public works. Among the more extrava-
gant of these were a giant swimming pool with three-story-high water
slides and waves, still incomplete in 1993; a gold plated, two-piece statue
celebrating the Araucan rodeo sport of *coleo;* a large chute for rodeo sports
(manga de coleo), used only about twice a year; a stadium; a bicycle race-
track; and a lavish new city hall complex. It was a common presumption
that many contractors were chosen for their political loyalty rather than
expertise, leading to some poor-quality public works that had to be recon-
structed afterward. It was also strongly suspected that some of the money
was simply disappearing into the pockets of county administrators and
contractors, which explains why Acosta's myriad public works succeeded
in gaining him the undying support of hosts of overpaid Araucan contractors and their employees.[85]

But Acosta also spent substantial sums on more basic public works
such as roads, schools, subsidized housing for schoolteachers, sewers, and
the installation of electricity and running water in marginal neighborhoods.[86] These expenditures bought him the loyalty of entire neighborhoods and demographic groups such as the urban poor, parents of school-
age children, and, as was grudgingly acknowledged by the Left-aligned
teachers' union president, a critical mass of Arauca County teachers. He
was also a man of his word in terms of honoring promises to reciprocate
his clients' support. For example, the head of a transportation cooperative explained to me that the cooperative had donated transportation to all
three county executive campaigns—Julio Acosta's in 1988, José Gregorio

González's in 1990, and Ricardo Alvarado's in 1992—but Acosta was the only one of the three that had helped the cooperative, with a county loan. And unlike those who followed him, Julio kept the same cabinet for his entire term, inspiring confidence in his followers.[87]

But Acosta did not stop at building his own constituency: he aspired to neutralize and then usurp oppositional constituencies. In the case of the UP, whose city council representative continued to adamantly oppose Acosta until he gave up in disgust in late 1989, Julio went straight to the base of the movement, buying the UP county council member's constituency out from under him. With Occidental's support, Acosta carried out the innovation of using the oil of Caño Limón to provide electricity twenty-four hours a day to urban Arauca and Arauquita. He was also quite helpful to the UP's squatter neighborhood, Pedro Nel Jiménez. He installed electricity, then subsidized its cost; built a school; provided water trucks for drinking water; and later installed pipes for running water (although because of shoddy workmanship and the dubious qualifications of the contractor, the pipes did not work). Nevertheless, he did enough for the neighborhood so that several UP activists bitterly claimed that all the residents now voted for "Julio," even though the UP had organized the neighborhood.[88] Through all these actions Acosta gained enough political capital to contemplate a formal break with the old guard LaTorristas.

1989–August 1990: Alliances with Political Newcomers Leave LaTorrismo Isolated

In the brief but crucial moment of regional history between early 1989 and August 1990, it seems all elite political actors in Arauca except the LaTorristas themselves recognized the altered regional balance of power and had positioned themselves to take maximum advantage of this new context. The key new allies to cultivate, the rising stars of Arauca, were clearly the Left and the new oil-linked incumbents led by Julio Acosta, while the old guard LaTorristas were increasingly seen as expendable and irrelevant. Contributing to this turning point were a number of changes. First, the new presidentially appointed military intendent of Arauca enhanced the influence of the new petrocrat faction and initiated a non-agression and public works agreement with the Patriotic Union. Second, by March 1990 the leader of the new petrocrat faction, Julio Acosta, broke away from LaTorre altogether to found his own political movement. Third, the other major elite factions of Arauca, independent Liberals and Conservatives, successfully allied with leftist sectors to take Arauca's two Senate seats. LaTorre, by failing to do the same, lost the Senate seat he had held since 1974.

The incipient schism between Julio Acosta and LaTorre had been deepened in May 1989, when President Barco responded to Arauca's escalating level of guerrilla combat by replacing the LaTorrista governor, Rosario Camejo, with a career military man not from Arauca, Colonel Fernando González Muñoz. Barco had assigned González Muñoz the mission of pacifying Arauca. González Muñoz, who aspired to be a general, aimed to please the president. His somewhat unconventional—but quite effective—way of carrying this out was to include, through cabinet appointments and the more equitable distribution of department fiscal resources, factions that were now the de facto powers of Arauca but that had been politically marginalized during the long LaTorrista era: the Patriotic Union and Julio Acosta's new faction.

First, González Muñoz negotiated an implicit nonaggression pact with the UP, facilitated by one of its top regional spokespersons, Octavio Sarmiento, who had previously been an Independent Liberal intendent. The military governor strongly discouraged violence against the UP, whether it was sponsored by the military or by paramilitary groups such as the notorious and purportedly LaTorrista-sponsored Gruciarar. Furthermore, González Muñoz spent more departmental resources on public works in Arauquita and Tame, the UP's departmental strongholds. The road between Saravena and Arauquita was finally paved, and repression against activists and civilians in the UP's stronghold counties fell dramatically.[89] In Arauquita, for example, repression fell from a level of 19.2 in 1988 to 0 in 1989, and in Arauca County it similarly fell from five assassinations in 1988 and early 1989 to none in the rest of 1989. The considerable drop in the level of repression, highly unusual in the Colombian context, continued through late 1992. Meanwhile, possibly by explicit agreement, although also reflecting a national trend, there were no peasant protests during 1989; nor were there any armed confrontations involving the FARC in Arauca or Arauquita (although the ELN remained active). However, both protests and combat resumed at their former level in 1990.

But intendent Colonel González Muñoz went further in his efforts to bring in the marginalized. Perhaps as another measure to weaken the

LaTorre-linked paramilitary groups, or perhaps as a means to befriend a county executive in charge of a generous county budget,[90] he also named to key positions in his cabinet several Liberals who owed their positions more to Julio Acosta than to LaTorre. This further weakened mainstream LaTorrismo and ensured the growth of Acosta's political movement.

His political capital thus further fortified by Colonel González Muñoz's support, Acosta officially broke with LaTorre in late 1989. His first act of independence was to declare his preference for one of his associates, José Gregorio (Goyo) González, as the Liberal candidate for county executive in Arauca County in 1990, though LaTorre preferred one of his own protégés, Marcos Ataya, whose family was among the plains cattle ranching elite. In a last attempt to reunify LaTorrismo, the two factions agreed to resolve the dispute by holding Arauca County's first primary election *(consulta popular)* in early 1990. Acosta's candidate, Goyo González, won the primary (with help from Venezuelan voters, according to some accounts);[91] it was to be the first of a series of defeats for old guard LaTorrismo.

The new petrocrat faction's success at the expense of LaTorrismo was evidenced in two other elections in March 1990. Goyo González easily won the county executive elections of Arauca with 66 percent of the vote, leaving the LaTorrista candidate with only 27 percent. On taking office, he appointed no LaTorristas to his cabinet, choosing Julio's followers instead. In the Intendential Council election, LaTorre's faction won only one seat, garnering just 8 percent of all votes for elected candidates, whereas Julio's faction won three seats and 34 percent of the vote.

Beyond the division of LaTorrismo and the clear advantage of the new oil-based Liberals, the March 1990 elections demonstrated that the Left remained very strong electorally and had even gained ground on some fronts. The UP won four of eleven Intendential Council seats, with 36 percent of the vote for elected councilors. The Saravena Liberals won 15 percent of the vote for elected candidates, with one councilor fully accountable to them and another who had won about half of his votes from the Saravena Liberals. At the county level the Left did best of all. The UP, running unopposed, won Arauquita with 100 percent of the vote (compared to 69 percent in 1988) and Tame with 58 percent (compared to 50 percent in 1988), and the Saravena Liberals won Saravena with 76 percent of the vote (compared to 67 percent in 1988).[92]

Finally, the crucial Senate and House elections of March 1990 revealed that Left-elite alliances were indeed the key to political success for elites; the old "elites alone" model of politics had become obsolete. In the Senate race both sectors of the Left were included in the electoral coalitions of the two successful candidates. The UP had supported the candidacy of the top vote winner (8,349 votes), Betty Camacho de Rangel, a traditional Liberal from the department of Meta (Arauca, as an intendency, had to share a senator with a department). The Saravena Liberals, as well as Julio Acosta himself, were similarly included among the sectors supporting Elías Matus, the Araucan Conservative who won the second largest number of votes (5,830). LaTorre, who allied with no leftist sectors, trailed a distant third in votes garnered (2,585 votes) and thus lost his all-important Senate seat, the top of the clientelist chain, which he had held since 1974. Meanwhile, the UP's Elsa Rojas de Fernández was easily reelected, with 50 percent of the vote, to Arauca's only seat in the House of Representatives, which she had held since 1986.[93]

Thus after March 1990 and especially after the inauguration in June 1990, old guard LaTorrismo found itself in a very weak position. Julio Acosta's new guard Liberals had split off from the old guard, taking with them virtually all state resources and therefore most of the electorate as well. Furthermore, with the respite afforded them by González Muñoz's tacit nonagression pact, the electoral Left was able to recover from the 1987–88 wave of repression and grew stronger. Those traditional party sectors that had allied with the Left were enjoying the fruits of power from their Senate seats; former Senator LaTorre was displaced.

The Araucan cattle ranchers, rural producers from a sparsely populated and marginal intendency, had always been considered nearly insignificant from the point of view of the national economy and the national Liberal Party directorate.[94] With the advent of oil, they had lost even their traditional status as unquestioned regional oligarchs and backbone of the regional economy. And after the loss of the Senate seat, the LaTorrista cattle ranchers had lost their last point of influence with the national government and hence had no more leverage with which to urge the increased militarization of the intendency (a task Occidental had not yet adopted either). Thus the incentives for the LaTorristas to form an electoral coalition with the Left—and the costs for not doing so—clearly favored the Left. By August 1990 Araucan LaTorristas found a pacted agreement with the Left the path that maximized their possibilities of maintaining access to the wealthy Araucan departmental government.

August 1990–August 1991: LaTorrista-UP Coalition and Pacted Peace, with Limits to Peasant Movement Success

The newly elected Intendential Council took office on June 1, 1990, with the four UP representatives alone in opposing the seven other representatives (among them a councilor from the Saravena Liberals). But by August 1990, as the LaTorristas at last recognized the advantages of alliances with the Left (especially the electorally more powerful UP), the coalition had changed to everyone against Julio Acosta. The four UP councilors led the new "group of 8" coalition, which included the Saravena Liberal, the councilor representing the Conservative-Saravena coalition, the single LaTorrista councilor, and one Liberal who was with neither LaTorre nor Julio. The UP-LaTorre electoral alliance held fast throughout 1990–92, with LaTorre and the UP sharing a gubernatorial candidate in October 1991 and being united (and alone) in the opposition coalition of the 1992–94 Departmental Assembly.[95] This coalition continued to protect the UP's activists from repression, prolonging the period of nonagression initiated by Colonel González through the end of 1992.[96]

Unlike the UP–González Muñoz pact, however, the agreement between the UP and the LaTorristas apparently involved only electoral coalitions and the promise of no political violence against coalition members; there was no implicit promise to minimize mobilizations or combat. Thus the largest peasant mobilization of the entire 1984–92 period was held in 1990, with another significant one held in 1992, and combat by both guerrilla groups resumed its level from before 1989. Nevertheless, violent repression against peasant activists remained minimal relative to its 1984–89 levels. In Arauca County there were no incidents of violence in 1990 and 1991, and then two people were assassinated in 1992. In Arauquita the trend was even more dramatic, with repression indexes of 0, 1, and 0 in 1990, 1991, and 1992, respectively—far below the maximum reform period level of 19.2 in 1988.

Although the ELN was generally more bellicose than the FARC at this moment, as shown in tables 6.2 and 6.3, it did not sabotage the UP's pact with the LaTorristas. First, neither guerrilla group had accepted the government's incentives to demobilize in exchange for guaranteed seats in the Constitutional Assembly, which was to be held from February to July 1991.[97] Second, the ELN was in the midst of arranging similar pacted electoral agreements with the Conservatives and soon the petrocrat Liberals. Thus the UP's pact with LaTorre did not awaken suspicions of treachery on the part of the ELN; rather, the ELN followed their lead.

Neither was the pact sabotaged by Occidental Petroleum. Although such electoral and tactical alliances between traditional parties and the Left were offensive to Occidental's regional management,[98] the corporation had neither regional political representation nor a means to conduct a tax boycott and therefore no direct veto power over the LaTorristas' pacting activities. Furthermore, Occidental had eschewed direct participation in local politics, preferring to pursue a friend-to-all strategy at the local level and seek serious political influence only at the national level, through the Executive Branch.

By late 1990, then, the situation for the UP and the UP-associated segment of the peasant movement was nearly ideal; both access to state resources and protection from repression were maximized. However, because the governor was still appointed by the president before October 1991, the Left and the peasant movement did not have direct influence on the governor's actions, an obstacle to peasant movement success.

An analysis of the pattern of peasant protests in Arauca reveals that from 1984 through 1988 the peasant movement was increasingly militant, as protests became longer, larger, and more frequent. This pattern was altered, however, from 1989 through 1992. In the new pattern more effort was put into organizing larger and more strategic mobilizations but with less frequency—once every other year—and with much more emphasis placed on preprotest negotiation and arbitration of grievances than before. This is similar to what one would expect in the case of an industrial labor conflict in a context with well-established arbitration rules and mechanisms (i.e., labor incorporation).

The end of the FARC-government peace agreement may have contributed to the reduction in the number of cross-regional protests in which Arauca participated. However, it is no coincidence that this first step toward the institutionalization of peasant conflict coincided with the pacted peace, when the Left was enjoying its first participation in the governing coalition in the Intendential Council. The Left now had access to institutional mechanisms with which to redirect departmental resources toward their peasant settler constituencies in the piedmont counties, making a more institutionalized approach possible for the first time.

Two protests, one massive and regional and one small and focused only on Arauquita, took place in the months after the June 1990 inauguration of county executives and the new Intendential Council. Both were quite well organized and received maximum support from the leftists who had just taken office. However, the souring of relations between the UP and Col. González Muñoz—a reflection of the hard-line counterinsurgency policies of the new president of the republic, César Augusto Gaviria (August 1990–August 1994)—predisposed the military intendent to absolute intransigence. The ultimate loser in the confrontation, however, was González Muñoz himself.

On September 11, 1990, the Fensuagro and the ANUC together organized a massive peasant protest in which 25,000 peasants camped out in the central squares of each piedmont county seat for six weeks. It was the largest and longest Araucan civic strike ever, and probably also the best organized. In addition to the traditional bread-and-butter demands— the paving of eight key routes in the piedmont and the two roads that connected the piedmont to the rest of Colombia; increased budget for the INCORA office in Saravena—the protest leaders presented three new ones directly related to demands for increased political rights and regional autonomy: the creation of a regional district attorney's office for the piedmont; the resignation of the army commander for Arauca, Colonel Santander; and the resignation of Intendent Colonel González Muñoz. The protesters also issued a telling denouncement of the "elitist, exclusive, anti-popular Constitutional Assembly orchestrated by Gaviria," underscoring the FARC's and the ELN's unified rejection of Gaviria's demobilization offers.

After receiving no response for the first four days, the protesters sent their negotiating committee to the Ministry of Agriculture in Bogotá. By early October the committee of sixty peasants, including the top leadership of Fensuagro and ANUC, had received no satisfactory response. They took over the Ministry of Agriculture and were summarily detained. In response the protesters who had been camping in the central squares of each of the county seats took over each county executive's office, the offices of the Telecom in each county seat (Telecom was the only place one could place phone calls in Arauquita), and each county's main church.

The directly elected leftist county executives from the region were helpful as usual, providing food and medical supplies. For example, Amos

Ríos, the UP county executive of Arauquita who had received 100 percent of the vote in March 1990, helped supply *ollas comunes,* or communal kitchens, for the protesters camped out in Arauquita for the length of the protest. He also supported another, smaller protest on June 4, 1990, after being in office for just three days. This was an urban-based countywide protest against the local military commander's policy of arbitrary and massive detentions of civilians suspected of sympathizing with the armed insurgencies. During the protest Ríos successfully negotiated an end to this method of harassment. Ríos's public works also demonstrated his loyalty to his own peasant constituency, as fully 74 percent were placed in rural areas influenced mostly by the UP. In addition, the intendential councilors sympathetic to the mobilization offered their services as mediators between the peasant protesters and the national government, as did the county councilors.[99]

Yet the protest was largely doomed by the more hostile national context and the lack of regional autonomy of the intendential government. President Gaviria, having taken office a month earlier, was anxious to demonstrate the hard line he would take with peasant protests in FARC and ELN war zones, mobilizations he viewed as guerrilla organized (a view shared by most of the military).[100] Thus, despite the massiveness of the protest and its extraordinary duration, after a month and a half of negotiations a commission from the national government offered only minimal concessions that were unsatisfactory to the protesters. Finally, in an effort to resolve the impasse, the president abruptly removed Colonel González Muñoz from his post, replacing him with a native Araucan from the plains—neither a LaTorrista nor aligned with Julio Acosta. Thus González Muñoz's resignation was the sole victory of this mobilization—but not an insignificant one, as it was at least a superficial concession to regional autonomy.[101]

It became clear that in this new era, although the UP's pact with LaTorrismo protected them from repression and guaranteed them access to many state resources, maximum success for the Araucan peasant movement was prevented by the continuing centralized control of the intendential executive. In this moment of presidential hostility toward leftist social movements in ELN and FARC war zones, peasant social movement success would require the loyalty of the governor. The advance toward increased regional autonomy would indeed occur in the next period, however, as an effect of the first direct election of governors.

August 1991–November 1992: The Peak of Peasant Movement Success

During this period, new Left-elite alliances and the direct election of governors maximized peasant social movement success. Alliances shifted as Liberals suffered yet another schism. Just as Julio Acosta had rebelled against his LaTorrista mentors and sponsors shortly before the March 1990 county executive elections—now Goyo González, elected with Julio Acosta's backing and campaign financing in early 1990, rebelled against the former county executive and founded his own line in 1991—just in time for the first direct election of governors in October. Since Goyo could count on the advantages of incumbency (i.e., control of the enormous oil-enhanced Arauca County budget), he was able to wrest control of the majority of the plains Liberal electorate from Julio Acosta.[102]

This new and fundamental division rearranged coalitions once again. Where the group of 8 coalition had been LaTorre, the UP, Conservatives, and Saravena Liberals versus Julio Acosta, the new coalitions for the first direct election of governors became the following: LaTorre and the UP supporting a LaTorrista candidate versus Goyo, Saravena Liberals, Conservatives, and Evangelical Christians supporting a Liberal candidate loyal to Goyo versus Julio Acosta alone. Goyo's new alliance, which was reminiscent of one of the winning coalitions for the March 1990 senatorial elections (Julio, Saravena Liberals, and Conservatives), won a narrow victory, edging out the coalition of LaTorre and the UP by just 156 votes but soundly defeating Acosta.[103] Significantly, although the alliances had been reshuffled, both sectors of the Left remained allied with important elite sectors, which continued to protect them against repression. More important still, one of these leftist sectors, the Saravena Liberals, now had significant influence over the governor, as 44 percent of his votes had come from the Saravena Liberals in the piedmont.

Other elections held in October 1991 also confirmed the Left's continued electoral strength. A new House of Representatives election was held, using the new ballot mandated by the Constitutional Assembly. The UP's candidate, Octavio Sarmiento, was elected, as was a LaTorrista candidate apparently running in coalition with at least one of the oil-Liberal factions, judging from his success (Arauca, which had been elevated to a department after the Constitutional Assembly, now had a right to two representatives instead of just one). A new Senate election was also held, now, as per the Constitutional Assembly's mandate, based on at-large national

lists rather than lists for each department. Among Araucan voters, the top
vote winners for the Senate were the UP's national senatorial candidate,
followed by Elías Matus, the Conservative–Saravena Liberal candidate,
with LaTorre trailing a distant third. All three were elected.[104]

In March 1992 the Left repeated its strong electoral showing at the
local and regional levels once again: the UP won two elections for county
executive, with 55 percent of the vote in Arauquita and 46 percent of the
vote in Fortul (a newly formed county, formerly a subdivision of Tame),
with most of the remainder going to the Saravena Liberals. The Saravena
Liberals themselves held on to the county executive post in Saravena with
43 percent of the vote. The Left also continued to control about half the
votes for the Departmental Assembly, as shown in table 6.4, although the
Saravena Liberals made some gains at the expense of the UP.[105] Thus by
early 1992 the peasant movement in general, between its two halves, had
an elected voice in Arauquita, Saravena, and Fortul and in the Departmental Assembly, governor's office, House, and Senate as well.

In addition, with the direct election of governors mandated by the
Constitutional Assembly, the long-standing demands of Araucans for more
control over their governors had finally been granted. Having received almost half his votes from the Saravena Liberals, the new governor, Alfredo
Colmenares, selected his gubernatorial cabinet to reflect this fact when he
assumed office in January 1992. In doing so, he was following the Colombian custom (post–La Violencia) of selecting cabinet members to reflect electoral coalitions. Furthermore, he voiced unambiguous support
for regional dialogues to reach a peace accord between the guerrillas, the
army, and representatives of civil society[106] and substantially redirected departmental spending toward the peasant sectors in the piedmont counties,
especially Saravena—the first time that spending was directed equally to
Left-dominated counties and the traditional flatlands Liberal-dominated
counties.[107]

The piedmont peasant movement's direct line to the governor's office
was clearly reflected in the success of an April 1992 peasant protest. In contrast to the massive but relatively unsuccessful civic strike of 1990, this
time the protest consisted exclusively of shutting down all businesses and
lasted only five days. Nonetheless, it was very successful. The written product of the negotiations was a list twelve pages long, enumerating all the
public works that the departmental government was to carry out in the

foothill counties. It was signed by the governor, key officials of the departmental administration, the senator representing the Conservative–Goyo Liberals–Saravena Liberals coalition, Arauca's two representatives to Congress, county executives, and finally by representatives of the protesters.[108]

Just as important as the peasant movement's influence over the governor and departmental administration, however, was the governor's possession of the fiscal wherewithal and the political autonomy to grant concessions to the peasant movement, despite the continuing national policy of giving no concessions to the peasant movement in war zones.[109] For example, the protesters had demanded an increased budget for INCORA in order to facilitate more loans with better conditions, as well as technical assistance. Faced with the president's refusal of this demand, the governor had directly supplemented INCORA's regional budget, thus sidestepping the president. However, because the president became increasingly hostile to the FARC and the ELN after the 1991 Constitutional Assembly—and they to him—he viewed with increasing suspicion the governor's perceived largesse with peasant constituencies sympathetic to these insurgencies. He would soon react.

CONCLUSION: OUTCOME OF
THE REFORM PERIOD IN ARAUCA

In Arauca a united and electorally powerful Left confronted what had once been a near-hegemonic party faction supported by wealthy cattle ranchers, the LaTorrista Liberals. The Left's electoral strength had been sustained in the face of years of repression, strengthened at its base as oil made the peasant movement more successful, and stimulated to participate electorally by the direct election of county executives. Although repression decreased slightly between 1985 and 1987 as a result of the national peace process between the government and the FARC, it climbed again to its former levels in 1988.

But the Araucan peasant movement based in the piedmont was able to withstand these successive waves of repression, and in this stability lay its bargaining power. The pacted solution that eventually emerged from 1989 through 1992 was considered as an option by the LaTorristas *only* because repression had not achieved its goal of erasing the political threat of the UP in the piedmont. The effect of social movement success on electoral stability became especially evident in 1987–88, when the peace euphoria of the FARC-government negotiations ended and a wave of repression ensued. Arauca's peasant regions resisted this repression, and their electoral strength survived intact for the first county executive elections in March 1988. The directly elected county executives then strengthened their base through aid to the peasant movement. In contrast, the unorganized sympathizers of urban Arauca who had voted for the UP in 1986 simply melted away when repression intensified, and the electoral strength of the Left fell sharply in that county.

The Araucan peasant movement's success (and consequently the electoral Left's as well) in turn derived from Arauca's fiscal wealth after 1987 and the Araucan peasant movement's ability, based on its regional political influence and absolute mobilizational strength, to win substantial concessions from the regional government when it was susceptible to Araucan political control, that is, either appointed or elected by Araucan political organizations.

Thus from 1985 to 1987, when the oil economy had begun to boom and the national government was inclined toward conciliation, the peasant movement was able to win concessions from both the intendential and the national government. In 1987 the national government cut off concessions, which in other regions of Colombia dealt a death blow to the peasant movement. However, the Araucan peasant movement could continue to demand and win concessions from its regional government. When in 1990 the national government instructed the centrally appointed military intendent to be intransigent with the peasant movement, all routes to concessions were cut off. But after late 1991, when Araucans could elect their governor directly, concessions flowed relatively abundantly once again, despite the increasing hostility of the national government toward the peasant movement it saw as a mere puppet of bellicose guerrilla movements uninterested in negotiations.

Oil and the direct election of county executives strengthened the peasant movement and the Left but reduced the influence of the large cattle ranchers and broke apart LaTorrista unity. By creating a fiscally wealthy county and departmental administration, oil created a new class of powerful incumbent politicians that eclipsed the traditional plains cattle ranching oligarchy that had sponsored them. The direct election of county executives provided this new class with the opportunity and the incentive to break away from their political patrons, as they were both able and eager to create their own political clientele.

A presidential appointment of a military intendent to the region determined the timing of the pacted peace that would come into being, as the military intendent not only negotiated a sort of yearlong nonagression pact with the UP but also divided the Liberals by promoting the petrocrats. The longer-lasting pact, August 1990 to late 1992, was between the leaders of the LaTorrista Liberals, who had links to the plains cattle rancher sponsors of paramilitary violence, and the Patriotic Union. It brought the LaTorristas continuing access to political power through electoral coalitions with the UP and brought a respite from repression to the leftist party. Later this LaTorre-UP pact was emulated by the other major leftist electoral force, the Saravena Liberals, who formed a parallel electoral alliance and pacted peace with the main petrocrat Liberal faction and the Conservatives.

The LaTorristas were forced to view a pact as their best option for maintaining power due to their political (and relative economic) weakness at the regional level and absolute voicelessness at the national level, having lost their crucial Senate seat in March 1990. The relative unity of the FARC and the ELN at the moment—both refused to demobilize and were viewed as outlaws by the government—made each movement less likely to sabotage the other's electoral coalition pacts with elite factions. The pact was also made possible by the autonomy of the LaTorristas from Arauca's economic mainstay, Occidental Petroleum, which opposed the pact.

Finally, the Left reached the apex of its regional power with the direct election of governors. The election itself not only cemented the two Left-elite electoral alliances; it also placed a governor in office who was both eager and able to be a firm advocate of the leftist peasant settle movement of the Araucan piedmont. The Saravena Liberal votes that had elected him created the incentive to be a peasant advocate; and his political autonomy from the central government and substantial budget made such advocacy possible.

ARAUCA IN THE COUNTERREFORM PERIOD

Human Rights Movements versus Selective Recentralization

The outcome for Arauca in the counterreform period was as exceptional as that in the reform period. By late 2008 Araucan social movements were strong, extremely well networked, unified with respect to social movement actions, and extraordinarily successful. This was despite the radical reversal of regional autonomy that decimated the electoral Left and broke up long-standing Left-elite alliances, the concerted attack from government forces augmented by U.S. military aid, and a late but deadly wave of paramilitarism. It was also despite the sometimes violent divisions between the ELN and the FARC and the guerrilla forces' increasingly frequent violation of international human rights norms. Their success was due in part to accidents of fate: the legacy of the oil-facilitated social movement success and Left-elite pacts of the late 1980s and early 1990s, for example, and the late entrance (2001) of paramilitary forces in the region. But it was also due to astute decisions on the part of social movement leadership, which helped them identify, connect with, and mobilize outside allies to match and counter the outside allies their political adversaries had brought to the region, as well as to adapt their strategy quickly to a rapidly shifting context. I divide the discussion into four periods: November 1992–97, the first counterreform period; late 1997–2001, the Pastrana peace negotiations era; 2002–4, the early Uribe era; and 2005–8, the late Uribe era.

CHRONOLOGY OF CHANGE

November 1992–October 1997: The First Counterreform Period

Although several of the key ingredients of the 1989–92 pacted peace had been reversed—most notably regional autonomy, an armed Left fully supportive of reform initiatives and electoral actions, and unity between the two leftist factions—Left-elite alliances held during this period, and Left electoral success remained almost unchanged. Nonetheless, there were key changes in the context: the strengthening of Julio Acosta's Liberal faction, hostile to Left-elite alliances; and an important shift in social movement strategy, from material demands aimed at the departmental government to human rights–focused demands targeting the national government.

National counterreform and de facto recentralization were deeply felt in Arauca, where regional autonomy had been exercised so dramatically during the pacted peace era. President Gaviria's November 1992 declaration of a State of Internal Commotion[1] authorized the removal from office of any local politician deemed to be "aiding guerrillas," broadly defined.[2] The measure was undoubtedly applauded by Occidental officials, who had vehemently denounced the Arauca governor's "collaboration with subversion" (i.e., appointment of Saravena Liberals to his cabinet) when I interviewed them in 1993.[3] Soon the governor was asked to purge leftist politicians from his cabinet or face removal from office. He did remove one UP cabinet member but also began to organize a movement of dissident governors.[4] In October 1993 the county executives of Saravena and Arauquita were detained for two months, for giving money to the rural Communal Action Committees—and, allegedly, the guerrillas. Their cases, based on the testimony of a secret witness, were later dismissed, the available evidence indicating that the budget had actually been spent on rural public works, as intended.[5] This pattern—accusation of the crime of "rebellion" based on secret testimony, relatively brief arrest, followed by acquittal due to lack of evidence—became increasingly prevalent for war zone county executives during this period.[6]

Militarization also increased, with bases placed in almost every county and ubiquitous military checkpoints.[7] Not surprisingly, repression intensified as well during the remaining Gaviria years (1993–94), diminished in the early years of Samper's administration when there were attempts at peacemaking, and intensified in the late Samper years with the arrival of paramilitarism via the state-sanctioned Convivir security cooperative. In Arauca, where there had been no incidents of repression in 1992, there were three assassinations in 1993 and one in 1994;[8] none in 1995–96; and seven in 1997.[9] All those killed were labor or leftist activists. Similarly, in Arauquita the repression index rose from 2.0 in 1992 to 3.75 in 1993, with one assassination in 1994: the sister of former UP Arauquita county executive and congresswoman Elsa Rojas, who thereafter eschewed political candidacy. The army also carried out several mass arrests: 43 peasants in Arauquita (October 1993) and 1,000 in Saravena (January 1994).[10] There were no incidents of rightist repression in 1995, but the army killed a peasant in 1996 and the Convivir killed two people in 1997. During this period the (pre-Chavez) Venezuelan National Guard was frequently denounced for harassing Araucan peasants as they traveled on the Arauca River.[11]

In response to this changed political context, the FARC and the ELN escalated combat actions significantly. The Gutiérrez database reports that guerrillas initiated half of the eight confrontations between guerrillas and the army in Arauquita from 1992 to 1994 and four of five of those that occurred in Arauca, demonstrating that they were the protagonists—and probably had the upper hand—in the conflict. Between 1995 and 1997 guerrillas in Arauca and Arauquita attacked military forces at least eight times, killing at least thirty-three soldiers. The most widely reported of these attacks occurred in June 1997, when guerrillas shot down a helicopter belonging to Ecopetrol, the national oil company, killing twenty soldiers.[12] In addition, the oil pipeline was attacked 20 times in 1993, 43 times in 1995, 44 times in 1996, and 65 times in 1997, the most since the pipeline's construction in 1986. The Araucan governor estimated that "at least 40 percent" of these attacks took place in the department of Arauca.[13]

Both guerrilla groups also began to engage more frequently in human rights violations, such as the FARC's assassination of an indigenous governor in April 1994 and more frequent killings of women who fraternized with police or soldiers, kidnappings, and threats to journalists.[14] In Arauca County from 1995 through 1997 there was an unprecedented upsurge in violence against elites or civilians judged to be allied with the Right by both the ELN and the FARC. Some of these people were longtime enemies: two Occidental security employees, a large landholder, a foundation director, and a Julio Acosta–linked public figure were assassinated, and an assassination attempt was made on Acosta. Others, though, were "former allies" of the Left, presumably targeted in retaliation for leaving or threatening to leave the coalition. These included an amnestied ELN guerrilla and Goyo González, a county executive in 1990–92, who was assassinated along with two of his bodyguards. In addition, the son of Adalberto Jaimes, congressman for the plains Liberal–Saravena Liberal coalition in 1994–97 was kidnapped.[15]

Although coca cultivation was incipient in Arauca,[16] its new presence, as well as the expanded guerrilla numbers that reflected national trends, exacerbated territorial competition between the FARC and the ELN. This led to overt conflicts, despite the similar postures of the two groups toward the government at this time. The ELN killed two UP activists in Arauquita in early 1994, an appointed Arauquita county official (from the UP) and her husband, and it was reported in 1997 that the FARC was beginning to elbow in on the ELN's traditional territories.[17]

The electoral arena reflected this period's trends toward a strengthened Araucan Right unallied with any leftist factions. Between the 1991 and 1994 gubernatorial contests, votes for Liberal candidates not allied with the Left increased from 15 percent to 38 percent of all votes for candidates. Julio Acosta, the most important of these candidates, had finished the 1991 governor's race a distant third after the two Left-elite alliances.[18] By March 1994, however, with 86 percent of his votes derived from the plains counties,[19] he managed to edge out the UP-LaTorrista candidate to claim one of Arauca's two seats in the House of Representatives.[20] Quickly creating powerful alliances in Congress, with his role as stalwart opponent of the Left an asset on the national level, Acosta was named vice president of the House soon after taking office.[21]

Also reflected in electoral events were this period's increased tensions between the two leftist political tendencies. The UP's gubernatorial candidate had lost to the Saravena Liberal–supported candidate by an extremely narrow margin not once but twice—13,624 to 13,780 votes in 1991 and 16,762 to 17,470 votes in 1994—raising the UP's suspicions and resentment against the Saravena Liberals.[22] As the 1997 gubernatorial election approached, the UP and the PCC expressed hostility toward the Saravena Liberals increasingly publicly and vehemently, even urging the national government to sanction the Saravena Liberal governor for spending irregularities.[23] Once again, however, the UP-LaTorrista candidate lost by a tiny margin in 1997—29,243 versus 27,760—as the Saravena Liberal–petrocrat Liberal coalition won its third governorship.[24]

However, the intensity of the leftist electoral rivalry, along with the near doubling of the department's population between 1990 and 2000,[25] had the result of dramatically boosting voter turnout for the gubernatorial elections in the piedmont as well as the plains, revealing the Left's continued faith in the efficacy of electoral action at this point. Total votes for governor rose from 35,680 in 1991 to 57,963 in 1994 to 61,315 in 1997.[26]

Electoral results from 1992 to 1997 offer incontrovertible proof that the electoral Left remained powerful in Arauca, in stark contrast to its decimation nationally.[27] The two Left-led Araucan coalitions, UP-LaTorrista and Saravena Liberal–petrocrat Liberal, were the top vote getters in the 1994 and 1997 races for governor, as well in the 1994 Senate race, where a traditional Liberal finished a distant third. The Saravena Liberal–allied 1994 House candidate received six thousand more votes than his closest competitor, Julio Acosta. And although in 1994 the UP lost the House seat it had held since 1986,[28] its electoral strength in the departmental assembly actually increased, from 29 percent of votes for elected candidates in 1992 to 37.8 percent in 1997. The UP retained control of the county executive's office in Arauquita and Fortul in 1994 and 1997 and in Arauquita increased its county council majority from eight to nine of thirteen. In Arauca County in both 1994 and 1997, the UP-supported LaTorrista county executive candidate was elected and the UP retained a member of the county council. The Saravena Liberals once again won the county executive seat in Saravena in 1994. (No information was available for 1997.) In 1997 four UP county council members were elected in Tame, six in Fortul, and two in Saravena.[29]

Finally, even if the guerrilla attacks on individual former elite allies hinted at serious tensions, the elections demonstrated that Arauca's Left-elite electoral alliances were still very much intact. It appears they had been solidified by regional backlash against both the Venezuelan National Guard and the president's repressive measures. Against a backdrop of increasingly frequent human rights denunciations against the Venezuelan National Guard (VNG) for abuses against Colombian civilians, many made by Arauquita's county executive,[30] in April 1997 the ELN shot at VNG troops from Arauquita, killing two. The Venezuelan minister of defense insisted Arauquita should be occupied by the military, a suggestion roundly and publicly denounced by Arauquita's UP county executive, Orlando Ardila. When Ardila was then called a "guerrilla auxiliary" by both a prominent Colombian right-wing columnist and the Venezuelan defense minister, the Araucan departmental assembly members unanimously leapt to his defense, exalting Ardila's "patriotic and courageous attitude . . . in defense of human rights." Defying this clear statement of regional political consensus, however, President Samper sent still more troops to Arauquita and met with Venezuelan president Rafael Caldera not to address VNG abuses against Araucan civilians but to better coordinate border security and intelligence.[31]

Responding to the new context of drastically reduced departmental autonomy and hostile responses from the national government, the peasant movement radically altered its protest repertoire by the end of this period. Mobilizations shifted from protests to strategic conferences and meetings, demands transitioned from state resources to respect for human rights, and targets changed from the departmental to the national government, making national and international allies more useful and sought after. In 1993–94, rather than protests, there were several forums, gatherings where lists of demands would be elaborated, to be presented later to authorities and disseminated to national allies. Most of these focused on the "old" demands—agrarian issues, education, health, and other material needs—but one in September 1993 instead focused on the rapidly deteriorating human rights situation and made demands of the national rather than departmental government. It raised national awareness of Arauca's human rights crisis, probably contributing to the writing of the Comisión Andina's 1994 book-length report.[32]

Similarly, in January 1994 community and church groups and regional elected officials formed a committee to denounce Arauca's human rights violations nationally and internationally, and a June 1994 negotiation between social movement organizations and the military high command tellingly yielded an agreement to allow social movements to follow up on human rights investigations, a major focus of social movement action in the years to come.[33] After a 1995 forum on old oil issues[34] and one last "old model" mobilization demanding resources from the departmental government in 1996,[35] four "new model" events with national targets and human rights demands were held in 1996 and 1997: a national anti-fumigation peasant protest in September 1996,[36] the "Town Meeting for the Right to Live" in Fortul in 1996, the "Public Hearing for the Life of the U'wa" in 1997, and the "Civic Strike for the Right to Live and Respect for Human Rights" in 1997.[37]

The new model was largely a response to the failure of the old model in the altered context of reduced Araucan political autonomy, increased UP/Saravena Liberal tensions, and fiscal contraction. Although both the 1991–94 and the 1994–97 governors had been elected by the Saravena Liberal–petrocrat Liberal alliance, the latter governor was much less predisposed to aid the piedmont settler movement, at least its UP-influenced sectors. An article in the Communist Party's newspaper regarding the October 1996 "old-style" protest, for example, denounces the governor's granting of about 1.2 billion pesos (about U.S.$1 million) to the military, his neglect of the population's needs, and his "authoritarian and intolerant language."[38] These accusations undoubtedly reflected the increased UP/Saravena Liberal tensions but likely also resulted from the president's restrictions of gubernatorial autonomy. The first elected governor had made his generous concessions to the peasant movement before the beginning of the counterreform; the governor during the period 1994–97 was under far greater pressure to support national military policy initiatives to avoid removal from office. A departmental fiscal crisis in 1997–98, after Occidental reduced production in response to escalating guerrilla attacks on the pipeline, would have further reduced gubernatorial largesse to the peasant movement.[39]

Araucan social movement activists also witnessed the successful implementation of the new strategy, as carried out by the U'wa indigenous community, located in the mountains of Saravena. Throughout Colombia the 1991 Constitution's new provisions for indigenous rights had spurred a wave of indigenous activism and electoral success, with most votes for indigenous parties coming from nonindigenous urban voters.[40] Making good use of this high public sympathy for the indigenous cause, the U'wa resisted Occidental's 1995 attempt to explore for oil on the U'wa reservation first by taking the case to the Defensoría del Pueblo in 1995[41] and then by organizing an August 1996 forum to which international NGOs and journalists were invited. Subsequently, the Colombian government invited the Organization of American States to mediate; the resulting report of September 1997 recommended that oil exploration be abandoned and the reservation enlarged.[42] The government had already taken some initial steps toward enlarging the U'wa and other Araucan indigenous reservations by initiating a small land purchase in April 1996.[43] Although the U'wa conflict with oil interests continued, their success had amply demonstrated the utility of national and international linkages.

In sum, from 1992 to 1997 Left electoral success continued as it had since 1986, even increasing slightly in 1997. However, this electoral success, even with the continuing elite-Left alliances, did not bring peace as it had in 1989–92 because the autonomy of coalition-elected officials was now seriously constrained by national policy, and the political violence against the Left was coming largely from actors outside the region: the Colombian government and army and the VNG. Furthermore, the unity between the two leftist factions that had characterized the pacted peace period (1989–92) was transformed into a more intense rivalry by increased territorial competition between the two guerrilla groups as well as intensified electoral competition between the two closely matched Left-elite alliances. However, the peasant movement's successful response to this changed situation allowed it to resist and remain relevant. Its shift toward developing national and international linkages and toward human rights demands aimed at the national government was reinforced by the failure of the old model, the success of the new model as demonstrated by the U'wa indigenous movement, and especially the growing threat of repressive violence.

October 1997–Late 2001: The Pastrana Peace Negotiations Era

Like Samper's administration, Pastrana's oversaw peace negotiations coinciding with a buildup of both paramilitary and guerrilla forces and expanded coca cultivation. Arauca reflected these trends, although the 2001 onset of paramilitarism was one of the nation's latest. Several trends continued from the previous period: guerrilla repudiation of institutional action and norms, as well as tension between the two guerrilla groups, became more noteworthy. Furthermore, the Left-elite alliances remarkably still held, despite the UP's diminished electoral strength. But the Araucan conflict became much more internationalized during this period, as both the expanded multinational oil presence and the vastly increased U.S. military role in Colombian counterinsurgency became blatant in the region. These "new enemies," however, increased awareness of Arauca's human rights plight among potential sympathizers in the industrial world. Seizing the opportunity, Araucan social movements learned to mobilize these supporters effectively, with the strategy yielding important human rights victories.

Andrés Pastrana (August 1998–August 2002) staked his presidency on peace with the FARC and the ELN. His peace with the former was formalized in a demilitarized zone in Meta/Caquetá from August 1998 to early 2002.[44] Negotiations with the ELN, while resulting in no formal agreements, were ongoing for most of his administration,[45] which meant the two guerrilla forces in Arauca once again shared the same posture toward the government. Although the level of guerrilla-army combat decreased during the negotiations, Pastrana's peace initiatives were otherwise unsuccessful, as evidenced by the rapid increase of guerrilla and paramilitary personnel and the coca expansion that financed it.[46] And even while seeking peace, Pastrana lobbied hard for the $1.3 billion mostly military U.S. aid package that was passed in mid-2000. However, the human rights certification that was tacked on to the bill would prove an important leverage point for Araucan activists.[47]

Parallel with (and in many ways facilitating) a heightened U.S. role in Colombian counterinsurgency was the increased involvement of Occidental and other oil multinationals in the Araucan conflict. After oil prices recovered from their 1998 slump and began their dizzying climb that continued through 2008 (see fig. 7.1), Araucan oil exploration expanded rapidly. In 1997 and 1998 concessions were granted to the Spanish Repsol for a total of 135,000 hectares, all in the piedmont counties; and Occidental was in the process of negotiating additional Arauca contracts.[48] Occidental's contributions to counterinsurgency increased concomitant with this expansion. From 1992 to 2000 it paid the obligatory $1.25 per barrel "war tax" to the Colombian government.[49] In 1997 it began making direct voluntary payments to the Colombian military, estimated at $650,000 per year.[50] Then, having taken the lead in forming the U.S.-Colombia Business Partnership, a consortium of mostly energy multinationals operating in Colombia, it lobbied for increased U.S. military aid to Colombia. Occidental's point person in Colombia, Larry Meriage, testified for this cause before the U.S. Congress in early 2000.[51]

Repression trends in Arauca reflected national events. Samper's Convivir initiative produced a spike of violence. Between November 1997 and

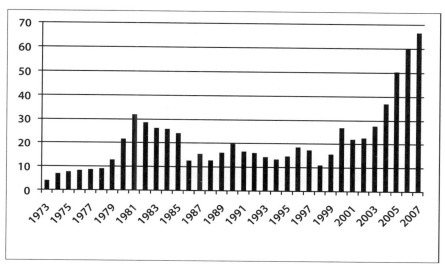

Figure 7.1. Average Global Crude Oil Prices, 1973–2007 (in dollars per barrel)

Sources: Energy Information Administration, "Crude Oil Price Summary (nominal dollars per barrel)," *Monthly Energy Review* (October 2008): table 9.1.

January 1998 a Convivir called "El Corral" became active in Arauca and was allegedly responsible for nineteen assassinations.[52] However, with the peace process under way and the Convivir abolished after mid-1998,[53] political violence against social movement activists and allies dropped. In Arauquita there were no incidents of this type in 1998, 1999, or the first nine months of 2000. Similarly, in Arauca there were no incidents in 1998, threats only in 1999, and one assassination in 2000. Meanwhile, the election of Hugo Chávez in Venezuela had nearly eliminated incidents of repression in Arauca perpetrated by the Venezuelan National Guard. There were no incidents of this kind in 1998–2001 in Arauquita or Arauca County. In 2001, however, as the peace process disintegrated, Arauca's repression index went up to 4.5, and Arauquita's rose to 7.25, a major repressive wave, with almost all incidents perpetrated by paramilitary forces.[54]

At first the paramilitary presence had been limited to sightings on the border with Casanare (February 1999)[55] and threats against the governor and Arauca county council members for having offered Arauca as a possible zona del despeje for ELN-government negotiations (April 1999).[56]

But by late 2000 paramilitary fighters killed an Arauquita fisherman and threatened to kill Arauquita's county officials unless they relinquished municipal funds.[57] In August 2001, as a May–September military operation was winding down, one thousand AUC members crossed into Tame from Casanare and established roadway checkpoints, despite the militarization of the region. Both Amnesty International and Latin America Working Group judged the paramilitary forces' apparent ease of movement to be a sign of the military's collusion.[58]

On the one hand, the paramilitary attack was aimed at the usual targets: social movement activists and peasants in guerrilla-influenced territories. Two of the four Arauca assassinations in 2001 and 6.75 of the 7.25 repression index for Arauquita that year were in this category,[59] and, by conservative estimates, the upsurge in violence against the peasant population induced 280 families to abandon their land in 2001.[60] On the other hand, the attacks for the first time targeted elite political allies of the Left. In March 2001 a former departmental assembly deputy whose evangelical Christian party had supported the 1997 UP-LaTorrista gubernatorial candidate, Octavio Sarmiento, was assassinated.[61] In early October 2001, in a devastating blow, Sarmiento himself and Luis Alfredo Colmenares Chía, Arauca's two representatives in the House at the time, were assassinated, Sarmiento at his ranch in Tame and Colmenares in Bogotá.[62] Both were members of the elite: Colmenares a plains petrocrat, Sarmiento a large rancher from Tame. Both had a long record of representing elite-Left alliances in high public office (Colmenares as petrocrat Liberal–Saravena Liberal governor and representative; Sarmiento as two-term UP-LaTorrista representative to the House). The AUC Web site was cited as claiming responsibility for both murders, accusing Sarmiento and Colmenares of links with the FARC and the ELN, respectively, and threatening further attacks on "guerrilla-allied" politicians."[63]

Araucan guerrilla actions also mirrored national trends. During the 1998–2001 period of peace negotiations, the level of guerrilla-army combats remained relatively low: 0, 2, 2, and 1 combats in 1998, 1999, 2000, and 2001, respectively in Arauquita; and 0, 0, 2, and 0 combats in the same years in Arauca.[64] However, in most other respects both guerrilla groups in Arauca grew more bellicose. Guerrilla numbers expanded nationally and presumably in Arauca as well. Hugo Chávez's 1998 election as president of Venezuela favored such expansion, as the FARC in Arauca perceived him as a potential ally and began to use Venezuelan territory as a refuge.[65] Furthermore, attacks on the oil pipeline, which took place overwhelmingly in Arauca, accelerated rapidly. There were 80 attacks in 1998, 77 in 1999, nearly 100 in 2000, and an all-time high of 112 in 2001— which actually halted pumping for 240 days that year.[66]

The FARC had long been the more "institutional" of the two guerrilla groups; it had launched the UP, had generally respected the need for UP county executives to comply with relevant laws, and had cultivated a good public image by focusing violent acts mainly on military targets. However, now the FARC's tactics began to converge with those of the ELN, which often flouted human rights and democratic norms. For example, the FARC began attempting to extort resources directly from municipal administrations, including those of the Patriotic Union.[67] Also, a new guerrilla tactic called the *paro armado,* or armed strike, emerged, with one occurring in June 1998. In contrast to the social movement–organized *paro cívico* of years past, guerrillas unilaterally demanded a halt to all transit, without consulting regional activists.[68] Although no guerrilla assassinations of Right-aligned civilians occurred in Arauquita, such incidents continued and escalated in Arauca County, with a political violence index for this category of 1.25 in 1998; 2.25 in 1999, including another attempt on Julio Acosta's life; 0 in 2000; and 5.0 in 2001.[69] But the most notorious example of the FARC's disregard for international norms occurred in March 1999, when the group killed three U.S.-based activists for indigenous rights working in solidarity with the U'wa cause.[70] Although the FARC later claimed the action was a "mistake," not authorized by the central command, only the direct perpetrators—not the regional commander—were punished, and with public service only.[71]

Even though ELN and FARC postures vis-à-vis government peace overtures were similar during this period and tactics were converging, tensions between the groups grew due to conflict over territories and resources. From 1986 through the late 1990s, only the ELN had carried out pipeline attacks—and collected extortion money from the contractors who came to repair it. However, in the late 1990s the FARC began blowing up the oil pipeline as well.[72] Furthermore, while the ELN had traditionally not allowed coca cultivation in Arauca before 1994, the FARC had no such prohibition.[73] Thus the late 1990s coca expansion—by late 2001 the UNODC reported 2,749 hectares of coca in Arauca—strengthened the FARC in Arauca relative to the ELN, increasing conflict between the two groups as the FARC elbowed in on the ELN's territories and sources of funding.[74]

The major trends apparent in the elections during this period—March 1998 House and Senate races and 2000 departmental and county elections—were surprising setbacks for Julio Acosta, the remarkable continuation of the department's Left-elite alliances, and the rapid atrophy of the UP's electoral strength. Although Acosta was the top vote getter in Arauca for Senate in March 1998, he overestimated his national constituency. Failing to garner enough votes to win one of the hundred seats (he came in 136th), he was thus shut out of national power for the time being. Similarly, Egdumar Chávez, the candidate who appeared to follow Acosta's "line," placed third after the candidates representing the two Left-elite alliances in both the March 1998 race for Arauca's two House seats and in the 2000 governor's race. Remarkably, both Left-elite alliances still held. The petrocrat Liberal–Saravena Liberal alliance was especially successful, winning 3,000 votes more than the LaTorrista-UP alliance in the March 1998 House election (11,350 vs. 8,386) and 11,497 more in the 2000 gubernatorial contest (23,951 vs. 12, 454).[75]

These figures, however, also reveal the rapidly declining electoral strength of the UP-LaTorrista coalition, which as recently as the October 1997 gubernatorial elections had missed victory by just 1,400 votes. Furthermore, the UP's Octavio Sarmiento, although as in 1991–94 elected to one of Arauca's House seats with LaTorrista support, in March 1998 listed his party affiliation as "coalition" rather than "Unión Patriótica," split the four-year term with his LaTorrista campaign adviser, Sirenia Saray, and occupied the office after her.[76] In other words, the UP-LaTorrista coalition was now LaTorrista dominated rather than UP dominated. In the October 2000 votes for assembly, county executive, and county council, the UP's decline was even more evident. Between 1997 and 2000 the number of UP deputies in the assembly declined from four to two, the UP's share of the Arauquita county executive vote for candidates was reduced from 62 percent to 45 percent, the number of UP county council members in Arauquita's thirteen-member county council fell from nine to five, and the UP lost the single county council seat in Arauca that it had held since 1986.[77]

Reasons for this precipitous decline could certainly include the Left's near-disappearance on the national level and the FARC's turn away from institutional politics. Although the UP's electoral success in Arauca had bucked both these trends before, this time the UP had great reason to be disillusioned with Araucan electoral politics in particular. In the 1997 gubernatorial election, the UP's vastly more experienced candidate, Sarmiento, had suffered his third narrow loss of the powerful governor's office, although Sarmiento's sure victory had been heralded in the mainstream press before the elections.[78] The UP alleged that 5,000 votes of people illegally registered in Saravena had been counted, giving Sarmiento's opponent the majority. The investigation was taken up by the National Electoral Council, but the decision was not changed.[79] Indicative of voter disillusionment, the total number of votes in the 2000 gubernatorial race was 53,270, down more than 8,000 votes from the 1997 governor's contest,[80] although the population in Arauca had grown from 177,000 to 216,000 between 1995 and 2000.[81]

In response to these electoral trends, which reduced the peasant movement's influence over the departmental government, and notwithstanding the post-1998 fiscal recovery that came in the wake of rapidly rising oil prices, which under other circumstances might have made state resources–focused mobilizations viable, social movements furthered the trends of the previous period. Responding as well to the growing threats of international military intervention and paramilitarism, they increasingly addressed human rights demands to national (and international) targets and sought elite regional and national and international allies, achieving their greatest success when international pressures were brought to bear on international actors and/or the Colombian government. Also noteworthy was the more direct and public distancing of these movements, especially the U'wa movement, from guerrilla tactics, as guerrilla actions became more extreme. These trends were apparent in Arauca's central human rights movement, the movement to seek justice in the aftermath of the Santo Domingo bombing, and the U'wa movement to prevent oil exploration on their lands.

The new model won an unusual success in the efforts to shut down the notorious Convivir El Corral, which had been accused of carrying out at least nineteen assassinations since its founding in late 1997. In January 1998 the Araucan radio journalist Efraín Varela, on the major Arauca radio station Meridiano 70, asked an El Corral leader why the vehicles of the Convivir had license plates from San Vicente de Chucurí, Santander, a hotbed of illegal paramilitary activity. The El Corral leader indignantly replied that the organization was operating in physical proximity to, and with the full knowledge of, the commander of the army's Eighteenth Brigade. The revelation caused a public uproar and made Efraín Varela, who was not a leftist but was known as a critical intellectual, a hero (and elite ally) of the human rights movement. In February 1998 a departmental paro cívico initiated by unions, peasant organizations, indigenous organizations, and other opposition groups called for an investigation of El Corral, among other human rights demands. The government agreed to investigate the Convivir (and other human rights violations), eventually revealing that the cooperative lacked proper licensing and forcing it to close down.[82] This was a major victory, highly unusual in Colombia.

Other mobilizations of the central human rights movement similarly demonstrated an increased interest in building new connections. An August 1998 event won the establishment of the Intersectoral Commission to Follow up on Human Rights Investigations in Arauca, which would include national NGOs and representatives of the Defensoría del Pueblo and the Procuraduría (Attorney General's Office) as well as Araucan social organizations.[83] The July 2000 "Indigenous-Peasant Mobilization" not only evidenced a peasant movement effort to build new regional alliances with the indigenous movement,[84] in a frontier region where peasant settlers and indigenous people historically competed for the same land. It also indicated new international alliances: a delegation led by a member of the European parliament and the president of the French Farmers' Confederation arrived in Arauca in time for the protest.[85]

The campaign to punish those responsible for the December 13, 1998, bombing of the hamlet of Santo Domingo in Tame, in which eighteen civilians were killed, demonstrated the way in which U.S. social movement linkages became especially crucial. Ironically, such linkages were promoted by the indirect involvement in the bombing of the U.S. government, Occidental, and another U.S. firm, as well as the passage of the Plan Colombia (mostly) military aid package. But these international actors could not have been mobilized without the initial organizational strength, astuteness, and persistence of Araucan social movements.

In the immediate aftermath of the bombing, the army insisted the bomb had been set off by guerrillas on the ground and quickly closed the investigation. But thirty villagers testified at great risk, evidence such as shrapnel had been carefully saved and documented, and the Araucan social movements persisted in calling for a full investigation. Breakthroughs came in June 1999 and February 2000, when the Procuraduría returned for a more thorough investigation and found that the bomb had been dropped from above (as the peasants had argued) and not exploded on the ground, as the army had alleged. By May 2000 an FBI ballistics test was ordered, which confirmed that the shrapnel fragments were from a specific type of U.S.-made cluster bomb used by the Colombian army. As the debate took place regarding the passage of Plan Colombia, and then whether to require human rights certification for this aid, the case gained prominence in both the United States and Colombia. Senator Patrick Leahy (D-Vt.) took a personal interest in it, and in September 2000 a mock trial held by the Human Rights Center at Northwestern University found the Colombian Air Force guilty.[86] As a result of these new developments, the Colombian Air Force commander in charge of the unit involved in the bombing, General Héctor Velasco, reinitiated the military investigation in December 2000.[87] Furthermore, in early 2001, as evidence emerged that the U.S. air surveillance firm hired by Occidental to monitor the pipeline, Airscan, may have helped the military pinpoint the target on the day of the bombing, the Procuraduría subpoenaed three former Airscan employees, all U.S. citizens.[88]

Meanwhile, the indigenous movement continued to have periods of success, using a similar strategy of mobilizing U.S. and national actors to pressure Occidental Petroleum, followed by new challenges. In the first wave of successes, the U'wa leader Berito Cobaría was awarded the prestigious Goldman Environmental Prize in 1998, in recognition of the U'was' traditional spirituality, pro-environmental stance, and support from human rights groups.[89] Then, in response to the 1997 OAS report recommending abandonment of oil exploration on U'Wa lands and enlargement of the U'wa reservation, Dutch Shell pulled out of its partnership with Occidental to explore on U'wa land, and the government increased the size of the U'wa reservation to 220,275 hectares.[90]

Then came the new challenges, followed by new success. Only one month later the government granted Occidental a contract to explore on land just 700 meters from the new borders of the U'wa reservation. Exploration began in January 2000.[91] The U'wa responded by calling in national allies—other indigenous communities as well as farmers and oil workers—to help them maintain peaceful (but nevertheless harshly repressed) blockades of the land under exploration and to block highways for nearly three months in early 2000. Meanwhile, in the United States, U'wa solidarity activism was noteworthy in 2000 and increased in 2001 as U.S. aid to Colombia gained a higher profile. The conflict was used to "seriously embarrass" the 2000 "environmental" presidential candidate—and major individual Occidental shareholder—Al Gore. Vigils were held outside the homes of Occidental executives, lawsuits were filed in Colombian and international courts, and shareholders' resolutions were presented. Furthermore, U'wa leaders traveled to the United States to lobby Congress and build support networks, and pro-U'wa individuals purchased land in and around the drilling sites. The project soon became a public relations nightmare for Occidental. Fidelity Investments, one of the largest shareholders in the company, divested from Occidental in 2000. In July 2001 Occidental announced that despite the high hopes raised by initial seismic studies, it had not found any oil, only water and gases, raising hopes that it would withdraw from the project altogether.[92]

During this period, social movements and leftist electoral forces began to make their first public statements repudiating guerrillas. Not surprisingly, the U'wa Web site denounces the February 1999 assassination of the three U.S. indigenous rights activists by the FARC and makes its own pacifist position—against *all* armed actors—clear: "The different armed actors have threatened and harassed the U'wa and their process of struggle . . . which has earned their repudiation and rejection of all these forms of violence." And in a first but telling example of the UP publicly distancing itself from the FARC, shortly before his assassination by paramilitary forces in 2001 UP congressman Octavio Sarmiento had expressed his opposition to a FARC-initiated *paro armado*.[93]

In sum, between 1997 and 2001 even more outside actors—the extraregional paramilitary forces like the El Corral Convivir and then the AUC itself in 2001, Occidental Petroleum, and especially the massive monetary aid of the U.S. government—joined the Araucan fray on the side of the military. Although Arauca's Left-elite electoral alliances still held, the electoral strength of the UP was undermined as the UP became disillusioned with regional electoral action and the FARC became overtly hostile to elections and other institutional expressions. By the end of the period, the shifting context created opportunities for new social movement strategies. Both the UP and U'wa representatives publicly repudiated specific human rights violations perpetrated by the FARC. More obviously, they had used the region's new international "enemies" to find new allies, creating national and international linkages that allowed them to effectively counteract the initiatives on the Right, with some rare successes.

2002–2004: The Early Uribe Era—Arauca's Moment in the National Spotlight

During the 2002–4 period national policies first ended peace processes with guerrillas and then, as oil prices escalated and new oil fields opened for exploration, suspended citizen rights and reversed Araucan regional autonomy. U.S. military aid and intervention in Arauca greatly increased, and the region became Uribe's top priority until FARC-influenced areas in the Amazon watershed took prominence after 2004. Paramilitary forces established a foothold in Tame and expanded toward the Venezuelan border. The repressive wave initiated in 2001, focusing on elite allies as well as social movements, thus continued and escalated in 2002. Left electoral success plummeted in 2003, the long-standing elite-Left coalitions disintegrated, and Julio Acosta at long last was elected governor. From 2003 to 2004 repression decreased dramatically in Arauca (where elite allies had been located) but not as much in Arauquita. Uribe's hard-line approach reduced guerrilla oil pipeline attacks and weakened the ELN, which explored negotiations with the government. In contrast, the FARC was driven further into an extreme anti-institutional stance. Araucan social movements continued and furthered the strategy of mobilizing outside allies and using the judicial tools provided by the 1991 Constitution to win major victories, with success that was exceptional in the Colombian context.

Several trends converged during 2002 to 2004 to give Arauca an unprecedented prominence in the national and international eye and to make these the most violent years ever in Araucan history. First, oil prices doubled between 1998 and 2001, then remained at the 2001 rate through 2004 (see fig. 7.1).[94] Oil earnings represented 30 percent of Colombia's foreign exchange, Arauca produced 20 percent of Colombia's oil, and there were signs this percentage would soon grow.[95] Four new oil exploration concessions were initiated between October 2001 and late 2003, covering a total of 726,055 hectares in the piedmont and involving Ecopetrol, Occidental, and France-based Hocol.[96] Oil was found in one of these concessions in 2005.[97] In 2004 Occidental extended its Caño Limón contract through 2018, when it expected the "economic life of the field" to end; the contract was originally set to expire in 2008.[98]

Second, U.S. military presence in Arauca increased dramatically. Occidental Petroleum, through intense lobbying efforts, succeeded in getting Arauca included in the U.S. military initiatives that were part of Plan Colombia. A $98 million package was dedicated to arming two new Colombian battalions whose primary mission was to protect the oil pipeline and sending sixty to one hundred U.S. officers to train them. Underscoring this new U.S. prioritization of the region, the U.S. ambassador visited Arauca, including the Caño Limón oil complex, twice in 2002.[99] But by late 2004 aid to Arauca was coming under fire in the United States as "corporate welfare" for Occidental.[100] It was further argued that Plan Colombia was supposed to fight drugs, not protect oil pipelines. Thus the Bush administration was pleased with President Uribe's announcement of Plan Patriota, which shifted the priority to fumigating coca crops and the geographic focus to fighting the FARC in its strongholds in southern Meta, Caquetá, and Putumayo.[101]

Third and most important, just as Pastrana had staked his reputation on negotiating peace with the FARC in the zona del despeje in Caquetá and Meta, Uribe intended to stake his on "retaking" Arauca. Having won by a landslide running on a "get tough" platform, he had the political capital[102]—and the regionally focused U.S. aid—to take on this goal, and he sought out every opportunity to publicize his intentions. In July 2003 he actually governed from Arauca for several days, giving pep talks to soldiers and announcing the guerrillas' imminent defeat, and by 2005 the number of troops in Arauca had increased from 5,766 to 7,839.[103]

Thus, in addition to initiating *national* measures reinstating a broadened State of Internal Commotion and policies dragging civilians into the war (e.g., live-at-home "peasant soldiers" and incentives for informers), Uribe implemented extreme restrictions on citizenship rights and coercive policies that were *regionally specific*.[104] Implemented only in Arauca, for example, the "Soldier for a Day" program required children to spend one day a week at the Saravena Battalion, swimming in the pool, eating treats, playing on the tanks, and seeing soldiers dressed as clowns.[105] More formally, in September 2002 Uribe declared Arauca-Arauquita-Tame and another subregion "zones of rehabilitation and consolidation (ZRC),"[106] where freedom of movement was restricted, the military could keep a registry of the population, and all foreigners needed to obtain permission eight days in advance of traveling to the region from the governor (Arauca) or the minister of the interior (Sucre/Bolívar).[107]

Uribe also went far beyond Gaviria in restricting the political and fiscal autonomy of Arauca's elected officials. The clear victory of Hector Gallardo (petrocrat-Saravena Liberal) in the October 2000 gubernatorial election was annulled by the president in September 2002; the vacant position was occupied by Uribe appointees until the elections of October 2003.[108] Similarly, when the Arauquita county executive resigned in 2002, he was replaced by an Uribe military appointee.[109] Perhaps most flagrantly, the national government then de facto determined the outcome of the October 2003 local and departmental elections by arresting, just five days before the election, virtually all the major contenders for governor and Arauca County executive that were not Acosta allies or Acosta himself, accusing them of links to guerrillas.[110] Finally, Uribe undermined the basic fiscal autonomy of the department in late February 2003, with a policy that mandated that the national government, rather than the department, would manage Arauca's (rapidly increasing) oil royalties.[111]

By 2003–4 a reaction to the excesses of 2002 on the part of Araucan social movements, judicial entities, human rights organizations, and even the U.S. military aid human rights certification process reined in the most extreme state violations of citizens' constitutional and political rights in Arauca.[112] For example, the Supreme Court declared many of the ZRC provisions illegal, refusing to renew either the ZRCs measure or the State of Internal Commotion in April 2003 (although some provisions of both measures still became law in late 2003), and the Procuraduría's serious concerns led to the dismantling of the "Soldier for a Day" program.[113]

Another changed direction in 2003–4 was the national emphasis on coca fumigation, implemented in Arauca as well. By the end of 2003, although official statistics noted only 2,214 coca hectares in Arauca in December 2002, the army claimed to have eradicated 15,000 to 17,000 hectares. Peasant and human rights organizations claimed more legal crops were fumigated than coca.[114] Although fumigation was widely condemned by peasant movements on economic and environmental grounds, it was both less lethal and less flagrantly offensive to human rights than the ZRC policies had been.

As these trends mitigated state-initiated repression in 2003–4, paramilitary consolidation and expansion during the same years increased "private" violence. Araucan paramilitary forces numbered about eight hundred in early 2003.[115] As the army's construction of the new Tame-Arauca "Route of the Liberators" proceeded (see fig. 8.1), funded by Arauca's now nationally controlled oil royalties, paramilitary forces consolidated control along this route, as well as in Tame's plains and urban center.[116] They even turned assassinated congressman Octavio Sarmiento's Tame ranch into a paramilitary base. Both military and paramilitary checkpoints—the paramilitary ones used to extort money from travelers—became commonplace along the roadway, as did reports of military-paramilitary collusion,[117] and they continued to be active through early 2006.[118]

Patterns in repression in Arauca reflected these trends in international and national policy and geographic paramilitary expansion. By the end of the period, Arauca, led by Tame, held the dubious distinction of being one of the most violent departments (per capita) in one of the most violent countries in the world.[119] The number of displaced people in Arauca was said to total 1,983 families, or 9,915 people, in early 2005—up from 520 families in 2002—probably an undercount given the dangers of denouncing the powerful violent actors.[120]

In both Arauca and Arauquita the overall levels of violence peaked in 2001 and 2002, with a clear reduction in 2003 and 2004 (see figs. 7.2 and 7.3). However, repression in the two counties differed both quantitatively and qualitatively. Between 2000 and 2002 Arauca experienced more than a twentyfold increase in its repression index (from 2.0 to more than 40.0), while Arauquita's repression index "merely" quadrupled, from 1.8 to 7.2. Furthermore, reflecting the greater elite presence in the plains county— both elite allies of the Left and elite paramilitary supporters resided there— Arauca County's repression in 2002–3 was overwhelmingly paramilitary and largely focused on the Left's elite allies, whereas Arauquita's was perpetrated primarily by public forces against the social movement leaders and base. Fully 23.6 of Arauca county's 2002 repression index of 41.7 focused on elite allies of the Left; the remaining 18.1 focused on those with only an indirect and weak presumed affiliation with the Left (e.g., individuals who attended the funeral of a labor leader, peasants residing in areas with guerrilla presence).[121]

Among the elite allies of the Left felled by paramilitary violence in Arauca County in 2002 were the Liberal vice president of Arauca's county council, the president of the chamber of commerce, and Efraín Varela, the Meridiano 70 radio station director (and former Saravena county executive)

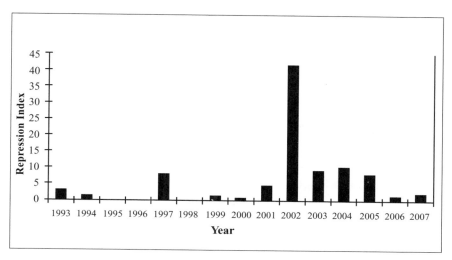

Figure 7.2. Political Violence in Arauca County, 1993–2007

Note: For explanation, operationalization, and sources for these data, see the methods section of chapter 1.

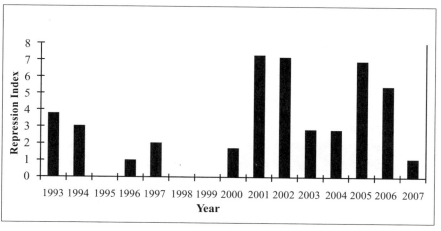

Figure 7.3. Political Violence in Arauquita, 1993–2007

Note: For explanation, operationalization, and sources for these data, see the methods section of chapter 1.

who had denounced the Convivir El Corral in 1998 (the latter murder was widely condemned by the national media). Days later Varela's most obvious replacement received paramilitary threats and abandoned the region. Not surprisingly, the incident had a significant chilling effect on Araucan media criticism of the military and paramilitary.[122] Also in 2002 paramilitary forces issued numerous death threats against the department of Arauca's political leadership. One threat against a list of more than two hundred individuals, most of them nonleftists, stated, "We want the politicians that represent Arauca to break all the commitments they have with [the FARC and the ELN]. . . . They will remain as military objectives until we accomplish their total eradication from the political map of Colombia." Another threat went further, targeting not those who chose to ally with leftist electoral forces but any county executive who might contemplate resigning in response to guerrilla threats.[123]

In 2003, with Left-elite alliances weakened, the repression index in Arauca County fell to 9.2, but the targeting of elite allies before the October gubernatorial elections and the predominance of paramilitary perpetrators were still noteworthy. All the incidents of repression (repression index 6.8) that took place before October were carried out by paramilitary forces, including the assassination of an electoral official and a journalist and threats against sixteen other journalists. Then, as described above, days before the gubernatorial elections, state security forces detained twenty-two leading Left-allied candidates for office in a new kind of "preventive" selective recentralization. After this incident, which definitively ruptured the elite-Left departmental coalitions, and through the end of 2004, repression remained roughly at 2003 levels and overwhelmingly private (85 percent of the repression index), but it refocused on the "old" targets: human rights, peasant, and leftist party activists.[124]

In contrast, in Arauquita repression in 2002–4 was exclusively social movement and peasant focused and more "public" than in Arauca County. In 2002 public forces accounted for 72 percent of the repression index. After Uribe's inauguration, as the ZRC period began, massive detentions by the military were common: nineteen people were arrested without warrants in Arauquita.[125] More notoriously, in Saravena, near the main piedmont military base with U.S. presence and funding, two thousand people were detained in a single incident. Fifty long-term arrests resulted, mostly of trade unionists.[126] Meanwhile, paramilitary attacks on social movement activists and leftist county administration officials continued in the piedmont: a key witness in the Santo Domingo bombing case was killed in Tame,[127] and in Arauquita, a former UP county council member and an appointed county administration official were assassinated.

By 2003–4, as the national government began shifting the focus of its counterinsurgency to southern coca-growing regions, levels of overall repression fell. Most incidents involved army harassment of peasants in the Panamá de Arauca area bordering Arauca in conjunction with a late 2003 coca fumigation campaign.[128] Although the presence of coca crops was the formal reason for targeting the area, one author suggests that the siting of a new oil field there contributed as well.[129] In addition to conducting fumigation campaigns, public forces tortured and arrested members of the UP-aligned Araucan Peasant Organization and a UP departmental assembly representative. Furthermore, paramilitary violence became more prominent, representing 34 percent of the repression index by 2003–4 as paramilitary forces began to move toward the Arauca River. In 2004 paramilitary incursions focused on peasants in the coca-growing (and potentially oil-producing) Panamá de Arauca area bordering Arauca County, as well as on the top social movement and leftist party leaders.[130]

Given the drastic change in national policy and the FARC's turn away from electoral politics, the major electoral trends of the period are not surprising: the electoral Left's (especially the UP-PCC's) continued decline; decreased voter participation, especially in the piedmont; and the final rupture of the two Left-elite alliances, which laid the groundwork for the electoral consolidation of the unallied Right. In October 2000 the UP still held two of eleven departmental assembly seats (18 percent), but by spring 2002 the Left-allied presidential candidate, Lucho Garzón, and the UP candidate for the House each won slightly more than 5 percent of the departmental vote for candidates; in contrast Alvaro Uribe won 53 percent of the Araucan vote for candidates in his presidential bid. Similarly, in the Senate races, votes for the Communist Party or its electoral vehicle declined from 1,966 (6.6 percent of the departmental vote for candidates) in 1998 to 345 (1.7 percent of Araucan votes for candidates) in 2002. In a closely related development, although population rose from 177,000 in 1995 to 216,000 in 2000 to 232,000 in 2005, voter participation in the House election declined from 32,902 in 1998 to 26,835 in 2002, and votes in the presidential election declined from 36,072 to 29,633 in the same years. This loss of votes derived disproportionately from the piedmont: voter participation in Arauquita's county executive race dropped from 6,201 to 3,684 (59 percent of its previous level) between 2000 and 2003; and in the county executive races in the capital, voter participation remained virtually identical, 20,362 in 2000 and 20,316 in 2003.[131]

The rupture of the Left-elite alliances was a logical consequence of the paramilitary targeting of elites and the weakening of the electoral Left. The first alliance to break was the UP-LaTorrista coalition for the House seat: in March 2002 the LaTorristas ran one candidate, who won a seat with 6,727 votes—fully 96 percent of them from the plains counties or Tame. The Communist Party ran its own candidate, who won only 1,185 votes (61 percent of these from Arauquita, Saravena, and Fortul) and was not elected. The Saravena Liberal–petrocrat Liberal alliance still appeared to be intact, however. Adalberto Jaimes won 7,232 votes and the second House seat, garnering 44 percent of his votes from Fortul, Arauquita, and Saravena; 11 percent from Tame; and the rest from the plains counties, Arauca, Puerto Rondón, and Cravo Norte.[132]

By the beginning of the 2003 gubernatorial campaign, however, the long-standing petrocrat Liberal–Saravena Liberal alliance had also broken. All the regional alliances then shifted, as Julio Acosta faced off against an all-piedmont candidate apparently supported by both sectors of the electoral Left. Fully 94 percent of Acosta's votes came from the plains (Arauca, Cravo Norte, Puerto Rondón) or the plains-piedmont county of Tame. Conversely, 64 percent of Helmer Muñoz's votes came from the piedmont counties or Tame.[133] Muñoz was a priest who ran the Ricardo Pampurí hospital, a medical facility supported largely by European NGOs and specializing in tropical diseases. It was located in the hamlet of La Esmeralda, a longtime peasant movement stronghold near the Arauquita–Saravena border, which roughly coincided with the line of demarcation between the FARC's and the ELN's zones of influence. Despite past conflicts with the guerrillas, Muñoz's humanitarian credentials, piedmont grassroots connections, and status as a "frequent critic of President Uribe's hard-line policies" made him an obvious choice to be an all-piedmont pro–social movement candidate.[134]

Muñoz was a leading contender for the governor's post. However, his victory was thwarted by his arrest and that of virtually all the major contenders for governor and Arauca county executive—with the glaring exception of Julio Acosta and his allies. Those arrested—including two former governors from 1997 to 2000 and 2000 to 2003, the leading La-

Torristas, the county executive of Arauca, and the most important petro-crat participants in the petrocrat–Saravena Liberal alliance—were accused of "rebellion," that is, aiding the FARC or the ELN. With this official blessing, Acosta handily won the elections with 20,090 votes, while Helmer Muñoz received just 12,711 votes. Similarly, the Arauca county executive race was won by one of the few candidates *not* detained just before the elections. Despite the fact that many human rights groups issued denunciations of the arrests before the election, the national government insisted that it had firm proof of complicity with guerrillas via an informer and stood by the process.[135] The era of Left-elite alliances had come to an abrupt end, and the Araucan Right had been greatly strengthened.

Although Uribe's selective recentralization strategy was clearly achieving its electoral goals, the post-2001 crackdown on guerrillas, which paralleled the electoral and political strategy, was having more mixed results. On the one hand, there were signs that the guerrillas were weakening. As the ELN's strongholds in and around the Middle Magdalena region came under attack from the AUC, the number of ELN fighters was reduced to about 80 percent of its high point by the end of 2004, and it began to explore peace talks with Uribe. A *Los Angeles Times* account reported that attacks on the Caño Limón–Coveñas oil pipeline on Araucan soil were reduced from an all-time high of 170 in 2001, 36 in 2002, and 34 in 2003 to only 5 by mid-2004.[136]

On the other hand, the strength, activity, and finances of guerrillas in Arauca, especially the FARC, seemed unaffected or even increased. In Arauquita the number of confrontations with fatalities increased from one to seven between 2002 and 2003, before dropping back to one in 2004. Similarly, in Arauca County, which had experienced one or two combats per year in the period 1996–2001, the number of combats between guerrillas and the army rose to five, four, and three in 2002, 2003, and 2004 respectively.[137] Furthermore, new economic sabotage tactics—bombings of the electrical infrastructure and "armed strikes"—emerged to replace the oil pipeline attacks. Attacks on electrical towers left most or all of the department without electricity in February, June, and September 2003 for four days to a week each time, while armed strikes by the ELN alone or with the FARC paralyzed all traffic in Arauca in February and one week in June. In 2004 the oil pipeline was bombed four times in Arauquita: three times by the FARC, once by the ELN.[138] Similarly, the government's late 2003 claims of victory over coca cultivation (assumed to contribute to guerrilla finances) turned out to be premature. The Observatorio de Drogas de Colombia reported that coca hectares had indeed declined to only 539 in late 2003 but then climbed to 1,552 by December 2004.[139]

Furthermore, the government's policies, by undermining the integrity of the electoral process as well as departmental autonomy and thereby weakening the electoral Left, helped push the FARC into an even more extreme defiance of democratic institutions, even while the ELN moderated its discourse. The tactic of killing elite-party politicians became more frequent. In Arauca guerrillas killed three high-level elite political officials in 2003: a consultant and an appointee to the Uribe-appointed governor and a Liberal departmental assembly deputy. In 2004, after the definitive demise of the LaTorre-UP coalition, the FARC was accused of assassinating the high-ranking LaTorrista Marcos Ataya and threatening Julio Acosta in December 2004.[140] In Arauquita between 2002 and 2003 guerrillas killed two Conservative county council members (one the president of the council) and a Liberal county council candidate. The FARC also threatened the Uribe-appointed acting county executive and made an assassination attempt on his replacement.[141] The exiled Uribe appointee, a retired general, resigned and left the region, denouncing the lack of protection he had received from the military because "90 percent of the soldiers are guarding the oil pipeline."[142] This suggests that the prioritization of pipeline protection allowed FARC advances on other fronts.

But beyond escalating this old tactic, the FARC broke new ground by sabotaging democratic institutions they had once respected or even promoted. In 2002 the FARC kidnapped an UP departmental assembly member and human rights activist, Martín Sandoval, along with six representatives of the Registraduría (national electoral institution), stealing voting materials. In 2003 sixteen leading Araucan journalists received death threats from the FARC. Proposing a link between rightist repression and the FARC's new direction, one version suggested the FARC aimed to force Araucan journalists to offer more critical coverage; since Efraín Varela's 2002 assassination, the journalists had limited themselves to reproducing official press releases.[143]

Perhaps most emblematic of the FARC's new orientation vis-à-vis institutional politics, in 2002 and 2003 the FARC issued death threats against

one of the UP's most popular county executives, Orlando Ardila, of Arauquita, as well as against all the other county administrations in the department.[144] Ardila soon resigned, followed by his entire county council and
shortly after the county executive and county council of Fortul, a long-
standing UP stronghold.[145] The FARC's threats were issued after Ardila's
October 2002 denunciation of the FARC's robbery of 200 head of cattle
(from an individual, presumably); 150 head of cattle from the Municipal
Technical Assistance Unit (UMATA) agricultural extension farm; and even
one million pesos from the municipal treasury. The chain of events reveals
the ways the logics of armed struggle and electoral action, viewed as com-
plementary by the reform period FARC, had now come to undermine each
other. The FARC's theft of private and especially municipal resources sabotaged Ardila's ability to carry out his electoral program and get reelected;
likewise, Ardila's defense of legal institutions interfered with the FARC's
ability to obtain resources to wage war. Thus began an open bifurcation
between leftist elected officials and social movements, on the one hand,
and guerrillas, on the other. As in 1997 Ardila's actions were applauded by
the departmental assembly: a farewell ceremony was held to express support for him after he resigned.[146] This time, however, the homage to Ardila
was an indirect censure of the FARC rather than of the president and
Venezuela's defense minister.

From the point of view of international humanitarian law, even more
egregious was that guerrillas, especially the FARC, increasingly killed ordinary civilians. In some cases the victims were perceived by the guerrillas
to be rightist sympathizers,[147] but there was an also increasing number of
deaths of civilians as "collateral damage." Guerrillas' use of land mines
and bombs became frequent after 2002. Land mines injured a child in
Arauquita in early 2004, a bomb set off by the FARC in Arauca killed a
police man and injured twenty-nine civilians in Arauca in August 2005,
and another bomb in Tame killed two and wounded thirty-seven in May
2004. Finally, as paramilitary forces began to consolidate control in rural
Tame, guerrilla abuses targeting peasants there escalated—a trend widely
condemned by regional, national, and international human rights organizations.[148]

Remarkably, even during and after the repressive assault of 2001–3,
Araucan social movements remained strong, with the repressive wave re-
affirming the emphasis on human rights demands targeting the national

government. The severity of national policies applied to Arauca and increased foreign presence drew the attention of national and international human rights entities alike to the region. Further facilitating alliances with these national and international advocacy groups, Araucan social movements increasingly distanced themselves from armed insurgencies as guerrilla actions became more extreme. The strengthened outside alliances boosted the success of three major campaigns that used Colombian civil rights protections to prosecute human rights offenders: justice for the Santo Domingo bombing victims; liberation of the peasant leader Luz Perly Córdoba; and bringing to justice the assassins of three regional activists killed in August 2004. Only the U'wa movement experienced one downside of international alliances—their fickleness—and refocused on national allies.

Araucan social movements in general during this period remained very strong, based on a dense web of organizations. Despite the 2001 paramilitary assault, in 2002 the Araucan social movements were described by a regional human rights report as demonstrating a "paradigm of social organization, with a great capacity for mobilization with respect to the rest of the country." A partial enumeration of Araucan social movement organizations included 57 cooperatives and peasant organizations, 14 labor organizations, 7 civic organizations, 1 student organization with 7 locals, 2 indigenous associations, 1 regional peasant association and branches of 2 national peasant organizations (ANUC, Fensuagro), 570 civic action committees, 7 municipal associations of civic action committees, 1 departmental association of civic action committees, 2 human rights committees (one regional, one a branch of a national organization), and the presence of many national NGOs. "The Araucan people's level of commitment is so high that it can be said with confidence that every resident belongs to at least one social organization."[149]

However, despite this strength and the moment of maximum intra- and intermovement unity, once national policy swung from negotiations toward a hard-line solution, continuing success would require social movements to mobilize international allies. A protest precisely at the moment of the policy shift in February 2002 is illustrative. Fully twenty thousand peasants and others, almost 7 percent of the department's population, occupied the town squares of Tame, Fortul, Saravena, Arauquita, and Arauca for several weeks under the motto "Against paramilitarism, U.S. military presence, and Plan Colombia." Unity was apparent in the intra-Left and Left-indigenous alliances. The indigenous movement, both "lines" of the peasant movement (ADUC and Fensuagro—Peasant Association of Arauca), all the labor organizations, and many national human rights organizations appeared on the signatory list of the press release about the protest, and about a third of the press release was devoted to the U'wa/ Occidental conflict. In the resulting "Cradle of Liberty Accords," Pastrana's (lame duck) administration promised to combat illegal armed groups in Tame, investigate alleged incidents of army and paramilitary complicity, and follow up on other human rights investigations via the Intersectoral Commission, among others. Results were disappointing, however. The Intersectoral Commission investigated fifty cases, but the report was neither finalized nor made public. Paramilitary forces were (temporarily) moved from Tame but took up residence in Cravo Norte, reportedly in the police barracks. Once Uribe took office in August 2002, the accords were ignored altogether.[150] It was clear a strategy adjustment was needed.

One new element emerged in later 2002 protests. As before, all the protests targeted national authorities. However, in contrast to earlier protests, many showed some signs of the same distancing from the guerrillas that the UP's Sarmiento and Ardila had expressed. Social organizations denounced specific human rights violations promptly and widely, whether these were committed by public or paramilitary forces or if they constituted violations against international humanitarian law by the guerrillas, such as bombings, kidnappings, and attacks on civilian property.[151] By early 2003, as national judicial entities reversed many of Uribe's selective decentralization measures, they were identified by Araucan social movements as key tools in their struggles against impunity—the second new element.

The third element, which gained prominence especially after 2003, was the mobilization of international allies via forums (rather than protests) and human rights reports. For example, a September 2004 forum in Saravena that called "For Life, Justice, and Defense of Territory" brought together hundreds of people, including national and international delegations. Detailed reports, on particular incidents or on the general Araucan human rights situation, were tools as well as products of the human rights movement and its allies. Amnesty International published its thirty-three-page "Laboratory of War" report in April 2004, and Araucan social organizations, together with national human rights NGOs and the European Network of Brotherhood and Solidarity, published a verification report on a May 2004 massacre perpetrated by the paramilitary in Tame in July 2004.[152] Creating these documents required non-Araucan Colombians and sometimes European or U.S. citizens to travel to Arauca and carry out extensive interviews, creating a wide-ranging network of connections and spokespersons for the region.

By the end of the period there was consensus that Arauca's social movements were still powerful and effective. In 2004 the attorney general of Colombia stated, with some admiration, "The relevant social activity of these social movement organizations in defense of human rights is well known nationally and internationally, which makes Araucan society one of the most organized and with the greatest capacity of denunciation."[153] The four main campaigns taken on by the Araucan social movements highlight this effectiveness—and its key ingredients.

First, the Santo Domingo case clearly demonstrates the ways the intervention of Occidental Petroleum and the U.S. government ironically generated U.S. human rights allies for the Araucan social movements and how these alliances, using the crucial tool of the human rights certification process for military aid, then facilitated the movement's success.

The Colombian military reopened its investigation of the incident as a result of U.S. pressure in December 2000, but the case then languished. Rapid progress began in early 2002, when another human rights certification was required to release U.S. military aid to Colombia. Senator Leahy's criticisms of Colombia's human rights record, specifically citing the Santo Domingo case, were gaining prominence.[154] A nineteen-page in-depth story on the history of the case published in the *Los Angeles Times* in March 2002 not only quoted Leahy but also revealed the roles of the United States and Occidental Petroleum in the bombing. In 1997 Occidental had originally contracted with an air surveillance firm, AirScan International, to use infrared technology to identify guerrillas who might be planning attacks on the oil pipeline. Later the Colombian army convinced AirScan to help it with other, non-pipeline-related, counterinsurgency operations, such as pinpointing the target for this bomb. The AirScan plane was present and videotaped the bombing; the tape would later become crucial evidence.[155]

The case became a major obstruction to U.S. military aid and a bone of contention between the two countries, but ultimately U.S. pressure to punish those (Colombians) responsible prevailed. When Colombia refused to fire General Velasco, the commanding officer in charge the day of the bombing, as per the U.S. request, the United States certified Colombian military aid in September 2002 but barred Velasco's unit from receiving it in January 2003. In February 2003 the case was finally transferred to the civilian justice system, and new evidence, including tapes of the pilots' voices as well as key civilian and military testimony, was to be included. Furthermore, the Airscan video was viewed by U.S. officials, as well as the *Los Angeles Times* journalist; it corroborated the peasants' version of the events and rebutted that of the military.[156]

In July 2003 the Bush administration once again demanded the resignation of Velasco; in the words of the U.S. ambassador to Colombia, Velasco had "moved heaven and earth to prevent the truth from emerging, and that has a price." Velasco resigned in late August 2003,[157] and more victories followed. In December 2003 Colombia's attorney general charged the crew of the military helicopter that had dropped the bomb with involuntary manslaughter.[158] By May 2004 an administrative tribunal in Arauca had ordered retribution for the family members of the eighteen peasants who had died, as well as for the twenty-two people injured in the incident[159]—a highly unusual outcome for Colombia's war victims in the Colombian context of widespread impunity. While U.S. pressure brought Colombian military personnel to justice, however, Occidental was left untouched, demonstrating the limitations of this strategy. In April 2003 the International Labor Rights Fund joined with the Human Rights Center at Northwestern University, the entity that had conducted the mock trial in late 2000, to sue Occidental for its role in the Santo Domingo bombing, but it appears the lawsuit was still pending as of July 2008.[160]

The second major campaign of this period, to liberate Luz Perly Córdoba, again used international alliances to pressure the Colombian government. In this case, however, the alliances were European and had been deliberately cultivated prior to their "deployment." Córdoba was president of the Peasant Association of Arauca and secretary general of Fensuagro, the Communist Party–influenced peasant organization. In September 2003 she attended the Second Platform for Human Rights Defenders in Dublin and then went on a European speaking tour to denounce human rights violations in Arauca. In February 2004 Córdoba, her lawyers, and Fensuagro's treasurer were arrested and accused of rebellion (i.e., supporting guerrillas) based on the testimonies of demobilized guerrilla informers and the declarations of her own state-provided bodyguards. A crop substitution program initiated by the Peasant Association of Arauca also earned her an accusation of drug trafficking. National and international human rights organizations, arguing she had been framed, took up the cause of her liberation. Her case soon gained prominence in Europe: on March 31, 2004, Córdoba was awarded the Danish Peace Prize; in October 2004 the European Parliament discussed her case, and a significant number of European parliamentarians, especially from the United European Left, decided to investigate the case and to question European aid to the Colombian military in general.[161]

The third campaign, to bring to justice the assassins of the trade unionists Jorge Prieto and Leonel Goyeneche and the peasant leader Héctor Alirio Martínez, stands out for its savvy use of the (new) Colombian judicial tools at its disposal. The three leaders, central in moving the Santo Domingo case forward, were killed on August 5, 2004, by the army battalion based in Saravena; the two witnesses were also arrested. Army spokespeople, as well as the vice president of the republic, claimed that the army was carrying out arrest orders in effect since 2003 and that the three had put up armed resistance.[162]

Araucan opposition organizations responded quickly, effectively, and with unity. Just one day after the assassinations a letter calling the army's story into question was signed by thirty-eight regional and national organizations—including the national labor federation CUT and all the major Araucan organizations—and sent to national and international human rights entities.[163] A day later a verification commission was organized to force a reexamination of the evidence. This included mostly Colombian human rights organizations but also the European Network of Brotherhood and Solidarity with Colombia and the U.S.-based Peace Brigades International. The commission report specifically credits the political pressure created by these organizations for getting the criminal investigator in Saravena to exhume the three bodies to conduct forensic tests.[164] The tests corroborated the witnesses' version: the three had been shot in the back at close range, and weapons had been placed near their bodies after their death.[165]

The fourth campaign, the continuing U'wa struggle against oil exploration, demonstrates both the utility and the dangers of reliance on international alliances. Especially after three U'wa children died fleeing from the army during a February 2002 protest, the U'wa cause was embraced by the Araucan peasant movement. Furthermore, Occidental's continued attempts to explore for oil near U'wa lands were met by ongoing high levels of U.S. activism: vigils outside Occidental executives' homes, lawsuits filed in Colombian and international courts, shareholder resolutions, U'wa visits to the U.S. Congress, and so on. Then came a major victory: in May 2002 Occidental withdrew from the exploration altogether and returned its concession to the Colombian government, insisting its decision was purely technical rather than a response to the protests. However, geologists found the company's abandonment of such a promising field after only one attempt highly unusual.[166]

The victory was short lived: the U'wa had won round 1 against Shell in the 1990s and round 2 against Occidental in 2002, but round 3 was against Ecopetrol, the Colombian state oil company, which initiated exploration in October 2002 on lands near the U'wa reservation. Amid signs that discovery of oil was imminent, the U'wa insistently called for solidarity in March and July 2003.[167] However, without the David-and-Goliath narrative "spiritual Colombian indigenous tribe fights Big U.S. Oil Company," and with the war in Iraq refocusing much U.S. activism, U.S. solidarity declined, in turn affecting U'wa mobilization. By August 2004 Ecopetrol found oil and natural gas in the wells near U'wa lands, though at only a fraction of the volume initially anticipated. It was clear the U'wa urgently required a new strategy and new allies to evict Ecopetrol from their region.[168]

Between 2002 and 2004 Uribe and his Araucan allies were strengthened by Pastrana's ending of the peace process, Uribe's reversal of regional democratic rights and autonomy, paramilitary consolidation and expansion, and increased U.S. military presence, all reinforced by skyrocketing oil prices and expanded exploration. As the changes radically reduced the Left's chances for electoral success—or autonomous action once elected—guerrillas responded with hostility toward *all* local officeholders. Arauca's social movements, though unified and still strong, ceased to see electoral action as a viable means to achieve their ends. Instead, Araucan social movements distanced themselves from the guerrillas, continued to focus on national human and cultural rights demands, and leveraged their rapidly growing knowledge of judicial procedures and especially their connections with (sometimes fickle) international actors to win impressive victories.

2005–2008: The Late Uribe Era—Setbacks for the Right and the Left

The period between 2005 and 2008 was characterized by widely fluctuating trends, in Arauca as well as in Colombia as a whole. The FARC experienced a resurgence and then weakened under Uribe's concerted attacks (as the ELN had earlier), with skyrocketing oil prices through late 2008 providing added incentive to government efforts. Paramilitary forces expanded, then (mostly) demobilized in late 2005, with some political allies such as Acosta subsequently exposed and banned from office. After the last period's relative unity, FARC-ELN relations hit a new nadir in 2006–7 as the ELN explored peace negotiations, with violent repercussions for Arauca's social movement activists. The Right achieved a moment of maximum electoral consolidation in early 2006, but the parapolítica scandal and related investigations boosted the Left slightly in the late 2007 local and departmental elections. Finally, social movements at first experienced a wave of victories in 2005, then were broadsided, disoriented, and divided by the FARC-ELN conflict, before experiencing a new wave of activity in late 2007. However, both disunity and the loss of the media spotlight inevitably lowered levels of activism.

The period yielded some clear and major gains for Uribe in Arauca. As skyrocketing oil prices and new Araucan oil finds provided ample incentive for President Uribe to keep the pressure on Araucan guerrillas, he did so and claimed some victories. Oil prices climbed quickly, from an average of $50.28 per barrel in 2005 to a high of 128.38 per barrel in July 2008 (see fig. 7.1).[169] Furthermore, one of the piedmont explorations initiated in 2001–3 had yielded oil by 2005, and despite the slated exhaustion of the Caño Limón oil field in 2018, Occidental still considered it one of the best reservoirs in the world in terms of productivity and recovery efficiency in October 2006.[170] These trends almost certainly influenced the targeting of the Araucan piedmont for a series of intense military operations from late 2006 through late 2008.[171] While harder to measure on the regional level, nationally the effects of such efforts on guerrilla combat strength were clear. By 2008 both the FARC and the ELN had been reduced to almost half their maximum number of fighters, and the ELN had actually engaged in peace talks from 2005 to 2007.[172] In addition, by the end of 2005 Arauca's Bloque Vencedores paramilitary group had formally demobilized, following the national trend.[173]

On the other hand, Uribe's national setbacks during this period also had direct repercussions in Arauca. In 2003 the high-circulation magazine *Semana,* modeled on *Time,* had published euphoric articles celebrating Uribe's "Reconquest of Arauca."[174] But after an embarrassing Araucan (and national) FARC resurgence in 2005, Uribe's 2002–3 strategy in Arauca came under intense scrutiny. By early 2006 a *Semana* article titled "Democratic Security Flunked in Arauca" enumerated his many failures: many still-active paramilitary forces extorting oil funds, despite their "demobilization" and the national government's control of Araucan oil royalties; FARC resurgence; the return of coca acreage to its pre-2003 levels (a claim verified by multiple sources); and an Araucan population increasingly resentful of an armed forces proven over and over again to be complicit in human rights violations.[175] The Polo Democrático's success in the early 2006 congressional and presidential elections, in conjunction with the "Justice and Peace" process that encouraged paramilitary confessions, further allowed the initiation of numerous investigations into Uribe allies', including his staunchest Araucan allies', complicity with paramilitary and drug trafficking interests. Finally, as Democrats gained ascendancy first in the U.S. Congress in the fall 2006 and then in the presidency by fall 2008, they pushed hard for human rights progress in Colombia, making Uribe more sensitive to foreign inquiries into the Araucan human rights situation.

Reflecting the vicissitudes of national policy, repression in Arauca varied both qualitatively and quantitatively over the period. In 2005 Uribe's shift in counterinsurgency focus to the southern coca-growing regions, coupled with the fact that Bloque Vencedores de Arauca was one of the last paramilitary groups to demobilize—only 207 of an estimated 1,000 or more fighters laid down arms, on December 23, 2005, just before the government-imposed deadline[176]—meant that 2005 was a high point for "privatized" repression in both Arauca and Arauquita, targeting social movement leaders. In Arauca repression decreased slightly from its 2004 level of 10.1 to 7.7 and was perpetrated entirely by paramilitary forces against apparently unaffiliated urban residents (seven assassinations) and top Communist Party and human rights movement leaders (seven threats). In Arauquita paramilitary incursions became more frequent and lethal. Repression rose from an index of 2.8 in 2004 to 6.9 in 2005, with 4.3 of these incidents perpetrated by paramilitary forces. With the exception of one urban merchant, all the victims were social movement leaders or war zone peasants.[177]

Despite the incompleteness of paramilitary demobilization, once it had taken place and Uribe's attention returned to Arauca in 2006—inspired both by the stinging criticisms and by oil prices—patterns of repression returned to "normal" (pre-1989): mostly "public" and affecting Arauquita much more than Arauca. Arauca's repression index dropped from 7.7 in 2005 to 1.2 in 2006, with no clear-cut cases of rightist political violence in 2007 or the first half of 2008. In Arauquita, in contrast, major military operations took place in the second half of 2006, the first half of 2007, and apparently all of 2008. Less lethal than paramilitary violence (rightist repression indexes for 2006, 2007, and the first half of 2008 of 5.4, 1.05, and 1.1, respectively), most of the incidents were detentions, torture, or threats affecting larger numbers of people than the targeted assassinations of 2005. In addition, fourteen major regional leaders were arrested by public forces in November 2008.[178]

Trends in guerrilla actions similarly swung from one extreme to another. At first, even as the ELN weakened on the national level and its activity in Arauca declined, the FARC experienced a resurgence.[179] Between 2004 and 2005 the number of combats with fatalities rose from one to four in Arauquita and from three to six in Arauca.[180] It was now clear that the ELN's loss had been the FARC's gain: there were three attacks on electrical towers in Arauquita and six in Arauca in 2005,[181] all by the FARC, which in addition called an armed strike that paralyzed the department for twenty-two days.[182] After military operations resumed in 2006, however, FARC-initiated combat and actions in Arauca were reduced to two in 2006 and one in 2007 but then expanded to five in January through mid-November 2008, all in Arauquita. In contrast, the ELN had no armed confrontations in either 2006 or 2007, probably due to the peace process as well as weakness, and only one aborted bombing attempt in Arauquita in 2008.[183] Despite the FARC's 2008 offensive, the military made clear regional military advances in late 2008, infiltrating a FARC unit and capturing armaments and two commanders.[184] By late 2008 one major Colombian daily stated, "No one doubts that the guerrillas have retreated and that attacks on the oil pipeline have been reduced to zero cases; and the insurgency no longer remains armed within urban outskirts."[185]

As guerrillas in Arauca faced their most serious military challenge ever, their actions became even more extreme. As before, guerrillas, especially the FARC, continued to target peasants living in zones of paramilitary influence. For example, in Tame in 2005 there were four guerrilla assassinations of civilians.[186] In addition, both FARC and ELN use of land mines continued in the region, as did attacks on elite-aligned politicians: in late 2006 the FARC made their seventh attempt on Julio Acosta's life.[187]

In a break with previous years, however, the long-standing tension between the FARC and the ELN erupted into the most overt and deadly conflict ever, with widespread consequences. Not only have armed confrontations between the two groups taken place since late 2005, but each group has also assassinated many social movement leaders and peasants from organizations or territories historically influenced by the other guerrilla group.[188] In Arauquita in 2006 four assassinations of this type occurred: two by the FARC, one by the ELN, and one by an unidentified guerrilla group. The Araucan Social Organizations in late 2006 denounced four other assassinations that had occurred in Tame, Saravena, and Arauca Counties as well.[189] In March 2006 the FARC went as far as to kill an activist from the Santo Domingo branch of the ADUC who was active in the bombing case.[190] In all, by September 2008 Amnesty International reported that "the dispute between the FARC and the ELN in Arauca Department has resulted in the killing of hundreds of civilians."[191] Not surprisingly, this has led to a peasant (and indigenous) exodus from the conflict zones to the piedmont cities, resulting in a sharp increase in the number of displaced people and a humanitarian crisis. The total displaced in Arauca now number 28,000—roughly 10 percent of the department's population.[192]

An initial cause of the ELN-FARC conflict was the ELN's peace negotiations with the Uribe government. Beginning in late 2005 and continuing through late 2007, with a last failed attempt in April 2008, these exacerbated relations with the still-belligerent FARC.[193] But even after the Uribe-ELN negotiations ended and the FARC and ELN once again shared a similar posture vis-à-vis the national government,[194] the conflict continued. First, the age-old territorial conflict over coca and oil lands remained.[195] Second, by 2008 the two insurgent groups had formed unstable nonaggression pacts with various reemergent paramilitary groups. In July 2006 as many as a thousand paramilitary fighters were still active in Arauca, especially Tame.[196] By late 2008 they had re-formed into smaller groups, one of which had reportedly formed an unstable nonaggression pact with the FARC, while the FARC fought another group, the Black Eagles. At the same time, in other regions of Colombia and possibly in

Arauca as well, the ELN had formed pacts with some paramilitary groups to combat the FARC.[197]

The contradictory national trends and unprecedented level of ELN-FARC conflict had similarly contradictory effects in the electoral arena. On the one hand, it was clear that the total electoral strength of the Araucan Left had continued to slip. Helmer Muñoz's cross-piedmont gubernatorial candidacy had garnered 36 percent of the departmental vote in 2003, but the Saravena Liberal and Polo candidates combined won just 31 percent of the gubernatorial vote in 2007, with only 25 percent of the vote going to Polo and Convergencia Ciudadana candidates combined in the assembly elections held on the same day. In the elections for the House of Representatives, the votes deposited for the Saravena Liberals (using Convergencia Ciudadana as their electoral vehicle in 2006) declined from 32 percent to 17 percent between 2002 and 2006, and those for the UP (2002) or Polo Democrático Alternativo (2006) stayed steady at 5 percent. Conversely, the electoral Right grew stronger. In the 2006–7 House of Representatives, Assembly, and gubernatorial races, Acosta's party won with ample leads of 32 percent, 29 percent, and 45 percent of valid votes, respectively. Even more dramatic was Alvaro Uribe's sweep of the May 2006 presidential vote in Arauca with 68 percent of the vote for candidates.[198]

Furthermore, with the possible exception of the 2007 Liberal gubernatorial candidate, who apparently derived about half of his votes from Convergencia Ciudadana, the Left had no alliances with elites in 2006 and 2007.[199] The re-creation of alliances was prevented by the 2005 imprisonment of ten of those arrested on the eve of the 2003 gubernatorial election, including the Saravena Liberal–petrocrat Liberal governors elected in 1997 and 2000 and Helmer Muñoz.[200] In addition, the FARC-ELN conflict impeded the formation of another all-piedmont coalition. Thus the two representatives elected by Araucans in March 2006 drew votes from, respectively, the plains and the piedmont, the latter oriented toward Saravena Liberals. The most successful candidate, from Julio Acosta's party Cambio Radical, drew 73 percent of his 10,859 votes from the plains counties of Arauca, Puerto Rondón, and Cravo Norte, and another 22 percent from the now largely "paramilitarized" Tame County. Also elected, with 5,504 votes, was José Vicente Lozano, former Saravena County executive and Saravena Liberal governor from 1994 to 1997. Fully 85 percent of his votes came from the piedmont counties of Arauquita, Saravena, and Fortul. A UP candidate ran against him for the Polo and won only 1,500 votes.[201] This last national political foothold for the Araucan Left was lost in mid-2008, however, when Lozano resigned after being accused of having ELN connections.[202]

In other ways, however, the electoral option for the Left was making a recovery. In the May 2006 presidential elections, Polo Democrático Alternativo was the second vote winner in Arauca as well as in the nation, with 26 percent of votes for candidates. The Polo appeared to be supported by both sectors of the Left, although with greater enthusiasm in the historic geographic base of the UP: 64 percent of Arauquita voters, 72 percent of Fortul voters, and 34 percent of Saravena voters supported Polo. And in late 2007, despite the FARC-ELN conflict and their extremist actions, the Left once again participated in county-level elections: the Saravena county executive candidate from the same party, and with the same two last names (i.e., probably a brother), as the 2006–10 Convergencia Ciudadano representative José Vicente Lozano narrowly lost in a near-three-way tie; Fortul elected a Polo county executive; and Arauquita elected a Polo county council majority, although not a Polo county executive.[203] Conversely, by mid-2008 Acosta's paramilitary connections had been fully revealed, and he went on the lam; the governor for the period 2008–11, his protégé, was accused of corruption and removed from office.[204]

Another sign of possible renewed faith in the electoral system was increased voter participation. Between 2002 and 2006 total votes in Arauca rose from 26,385 to 40,034 in the House of Representatives elections, from 26,782 to 40,995 in the Senate elections, and from 29,633 to 47,421 in the presidential elections. Similarly, between 2003 and 2007 votes for gubernatorial candidates rose from 41,779 to 64,441, and votes for assembly rose from 41,911 to 76,720.[205] This approached the levels of participation of 1997 in terms of the proportion of the population voting.[206]

The fortunes of Arauca's social movements rose, then fell, then rose again, as the movements scrambled to find new responses to the rapid, successive changes that buffeted the region. First came a wave of successes that derived from the groundswell of activity and international solidarity and the strategy perfected from the mid-1990s through 2005. The 2004–5 campaign to liberate the peasant leader Luz Perly Córdoba was the first to yield fruit. Thanks in great part to the national and international pressure on her behalf, Córdoba and the Peasant Association of Arauca's treasurer were granted conditional liberty on March 16, 2005, after they posted bail.[207] Córdoba was one of twelve Colombian women nominated for the Nobel Peace Prize in June 2005, but by then she had left the country due to paramilitary threats.[208]

Next, an unprecedented victory was won in the effort to prosecute the assassins of the late UP congressman and gubernatorial candidate Octavio Sarmiento, who was killed in 2001. Although a regional court had earlier absolved the paramilitary leader Emiro Pereira, an August 2005 judgment by a national entity reversed this ruling.[209] In mid-May 2007 Pereira was sentenced to forty years in prison. Of the seven assassinated UP parliamentarians whose cases were being followed by the Inter-Parliamentary Union, Sarmiento's was the only one that had resulted in a sentencing, highlighting once again the exceptional success of the Araucan social movements.[210]

The expertly implemented campaign to prosecute the assassins of the three regional activists killed in August 2004 also met with success during this period. Possibly influenced by the human rights pressures deriving from the U.S. political shift, in mid-May 2007 the attorney general's investigation concluded that the assassinations had in fact been carried out by the army, as the human rights movement had long alleged.[211] In August 2008 unusually long sentences were imposed: forty years in prison for five of the lower-ranking perpetrators and twenty years of removal from his post for the commander of Colombia's special forces, Luis Francisco Medina Corredor.[212]

Similarly, in January 2005 Araucan social movement leaders traveled to Brazil to attend an international conference for oil-region activists, returning with a clarified agenda for action. In April 2005 a team of investigators from the Spain-based Comisión Valenciana de Verificación de Derechos Humanos visited Arauca, then published an in-depth report, focusing especially on army complicity with paramilitary forces. In August 2005 the three-day Social Humanitarian Forum in Saravena yielded a fifty-one-page collectively written report and action points. The same month, an NGO called the International Peace Observatory, staffed by international volunteers, answered the Araucan Peasant Association's call and began an "accompaniment" project (with volunteers acting as unarmed bodyguards) in Arauca.[213]

However, these successes came to an end with the internecine warfare between the ELN and the FARC, which devastated social movements by assassinating top leaders. Overall social movement activity dropped precipitously in 2006, with evidence of only one major campaign, to boost the accompaniment presence of foreign solidarity workers, and just three events, in June, August, and October.[214] Faced with this catastrophic assault, social movements initially chose to openly denounce the insurgent organizations and appeal to them directly to obey international humanitarian law. During this period, the Noche y Niebla database reported guerrilla perpetrators of political assassinations against social movement activists, suggesting the press releases sent to Bogotá by the organizations had similarly implicated guerrillas as perpetrators rather than using the vaguer phrase "armed actors." In April and June the Organizaciones Sociales de Arauca posted prominently on their Web site a press release denouncing ELN attacks on UP-PCC activists as well as FARC attacks on ADUC activists, although they were signed only by outside Colombian and European allies, respectively, not by the Araucan organizations themselves.[215] Similarly, a June 2006 accompaniment mission by an Italian group created a slide show documenting the ways both the FARC-ELN war and the army harassment was harming the population.[216]

However, it is likely this strategy was divisive and played into the hands of the military. Furthermore, once the guerrilla-paramilitary nonaggression pacts emerged, identifying perpetrators would have become even more complex. Thus in 2007 an adjusted social movement strategy emerged, as did a revival of movement activity, complete with a redesigned Web site with YouTube video links. Incidents of violence were denounced thoroughly and extensively but now without identifying the presumed perpetrator, *unless* it was clearly the Colombian armed forces. For example, Noche y Niebla began reporting most assassinations as perpetrated by "armed groups." Similarly, an October 2007 press release listed the times, dates, and places of five violent incidents that had occurred in the previous two weeks without identifying perpetrators, then added: "We demand of the state organizations of justice and control that they initiate investigations of these incidents immediately. Of the actors in the armed conflict, we demand that they not involve civilians in their actions . . . and that they respect and obey the principles and norms of international humanitarian law." An additional strategy shift was a direct call to Araucans to desist from coca cultivation, due to the crop's nefarious effects on community solidarity and petty crime.[217]

Social movement activity increased greatly in 2007, with the visit of an international verification commission in January; a June 2007 conference in Spain focused on the Spain-based oil corporation Repsol's misdeeds in

Arauca; an August People's Court (Tribunal Popular del Pueblo) in Bogotá focused on multinational complicity in state political violence, one
in a series of international meetings with one hundred to two hundred
respected NGO leaders; a major congressional hearing in September held
in Arauca and attended by almost four thousand people, which yielded a
statement signed by five Polo Democrático members of congress and two
congressmen from other parties requesting that the national government
act; and the visit of another international observation mission in October.[218] Despite 2008's intensification of intraguerrilla and paramilitary
violence and the resulting humanitarian crisis, activity levels remained
similar. Five events took place, all between July and December (interestingly, after the ELN had returned to a more bellicose posture). There were
two human rights hearings in Arauquita, one featuring a visit from members of congress, the other bringing UN officials; a municipal peasant forum
in Saravena; a commemoration of the anniversary of the assassination of
the three union leaders, with two thousand participants; an indigenous
civic strike; and a general civic strike that claimed the support of 70 percent of the population.[219]

In fact, in some respects 2008 seemed to replay the high violence/
high visibility/high mobilization/high success pattern of 2002–4. First,
Arauca's internal refugee crisis greatly increased the presence of international relief agencies in Arauca, putting added pressure on Uribe. The UN
High Commissioner for Refugees even opened a new regional office in
Saravena. In late October 2008 the High Commissioner himself spoke to
the president before traveling to Arauquita for the hearing; Uribe chose
the occasion to very publicly scold the high military command for their
lack of improvement in human rights matters.[220] Second, press coverage
of Arauca was once again approaching the 2003 levels. A search with the
parameter "Arauca" on ElTiempo.com resulted in a high of 729 articles
for 2003, a low of 356 for 2006, and 580 and 492 for 2007 and the first
eleven months of 2008, respectively.

The U'wa struggle to impede oil exploration on their lands, meanwhile, faced new challenges as booming oil prices increased Ecopetrol's
resolve to begin exploration there and elsewhere. A November 2006 U'wa
press release quoted President Uribe as saying, "The oil from U'wa territory will be taken out because it has to be taken out, no matter how we
have to do it" (Se saca porque se saca, como sea).[221] By 2008 Ecopetrol

was aggressively seeking foreign investment by trading 10 percent of its shares on the New York Stock Exchange. Uribe boasted that the number of oil wells explored by Ecopetrol had increased from ten to one hundred between 2002 and 2008. In response to this situation, the U'wa at first intensified the same strategy initiated at the close of the previous period: they stalled exploration on their reservation by refusing to participate in the "prior consultation" process[222] and seeking out and strengthening national indigenous alliances while maintaining some international ties. In July 2005 U'wa women joined in an act of solidarity with indigenous women in Cauca Department (Colombia's historic indigenous movement stronghold). In October 2005 a top U'wa leader, Roberto Cobaría, traveled to the United States on a speaking tour; he also went on speaking tours to Europe.[223]

As Ecopetrol's exploration attempts grew more imminent in late 2006, however, the U'wa began to appeal directly to public (nonindigenous) opinion. Press releases threatened collective suicide if exploration took place (December 2006) and denounced Ecopetrol for bribing U'was with market baskets (May 2007). Signs of their success included largely sympathetic coverage in mainstream venues such as *Semana* highlighting the U'was' widely admired cultural autonomy and pride and a major sculpture erected in July 2007 in the Güicán town plaza (near U'wa territory) commemorating the U'was' legendary mass suicide when faced with the prospect of enslavement by the conquistadors.[224] A third phase, with a return to a more international focus, began in late 2008. In October one thousand U'was participated in a three-day mobilization in defiance of military orders. In November U'wa leaders traveled to New York to urge major U.S. investment firms not to invest in Ecopetrol, apparently the beginning of a new U.S.-focused campaign.[225]

In sum, during 2005–8, even though paramilitary violence decreased, Araucan social movements faced some of their most difficult challenges ever. Deprived of most of the electoral representatives that had long advocated for them and with a reduced media spotlight, they were still under attack by the military, and the assault on social movements by the insurgencies themselves devastated their leadership and destroyed what remained of the fragile unity of 2002–4. In this context the achievements of the period are remarkable. Social movements brought older campaigns for justice to fruition, and after a quick adjustment of the initial, failed strategy to repudiate guerrilla violence explicitly, they seized on the few new opportunities that the period presented: Repsol's and Ecopetrol's increased roles in the region yielded new solidarity campaigns in Spain and creative appeals to Colombian public opinion; Polo Alternativo's national success in 2006 was used to organize a congressional hearing on Araucan human rights; and the increased presence of international relief organizations was used to put pressure on Uribe for human rights improvements. It seems possible that they will manage, once again, to defeat the odds.

CONCLUSION

In the late reform period of the early 1990s, the electoral Left found success through a strategy that relied on alliances with regional elites both to reduce repression and to bolster the social movements' material success. This succeeded when Arauca had full regional self-determination but was ultimately doomed when the national government began to override regional autonomy through selective recentralization. By 2003, motivated both by Arauca's oil wealth and by the power of the Araucan electoral Left, such selective recentralization was taken to extreme lengths: elections were annulled, candidates were arrested days before the elections, and departmental budgetary decisions were overridden by national prerogatives. National and international actors—the Colombian government, Occidental Petroleum, and the U.S. government—had transformed a once-regional conflict into a national or even global one. And Araucan social movements followed suit, quite successfully.

Araucan social movements had moments of extraordinary success in the counterreform period, as in the reform period. This success was a result of luck and the astute use of each opportunity. Their luck consisted first in the political economy of their region, which allowed Araucan social movements to begin the counterreform period in a position of unusual organizational strength, and second in the fact that the major wave of repression came late to Arauca, allowing the movements to apply strategies tested in other regions and receive support from a growing urban Left.

But beyond luck, Araucan social movements made good decisions that helped them adapt quickly to the changing conditions of the counterreform period. Once regional autonomy was reduced and governors could no longer be as useful to the piedmont peasant movement in procuring state resources, social movements adopted a human rights–focused strategy, with the national government as the target. When the intervention of the U.S. government and Occidental Petroleum into the regional context became notorious, these linkages were used to build alliances with U.S. supporters. Even the region's terrible humanitarian crisis had a hidden opportunity: the increased presence of international relief organizations, which increased the visibility of the region's human rights movement. When international solidarity from a certain source waned, social movements turned to national allies. Finally, when the FARC and the ELN began to violate international humanitarian law with considerable frequency—due to their competition for territories with each other and with paramilitary groups and their differing relationships to the peace process—social movements distanced themselves from these groups and sought to find redress through national and international judicial processes. And after the FARC-ELN conflict spilled over into the murder of social movement activists, the social movements first engaged in direct denunciations of specific groups but then adjusted the strategy to avoid having these denunciations become tools for the military.

Throughout every stage of history described here, Araucan social movements have been extraordinarily successful. There is reason to hope that this will continue.

CONCLUSION

This study has aimed to document and then theorize the process of democratization/decentralization and social movement response, elite reaction, and counterreform in rural areas of the Third World. It has focused in particular on a case with weak state mediation mechanisms, powerful social movements, and armed insurgencies, but its conclusions may be generalizable to a broader set of contexts. Most studies of democratization and decentralization to date have not focused on such contexts, defined either broadly or narrowly. Conversely, most studies of rural social movements have not analyzed the effects of changing political institutions. Finally, in general, the recent literature on alliances between social movements of the global South and transnational activist networks based in the global North has not systematically compared successful and failed attempts to form such alliances. This study has aimed to complement and extend all three of these literatures. To do so, I address two central sets of questions: explaining the common evolution of the regions over time and identifying the causes of contrasting regional outcomes.

The first set of questions aims to identify the relationship between processes of democratization/decentralization and counterreform/recentralization on the national level and patterns of social movement and elite responses on the local level. What are the effects of these reforms and counterreforms on social movement tactics, level of activity, unity, and success? How are local elite interests affected by these national trends and local social movement responses, and how do elites then react? The answers to these questions provide not only an understanding of the unique nature of the Colombian context of violent democratization but also a comparison to other national cases that are more urban or that have stronger states, weaker social movements, or no armed insurgencies.

My analysis of the common evolution of the three case study regions over the course of the reform period implicitly compares Colombia's process of violent democratization with other national patterns of democratization. While each national pattern contrasts in some ways with Colombia, each also has essential commonalities with Colombia's contradictory process of violent democratization. Thus new insights drawn from the Colombian case can be fruitfully applied to each alternative pattern of violent democratization.

Colombia's pattern of simultaneous elite-led democratization and backlash, with its echo on the Left in the simultaneous use of contradictory tactics (armed struggle, social movement activity, and electoral participation), is clearly different from the paradigmatic, more clearly unilinear progress toward consolidated democracy in Argentina and Chile (with weakened social movements). Even so, in these cases as well as in Colombia, the reform process created deep divisions among both elites and the Left, overcome in favor of soft-liners in the Southern Cone but becoming permanent in Colombia.

Colombia's contradictory process of democratization can also be instructive for an analysis of post–Cold War Central America. In El Salvador, Nicaragua, and Guatemala, unlike Colombia, international intervention brought a successfully negotiated peace with democratization. However, in all four cases powerful guerrilla movements, with some links to strong social movements, have had to face the dilemmas of electoral participation after reform. If they abstain from the electoral process, they lose an opportunity to build alliances and gain access to state resources for their constituencies; but if they participate, the candidates and their support base may face paramilitary violence.

Other models approximate the Colombian pattern, even while still exhibiting important contrasts. In 1980s Peru as in Colombia, democratization initially coincided with rapidly escalating armed insurgency and repressive violence, which then provided an impetus for national counterreform as hard-liner elites took the upper hand. In Peru this counterreform led to the defeat of the armed insurgency, but such a rapid defeat of guerrillas seems highly unlikely in Colombia, where guerrillas have resisted almost fifty years of counterinsurgency. With Colombia's long history of formal democracy, it is also unlikely that an overtly unconstitutional elimination of congressional power, such as that carried out in Peru, would be tolerated by Colombian elites.[1] Then again, Colombia's pattern of constitutional governments tolerating rampant paramilitary activity has often meant that unconstitutional counterinsurgency measures (e.g., widespread extrajudicial executions of social movement activists) can take place without suspending the Constitution.

Rural Brazil in the 1980s shares with Colombia a similar postreform pattern of private elite-sponsored paramilitary violence against organized peasants, tolerated by the government despite formal moves toward democratization. However, because a revival (or creation) of armed insurgency did not occur in Brazil, the absolute level of repressive violence in Brazil has remained lower than in Colombia, and reforms have not been reversed. A similar state-elite constellation of forces in Mexico has indeed stimulated the Zapatista insurgency, resulting in increased repressive violence. However, the Zapatista insurgency is considerably weaker militarily and with much smaller geographic presence than Colombian guerrillas, and with much greater levels of support and sympathy from transnational publics.

The second set of questions addressed in this study, based on cross-regional contrasts, aims to explain the dramatic variation in material and political gains for, and levels of repression against,[2] social movements during the reform period as well as the counterreform period. These comparisons reveal what courses of action social movement activists might best take and what contexts are most likely to facilitate their efforts. They also highlight the many ways that resourceful, strategic, and creative use of a very brief, very narrow, and yet very important window of opportunity might be used to derive the maximum long-term benefit for the social movement constituencies that have long sought social justice in the rural Third World. They also reveal how, even in the most demoralizing context of political closing and physical extermination, social movement activists at times can succeed in mobilizing outside support not just for movement and individual survival but also to win remarkable collective victories.

CASE STUDY COMPARISON

The Reform Period

All the regional case studies were chosen based on the presence of a powerful rural social movement facilitated by their location in a colonization zone or the presence of a continuous-harvest plantation crop, or both. All three regions had been characterized by political violence and guerrilla activity, which both reflected and exacerbated the weakness of the Colombian state, in particular, with respect to its conflict mediation capabilities. Before democratic reforms were implemented, the regional social movement's power and success had been severely limited by a context where labor movements had little recourse to official mediation mechanisms—which led to guerrilla intervention in labor conflicts—and the peasant movements even less, due to the shallowness of Colombia's incorporation process. This was the case even when rapid economic growth should have favored social movement success.

Reform and political opening, however, not only allowed guerrilla groups to declandestinize, spurring additional social movement mobilization, success, and even some tentative steps toward incorporation. It also facilitated the Left's electoral expression and consequent displacement of the elite political faction that had once dominated local political institutions, monopolizing the political and fiscal resources of the local state for its own partisan purposes.

On taking office, newly elected leftist officials aided their movements more than traditional party county executives did, using both the power of the office (for mediation and advocacy) and its fiscal resources. The latter function was used especially when fiscal resources were greater (Arauquita and to a lesser extent Apartadó, in contrast to Cartagena del Chairá's meager county budget). However, these leftist county officials were then targeted for repression more than either their traditional party counterparts or other leftists in noninstitutional positions. Furthermore, their political affiliation interfered with their ability to collect fiscal resources. In Urabá banana plantation owners paid taxes without protest to the Liberal-dominated county administration in Carepa, yet went to great lengths to avoid paying similar taxes to Left-dominated Apartadó. Leftists in Arauquita denounced similar inequities in Occidental Petroleum's royalty payments to their county, as compared with the contiguous, Liberal-dominated county of Arauca. In all regions except Arauca, where the Left had considerable influence at the departmental level, leftist county executives complained of the departmental government's refusal to pass on the full amount of state resources due them by law.

Even when they were from traditional parties, directly elected county executives were more responsive to social movements than their appointed predecessors had been, although still less responsive than leftist county executives. Direct election, by creating a direct candidate-electorate relationship, also created the conditions for traditional county executives to break away from their erstwhile regional political bosses and in some cases form new coalitions with the Left. The first directly elected county executive in Arauca County exemplified both of these patterns.

The reform period gains for social movements and the Left were a loss for displaced regional bosses, who sponsored a violent elite backlash in which leftist elected officials and social movement activists were assassinated with impunity. During the reform period, it was invariably the elite sector that was being politically displaced by the Left, rather than the one that was being materially challenged by the social movement (when these were separate entities), which led repressive efforts and was aided in this task by its ties to the police, the army, and paramilitary groups. Unlike the social movement's elite target, or "concession sponsor," which tended to be a national elite with considerable capital, the politically displaced local elite sector was likely to require access to local state resources and a local electorate in order to defend its economic and political position.

In response to the contradictory cues of simultaneous reform and backlash, some guerrilla movements moved toward demobilization, while others became more bellicose—even while continuing to support electoral actions in some cases. This exacerbated already existing tactical divisions within the guerrilla movement. Finally, in the early 1990s economic opening caused further shifts in each region's balance of power, as export sectors were strengthened economically and fortified militarily on both the regional and national levels.

All the above processes occurred in all the regions, yet reform period regional outcomes—social movement gains and repression—varied greatly across regions. The contrasting outcomes at different moments in each region are illustrated in figure 8.1. Cases are presented in descending order

Figure 8.1 Reform Period Outcomes: Three Regions

Social Movement Gains

		Low	High
Level of Repressive Violence	*Low*	The Caguán, 1989–92	The Caguán, 1984–87 Arauca, 1989–92
	High	The Caguán, 1988	Arauca, 1984–88 Urabá, 1984–92

by level of violence experienced during the reform period. Urabá presented the most violent outcome: the level of violence escalated constantly after reform, yet the stable success of the banana workers' movement through 1992 allowed the electoral Left to resist this onslaught. Cartagena del Chairá, in the Lower and Middle Caguán Valley, presented two outcomes: a negotiated agreement with the national government that brought both peace and social movement gains (1984–87), then an end to concessions to the peasant movement, and, after the repressive wave of 1988, defeat of the peasant movement, with neither mobilization nor gains, or need for further repression. The most positive outcome was that of Arauca: social movements resisted a long repressive wave before 1989 and emerged still successful, winning a peace with considerable social movement gains from 1989 to 1992.

In general, those conditions that maximized the Left's bargaining power relative to repression-sponsoring elites in the regional balance of power facilitated a regional pacted peace with social movement gains. For this outcome to occur, it was crucial that the Left's leverage with respect to elites be expressed *electorally.* Left-elite electoral coalition was the mechanism through which such a pact was initially negotiated and formalized, with peace a corollary of power sharing. Elites entered into such an agreement only when alliance with leftist electoral forces was their sole means of retaining access to state resources. Thus essential preconditions for such a pact (besides the regional autonomy of the reform period) include the nearly complete and *sustainable* electoral displacement of repression-sponsoring elites, made possible by the combination of social movement strength (itself derived from social movement success and Left unity) and repression-sponsoring elite weakness (derived from their absolute or relative economic decline) and leftist unity (see fig. 1.4).

One of the factors that most enhanced the electoral strength and stability of the Left was continuous social movement success. Interestingly, in all cases repression did not deter the mobilization of a successful movement but was devastating to an unsuccessful movement. Unlike elite parties, which derive their strength from the economic influence of their most powerful supporters, leftist parties depend on a large, powerful, active, and well-organized social movement to garner votes for an agenda that directly challenges the status quo. Thus the electoral fortunes of the Left closely mirrored the fortunes of the social movement in the region. For peasant movements that targeted the state, social movement success was facilitated by either political opening or the fiscal prosperity of the state target, or both. For labor movements, similarly, success was facilitated by the economic prosperity of the employing sector, but it was largely determined by political opening.

In both Arauca and Cartagena del Chairá, national political opening facilitated noteworthy peasant social movement success from 1984 to 1987. After 1987 national concessions ceased. With no alternative concession sponsor in sight—the Caquetá departmental government was both fiscally poor and politically hostile—the success and strength of Cartagena del Chairá's movement quickly faded. A wave of repression in 1988 quickly defeated the peasant movement and reduced the Left's electoral strength at both the county and departmental levels to a fraction of its former strength. In contrast, the Araucan peasant movement remained successful even after 1987 by reorienting its demands toward the departmental government, which was fiscally wealthy and strongly Left influenced.

Due to the stability of the concession-granting elite sector (banana plantations) and the occasional positive intervention of government entities, the main labor movement in Urabá remained successful throughout the reform period. The urban civic and squatters movements in this region were successful through the same period, as they benefited directly from their links with the successful labor movement, the increased demand for low-cost urban housing that came with an expanded workforce and decreased reliance on work camps for housing, and more sympathetic municipal governments after the direct election of county executives.

Finally, a key to the Left's bargaining leverage relative to elites was unity, put to the test by the bifurcation of the guerrilla movement in the early 1990s. Regions where the Left drew its support from plantation labor movements suffered much greater intra-Left antagonism than did regions where the Left was peasant based. In the worker region Urabá, some guerrilla groups demobilized and subsequently were portrayed as model citizens by the government, while others remained militarily active, with social movements in their areas of influence labeled as subversive, breaking previously existing intra-Left alliances. In the two peasant regions, on the other hand, no guerrilla groups demobilized; therefore, antagonisms over tactical choices were minimized. Possible reasons for this contrast are discussed at greater length below.

Thus after reform the leverage of the Left is maximized in regional contexts where a peasant-based social movement maximizes leftist unity; and where fiscal wealth, political opening, and/or the prosperity of the concession-sponsoring elite sector enhance social movement success, which then boosts the electoral strength and stability of the Left. The key, however, to an outcome that includes gains for the Left *and* peace is not just the leverage of the Left but its leverage *relative* to those elites who had formerly sponsored repression against the social movement.

The political leverage of repression-sponsoring elites depended primarily on the prosperity of the economic sector that undergirded that elite political faction. Sectoral economic decline reduced the repression-sponsoring elite's ability to hire employees or buy votes and election day free lunches or otherwise spend sectoral wealth in politically conditioned ways in order to create a loyal clientele. It also increased the possibility that a different economic sector, led by different elites, would be seen as the primary source of employment, causing a shift in loyalties. Eventually, then, sectoral decline would cause the electoral atrophy of the elite sector that had once dominated local political institutions—a process accelerated by democratization as direct votes became more important to determining control of the local state than regional elite connections to national political brokers.

As the previous discussion implies, the most favorable balance of power for rural social movements (Arauca) occurred where the Left was successful and therefore strong and unified, and the social movement's target for material concessions (the national government, then the petrocrat-dominated departmental government) was an elite sector *other* than the one that had formerly dominated political institutions (the LaTorrista cattle-ranching Liberals); that is, the repression-sponsoring elite and the concession-sponsoring elite/state sector were distinct entities. In this context social movement success and strength were boosted by both political opening and fiscal wealth and continued undeterred by repression before 1989. At the same time, although there was no economic decline of La-Torristas in absolute terms, the oil boom after 1986 vastly increased the ability of competing elites—non-LaTorrista petrocrats—to finance much more powerful electoral machines and offer more lucrative state jobs. This made the relatively meager electoral campaign funds of the cattle ranchers virtually irrelevant, without reducing social movement success. Once the direct election of county executives divided Liberals, the stage was set for each faction to ally with a different leftist sector.

A somewhat contradictory situation arose in Urabá, where the orthodox Marxist prediction was in fact reality: an elite sector (not the state) was the main material antagonist of the rural social movement (concession-sponsoring elite) *and* the main political antagonist (repression-sponsoring elite). In this situation, while economic prosperity of the concession-sponsoring elite sector brought social movement success, enhancing the social movement's electoral success and leverage, it also enhanced elite leverage, creating incentives for the elite to violently repress the Left rather than negotiate to share political control of the region. In this case, the plantation owners' strength was enhanced by the entrance of narco cattle ranchers into the zone, as well as the post-1990 national emphasis on exports, increasing their influence over the national government and resulting in increased militarization of the region. This resulted in a stalemate: the Left was able to make continuous material gains and retain both movement and electoral strength despite repression, but it was unable to impose a pacted peace.

A parallel situation but with different results was presented in Cartagena del Chairá, Caquetá, where the national government was both the concession sponsor and the repression sponsor. In this region, with strong social movements but incipient or very weak elites, repression was necessarily organized directly by the military, and social movement demands were aimed at the wealthiest and most sympathetic state target: the national government during the peace process with the FARC. Here, wide boom-and-bust cycles in the fortunes of these social movement resulted: in times of political opening (1984–87) there were both social movement gains and a minimum of repression; in times of political closing (1988–92) so-

cial movements gains ceased, military aggression escalated, and Left electoral success plummeted. After 1987 the briefly displaced Turbayista Liberal elites thus regained uninterrupted access to state resources *without*
having to form any electoral coalitions with the Left.

Simply stated, in contrast to the process in Arauca, the repression-
sponsoring elites of Urabá and Caquetá did not form regional pacts with
the Left because they had no need to do so in order to retain access to key
state resources. Despite the ways the reform period strengthened the Left
in both regions, economically stable repression-sponsoring elites recovered lost ground either electorally (the Caguán and Caquetá as a whole)
or through increased access to higher levels of government and strengthened regional elite presence (Urabá), regaining their temporarily reduced
bargaining power relative to the Left.

Another implication of different repression sponsors concerns "public" and "private" violence. Where elites had an established presence
(Urabá), private (paramilitary) repression with army collusion predominated, with more lethal results and especially targeting institutional figures (county executives, social movement leaders, etc.). In frontier zones
with incipient elites, however, such as Arauquita (where elites were present only in the next county) and especially Cartagena del Chairá, violence
was overwhelmingly public, carried out directly by the army, although
with active support from elites in neighboring areas (the Turbayistas and
pre-pact LaTorristas). This public violence was less lethal than "private"
(paramilitary) violence and tended to target "anonymous" war zone peasants in particular, although institutional figures were often harassed or
"preventively detained."

The Postreform Period

By 1992 the counterreform had begun; political closing and an end to
government-guerrilla negotiations ensued. In all regions this was accompanied by a cutoff of material concessions to social movements associated
(in the government's conception, at least) with still-active leftist insurgencies. (The now right-wing, Esperanza-affiliated Sintrainagro banana workers' union, in contrast, experienced this shift as an expansion of political
opportunities, with the increased social movement and electoral success
this implies). All three regions experienced their most massive wave of

rightist violence ever, spearheaded either by paramilitary forces or by the military itself. This forced the reclandestinization of the Left, weakening leftist parties and social movements. Electoral success plummeted, destroying the possibility of a regional pacted peace by removing its second essential ingredient—the first was regional autonomy. It also reaffirmed the choice, for the still-armed FARC and ELN, to escalate combat and made existing "good guerrilla"/"bad guerrilla" tensions explode into vicious violence. Guerrillas who had once aimed to cultivate a good public image now routinely used land mines, destroyed infrastructure, and assassinated noncombatants. Armed insurgencies that had once actively participated in elections now sabotaged elections and elected officials—even leftist ones—aiming instead to influence their actions directly through threats.

In all regions the government also selectively reversed the previous decade's decentralizing and democratizing reforms by several different methods, effectively destroying the extraordinary autonomy experienced in the previous period and overriding any pacted regional agreements that had been made. Accentuating the loss of local and regional autonomy resulting from these measures, actors outside the locality, region, or even the nation, including the U.S. government, joined the fray on the side of elites and other right-wing forces. Social movements of the Left in turn responded to the new political context by shifting from material demands, which were now rarely met (except when coming from the right-wing Sintrainagro), to human rights demands, a tactic that met with more success in the post–Constitutional Assembly juridical context. They also distanced themselves from the increasingly extremist guerrilla movements. These two shifts facilitated, and created incentives for, the forming of closer alliances with organizations in other regions, in Bogotá, and in the industrialized world. This trend was reinforced by the resurgence of the moderate, urban Left after 2000, which strengthened these regional movements' urban allies.

Despite these commonalities, however, there were markedly different outcomes in the three regions in terms of social movement attainment of goals. In ascending order of success, the UP in Urabá was destroyed; the peasant movement in the Caguán received only national solidarity until very recently and no concrete concessions; the Esperanza-led Sintrainagro banana workers' union succeeded in making material gains until 2003 but then confronted many obstacles as the political context became more hostile. Likewise, the U'wa movement against oil extraction in Arauca experienced unprecedented success when its foe was Occidental Petroleum but could achieve only stalemate once it confronted the Colombian oil company Ecopetrol. The most clear-cut examples of success were the Chocaguán crop substitution program in Cartagena del Chairá, which expanded greatly after 2000 with international funding; the San José de Apartadó Peace Community, which in late 2008 was well on its way to winning the prosecution of military personnel for a February 2005 massacre; and the Araucan peasant movement, which won the liberation of its leader Luz Perly Córdoba, the prosecution of Colombian military personnel involved in the Santo Domingo bombing, and the decertification for U.S. military aid of the military unit involved, the prosecution of paramilitary forces for the assassination of two Left-allied Araucan congressmen, and the prosecution of military personnel implicated in the assassination of three regional labor-peasant leaders.

In this recentralized era, these outcomes were no longer determined strictly by the relative leverage of regional actors themselves but rather by the relative ability of regional actors to recruit outside allies to their side in order to alter national policy. A central goal, therefore, became to identify the factors that allowed social movements (and some elites) to mobilize more outside support than others for their cause.

The argument that emerged from my analysis of the three cases is summarized in figure 1.5. The two major determinants of a social movement's ability to win outside allies (which in turn made it more successful in winning concessions in the postreform period) were its strength immediately after the major postreform period repressive wave, which allowed it to dedicate time and resources to the cultivation of allies, and a series of movement and target characteristics that made the cause more visible and attractive to outside supporters.

Some of the sources of basic social movement strength continued to be very similar to those in the reform period. Obviously, starting the counterreform period from a position of strength (Urabá, Arauca) and not weakness (Cartagena del Chairá) facilitated such strength. Furthermore, where there were weaker elites—usually in the south of Colombia—the massive repressive wave was not only more public and thus less lethal but also later (2004–5 in Cartagena del Chairá; 2001–3 in Arauca). This was much more advantageous than an early repressive wave (1992–95 for Esperanza in Urabá; 1995–96 against the UP in Urabá). It allowed activists to learn from both the tragic and the successful experiences of other regions, connect with urban allies who were stronger by the Uribe years, and prepare for the onslaught. Finally, as in the reform period, political opportunity or prosperity in the concession sponsor that made a target more likely to grant success greatly facilitated social movement strength. This was present for Sintrainagro in the form of both banana sector economic growth and regional and national political opportunity through 2003; for Arauca, in the form of continuing peasant organizational strength and Left electoral strength through 2003; and for the U'wa movement in Arauca, in the form of the national indigenous resurgence in the late 1990s. The national decimation of the UP and the war against the FARC, however, further weakened the peasant movement of Cartagena del Chairá early in the postreform period, and the early and massive repressive wave eliminated the UP in Apartadó.

Social movement strength was essential to making the transition from the leftist reform period strategy of making material demands only to the leftist postreform strategy of making human rights demands, because such a transition required retraining of movement leaders in judicial processes and strategies as well as the creation of a new network of allies. Thus stronger movements were able to make this transition earlier (San José de Apartadó Peace Community and the Araucan peasant movement both moved to the new strategy in the mid-1990s) than weaker ones (the Caguán peasants took up human rights demands in 2005). The U'wa movement, the Chocaguán crop substitution project, and the Sintrainagro labor movement did not change demands during the postreform period: the former two adopted "new" demands (environmentalism, honest livelihood) from the start, and the latter continued to focus mainly on material demands, although emphasizing the "shared value" of their common struggle against the FARC in communications with management.

Being strong enough to survive the first massive wave of repression, though, was not enough to guarantee ultimate success; movements with characteristics that better enabled them to attract external allies were much more able to succeed in their goals, as social movements could then ask allies in Bogotá, or Europe, or the United States to help them pressure the Colombian government. A full discussion and exemplification of the ways these trends manifested in the three regions is included in the theory section. In overview, any one of these characteristics could facilitate a movement's efforts to attract outside allies:

1) It faced a more visible target, or one more vulnerable to political pressure or negative publicity.
2) It could frame its demands in terms of values that the allies being recruited shared (e.g., human rights, peace, democracy, national sovereignty, an honest livelihood, environmentalism—or for Esperanza, an anti-FARC agenda) and/or had leaders or important national allies that were of a relatively high educational level and/or affiliated with the church to aid in this (re)articulation of demands.
3) It distanced itself from guerrillas and was explicitly pacifist.

Yet the first and last factors themselves need explanation. Distance from guerrillas could facilitate a social movement's national and international alliances, especially with religious and U.S-based organizations. (European, Colombian, and leftist organizations were more tolerant of lingering affinities.) However, social movements in zones of guerrilla influence may refrain from condemning guerrilla actions either because they are still deriving some benefits from guerrilla presence or because movement members are vulnerable to guerrilla coercion and fear retaliation. Guerrilla behavior is a key determinant of which way social movements lean on this delicate issue. Where guerrillas have more flagrantly and widely engaged in human rights violations, such as killing alleged informers or elected officials, planting mines, and setting off bombs that kill civilians, social movements are more likely to take a stance against them. The following two conditions maximize the possibility that guerrillas will carry out such acts: (1) guerrilla political divisions are acute (e.g., one is in peace negotiations while the other is engaged in all-out war); and/or (2) in a context with fluid rather than static territorial boundaries between the zones of influence, the guerrilla group is competing for control of the population and territory with other armed actors. This second condition maximizes the possibility that noncombatants will be suspected of being "enemy agents."

Targets were more vulnerable to political pressure or negative publicity for several reasons. Foreign corporations were more easily vilified as agents of imperialism and also more easily prosecuted via judicial mechanisms on their home turf. Furthermore, repressive waves that were more overtly mandated and funded by the United States (Arauca in 2002–3; the Caguán after 2004) provoked more anti-imperialist outrage than private repressive waves (Urabá). Relative to paramilitary forces, military officials were more easily identified and captured and were held to higher standards of conduct, including by the U.S. human rights certification process for military aid.

Greater visibility of the target's misdeeds also increased target vulnerability. Regional humanitarian crises drew international relief agencies and press attention to the zone (Arauca and the Caguán after 2006), embarrassing the government. Similarly, more drastic government curtailment of civil rights in a region via more extreme selective recentralization measures drew the attention and condemnation of transnational human rights advocacy groups (e.g., the many human rights reports about Arauca during the zones of rehabilitation and consolidation policies of 2002–3). Recentralization measures were more extreme and extensive in regions that were wealthier and had greater institutional representation of the Left: Arauca more than Apartadó, with the least extensive measures in Cartagena del Chairá.

Thus political and economic opportunity, together with a later and more public repressive wave, created a movement that was stronger after the massive wave of counterreform period repression, especially if the movement ended the reform period strong. This strength allowed the movement to dedicate personnel and resources to the mammoth task of shifting to "shared value" demands and cultivating alliances beyond the region. If this strength was combined with factors that facilitated the existence and effectiveness of transnational alliances—movement values that were consistent with those of transnational advocacy networks; vulnerability and visibility of the target (itself ironically a result of more extreme selective recentralization measures, more dire humanitarian crises, and more overt U.S. intervention, among other things); and social distancing from guerrillas (itself a result of more extremist guerrilla behavior)—then the movement will have a greater likelihood of recruiting outside allies. Consequently, it will be more successful, as the outside allies help pressure the Colombian government to change policies.

Theoretical Implications

Studies of rural regions with powerful social movements, guerrilla insurgencies, and weak states necessitate a reexamination and extension of existing theories of democratization/decentralization, social movements, transnational activism, guerrillas, and political violence in several ways. In the following discussion, I first address analyses of political processes, institutional change, and globalization (trends over time), considered from the perspective of the state and elites ("from above") and from the perspective of social movements and guerrillas ("from below"); and then discuss analyses of the factors that determined the contrasting regional outcomes.

THEORIZING NATIONAL POLITICAL PROCESSES AND MOVEMENT RESPONSES: COMMON OUTCOMES

Effects of Reform and Counterreform on Elite and State Actions

O'Donnell and Schmitter drew their analysis primarily from the democratic transition during the early 1980s in the Southern Cone, where social movements had been severely weakened by years of dictatorship, especially in Argentina, and laws were widely enforced, especially in Chile.[3] They suggest that in a delicate moment of transition to democracy two outcomes were possible: democratic consolidation or involution, that is, return to military rule. However, in applying O'Donnell and Schmitter's framework to the Colombian context, where social movements and armed insurgencies are strong rather than nearly defeated and the state is weak relative to private elite actors rather than strong as in Chile and Argentina, I find that democratization and involution may actually occur simultaneously rather than as chronologically distinct phases. While softliner elites are strong enough to impose democratic reforms at the national level, they are either unable (due to insufficient control over private elites and antireformist military) or unwilling (due to their essential agreement with the aims of dirty war) to put a stop to private elite-sponsored paramilitary activities that operate with military complicity. Neither did Colombia's counterreform period resemble O'Donnell and Schmitter's "involution." Few reforms were reversed outright via national legislation; rather, counterreform took place through ad hoc presidential decrees and actions, many of them affecting only certain regions.

O'Donnell draws attention to such regional dynamics when he addresses the special characteristics of democratization in contexts of weak national states, or "brown" regions (i.e., with weak state institutions) within nations having otherwise strong states.[4] In such contexts he predicts that democratization may well lead to local elite colonization of the state, where local elites effectively monopolize not just electoral power but also key state resources such as the police and judiciary. In these cases, with democratization the urban or rural poor will have gained the right to vote, but their de facto access to state resources will remain virtually unchanged in a phenomenon O'Donnell calls "low intensity citizenship." Although some regions of Colombia resemble this elite-dominated model, my three case study regions had strong social movements, at least during the reform period. Thus democratization allowed the social movements to make real gains in political representation, with which they could make significant material gains. However, the continuing lack of access to the judiciary that O'Donnell's model predicted has generally prevented the movements from prosecuting elites and military actors who assassinated their newly elected representatives.

Notably, though, after the Constitutional Assembly created a greater array of national legal institutions designed for the defense of the citizenry, social movements in these regions have sometimes been able to win redress to their grievances via national rather than regional judicial institutions. Such gains, as well as the backlash against rural social movements benefited in the regional balance of power by democratization, are in fact predicted by Fox, although the process through which this takes place is not fully explained.[5]

Romero's study of the rise of paramilitary organizations in Colombia from 1982 to 2003 theorizes simultaneous peasant gains and backlash in the context of democratic reform, as well as the regionalization of this phenomenon hinted at by O'Donnell's low intensity citizenship concept.[6] In those peripheral (newly settled) regions where local elites had previously dominated local state institutions but social movements were electorally strong enough to displace them under the new rules, decentralizing democratic reforms and peace processes initiated by elites from the center threatened peripheral elite domination of the local balance of power. To reestablish the regional status quo, peripheral elites organized paramilitary groups to eliminate leaders of the emergent movements. As the reform process progressively fragmented the state between reformists and hard-liners, with most of the military falling in the latter category and forming alliances with peripheral elites on the regional level, such elite actions were rarely prosecuted.[7] Thus increased political murders by paramilitary groups during moments of reform and peace processes—and conversely, decreased paramilitary murders of political activists during moments of counter-reform and all-out war—are not anomalous, as O'Donnell and Schmitter's argument might imply, but rather are predicted by Romero's model. His analysis also highlights the center/periphery tensions inherent in the dynamics of Colombia's violence.[8]

Such center/periphery tensions have received increasing attention in recent years, as almost all Latin American countries joined a new wave of decentralization between the 1980s and the 2000s. These reforms, to varying degrees, redistributed political and fiscal autonomy from central to state and local governments.[9] Much of the copious literature on this trend is sponsored by international development agencies such as the World Bank and the Inter-American Development Bank, which encouraged decentralizing reforms to bring about greater fiscal efficiency and political transparency.[10] Although some of these analyses have examined the political motives for decentralization,[11] the main objective of this literature is to evaluate specific cases to pinpoint the most effective implementation strategies with which to achieve the stated goals. This approach contributes key insights, such as the finding that localities with stronger and more autonomous organized civil society groups acting as "monitoring influences" are likely to experience better responsiveness to citizen demands,[12] as was demonstrated in my cases as well. However, in contrast to Romero's perspective and belying the intense debate on decentralization in Colombia, the approach tends to conceptualize decentralization mostly as a "win-win" situation for all parties.[13]

More recently, research in political science has sought to explain the political causes of decentralization rather than its economic outcomes, zeroing in on a particular puzzle: "Why would [central] politicians surrender power [to politicians from the periphery]?"[14] While some suggest that the reform is promoted by party leaders in the center who stand to gain electorally from decentralization,[15] this neglects bottom-up factors and makes the subsequent selective recentralization efforts of Presidents Gaviria and Uribe seem anomalous. Why would the national government find the results of a reform promoted from above so threatening?

In contrast, Eaton describes two distinct paths to decentralization, one top-down and the other bottom-up.[16] In this view decentralization is not always fully compatible with the interests of the party in power nationally; rather, it is the outcome of a conflictive process. In the bottom-up path, which in my view is the one Colombia has taken, democratization strengthens opposition groups, which then advocate decentralization as a way to further their electoral growth. Decentralizing reform is passed grudgingly by a recalcitrant national elite, which then seeks every opportunity to reduce the impact of the reform. This has often occurred through the passage of national recentralizing legislation applicable throughout the nation, although such a strategy is more difficult to carry out in democratic contexts.[17]

In contrast to Eaton's recentralization examples, though, Colombia's recentralization has been selective: it has applied only to certain war zone localities and regions. Why are some regions targeted when others are not? The authors in Cornelius, Eisenstadt, and Hindley's edited volume examine the effects of decentralization on national politics in Mexico, finding that in some cases decentralization gave opposition parties such as the PAN toeholds with which to accumulate national power (Eaton's bottom-up path), but in other cases it strengthened the incumbent PRI.[18] Clearly, decentralization will have more threatening effects for the nationally governing party in regions where the opposition is strong. A corollary is that some regions — notably those with the potential for a substantial regional tax base (e.g., Bolivia's prosperous Santa Cruz region) — have more to gain from decentralization than others and the central government more to lose when those departments gain fiscal autonomy.[19]

Decentralization amid civil war also brings to the fore a policy debate that has raged for two decades in Colombia, where powerful armed actors are capable of influencing the actions of local and departmental elected officials or even extorting money from them. Should governments facing such a challenge avoid decentralization altogether in order to prevent the risk, pointed out by Eaton, of such armed actors gaining additional fiscal and political resources with which to continue waging war?[20] Or, to the contrary, would the failure to democratize local governments legitimate violent tactics on the part of insurgencies, as the writings of Jaime Castro, an architect of Colombia's decentralization process, have often implied?[21]

Colombian presidents since 1988 have chosen to resolve this security dilemma, as well as the parallel political dilemma of decentralization creating a foothold for the leftist opposition, with different forms of de facto or de jure selective decentralization. This leaves the nationally legislated decentralizing reform intact but reverses its effects in regions where armed actors, especially leftist guerrillas, are said to be most able to extract material benefits from local and departmental governments. In fact, such measures have been applied not necessarily where guerrillas are strongest but where the electoral Left is most successful and the regional state wealthiest. Thus the most radical recentralization measures were applied to Arauca, a region that had significant leftist electoral influence *and* that controlled considerable oil royalties. While all three regions witnessed arrests of leftist elected officials and/or candidates, sometimes on the eve of elections—and subsequent acquittals due to lack of evidence—these were more extensive in Apartadó and especially Arauca than in Cartagena del Chairá. And only Arauca, with its oil-enhanced budget and strong electoral Left through 2003, experienced direct interference in the autonomy of directly elected regional officials, such as threats of removal from office to force governors to alter their cabinet choices or a national takeover of departmental oil royalties. Likewise, only Araucan citizens faced de jure restrictions on their civil rights.

This solution, however, re-creates the problem that Colombian decentralization, proposed as part of the peace process with insurgent groups, was intended to address. By eliminating the possibility for oppositional political forces in war zones to gain access to local and departmental government via the electoral process, selective recentralization may relegitimate armed struggle in the eyes of war zone residents. Roldán, in her study of Antioquia during La Violencia, eloquently describes a parallel phenomenon in the past.[22] A peripheral region's perceived history of rebelliousness and (cultural/racial difference) led central authorities to respond to grievances with repression and political exclusion rather than negotiation, in contrast to the opposite pattern in central regions. Such exclusionary treatment in turn made the population more willing to accept violence as a legitimate political tool. Pizarro agrees that restriction of democracy legitimates guerrilla movements in the eyes of some and that aggressive military harassment of certain regions backfires by boosting peasant support for guerrillas.[23] However, unlike Roldán, he stops short of positing that democracy is *more* restricted in war zones than in the mainstream rural areas or urban centers. Tellingly, two of the peripheral, dissident, and violent regions in Roldán's study, Urabá and the Magdalena Medio, continue to be violent and dissident regions today. Pizarro also concurs that the map of violent regions in La Violencia overlaps almost perfectly with a map of violent regions today.[24]

The regionalization of citizenship described by Roldán is reminiscent of what Tilly and Tarrow call "composite regimes" (South Africa during apartheid, Israel, Northern Ireland), in which "different systems of rule shape the contentious repertoires of different populations" within the same nation-state.[25] Thus one conflict — Israeli settlers versus the Israeli state, for example, or Antioquian peasants of the central municipalities versus the departmental government — engages in social movement repertoires with the state (nonviolent protests, petitions, use of the media, etc.), and the state responds with negotiation. Meanwhile, another, more politically excluded population — the Palestinians in their interactions with Israel, for example, or the citizens of the peripheral zones of Antioquia versus the state in Roldán's study — engages largely (although not entirely) in lethal politics as their response to violent state repression.

An even more stark and explicit juridical divide between Algerian colonizers and natives is denounced in Frantz Fanon's influential *The Wretched of the Earth.* In his view such a dehumanizing deprivation of citizenship rights demands a violent response on the part of the natives, both as a rational decolonizing political action and as a psychologically healing one.[26] But the more ambiguous Colombian context, where such differentially repressive treatment of "red zone" citizens is more often de facto than de jure, complicates this schema in several ways. First, red zone citizens continue to engage in social movement repertoires, in the hope of exercising their de jure rights as Colombian citizens, even while lethal politics of both the Right and the Left roil around them. Second, in the Colombian context the political exclusion experienced by red zone citizens is nearly invisible to the citizens of the center and mainstream rural zones. This not only means that many of the latter perceive armed insurgency as illegitimate and despicable, with no connection to social conflict. It also means — in an apparent but oft-articulated contradiction — that even the nonviolent social movement actions of the red zone citizens are seen as tainted by guerrilla influence rather than as originating from legitimate grievances. Entire regional populations are seen as guerrilla auxiliaries, even while guerrillas are seen as having no popular support.

Social Movement and Guerrilla Responses to Reform,
Counterreform, and Globalization

McAdam, Zamosc, Wickham-Crowley, Pizarro, Tilly and Tarrow, Tilly,
and Keck and Sikkink all examine institutional changes from below, addressing the ways that reform and counterreform affect the level and type of
social movement or guerrilla mobilization, success, or tactical/ideological
unity.[27] McAdam and Zamosc address social movements with few or no
links to leftist electoral parties or guerrilla movements, that is, reformist
movements; Wickham-Crowley's and Pizarro's analyses focus primarily on
armed insurgencies; and Tilly and Tarrow consider the relationship between these two repertoires. Tilly and Keck and Sikkink explore the ways
in which the trend toward globalization since the 1990s has altered the
terrain and available strategies for social movements.

The major predictions of these theories have been confirmed by this
study. McAdam and Zamosc argue that political opening brings a mod-
eration of social movement tactics and ideology, social movement unity,
increased mobilization, and success and steps toward more institutional
expressions of conflict, as occurred in all the regions in this study from
1984 to 1988, whereas political closing brings radicalization of tactics and
factionalism, decreased mobilization, and failure, as occurred in most of
my study regions in the early counterreform period, with the exception of
the Right-allied Sintrainagro, which experienced the counterreform period as a political opening. (The late reform period is discussed below.)
Wickham-Crowley conversely argues that moves toward democracy and
away from dictatorship weaken and divide guerrilla movements, whereas
dictatorship facilitates guerrilla strength and victory. In general, this argument was also verified by the Colombian case: moments of peace negotiation reduced the perceived legitimacy of the guerrilla movement and induced some to demobilize, whereas moments of counterreform brought
about tactical unity among guerrillas, military buildup and offensives, and
rapid moves away from respect for institutional and international norms.

However, all three theories still need to be adjusted to apply to the
Colombian context of the late 1980s through late 2008, as each assumes
state actions can easily be classified as demonstrating either political opening or closing, dictatorship or democracy. In fact, after 1987 reforms and
peace processes indicated a continuing trend toward democratization,

while escalated counterinsurgency and paramilitary activity and the cessation of material concessions to war zone social movements indicated a clear political closing. Violent democratization, and later selective recentralization with continuation of many national reform gains, presented both guerrillas and social movements in the case study regions with a difficult dilemma: which of these contradictory trends should inform their responses?

In *Insurgencia sin revolución,* Pizarro addresses the guerrilla response to this situation of neither dictatorship nor democracy but rather "restricted democracy."[28] He argues that the existence of some elements of democracy prevents guerrilla groups from taking state power, yet the limited nature of democracy—together with a weak state and the long established repertoire of guerrilla activity in some regions—keeps Colombia's "chronic insurgency" going and its links to social movements intact.

Regarding social movement response to this ambiguous political context, generally, my cases did show that political opening promoted a greater emphasis on legal/institutional tactics, as McAdam, Zamosc, and Wickham-Crowley all predict, and political closing drove guerrillas toward a renewed emphasis on armed struggle and away from support of electoral/social movement strategies. However, at all times the three tactics coincided in the same territories and based on the same populations. In other words, the state's mixed signals of violent democratization were met by the dissident regions' own mixed signals. Tilly and Tarrow's analysis of repertoires of contention in "horizontally segmented regimes" such as Northern Ireland, a subcategory of composite regimes, describes this territorial coincidence of social movement repertoires and lethal tactics as a response to the ambiguous legal setting.[29]

Through the middle of the reform period such simultaneous use of social movement and lethal politics repertoires was planned by some ideological tendencies, a phenomenon the Colombian Communist Party at one point called the "combination of all forms of struggle."[30] In the counterreform period, however, as guerrilla actions became more extreme, in most regions social movements distanced themselves so much from the insurgencies that they could not be considered part of the same movement at all (e.g., Arauca after 2000). Even in that case, however, they still shared a support population and territories. In turn, the mixed signals from the dissident regions are used to justify continued debate and vacillation on the part of the state: soft-liners advocate further democratic reforms and peace negotiations, and the latter push for full-scale counterinsurgency, and neither faction dominates fully for an extended period.

Beyond the trends toward reform or counterreform on the national level, the social movements in this study also faced trends that brought regional, supraregional, national, and transnational actors into each region's conflict, especially after the early 1990s. On the state-elite side, paramilitary groups once organized on the municipal level became regional, then supraregional, then national, as described by Romero.[31] The Colombian state's recentralization measures made the national Executive Branch a more active participant in each region's conflicts. International, especially U.S.-based, corporations already present in the regions became more implicated in regional conflicts by sponsoring paramilitary groups (Chiquita and Coca-Cola in Urabá), collaborating with military initiatives, or pushing for increased U.S. military aid to the region where they were based (Occidental Petroleum in Arauca). Finally, the U.S. government massively increased military aid, supporting military offensives especially in Arauca and the Lower Caguán.

Although none of these trends on the state-elite side were due to "globalization" per se, they did present social movements with a new set of powerful enemies from beyond the local or regional setting. Meanwhile, however, the increased availability, after the early 1990s, of what Keck and Sikkink call transnational advocacy networks presented a new set of strategic possibilities, leading in every region to new social movement repertoires.[32] Thus increased U.S. military aid to Colombia created new hardships for war zone peasants but also led to greater U.S. scrutiny of the Colombian military's human rights record and even of the paramilitary demobilization process. Social movements in Arauca then used the human rights certification process to speed prosecutions of military personnel in the Santo Domingo bombing case, and U.S. dismay at the impunity of notorious drug traffickers among still un-demobilized paramilitary leaders forced the Colombian government to pressure for a speedier paramilitary demobilization, facilitating the prosecution of paramilitary leaders in Urabá and Arauca.

Therefore, as Tilly wrote of globalization in general, the increased U.S. involvement in these regional conflicts provided both new threats and new opportunities for social movements.[33] To this "pull factor" explaining a shift of movement demands, targets, and tactics I might add a "push factor": the failure of the "old" strategies to work in the new context of counterreform and supraregional enemies made a strategic shift not an option but an imperative. Consequently, in all regional cases in the counter-reform period, social movements shifted their focus increasingly from the local or regional level to the national level and attempted to mobilize suffi-cient national and international allies to induce the government to meet regional social movement demands. Such a use of international (usually from the global North) allies to influence domestic (usually from the global South) policy is termed by Keck and Sikkink "the boomerang pattern."[34]

EXPLAINING REGIONAL CONTRASTS IN THE BALANCE OF POWER AND THE NATIONAL LEVERAGE OF REGIONAL ACTORS

The above analysis has emphasized the ways in which events in all three regions evolved in parallel ways over the course of the period of study. However, factors rooted in the regional political economy as well as other factors promoting or hindering international alliances determined the di-verging fate of the three regions in terms of social movement survival, gains, and repression.

Overarching Principles That Determined Regional Outcomes

The Reform Period: Balance of Power between Elites
and Regional Social Movements
Two main positions can be identified with respect to the effect of regional social movement/elite balance of power on postdemocratization peace and social movement gains. On the one hand, O'Donnell and Schmitter and Moore, who were mainly concerned with attaining formal (political gains only) rather than substantive democracy (political and material gains), argue that a balance of power that favors labor or the peasantry too much will cause an undemocratic outcome—either involution (O'Donnell and Schmitter) or communism (Moore).[35] On the other hand, scholars con-cerned with obtaining social movement gains only (Paige)[36] or demo-cratic political institutions *with* substantive gains for subordinate classes

(Rueschemeyer, Stephens, and Stephens)[37] have argued that this outcome was more likely if social movements were in a very strong bargaining position relative to elites, either clearly dominant[38] or at least stalemated.[39]

Without a doubt, the experience of the three case study regions verified the second position more than the first, as the optimal reform period outcomes for social movements—social movement gains with peace—occurred when and where social movement leverage relative to elites was maximized. In contrast, where elites dominated social movements in the regional balance of power, there was peace but no social movement gains or even a reversal of previous social movement victories, that is, social movement *defeat* (e.g., the Caguán from late 1988 through the end of the reform period).

My cases are different from those studied by Paige and Rueschemeyer, Stephens, and Stephens in key ways, however. Stalemated situations (El Salvador and Guatemala in the 1990s; Europe prior to the extension of suffrage) eventually produced peace with social movement gains in the contexts examined by these authors—due, I would argue, to either international mediation (Central America) or more effective national mechanisms for the mediation of social conflict (Europe). However, regional stalemate in Colombia during the reform period (e.g., Urabá) produced social movement gains but with endemic violence, as the region benefited neither from outside mediation nor effective institutional mechanisms for conflict resolution. Richani argues that Colombia as a whole in the 1990s could be described as a stalemate between guerrillas and the military.[40] Both sides were strong, few mediation mechanisms existed, and those that did exist were often ineffective and unenforceable. Furthermore, the main international source of military aid, the United States, continued to both subsidize the military and press for a military solution.

Therefore, in my study, only in contexts where social movements dominated the regional balance of power during the reform period could social movements use the existing structures of electoral democracy—rather than nonexistent national or international institutions specifically designed for conflict mediation—to form a Left-dominated electoral coalition, composed of leftist and elite parties, with a corollary antirepression pact (e.g., Arauca from 1989 to 1992, Urabá in 1991–92). Unfortunately, in contrast to the mediated solutions described by Paige and Rueschemeyer, Stephens, and Stephens, the pacted peace agreements in my case study regions, as well as the negotiated peace of the Caguán, depended on the political moment and were not institutionalized power-sharing agreements.[41] They were therefore more ephemeral than democracy in Central America after the late 1990s or the welfare state in Europe.

The Counterreform Period: Social Movement Leverage over the National Government

The literature on social movements typically assumes that a movement's ability to affect the national government's actions—that is, its leverage relative to the government—is a principal determinant of its likelihood of surviving and succeeding, and that allies outside the movement are a crucial element of movement leverage. This argument is central to the analyses of McAdam on the Civil Rights movement, Zamosc on the Colombian peasant movement, the Colliers' analysis of Latin American labor movements, and many others.[42] Thus that this is also true for my three case study regions during the postreform period is unsurprising. It is important to note, though, that this "normal" situation was a marked departure from the extraordinary moment that took place after the implementation of democratizing and decentralizing reforms and before the beginning of the counterreform, from about 1986 to 1992.

During that short window of time, the municipalities and regions had exceptional autonomy to carry out informal pacted peace agreements. The autonomy derived from the decentralizing reforms themselves, as well as from the fact that the conflict was still by and large limited to the municipal or regional level. Once the decentralizing reforms were selectively reversed in those prosperous regions where the Left had been most successful; and once supraregional, national, and international actors began to enter into these previously local/regional conflicts as elite allies; local social antagonists lost their ability to resolve the conflict among themselves via informal pacts facilitated by the electoral process. Even a Left-dominated regional balance of power could be overridden by the actions of outside state and elite actors. For social movements, success and even survival then became contingent on the ability to successfully apply the "boomerang pattern";[43] to mobilize allies in other regions and even in other nations to press the national government for more favorable actions, policies, and resources. Although a radical departure from the previous decade, this situation was just a slightly more transnationalized variation of "normal" social movement politics.

Sources of Social Movement Leverage

The Reform Period

The two major components of social movement strength within the regional balance of power were social movement success (which translated into reform period electoral success) and unity. Social movement success depended on the willingness and ability of the social movement's target to grant concessions. But who was the target? Much of the U.S. social movements literature, especially that written in the political process vein,[44] has assumed social movements primarily confront state targets; thus their success depends largely on political opportunity. On the other hand, analyses of Third World social movements, especially those written from a perspective closer to orthodox Marxism, assume peasants and workers confront their material antagonists (the bourgeoisie or landed elites) directly. Success then depends largely on economic, more than political, conditions affecting the target elite. Bergquist emphasizes the ways economic growth and, therefore, labor shortage facilitate labor success, whereas Paige argues that the structural weakness of landed elites without capital-derived income make them vulnerable to agrarian (peasant) revolution.[45]

A third position combines elements of these first two. Zamosc argues that different types of agrarian movements have different targets: smallholder peasants aim their demands—for improved credit, infrastructure, services, and so forth—at the state; landless peasants must confront both the state and landowners in order to successfully force land redistribution; and rural workers must confront rural capitalists alone. From Zamosc's perspective, then, political opportunity is indeed relevant to the success of the first two categories of movements.[46]

My cases show that Zamosc's analysis is the most relevant. In both Arauca and the Caguán during the reform period, the most active movements were those of peasant settlers that aimed their demands strictly against the state, not against local elites, at both the national and departmental levels, and both movements were greatly affected by political opening and closing at both levels. I would add to Zamosc's analysis, though, that fiscal opportunity can be as determinant of peasant social movement success as political opportunity for state-focused movements. In Arauca the rapidly growing post–oil boom fiscal pie meant peasant demands could be granted *without* adversely affecting other constituencies. This departmental fiscal prosperity, in combination with the departmental electoral strength of the Left, meant the Araucan peasant movement continued to thrive long after the national political closing had defeated the Caguán's peasant movement.

As Paige, Bergquist, and Zamosc all agree, rural workers mainly confront rural capitalists, and their success depends primarily on sectoral prosperity and expansion. However, political opening also greatly promotes the success of this constituency; without it, labor activists even in Urabá's fast-growing banana sector in the 1960s and 1970s were repressed and unable to build a strong organization. Democratization and the peace process allowed the declandestinization of the labor movement in Urabá, boosted labor activism, and facilitated the more sympathetic mediation of the national government. It also made possible the pro-labor intervention of leftist county executives and transformed labor conflict patterns from constant small strikes to an industry-wide negotiation every two years. The postreform Esperanza-led banana workers' union in Urabá was spared from destruction only because it aligned itself, for the purposes of departmental and national politics, with the right-wing banana plantation owners: political closing for the rest of the labor movement was actually political opening for them.

Finally, rural squatters on private land, as Zamosc points out, confront both landlords and the state. Their success depends on political opening (Zamosc), as well as the weakness of the landlords in question, both politically (Zamosc) and economically (Paige). This finding may also be applied to urban squatters, as the evidence from Urabá reveals. The huge La Chinita squatter settlement was legalized especially quickly because the land was owned by a (vulnerable) elected official and the state was anxious to appease the newly demobilized Esperanza.

How does rural worker, peasant, and squatter movement success then translate into votes for leftist parties? My findings support an elaboration of a hypothesis suggested by the analysis of Fox: stronger social movements have greater electoral potential.[47] Specifically, I found that while elite electoral strength generally reflects the prosperity of the undergirding economic sector, leftist electoral strength usually reflects the strength and success of the social movement that forms its base, *regardless of the level of repression*. During the reform period, successful and well-organized social movements continued to be electorally successful despite even very high levels of repression (Apartadó and Arauquita); but unsuccessful or loosely organized social movements (UP votes in urban Arauca after 1986; the Caguán after 1988) quickly lost electoral strength after the first repressive wave.

How does such electoral success in turn affect these rural peasant, worker, and squatter movements? My findings support another hypothesis derived from Fox's analysis: institutional political gains by social movement representatives further strengthen the movement. In my case study regions, once social movement–based leftist political parties attained power via electoral means, state actions and resources were directed toward reinforcing social movement strength in three ways.[48] First, leftist incumbents in local government used the county budget to build movement-focused public works such as union halls, peasant producer/consumer cooperatives, and schools, roads, electricity, and so forth, for newly settled *zonas de colonización,* recently recuperated peasant land invasions or urban squatter settlements. However, the number and magnitude of the public works and the proportion of all public works underwritten by the county budget were much more noteworthy in those counties with significant local tax bases: Apartadó and Arauquita. The "Esperanza" administrations in Apartadó continued this labor advocacy via public works even as a right-wing party.

Second, leftist county executives used political membership in the leftist party as a criterion for county employment, in what I have termed clientelism from below. Although this lamentably replicated an aspect of the old politics that was supposed to be left behind, it also provided a rare selective incentive for movement membership that began to offset the more common perception of movement membership as a quick way to get killed. Again, though, the importance of this source of employment depended on the size of the total county budget.

The poorest counties were limited to the third form of pro-movement action: advocacy. This might be for fund-raising purposes (e.g., applying for state or NGO/private grants for public works, as in Cartagena del Chairá); to advance movement interests before the movement's targets (e.g., attempting to resolve disputes between urban squatters and the owners of the invaded property or between the military and the banana workers in Apartadó; efforts to negotiate less abusive military or Venezuelan National Guard policies toward Arauquita residents); to push along the prosecution of human rights cases or denunciations of abuses (largely but not exclusively carried out by the personero, who was part of each county's administration); and to participate in the brokering of informal regional peace pacts (Arauca) or more formal peace agreements (e.g., the Gloria Cuartas administration in Apartadó).[49]

In short, leftist local and departmental elected officials could benefit from all the privileges of incumbency outlined by Bergquist in his study of nineteenth-century rural Colombian elites (especially control of state fiscal resources) *except* control over the judiciary, police, or local army commander, which remained at all times firmly under national or local elite control.[50] Nonetheless, the state resources that passed from elite to leftist or social movement hands after the passage of decentralizing reforms represented a significant threat to the regional status quo, which for Romero is key to explaining why the years immediately after the decentralizing measures were passed, 1988–95, were among Colombia's most violent ever.[51]

The third major source of social movement leverage in the regional balance of power, unity, was defined both as fewer ideological tendencies in each region ("numerical unity") and as unified guerrilla responses vis-à-vis government peace offers ("tactical unity"). It is well established in the social movement literature that unity boosts success,[52] and my cases were not an exception to the rule. Numerical unity among leftist tendencies boosted the strength of social movements relative to elites by creating fewer bargaining agents, thus making a pacted peace more likely.

Tactical unity also greatly increased the likelihood of success of pacted agreements that were reached. If both guerrilla groups in the region had chosen the same response to government peace offers, each was less likely to sabotage the pacted peace initiated by the other (e.g., in Arauca, the FARC and ELN from 1989 to 1992 respected the other tendency's regional pact). Conversely, as Urabá's experience in the 1990s and Arauca's experience after 2006 tragically demonstrates, when one guerrilla group demobilizes, or even begins to discuss demobilization, and the other does not, the still-active insurgency is likely to view the demobilized group as traitors. This is especially true if the two groups shared military operations in the past (Arauca and Urabá) or if the demobilized sector experiences greater material success than the nondemobilized sector after demobilization (Urabá).

My cases showed that there were fewer different ideological tendencies in the peasant regions than in Urabá (in the Caguán, only the FARC; in Arauca, the FARC and the ELN; in Urabá, FARC, ELN, and EPL, which subdivided into EPL dissidence and Esperanza, Paz y Libertad after

1990). Voting results by precinct verified that among rural populations, political affiliation corresponded quite strictly with geography. In guerrilla-dominated rural areas, it is common for the guerrilla group to act as a parallel state, offering police and conflict-resolution functions as well as organizing collective public works projects (this was especially noteworthy in the Lower Caguán). The guerrilla group defended the controlled territory not only from encroachment by the army, the paramilitary, and fumigation planes but also from encroachment by competing guerrilla groups (e.g., Arauquita). In contrast, in Urabá, where the population was urbanized or living in work camps, recruitment to leftist parties and mass organizations was not as territorial but rather was closer to a free-for-all within each territorial unit (urban neighborhood, plantation, etc.). Guerrilla groups cannot defend territory as effectively against encroachment in this context, which allows more tendencies to enter and compete.

That such territorial military control would further consolidate the guerrilla group's political control over the region is consistent with Wickham-Crowley's study. He argues that guerrilla movements are more able to establish vertical ties with peasants, and therefore more easily access peasant resources, where there are no competing political forces—elite or otherwise—that have previously established alliances with the peasantry. However, he does not specifically identify territorial military control, or coercive factors, as favoring the establishment of such ties,[53] but Pizarro does, adding that para-state functions of guerrillas in peasant regions further reinforce such territorial control.[54] Pizarro further suggests that in regions where disputes for territorial control are more intense, guerrilla abuses of the population—and of other guerrillas—are more likely to occur. This is an important insight, and goes far toward explaining why guerrilla abuses of the population, as well as violent attacks on other guerrilla groups, were most rampant in the regions and at the moments with greatest territorial competition between guerrilla groups (Urabá 1992–96, Arauca 2006–8) or between guerrilla groups and paramilitary forces (Arauca 2001–6) and least frequent in the monochromatic FARC-controlled political landscape of the Middle and Lower Caguán before 2004.

To this insight, Richani adds a corollary: guerrillas and paramilitary groups use military control of territories not just to obtain the support of the population but also to control resources (coca fields, oil pipelines, gold mines) with which to finance their operations. Territorial control, enabling rent extraction, is crucial to what Richani calls the FARC's and the ELN's "positive political economy," which has contributed to preventing their demobilization to date.[55] In response to this positive political economy, however, the government has focused nearly exclusively on offering material incentives for guerrilla groups, or individual fighters, to demobilize and serve as informers. Thus the continuing political and social exclusion of social movements in these regions—the other major facilitating factor for armed insurgency—has remained unaddressed. As a result the demobilization of four of Colombia's six major insurgencies in the early 1990s did *not* lower Colombia's overall level of armed conflict. The still-active insurgencies immediately moved into the regions abandoned by the demobilized groups and engaged in a military buildup.

What explains why some regions, and some types of social struggles, seem to historically present more guerrilla activity than others? The contrast in response to government peace offers by the national guerrilla organizations reflects to a large degree the difference in their social bases. The FARC and the ELN are not just larger and militarily stronger; they are based primarily on new peasant settler zones. But the smaller and militarily weaker M-19 and EPL had a greater proportion of their territory and influence in areas of traditional latifundio, plantation regions, or urban unions. This national correlation of demobilized groups with urban/worker bases and still-active insurgencies with peasant regions verifies Paige's conclusions that plantation regions are more reformist than peasant regions with latifundio.[56]

The findings within each region, however, call into question some of Paige's conclusions. Paige erroneously predicts no guerrilla movements in either settler regions or plantation regions, when in fact they were present in both in my cases. This is because he focuses entirely on economic structure, failing to take into account state institutions and local political-military realities that also shape social movements' available repertoires.[57]

Specifically, Paige argued that both smallholder peasant movements (e.g., the Caguán and Arauca) and plantation labor movements (e.g., Urabá) would be reformist (i.e., with no guerrillas present), as both economic structures involve cultivator confrontation with noncultivating classes (intermediaries and plantation owners, respectively) that derived their income from capital rather than land.[58] The case studies from which Paige derives this argument, the coffee region in Colombia and sugar plantations in Peru, differ markedly from my case study regions in terms of the state's ability to mediate class conflicts through institutional means. Colombia's coffee regions have a powerful para-state in the Federation of Coffee Growers (Fedecafé), which regulates coffee prices and provides relatively ample infrastructure. Guerrilla activity and leftist politics are indeed rare there. In contrast, though also populated by smallholders, Colombia's settler regions had minimal infrastructure, and cries for improvements were met mostly with repression, producing radical movements.[59]

Similarly, Peru's coastal sugar regions benefited from one of the most radical labor incorporation processes in Latin America, leading to extensive material gains, labor rights, and state mediation mechanisms for organized labor. In contrast, as Collier and Collier note, Colombia (with Uruguay) had one of the least inclusive labor incorporation periods in Latin America, and rural labor benefited even less than urban labor due to colonization of the rural state by local elites.[60] Thus before the reform period plantation owners in Urabá frequently ignored even the few legally mandated arbitration mechanisms, frustrating all legal efforts to organize and eventually leading to the desperate tactic of "armed trade unionism" in Urabá and in other Colombian regions with continuous-harvest plantation labor movements.[61]

In the postreform period the banana workers' union in Urabá did in fact become "reformist"—but not for the reasons predicted by Paige. As they aligned with the right-wing banana plantation owners and against the FARC, they were in effect incorporated—given both political and material benefits—and not only electorally mobilized but militarily mobilized as well against members of the Patriotic Union. In effect, the state and elites decided to strengthen them because they were politically and militarily useful—at least during a certain conjuncture through 2003—an incorporation based on strategic geopolitical factors, not economic ones.

Whereas Paige sees smallholder peasants and plantation labor movements as equally prone to reformist tendencies, Collier and Collier argue that throughout Latin America peasants are less incorporated than are workers, with few guaranteed rights for resolution of collective disputes with landed elites and intermediaries and dismal material conditions. In fact, they are incorporated at all only in Venezuela and Mexico and excluded almost entirely in the other countries. For example, in Colombia, although the INCORA was established in the 1960s to redistribute land

and credit to peasants, its resources became so meager that its effectiveness as mediator was severely compromised. Therefore, for Collier and Collier, it is not an anomaly that guerrillas with a worker base have been more likely to demobilize than smallholder-based guerrillas.[62]

Wickham-Crowley also predicts greater peasant than worker receptiveness to guerrillas, not only in areas where guerrillas are able to establish vertical ties with peasants, as discussed earlier, but also in areas of precarious peasant landownership, because in this context guerrillas can physically defend threatened landholdings.[63] This protection rationale for the armed insurgency was most clearly in evidence in the Caguán, where peasants were both occupying the land illegally and growing illegal crops.

Finally, insights about the greater importance, to guerrillas, of territorial military control in peasant regions and the lower degree of political incorporation in peasant regions may be combined to explain why worker-based guerrillas might gain more from demobilization than peasant-based groups.[64] With the loss of the military control of the region, settler region guerrillas could not function as effectively as the parallel state, reducing their ability to derive political support from the peasant population and financial resources from elites. Furthermore, demobilized settler region guerrillas would not gain access to institutionalized forms of conflict resolution for peasants, as there are none. In worker regions, however, where armed defense of political and geographic territory is less effective, urban territory is less likely to be lost through demobilization, while electoral success is enhanced by the perception that voting for a demobilized group is "less dangerous" (e.g., Esperanza in Apartadó). And while the EPL lost access to the tactic of armed trade unionism, it gained greater access to the arbitration mechanisms of the state and reduced its own vulnerability to elite-sponsored repression.

=

Social movement success and unity thus facilitated the formation of a pact between leftist parties and the repression-sponsoring elite, via the mechanism of an electoral coalition supporting a candidate for local or departmental office. Such a pact lowered repressive violence considerably. Unity, especially tactical unity, then allowed the pact to continue unsabotaged by other leftist sectors. That such a similar pact was negotiated in Arauca during a period (1989–92) when the Patriotic Union often ran in coalition with elite sectors makes it seem likely that the tactic was an innovation added to the repertoire of the electoral Left and its associated social movements. Such a repertoire had not been available earlier. Local and departmental elections and the ensuing local and regional autonomy, made possible only by decentralizing reform, provided the central incentive for the pact as well as the mechanism through which the pact was carried out.

But as Tilly also argues, as political opportunities shift, old repertoires that have become unsuccessful die out. Once selective recentralization, paramilitary violence, and the end of the peace process with the FARC severely weakened the electoral Left and/or prevented leftist electoral officials from carrying out their mandate, the "pacted peace" repertoire had to be shelved, and the search for the next innovation came soon after.[65] In every region social movements began to seek national and international allies to help them pressure the national government for less punitive political and military policies.

The Postreform Period

The literature on transnational advocacy networks (TANs) has expanded exponentially in recent years.[66] Its very newness, however, has meant that much of the work consists of inspiring success stories from which the shared ingredients of success are derived. As Tarrow notes, there has been much more "lumping than splitting": critical disaggregation is now needed.[67] A central argument, addressed largely to northern TANs and their sympathizers, is that transnational support can be crucial for southern movement success, if care is taken to avoid pitfalls.[68] Because few examine what might make one southern movement more attractive to support than another, or systematically compare successful and failed attempts to attract TAN solidarity, I derived arguments indirectly from the existing literature or directly from my own case studies.

Several factors might facilitate solidarity. First, social movements must survive the initial repressive wave and have sufficient strength to garner outside support. Dead activists and decimated southern social movements cannot recruit allies. This seemingly obvious point goes largely unaddressed in the current literature. Seeking allies requires significant initiative, discussion, adjustment of demands and discourse, and planning, as well as investment of time and money for organizing and attending conferences, hosting visiting delegations, traveling to the capital to connect with NGOs and activists from other regions, setting up Web sites and establishing e-mail access for leaders, and so forth. Likewise, TANs are not attracted to lost causes when so many winnable causes compete for their attention.

Second, given equal strength and viability, movements that articulate values shared by transnational publics will be more likely to gain the support of northern constituencies. Many analyses of recent transnational social movement activism agree that it is distinguished from former waves in its emphasis on the "soft power" of values or ideological propositions shared by the TANs and the southern movements.[69] In practice, of those issues relevant to my cases, this has meant that human rights and peace issues have received by far the most international solidarity action, with environmental issues close behind, then ethnic self-determination and "development."[70]

In general terms, movements whose demands can be framed in terms of "right and wrong" and whose grievances can be attributed to the actions of an identifiable actor (e.g., specific military units) are much more likely to gain international allies than ones based solely on material concerns.[71] Responding to this new requirement, workers from the Global South who have successfully mobilized transnational labor solidarity reframed their material demands (e.g., for higher wages) as demands for basic rights, a fulfillment of the social contract, and democratic governance.[72] But, Keck and Sikkink admit, the grievances of some movements are "irremediably structural" (e.g., the demand for land reform), and these movements "will have difficulty reframing their demands in a way that resonates with transnational publics."[73]

Environmental demands and often closely related indigenous people's demands also facilitate international solidarity. Framing his movement as "green"—that is, promoting the preservation of their rainforest environment—was crucial to the success of Chico Mendes's Brazilian rubber tappers in garnering international support for his cause and winning their demands.[74] In Latin America international solidarity for indigenous groups has frequently been tied to such environmental concerns, as it is assumed that indigenous groups are better custodians of the environment than are nonindigenous peasants. Such solidarity can be celebrated for leading to important and groundbreaking victories for people suffering multiple forms of oppression, even if it is not necessarily true that indigenous people are "greener" or if such an expectation is always in their interest.[75]

Regardless, it is clear that, other things being equal, an indigenous struggle is more likely to elicit international support than a peasant one at this moment in time.[76]

Third, a movement's ability to gain international allies may be shaped not just by the content of its message, but by the messenger. A social movement actor in search of international alliances must be "capable of transmitting the message,"[77] but, as Olesen puts it, "generating transnational resonance is no easy task." Beyond technological resources, this usually requires a media-savvy and cosmopolitan leadership, capable of understanding the way publics of the global North might think, and this is usually associated with individuals with a high educational level, such as Comandante Marcos.[78] I would add that universally recognized credentials—professional, clerical, and university degrees—might also make the actor more credible to transnational audiences regardless of how talented a "framer" he or she might be. Clergy, by belonging to international churches, are in addition already part of a transnational network.

Another clear bias in post–Cold War transnational advocacy favors pacifist groups over armed groups. Amnesty International, for example, will not adopt as a "prisoner of conscience" any person who has advocated violence,[79] and several religious (e.g., Quaker, Mennonite) and most peace groups are also explicitly pacifist. Cognizant of this fact, although his rubber tappers' movement was victim to increasing death squad attacks, Chico Mendes urged his movement to remain nonviolent so as to retain the moral high ground, and his decision fed a groundswell of international support.[80] While the outpouring of international support for the Zapatista uprising may appear to violate this rule, the group's guns have played a mostly symbolic role since 1994; the group is now known for its rhetorical rather than military prowess.[81]

Related to this point, since armed groups generally have a clear hierarchical structure, is the preference for supporting movements that exemplify "new left" forms of participatory democracy, which Evans calls one of the "political foundations of counter-hegemonic globalization."[82] The Zapatistas, on identifying "global civil society" as their most important ally, quickly shifted from armed struggle to social and political transformation.[83] Specifically, they adopted a "master frame" of democratic participation through dignity, diversity, flexibility, and dialogue. For Olesen, this concept of radical democracy is key to explaining the Zapatistas' appeal to activists from the global North, who see visits to Chiapas not just as support missions but also as inspiring training workshops with which to acquire new tools to apply at home.[84]

Beyond movement strength, shared values, especially pacifism and distance from armed actors, and the ability to articulate such values, a fourth crucial factor facilitating transnational solidarity with movements of the global South is the vulnerability of the target. Keck and Sikkink note that TANs are most useful, and most likely to be sought out, in situations in which the southern movement target is vulnerable to material incentives, pressure from outside actors, or accusations of contradictions between stated normative values and actions.[85] But what makes a target vulnerable?

Tesh's analysis of a peasant anti-canal expansion movement in today's Panama addresses the ways a domestic enemy can ironically be less vulnerable than an international one, hindering the development of a movement-TAN alliance.[86] While fighting such an expansion when the canal was U.S.-controlled would have been seen as an anti-imperialist act, it is now described by pro-expansion Panamanians as an assault on national economic progress (although the peasants see the expansion as economic folly). U.S. allies in such a context would only exacerbate such a perception of the movement and were thus not sought out by the movement. Similarly, U.S.-based TANs might be hesitant to support the movement, even if they were invited, for fear of being seen as imperialist.

Beyond the greater vulnerability of foreign targets, my cases showed clearly that military personnel were far more vulnerable to prosecution than paramilitary individuals, due to the greater ease of identifying and capturing them, as well as the state's greater accountability for their actions (and conversely the greater potential for military personnel's actions to tarnish the reputation of the Colombian government). Paramilitary forces were absolutely invulnerable until late in the demobilization process (after 2004). Furthermore, any situation that drew negative national or international attention to the region—whether this be extreme selective recentralization measures or acute regional humanitarian emergencies—not only created greater potential to embarrass the Colombian government, increasing its vulnerability, but also facilitated links between external publics and regional movements.

Although international support can be crucial to the success of some movements, there are some drawbacks to receiving it. Understanding these drawbacks—and avoiding the tendency to "exaggerate the virtues and power" of existing transnational groups and networks—is an "essential first step toward real understanding of their potential power."[87] One such pitfall is internal stratification of the movement, which may arise when the premium placed on articulating issues in a way that "resonates transnationally" makes the most cosmopolitan and educated members rise to the top of the movement's internal hierarchy.[88] Conversely, other movements, either due to the low educational level of their leaders or the real constraints on the framing of their demands, will simply not be able to garner international support.

Other pitfalls derive from the fundamental asymmetry of power between the many movements of the global South seeking international support and the TANs of the global North that decide which few will actually receive it. First, the bias toward movements that combine several attractive features, such as shared values, identifiable enemies, and winnable campaigns, could mean that a movement suddenly loses international support when conditions shift. Such fickleness was experienced by the Zapatistas, who found international support waned between 2001 and 2003 without constant "flashpoints" of repressive violence to denounce.[89]

Second, the touted "diffusion of discourse" via transnational social movement links may be consensual, but it is not symmetrical. As Thayer noted in her study of Brazilian women's organizations' use of the U.S. feminist book *Our Bodies, Ourselves,* discursive "flows from North to South [occur] far more easily than in the reverse direction."[90] Leaders of southern movements may consequently be tempted to stretch the truth in their efforts to "market" their movement's struggles transnationally or nationally. For example, the Pataxó indigenous group in Brazil, which had never traditionally worn feathered headdresses, suddenly adopted the practice to appear more "Indian" to win a land claim. Such "staged authenticity" can backfire later when international supporters feel betrayed by the deception or if the social movement's base feels the image (and framing) projected by leaders undermines their dignity and that of the cause.[91]

Third, when the international aid is material and substantial, struggles over its distribution can cause or exacerbate internal divisions. Responding to a situation that was moving in this direction, the Zapatistas in 2003 established new rules to impose greater movement control over the ways international aid was spent in their communities.[92]

How did these patterns play out in the various social movements studied? I address these in ascending order of success. Despite its strength and exceptional success during the reform period, the Patriotic Union in Apartadó was caught unprepared and was decimated by the early, overwhelming repressive wave. Those who survived were exiled from the region and dispersed. Only the peasant settlers of San José de Apartadó, which was not hit as hard by the paramilitary bloodbath because of its mountainous location and stronger guerrilla presence, managed to survive and maintain their organization long enough to create effective international connections.

The peasant movement of Cartagena del Chairá fared just slightly better. Although they benefited from a very late (2004) and public repressive wave that allowed them to learn from other movements and ally with a stronger urban human rights movement, the peasant movement had atrophied after years of all-out war and then exclusion of the county from the demilitarized zone. And although U.S. funding and political pressure were key to the 2004–5 Plan Patriota assault on the region—and probably crucial to the movement's success in finding at least Colombian supporters—there were neither U.S. corporations nor U.S. personnel in the zone to attract international press coverage. The movement focused on egregious human rights violations but otherwise faced numerous additional symbolic obstacles to garnering international support: the region's peasants did not condemn the FARC and in some cases appeared sympathetic (that relatively few FARC abuses had occurred in the Caguán can help explain the social movement's lack of explicit distancing); it did not openly distance itself from the region's coca economy; and its leaders were peasants, not intellectuals. If the movement felt any temptation to alter its discourse to gain outside support, it clearly resisted such pressure in order to remain faithful to local conditions. But as a result, only in 2008, when Cartagena del Chairá became one of the nation's leading sources of internal refugees, did international agencies make their first postreform period appearance in the town. Beyond some sympathetic press stories, the movement has won no concrete successes.

The Esperanza-led Sintrainagro labor movement, as a Right-allied union, does not entirely fit the mold described in this section. However, it did seek outside allies—at first exclusively rightist ones (paramilitary, military, and plantation owners) and then more oppositional ones (the national labor federation) as the political context became more hostile. In seeking out these varied allies, it articulated shared values: the struggle against the FARC, on the one hand, and the struggle against banana plantation owners and for wage justice, on the other. Its struggle in the latter phase was hindered by the invulnerability of the Colombian banana plantation owners, considered heroes of national development in Colombia.

The U'wa struggle against oil extraction benefited not only from Arauca's late repressive wave but also from the timing of its initial confrontation with Occidental, which coincided with a wave of indigenous party electoral success of the late 1990s. It encapsulated several "pro-transnational solidarity" features: the U'was were a very spiritual and traditional indigenous tribe with clearly environmental demands, and they were facing a very visible, easy to vilify, and thus vulnerable target, Occidental Petroleum, which at that time had a very susceptible shareholder in the 2000 presidential candidate, Al Gore. Massive U.S.-based protests erupted, mostly bent on shaming Occidental. But once Occidental abandoned the site and Ecopetrol moved in, international solidarity with the antiexploration movement nearly evaporated, and the movement had to quickly shift tactics and alliances, illustrating the potential instability of transnational alliances.

Chocaguán, the Italian priest's crop substitution and community development project in the Lower Caguán, was not a social movement strictly speaking but nonetheless demonstrated many of the same principles that apply to transnational solidarity. It benefited from a solid institutional base: the priest had begun the project in the 1980s, and his salary derived from the church. Furthermore, the project benefited from a credible, cosmopolitan, and charismatic interlocutor who already belonged to a transnational network (the Catholic Church); a clear distancing from both the coca economy and all violent actors in the region; a "green" element in that cacao, which was being grown organically, was a sustainable crop native to the rainforest; and an unthreatening and politically neutral "development for peace" rhetoric, in contrast to the competing antigovernment peasant movement of the Caguán. It had received steadily increasing funding from church and other international sources since the early 1990s, the project had expanded, and the priest won the Colombian Peace Prize in 2004. However, the advantage of the priest's continuous centrality to the project and credibility vis-à-vis transnational publics became a liability in 2008, when he returned to Italy for health reasons, leaving the project to an uncertain future. Furthermore, his departure from the zone is likely to both decrease donations and stimulate struggles over the allocation of those that continue.

The San José de Apartadó Peace Community consisted of only about 1,400 people, but it was built on the strong foundation of the UP-influenced Urabá peasant settler movement. Although the peasants of San José, like the UP in flatland Urabá, were hit by the repressive wave, most of the deaths occurred after the 1995–97 wave, giving the community time to transition to a new strategy. The community's post-1997 steadfast radical neutrality against both guerrillas and paramilitary forces and the prominence of a priest in its leadership has won it international peace prizes and has provided an inspiring and powerful impetus for many pacifist international accompaniment missions, among them Fellowship of Reconciliation, a U.S.-based interfaith group promoting nonviolence, and Peace Brigades International. Although nearly two hundred community members have been killed and the movement has long faced invulnerable paramilitary leaders, with the support of U.S. Senator Leahy it has recently won success in the prosecution of the military perpetrators of a 2005 massacre: temporary decertification of U.S. military aid in 2005 and the prosecution of the military personnel implicated.

Also in Urabá, the changing political climate of the second Uribe administration, with much increased public pressure to prosecute paramilitary forces, facilitated other victories. Notably, however, the rules of vulnerable targets still apply: foreign corporations are much more likely to be prosecuted for paramilitary links than are Colombian ones. The Carepa local of the Coca-Cola union, which was decimated by the overwhelming paramilitary assault of 1994–96, has nonetheless benefited from the existence of an international network in solidarity with Colombian Coca-Cola workers. This allowed leaders of the Colombian Coca-Cola workers' union to file suit against Coca-Cola in the United States and also allowed one of the exiled union leaders from Carepa to go on a speaking tour in the United States. Similarly, although paramilitary leaders' confessions have made clear that all banana plantation owners supported the paramilitary forces, only Chiquita banana has been sued—in a U.S. court, by U.S. allies of Colombian human rights activists—and slapped with a multimillion-dollar fine.

Finally, the Araucan peasant movement was the most successful, in the postreform as well as the reform era. Starting from a position of strength in the early 1990s and benefiting from a late repressive wave (2001), the movement transitioned by the mid-1990s to a human rights–focused strategy. The Araucan movement further benefited from more visible and vulnerable targets: U.S. trainers in the region, Occidental Petroleum, overt and de jure recentralization that drew the attention of many transnational human rights advocacy groups, and, in 2008, the presence of international refugee agencies. Due to increasing guerrilla abuses against civilians in the region, the social movement had distanced itself from the insurgent organizations. However, as guerrilla violence against movement activists became more extreme after 2006, condemnation has become less overt. Exemplifying Keck and Sikkink's insight about articulating specific solvable problems, the movement devised separate campaigns to investigate and punish those responsible for the Santo Domingo bombing and the assassination of the three union leaders, as well as to free leader Luz Perly Córdoba. Each mobilized international support and succeeded. The Santo Domingo case was a textbook example of the "boomerang pattern": Araucan human rights activists alerted U.S.-based human rights TANs, which pressured U.S. senators, who succeeded in making the U.S. government withhold further military aid from the Colombian government until the massacre was fully investigated and the guilty officer removed from his post. The antiparamilitary sentiments of the second Uribe term even facilitated the rare prosecution of paramilitary forces for the assassination of two Araucan congressmen.

In summary, during the counterreform period, social movements were most likely to gain international allies, and thus prevail, when their previous success and a later repressive wave facilitated a more rapid transition to a human rights–focused strategy and a more concerted effort to build new alliances. Such allies were more attracted to movements, however, when these demonstrated distance from guerrillas or other shared values, were led by intellectuals, and faced a visible and vulnerable target. Pitfalls related to the overreliance of movements on certain intellectual leaders and the instability of transnational solidarity.

Sources of Elite Leverage

During the reform period social conflicts in all regions (with the partial exception of the Caguán's conflict, which was closely linked to the national government–FARC peace process) were truly local or regional. The movement's demands were presented to local or regional targets, who had the autonomy to decide how to respond, and the repressor was also locally based. The same national trends that worked in favor of the Left—local and regional elections, local and regional autonomy, the peace process—were seen by elites as serious threats.

Within this unusually autonomous, localized, and pro-social movement context of the reform period, what conditions made elites more likely to pursue repressive violence as an exit strategy, and, conversely, which made them more amenable to electoral alliances with the Left? Repression-sponsoring elites, those displaced from local political institutions, were most likely to peacefully share power with the Left when they were weakest relative to the Left, as Left-dominated coalitions with elites then became elites' last chance for retaining access to state resources. On the other hand, they were most likely to pursue repression as a strategy to regain access to state resources when they were strongest relative to social movements. Therefore, the ideal situation for a social movement is one where (1) the concession sponsor and the repression sponsor are not the same elite faction or state entity; (2) the concession sponsor is prosperous (if a private elite) or politically open and/or fiscally prosperous (if a state target); and (3) the repression-sponsoring elite is weak.

Who are the repressors during the reform period, and what are their motives? Four main positions emerge in response to this question. Paige, representing the position closest to orthodox Marxism, suggests that the main repressors of social movements are the movement's material antagonists: plantation owners repress labor movements, large landowners repress movements of landless peasants proposing land reform, and intermediaries repress smallholders.[93] Their primary motive is therefore the defense of their material interests. He emphasizes, however, that of these three types of agrarian elites, it is the landowners confronting landless peasants who are likely to generate the highest levels of repression due to the zero-sum nature of the conflict.

Romero, in contrast, argues that paramilitary violence exploded in the 1980s not because of increased land conflicts but precisely as a rural elite reaction to displacement from local political institutions via the peace process and decentralizing reforms.[94] He implies that their main motive is retaining political domination over certain *territories*. Fox concurs that elites faced with displacement from political institutions, that is, incumbent political elites, are major repressors but argues their main motive is to prevent change in state *policy*.[95] Bergquist also argues that elite political incumbents (as well as material antagonists of movements) are culprits in repressive backlash, but he emphasizes loss of access to state *resources* (state employment, control of police and judiciary), rather than policy, as their main fear.[96]

My cases during the reform period provide a clear refutation of the orthodox Marxist explanation of repression and confirm the hypotheses suggested by Romero, Fox, and Bergquist. If there were several well-established elite sectors in a region, the elite sector that formerly controlled state institutions—which was often *not* the material antagonist of the social movement—was the main sponsor of repression, with control over state resources (and to a lesser extent policy) a main object. In Arauca the displaced cattle-ranching LaTorrista Liberals, with whom the Araucan peasant settler movement had no direct *material* conflict (although they struggled over departmental expenditures), sponsored Arauca's first paramilitary group. Bergquist's point that elites that control local state institutions also control (de facto if not de jure) local judiciary, police, and army institutions is also borne out by the evidence (e.g., the LaTorristas' and bananeros' close relationships with army and police commanders). Such connections to coercive state institutions help explain the mechanisms through which recently displaced elites initiate repressive efforts.

In Urabá, where the displaced elites (Guerrista Liberals) were also the concession-sponsoring banana plantation owners, the situation was less clear-cut, but some evidence still points to the predominance of the political motive (Fox and Bergquist) over the strictly material one (Paige).[97] In the late 1980s the UP-affiliated banana workers' union represented a minority of the union movement (most were affiliated with the Frente Popular), but the UP represented 75 percent of the electoral Left—and a far greater proportion of political assassinations against leftists after 1986. A strict defense of material interests would have mandated that most political assassinations target the Frente Popular–affiliated union members.

The independent role of the military in repression is not directly addressed by Fox, Paige, or Bergquist, perhaps because none of these theorists drew conclusions from contexts with active armed insurgencies. Generally, as suggested by Romero's analysis of the rise of paramilitary groups in Urabá and the evidence from my other cases, the military played a supporting role in the regional repressive division of labor, enabling the privatized violence initiatives taken by the repression-sponsoring elite (e.g., Urabá).[98] This presented the advantage, to the military, of avoiding being caught red-handed engaged in human rights violations such as the killing of leaders of legally chartered unions. A high-ranking officer interviewed by Richani, for example, said regarding army collaboration with paramilitaries, "As long as they are fighting our enemy we have no interest in fighting them."[99]

However, in regions where the repression-sponsoring elite had no political base within the guerrilla-controlled areas (the Lower Caguán, Arauquita), repression-sponsoring elites from outside the region would encourage or pay the army to carry out repression. Beyond responding to local or regional elites, however, the army also responded to national directives (e.g., to retake the Caguán after the collapse of both peace processes), giving these conflicts a supraregional or national dynamic even during the reform period. Furthermore, the army had its own reasons for opposing leftist county executives and the social forces that elected them: to prevent any possibility of guerrillas benefiting materially or politically from county expenditures in guerrilla-controlled territories.

The main sponsor and initiator of repression, then, is the elite faction that has just been displaced from local political power. It is this faction's strength or weakness that must be determined to judge the regional social movement/elite balance of power. As Bergquist has argued, the main determinant of elite electoral strength—which is ultimately the source of its bargaining position relative to the social movement—is the economic prosperity of the undergirding economic sector.[100] Prosperity facilitated the elite's electoral success as it provided more private resources to be dispensed in a politically conditioned fashion, a system clearly illustrated by the prereform LaTorrista political machine. The rapid parallel decline in economic and electoral fortunes of LaTorrista Liberals in Arauca is a clear example of how these phenomena are linked, facilitating elite pacts with the Left. Conversely, the economic stability of banana plantation owners and Turbayista Liberals in Caquetá made it unnecessary for them to pursue a pacted agreement with the Left; they pursued repression instead. The evidence also verifies Bergquist's argument that changes in national policy can alter the regional balance of power. Counterreform and increased militarization strengthened elites in all three case study regions at the end of the reform period, and a national shift to an export-oriented development strategy boosted the standing of Urabá's banana plantation owners with the president.

During the reform period, displaced elites were for the most part abandoned by outside actors, left to repress or negotiate as they saw fit, with neither help nor interference from outside. In marked contrast, in the post-reform period the national government rolled back many of its pro–social movement policies, and elite rescuers from far and near appeared in conflictive zones in many different guises, invited or not. Local elites no longer needed pacts to survive for the most part; even if they desired to maintain the Left-elite pacts, as in Arauca, these were universally overridden by outsider elites in the counterreform period.

First, paramilitary groups became interregional and then national. Starting in the regions closer to the Atlantic coast and working their way inland, paramilitary groups began to agglomerate and grow more aggressive in their ambitions after 1994. Their goal was to accumulate financially and geopolitically strategic territories from which to build political power, giving priority to territories with a critical mass of large landowners.[101] Whereas banana plantation owners and Urabá cattle ranchers in 1988 could call only on Muerte a Revolucionarios del Nordeste (Death to Revolutionaries of the Northeast), an Antioquia-based group, to carry out repression on their behalf, by 1994 they could count on the seminational ACCU and by 1997 on the national Autodefensas Unidas de Colombia.[102] And whereas the Gruciarar of the late 1980s was purely Araucan, the paramilitary forces that arrived in Arauca in 2001 were part of the national AUC and overrode the still-existing Left-elite pacts by killing their two main representatives.

Another postreform change was the much more overt and aggressive role in repression for previously untarnished concession-sponsoring elites. In the reform period it was only rumored that Occidental Petroleum had lobbied the Colombian government for greater levels of militarization in their respective regions. By the 1990s, however, Occidental—a concession-sponsoring elite in the sense that it underwrote the departmental budget—not only publicly lobbied the U.S. Congress for more military aid for Colombia and specifically new bases and U.S. trainers for Arauca but also directed its personnel to aid the army's counterinsurgency missions. This finding shows that in this more "normal" context of counterreform, material interests do indeed motivate repressors, as would follow from a Marxist argument.[103]

In the postreform era and in the context of rapidly expanding paramilitary forces, the military appeared to refine a division of labor with paramilitary groups: paramilitary groups focused on the north of Colombia while the military focused on the south. But perhaps the most noteworthy contrast between the military's role during the two eras was the greatly increased proportion of the military budget that came from U.S. military aid after 2000. This increased the military budget, troop numbers, and level of activity, but it also meant the military, and the Colombian government as a whole, was more subject to the will of the United States. This came to bear in the regionalization of aid: new bases were built in Arauca, and Plan Patriota sent troops into the southern coca-growing zones to eradicate the crop. In short, the postreform moment was overwhelmingly a positive shift for elites, who were able to establish connections with different types of wealthy and armed allies from outside the region and the country.

PROSPECTS FOR SOCIAL MOVEMENTS IN WAR ZONES: GAINS, LOSSES, AND NEW STRATEGIES

As the three case studies have demonstrated, even the most successful pacted regional peace with social movement gains is unsustainable in the context of violent democratization and less so in the context of counterreform. First, even while the reform period lasts, if the peace depends on the economic decline of repression-sponsoring elites it will inevitably be ephemeral. Eventually, the economic decline of a key elite group in a region will tend to weaken the entire region economically, affecting the Left's ability to extract concessions via social movement mobilization and thus its bargaining power. Or an elite sector that declines permanently will be replaced with a new economic activity, with its own set of elites. The Left's pacted peace with the now nonexistent elite sector would thus become irrelevant.

Beyond the vagaries of boom-and-bust cycles, however, there are additional drawbacks to a peace agreement pacted informally at the regional level. Even when the local political economy, the Left, and repression-sponsoring elites continue to favor a regional pact, the pact may be actively sabotaged by regional actors that previously played a secondary role in repressive efforts, such as Occidental in Arauca in the early 1990s. Finally, a regionally based, conjunctural and informal pacted peace, that is, one that emerges from a fortuitous and temporary confluence of political circumstances, depends on the tolerance or support of the national government and can take place only while the democratization measures that benefited the Left are still in effect. The dependence of the pacted peace on the national political context was also central in Cartagena del Chairá during the reform period.

Ultimately, then, a regional pacted peace cannot coexist with counterreform. Regional peace pacts such as the ones described in this study during the reform period will thus tend to be both exceptional and temporary, depending on an unusual political moment and the unusual confluence of economic factors needed to ensure an overwhelmingly pro–social movement regional balance of power.

With counterreform and the paramilitary backlash in the 1990s, much of the gains of the late 1980s and early 1990s seemed to have been violently swept away forever. In Urabá hundreds were killed by paramilitary forces, accused of being guerrilla sympathizers, and the Left (not including Esperanza) lost all electoral influence within the space of a few years. In the Caguán, where the peasant movement had already been weakened by the early 1990s, the exclusion of Cartagena del Chairá from the demilitarized zone during the Pastrana government further demoralized the remaining peasant activists, and Plan Patriota drove many from the region. Even in stalwart Arauca, continuous legal, political, and military/paramilitary attacks on the leaders of the two alliances chipped away at the remnants of the Left-elite alliances until they finally ceased to exist.

Which gains, if any, remain from the earlier period, and what lessons can be learned? The achievements made by the social movements, leftist parties, and county executives during the reform period were nothing less than remarkable, and they stand as a testament to what can be done when the moment is right. Despite the very real obstacles of violent repression, meager fiscal resources, and the ineffectiveness of formal state mediation mechanisms, social movements and leftist parties in these regions made remarkable gains, many of which far outlasted the brief window of opportunity in which they were won. Surely, then, their experience could be instructive for both analysts and activists aiming to understand how social movements might make the most of the mixed blessings of violent de-mocratization.

Future activists may want to emulate the way social movement activists in all three regions took full advantage of an unusual conjuncture to rapidly declandestinize and make tremendous gains, many of them permanent. The Caguán settlers won the cancellation of the wildlife reserve; the Araucan settlers won important transportation and education infrastructure; in Urabá, many bread-and-butter labor gains were made that hold to this day, and erstwhile urban squatters continue to have the public services first won under leftist administrations.

Leftist parties also made the most of the brief window of opportunity. With meager campaign resources, faced by relentless and lethal repression that sometimes forced them to replace their candidates in the middle of campaigns, and with no previous experience in running candidates for this office, leftist parties nonetheless successfully organized county executive campaigns. These examples reveal a savvy recognition on the part of leftist electoral forces of the unusual possibilities for change that existed at that precise moment in time, as well as an extraordinary and altruistic commitment to their constituencies.

On taking office, the leftist county executives carried out actions that left traces far beyond their brief time in office: the public works legacy, the legalization of squatters' neighborhoods and rural landholdings, labor gains won through mediation, and some international connections that bore fruit later on. Finally, there is the new model of informal diplomacy itself, as manifested in the pacted peace agreements, and the administrative and political experience gained by the parties, which will be of use when the next window of opportunity arises.

In fact, the opening may not be so far away. Although the moment is no longer right for social movement material gains, electoral gains, or Left-elite electoral coalitions in the war zones, in many ways the political moment on the national and international levels is favoring social movements and the Left in the case study regions more than in many years. Left-leaning Latin American governments have left Uribe isolated on the national level and have provided the Colombian Left with paths to follow, while the Democrat-dominated U.S. Congress is pressuring President Uribe for progress on human rights cases and reducing military aid. The Polo Democrático Alternativo has decided to apply crucial lessons from the experience of the 1980s and 1990s, both the successes and the failures. To avoid a replication of the mass assassinations against the leftist electoral experiments of the reform period, the Polo has expressed greater distance from the armed insurgencies without playing into the hands of Uribe. To avoid being co-opted by traditional parties, up to now it has maintained a certain distance from these as well. As a result, the Polo is now a critical mass in the Colombian Congress. There it is keeping the heat on Uribe and his political allies for their links to paramilitary forces, among other things. The Polo's gamble has succeeded so far: it has won important posts, such as the mayor of Bogotá, helping to build the urban Left into a stronger ally for the regional social movements of the war zones—if it can maintain its fragile unity.

Meanwhile, nearly twenty years after the passage of the Constitutional Assembly and its new measures for defending human rights, Colombian NGOs have become expert at using the new resources as well as old ones such as the Colombian Supreme Court. Similarly, after two decades of focusing on human rights demands, regional social movements have forged solid links with national NGOs. Through these, they ally with international NGOs as well, combining forces to pressure the Colombian judiciary to live up to its promise. A new type of expertise and experience is beginning to accumulate, and each human rights victory, each prosecution of the assassin of a "red zone" social movement activist, each judicial decision to make the state pay indemnization for wrongful death of a peasant at the hands of the military, chips away at the "composite state" that has prevented social movement incorporation in the war zones. Slowly, as small steps are being made to bring the laws of the center even to the red zones, the peasant and labor movements of the war zones are acquiring the rights of citizenship.

N O T E S

One. Introduction

1. I will focus especially on the reforms allowing the direct election and increased fiscal autonomy of county executives *(alcaldes)* and governors, as well as the peace process with guerrilla groups, and other reforms meant to weaken clientelist practices and increase the ability of civilians to rein in abuses of the state.

2. In my cases, usually this consisted of elite-backed paramilitary violence against social movement and Leftist political party activists.

3. This consisted of ad hoc, temporary, or region-specific suspensions of the Constitution of 1991 for the purposes of facilitating counterinsurgency, as well as an end to material gains for war zone peasant movements, a hardening of the government position vis-à-vis guerrilla groups, and escalating military attacks on guerrillas.

4. Movements of unarmed peasant, labor, and urban movements calling for material gains, political representation, or human rights demands.

5. Throughout this study, I have translated *alcalde* as "county executive" rather than "mayor," as the latter term connotes urban contexts while the fomer connotes rural settings.

6. Skocpol, "Bringing the State Back In."

7. The exception might be the apparent ability of the Colombian state to manage the economy effectively. This derives in part from the Colombian state's autonomy with respect to foreign capital, which has implied successful extraction of resources from foreign investments. However, it might also be argued that the Colombian state has *delegated* a great part of this economic management function to competent industrial organizations such as the Colombian Federation of Coffee Growers and the National Association of Industrialists, and has then refrained from interfering with these organizations' parallel-state activities and initiatives.

8. Migdal, *Strong Societies and Weak States.*

9. Leal and Dávila, *Clientelismo*; Romero, *Paramilitares y autodefensas.*

10. Richani, *Systems of Violence,* 69.

11. Hartlyn, "Colombia: The Politics of Violence and Accommodation."

12. Zamosc, "Peasant Struggles of the 1970s in Colombia," 106–7; Bergquist, *Labor in Latin America,* 290–93.

13. Hartlyn, *The Politics of Coalition Rule in Colombia.*

14. Hartlyn, *The Politics of Coalition Rule in Colombia,* 16–30.

15. Hartlyn, "Colombia: The Politics of Violence and Accommodation."

16. Collier and Collier, *Shaping the Political Arena,* 323, 289–313.

17. This phenomenon was especially prevalent in Urabá, the banana-growing region on Colombia's border with Panamá settled after the 1950s (see Uribe de Hincapié, *Urabá: ¿Región o territorio?* Botero Herrera, *Urabá: Colonización, violencia y crisis del estado*; and Martin, "Desarrollo económico, sindicalismo, y proceso de paz en Urabá"), but it occurred in San Alberto (Cesar) and other unionized rural labor movements as well.

18. Collier and Collier, *Shaping the Political Arena,* 323, 289–313.

19. LeGrand, *Frontier Expansion and Peasant Protest in Colombia,* 164.

20. LeGrand, *Frontier Expansion and Peasant Protest in Colombia,* 169; Richani, *Systems of Violence.* On the movements of the 1930s, see LeGrand, *Frontier Expansion and Peasant Protest in Colombia*; and Marulanda, *Colonización y conflicto.* Zamosc, *The Agrarian Question and the Peasant Movement in Colombia,* gives a comprehensive account of the peasant movements of the 1970s; and Alain de Janvry's influential analysis in *The Agrarian Question and Reformism in Latin America* places the Colombian land reform during this era in comparative Latin American perspective. Richani, *Systems of Violence,* offers a pessimistic assessment of the trends toward rapid concentration of land tenure in the 1980s and 1990s.

21. Zamosc, "Peasant Struggles of the 1970s in Colombia."

22. Unless otherwise noted, qualitative historical details about each guerrilla group are from Pizarro, "Revolutionary Guerrilla Groups in Colombia." Numerical estimates of the numbers of fighters as of the early 1980s are derived from a government brochure (Ministerio de Gobierno de Colombia, *Política de paz del Presidente Betancur*) in possession of Marc Chernick, who kindly shared the figures with me.

23. Peñate, "Arauca: Politics and Oil in a Colombian Province," 50–81.

24. Molano, "Violence and Land Colonization."

25. Pizarro, "Revolutionary Guerrilla Groups in Colombia"; Molano, "Violence and Land Colonization."

26. Pizarro, "Revolutionary Guerrilla Groups in Colombia."

27. Zamosc, *The Agrarian Question and the Peasant Movement in Colombia,* 113–21.

28. Pizarro, "Revolutionary Guerrilla Groups in Colombia"; Chernick and Jiménez, "Popular Liberalism, Radical Democracy, and Marxism."

29. Pizarro, "Revolutionary Guerrilla Groups in Colombia."

30. Chernick, "Negotiating Peace amid Multiple Forms of Violence."

31. CIJP, "1981–1994: Trece años en búsqueda de paz," 7–23.

32. Arizala, "Las experiencias alternativas de tipo partidistas, independientes del bipartidismo."

33. Pizarro, "Revolutionary Guerrilla Groups in Colombia."

34. CIJP, "1981–1994: Trece años en búsqueda de paz"; Hartlyn, "Colombia: The Politics of Violence and Accommodation"; Chernick, "Negotiating Peace amid Multiple Forms of Violence."

35. Richani, *Systems of Violence,* 34.

36. Romero, *Paramilitares y autodefensas.*

37. Jaramillo, Mora, and Cubides, *Colonización, coca y guerrilla.*

38. Richani, *Systems of Violence,* 59–91.

39. Ministerio de Gobierno de Colombia, *Política de paz del Presidente Betancur;* Arnson, "Summary of Conference Presentation by Alberto Chueca Mora," 4, citing Ministry of Defense figures.

40. Chernick, "Negotiating Peace amid Multiple Forms of Violence."

41. Chernick, "Negotiating Peace amid Multiple Forms of Violence"; Hartlyn, "Colombia: The Politics of Violence and Accommodation."

42. Willis, Garman, and Haggard, "The Politics of Decentralization in Latin America."

43. Carroll, "Backlash against Peasant Gains in Rural Democratization."

44. Chernick and Jiménez, "Popular Liberalism, Radical Democracy, and Marxism"; Romero, *Paramilitares y autodefensas.*

45. In 1980 the estimated number of extrajudicial executions of civilians for political or presumably political reasons (not including drug-related violence) was ninety-two; by 1989 the number had been multiplied by twenty (CAJSC, *Detrás del terrorismo y la guerra al narcotráfico*).

46. Americas Watch, *The Drug War in Colombia,* 32–41.

47. Human Rights Watch, *State of War,* 8, citing Defensoría del Pueblo, *Estudio de caso de homicidio de miembros de la Unión Patriótica y Esperanza, Paz y Libertad* (Santafé de Bogotá: Informe para el Congreso, el Gobierno, y el Procurador General de la Nación, 1992), 1–172.

48. Pécaut, "Guerrillas and Violence," 234–36.

49. In 1994 another very small group, a dissident group within the ELN called Corriente de Renovación Socialista, also demobilized. CIJP, "1981–1994: Trece años en búsqueda de paz," 1–23.

50. CIJP, "1981–1994: Trece años en búsqueda de paz"; Chernick and Jiménez, "Popular Liberalism, Radical Democracy, and Marxism," 75; Presidencia de la República, *Constitución Política de Colombia.*

51. On demobilization, see CIJP, "1981–1994: Trece años en búsqueda de paz," 16–19; for estimates of "guerrilla manpower," see Arnson, "Summary of Conference Presentation by Alberto Chueca Mora," 5; for figures on guerrilla-army combat, see Consejería de la Paz (president's ad hoc task force on peace), a database on armed confrontations between the guerrillas and the army for the period 1985–91 that was developed and given to me by Alejandro Reyes Posada of the National University of Colombia. For 1992–95 figures on combat, see *Justicia y Paz* 5–8 (1992–95), statistical appendix for each year. For information on the December 1990 bombing of the FARC headquarters, see CIJP, "1981–1994: Trece años en búsqueda de paz."

52. Human Rights Watch, *State of War,* 3–7.

53. Zuluaga Nieto, "De guerrillas a movimientos políticos," 40–42.

54. Human Rights Watch, *State of War,* 3–7; García, "Guerra y paz con la guerrilla"; *Justicia y Paz* 7, no. 4 (1994): 139.

55. CIJP, "1981–1994: Trece años en búsqueda de paz," 20–21; Human Rights Watch, *State of War,* 20–24.

56. Human Rights Watch, *State of War,* 18–21.

57. Ocampo, "Reforma del estado y desarrollo económico y social en Colombia"; Misas Arango, "Apertura económica y apertura política: Dos escenarios no siempre coincidentes"; Aguilar Z., "Sustitución de importaciones y apertura económica."

58. Brooke, "Despite Violence, Colombia Surges."

59. Vincent, "Liberal Candidate Leads in Colombia Election."

60. Chernick, "Negotiating Peace amid Multiple Forms of Violence," 183–85.

61. Arnson, "Summary of Conference Presentation by Alberto Chueca Mora," 9.

62. Human Rights Watch, *State of War.*

63. Romero, *Paramilitares y autodefensas,* 101–2, 92.

64. One hectare is equivalent to 2.2 acres.

65. Arnson, "Summary of Conference Presentation by Alberto Chueca Mora," 4.

66. Richani, *Systems of Violence,* 130.

67. Priest, "U.S. May Boost Military Aid to Colombia's Anti-Drug Effort."

68. Pizarro, "Las terceras fuerzas en Colombia hoy."

69. Amnesty International, *Colombia: Un laboratorio de guerra,* 33–36.

70. Pizarro, "Las terceras fuerzas en Colombia hoy."

71. Van Cott, *From Movements to Parties in Latin America,* 177–211.

72. "Upsurge in Violence Leads to State of Emergency"; Collier, "Drug War in the Jungle."

73. Romero, *Paramilitares y autodefensas,* 101, 92.

74. Arnson, "Summary of Conference Presentation by Alberto Chueca Mora," 4–5; Observatorio de Drogas de Colombia, "Cultivos ilícitos en Colombia, 1989–2004."

75. "El otro despeje"; "Peace Recedes."

76. Richani, *Systems of Violence,* 45.

77. Bagley, "Drug Trafficking, Political Violence, and U.S. Policy in Colombia under the Clinton Administration," 38–44. Five-year projected total aid from Collier, "Drug War in the Jungle."

78. "Upsurge in Violence Leads to State of Emergency."

79. Romero, *Paramilitares y autodefensas,* 193–222; "Upsurge in Violence Leads to State of Emergency."

80. In the ZRCs, for example, searches, wiretaps, and "preventive arrests" could be carried out without warrants. LAWGEF, "The Wrong Road"; "Weekly Assesses Performances of Colombia's Ministries in 2004."

81. HVCJ, *Informe de derechos humanos Arauca 2002,* 40–41, 53–55; Amnesty International, *Colombia: Un laboratorio de guerra,* 9–13; "E. U., tras la cabeza del comandante de la Fuerza Aérea Colombiana (FAC), general Héctor Fabio Velasco."

82. "Armed Conflict Enters Key Phase."

83. Allen, "Bush Stops in Colombia, Pledges Aid for War."

84. Allen, "Bush Stops in Colombia, Pledges Aid for War."

85. "U.S. Approves Troop Increase."

86. "William, dos años metido en las selvas del Patriota"; Forero, "Colombia's Coca Survives U.S. Plans to Uproot It"; Coronell, "El mapa del fracaso."

87. Results for 2006 presidential elections obtained from www.registraduria .gov.co. My conclusion that Uribe's combat efforts shifted away from southern coca-growing regions and toward Arauca during the period 2006–8 is derived from my analysis of the ElTiempo.com archive for these years, using the search parameters "Arauca" and "Cartagena del Chairá." For the shift toward infiltration and buying desertions, see "Interview: Ingrid Betancourt"; and "Cash Persuades Guerillas to Give Up."

88. Arnson, *Colombia's Peace Processes,* 1; Arnson, "Editor's Introduction," 1; Flamini, "Analysis: Tide Slowly Turning in Colombia."

89. Human Rights Watch, *Breaking the Grip?* 4.

90. For the decline in kidnappings: "Pass the Pact: U.S. Economic Woes Strengthen the Case for Free Trade in Colombia." For the decline in homicides and improved urban safety: Kushner, "The Truth about Plan Colombia."

91. ELN negotiation dates: "Colombian Government Announces New Talks with Rebels to Set Formal Peace Process Agenda"; "Colombian leader calls on

FARC, ELN rebels to choose path of peace." FARC numbers in 2000: Arnson, "Summary of Conference Presentation by Alberto Chueca Mora," 4–5; ELN numbers at their high point: PNUD-Colombia, "¿Cómo va el ELN?" citing Minister of Defense. Numbers for 2008 for both groups: Hanson, "Backgrounder— FARC, ELN: Colombia's Left-Wing Guerrillas."

92. Council on Hemispheric Affairs, "Colombia: The Betancourt Rescue and Beyond"; "Interview: Ingrid Betancourt."

93. Kushner, "The Truth about Plan Colombia." It is important to note, however, that those polled were generally urban and middle class.

94. Sources from across the political spectrum agree that impunity for human rights violators is widespread in Colombia and convictions extremely rare. See, e.g., U.S. Department of State, "Colombia: Country Reports on Human Rights Practices"; USLEAP, "Colombia Fact Sheet: Murders of Trade Unionists and Impunity under Uribe"; Human Rights Watch, "Colombia's Checkbook Impunity—A Briefing Paper"; Amnesty International, "Colombia," 93–95.

95. "La guerra de la tierra."

96. Kraul, "In Colombia, Paramilitary Groups Still Spreading Terror."

97. Human Rights Watch also expresses concern that the May 2008 extradition to the United States of almost all the most powerful paramilitary leaders before they had finished confessing has interrupted the process of uncovering the full extent of complicity. See Human Rights Watch, *Breaking the Grip?* 6–7, 82–84.

98. Human Rights Watch, *Breaking the Grip?* 44–45; "Scandals Undermined Support for Colombian President in 2008."

99. O'Neil and Chaskel, "Holding up Trade Deal Won't Solve Colombia's Woes"; "Colombian Leader Urges Mayors to Support Free Trade Deal."

100. "Scandals Undermined Support for Colombian President in 2008."

101. "Embajador de E. U. precisa alcances de veto a comandos de unidades militares."

102. Kushner, "The Truth about Plan Colombia"; Kraul, "Bush Pushes Trade Pact to Aid Colombia and His Legacy"; "Porque sí a las bases"; Arostegui, "US Bases Deepen Rift."

103. "Colombia Aislada."

104. "Muerto de la risa." In 2005 a first constitutional amendment allowed Uribe to run for reelection in 2006; Muse, "With Landslide Win, Colombia's Uribe Looks to 4 More Years Combating Violence, Boosting Economy."

105. LAWGEF, "The Wrong Road: Colombia's National Security Policy."

106. "Exterminio de UP, otro caso en le impunidad que empieza a moverse." Yezid Campos's *Memoria de los silenciados* presents documents from this court

case as well as moving testimonies from some of the survivors of this attack in both book and video (under the title *El baile rojo*) versions.

107. Arnson, "Colombia, el Congreso de los Estados Unidos, y el TLC," 1; "Colombia: A Hero at Home, a Villain Abroad."

108. Amnesty International, *Colombia: Un laboratorio de guerra,* 33–36.

109. Wilson and Carroll, "The Colombian Contradiction."

110. "La gran encuesta de la parapolítica."

111. "Fiscalía abre proceso de 'Farcopolítica.'"

112. DANE, *Colombia estadística, 1988.*

113. Registraduría Nacional del Estado Civil, *Estadísticas electorales 1990, marzo 11 de 1990.* In two other counties, however—Leiva (Nariño) and Yondó (Antioquia)—leftist county executives were elected in coalition with other forces (Carroll, "Backlash against Peasant Gains in Rural Democratization").

114. Registraduría Nacional del Estado Civil, *Estadísticas electorales 1990, marzo 11 de 1990.* As county council electoral results were not available for rural counties in 1990 and only elected county executive candidates were recorded and not the unsuccessful candidates, this was the best available measure of leftist electoral strength for this election. San Alberto's county executive appears as "Frente Popular" in this source because the M-19, which had demobilized only days before the election and did not yet have a *personería jurídica,* or charter, borrowed that of the other party, as was explained to me by my San Alberto interviewees (Carroll, "Violent Democratization").

115. CSV, *Pacificar la paz*; DANE, *Colombia estadística, 1989,* 2: 295–306.

116. LeGrand, *Frontier Expansion and Peasant Protest in Colombia*; Marulanda, *Colonización y conflicto*; Bergquist, *Labor in Latin America.*

117. Carroll, "Backlash against Peasant Gains in Rural Democratization."

118. County of Palestina, Huila, "Nuestro municipio"; Marulanda, *Colonización y conflicto,* 21–34.

119. Pizarro, "Revolutionary Guerrilla Groups in Colombia"; Molano, "Violence and Land Colonization."

120. Marulanda, *Colonización y conflicto,* 18.

121. Zamosc, *The Agrarian Question and the Peasant Movement in Colombia.*

122. Zamosc, "Peasant Struggles of the 1970s in Colombia."

123. LeGrand, "The Colombian Crisis in Historical Perspective," 4.

124. There are sixteen counties in this category. In Urabá/Alto Sinú Valley/ Atrato Valley are Valencia, Córdoba; Mutatá and Murindó, Antioquia; Riosucio, Bojayá, and Acandí, Chocó. In the Middle Magdalena Valley/Norte de Santander are Yondó, Antioquia; San Pablo, Bolívar; Florián, Santander, and Tibú, Norte de Santander. In the piedmont of the eastern plains, from north to south, are Arauquita, Tame, and Saravena, Arauca; El Castillo and San Juan de Arama, Meta; and

Puerto Rico, Caquetá. See Marulanda, *Colonización y conflicto,* 28; Delgado, "Una baba espesa"; Municipio de Florián, Santander, "Datos generales" and "Hidrografía"; and Municipio de Valencia, Córdoba, "Económica," "Geográfica," and "Histórica." Further evidence for this categorization is drawn from fieldwork for this book, carried out in 1992–93; and fieldwork for my 1994–95 article, "Backlash against Peasant Gains in Rural Democratization," carried out in 1989, for which I visited Mutatá (adjacent to Murindó), Yondó, San Pablo, Mesetas, and Lejanías (contiguous to El Castillo) and conducted interviews regarding the settlement history of San Juan de Arama.

125. Election results, March 1988, 1990, and 1992: Registraduría Nacional del Estado Civil, *Estadísticas electorales 1988*; Registraduría Nacional del Estado Civil, *Estadísticas electorales 1990, marzo 11 de 1990*; Registraduría Nacional del Estado Civil, *Estadísticas electorales: Elecciones del 8 de marzo de 1992.*

126. The other six counties in this category are, from south to north, Leiva, Nariño (Municipio de Leiva, Nariño, Web site, and UNODC, "Coca Cultivation in the Andean Region," 10 (map of coca-growing regions); La Macarena, Vista Hermosa, Puerto Rico, Puerto Lleras, and Puerto Gaitán, Meta (UNODC, "Departamento de Meta: Cultivos ilícitos de coca, Censo 31 de diciembre de 2004"). For Vistahermosa, see also Carroll, "Backlash against Peasant Gains in Rural Democratization."

127. Collier and Collier, *Shaping the Political Arena.*

128. Delgado, *Política y movimiento obrero.*

129. For Urabá counties, see *Augura* 9, no. 3 (1983): 12. For Segovia, Remedios, and Sabana de Torres: Carroll, "Backlash against Peasant Gains in Rural Democratization"; and Municipio de Sabana de Torres Web site. For San Alberto: Carroll, "Violent Democratization," 282–406.

130. Paige, *Agrarian Revolution.*

131. Marulanda, *Colonización y conflicto,* 26–28.

132. Helmsing, *Firms, Farms, and the State in Colombia,* 250–251.

133. Zamosc, "Peasant Struggles of the 1970s in Colombia."

134. Carroll, "Backlash against Peasant Gains in Rural Democratization."

135. Zamosc, *The Agrarian Question and the Peasant Movement in Colombia*; Escobar, "Clientelism, Mobilization, and Citizenship," 351–432.

136. The definitive work on Puerto Boyacá's transformation is Medina Gallego, *Autodefensas, paramilitares y narcotráfico en Colombia.*

137. A similar bloodbath occurred in San Alberto (Cesar) shortly after I completed interviews there in the summer 1993. Though not presented in this book for reasons of space, this case is documented in Carroll, "A Window of Opportunity for the Left Despite Trade Liberalization"; and Carroll, "Violent Democratization," 282–406. The extreme danger my surviving interviewees still

face and considerations regarding human subjects prevent me from making my interview notes accessible to the public. I did not tape-record, also as a precaution for my interviewees' safety, as well as their comfort during the interview.

Two. Urabá in the Reform Period

1. In 1986 Medellín's population was 1,480,382; Bogota's population was 4,236,490. DANE, *Colombia estadística 1989,* vol. 2: *Municipal.*

2. Interviews 40, 47.

3. Location of banana plantations derived from a map given to me by Esperanza leaders. On plantain farmers: interviews 40, 47.

4. Interview 39. Voting results by precinct for 1990 and 1992 also demonstrate the contested nature of urban electoral politics. In Apartadó no party won more than 43 percent of the vote of the urban population in either year. Reformist Liberal factions drew over 90 percent of their votes from the urban population. Election results obtained from Registraduría Municipal del Estado Civil de Apartadó.

5. Interviews 38, 4.

6. Population statistics from DANE, *Colombia estadística 1989,* vol. 2: *Municipal,* 81–82.

7. On banana workers' residential patterns and squatters' organization office location: interview 39. On relative strength of Apartadó labor and on labor and Left party office locations: interviews 43, 44, 45. On peasant office location: interview 40. On Left electoral strength in the four banana axis counties: Registraduría Nacional del Estado Civil, *Estadísticas electorales 1988: Asambleas, Consejos Intendenciales, Consejos Comisariales, Concejos Municipales, Alcaldías* (March 13, 1988).

8. AUGURA participation: interview 44. Liberal political factions: interview 41 and county council results for 1986, 1988, 1990, and 1992 from Registraduría Municipal de Apartadó. On Carepa Liberal factions as a comparison: interviews 47, 48, 49, 51.

9. Botero Herrera, *Urabá,* 27–30; Uribe de Hincapié, *Urabá: ¿Región o territorio?* 215–16; Bejarano, "La violencia regional y sus protagonistas," 43–44.

10. Frutera de Sevilla wished to avoid direct landownership because only 15 percent of the consumer price of bananas went to the landowner, and the corporation's sugar plantations in Cuba had just been confiscated; "Gracias y desgracias de una región." On settler–plantation owner relations: Botero Herrera, *Urabá,* 76; and "Gracias y desgracias de una región." Production statistics: Botero Herrera, *Urabá,* 35–36; see also table 2.3.

11. Bejarano, "La violencia regional y sus protagonistas," 44; Botero Herrera, *Urabá*, 81.

12. Botero Herrera and Sierra Botero, *El mercado de fuerza de trabajo en la zona bananera de Urabá*, 106; García, *Urabá*, 25–27.

13. Ramírez G., "Consolidación de la actividad bananera de Urabá," 77. See table 2.3 for sources.

14. Paige, *Agrarian Revolution*.

15. Estimate in interview 45, from a board member of the largest banana workers' union, Sintrainagro; "Gracias y desgracias de una región."

16. Originally, the full title of the organization was Asociación de Ganaderos y Agricultores de Urabá (Association of Cattle Ranchers and Farmers of Urabá), but by 1966, given the rapid expansion of the banana sector and its increased importance relative to other sectors in the region, the association reformed its statutes to become Asociación de Bananeros y Agricultores de Urabá (Association of Banana Producers and Farmers). See Alvarez de Gil, "Historias de Urabá y AUGURA en su contexto," 35–38.

17. Alvarez de Gil, "Historias de Urabá y AUGURA en su contexto," 80–85.

18. Henríquez Gallo, "El papel de las empresas nacionales en la comercialización del banano y el caso colombiano," 81.

19. Ramírez G., "Consolidación de la actividad bananera de Urabá," 91.

20. Standard Fruit continued to carry out the final stage of marketing for Proban. Ramírez G., "Consolidación de la actividad bananera de Urabá," 91; Botero Herrera, *Urabá*, 100–103; Henríquez Gallo, "El papel de las empresas nacionales en la comercialización del banano y el caso colombiano," 81–85.

21. Botero Herrera, *Urabá*, 88–89.

22. Alvarez de Gil, "Historias de Urabá y AUGURA en su contexto," 35–39; Henríquez Gallo, "El papel de las empresas nacionales en la comercialización del banano y el caso colombiano," 81; Ramírez G., "Consolidación de la actividad bananera de Urabá," 91. Electoral results for March 1982 and March 1984: Registraduría Nacional del Estado Civil, *Estadísticas electorales, Marzo 1982*; Registraduría Nacional del Estado Civil, *Estadísticas electorales: Asambleas Departamentales, Consejos Intendenciales, Consejos Comisariales, Concejos Municipales, marzo 11 de 1984*.

23. Alvarez de Gil, "Historias de Urabá y AUGURA en su contexto," 35–39; Henríquez Gallo, "El papel de las empresas nacionales en la comercialización del banano y el caso colombiano," 81; Ramírez G., "Consolidación de la actividad bananera de Urabá," 91.

24. Santamaría and Luján, *Proceso político en Colombia*, 55.

25. Santamaría and Luján, *Proceso político en Colombia*, 56–57.

26. Botero Herrera, *Urabá,* 161–62.

27. Botero Herrera, *Urabá,* 161–62.

28. Botero Herrera, *Urabá,* 163.

29. "Gracias y desgracias de una región"; Botero Herrera, *Urabá,* 164; CAJSC, *Urabá,* 68.

30. Pécaut, *Política y sindicalismo en Colombia,* 96–97; "Renace, Ciénaga, renace," 24; Botero Herrera, *Urabá,* 164; Uribe de Hincapié, *Urabá: ¿Región o territorio?* 197.

31. Martin, "Desarrollo ecónomico," cited in Botero Herrera, *Urabá,* 163.

32. Martin, "Desarrollo ecónomico," cited in Botero Herrera, *Urabá,* 163.

33. Above examples from Martin, "Desarrollo ecónomico," cited in Botero Herrera, *Urabá,* 161–66.

34. "Informe especial: La contra-revolución en Urabá," 32; Registraduría Nacional del Estado Civil, *Estadísticas electorales, marzo 1982;* Botero Herrera and Sierra Botero, *El mercado de fuerza de trabajo en la zona bananera de Urabá,* 96.

35. Alvarez de Gil, "Historias de Urabá y AUGURA en su contexto," 38.

36. Martin, "Desarrollo ecónomico," 30–32, cited in Bejarano, "La violencia regional y sus protagonistas," 48; Botero Herrera and Sierra Botero, *El mercado de fuerza de trabajo en la zona bananera de Urabá,* 92; report of Sintrabanano, cited in "Gracias y desgracias de una región."

37. Botero Herrera, *Urabá,* 173–75.

38. Peasants *(parceleros)* resided in long-settled areas of Urabá, especially the flatlands, and tended to have landholdings smaller than 10 hectares. Settlers *(colonos),* in contrast, generally had arrived more recently (1965–75), lived in mountainous areas, and had somewhat larger landholdings (10–20 hectares); interview 40. See also Botero Herrera, *Urabá,* 173–75; Martin, "Desarrollo ecónomico," 30–32.

39. Botero Herrera, *Urabá,* 173–75, citing Martin, "Desarrollo económico"; Uribe de Hincapié, *Urabá: ¿Región o territorio?* 162–65; León Zamosc, the central authority on this movement of the 1970s, argues that leftist activists tended to join and fortify these movements well after they were under way; see Zamosc, *The Agrarian Question and the Peasant Movement in Colombia,* 79.

40. Nationwide, the level of peasant mobilization had also slowed considerably. Uribe de Hincapié, *Urabá: ¿Región o territorio?* 162–65; Zamosc, "Peasant Struggles of the 1970s in Colombia," 119–23; CAJSC, *Urabá,* 68.

41. Interview 39.

42. Botero Herrera, *Urabá,* 82–83. According to Botero Herrera, 1,200 families resisted eviction (45). Information in paragraph also derived from interviews 45, 47, 50, 3, 39.

43. For names of county council members: Registraduría Nacional del Estado Civil, *Estadísticas electorales: Asambleas Departamentales, Consejos Intenden-*

ciales, Consejos Comisariales, Concejos Municipales, marzo 11 de 1984; for movements with which interviewees were involved, see interviews 38, 39, 40, 44, 45, 46.

44. Uribe de Hincapié, *Urabá: ¿Región o territorio?* 223–24. The MRL was used by the Communist Party as an electoral front because the National Front, a power-sharing agreement between Liberals and Conservatives that was in effect from 1956 through 1974, presented a serious obstacle to third-party political participation; Hartlyn, "Colombia: The Politics of Violence and Accommodation," 308–10.

45. Uribe de Hincapié, *Urabá: ¿Región o territorio?* 225–26; "Informe especial: La contra-revolución en Urabá," 32; Botero Herrera and Sierra Botero, *El mercado de fuerza de trabajo en la zona bananera de Urabá,* 96. For county council election results: Registraduría Nacional del Estado Civil, *Estadísticas electorales, Marzo 1982.*

46. See table 2.2 for sources. Figures for 1984 and 1985 (when Colombian firms controlled all stages of marketing for 78 percent of the bananas from Urabá and 100 percent of the bananas for the first stage) and for 1987 (78.8 percent and 100 percent, respectively) are from Botero Herrera, *Urabá,* 104. Figures for 1992 (79 percent and 100 percent, respectively) were estimates given by an employee of AUGURA on November 27, 1992.

47. Botero Herrera, *Urabá,* 175; CAJSC, *Urabá,* 56. See also table 2.2.

48. In *Urabá: Región, actores y conflicto,* 123–28, García confirms this "dead end" that preceded guerrilla entrance into the banana-sector labor conflict.

49. Interview 43.

50. Botero Herrera, *Urabá,* 175–76.

51. Interview 44 provided data on the Apartadó strike and the regional overview; Botero Herrera, *Urabá,* 168.

52. Botero Herrera, *Urabá,* 62; interview 42. This list clearly indicates the emergence of a new type of labor mobilization in Urabá during this period: the one-day work stoppage to protest violence. Labor leaders (see, e.g., interview 38) make a clear distinction between these *paros* and *huelgas,* or full-blown strikes. Paros usually last only one day and are done for political reasons or to protest violations of a current contract. They frequently involve only one or a few plantations. On the other hand, huelgas tend to be both larger in scope and longer and have as their central purpose bringing the plantation owners, or AUGURA as a whole, to the negotiating table.

53. Interview 43.

54. CAJSC, *Urabá,* 56–57; interview 43; "Gracias y desgracias de una región"; Martin, "Desarrollo económico," cited in Botero Herrera, *Urabá,* 168. Apartadó membership figures: interview 44.

55. Interview 79; Botero Herrera, *Urabá,* 167. The cost of living rose 22.5 percent in 1985, according to data cited in Rey de Marulanda and Córdoba Garcés,

El sector bananero de Urabá, 32. Interview 44 provided information about the Apartadó strike; interview 42 provided data on the Carepa strike. See also interview 43.

56. Arenas, *Cese el fuego,* 11; Arizala, "Las experiencias alternativas de tipo partidistas, independientes del bipartidismo"; Uribe de Hincapié, *Urabá: ¿Región o territorio?* 227; CSV, *Pacificar la paz,* 100.

57. For 1984 electoral results: Registraduría Nacional del Estado Civil, *Estadísticas electorales: Asambleas Departamentales, Consejos Intendenciales, Consejos Comisariales, Concejos Municipales, marzo 11 de 1984.* For 1986 county council results, Registraduría Nacional del Estado Civil, *Estadísticas electorales: Senado-Cámara, Concejos Municipales, Consejos Comisariales, Consejos Intendenciales, Asambleas Departamentales, marzo 9 de 1986.* Names of elected Apartadó county council members in 1986 obtained from "Actas electorales," found at Registraduría Nacional del Estado Civil. For the social movement affiliation of Apartadó county council members, interview 41.

58. Interviews 74, 1, 38, and 4; certificates of inauguration at the Apartadó courthouse show dates of inauguration.

59. Interview 39.

60. Interview 47 revealed that only in 1992 was neighboring Carepa updating its rural appraisals, using funds provided by the department of Antioquia. The attempts of county administrations, especially those dominated by the UP, to update appraisals of rural property created additional tensions between them and AUGURA members; see CAJSC, *Urabá,* 37–38.

61. Interview 4.

62. Henríquez Gallo, "Parliamentarians and Banana Production," 106.

63. Henríquez Gallo, "Parliamentarians and Banana Production," 106; "Ocampo Madrid, Sergio"; interview 4.

64. Registraduría Nacional del Estado Civil, *Estadísticas electorales: Asambleas Departamentales, Consejos Intendenciales, Consejos Comisariales, Concejos Municipales, marzo 11 de 1984;* Registraduría Nacional del Estado Civil, *Estadísticas electorales: Senado-Cámara, Concejos Municipales, Consejos Comisariales, Consejos Intendenciales, Asambleas Departamentales, marzo 9 de 1986.*

65. Henríquez Gallo, "Parliamentarians and Banana Production," 103–7.

66. Henríquez Gallo, "Parliamentarians and Banana Production," 103–7; CAJSC, *Urabá,* 37–38.

67. Martin, "Desarrollo económico," cited in Botero Herrera, *Urabá,* 168.

68. See methodological section of the introduction for sources and operationalization; see table 2.4 for full series of repression indexes, 1984–92.

69. This finding is consistent with Romero's argument that paramilitary violence against social movement activists increases during moments when the gov-

ernment is most actively negotiating peace with guerrillas. Romero, *Paramilitares y autodefensas*, 90–93.

70. Interviews 75, 76.

71. Arenas, *Cese el fuego*, 11; Arizala, "Las experiencias alternativas de tipo partidistas, independientes del bipartidismo"; Uribe de Hincapié, *Urabá: ¿Región o territorio?* 227; CSV, *Pacificar la paz*, 100.

72. Botero Herrera, *Urabá*, 170–78. The Partido Comunista Marxista-Leninista was a Maoist offshoot of the Colombian Communist Party in 1965.

73. Uribe de Hincapié, *Urabá: ¿Región o territorio?* map 7; Botero Herrera, *Urabá*, 177. Federal employees in the Registraduría of Apartadó with whom I spoke in late 1992 were not from the region and were not politically active, yet they were quite well informed about guerrilla zones of influence, as any resident of the region must be to safeguard his or her safety. During the 1980s a third guerrilla group, the Ejército de Liberación Nacional (ELN), also entered Urabá and apparently had its greatest influence in the banana axis; see CAJSC, *Urabá*, 52. However, it represented only a small proportion of the armed movement in Urabá. On "patchwork quilt" of plantation affiliations: interviews 43, 44.

74. For example, in Apartadó between 1987 and 1988, the number of armed confrontations involving the FARC increased from 0 to 3, while those involving the EPL increased from 2 to 15 (see table 2.4). On the FARC, the EPL, and the peace process, see CAJSC, *Urabá*, 58–59.

75. Previous two paragraphs: interview 5; Sarmiento, "Se madura conflicto en Urabá"; interviews 42, 38; Botero Herrera, *Urabá*, 63; "Urabá: ¿Qué te AUGURAn?" 35.

76. Interview 42 documents the Carepa strikes. For other mobilizations, see Rey de Marulanda and Córdoba Garcés, *El sector bananero de Urabá*, 32; "Renace, Ciénaga, renace," 24–25; and Botero Herrera, *Urabá*, 63. An exodus is a mobilization in which peasants flee the countryside and concentrate in the cities both to escape military operations/bombings and to call attention to their plight. "Urabá: ¿Qué te AUGURAn?" 35.

77. "Semana de pasión," 55; "Urabá: ¿Qué te AUGURAn?" 32–35; García, *Urabá*, 158–59; interviews 38, 42, 45.

78. "Semana de pasión," 55; "Arcano tres tuvo que retroceder."

79. Interview 38; "Semana de pasión," 55.

80. Rey de Marulanda and Córdoba Garcés, *El sector bananero de Urabá*, 33; "Asesinado otro líder sindical en Urabá"; interview 38; "Urabá: Página histórica del movimiento sindical"; Sarmiento, "Se madura conflicto en Urabá."

81. Botero Herrera, *Urabá*, 63; "Urabá: ¿Qué te AUGURAn?" 35.

82. Interview 38; "Algo nuevo está pasando"; Sarmiento, "Se madura conflicto en Urabá."

83. Interview 38; "Algo nuevo está pasando," 35.

84. CAJSC, *Urabá*, 41; "Algo nuevo está pasando," 35; interview 38.

85. "Algo nuevo está pasando," 35; CAJSC, *Urabá*, 41; CSV, *Pacificar la paz*, 33–34; interviews 38, 42.

86. Botero Herrera, *Urabá*, 63; "Urabá: ¿Qué te AUGURAn?" 35.

87. See table 2.1 for full series of unionization figures by tendency in Apartadó and Urabá and sources; overview of regional unionization: Uribe, *Urabá: ¿Región o territorio?* 201–2.

88. Interview 42. Rey de Marulanda and Córdoba Garcés, *El sector bananero de Urabá*, 32. On banana worker organizing in other regions: "Renace, Ciénaga, renace," 24–25.

89. Interview 3. For the number of county council members elected from each party, see Registraduría Nacional del Estado Civil, *Estadísticas electorales 1988: Asambleas, Consejos Intendenciales, Consejos Comisariales, Concejos Municipales, Alcaldías [marzo 13 de 1988]*. Names of candidates and exact number of votes won by each obtained from Registraduría Municipal del Estado Civil de Apartadó.

90. Registraduría Nacional del Estado Civil, *Estadísticas electorales 1990: Senado-Cámara, Asambleas, Consejos Intendenciales, Consejos Comisariales, Concejos Municipales, Alcaldes, Consulta Popular [marzo 11 de 1990]*. Details of the coalition from interview 41.

91. Names of county council candidates and whether each was elected, number of votes obtained by each, and party affiliation obtained from Registraduría Municipal del Estado Civil de Apartadó.

92. About 20 percent of organized workers were affiliated with smaller unions in 1988, according to Rey de Marulanda and Córdoba Garcés, *El sector bananero de Urabá*, 32. Interview 44 corroborated the approximate proportion of workers belonging to each union.

93. Interviews 39, 43.

94. Interviews 39, 43.

95. Interviews 38, 4, 3, 39, 41.

96. Interviews 3, 5.

97. Interview 38; "Semana de pasión," 55.

98. Rey de Marulanda and Córdoba Garcés, *El sector bananero de Urabá*, 33; "Asesinado otro líder sindical en Urabá"; interview 38; "Urabá: Página histórica del movimiento sindical," 28–30.

99. CAJSC, *Urabá*, 41; "Algo nuevo está pasando," 35; interview 38.

100. Interviews 3, 1.

101. In Colombia at this time each political tendency presented not a single candidate but a slate of ranked candidates for each political body (Departmental Assembly, county council, Senate, etc.). A very successful slate, for example, would

elect the top five candidates; a less successful slate would elect only the head of the list. Results for 1988 Departmental Assembly: Registraduría Nacional del Estado Civil, *Estadísticas electorales 1988: Asambleas, Consejos Intendenciales, Consejos Comisariales, Concejos Municipales, Alcaldías [marzo 13 de 1988]*. House and Senate 1990 results: Registraduría Nacional del Estado Civil, *Estadísticas electorales 1990: Senado-Cámara, Asambleas, Consejos Intendenciales, Consejos Comisariales, Concejos Municipales, Alcaldes, Consulta Popular [marzo 11 de 1990]*.

102. *AUGURA* 12, no. 1 (1986): ii; AUGURA, *Actividad bananera de Urabá*, 21.

103. Uribe de Hincapié, *Urabá: ¿Región or territorio?* 252; CAJSC, *Urabá*, 72–73; "Pura sangre," 29; interviews 75, 76.

104. "Pura sangre," 28–29; "El narco-agro: Mas de un millón de hectáreas estan en manos de los narcotraficantes." Unpublished map titled "Predios decomisados por el INCORA a narcotraficantes" given to me by Alejandro Reyes Posada.

105. Interview 3; Americas Watch, *The Drug War in Colombia*, 22–23. A deserter cited by Americas Watch gave the number of Castaño's men as 120 (22).

106. Americas Watch, *The Drug War in Colombia*, 32–41.

107. CSV, *Pacificar la paz*, 140; Americas Watch, *The Drug War in Colombia*, 21; Bejarano, "La violencia regional y sus protagonistas," 52.

108. "El dossier de Urabá," *Semana*, May 3, 1988, 27–34; Americas Watch, *The Drug War in Colombia*, 21–23.

109. WOLA, *Colombia Besieged*, 71–72. The conversion of Puerto Boyacá from a Communist Party stronghold to a hegemonic narco-paramilitary stronghold in the 1980s is thoroughly documented by Medina Gallegos in his *Autodefensas, paramilitares y narcotráfico en Colombia*.

110. CAJSC, *Urabá*, 71–73, 104; Americas Watch, *The Drug War in Colombia*, 22, 90. The date, places, and number of persons killed in the incidents are the following: August 29, 1988, Chigorodó, 4 peasants; September 30, 1988, Turbo, 5 workers; January 3, 1989, Apartadó, 4 workers; June 3, 1989, Turbo, 4 peasants; June 16, 1989, Apartadó, 4 workers.

111. Botero Herrera, *Urabá*, 182.

112. See table 2.4 for full series.

113. Interview 43; CAJSC, *Urabá*, 59–60; Editora Lesi, *Nueva constitución política de Colombia*, 126–27; Americas Watch, *The Drug War in Colombia*, 119; CSV, *Pacificar la paz*, 135, 268.

114. The April massacre took place in the vereda Mejor Esquina, Buenavista County, Córdoba. Six of the victims were Frente Popular activists (*Justicia y Paz* 1 [April–June 1988]). According to subsequent investigations, narco paramilitary groups from Puerto Boyacá were behind this massacre, although Fidel Castaño was also implicated. Americas Watch, *The Drug War in Colombia*, 22–23.

115. Interview 43; CAJSC, *Urabá,* 59–60; Editora Lesi, *Nueva constitución política de Colombia,* 126–27; Americas Watch, *The Drug War in Colombia,* 119; CSV, *Pacificar la paz,* 135, 268.

116. Uribe de Hincapié, *Urabá: ¿Región o territorio?* 232–53; Americas Watch, *The Drug War in Colombia,* 123–24; interview 6.

117. Interviews 43, 6; CAJSC, *Urabá,* 59–60; Editora Lesi, *Nueva constitución política de Colombia,* 126–27; Americas Watch, *The Drug War in Colombia,* 119, 123–24; CSV, *Pacificar la paz,* 135, 268; Uribe de Hincapié, *Urabá: ¿Región o territorio?* 232–53.

118. Figures for Urabá: interview 43; figures for Apartadó: interview 44; figures for Carepa: interview 42.

119. Enrique Santos Calderón, August 1990, cited in Arango Zuluaga, *De Cravo Norte a Tlaxcala,* 26; Americas Watch, *The Drug War in Colombia,* 123–24; Uribe de Hincapié, *Urabá: ¿Región o territorio?* 232, 253; *Justicia y Paz* 4, nos. 1–2 (October–December 1991): 25; CAJSC, *Urabá,* 60, 106–7; interview 6.

120. Junta Directiva Sintrainago (Sintrainago Executive Board), letter addressed to the participants at the 1991 Congreso Bananero, 133, in AUGURA, "Congreso Bananero 1991, memorias," *Revista AUGURA,* año 17, no. 1 (1991).

121. AUGURA, "Sector bananero, crisis económica 1991–1992," 133–34 (document obtained from regional office of AUGURA in Carepa); Ramírez Tobón, "Estado y crisis regional," 30; CSV, *Pacificar la paz,* 33–34.

122. Interview 38 provided information about small strikes in Apartadó and overall negotiations. See table 2.3 for sources on productivity figures.

123. Enrique Santos Calderón, August 1990, cited in Arango Zuluaga, *De Cravo Norte a Tlaxcala,* 26; Americas Watch, *The Drug War in Colombia,* 124; CAJSC, *Urabá,* 60, 106–7.

124. Arango Zuluaga, *De Cravo Norte a Tlaxcala,* 11, 160, 199–210; *Justicia y Paz* 3–4 (1990–91).

125. Interviews 44, 45.

126. Concejo Municipal de Apartadó (County Council of Apartadó), "Acuerdo #008 de 23 noviembre 1990, sobre presupuesto de ingresos y egresos para el período fiscal del 1 de enero al 31 de diciembre de 1991" (Agreement #008 of November 23, 1990, about Budget Revenue and Expenditures for the Fiscal Period 1 January to 31 December 1991). There was a public interest angle to the popular cable repeater: Urabá had no TV stations of its own and was too far from Medellín or Montería (Córdoba) to receive their broadcasts. Interview 49 provided information about this public work and relations with the army and diocese.

127. Interview 76; Uribe de Hincapié, *Urabá: ¿Región o territorio?* 232.

128. *Justicia y Paz* 3, no. 4 (October–December 1990): 75; Registraduría Nacional del Estado Civil, *Estadísticas electorales 1990 [marzo 11 de 1990],* 51.

See methodology section of chapter 1 for information on operationalization and sources.

129. *Justicia y Paz* 4 (1991).

130. UP version: interviews 38, 39. Interview 43 provided information about the Esperanza version; the interviewee also placed the number of participating families at 950 rather than 1,500.

131. *Justicia y Paz* 4, no. 4 (October–December 1991): 25; CAJSC, *Urabá,* 60, 106–7.

132. CAJSC, *Urabá,* 60, 106–8; interview 43. *Justicia y Paz* (4, no. 4 [October–December 1991]: 25) reported that on October 12, 1991, more than forty demobilized EPL guerrillas had been killed nationwide; and *Justicia y Paz* (5, no. 2 [April–June 1992]: 21) reported that the total was 96 on April 27, 1992. CAJSC, *Urabá,* 108.

133. *Justicia y Paz* 4–5 (1991–92). According to CAJSC, *Uraba,* 106–11, while some assassinations in 1992 were clearly carried out by the EPL dissidence, with others it was difficult to judge which sectors might be implicated.

134. *Justicia y Paz* 4, no. 3 (July–September 1991): 20; CAJSC, *Urabá,* 61, 114. Interview 74 provided information about the UP view of Esperanza.

135. Comisión Verificadora, *Informe final sobre Urabá,* 26; Arango Zuluaga, *De Cravo Norte a Tlaxcala,* 11, 34, 160, 199–210.

136. Comisión Verificadora, *Informe final sobre Urabá,* 26; *Justicia y Paz* 4–5 (1991–92).

137. Interviews 42, 44, 38.

138. AUGURA, *Carta Informativa* 7 (August 1992): 4, 10; AUGURA, "Sector bananero, crisis económica 1991–1992"; CAJSC, *Urabá,* 62. Interview 43 provided information about regional membership; interview 44 provided information about Apartadó membership.

139. Interviews 39 and 35 provided the basic chronology and the UP perspective in this and the previous paragraph. Interview 43 provided the Esperanza perspective on the La Chinita invasion.

140. For number of county council members elected from each party in 1988, see Registraduría Nacional del Estado Civil, *Estadísticas electorales 1988: Asambleas, Consejos Intendenciales, Consejos Comisariales, Concejos Municipales, Alcaldías [marzo 13 de 1988].* Names of candidates and exact number of votes won by each obtained from Registraduría Municipal del Estado Civil de Apartadó. All county council data for 1990 obtained from Registraduría Municipal del Estado Civil de Apartadó. County council and county executive results for 1992 obtained from Registraduría Nacional del Estado Civil, *Estadísticas electorales: Elecciones del 8 de marzo de 1992,* vol. 1: *Alcaldes, Concejales, Diputados, Ediles.* Interview 41 provided information that clarified coalitions.

141. Interview 40.

142. Names of elected county council members and votes per party for 1984 obtained from Registraduría Nacional del Estado Civil ("Actas electorales"). County council and Departmental Assembly results from 1992 from Registraduría Nacional del Estado Civil, *Estadísticas electorales: Elecciones del 8 de marzo de 1992,* vol. 1: *Alcaldes, Concejales, Diputados, Ediles.* Interview 41 provided information about party factions and coalitions in 1984 and in the 1992 county council. House, Senate, and Departmental Assembly results for October 1991 from Registraduría Nacional del Estado Civil, *Estadísticas electorales: Elecciones del 27 de octubre de 1991,* vol. 1: *Senadores, Representantes, Gobernadores.* The post–Constitutional Assembly era's explosion of new parties and political movements brought an extreme fragmentation of the vote. Thus many candidates, like Guillermo Gaviria, took office having won only a very small proportion of the total vote.

143. De la Calle Lombana, "Palabras del Ministro del Gobierno Delegatorio de funciones presidenciales Humberto de la Calle Lombana en el Congreso Bananero," 23–27; Gaviria Trujillo, "Mensaje del Presidente de la República, Gaviria Trujillo, al Congreso Bananero 1991," 28–29; AUGURA, *Carta Informativa* 7 (August 1992): 4, 11.

144. CAJSC, *Urabá,* 62; interview 76.

145. CIJP, "Trece años en búsqueda de paz," 1–23.

146. Interview 75.

147. CSV, *Pacificar la paz,* 35; Comisión Verificadora, *Informe final sobre Urabá,* 41; CAJSC, *Urabá,* 156.

148. See the methodology section in chapter 1 for information about operationalization and sources for the repression index.

Three. The Counterreform Period in Urabá

1. For date of incident, see *Justicia y Paz* 6, nos. 1–3 (1993): 64. Interview 75 provided information about the involvement of Comandos Populares.

2. United Nations Working Group on Arbitrary Detention, "Civil and Political Rights, including the Questions of Torture and Detention," 78.

3. The escalation of political violence would have been even more noteworthy had I derived all the data from the same source. For Urabá, my data from 1992 and before were from *Justicia y Paz,* which includes press reports of political violence of all kinds, while the data from 1993 and beyond is from the more stringent database on lethal political violence elaborated by Francisco Gutiérrez of the National University of Colombia. It draws from the same newspapers but tracks only lethal violence, not assassination attempts, arrests, tortures, etc. See methodological index for details.

4. De Urbina and Kuntz, "Gloria Cuartas, Colombia's Messenger of Peace"; interview 80; Romero, *Paramilitares y autodefensas,* 206.

5. Previous two paragraphs: Romero, *Paramilitares y autodefensas,* 206–11.

6. Romero, *Paramilitares y autodefensas,* 215.

7. Lapan, "Killer Cola?"

8. "Entrevista con el Secretario General del regional del Partido Comunista de Urabá."

9. "Elecciones en Urabá serán ilegítimas."

10. Romero, *Paramilitares y autodefensas,* 216.

11. Political violence through 2004: Gutiérrrez, "Assassinations in Apartadó, Cartagena del Chairá, Arauca, and Arauquita, 1975–2004." Data for 2005 derived from the Noche y Niebla database.

12. Kraul, "Village's Unarmed Rebellion"; Zamarra, "San José de Apartadó"; Fellowship of Reconciliation, "Update on the Massacre in San José de Apartadó, Colombia."

13. Political violence and combat statistics from 1998 to 2004: Gutierrez, "Assassinations in Apartadó, Cartagena del Chairá, Arauca, and Arauquita, 1975–2004." Political violence 2005–7 and combat 2005: Noche y Niebla database; and combat 2006–8: ElTiempo.com archive, search term "Apartadó." Regional FARC leader: "Por ela ofrecían un millón de dólares entrega de 'Karina' en Antioquia, otro duro golpe a moral de las Farc." The number of community members killed by early 2008 was provided by the documentary film by Contravía, *San José de Apartadó: 3 años después.* On Uribe's position and the perpetrators of violence, see Kraul, "Village's Unarmed Rebellion."

14. Kraul, "Village's Unarmed Rebellion." For Giraldo as the spokesperson for the peace community and the pressure from fifty-nine members of the U.S. Congress, see "El acoso sigue en S. J. de Apartadó"; and Leahy, "Statement of Senator Patrick Leahy on the Massacre at San José de Apartadó."

15. "Son 69 los militares que deben responder en indagatoria por la masacre de San José de Apartadó."

16. "Captura para 15 militares por masacre de Apartadó"; "Llaman a Gloria Cuartas y al padre Javier Giraldo para declarar en caso contra el general Del Río"; "Del Río, a juicio por crimen de paras."

17. For the number of members, see Iturralde, "Una masacre anunciada"; and Fellowship of Reconciliation, "FOR Peace: The Blog of the Fellowship of Reconciliation."

18. Citations for the San José de Apartadó Peace Community media coverage described in this paragraph are the following: *Toronto Star,* Ward, "Bloodbath in a Peaceful Village"; *Los Angeles Times,* Kraul, "Village's Unarmed Rebellion"; documentary films: *Howard County Calendar: Community Events*; EEC-funded Contravía, *San José de Apartadó: 3 años después*; *Estreno del documental "Hasta la*

última piedra"; photo essay: "Jesús Abad Colorado, uno de los distinguidos con el 2006 International Press Freedom Award."

19. Fellowship of Reconciliation Colombia Program, "San José Community Awarded Peace Prize"; "Nominan a Nobel de Paz a 2 comunidades colombianas"; Knox, "Moral Suasion, not Courts, Works for Rights Winner Priest 'Given up on Colombian Justice' in Fight for Political Victims"; "Otorgan Premio Nantes 2008 a Gloria Cuartas."

20. Lapan, "Killer Cola?" 6; Blanding, "The Case against Coke."

21. "Banana Para-Republic"; "'H H' dice que 'para' que participó en asesinato de Manuel Cepeda está libre."

22. "173 Victims' Families File Suit Demanding Chiquita to Pay Reparations."

23. Romero, *Paramilitares y autodefensas,* 101–2, 218–19.

24. "La presencia paramilitar." On Urabá demobilizations, see "Camuflados de ex paramilitares, una peligrosa moda en Urabá." For extradition and foot-dragging, see Arnson, "Editor's Introduction."

25. "Las guerras de los narcos de 'Tercera Generación.'"

26. Ramírez, "Sólo San Isidro no salió a votar."

27. "Los 'esperanzados' en homenaje a Del Río"; Romero, *Paramilitares y autodefensas,* 193–94.

28. "Corto paro de Sintrainagro."

29. "Capturan al jefe de las 'Águilas Negras' en Antioquia, acusado de 400 asesinatos"; "Detenidos lugarteniente de 'don Mario' y 2 escoltas que iban en vehículo del ministerio del Interior."

30. Ramírez, "Sintrainagro, en paro indefinido desde el jueves"; Inter-American Commission on Human Rights, "Admissibility: María del Consuelo Ibarguen Rengifo, et al., Colombia."

31. Bedoya Madrid, "Los trabajadores bananeros suspenden el paro indefinido."

32. Interview 81.

33. AUGURA, "Coyuntura Bananera Colombiana: Primer semestre de 2001," 31.

34. AUGURA, "Coyuntura Bananera Colombiana [Segundo semestre de año] 2003," 15; AUGURA, "Coyuntura Bananera Colombiana: 2007," 15–16.

35. Effects of peso revaluation, Urabá palm growth: "Por caída del dólar, bananeros han perdido $1,24 billones"; Fedepalma, "The Oil Palm Agroindustry in Colombia," 4, 18; Fedepalma, "Distribution of Oil Palm Planted Area According to Zones (in Hectares)."

36. Ramírez, "El gobierno promete $5.000 millones a los bananeros"; Rivera Zapata, "Inminente cese de actividades de trabajadores bananeros"; Rodríguez, "La CUT saluda el acuerdo laboral entre Sintrainagro y el sector bananero."

37. Gómez, "Acuerdo bananero asegura la paz laboral en Urabá."

38. Cañas, "Inminente paro bananero"; Bedoya Madrid, "Paralizada Urabá por huelga bananera."

39. Ramírez, "La mediación de mintrabajo evitó un paro y una huelga."

40. Interview 43 provided information on union membership in 1992. Rivera and Torres, letter to John Sweeney, April 11, 2008, provided data on membership in 2008. For the 2006 strike, see Delgado, "Sindicatos de paramilitares?" All COL data in this paragraph are from Banco de la República, "Indices de precios al consumidor y del productor." For the one-plantation strike in 2008, see Giraldo and Triana, "Apoyamos la huelga en Banur s.a y reclamamos pronta solución."

41. AUGURA, *Informe de actividades, 1997,* 19.

42. "Paro bananero en la región de Urabá"; Ramírez, "En pliego bananero, el llamado es a concertar"; Ramírez, "Sintrainagro alerta contra el arancel de la Unión Europea"; Ramírez, "Bananeros y trabajadores persiguen un Pacto Social"; Romero, *Paramilitares y autodefensas,* 185–87.

43. Ramírez, "Trabajadores bananeros amenazan con huelga"; Pérez and Hurtado, "Sin acuerdo el pliego bananero"; Ramírez, "La huelga, un suicidio para los bananeros"; Ramírez, "Obreros bananeros votan la huelga"; Gómez, "Acuerdo bananero asegura la paz laboral en Urabá."

44. Ramírez, "La mediación de mintrabajo evitó un paro y una huelga"; Delgado, "¿Sindicatos de paramilitares?"

45. AUGURA, *Informe de actividades, 1997,* 19; Cañas, "Inminente paro bananero."

46. Ramírez, "Bananeros mantienen los diálogos laborales."

47. Rivera Zapata, "Referencia: Denuncia nacional e internacional. Asunto."

48. On divide-and-conquer tactics, see Rivera et al., "Comunicado Público: Apartadó, 31 de julio de 2008." For plantation layoffs of banana workers and the substitution of African palm cultivation for banana growing, see Sánchez, "Forum in Defense of Employment Concludes with Great Success." For the threats in late 2006, see Noche y Niebla database. For the assassination of Carmen Cecilia Santana early in 2007, see "Otra víctima de 'paras' asesinada no alcanzó a denunciar en justicia y paz"; Apartadó county executive, "Gobierno rechaza intimidación de bandas criminales en el Urabá."

49. Delgado, "¿Sindicatos de paramilitares?"

50. Rivera and Torres, Letter to John Sweeney et al., AFL-CIO, dated April 11, 2008.

51. Delgado, "Sindicatos de paramilitares?"; Programa de Gobierno 2008–2011 de Oswaldo Cuadrado Simanca" (Apartadó county executive).

52. County council and county executive election results for March 1994 obtained from Registraduría Nacional del Estado Civil.

53. County council and county executive election results for 1997 and departmental assembly results for 1994 obtained from Registraduría Nacional del Estado Civil.

54. Romero, *Paramilitares y autodefensas,* 184; county executive and county council election results, March 2000, obtained from Registraduría Nacional del Estado Civil.

55. Pizarro, "Las terceras fuerzas en Colombia hoy," 212–13.

56. Delgado, "¿Sindicatos de paramilitares?"

57. Registraduría Nacional del Estado Civil, electoral results for Apartadó county executive elections 2003 and 2007 and county council 2007, available on-line at www.registraduria.gov.co.

58. Rivera Zapata, "Inminente cese de actividades de trabajadores bananeros"; Ramírez, "El gobierno promete $5.000 millones a los bananeros"; Rodríguez, "La CUT saluda el acuerdo laboral entre sintrainagro y el sector bananero."

59. Romero, *Paramilitares y autodefensas,* 174.

Four. The Caguán in the Reform Period

1. Artunduaga, *Historia general del Caquetá,* 15–16, 127–31; Delgado, *Luchas sociales en el Caquetá,* 6–16; González and Ramírez, "Aspectos de la violencia en el Caquetá," 83–84.

2. Artunduaga, *Historia general del Caquetá,* 40–42, 131–40, 152–54; Delgado, *Luchas sociales en el Caquetá,* 9–15, 16–33, 145–48; González and Ramírez, "Aspectos de la violencia en el Caquetá," 91.

3. Delgado, *Luchas sociales en el Caquetá,* 44, 96–97, 145–48; Artunduaga, *Historia general del Caquetá,* 146.

4. Delgado, *Luchas sociales en el Caquetá,* 72–79, 113–24, 142, 169; Artunduaga, *Historia general del Caquetá,* 173–78; Valencia, "Marco institucional de la colonización reciente en el Caquetá," 40–42, 52–57; González and Ramírez, "Aspectos de la violencia en el Caquetá," 98; Colombian Solidarity Committees of North America, *Death and Torture in Caquetá.*

5. CIJP, "1981–1994: Trece años en búsqueda de paz," 8–10; Pedraza, "Departamento Nacional de Planeación: El proceso de paz en el Caquetá (caso del Caguán)," 6–10; Jaramillo, Mora, and Cubides, *Colonización, coca y guerrilla,* 1–33; Artunduaga, *Historia general del Caquetá,* 180–84.

6. Artunduaga, *Historia general del Caquetá,* 175; Pedraza, "Departamento Nacional de Planeación: El proceso de paz en el Caquetá (caso del Caguán)," 7.

7. Jaramillo, "Estudio del proceso de colonización en el Bajo y Medio Caguán," 44–49; Artunduaga, *Historia general del Caquetá,* 155.

8. For economic and demographic trends prior to the late 1970s, see Jaramillo, "Estudio del proceso de colonización en el Bajo y Medio Caguán," 53–56; interview 20; Pedraza, "Departamento Nacional de Planeación: El proceso de paz en el Caquetá (caso del Caguán)," 3; Jaramillo, Mora, and Cubides, *Colonización, coca y guerrilla,* 3–57. Population data: interview 19. For coca prices, see Jaramillo, Mora, and Cubides, *Colonización, coca y guerrilla,* 127, 145–59, 197, 212, 219, 225; Valencia, "Marco institucional de la colonización reciente en el Caquetá," 8; interviews 24, 74. Exchange rates (pesos/dollar) used for conversion throughout this chapter are the following: 1980–81, 50; 1982, 67; 1983, 84; 1984, 100; 1985, 170; 1986, 240; 1987, 310; 1988, 380; 1989, 450; 1990, 520; 1991, 590; 1992, 650; 1993, 767; 1994, 884; 1995, 1,000.

9. Jaramillo, Mora, and Cubides, *Colonización, coca y guerrilla,* 246–47; interview 76; Pedraza, "Departamento Nacional de Planeación: El proceso de paz en el Caquetá (caso del Caguán)," 3; interview 33; Valencia, "Marco institucional de la colonización reciente en el Caquetá," 72; interview 36.

10. Jaramillo, Mora, and Cubides, *Colonización, coca y guerrilla,* 62, 104, 111, 129, 149, 246–47, 251–53, 277, 283; Pedraza, "Departamento Nacional de Planeación: El proceso de paz en el Caquetá (caso del Caguán)," 3; interviews 73, 25, 31, 33, 74, 34.

11. Pedraza, "Departamento Nacional de Planeación: El proceso de paz en el Caquetá (caso del Caguán)," 10–14; interviews 73, 25, 19, 74; Jaramillo, Mora, and Cubides, *Colonización, coca y guerrilla,* 66–70, 84, 169.

12. Andreas and Youngers, "U.S. Drug Policy and the Andean Cocaine Industry," 529–35.

13. Interview 73; Andreas and Youngers, "U.S. Drug Policy and the Andean Cocaine Industry," 545–51.

14. Andreas and Youngers, "U.S. Drug Policy and the Andean Cocaine Industry," 529–62.

15. Andreas and Youngers, "U.S. Drug Policy and the Andean Cocaine Industry," 536–40; "El Narco-agro—Mas de un millón de hectáreas están en manos de los narcotraficantes," 34–38; INCORA, "Tierras confiscadas a narcotraficantes por el INCORA."

16. Artunduaga, *Historia general del Caquetá,* 184; Delgado, *Luchas sociales en el Caquetá,* 158, 186; Pedraza, "Departamento Nacional de Planeación: El proceso de paz en el Caquetá (caso del Caguán)," 8; Comité Permanente de Derechos Humanos, "Incumplen convenio de paz"; interview 17; document from early 1984, archive of the Colonization Committee.

17. For the source for this and all other electoral data, except where otherwise noted, please refer to departmental and county electoral summaries, tables 4.1, 4.2, and 4.4.

18. Interview 73; Delgado, *Luchas sociales en el Caquetá,* 95, 162.

19. For repression figures, see Comité Permanente de Derechos Humanos, "Incumplen convenio de paz"; clippings from the CINEP press archive. Mobilizations, guerrilla presence: interview 33; Pedraza, "Departamento Nacional de Planeación: El proceso de Paz en el Caquetá (caso del Caguán)," 7; interview 74; Delgado, *Luchas sociales en el Caquetá,* 56; interview 36; Jaramillo, Mora, and Cubides, *Colonización, coca y guerrilla,* 278.

20. CIJP, "1981–1994: Trece años en búsqueda de paz," 9–10; Jaramillo, Mora, and Cubides, *Colonización, coca y guerrilla,* 133; Pedraza, "Departamento Nacional de Planeación: El proceso de paz en el Caquetá (caso del Caguán)," 9–10.

21. Data on armed confrontations between guerrillas and the army from Consejería de Paz, database elaborated by Alejandro Reyes Posada; data on repression from CPDH, *Boletín de Prensa,* 1985–86. For tolerance by army commanders, see Pedraza, "Departamento Nacional de Planeación: El proceso de paz en el Caquetá (caso del Caguán)," 14; interview 78; and Jaramillo, Mora, and Cubides, *Colonización, coca y guerrilla,* 283.

22. Interviews 19, 25.

23. Pedraza, "Departamento Nacional de Planeación: El proceso de paz en el Caquetá (caso del Caguán)," 10–14; Jaramillo, Mora, and Cubides, *Colonización, coca y guerrilla,* 119, 162, 242, 261–62; interviews 20, 22.

24. Pedraza, "Departamento Nacional de Planeación: El proceso de paz en el Caquetá (caso del Caguán)," 14–17; Jaramillo, Mora, and Cubides, *Colonización, coca y guerrilla,* 134, 153–55; interview 74; *Unión Patriótica* 1, no. 1 (July 1985): 4 (the newspaper of the Caquetá Patriotic Union in Florencia); interview 78.

25. Jaramillo, Mora, and Cubides, *Colonización, coca y guerrilla,* 237; CIJP, "1981–1994: Trece años en búsqueda de paz," 12; Delgado, *Luchas sociales en el Caquetá,* 162.

26. Pedraza, "Departamento Nacional de Planeación: El proceso de paz en el Caquetá (caso del Caguán)," 18–19, 24–25; Jaramillo, Mora, and Cubides, *Colonización, coca y guerrilla,* 40, 119, 156–57, 188–91, 198, 243, 282; *Unión Patriótica* 1, no. 1 (July 1985): 8; interview 22; Delgado, *Luchas sociales en el Caquetá,* 163–64; interview 20.

27. Pedraza, "Departamento Nacional de Planeación: El proceso de paz en el Caquetá (caso del Caguán)," 18–19, 26–33; Jaramillo, Mora, and Cubides, *Colonización, coca y guerrilla,* 86–88, 157, 166, 169, 190–91, 198–99; interview 20.

28. Pedraza, "Departamento Nacional de Planeación: El proceso de paz en el Caquetá (caso del Caguán)," 18, 20–22, 26–29, 30–33; *Unión Patriótica* 1, no. 1 (July 1985): 4; interview 78; Jaramillo, Mora, and Cubides, *Colonización, coca y guerrilla,* 199–204.

29. Jaramillo, Mora, and Cubides, *Colonización, coca y guerrilla,* 205–9; Delgado, *Luchas sociales en el Caquetá,* 168; "Colombia: Announces Extended Peace Pact with Main Rebel Group."

30. Jaramillo, Mora, and Cubides, *Colonización, coca y guerrilla,* 13–14, 209–13, 216–18; Pedraza, "Departamento Nacional de Planeación: El proceso de paz en el Caquetá (caso del Caguán)," 18–19, 26–29; interview 22.

31. CIJP, "1981–1994: Trece años en búsqueda de paz," 8–10; Delgado, *Luchas sociales en el Caquetá,* 156; Pedraza, "Departamento Nacional de Planeación: El proceso de paz en el Caquetá (caso del Caguán)," 10–14.

32. Pedraza, "Departamento Nacional de Planeación: El proceso de paz en el Caquetá (caso del Caguán)," 14–15, 20, 26–29, 30–32, 37–39; interview 77; Delgado, *Luchas sociales en el Caquetá,* 146; Jaramillo, Mora, and Cubides, *Colonización, coca y guerrilla,* 199–210.

33. Interview 78; Pedraza, "Departamento Nacional de Planeación: El proceso de paz en el Caquetá (caso del Caguán)," 14, 26–29, 32, 37–39.

34. CIJP, "1981–1994: Trece años en búsqueda de paz," 11–13; Pedraza, "Departamento Nacional de Planeación: El proceso de paz en el Caquetá (caso del Caguán)," 33; interview 78; Jaramillo, Mora, and Cubides, *Colonización, coca y guerrilla,* 213.

35. Jaramillo, Mora, and Cubides, *Colonización, coca y guerrilla,* 213–15.

36. Jaramillo, Mora, and Cubides, *Colonización, coca y guerrilla,* xii–xiii, 94, 213–16, 219–20, 276; Pedraza, "Departamento Nacional de Planeación: El proceso de paz en el Caquetá (caso del Caguán)," 39; "Farc han declarado la guerra al liberalismo"; "Caquetá: Gremios prueban violación de tregua por parte de las Farc."

37. Jaramillo, Mora, and Cubides, *Colonización, coca y guerrilla,* 216; interviews 74, 17.

38. Jaramillo, Mora, and Cubides, *Colonización, coca y guerrilla,* 216–18, 274–75; interviews 22, 73, 74, 77, 78.

39. Interview 25; Henry Millán, text of speech given on July 17, 1988, in *Acuerdo del gobierno y los campesinos del Caquetá* (Millán, from the Patriotic Union, was one of Caquetá's two representatives to the House of Representatives, 1986–90 and 1990–92); interview 74; Jaramillo, Mora, and Cubides, *Colonización, coca y guerrilla,* 216–18; Delgado, *Luchas sociales en el Caquetá,* 174.

40. Jaramillo, Mora, and Cubides, *Colonización, coca y guerrilla,* 218–19, 274; Delgado, *Luchas sociales en el Caquetá,* 174; Pombo, "Barco rediseñó el proceso de paz"; interview 78.

41. Interviews 78, 17, 22, 74. See also Convenio de Florencia (August 1987); "Documento final del diálogo de las fuerzas vivas del Caquetá" (October 1987); and Henry Millán, text of speech given July 17, 1988; all in the pamphlet *Acuerdo del gobierno y los campesinos del Caquetá.*

42. Interviews 20, 25; Jaramillo, Mora, and Cubides, *Colonización, coca y guerrilla,* 293; interviews 22, 23, 30, 21.

43. Jaramillo, Mora, and Cubides, *Colonización, coca y guerrilla,* 284–85; interviews 25, 20.

44. Approved county budgets for calendar years 1987, 1989, 1990, county council, Cartagena del Chairá; dates county executives assumed office from County Courthouse of Cartagena del Chairá; interviews 31, 28, 35.

45. Interviews 32, 19, 28, 20, 25, and 26 document discrimination against UP county executives in allocating departmental resources. On departmental funds allocated to UP county executives as compared to Turbayista Liberal ones, see approved county budgets for calendar years 1987, 1989, 1990, and 1991, county council, Cartagena del Chairá; interview 17. Other signs of departmental disregard for the UP county executive included threats by military personnel and the fact that he was not invited to the inauguration ceremony for the Paujil-Cartagena road in 1988; Jaramillo, Mora, and Cubides, *Colonización, coca y guerrilla,* 116, 219; Henry Millán, text of speech given July 17, 1988.

46. *Justicia y Paz* 2–5 (1989–92); Jaramillo, Mora, and Cubides, *Colonización, coca y guerrilla,* 280.

47. "Caquetá: El liberalismo asegura haber perdido 35 de sus miembros en época pre-electoral y la UP exhibe una lista de 22 asesinados," *El Tiempo,* March 13, 1988, cited in Beaufort, "La elección de alcaldes en el Caquetá y su contexto político," 16; "DLN garantiza seguridad a liberales del Caquetá"; "Caquetá: Experimento piloto de la subversión," quoted in Jaramillo, Mora, and Cubides, *Colonización, coca y guerrilla,* 220; other examples of this type of rhetoric are provided by Jaramillo, Mora, and Cubides: xii–xiii, 94, 219–20; Pedraza, "Departamento Nacional de Planeación: El proceso de paz en el Caquetá (caso del Caguán)," 39.

48. "Caquetá: El liberalismo asegura haber perdido 35 de sus miembros en época pre-electoral y la UP exhibe una lista de 22 asesinados," *El Tiempo,* March 13, 1988, cited in Beaufort, "La elección de alcaldes en el Caquetá y su contexto político," 16; interviews 74, 20.

49. "Nuevos hechos de violencia en el Caquetá"; interviews 21, 35, 17; dates of tenure in office for all county executives since January 1986, County Courthouse, Cartagena del Chairá; Henry Millán, text of speech given on July 17, 1988; interviews 25, 22, 20.

50. Interviews 73, 22, 35; Jaramillo, Mora, and Cubides, *Colonización, coca y guerrilla,* 272; *Justicia y Paz* 1, no. 3 (1988); interviews 20, 27, 23.

51. Interviews 74, 33; Jaramillo, Mora, and Cubides, *Colonización, coca y guerrilla,* 246, 277–78; interview 36; Valencia, "Marco institucional de la colonización reciente en el Caquetá," 72; interviews 34, 76.

52. Interviews 18, 17, 34, 74.

53. Jaramillo, Mora, and Cubides, *Colonización, coca y guerrilla,* 127, 145–48, 151, 159, 219, 225; interview 19; Valencia, "Marco institucional de la colonización reciente en el Caquetá," 84; "Anteproyecto de desarrollo agropecuario de sustitución de cultivos ilícitos para el Bajo Caguán."

54. Interview 74; Jaramillo, Mora, and Cubides, *Colonización, coca y guerrilla,* 59–63, 119–21, 125–26, 151.

55. Interview 74.

56. Interviews 74, 78, 17, 33, 29; list of all titles from INCORA office in Florencia and information on reselling of titles from the Registro de Instrumentos Públicos (Registry of Public Documents), Florencia; interview 34.

57. Valencia, "Marco institucional de la colonización reciente en el Caquetá," 32.

58. Ministerio de Agricultura, *Anuario: Estadísticas del sector agropecuario 1992,* 105, 108; Federación Nacional de Ganaderos, *Carta Fedegan* 33 (April–May 1995): 30; Visbal Martelo, *Intervención del Doctor Jorge Visbal Martelo,* 45.

59. Delgado, *Luchas sociales en el Caquetá,* 96–97.

60. *Acuerdo del gobierno y los campesinos del Caquetá;* Jaramillo, Mora, and Cubides, *Colonización, coca y guerrilla,* 275–76; interview 74.

61. Interviews 22, 74, 20, 25, 29, 23; Jaramillo, Mora, and Cubides, *Colonización, coca y guerrilla,* 293; interview 29; "Anteproyecto de desarrollo agropecuario de sustitución de cultivos ilícitos para el Bajo Caguán," appendix; interview 23.

62. Interviews 33, 28, 30, 20 document the view that the National Rehabilitation Plan, the army, and the priest's investments weakened the peasant social movement. See also Jaramillo, Mora, and Cubides, *Colonización, coca y guerrilla,* 221–25. According to interview 23 and approved county budgets for 1989–92, County Council, Cartagena del Chairá, the priest's crop substitution project spent more than $70,000 between 1989 and 1992—about the same as the county budget in those same years. Interview 21 documents the change of allegiance of the former president of the Colonization Committee.

63. Jaramillo, Mora, and Cubides, *Colonización, coca y guerrilla,* 113–18, 220–21, 24, 102, 26, 28; "Anteproyecto de desarrollo agropecuario de sustitución de cultivos ilícitos para el Bajo Caguán"; interviews 20, 21, 22, 23, 24, 25.

64. *Justicia y Paz* 2–5 (1989–92); Jaramillo, Mora, and Cubides, *Colonización, coca y guerrilla,* 280.

65. The most detailed account of the perestroikos vs. mamertos division is Dudley, *Walking Ghosts,* esp. 127–41. For Iván Marquez's return to armed insurgency, see Jaramillo, Mora, and Cubides, *Colonización, coca y guerrilla,* 278; for the FARC's participation in local electoral campaigns, interview 74; for the evolution of FARC-government relations in 1990, see CIJP, "1981–1994: Trece años en búsqueda de paz," 16–17.

66. Interviews 18, 20, 33, 34.

67. Based on precinct-level voting results for county executive in March 1988, for the Senate in October 1991, and for the county council in March 1992. March 1990 electoral results by precinct were not available. All precinct-level voting results were obtained from Registraduría Municipal del Estado Civil, Cartagena del Chairá.

68. Interviews 74, 18, 33; *Justicia y Paz* 2–5 (1989–92).

69. Planned county budget for 1991: Municipio de Cartagena del Chairá; interview 28. For electoral statistics and sources, see tables 4.1, 4.2, and 4.4.

70. See table 4.1 for chronology and sources.

71. On Turbayista domination from the 1960s to the early 1980s, see Delgado, *Luchas sociales en el Caquetá,* 44, 96–97, 145–48; Artunduaga, *Historia general del Caquetá,* 146. On electoral trends from 1987 to 1992, see tables 4.1 and 4.4.

Five. The Counterreform Period in the Caguán

1. "Bloqueo a marchas campesinas"; CIJP, "1981–1994: Trece años en búsqueda de paz," 21; interview 74.

2. Chernick, "Negotiating Peace amid Multiple Forms of Violence," 183–85.

3. Observatorio de Drogas de Colombia, "Estimativos de cultivos de coca en Colomba por principales áreas de cultivo, 1991–1998 (hectáreas)."

4. Arnson, "Summary of Conference Presentation by Alberto Chueca Mora," 5.

5. CIJP, "1981–1994: Trece años en búsqueda de paz," 90.

6. "El coco de los diálogos regionales"; "Turbay Cote, un año secuestrado"; "FARC asesinan al gobernador de Caquetá"; Observatorio de los Derechos Humanos en Colombia, "Kidnapping and Death of Congressman Rodrigo Turbay Cote."

7. Richani, *Systems of Violence,* 130.

8. Schemo, "Colombian Rebels Release 70 Soldiers and Marines"; "Los desertores."

9. For the closing of the base in 1997, see Restrepo, "Militares echaron candado a su base." For data on political violence and combat, see Gutiérrez, "Assassinations in Apartadó, Cartagena del Chairá, Arauca, and Arauquita 1993–2004"; *Justicia y Paz* 5–8 (1992–June 1996); *Noche y Niebla* (July 1996–99).

10. Rodríguez, "Remolinos: Un día de narcomercado"; Restrepo, "Militares echaron candado a su base."

11. "Terminó paro en Cartagena del Chairá."

12. Interview 74.

13. Electoral results for local authorities in March 1992 and October 1994 obtained from Registraduría Nacional del Estado Civil.

14. Registraduría Nacional del Estado Civil, *Estadísticas electorales, March 1992*; and *Elecciones Senadores, Cámara y Consulta Liberal*, March 1994.

15. Interview 80; "Libres Victor Oime y su hijo."

16. Murillo, "Yo recibí una orden del grupo de las FARC."

17. Murillo, "Por fin, alcalde en C. del Chairá."

18. Electoral results for Departmental Assembly in Caquetá in 1997 and for the House of Representatives, Senate, and president in 1998 obtained from Registraduría Nacional del Estado Civil.

19. Ministerio de Agricultura y Desarrollo Rural, *Anuario estadístico del sector agropecuario 2003*, 193, 195.

20. Election results for House of Representatives in Caquetá in 1998 obtained from Registraduría Nacional del Estado Civil.

21. "Upsurge in Violence Leads to State of Emergency."

22. "La ley del Caguán: Semana revela el documento que ha servido de base a las exigencias de las FARC en la zona del despeje"; "La otra Cartagena"; FARC-EP, "Propuesta de las FARC-EP a la Audiencia Especial con representación de 21 países."

23. On aerial fumigation, see Permanent Peoples' Tribunal Session on Colombia, "Accusation against the Transnational Dyncorp," 40–48. For documentation of political violence, see Gutiérrez, "Assassinations in Apartadó, Cartagena del Chairá, Arauca, and Arauquita, 1993–2004"; *Noche y Niebla* (July 1996–99); and Noche y Niebla database, 2000–2002.

24. Interview 84.

25. Penhaul, "En Cartagena del Chairá"; Murillo, "Por fin, alcalde en C. del Chairá"; "Singulares elecciones en Cartagena del Chairá."

26. Interviews 84, 83.

27. Although some sources attributed the murder to paramilitary groups (see "Paramilitary Massacres across the Land") and others to "unknown assailants" (see Gutiérrez, "Assassinations in Apartadó, Cartagena del Chairá, Arauca, and Arauquita, 1993–2004"; "Violencia tiene acorralados a los alcaldes de Caquetá"; and "Perpetran masacres en Colombia"), later and more detailed accounts attributed it to the FARC (see, e.g., "Estamos dando resultados positivos para el país"). The lack of outrage about the murder on the part of leftist peasant movement activists (interviews 82, 83, 84, 86), coupled with their mention of how the local official had "broken promises" to the movement, also supports the interpretation that the FARC killed him.

28. Kotler, "Killings Provoke Outrage, but Colombia Peace Efforts Go On"; "Top Colombian 'Peacemaker' Gunned Down."

29. "FARC Comments on Murders of Congressman Turbay and of His Companions."

30. Arnson, "Summary of Conference Presentation by Alberto Chueca Mora," 5.

31. *Noche y Niebla* 11 (January–March 1999): 89.

32. Collier, "Drug War in the Jungle."

33. Observatorio de Drogas de Colombia, "Cultivos de coca en Colombia por departamentos, 1999–2006 (hectáreas)."

34. Collier, "Lure of Coca Money Hard for Farmers to Resist."

35. "Upsurge in Violence Leads to State of Emergency"; results for presidential election of May 2002, Registraduría Nacional del Estado Civil, accessed December 12, 2006, at www.registraduria.gov.co.

36. "Plan Patriota."

37. Forero, "Colombia's Coca Survives U.S. Plans to Uproot It"; interview 84.

38. "Plan Patriota: Recuperar el territorio considerado por años la retaguardia profunda de las FARC es el objetivo de la ofensiva de las fuerzas armadas"; Lozano, "Cinco años para derrotar a las FARC."

39. On the exodus of top FARC leadership from the zone, see Ruíz, "Semana en el corazón de la guerra." For cattle ranching in Cartagena del Chairá, see "William, dos años metido en las selvas del Patriota." For control of the Caguán River, see "Fin del Plan Patriota, llega el Plan Victoria." For army control of the Caguán River, see "Desmantelamos célula de las Farc: Santos."

40. "Desmantelamos célula de las Farc: Santos."

41. "De Navidad, llegó la luz a Cartagena del Chairá."

42. Gutiérrez, "Assassinations in Apartadó, Cartagena del Chairá, Arauca, and Arauquita, 1993–2004"; Noche y Niebla, "Base de datos."

43. Ruiz, "El río de la guerra: Con el Plan Patriota las fuerzas armadas se metieron a la madriguera de las FARC."

44. Interviews 83, 84.

45. 2007 FARC assaults: "A las Farc atribuyen asesinato de aspirante a alcaldía en Caquetá"; "De concejal en Caquetá a obrero raso en Bogotá"; "Farc vuelan lancha en Cartagena del Chairá"; "Secuestrados tres agentes por rebeldes de las Farc"; "No cede la violencia pre-electoral: asesinan a dos candidatos en Caquetá." 2008 FARC assaults: "Baleado concejal de Cartagena del Chairá"; "Baleado este domingo el concejal Hair Guerrero Orozco, de Cartagena del Chairá (Caquetá)"; "Noticias breves de justicia"; "Comprende escolta y ayuda económica protección a concejales de Cartagena del Chairá."

46. Noche y Niebla, "Base de datos" (October 6, 2003); "La gran redada."

47. Noche y Niebla, "Base de datos"; Raigozo, "Chino, a usted lo matan hoy."

48. Lozano, "Cinco años para derrotar a las FARC"; Noche y Niebla, "Base de datos."

49. Noche y Niebla, "Base de datos."

50. "Detenido dirigente agrario en el Caquetá"; "Detenciones masivas en Caquetá"; Endrezzi, "Apéndice," 310–17. Endrezzi's addendum was the epilogue to the book by Father Jacinto (Giacinto Franzoi), *Dios y cocaína: De cómo un misionero sobrevivió en el Caguán.* The work was published after the manuscript of my book was finalized but provides a detailed and fascinating account of the priest's experience and reflections on his thirty years in the Lower Caguán.

51. For displacement figures, see "Aumento del desplazamiento en diferentes regiones del sur occidente colombiano." For the population of Cartagena del Chairá in 2005, see DANE, *Censo general 2005,* 41. For population loss in Peñas Coloradas: Emanuelsson, "Un viaje al ojo del huracán del Plan Patriota"; "La Julia, otro 'santuario' de las Farc que languidece sin la coca."

52. "Primera Asamblea Comunitaria Municipio de Cartagena del Chairá."

53. Emanuelsson, "Un viaje al ojo del huracán del Plan Patriota."

54. Vieira, "El sur del país va a explotar"; García, "Plan Patriota: Violencia, desplazamiento, y miseria"; Lozano, "Cinco años para derrotar a las FARC"; "Campesinos, víctimas del Plan Patriota."

55. "Misión de observación al corazón del Plan Patriota."

56. "El Plan Patriota"; Ruiz, "El río de la guerra: Con el Plan Patriota las fuerzas armadas se metieron a la madriguera de las FARC."

57. Forero, "Colombia's Coca Survives U.S. Plans to Uproot It"; Coronell, "El mapa del fracaso."

58. Comunidad de Paz de San José de Apartadó, "Breve historia y estado de la Red de Comunidades y la Universidad Campesina de la Resistencia."

59. I considered the Polo's votes as a percentage of all votes for candidates (i.e., not taking into account blank and invalid ballots). All electoral results from Registraduría Nacional del Estado Civil; accessed December 12, 2006, at www .registraduria.gov.co. The results of the 2003 county elections were not available for Cartagena del Chairá. Attribution of the Polo's decline to repression and loss of population: interviews 82, 83.

60. "Grave crisis humanitaria generada por el Ejército nacional en poblaciones del Bajo Caguán, Caquetá, denunció misión humanitaria."

61. Interview 84; "Ocho Premios Nacionales de Paz continúan y fortalecen sus iniciativas"; UNODC, "Chocagüán: Comité de Cacaoteros de Remolino del Caguán y Suncillas"; "Cura para la paz: Al cumplirse 40 años de la muerte de Camilo Torres, la Iglesia de hoy ha renunciado a las armas, pero no a la transformación social"; "El cura más popular del Caguán."

62. "Fábrica de chocolates que funciona en Remolino del Caguán, espera vender sus productos en Italia."

63. Naciones Unidas, Oficina contra la Droga y el Delito, "Presentan productos del desarrollo alternativo de la zona del Caguán."

64. "Premio Nacional de Paz reconoce esfuerzos e iniciativas en pro del bienestar de las comunidades."

65. "Fábrica de chocolates que funciona en Remolino del Caguán, espera vender sus productos en Italia."

66. "El cura más popular del Caguán."

67. Asociación de Juntas de Cartagena del Chairá, "Militarización e impactos social del Plan Patriota en el sur del país"; Banco de Datos de Derechos Humanos y Violencia Política del CINEP, "Estadísticas de derechos humanos y DIH, Cartagena del Chairá, Caquetá, del 1 de enero 2004 al 5 de julio 2005," handout distributed by activists from the Caguán at the press conference to protest Plan Patriota, Bogotá, July 28, 2005, in author's possession.

68. Lozano, "Cinco años para derrotar a las FARC."

69. Vieira, "El sur del país va a explotar."

70. Noche y Niebla, "Base de datos."

71. Ruiz, "El río de la guerra: Con el Plan Patriota las fuerzas armadas se metieron a la madriguera de las FARC"; Lozano, "Cinco años para derrotar a las FARC."

Six. Arauca in the Reform Period

1. Oil did not create a strong or leftist movement of Araucan oil workers, as the Araucan oil operation consisted solely of high-tech oil wells and a pipeline. The oil workers, though unionized, were highly skilled, highly stratified, and not radical (interview 55).

2. The electoral front associated with the ELN disguised its candidates as Liberals or Conservatives throughout the entire period of study. The precursor of the UP also did so in 1984. Flatlands Liberals and Conservatives were not fooled and instantly knew the difference between real Liberals and Conservatives and the ones from the piedmont, where the Left is strongest (thus the name "Saravena Liberals," after the most populous county in the piedmont and stronghold of the ELN). In 1986 and thereafter, however, the leftist political party associated with the Communist Party opted for overt electoral participation via the Patriotic Union. See table 6.1.

3. Interview 59.

4. The hierarchy of Colombian territorial subunits, before the Constitutional Assembly of 1991, was as follows: the most populous were departments,

with their own senators and representatives (the total number of the latter depending on population size); next, intendencies *(intendencias),* along with the category ranked below them, commissaries *(comisarías),* shared senators and representatives with contiguous departments. For example, the two senators and three representatives for the intendency of Arauca from 1986 to 1990 also represented and were elected by voters in the department of Meta and the commissaries of Guainía, Guaviare, Vaupés, and Vichada. After the Constitutional Assembly, all intendencies (but not commissaries) were elevated to the level of department, enabling them to elect their own governors in 1991 and their own representatives thereafter. However, senators were then elected via proportional representation, increasing the representation of urban voters at the expense of regions such as Arauca.

5. Matus Caile, *Historia de Arauca, 1818–1819,* 91.

6. Interview 14.

7. Zamosc, *The Agrarian Question and the Peasant Movement in Colombia*; Pérez Bareño, "Arauca: Colonización y petróleo," 67. Figures collected by the Araucan section of the National Health Ministry for 1981 calculate the population of the four piedmont counties as 57,755 and that of the three plains counties as 20,186, yielding a total of 78,411 (population tables for 1981–93 obtained from Ministerio Nacional de Salud, Servicio Seccional de Salud de Arauca, Sección Información).

8. Interviews 9, 12. Only 13 percent of holdings in Arauquita were larger than 100 hectares. Twenty-two percent were from 50 to 100 hectares, 32 percent (the median category) ranged from 20 to 50 hectares, and 33 percent were smaller than 21 hectares. Ministerio de Agricultura, Intendencia Nacional de Arauca, Plan Nacional de Rehabilitación, "Análisis veredal de los municipios de la intendencia de Arauca," Arauca, 1984 (survey conducted by Plan Nacional de Rehabilitación on demography and public services in rural neighborhoods).

9. Peñate, "Arauca: Politics and Oil in a Colombian Province," 17.

10. Interviews 9, 12; Peñate, "Arauca: Politics and Oil in a Colombian Province," 17–18.

11. Interviews 9, 12.

12. Peñate, "Arauca: Politics and Oil in a Colombian Province," 19–20; interview 9.

13. Interview 61; Pérez Bareño, "Arauca: Colonización y petróleo," 69, 86.

14. For schoolhouses as "social nuclei" and symbols of autonomy for rural veredas, see Urueta, "Colonización y territorialidad en el Guaviare"; for demands of the peasant movement, see Peñate, "Arauca: Politics and Oil in a Colombian Province," 30; on the 1972 civic strike, see Pérez Bareño, "Arauca: Colonización y petróleo."

15. Peñate, "Arauca: Politics and Oil in a Colombian Province," 32–33.

16. Peñate, "Arauca: Politics and Oil in a Colombian Province," 28–31.

17. Peñate, "Arauca: Politics and Oil in a Colombian Province," 54–57; Pérez Bareño, "Arauca: Colonización y petróleo," 71–72.

18. Interviews 9, 12, 14.

19. Interviews 9, 57.

20. Interviews 9, 7, 63.

21. Quotation marks are used because the two political movements ran as the second candidate, or the alternate for the first candidate, on two lists led by traditional plains politicians. In the system of proportional representation for Intendential Councils each party or party faction would have not just a single candidate but rather an ordered list of candidates. A successful list might have the first three candidates elected; a less successful list would manage to elect only the lead candidate. See table 6.4 for sources and operationalization for 1984 intendential council results.

22. Registraduría Nacional del Estado Civil, *Estadísticas electorales: Asambleas Departamentales, Consejos Intendenciales, Consejos Comisariales, Concejos Municipales, marzo 11 de 1984*; interviews 11 and 53.

23. See the methods section of chapter 1 for operationalization, formation of indexes, and sources.

24. Interviews 56, 62, 70.

25. Population data for 1981–93 obtained from Ministerio Nacional de Salud, Servicio Seccional de Salud de Arauca, Sección Información.

26. Interviews 64, 13, 14; population data for 1981–93 obtained from Ministerio Nacional de Salud, Servicio Seccional de Salud de Arauca, Sección Información.

27. Arizala, "Las experiencias alternativas de tipo partidistas, independientes del bipartidismo"; Peñate, "Arauca: Politics and Oil in a Colombian Province," 62.

28. Comité Coordinador del Primer Foro por la Paz y el Desarrollo, *Primer Foro por la Paz y el Desarrollo.*

29. Registraduría Nacional del Estado Civil, *Estadísticas electorales: Senado-Cámara, Concejos Municipales, Consejos Comisariales, Consejos Intendenciales, Asambleas Departamentales, marzo 9 de 1986*; electoral acts, Registraduría Intendencial de Arauca. For "political line" of candidates, interviews 15, 53, 56.

30. Barco was president from August 1986 to August 1990.

31. Registraduría Nacional del Estado Civil, *Estadísticas electorales: Senado-Cámara, Concejos Municipales, Consejos Comisariales, Consejos Intendenciales, Asambleas Departamentales, marzo 9 de 1986*; Tame was not subdivided into Tame and Fortul until shortly before the March 1990 elections. On Barco's directive, interview 74.

32. Interview 60; "La Occidental: Un coloso en apuros"; Ecopetrol, *Informe annual 1986,* 45; Occidental Petroleum, "Cravo Norte y el contrato de asociación" (corporate public relations document), 1992, in author's possession.

33. By Colombian law (Law 20 of 1969, Decrees 1246 and 2310 of 1974, and Law 75 of 1986), oil companies are obligated to pay 2.5 percent of the value of the total annual oil extraction to the county in which the wells are located, 9.5 percent to the department, and 8 percent to the nation; see de Angulo Piñeros, "Producción de petróleo y desarrollo regional," 303–5. According to the relevant planned county budgets of Arauca, Arauca's county budget in fiscal year 1986 was 73.1 million pesos; in FY 1987, it was 1.994 billion pesos. Figures on Arauquita budget from interviews 2 and 11.

34. "Guerrilla Attacks Force Colombia to Import Oil"; Miller, "The Politics of Petroleum."

35. Peñate, "Arauca: Politics and Oil in a Colombian Province," 38–40, 70.

36. Interview 55.

37. Interviews 7, 8, 9, 12.

38. Interviews 59, 61.

39. Interviews 61, 60.

40. Interviews 7, 9, 12, 11.

41. Interviews 7, 9, 11, 12; Registraduría Nacional del Estado Civil, *Estadísticas electorales, marzo 9 de 1986.*

42. Interviews 7, 9, 12, 11.

43. Interviews 7, 9, 12.

44. Interviews 8, 9, 12.

45. Miller, "The Politics of Petroleum"; interviews 60, 8, 7, 9, 10, 11, 12.

46. Interviews 7, 8, 9, 12.

47. Comité Negociador, Marcha Campesina a Arauca, *Arauca paró por paz y progreso.*

48. Comité Negociador, Marcha Campesina a Arauca, *Arauca paró por paz y progreso.*

49. Interviews 7, 8, 9, 12.

50. Jaimes, "Acuerdos en Ocaña y Saravena."

51. García V., *Las cifras de las luchas cívicas,* provides information about mobilizations, demands, dates, and participating counties. CINEP press summaries and clippings files provide data on demands and the number of participants at protests. Interviews 7, 8, 9, and 12 verified and supplemented information from other sources, including concessions made and details about the interventions of county executives in protests.

52. Peñate, "Arauca: Politics and Oil in a Colombian Province," 64.

53. County council results for Arauca County, 1990 and 1992, by precinct, obtained from Registraduría Municipal del Estado Civil de Arauca; interviews 57, 58.

54. Interviews 55, 68.

55. The rumor of FARC control of the neighborhood was still alive as of July 1993. Returning from my interview with the regional management of Occidental, I overheard the helicopter pilot explain to another passenger as we flew over the neighborhood where my research assistant and I had been welcomed by residents four nights earlier: "That squatter invasion is run by the FARC. Nobody but guerrillas can go there."

56. Interview 65.

57. William Gamson uses the term *preemption* to describe a situation in which the state responds to popular demands for resources and legislation (new advantages) and political power (acceptance) by granting the desired resources to the movement's constituents while denying any autonomous political representation to the movement's leaders. This is contrasted to co-optation, where movement leaders are given acceptance with no new advantages; full response; and collapse or outright failure. Gamson, *The Strategy of Social Protest*, 27–37.

58. Interview 65.

59. Registraduría Nacional del Estado Civil, *Estadísticas electorales, marzo 13 de 1988*; and *Estadísticas electorales, marzo 11 de 1990*.

60. Voting results by precinct for county council elections of 1988, 1990, and 1992 obtained from Registraduría Municipal del Estado Civil de Arauquita.

61. García V., *Las cifras de las luchas cívicas*. For number of participants for protests and demands: CINEP press summaries and clippings files. For verification and supplementation of information from other sources, concessions made, and details on county executive intervention in protests: interviews 7, 8, 9, 12.

62. However, by 1992–93 all of my peasant interviewees in Arauca County as well as the president of the chamber of commerce concurred that these loans were frequently distributed according to political loyalties rather than need; interviews 57, 58, 59. On Elsa Rojas's elected position: Registraduría Nacional del Estado Civil, *Estadísticas electorales, marzo 9 de 1986*.

63. Interviews 7, 8, 9, 12.

64. Election results for county executive elections of March 1988: Registraduría Nacional del Estado Civil, *Estadísticas electorales 1988*; and interview 53.

65. Interview 14.

66. Registraduría Nacional del Estado Civil, *Estadísticas electorales 1988*; Registraduría Nacional del Estado Civil, *Estadísticas electorales 1990: Senado-Cámara, Asambleas, Consejos Intendenciales, Consejos Comisariales, Concejos Municipales, Alcaldes, Consulta Popular*; Registraduría Nacional del Estado Civil, *Estadísticas electorales: Elecciones del 8 de marzo de 1992*; and interview 53 provided data on results of the elections of March 1988, 1990, and 1992 (including elections to Intendential Council).

67. Interviews 7, 8, 9, 12.

68. The county registrar of Arauquita told me that the incident had caused quite a chilling effect: no one wanted to have a citizen identification card from Arauquita. While in the registrar's office, I witnessed a woman urgently requesting that the county registrar record Arauca instead of Arauquita as her hometown on the ID card, but the registrar could not legally comply.

69. Interviews 7, 8, 9, 12, 2.

70. The geographic location of public works was derived from my analysis of the public works component of the county budget for Arauquita for fiscal years 1988–89 and 1989–90. Political orientation of different rural neighborhoods and information on the mayor's fiancé were derived from interviews 7, 8, 9, 12, and 2.

71. Chronology of guerrilla attacks was derived from *Justicia y Paz* 1–5 (March 1988–June 30, 1992); impression of military superiority of guerrillas from interview 72.

72. De Angulo Piñeros, "Producción de petróleo y desarrollo regional," 305. Arauca County's budget increased from 73 million pesos in FY 1986–87 to 1,994 million pesos in FY 1987–88, an absolute increase of 2,700 percent, or 2,100 percent in dollars (using 240 and 310 pesos/dollar as the average exchange rate in 1986–87 and 1987–88, respectively); Arauca County Planned Budget for fiscal years 1986–87 to 1992–93.

73. Analysis of sources of revenue from Arauca County Planned Budget for the years 1986 and 1987.

74. Interviews 15, 16, 59, 61.

75. Cesar Ataya, a close relative of the LaTorrista county executive candidate Marco Ataya, was manager of the Fondo Ganadero de Arauca, a lending institution for large cattlemen, in 1986, and in that capacity he attended the First Forum for Peace and Development in Arauca in August 1986; Comité Coordinador del Primer Foro por la Paz y el Desarrollo, *Primer Foro por la Paz y el Desarrollo.* According to an article in the regional magazine of the Association of Araucan Professionals, the Araucan Cattle Ranchers' Committee was founded by, among others, Eduardo and Julio LaTorre and Francisco Luís Meza Mejía (Camilo Meza LaTorre, a close relative of former Senator LaTorre, was the lone LaTorrista intendential councilor in the 1990–92 Intendential Council). Other founders included Vicente Loyo, head of the LaTorrista list for the Intendential Council in 1984, and Nereo Guerrero; "Comité de ganaderos de Arauca se crece," 6. Guerrero was one of the largest of the cattle ranchers, according to several of my interviews with independent Liberals, and was related to Stella Torres de Guerrero, the intendent appointed by LaTorre in late 1988 and displaced by Colonel González Muñoz.

76. Interviews 64, 62, 70, 71.

77. Interview 66.

78. "Comité de ganaderos de Arauca se crece," 13.

79. Names of appointed intendents and dates of their appointments obtained from records archived in the intendential courthouse in Arauca. Interview 66 provided information about the political affiliation of each.

80. Interview 66.

81. Interviews 15, 65, 54, 67, 69, 62, 13.

82. Arauca County Planned Budget for 1988. Based on my records during fieldwork for that period, the 1988 exchange rate is assumed to be 380 pesos/dollar.

83. Population figures from Ministerio Nacional de Salud, Servicio Seccional de Salud de Arauca, Sección Información. Budget figures for 1988 from Arauca County Planned Budget for 1988. Fiscal resources/capita figures from DANE, *Estadísticas Municipales de Colombia, 1990,* 181–201.

84. Analysis of Arauca County Planned Municipal Budgets for the years 1988–90; Fiscal Code, November 1988, obtained from Alcaldía Municipal de Arauca; interviews 15, 16.

85. Analysis of Arauca County Planned Municipal Budgets for 1986–87 and 1988–90; interviews 62, 15, 59.

86. Analysis of Arauca County Planned Budgets 1988–90; interview 66.

87. Interviews 61, 66, 68.

88. Interviews 66, 65.

89. Interviews 71, 56, 62, 70, 72.

90. Interview 74 shed light on Gonzalez's possible material motives for such a friendship, stating that in June 1995 Fernando González Muñoz—by then a two-star general—was accused by the Colombian Attorney General's Office (Fiscalía) of having participated in illicit enrichment, i.e., embezzlement, during his time in Arauca. The Supreme Court ordered him removed from his post.

91. Interviews 71, 56, 62, 70, 72, 66.

92. Electoral results for March 1990: Registraduría Nacional del Estado Civil, *Estadísticas electorales 1990: Senado-Cámara, Asambleas, Consejos Intendenciales, Consejos Comisariales, Concejos Municipales, Alcaldes, Consulta Popular.* Interviews 53, 70, and 66 identified coalitions and factions.

93. Electoral results for March 1990: Registraduría Nacional del Estado Civil, *Estadísticas electorales 1990: Senado-Cámara, Asambleas, Consejos Intendenciales, Consejos Comisariales, Concejos Municipales, Alcaldes, Consulta Popular.* Interviews 53, 70, and 66 identified coalitions and factions.

94. Interview 66.

95. Interview 53.

96. Interviews 53 and 56 provided information about coalitions and their implications for repression.

97. CIJP, "1981–1994: Trece años en búsqueda de paz," 1–23.

98. Interview 60.

99. Interviews 9, 12; Arauquita executed municipal budget for 1990–91.

100. CIJP, "1981–1994: Trece años en búsqueda de la paz," 1–23.

101. Interviews 72, 8, 9, 12; CINEP press summaries (1989–92) and clippings files (1984–89) for political violence and mobilizations in Arauca.

102. Interviews 66, 53, 70.

103. Registraduría Nacional del Estado Civil, *Estadísticas electorales: Elecciones del 27 de octubre de 1991*, vol. 1. For coalitions: interviews 66, 53, 54, 70.

104. Registraduría Nacional del Estado Civil, *Estadísticas electorales: Elecciones del 27 de octubre de 1991*, vol. 1; for coalitions, interview 53.

105. Registraduría Nacional del Estado Civil, *Estadísticas electorales: Elecciones del 8 de marzo de 1992*; interview 53.

106. Not only Arauca's governor but many directly elected governors with primarily rural constituencies faced an overwhelming consensus in favor of such "regional dialogues," since both their elite and their subordinate constituents required a modicum of social peace to progress or even survive economically. However, the dialogues were steadfastly opposed by the president, who argued that they would undermine the position of the Executive and strengthen the insurgency. See, e.g., "President Gaviria on Drug Trafficking, Guerrillas, and Latin American Integration."

107. Interviews 11, 66.

108. "Acta de compromiso entre el gobierno y las comunidades del departamento (de Arauca), Jornada Agraria, abril de 1992," signed in Saravena, Arauca, on May 2, 1992 (document in author's possession).

109. Note that this civic strike piggybacked on the nationwide Telecom workers' strike. Protesting privatization, Telecom's workers cut off all international phone communications, paralyzing Colombia's financial sector. When the oil workers of Colombia's major refineries joined in the strike and it threatened to become a national general strike, President Gaviria's hard no-negotiations line softened quickly, perhaps contributing to the success of the 1992 Arauca civic strike as well.

Seven. Arauca in the Counterreform Period

1. Estado de Conmoción Interna, which could be declared for only three months at a time, replaced the longer-term Estado de Sitio after the 1991 Constitutional Assembly.

2. "Decretan conmoción interna"; "Congreso dará prioridad a estados de excepción"; "Prohiben a alcaldes y gobernadores diálogos con la CG"; "Emboscada legal a la guerrilla."

3. Interview 60.

4. "Emboscada legal a la guerrilla."

5. CAJSC, *Arauca: Serie informes regionales de derechos humano,* 80.

6. Human Rights Watch, *State of War,* 21.

7. CAJSC, *Arauca: Serie informes regionales de derechos humanos,* 115.

8. *Justicia y Paz* 6, no. 2 (1993): 30 documents the 1993 incident; CAJSC, *Arauca: Serie informes regionales de derechos humanos,* 55, 98–105, documents the 1994 incident.

9. Gutiérrez, "Assassinations in Apartadó, Cartagena del Chairá, Arauca, and Arauquita"; *Noche y Niebla* 3 (January–March 1997): 62; *Noche y Niebla* 4 (April–June 1997): 74, 51; *Noche y Niebla* 6 (October–December 1997): 51.

10. Political violence incidents from 1993–94 are drawn from Gutiérrez, "Assassinations in Apartadó, Cartagena del Chairá, Arauca, and Arauquita"; *Justicia y Paz* 6, no. 2 (1993): 27, 30; *Justicia y Paz* 6, no. 3 (1993): 121; *Justicia y Paz* 7, no. 2 (1994): 121; and *Justicia y Paz* 7, no. 1 (1994): 25. For mass arrests, see *Arauca: Serie informes regionales de derechos humanos,* 87.

11. On 1995–97 incidents of political violence, see *Noche y Niebla* 2 (October–December 1996): 72; and *Noche y Niebla* 6 (October–December 1997): 50. On the Venezuelan National Guard, see CAJSC, *Arauca: Serie informes regionales de derechos humanos,* 106–9; and "Borracho prendió la frontera."

12. Gutiérrez, "Assassinations in Apartadó, Cartagena del Chairá, Arauca, and Arauquita"; "Otra masacre en Arauca"; "Combates con el ELN en Arauca: 22 muertos."

13. For attacks in 1993, see CAJSC, *Arauca: Serie informes regionales de derechos humanos,* 21, 115–21. For attacks in the period 1995–97, see "Alarmante terrorismo petrolero"; "Colombia Reports Record Oil Exports"; and "Rebels Dynamite Oil Pipeline." For the governor's estimate, see "Arauca está al borde de la quiebra."

14. CAJSC, *Arauca: Serie informes regionales de derechos humanos,* 21, 115–21.

15. Gutiérrez, "Assassinations in Apartadó, Cartagena del Chairá, Arauca, and Arauquita." *Justicia y Paz* 9, no. 1 (1996): 60; and interview 56 document the murder of Goyo González; *Noche y Niebla* 3 (January–March 1997): 62 documents the kidnapping of the son of Congressman Jaimes.

16. Although several sources reported artisanal laboratories in Arauquita ("Colombia: Two Cocaine Laboratories Dismantled") or Saravena ("Campesinos huyen de las balas") or ELN-owned coca farms in the region (Brooke, "Colombia's Rebels Grow Rich from Banditry"), the national entity charged with monitoring regional acreage of illicit crops reported no coca acreage in Arauca before 1999 (Observatorio de Drogas de Colombia, "Estimativos . . . por área, 1991–1998").

17. On the presence of coca and its effects on the rivalry between FARC and ELN, see CAJSC, *Arauca: Serie informes regionales de derechos humanos,*

112–17; and Torchia, "Colombia's Rebel Groups Share Leftist Ideology, Simmering Rivalry." On the ELN's assassination of UP activists, see "Assassinations in Apartadó, Carepa, Cartagena del Chairá, Arauca, and Arauquita, 1992–2004."

18. Results for elections of local authorities, 1994, obtained from Registraduría Nacional del Estado Civil; Registraduría Municipal del Estado Civil, *Estadísticas electorales: Elecciones del 27 de octubre de 1991,* vol. 1.

19. This was demonstrated by electoral results by county for this election, obtained from Registraduría Nacional del Estado Civil. Tame, which includes both plains and piedmont sectors, was counted as a plains county.

20. Registraduría Nacional del Estado Civil, *Elecciones de Senadores, Cámara, y Consulta Liberal, marzo 13 de 1994,* vol. 1. Interview 56 documented alliances in this election.

21. "Atentado a congresista con carro bomba."

22. Results for elections of local authorities, 1994, obtained from Registraduría Nacional del Estado Civil; Registraduría Municipal del Estado Civil, *Estadísticas electorales: Elecciones del 27 de octubre de 1991,* vol. 1, for 1991 governor results.

23. "En Arauca, PCC fija posición ante sanción a gobernador."

24. Results of the 1997 gubernatorial election obtained from Registraduría Nacional del Estado Civil.

25. The department's population rose from 138,000 in 1990 to 216,000 in 2000 (DANE, "Arauca: Indicadores demográficos 1985–2005").

26. Results for elections of governor for 1994 and 1997 obtained from Registraduría Nacional del Estado Civil; 1991 reulsts from Registraduría Municipal del Estado Civil, *Estadísticas electorales: Elecciones del 27 de octubre de 1991,* vol. 1.

27. Neither the M-19 nor the UP had a single senator by then. Pizarro, "Las terceras fuerzas en Colombia hoy," 311–13.

28. Registraduría Municipal del Estado Civil, *Elecciones de Senadores, Cámara, y Consulta Liberal, marzo 13 de 1994,* vol. 1.

29. The following election results were obtained from Registraduría Nacional del Estado Civil: results for Departmental Assembly in 1994 and 1997, Arauquita and Arauca county executive in 1994 and 1997, Saravena county executive in 1994, and Arauquita and Arauca county council in 1994. "El Arauca vibrador" provided data on UP county executives in 1997; and "Arauca a todo vapor" provided data on UP county council members in 1997.

30. "Borracho prendió la frontera."

31. "Venezuela pide ocupación militar de Arauquita"; "Imprudencia"; "Una semana de cierre completó la frontera"; "En Arauca rechazan declaraciones sobre alcalde"; "Acuerdan estrategia de seguridad para la frontera."

32. HVCJ, *Informe de derechos humanos Arauca 2002,* 23; CAJSC, *Arauca: Serie informes regionales de derechos humanos,* 105, 147–48.

33. CAJSC, *Arauca: Serie informes regionales de derechos humanos,* 104, 148 (January 1994 event); 149 (June 1994 event).

34. HVCJ, *Informe de derechos humanos Arauca 2002,* 23.

35. "Arauca: La hora de protestar."

36. "Colombian Rebels Extend Highway Blocks."

37. HVCJ, *Informe de derechos humanos Arauca 2002,* 23.

38. "Arauca: La hora de protestar."

39. Haven, "Crews Clean up after the Latest Attack on Oil Pipeline"; "Multinational Oil Company Forced to Suspend Production after Attacks"; "Arauca pediría declarar la emergencia económica."

40. Van Cott, *From Movements to Parties in Latin America,* 190–211.

41. The Defensoría del Pueblo is the national Ombudsman's Office established by the Constitutional Assembly.

42. "Los abusos de Riowa."

43. "Tierra para indígenas de Arauca."

44. "Upsurge in Violence Leads to State of Emergency."

45. "Colombia: Government Gives Go-Ahead to Arrange ELN Convention"; Johnson, "Analysis: Few Prospects for Colombia Peace."

46. Between 1997 and 2000 the number of guerrilla fighters rose from 14,000 to more than 20,000, and coca hectares increased from 100,000 to 160,000 hectares (Arnson, "Summary of Conference Presentation by Alberto Chueca Mora," 5), financing the armed actors (Richani, *Systems of Violence*). Paramilitary personnel increased from about 3,800 to slightly over 8,000 (Romero, *Paramilitares y autodefensas,* 101–5).

47. Bagley, "Drug Trafficking, Political Violence, and U.S. Policy in Colombia under the Clinton Administration," 38–44; Schmitt, "$1.3 Billion Voted to Fight Drug War among Colombians."

48. Foro Social Humanitario, *Efectos del Plan Colombia y la seguridad democrática en la región del Arauca y el Oriente*; Occidental, "Colombia: Technology."

49. For the war tax, see "Colombian Security"; and "Trying to Attract the Foreign Companies."

50. Richani, "Multinational Corporations, Rentier Capitalism, and the War System in Colombia," 127–28; Miller, "A Colombian Village Caught in a Cross-Fire."

51. Loewenberg, "Big Guns Back Aid to Colombia."

52. Amnesty International, *Colombia: Un laboratorio de guerra,* 19.

53. "As Colombia Picks New Chief, Rebels Voice Their View."

54. Gutiérrez, "Assassinations in Apartadó, Cartagena del Chairá, Arauca, and Arauquita"; *Noche y Niebla* 15 (January–March 2000): 85; *Noche y Niebla* 17 (July–September 2000): 142; *Noche y Niebla* 12 (April–June 1999): 61, 81; *Noche y Niebla* 16 (April–June 2000): 96; Noche y Niebla, "Base de datos."

55. "Operación aérea con linternas y faroles."

56. *Noche y Niebla* 12 (April–June 1999): 61, 81.

57. *Noche y Niebla* 17 (July–September 2000): 42.

58. Amnesty International, *Colombia: un laboratorio de guerra*, 19–20; LAWGEF, "The Wrong Road," 15, citing *Report of the United Nations High Commissioner for Human Rights on the Human Rights Situation in Colombia* (UN Document E/CN.4/2003/13, February 24, 2003).

59. Arauca County incidents in this category are documented in DC-Indymedia, "Human Rights Abuses against Trade Unionists Worsen in Colombia." Incidents in Arauquita in 2001 were documented by Gutiérrez, "Assassinations in Apartadó, Cartagena del Chairá, Arauca, and Arauquita"; "Masacre en Arauquita"; and Noche y Niebla, "Base de datos" (July 20 and December 31, 2001).

60. Figures from the 2004 Departmental Development Plan, the writing of which was overseen by Julio Acosta, governor from 2003 to 2006. Departmento de Arauca, *Plan de desarrollo departamental 2004–2007*, 5.

61. "Arauca a todo vapor"; Noche y Niebla, "Base de datos" (March 11, 2001).

62. "Colombia: Otro congresista asesinado."

63. "Far Right Colombian Group Admits to Killings"; "Former Parliamentarian Murdered in Colombia."

64. Gutiérrez, "Assassinations in Apartadó, Cartagena del Chairá, Arauca, and Arauquita."

65. "FARC Invites President-Elect Chávez, Other Venezuelans, to Peace Talks"; "'Enemies' of Peace Killed Americans" reports that FARC kidnap victims were held and killed in Venezuela.

66. "Rebels Blew up Colombia's Main Oil Pipeline 586 Times since 1982" documents attacks in 1998; "World in Brief" documents attacks in 1999; and "Rebels Sabotage Oil Pipeline," in 2000. For the predominance of incidents in Arauca in 2001, see Departmento de Arauca, *Plan de desarrollo departamental, 2004–2007*.

67. Richani, "Multinational Corporations, Rentier Capitalism, and the War System in Colombia," 129.

68. "Arauca está al borde de la quiebra."

69. Gutiérrez, "Assassinations in Apartadó, Cartagena del Chairá, Arauca, and Arauquita"; *Noche y Niebla* 11 (January–March 1999): 62; *Noche y Niebla* 14 (October–December 1999): 65; Noche y Niebla, "Base de datos."

70. "'Enemies' of Peace Killed Americans."

71. Johnson, "Colombian Rebel." The regional FARC commander at the time was Germán Briceño, brother of the hard-line FARC commander, Jorge Briceño; see "Operación aérea con linternas y faroles."

72. Miller, "The Politics of Petroleum"; "Arauca está al borde de la quiebra."

73. CAJSC, *Arauca: Serie informes regionales de derechos humanos,* 53–54.

74. Observatorio de Drogas de Colombia, "Cultivos de coca en Colombia por departamentos 1999–2006 (hectáreas)"; Miller, "The Politics of Petroleum"; "¿Saldo en rojo?"

75. For the results of the 1998 election to the Senate and the House and the number of votes cast for each candidate (nationally and in Arauca), see Registraduría Nacional del Estado Civil, available at www.registraduria.gov.co. My speculation on Egdumar Chávez's political allegiance to Acosta is based on the fact that he won 7,053 votes (close to the number Acosta won in Arauca on the same day) and that he belonged to neither of the two Left-elite coalitions. For the UP-LaTorrista alliance, see "Arauca a todo vapor." Election results for governor by department, 2000, obtained from Registraduría Nacional del Estado Civil. The lack of data by county for the 1998 and 2000 elections, however, makes it impossible for me to judge what percentage of the petrocrat Liberal–Saravena Liberal votes came from the piedmont and what percentage came from the plains.

76. Registraduría Nacional del Estado Civil, *Estadísticas electorales: Elecciones del 27 de octubre de 1991,* vol. 1; "Arauca a todo vapor"; and Saray de Ataya, Sirenia Web site document the UP-LaTorrista alliance. Results of the 1997 gubernatorial election obtained from Registraduría Nacional del Estado Civil. Results of the 1998 House election from Registraduría Nacional del Estado Civil, at www .registraduria.gov.co.

77. Election results for Arauca Departmental Assembly and Arauca and Arauquita county council and county executive, 1997 and 2000, obtained from Registraduría Nacional del Estado Civil.

78. "Arauca."

79. Results from 1997 and 2000 gubernatorial elections obtained from Registraduría Nacional del Estado Civil. Several of my attempts to obtain the 1997 Arauca gubernatorial electoral results broken down by county were denied by the Registraduría, even though this information was published in books for elections through 1994 and is posted on the Registraduría Web site for elections after 1997. On accusations of electoral fraud, see "El Arauca vibrador."

80. Results from 1997 and 2000 gubernatorial elections obtained from Registraduría Nacional del Estado Civil.

81. DANE, "Arauca: Indicadores demográficos 1985–2005."

82. Amnesty International, *Colombia: Un laboratorio de guerra,* 19.

83. Foro Social Humanitario, *Efectos del Plan Colombia y la seguridad democrática en la región del Arauca y el Oriente,* 6; HVCJ, *Informe de derechos humanos Arauca 2002,* 24.

84. HVCJ, *Informe de derechos humanos Arauca 2002,* 23.

85. "Internacionales: Parlamentarios europeos apoyan campesinos colombianos."

86. Miller, "A Colombian Village Caught in a Cross-Fire"; Organizaciones Sociales de Arauca, "Acción urgente Arauca."

87. Kotler, "Colombia Military Investigating Bomb Deaths following FBI Report."

88. "U.S. 'Outsourcing' War on Drugs."

89. Goldman Environmental Prize, "Recipients by Year"; Goldman Environmental Prize, "Berito Kuwaru'wa: Colombia: Oil and Mining."

90. "Los abusos de Riowa"; Soltani and Koenig, "U'Wa Overcome Oxy."

91. "Los abusos de Riowa."

92. For repression of U'wa mobilization in early 2000, see Foro Social Humanitario, *Efectos del Plan Colombia y la seguridad democrática en la región del Arauca y el Oriente,* 40–43. For U.S. and Colombian activism and Fidelity's divestment, see Soltani and Koenig, "U'Wa Overcome Oxy." Vidal, "Colombia's U'Wa Have Their Prayers Answered," documents that Occidental did not find oil after drilling to 3,600 meters, despite studies promising 1.4 billion barrels. On the visits of U'wa leaders' to the United States, see Twomey, "An Unnatural Journey for Nature's Cause."

93. For the U'wa position, see "Los abusos de Riowa." For Sarmiento's position, see Baig, "Asesinan a parlamentario Colombiano."

94. Energy Information Administration, "Monthly Energy Review: Petroleum," December 2007.

95. Miller, "The Politics of Petroleum."

96. Foro Social Humanitario, *Efectos del Plan Colombia y la seguridad democrática en la región del Arauca y el Oriente,* 46; "Hocol: About the Company"; "Maurel & Prom: History."

97. "New Oil Deposits Found in Northwest Colombia."

98. Occidental Petroleum, "Occidental Receives Contract Extension in Colombia."

99. Richani, "Multinational Corporations, Rentier Capitalism, and the War System in Colombia," 131–32. For the visits of the U.S. ambassador, see Foro Social Humanitario, *Efectos del Plan Colombia y la seguridad democrática en la región del Arauca y el Oriente,* 9.

100. Miller, "The Politics of Petroleum."

101. "Bush Stops in Colombia, Pledges Aid for Drug War"; "Rights Abuses in Colombia Worst in Region—Human Rights Watch."

102. Restrepo, "La difícil recomposición de Colombia."

103. For Uribe governing from Arauca, see "La toma de Arauca"; for troop numbers, see "¿Saldo en rojo?"

104. LAWGEF, "The Wrong Road: Colombia's National Security Policy," 2; Amnesty International, *Colombia: Un laboratorio de guerra,* 9–12.

105. Amnesty International, *Colombia: Un laboratorio de guerra,* 11–13; HVCJ, *Informe de derechos humanos Arauca 2002,* 40–41, 53–55.

106. The other subregion was a cluster of twenty-six counties straddling the border of Bolívar and Sucre Departments (Amnesty International, *Colombia: Un laboratorio de guerra,* 11–13).

107. Amnesty International, *Colombia: Un laboratorio de guerra,* 9–13. The specific provisions were to allow the armed forces to carry out arrests, search homes, and intercept communications without warrants.

108. Amnesty International, *Colombia: Un laboratorio de guerra,* 22; HVCJ, *Informe de derechos humanos Arauca 2002,* 39–40.

109. Noche y Niebla, "Base de datos" (March 7, 2003).

110. Noche y Niebla, "Base de datos" (October 21, 2003); "Hierven las campañas en Arauca."

111. HVCJ, *Informe de derechos humanos Arauca 2002,* 40; "La reconquista de Arauca."

112. HVCJ, *Informe de derechos humanos Arauca 2002,* 40–41, 53–55; Amnesty International, *Colombia: Un laboratorio de guerra,* 9–13; "E. U., tras la cabeza del comandante de la Fuerza Aérea Colombiana (FAC), general Héctor Fabio Velasco."

113. Amnesty International, *Colombia: Un laboratorio de guerra,* 9–13. HVCJ, *Informe de derechos humanos Arauca 2002,* 40–41, 53–55.

114. For official figures for number of coca hectares in Arauca, see Observatorio de Drogas de Colombia, "Cultivos de coca en Colombia por departamentos 1999–2006 (hectáreas)." For the claim that legal crops were fumigated, see Fensuagro, "¡Alto a las fumigaciones en Arauca!"; and Comisión Valenciana de Verificación de Derechos Humanos, "Colombia: Rompiendo el silencio. Valencia (España)." For official claims of how many coca hectares were eradicated, see Departamento de Arauca, *Plan de desarrollo departamental 2004–2007.*

115. "La reconquista de Arauca."

116. "Masacre: Invasiones bárbaras"; "¿Saldo en rojo?"; Foro Social Humanitario, *Efectos del Plan Colombia y la seguridad democrática en la región del Arauca y el Oriente,* 21.

117. Comisión Valenciana de Verificación de Derechos Humanos, "Colombia: Rompiendo el silencio. Valencia (España)," 45–50; Organizaciones Sociales del Departamento de Arauca, "Masacres borrascosas," 1–6.

118. "La presencia paramilitar"; "¿Saldo en rojo?"; "Undemobilized Paramilitary Blocs Control Bulk of Drug Crops."

119. Miller, "The Politics of Petroleum." *Semana*'s January 2005 article "Masacre: Invasiones bárbaras" includes all assassinations in its count, including

nonpolitical ones. It reported these numbers for murders in Tame: 43 in 2000, 74 in 2001, 138 in 2002, 210 in 2003, and 202 in 2004.

120. Comisión Valenciana de Verificación de Derechos Humanos, "Colombia: Rompiendo el silencio. Valencia (España)," 52–53.

121. Gutiérrez, "Assassinations in Apartadó, Cartagena del Chairá, Arauca, and Arauquita"; and Noche y Niebla, "Base de datos."

122. Gutiérrez, "Assassinations in Apartadó, Cartagena del Chairá, Arauca, and Arauquita"; and Noche y Niebla, "Base de datos"; "Amenazados tres comunicadores en Arauca"; "Paras posibles autores"; "Autoridades atribuyen a paramilitares crimen del periodista Efraín Varela en Arauca"; HVCJ, *Informe de derechos humanos Arauca 2002,* 55–59.

123. Noche y Niebla, "Base de datos" (Arauca, June 21 and September 24, 2002).

124. Gutiérrez, "Assassinations in Apartadó, Cartagena del Chairá, Arauca, and Arauquita"; Noche y Niebla, "Base de datos."

125. Gutiérrez, "Assassinations in Apartadó, Cartagena del Chairá, Arauca, and Arauquita"; Noche y Niebla, "Base de datos."

126. Hilton, "Colombia's Oil Pipeline Is Paid for in Blood and Dollars"; Amnesty International, *Colombia: Un laboratorio de guerra,* 10.

127. HVCJ, *Informe de derechos humanos Arauca 2002,* 61.

128. Miller, "The Politics of Petroleum."

129. For repressive incidents, see Gutiérrez, "Assassinations in Apartadó, Cartagena del Chairá, Arauca, and Arauquita"; and Noche y Niebla, "Base de datos." For the start date of the September 2003 fumigation campaign, see Fensuagro, "¡Alto a las fumigaciones en Arauca!" For the approximate end date in November 2003, see LAWG, *Informe 2005.*

130. Gutiérrez, "Assassinations in Apartadó, Cartagena del Chairá, Arauca, and Arauquita"; Noche y Niebla, "Base de datos."

131. In the county executive, county council, and departmental assembly races of 2003, candidates ran with new party names, making it impossible to identify leftist tendencies with confidence. Election results for Arauca Departmental Assembly and Arauquita and Arauca county executive, 2000, obtained from Registraduría Nacional del Estado Civil. Election results for House and Senate 1998 and 2002 and president 2002, as well as for Arauca and Arauquita county executive 2003, accessed at www.registraduria.gov.co. Population figures from DANE, "Arauca: Indicadores demográficos 1985–2005."

132. Results for elections to House, 2002, Registraduría Nacional del Estado Civil, accessed at www.registraduria.gov.co.

133. For the results of the 2003 gubernatorial election in Arauca, see Registraduría Nacional del Estado Civil: www.registraduria.gov.co.

134. "Misioneros de guerra"; Miller, "The Politics of Petroleum."

135. For arrests, the reactions of human rights groups, and the response of the government, see Noche y Niebla, "Base de datos" (October 21, 2003); and "Hierven las campañas en Arauca." Election results for governor and county executive in Arauca County in 2003 obtained from Registraduría Nacional del Estado Civil, www.registraduria.gov.co.

136. The Defense Ministry estimated ELN personnel declined from 4,533 in 2000 to 3,655 in late 2004; see PNUD-Colombia, "¿Cómo va el ELN?" For peace overtures by the ELN, see "Details of Uribe's Meeting with ELN Revealed"; and "Colombia: Uribe on Relations with USA, Peace Processes, Economy, Other Issues." For attacks on the oil pipeline, see Miller, "The Politics of Petroleum."

137. Gutiérrez, "Assassinations in Apartadó, Cartagena del Chairá, Arauca, and Arauquita."

138. For attacks on Arauca County's infrastructure and for armed strikes, see "Paro armado llega a Arauca"; "Atentan contra diputado araucano"; "Forced Strike Imposed by Rebels Creates Humanitarian Crisis in Arauca"; "Arauca, sin luz"; and "Siguen ataques en Arauca." For attacks on the oil pipeline, see Noche y Niebla, "Base de datos."

139. Observatorio de Drogas de Colombia, "Cultivos de coca en Colombia por departamentos 1999–2006 (hectáreas)."

140. Noche y Niebla, "Base de datos"; "Buscan a asesinos de ex-alcalde de Arauca"; "Gobierno no entra en polémica de gobernador con congresista."

141. Gutiérrez, "Assassinations in Apartadó, Cartagena del Chairá, Arauca, and Arauquita"; Noche y Niebla, "Base de datos." For the political affiliation of the October 2003 county council candidate, see Aznárez, "Votando entre asesinatos, secuestros, y extorsiones."

142. "Arauquita se quedó al garete."

143. Noche y Niebla, "Base de datos."

144. Gutiérrez, "Assassinations in Apartadó, Cartagena del Chairá, Arauca, and Arauquita"; Noche y Niebla, "Base de datos."

145. Amnesty International, *Colombia: Un laboratorio de guerra,* 22; "Renuncia masiva en Arauquita"; "Renuncias en zona de rehabilitación"; "UP amenazada por FARC"; "Municipio de Arauquita quedó sin concejales"; "Arauquita se quedó al garete."

146. "Renuncias en zona de rehabilitación" documents Ardila's condemnation of FARC thefts; "UP amenazada por FARC" documents the homage to Ardila.

147. Examples include the killing of an off-duty soldier and the kidnapping of the owner of a taxi business in 2002; see Gutiérrez, "Assassinations in Apartadó, Cartagena del Chairá, Arauca, and Arauquita"; and Noche y Niebla, "Base

de datos." On the trend toward increasing violence, see Amnesty International, *Colombia: Un laboratorio de guerra,* 22.

148. Assassinations of this type in Tame: 8 in 2002, 11 in 2003, and between 11 and 28 in 2004. These data and land mine and bombing incidents from Noche y Niebla, "Base de datos." Noche y Niebla attributes an especially notorious incident on New Year's Eve, 2004, in Tame—a massacre of thirteen adults and four children—to paramilitary forces, but most sources attribute it to the FARC. See, e.g., "Masacre: Invasiones bárbaras."

149. HVCJ, *Informe de derechos humanos Arauca 2002,* 22–23.

150. Tame is known as the "cradle of liberty" because of its prominence in the War of Independence against Spain. For the February 2002 protest, see HVCJ, *Informe de derechos humanos Arauca 2002,* 24–26. For the press release about the protest, see Organizaciones Sociales de Arauca, "Acción urgente Arauca."

151. HVCJ, *Informe de derechos dumanos Arauca 2002,* 25.

152. Saravena Forum: Rueda, "¡Arauca existe, insiste, y resiste!"; Amnesty International, *Colombia: Un laboratorio de guerra;* Organizaciones Sociales del Departamento de Arauca, "Masacres borrascosas."

153. Comisión Valenciana de Verificación de Derechos Humanos, "Colombia: Rompiendo el silencio. Valencia (España)," 53.

154. "E. U., tras la cabeza del comandante de la Fuerza Aérea Colombiana (FAC), general Héctor Fabio Velasco."

155. Miller, "A Colombian Village Caught in a Cross-Fire." As Occidental Petroleum is headquartered in the Los Angeles area, the story had a local angle.

156. "E. U., tras la cabeza del comandante de la Fuerza Aérea Colombiana (FAC), general Héctor Fabio Velasco"; Purdum, "U.S., Citing Better Human Rights, Allows Aid to Colombia Military"; Miller, "A Colombian Village Caught in a Cross-Fire."

157. LaTorre, "Colombia: Renuncia polémico militar."

158. "Colombia Charges Three Military Airmen for Bomb That Killed 17 Civilians during Rebel Attack."

159. "Estado deberá pagar a familiares de víctimas del bombardeo en Santo Domingo."

160. Lobe, "U.S. Oil Firm Occidental Sued for 1998 Colombia Bombing"; Rohter, "McCain Heads Today for Colombia, Where Adviser Has Long Had Ties."

161. Comisión Valenciana de Verificación de Derechos Humanos, "Colombia: Rompiendo el silencio. Valencia (España)," 27–29; "Eurodiputados enviarían misión de verificación por judicialización de Luz Perly Córdoba."

162. Comisión Valenciana de Verificación de Derechos Humanos, "Colombia: Rompiendo el silencio. Valencia (España)," 55–56.

163. CIJP, "Ante el exterminio en Arauca, Verdad y Justicia."

164. Comisión de Verificación de la Ejecución de los Líderes Araucanos Héctor Alirio Martínez, Leonel Goyeneche, y Jorge Prieto, "Crónica de otra muerte anunciada en Arauca."

165. Comisión Valenciana de Verificación de Derechos Humanos, "Colombia: Rompiendo el silencio. Valencia (España)," 55–56.

166. "Los abusos de Riowa"; Twomey, "An Unnatural Journey for Nature's Cause"; Soltani and Koenig, "U'Wa Overcome Oxy"; Vidal, "Colombia's U'Wa Have Their Prayers Answered."

167. Soltani and Koenig, "U'Wa Overcome Oxy"; Vidal, "Colombia's U'Wa Have Their Prayers Answered"; "Colombia: U'Wa Indians Complain about Actions of Occidental Petroleum"; "Colombia: Review."

168. Interview 85 documents the decline in U.S. solidarity, the reasons for this decline, and the need for a new strategy. "Colombia: Ecopetrol Discovers 15 Mln Barrels Crude in Gibraltar" provided information on the existence and magnitude of the August 2004 find.

169. Energy Information Administration, "Monthly Energy Review: Petroleum," October 2008.

170. Occidental, "Colombia: Technology"; "New Oil Deposits Found in Northwest Colombia."

171. Noche y Niebla, "Base de datos."

172. Hanson, "Backgrounder—FARC, ELN," cites the FARC high point as 16,000. In 2008 the FARC and the ELN are said to have 9,000 and 2,200 to 3,000 fighters, respectively. PNUD-Colombia, "¿Cómo va el ELN?" gives the ELN's high point as up to 4,500 fighters. "Colombian Government Announces New Talks with Rebels to Set Formal Peace Process Agenda" and "Colombian Leader Calls on FARC, ELN Rebels to Choose Path of Peace" provide information about ELN negotiation dates.

173. "La presencia paramilitar."

174. "La reconquista de Arauca"; "La toma de Arauca."

175. "¿Saldo en rojo?" claimed Arauca produced one ton of coca per month in early 2006. The government's agency for illicit drug statistics similarly reported a recuperation of coca acreage after 2003; 2001 coca hectares reported as 2,749; 2003, 539; and late 2005, 1,883 (Observatorio de Drogas de Colombia, "Cultivos de coca en Colombia por departamentos 1999–2006 [hectáreas]"). The Social Organizations of Arauca put the number of total hectares of coca in Arauca at 20,000 in August 2005; Foro Social Humanitario, *Efectos del Plan Colombia y la seguridad democrática en la región del Arauca y el Oriente,* 20. A map comparing coca cultivation areas in 2000 and 2005 based on U.S. State Department and UN Office on Drugs and Crime data also indicates similar or increased acreage. Forero, "Colombia's Coca Survives U.S. Plans to Uproot It"; Coronell, "El mapa del fracaso."

176. "La presencia paramilitar"; "¿Saldo en rojo?"; "Undemobilized Paramilitary Blocs Control Bulk of Drug Crops."

177. Gutiérrez, "Assassinations in Apartadó, Cartagena del Chairá, Arauca, and Arauquita"; Noche y Niebla, "Base de datos."

178. Noche y Niebla, "Base de datos." For the arrests in November 1998, see Comité Permanente por la Defensa de los Derechos Humanos, "Detenido Martín Sandoval y un grupo de 13 dirigentes sociales en Arauca."

179. For the resurgence of FARC, see "Re-election: Colombia's Gamble on Uribe." The Ministry of Defense estimated that the number of ELN fighters decreased from 4,533 to less than 3,500 by the end of 2005. PNUD-Colombia, "¿Cómo va el ELN?"; "Colombian Government Announces New Talks with Rebels to Set Formal Peace Process Agenda."

180. Gutiérrez, "Assassinations in Apartadó, Cartagena del Chairá, Arauca, and Arauquit."

181. Noche y Niebla, "Base de datos."

182. Noche y Niebla, "Base de datos"; "¿Saldo en rojo?"

183. Noche y Niebla stopped publishing data on guerrilla actions and combat in 2006. For this finding, I searched the ElTiempo.com archive by "FARC Arauca" and "ELN Arauca," recording each news item that reported a confrontation initiated by an insurgent group in Arauca or Arauquita County in 2006, 2007, or January–November 2008.

184. "Caen campamentos de las FARC y el ELN en Arauca"; "Muerto en combate hombre de confianza de 'Grannobles, hermano del 'Mono Jojoy'"; "Cayó en combates 'Pacho Calvo,' reemplazo de 'Jurga' en las Farc"; "Caen 34 guerrilleros en operativos en Arauca y Cauca."

185. From *El Espectador,* as reported by the BBC in "Colombia's Arauca under Siege by Paramilitaries, Rebels—Daily."

186. Noche y Niebla, "Base de datos."

187. International Campaign to Ban Land Mines notes that Arauca is one of the most mined regions in Colombia, with both insurgent organizations and the military implicated. "Landmine Monitor Report 2007: Colombia"; "Landmine Monitor Report 2008: Colombia"; Noche y Niebla, "Base de datos"; "Gobierno no entra en polémica de gobernador con congresista."

188. "Enemigos íntimos"; "FARC contra ELN."

189. Noche y Niebla, "Base de datos."

190. El Observatorio para la Protección de los Defensores de Derechos Humanos, "Acción urgente: Asesinato, Colombia."

191. Amnesty International, *Blood at the Crossroads,* 3.

192. For the destinations of the refugees, see UNHCR, "UNHCR Briefing Notes." For numbers of internally displaced, see Relief Web, "Colombia: Key Facts on Recent Displacement in Arauca."

193. "Colombian Government Announces New Talks with Rebels to Set Formal Peace Process Agenda"; "Immediate Resumption of Talks with Colombian ELN Rebels Said Unlikely."

194. "Colombian Leader Calls on FARC, ELN Rebels to Choose Path of Peace."

195. "Enemigos íntimos."

196. "La presencia paramilitar"; CCMA, "El día de ayer."

197. "Colombia's Arauca under Seige by Paramilitaries, Rebels—Daily"; "Colombian Daily Says FARC Rebels Have Pacts with Other Armed Groups."

198. All percentages were calculated by dividing votes for the candidate/party by total votes for candidates. Election results for governor, 2003 and 2007, House of Representatives 2002 and 2006, assembly 2007, and president 2006 from Registraduría Nacional del Estado Civil, www.registraduria.gov.co. I assumed that Adalberto Enrique Jaimes Ochoa was the Saravena Liberal gubernatorial candidate in 2007, as he had long represented this political tendency, most recently as representative to the House for the 2002–6 term.

199. This inference is drawn from the fact that Convergencia Ciudana won 13 percent of the votes for Departmental Assembly in 2007 and the Liberal Party won 24 percent; that there was no Convergencia Ciudadana candidate for governor; and that the Liberal gubernatorial candidate, Adalberto Jaimes, who had served many years as elite ally to the Saravena Liberals, won 25 percent of votes for candidates on the same day.

200. "Condenas en Arauca por vínculos con ELN."

201. Results for election to House of Representatives for the department of Arauca and each of the seven Araucan counties, 2006, Registraduría Nacional del Estado Civil, www.registraduria.gov.co. Votes for senators in 2006 in Arauca were dispersed among too many candidates to make analysis productive.

202. "Corte estudia renuncia por 'Elenopolítica'"; "Ahora, la Farcpolítica."

203. Percentages are derived by dividing votes for the Polo by total votes for candidates. Election results for president for 2006 in the department of Arauca and the counties of Arauquita, Fortul, and Saravena and for county executives (alcaldías) in 2007 from Registraduría Nacional del Estado Civil, www.registraduria.gov.co.

204. "No descartan que Julio Acosta esté en el exterior"; "Cayó gobernador de Arauca."

205. Arauca election results for House, Senate, and president in 2002 and 2006 and for governor and Departmental Assembly in 2007 and 2007 obtained from Registraduría Nacional del Estado Civil, www.registraduria.gov.co.

206. Results of the 1997 gubernatorial election obtained from Registraduría Nacional del Estado Civil. My calculation of voters as percentage of total population was derived from DANE, "Arauca: Indicadores demográficos 1985–2005,"

which reports the Araucan population in 1995, 2000, and 2005 as 177,000, 216,000, and 232,000, respectively.

207. Comisión Valenciana de Verificación de Derechos Humanos, "Colombia: Rompiendo el silencio. Valencia (España)," 27–29; "Eurodiputados enviarían misión de verificación por judicialización de Luz Perly Córdoba."

208. "Doce mujeres colombianas que trabajan en contra de la guerra aspiran al Premio Nobel de Paz."

209. Colprensa, "Jefe paraco sí ordenó asesinatos."

210. Inter-Parliamentary Union, "Colombia: Case No. CO/01—Pedro Nel Jiménez Obando; Case No. CO/02—Leonardo Posada Pedraza; Case No. CO/03—Octavio Vargas Cuéllar; Case No. CO/04—Pedro Luís Valencia Giraldo; Case No. CO/06—Bernardo Jaramillo Ossa; Case No. CO/08—Manuel Cepeda Vargas; Case No. CO/139—Octavio Sarmiento Bohórquez."

211. "Procuraduría abre pliego de cargos contra militares por la muerte de los sindicalistas en Arauca."

212. On the sentences for the lower-ranking perpetrators, see Humanidad Vigente, "Masacre de Caño Seco (Arauca)." On the removal of Luis Francisco Medina Corredor, see "Por muerte de sindicalistas en Arauca, destituido 20 años un coronel del Ejército."

213. For the 2005 conference of activists in Brazil, see Mesa por Arauca, "Campaña internacional denuncia explotación petrolera en Arauca"; and Comisión Valenciana de Verificación de Derechos Humanos, "Colombia: Rompiendo el silencio. Valencia (España)." For the Saravena forum, see Foro Social Humanitario, *Efectos del Plan Colombia y la seguridad democrática en la región del Arauca y el Oriente*; and International Peace Observatory, "What Is IPO?"

214. Interview 85 documents the decline in Araucan activism in 2006. Social movement activities in 2006 were documented by Organizaciones Sociales de Arauca, "Misión de Acompañamiento y Solidaridad 14/17 Junio 2006 por Oscar Paciencia"; Organizaciones Sociales de Arauca, "Acompañamiento permanente"; Asociación Campesina de Arauca, "Declaración final del encuentro por la memoria y la dignidad del pueblo de Arauca."

215. Noche y Niebla database, incidents for 2006; Organizaciones Sociales de Arauca, "Carta abierta a la opinión pública." Most signatories were prominent Colombian human rights NGOs, with the exception of the Red de Hermandad y Solidaridad con Colombia. This international solidarity organization authored the second press release, "Llamado europeo a la insurgencia colombiana" (European Appeal to the Colombian Insurgency), signed by twenty-one smaller European human rights groups.

216. Organizaciones Sociales de Arauca, "Misión de Acompañamiento y Solidaridad 14/17 Junio 2006 por Oscar Paciencia."

217. Noche y Niebla, "Base de datos"; Organizaciones Sociales de Arauca, "La vida no vale nada"; Organizaciones sociales de Arauca, "Cultivos de uso ilícito: No!"

218. Organizaciones Sociales de Arauca: "Misión de verificación"; "Audiencia preliminar petrolera"; "Audiencia petrolera"; "Audiencia pública de la comisión de DDHH del senado de la República"; "Constancia Pública del Senado"; "Informe preliminar de la Misión de Observación sobre Ejecuciones Extrajudiciales e Impunidad en Colombia [1]." Party affiliation of the Polo signatories to the October 3, 2007, "Constancia Pública del Senado," document were derived from analysis of Senate 2006 election results from the Registraduría Nacional del Estado Civil, www.registraduria.gov.co.

219. Asociación Nacional de Ayuda Solidaria, "Audiencia por los derechos humanos en Arauquita, Arauca"; Hernán Durango, "Durante el gobierno Uribe han sido encarcelados tres mil araucanos"; Asojuntas-Saravena, "Declaración Foro Comunal en Saravena"; ONIC, "La Minga sigue . . . , en Arauca y en la Univ. Nacional"; Organizaciones Sociales de Arauca, "Reporte paro 24 horas."

220. Relief Web, "Colombia: Key Facts on Recent Displacement in Arauca"; "Uribe les jala las orejas a militares."

221. Autoridades Tradicionales, Cabildo Mayor y Pueblo U'wa, Resguardo Indígena Unido U'wa, "Ecopetrol S. A. reinicia actividades petroleras en territorio U'wa."

222. Beeson, "U'wa Fight New Oil Exploration."

223. Vieira, "Colombia: Indigenous Women Brave War Zone to Express Solidarity"; "Take Action: U'wa Leaders in San Francisco, DC & Chicago!"

224. For Ecopetrol's bribing of the U'was, see "Indígenas u'wa dicen que Ecopetrol busca comprar con mercados su apoyo a exploración petrolera." For *Semana*'s coverage of the U'was, see Restrepo, "Por qué el pueblo U'wa se niega a la exploración petrolera en su territorio." For the mass suicide of the U'was, see "Defenderemos la tierra con la vida: U'was." For the sculpture, see "Monumento a la libertad U'wa se presentará el 16 de julio en el parque principal de Güicán."

225. For the October protest, see Beeson, "U'wa Fight New Oil Exploration." For the U'was' trip to New York, see Miller and Beeson, "Colombian Indigenous Travel to New York to Urge Investors Not to Buy Shares of Colombian State Oil Company Ecopetrol."

Eight. Conclusion

1. Notwithstanding President Uribe's successful masterminding of the constitutional amendment to allow presidential reelection (specifically, his own in 2006).

2. As noted earlier, following the social movement literature, repression is conceptualized as an elite response to social movement activity meant to dissuade activists from further participation. In the case studies examined here, the most common form of repression is the assassination of movement activists, but arrest, torture, and death threats are also common.

3. O'Donnell and Schmitter, *Transitions from Authoritarian Rule.*

4. O'Donnell, "On the State, Democratization, and Some Conceptual Problems."

5. Fox, "Editor's Introduction."

6. Romero, *Paramilitares y autodefensas*; O'Donnell, "On the State, Democratization, and Some Conceptual Problems."

7. Romero, *Paramilitares y autodefensas,* 15–31.

8. O'Donnell and Schmitter, *Transitions from Authoritarian Rule*; Romero, *Paramilitares y autodefensas,* 90–93.

9. Burki, Perry, and Dillinger, "Prologue," 2.

10. Eaton, *Politics beyond the Capital,* 210.

11. See, e.g., Angell, Lowden, and Thorp, *Decentralizing Development*; Manor, *The Political Economy of Democratic Decentralization.*

12. Angell, Lowden, and Thorp, *Decentralizing Development,* 66; Peterson, *Decentralization in Latin America,* 31–32.

13. See, e.g., Peterson, *Decentralization in Latin America*; Campbell, *Decentralization and the Rise of Political Participation in Latin American Cities*; and Campbell and Fuhr, *Leadership and Innovation in Subnational Government.*

14. Eaton, *Politics beyond the Capital,* 7; see also O'Neill, *Decentralizing the State,* 15.

15. Willis, Garman, and Haggard, "The Politics of Decentralization in Latin America"; O'Neill, *Decentralizing the State.*

16. Eaton, *Politics beyond the Capital,* 3–8.

17. Eaton, *Politics beyond the Capital,* 212; Eaton and Dickovick, "The Politics of Recentralization in Argentina and Brazil."

18. Cornelius, Eisenstadt, and Hindley, *Subnational Politics and Democratization in Mexico.*

19. Eaton, "Backlash in Bolivia."

20. Eaton, "The Downside of Decentralization."

21. Castro, "La reforma política," 21–22, 35–39, 40–43; Castro, *Elección popular de alcaldes,* 5–9; Castro, *Proceso a la violencia y proceso de paz*; Castro, *Respuesta democrática al desafío guerrillero.* Although he granted that paramilitary and guerrilla leaders were in some cases deriving such benefits from local governments, Castro did not suggest recentralizing. Instead he proposed stricter vigilance by independent local *personerías* (roughly equivalent to district attorneys)

and a territorial reorganization that would aggregate departments into regions. Castro, *Decentralizar para pacificar,* 31–33, 103–13; Castro, *La cuestión territorial,* 169–71, 71–103.

22. Roldán, *Blood and Fire,* 291–98.

23. Pizarro, *Insurgencia sin revolución,* 116–23.

24. Pizarro, *Insurgencia sin revolución,* 114–16.

25. Tilly and Tarrow, *Contentious Politics,* 163–81, quote on 163.

26. Fanon, *The Wretched of the Earth,* 35–95.

27. McAdam, *Political Process and the Development of Black Insurgency;* Zamosc, "Peasant Struggles of the 1970s in Colombia"; Wickham-Crowley, "Winners, Losers, and Also-Rans"; Pizarro, *Insurgencia sin revolución;* Tilly and Tarrow, *Contentious Politics;* Tilly, *Social Movements, 1768–2004;* Keck and Sikkink, *Activists beyond Borders.*

28. Pizarro, *Insurgencia sin revolución,* 116–23.

29. Tilly and Tarrow, *Contentious Politics,* 163–81.

30. Dudley, *Walking Ghosts,* 129.

31. Romero, *Paramilitares y autodefensas.*

32. Keck and Sikkink, *Activists beyond Borders.*

33. Tilly, *Social Movements, 1768–2004,* 101.

34. Keck and Sikkink, *Activists beyond Borders,* 13–14.

35. O'Donnell and Schmitter, *Transitions from Authoritarian Rule;* Moore, *Social Origins of Dictatorship and Democracy.*

36. Paige, *Agrarian Revolution.*

37. Paige, *Coffee and Power;* Rueschemeyer, Stephens, and Stephens, *Capitalist Development and Democracy.*

38. Paige, *Agrarian Revolution.*

39. Paige, *Coffee and Power;* Rueschemeyer, Stephens, and Stephens, *Capitalist Development and Democracy.*

40. Richani, *Systems of Violence,* 152–55.

41. Paige, *Coffee and Power;* Rueschemeyer, Stephens, and Stephens, *Capitalist Development and Democracy.*

42. McAdam, *Political Process and the Development of Black Insurgency;* Zamosc, "Peasant Struggles of the 1970s in Colombia"; Collier and Collier, *Shaping the Political Arena.*

43. Keck and Sikkink, *Activists beyond Borders,* 13–14.

44. For example, McAdam, *Political Process and the Development of Black Insurgency.*

45. Paige, *Agrarian Revolution;* Bergquist, *Labor in Latin America.*

46. Zamosc, "Peasant Struggles of the 1970s in Colombia."

47. Fox, "Editor's Introduction."

48. Fox, "Editor's Introduction."

49. See Carroll, "Backlash against Peasant Gains in Rural Democratization," for more examples of UP county executive actions during the reform period.

50. Bergquist, *Labor in Latin America.*

51. Romero, *Paramilitares y autodefensas,* 34–39.

52. See, e.g., Gamson, *The Strategy of Social Protest,* 99–107.

53. Wickham-Crowley, "Winners, Losers, and Also-Rans."

54. Pizarro, *Insurgencia sin revolución,* 116.

55. Richani, *Systems of Violence,* 59–81.

56. Paige, *Agrarian Revolution.*

57. Tilly, *Regimes and Repertoires,* 35–59.

58. In my study, plantation labor movements did in fact target plantation owners. However, peasant settlers targeted the state rather than intermediaries. And although in all three regions social movements confronted landed elites (repression sponsors) *politically,* they did not confront these elites economically.

59. Zamosc, "Peasant Struggles of the 1970s in Colombia."

60. Collier and Collier, *Shaping the Political Arena.*

61. See Carroll, "A Window of Opportunity for the Left Despite Trade Liberalization," for a detailed discussion of "armed trade unionism" in the palm workers' union in San Alberto (Cesar). Because armed trade unionism greatly intensified repression of the labor movement in both San Alberto and Urabá in later years, it is easy to condemn it now with 20/20 hindsight. However, given the absolute failure of prior legal means and the presence of guerrillas in both zones, it must have seemed like a logical choice. In fact, in both regions it won union recognition as well as bread-and-butter labor gains where nonviolent means had failed. As Tilly writes, "We should resist the temptation to label one . . . repertoire more efficient, more political, or more revolutionary than the other. . . . We must recognize that repertoires of contention are sets of tools for the people involved" (*Regimes and Repertoires,* 54–55).

62. Collier and Collier, *Shaping the Political Arena.*

63. Wickham-Crowley, "Winners, Losers, and Also-Rans."

64. Pizarro, *Insurgencia sin revolución*; Richani, *Systems of Violence,* 59–81; Collier and Collier, *Shaping the Political Arena.*

65. Tilly, *Regimes and Repertoires,* 35–59.

66. Keck and Sikkink, *Activists beyond Borders.*

67. Tarrow, "From Lumping to Splitting."

68. See, e.g., Brecher, Costell, and Smith, *Globalization from Below.*

69. See, e.g., Keck and Sikkink, *Activists beyond Borders,* 2; Evans, "Counter-hegemonic Globalization," 658; Florini, *The Third Force,* 7.

70. Keck and Sikkink, *Activists beyond Borders,* 11; Smith, Chatfield, and Pagnucco, *Transnational Social Movements and Global Politics,* 47; Lipschutz, "Reconstructing World Politics," 241–44.

71. Keck and Sikkink, *Activists beyond Borders,* 2.

72. Evans, "Counterhegemonic Globalization," 660–63.

73. Keck and Sikkink, *Activists beyond Borders,* 27.

74. Mendes, *Fight for the Forest*; Evans, "Counterhegemonic Globalization," 667.

75. See, e.g., Rudel, Bates, and Machinguiashi, "Ecologically Noble Amerindians?" Furthermore, Kent Redford, in "The Ecologically Noble Savage," argues that such an apparently positive stereotype can lead to harmful policies as indigenous people are viewed as unchanging in their ways and needs.

76. Tesh, "Resisting the Expansion of the Panama Canal," 15.

77. Keck and Sikkink, *Activists beyond Borders,* 28.

78. Olesen, "The Zapatistas and Transnational Framing," 193–94.

79. Keck and Sikkink, *Activists beyond Borders,* 15.

80. Mendes, *Fight for the Forest.*

81. Olesen, "The Zapatistas and Transnational Framing," 180; Earle and Simonelli, "The Zapatistas and Global Civil Society," 119–20.

82. Evans, "Counterhegemonic Globalization," 659.

83. Earle and Simonelli, "The Zapatistas and Global Civil Society," 120.

84. Olesen, "The Zapatistas and Transnational Framing," 182–87.

85. Keck and Sikkink, *Activists beyond Borders,* 29.

86. Tesh, "Resisting the Expansion of the Panama Canal," 14–15.

87. Evans, "Counterhegemonic Globalization," 657.

88. Conklin, "Body Paint, Feathers, and VCRs," 725.

89. Earle and Simonelli, "The Zapatistas and Global Civil Society," 122.

90. Thayer, "Traveling Feminisms," 229.

91. Conklin, "Body Paint, Feathers, and VCRs," 727–29.

92. Earle and Simonelli, "The Zapatistas and Global Civil Society," 121–24.

93. Paige, *Agrarian Revolution.*

94. Romero, *Paramilitares y autodefensas,* 39–40.

95. Fox, "Editor's Introduction."

96. Bergquist, *Labor in Latin America.*

97. Fox, "Editor's Introduction"; Bergquist, *Labor in Latin America;* Paige, *Agrarian Revolution.*

98. Romero, *Paramilitares y autodefensas,* 159–219.

99. Richani, *Systems of Violence,* 103.

100. Bergquist, *Labor in Latin America.*

101. Romero, *Paramilitares y autodefensas,* 39, 228.

102. Romero, *Paramilitares y autodefensas.*

103. Paige, *Agrarian Revolution.*

BIBLIOGRAPHY

ARCHIVES

Centro de Investigación y Educación, Popular Library and Press Archive, Bogotá.

DATABASES

Gutiérrez, Francisco. "Assassinations in Apartadó, Cartagena del Chairá, Arauca, and Arauquita, 1975–2004." Unpublished database, courtesy of Francisco Gutiérrez, Instituto de Estudios Políticos y Relaciones Internacionales, National University of Colombia.

INCORA (Instituto Colombiano para la Reforma Agraria). "Tierras confiscadas a narcotraficantes por el INCORA." 1989–90.

Noche y Niebla. "Base de datos: Casos de violencia política en Colombia." January 2001–December 2006. Accessed at www.nocheyniebla.org/menubasedatos .html.

Reyes Posada, Alejandro. "Armed Confrontations between Guerrillas and the Colombian Army, 1985–1991." Data provided by Consejería de la Paz (President's Ad Hoc Task Force on Peace).

El Tiempo archive. Accessed at www.eltiempo.com/archivo.

DOCUMENTARY FILMS

Campos Zornosa, Yezid. *El baile rojo: Memoria de los silenciados.* Produced by CEICOS. 2003.

Contravía. *San José de Apartadó: 3 años después.* Accessed at www.contravia.tv/ ?p=38 on December 26, 2008.

JOURNALS

Boletín de Prensa, 1984–88. Published by CPDH (Comité Permanente por la Defensa de los Derechos Humanos).

Justicia y Paz 1–9 (1988–96). Published by CIJP (Conferencia de Religiosos de Colombia, Comisión Intercongregacional de Justicia y Paz).

Noche y Niebla 1–18 (July–September 1996 to October–December 2000). Published by CIJP and CINEP Banco de Datos.

MUNICIPAL AND FEDERAL GOVERNMENT STATISTICAL DATA

DANE (Departamento Administrativo Nacional de Estadística). "Arauca: Indicadores demográficos 1985–2005." Excel spreadsheet, 2006. Accessed at www.dane.gov.co/files/investigaciones/poblacion/ITMoDto1985_2005/Arauca.xls on 27 December 2007.

———. *Censo general 2005.* Bogotá: DANE, 2008.

———. *Colombia Estadística, 1988.* Vol. 2: *Municipal.* Bogotá: DANE, 1988.

———. *Colombia Estadística, 1989.* Vol. 2: *Municipal.* Bogotá: DANE, 1989.

———. *Estadísticas Municipales de Colombia, 1990.* Bogotá: DANE, 1992.

Energy Information Administration. "Monthly Energy Review: Petroleum." October 2008. Table 9.1, "Crude Oil Price Summary." Accessed at www.eia.doe.gov/emeu/mer/petro.html on 11 November 2008.

Gobernación del Caquetá, Secretaría de Planeación Departamental, División Estudios Regionales. *Anuario estadístico Caquetá 1989.* Florencia, Caquetá, Colombia, 1990.

Ministerio de Agricultura y Desarrollo Rural. *Anuario estadístico del sector agropecuario 1991.* Bogotá: Ministerio de Agricultura, 1992.

———. *Anuario estadístico del sector agropecuario 2003.* Bogotá: Ministerio de Agricultura, 2004.

———. *Anuario: Estadísticas del sector agropecuario 1992.* Santafé de Bogotá, D.C., 1993.

Ministerio Nacional de Salud, Servicio Seccional de Salud de Arauca, Sección Información. Population tables, 1981–93.

Observatorio de Drogas de Colombia. "Cultivos de coca en Colombia por departamentos 1999–2006 (hectáreas)." Accessed at http://odc.dne.gov.co/spip.php?rubrique7 on 1 March 2008.

———. "Cultivos ilícitos en Colombia, 1989–2004." Accessed at http://odc.dne.gov.co/sidco/publicaciones.do?acion=veEstadísticas on 23 June 2006.

———. "Estimativos de cultivos de coca en Colomba por principales áreas de cultivo, 1991–1998 (hectáreas)." Accessed at http:/odc.dne.gov.co/IMG/xls/PUBLICACION_26.xls on 12 December 2006.

Registraduría Nacional del Estado Civil. *Estadísticas electorales, marzo 1980: Asambleas Departamentales, Consejos Intendenciales, Consejos Comisariales.* Bogotá: Registraduría Nacional del Estado Civil, República de Colombia, 1980.

————. *Estadísticas electorales, marzo 1982: Senado-Cámara, Asambleas Departamentales, Consejos Intendenciales, Consejos Comisariales.* Bogotá: Registraduría Nacional del Estado Civil, República de Colombia, 1982.

————. *Estadísticas electorales: Asambleas Departamentales, Consejos Intendenciales, Consejos Comisariales, Concejos Municipales, marzo 11 de 1984.* Bogotá: Registraduría Nacional del Estado Civil, República de Colombia, 1984.

————. *Estadísticas electorales: Senado-Cámara, Concejos Municipales, Consejos Comisariales, Consejos Intendenciales, Asambleas Departamentales, marzo 9 de 1986.* Bogotá: Registraduría Nacional del Estado Civil, República de Colombia, 1986.

————. *Estadísticas electorales 1988: Asambleas, Consejos Intendenciales, Consejos Comisariales, Concejos Municipales, Alcaldías [marzo 13 de 1988].* Bogotá: Registraduría Nacional del Estado Civil, República de Colombia, 1988.

————. *Estadísticas electorales 1990: Senado-Cámara, Asambleas, Consejos Intendenciales, Consejos Comisariales, Concejos Municipales, Alcaldes, Consulta Popular [marzo 11 de 1990].* Bogotá: Registraduría Nacional del Estado Civil, República de Colombia, 1990.

————. *Estadísticas electorales 1990.* Vol. 1: *Presidente de la República, Congreso de la República [mayo 27 de 1990].* Bogotá: Registraduría Nacional del Estado Civil, República de Colombia, 1990.

————. *Estadísticas electorales 1990.* Vol. 1: *Asamblea Constituyente* [9 diciembre 1990]. Bogotá: Registraduría Nacional del Estado Civil, 1991.

————. *Estadísticas electorales: Elecciones del 27 de octubre de 1991.* Vol. 1: *Senadores, Representantes, Gobernadores.* Bogotá: Registraduría Nacional del Estado Civil, República de Colombia, 1991.

————. *Estadísticas electorales: Elecciones del 27 de octubre de 1991.* Vol. 2: *Senadores, Representantes, Gobernadores.* Bogotá: Registraduría Nacional del Estado Civil, República de Colombia, 1991.

————. *Estadísticas electorales: Elecciones del 8 de marzo de 1992.* Vol. 1: *Alcaldes, Concejales, Diputados, Ediles.* Bogotá: Registraduría Nacional del Estado Civil, República de Colombia, 1992.

————. *Elecciones de Senadores, Cámara, y Consulta Liberal, marzo 13 de 1994.* Vol. 1. Bogotá: Registraduría Nacional del Estado Civil, República de Colombia, 1994.

INTERVIEWS

Summer 1989

1. National leaders of the UP, Bogotá, June 1989.
2. Arauquita's county executive for the 1988–90 term, Bogotá, July 1989.
3. County manager of Apartadó, Apartadó, 24 July 1989.

4. Acting county executive of Apartadó, Apartadó, 24 July 1989.
5. Leader of Sintrainagro (regional level) and former Sintrabanano activist, county council member for the UP 1988–90, Apartadó, 24 July 1989.

January–August 1992 (Bogotá)
6. Consultant to Bernardo Gutiérrez, demobilized EPL guerrilla and representative to the Constitutional Assembly for Esperanza, Paz y Libertad, Bogotá, April 1992.

August–September 1992 (Arauca)
7. Three regional peasant activists affiliated with the UP, Arauca City, 25 August 1992.
8. UP peasant activists in Fortul, 27 August 1992.
9. UP (Fensuagro) peasant activist and founding settler from Arauquita, 30 August 1992.
10. Former UP county council member for 1986–88 for Arauquita, 30 August 1992.
11. Elsa Rojas de Fernández, Arauquita's county executive for the 1992–94 and 1984–86 terms and representative to the House for the UP, 1986–88, 31 August 1992.
12. UP (Fensuagro) peasant activist and labor leader, founding settler, Arauquita (not the same person interviewed 30 August 1992), 2 September 1992.
13. UP county council representative for the 1992–94 term for Arauca County, 4 September 1992.
14. Conservative Party leader, Arauca, 4 September 1992.
15. Former intendential councilor from the UP, Arauca, 5 September 1992 (also interviewed 14 and 17 July 1993).
16. Auditor for Arauca County, 5 September 1992.

September–October 92 (Cartagena del Chiará)
17. UP activist, former county council member, and county executive candidate for the UP in Cartagena del Chairá, urban Cartagena del Chairá, 16 September 1992.
18. UP activist and leader of the urban communual action committees in Cartagena del Chairá, urban Cartagena del Chairá, 18 September 1992.
19. Official from the Cartagena del Chairá office of the Malaria Eradication Service, Cartagena del Chairá, urban Cartagena del Chairá, 18 September 1992.
20. Founding settler and current appointed local official in charge of Remolino and one of the founding leaders of the colonization committee (shared interview), Remolino del Caguán, 19 September 1992.

21. Former president of the Colonization Committee, Remolino del Caguán, 20 September 1992.

22. A founding leader of the Colonization Committee (same person interviewed on 19 September 1992) and UP county council member and colonization committee activist in Remolino del Caguán (shared interview), 20 September 1992.

23. Italian priest of the Remolino parish who ran a crop substitution program in the Lower Caguán, Remolino del Caguán, 20 September 1992.

24. Colonization Committee and Communist Party activist, Remolino del Caguán, 20 September 1992.

25. Founding settler who was an appointed local official in charge of Remolino (also interviewed 19 September 1992), Remolino del Caguán, 20 September 1992.

26. Two FARC guerrillas on patrol in Remolino del Caguán, 20 September 1992.

27. Peasant who was harassed by the army, Remolino del Caguán, 20 September 1992.

28. County executive of Cartagena del Chairá (Turbayista Liberal) for the June 1992–January 1995 term, urban Cartagena del Chairá, 21 September 1992.

29. Official from the Cartagena del Chairá office of the Colombian Institute for Agrarian Reform (INCORA), urban Cartagena del Chairá, 21 September 1992.

30. Commander of the Cartagena del Chairá military base, urban Cartagena del Chairá, 21 September 1992.

31. UP activist, former county council member, and county executive candidate for the UP in Cartagena del Chairá (same person interviewed 16 September 1992), urban Cartagena del Chairá, 21 September 1992.

32. County council representative (Turbayista Liberal) in Cartagena del Chairá for several terms and former peasant activist, urban Cartagena del Chairá, 21 September 1992.

33. UP activist, former county council member, and county executive candidate for the UP in Cartagena del Chairá (same person interviewed 16 September and 21 September 1992), urban Cartagena del Chairá, 22 September 1992.

34. County council representative (Liberal Turbayista) in Cartagena del Chairá for several terms and former peasant activist (same person interviewed 21 September 1992), Florencia, Caquetá, 23 September 1992.

35. Former UP county council member in Cartagena del Chairá (several terms), Florencia, Caquetá, 23 September 1992.

36. Social scientist who designed an urban plan for Remolino during the Laboratory of Peace era, Bogotá, October 1992.

November–December 92 (Urabá)

37. Director of urban planning of Apartadó, 24 November 1992.
38. Member of board of directors of the Apartadó local of Sintrainagro, former Sintrabanano activist (UP line), 25 November 1992.
39. Representative of the Communist Party housing organization, Centro Nacional de Provivienda (Cenaprov), Apartadó, 28 November 1992.
40. Regional peasant leader for the UP in Apartadó, 30 November 1992.
41. County executive of Apartadó for the UP, 1992–94 term, county council member 1990–92, and longtime Sintrabanano-Sintrainagro-PCC activist, Apartadó, 1 December 1992.
42. Two members of the board of directors of the Carepa local of Sintrainagro (Esperanza line), former Sintagro activists, one of whom was an Esperanza county council member in Carepa, Apartadó, 3 December 1992.
43. Regional leader of Esperanza, Paz y Libertad, Apartadó, 3 December 1992.
44. Member of board of directors of Apartadó local of Sintrainagro (UP line), former activist in Sintrabanano (same activist interviewed 25 November 1992), Apartadó, 4 December 1992.
45. Member of the board of directors of the Carepa local of Sintrainagro who was a UP county council representative in Carepa, Carepa resident, former Sintrabanano activist, and activist in the peasant and urban land invasion movements in Carepa, Apartadó, 5 December 1992.
46. Representatives of the Cooperativa de San José de Apartadó (rural Apartadó), 6 December 1992.
47. Longtime resident of Carepa and Liberal activist (aligned with the reformist Federiquista faction), Carepa, 8 December 1992.
48. Carepa county council members (1992–94 period) from the following orientations: Guerrista Liberal, evangelical Christian, Independent Liberal–Esperanza Coalition, and New Liberal Generation, Carepa, 7 December 1992.
49. Non-UP Apartadó schoolteachers' union activist, Apartadó, 7 December 1992.
50. Guerrista Liberal county executive of Carepa for the 1992–94 term, Carepa, 7 December 1992.
51. Two housing activists from Carepa, 8 December 1992.
52. First directly elected county executive of Carepa, Liberal Guerrista, 8 December 1992.

July 1993 (Arauca)

53. Former UP intendential councilor (equivalent to Departmental Assembly representative), Arauca, 14 July 1993.
54. Arauca county council representative for 1992–94 term representing evangelical Christians (for the Unión Cristiana party), Arauca, 15 July 1993.

55. Leaders of SintraOxy, the oil workers' union, Arauca, 17 July 1993.

56. Former UP intendential councilor, Arauca, 17 July 1993.

57. Three founding settlers from the settler-populated Bocas del Ele and Lipa rural precincts (Inspección de Policía) on the border with Arauquita, Arauca County, hamlet of Bocas del Ele, 17 July 1993.

58. Precinct representative to the Arauca County government (Inspector de Policía) from Bocas del Ele/Lipa, hamlet of Bocas del Ele, 17 July 1993.

59. President of the Arauca City Chamber of Commerce, Arauca, 20 July 1993.

60. Occidental District Management, Caño Limón extraction complex, Arauca County, 20 July 1993.

61. Representative of Cootransefluarauca, the Cooperative of River Transporters of Arauca, city of Arauca, 21 July 1993.

62. Arauca county council representative, 1988–90 term, representing Independent Liberals, Arauca City, 21 July 1993.

63. UP (Fensuagro) peasant activist, Saravena, 23 July 1993.

64. Regional representative of the INCORA, Saravena, 23 July 1993.

65. UP urban housing activist associated with the Pedro Nel Jiménez neighborhood, Arauquita, 24 July 1993.

66. Julio Acosta, first directly elected county executive of Arauca (1988–90) and former LaTorrista, Arauca, 25 July 1993.

67. Arauca county council representative for the 1992–94 term representing El Porvenir, an urban neighborhood populated mostly by Afro-Colombians from the department of Cauca, Arauca City, 25 July 1993.

68. President of the regional teachers' union ASEDAR, Arauca City, 26 July 1993.

69. Arauca county council representative for the 1992–94 term representing disabled people, Arauca City, 26 July 1993.

70. Independent Liberal activist in Arauca County, Arauca City, 27 July 1993.

71. An assistant to the UP representative from Arauca, who was also a former intendent, Bogotá, 29 July 1993.

72. Two Araucan peasant activists from the UP (both also interviewed 25 August 1992), Bogotá, 4 August 1993.

1995

73. Former coca harvester (raspador) who was present when the presidential councilor visited Remolino in late March 1987, Ibagué, Tolima, 19 June 1995.

74. Member of the Central Committee of the PCC and former departmental assembly member from Caquetá, Ibagué, Tolima, 4 July 1995.

75. Human rights activist and educator who authored a report (that of the Comisión Verificadora) on Urabá, Bogotá, 24 July 1995.

76. Army general connected with the National Council on Security and a presidential security adviser at the Consejería Presidencial por la Seguridad, Bogotá, 27 July 1995.
77. Researcher from Communist Party research institute, Bogotá, 28 July 1995.
78. Former official of the INCORA in Caquetá who was very involved in the Middle and Lower Caguán peace process of 1984–86, Bogotá, 29 July 1995.
79. Union official from the national office of Sintrainagro (UP line), Bogotá, 31 July 1995.
80. Former member of the Central Committee of the PCC, Bogotá, 20 July 2005.
81. Leader of the Comité Permanente para la Defensa de los Derechos Humanos, Bogotá, 27 July 2005.
82. Communist Party activist from Cartagena del Chairá at a press conference denouncing Plan Patriota in Bogotá, 28 July 2005.
83. Activist from Remolino del Caguán at a press conference denouncing Plan Patriota in Bogotá, 28 July 2005.
84. President of Remolino Communal Action Committee at a press conference denouncing Plan Patriota in Bogotá, 28 July 2005.
85. U'wa project coordinator at Amazon Watch, by telephone, 8 November 2006.
86. Former Communist Party leader from Caquetá, Bogotá, 26 June 2007.

NEWSPAPER ARTICLES AND PRESS RELEASES

"173 Victims' Families File Suit Demanding Chiquita to Pay Reparations." *International Rights Advocates Newsletter,* September 2007, 3. Accessed at www.iradvocates.org on 26 October 2007.
"A las Farc atribuyen asesinato de aspirante a alcaldía en Caquetá." *El Tiempo,* 16 February 2007, 1–5.
"Acuerdan estrategia de seguridad para la frontera." *El Colombiano,* 23 April 1997, 8A.
"Ahora, la Farcpolítica." *El Tiempo,* 24 May 2008. Accessed at www.eltiempo.com on 22 November 2008.
"Alarmante terrorismo petrolero." *El Tiempo,* 19 November 1995, 8C.
"Algo nuevo está pasando." *Opción,* December 1989, 35.
Allen, Mike. "Bush Stops in Colombia, Pledges Aid for War." *Washington Post,* 22 November 2004, A23.
"Amenazados tres comunicadores en Arauca: Continúan ataques contra emisora." *El Tiempo,* 3 July 2002, 1–4.

"Arauca." *El Nuevo Siglo,* 26 July 1997, 9.

"Arauca a todo vapor." *Voz,* 30 July 1997, 13.

"Arauca está al borde de la quiebra: Gobernador." *El Espectador,* 1 July 1998, 3B.

"Arauca pediría declarar la emergencia económica." *La República,* 17 July 1997, 4A.

"Arauca, sin luz." *El Tiempo,* 16 September 2003, 1–3.

"Arauca: La hora de protestar." *Voz,* 9 October 1996, 5.

"Arauquita se quedó al garete." *El Tiempo,* 8 March 2003: 1:7.

"Arcano tres tuvo que retroceder." *Opción,* October 1988, 14–16.

"Armed Conflict Enters Key Phase." *Latin American Weekly Report,* 8 June 2004. Accessed via LexisNexis Academic on 18 November 2006.

Arostegui, Mario. "U.S. Bases Deepen Rift; Colombian Granting of Access Has Chavez Angry." *Washington Times,* 27 August 2009. Accessed via LexisNexis Academic on 14 October 2009.

"As Colombia Picks New Chief, Rebels Voice Their View." *New York Times,* 21 June 1998, A3.

"Asesinado otro líder sindical en Urabá." *El Espectador* (Bogotá), 23 January 1989.

Asociación Campesina de Arauca. "Declaración final del encuentro por la memoria y la dignidad del pueblo de Arauca." 29 October 2006. Accessed at www .prensarural.org/spip/spip.php?article108 on 11 November 2008.

Asociación Nacional de Ayuda Solidaria. "Audiencia por los derechos humanos en Arauquita, Arauca." Agencia Prensa Rural. Accessed at www.prensarural.org/ spip/spip.php?article1396 on 11 November 2008.

"Atentado a congresista con carro bomba." *El Tiempo,* 29 April 1997, 11A.

"Atentan contra diputado araucano." *El Tiempo,* 17 February 2003, 1–4.

"Aumento del desplazamiento en diferentes regiones del sur occidente colombiano." www.eltiempo.com, 3 April 2008. Accessed on 30 December 2008.

"Autoridades atribuyen a paramilitares crimen del periodista Efraín Varela en Arauca." *El Espectador,* 30 June 2002, 15B.

Baig, José. "Asesinan a parlamentario Colombiano." www. BBCMundo.com, 2 October 2001. Accessed at http://news.bbc.co.uk/hi/spanish/latin_america/ newsid_1576000/1576190.stm on 8 August 2006.

"Baleado concejal de Cartagena del Chairá." www.eltiempo.com, 18 February 2008. Accessed on 30 December 2008.

"Baleado este domingo el concejal Hair Guerrero Orozco, de Cartagena del Chairá (Caquetá)." www.eltiempo.com, 18 February 2008. Accessed on 30 December 2008.

"Banana Para-Republic." www.semana.com, 17 March 2007. Accessed on 14 June 2007.

Beeson, Bart. "U'wa Fight New Oil Exploration." NACLA on-line news, 29 October 2008. Accessed at http://nacla.org/print/5151, 8 December 2008.

"Bloqueo a marchas campesinas." *El Tiempo,* 8 October 1992, 8C.

"Borracho prendió la frontera." *El Tiempo,* 9 June 1996, 6A.

Brooke, James. "Colombia's Rebels Grow Rich from Banditry." *New York Times,* 2 July 1995.

———. "Despite Violence, Colombia Surges." *New York Times,* 10 February 1994, D1.

"Buscan a asesinos de ex-alcalde de Arauca: Sindican a las FARC." *El Tiempo,* 23 January 2004, 2–8.

"Bush Stops in Colombia, Pledges Aid for Drug War." *Washington Post,* 23 November 2004, A23.

"Caen Campamentos de las FARC y el ELN en Arauca." *El Tiempo,* 7 September 2008. Accessed on 14 November 2008.

"Caen 34 guerrilleros en operativos en Arauca y Cauca—infiltrados de la policía hasta tomaron cerveza con jefes de Farc." *El Tiempo,* 3 August 2008. Accessed on 22 November 2008.

"Campesinos huyen de las balas." *El Tiempo,* 24 November 1995, 14A.

"Campesinos, víctimas del Plan Patriota." *Voz,* 31 August 2005, 10.

"Camuflados de ex paramilitares, una peligrosa moda en Urabá." *El Tiempo,* 7 November 2006. Accesssed on 28 December 2008.

Cañas, Elizabeth. "Inminente paro bananero." *El Espectador,* 7 July 1998, 4B.

"Captura para 15 militares por masacre de Apartadó." www.eltiempo.com, 27 March 2008. Accessed on 28 December 2008.

"Capturan al jefe de las 'Águilas Negras' en Antioquia, acusado de 400 asesinatos." www.eltiempo.com, 18 September 2008. Accessed on 27 December 2008.

"Caquetá: Gremios prueban violación de tregua por parte de las Farc." *El Tiempo,* 23 February 1987.

"Cash Persuades Guerillas to Give Up." *Daily Telegraph* (London), 1 December 2008. Accessed via LexisNexis Academic on 10 January 2009.

"Cayó en combates 'Pacho Calvo,' reemplazo de 'Jurga' en las Farc." www.eltiempo .com, 29 October 2008. Accessed on 22 November 2008.

CIJP (Comisión Intereclesial de Justicia y Paz). "Ante el exterminio en Arauca, Verdad y Justicia." Agencia Prensa Rural, 6 August 2004. Accessed at www .prensarural.org/arauca20040806.htm on 1 September 2006.

"Cayó gobernador de Arauca." www.eltiempo.com, 25 October 2008. Accessed on 5 December 2008.

Collier, Robert. "Drug War in the Jungle." *San Francisco Chronicle,* 17 December 2000.

———. "Lure of Coca Money Hard for Farmers to Resist: Government Officials Admit That Crop Substitution Is a Tough Sell in Impoverished Countryside." *San Francisco Chronicle,* 17 December 2000.

"Colombia: A Hero at Home, a Villain Abroad: The Paradox of Colombia's Uribe." *Economist,* 12 July 2007. Accessed at www.economist.com on 20 August 2007.

"Colombia: Announces Extended Peace Pact with Main Rebel Group." Inter Press Service, 30 December, 1985. Accessed via LexisNexis Academic on 13 March 2008.

"Colombia: Ecopetrol Discovers 15 Mln Barrels Crude in Gibraltar." *Latin American News Digest,* 26 August 2004. Accessed via LexisNexis Academic on 20 November 2006.

"Colombia: Government Gives Go-Ahead to Arrange ELN Convention." BBC, 21 November 1998, accessed via LexisNexis Academic on 8 October 2006.

"Colombia: Otro congresista asesinado." www. BBCMundo.com, 8 October 2001. Accessed at news.bbc.co.uk/hi/spanish/latin_america/newsid_1587000/1587850.stm on 8 August 2006.

"Colombia: Review." Quest Economics Database, 29 September 2003. Accessed via LexisNexis Academic on 20 November 2006.

"Colombia: Two Cocaine Laboratories Dismantled." BBC, 4 February 1993. Accessed via LexisNexis Academic on 27 December 2007.

"Colombia: Uribe on Relations with USA, Peace Processes, Economy, Other Issues." BBC Worldwide Monitoring, 11 November 2004. Accessed via LexisNexis Academic on 1 November 2008.

"Colombia: U'wa Indians Complain about Actions of Occidental Petroleum." BBC, 12 March 2003. Accessed via LexisNexis Academic on 17 September 2006.

"Colombia aislada." *Semana,* 29 August 2009. Accessed via LexisNexis Academic on 14 October 2009.

"Colombia Charges Three Military Airmen for Bomb That Killed 17 Civilians during Rebel Attack." Associated Press, 20 December 2003. Accessed via LexisNexis Academic on 20 November 2006.

"Colombia Reports Record Oil Exports." United Press International, 23 December 1996. Accessed via LexisNexis Academic on 4 October 2006.

"Colombian Daily Says FARC Rebels Have Pacts with Other Armed Groups." BBC, 21 October 2008. Accessed via LexisNexis Academic on 18 November 2008.

"Colombian Government Announces New Talks with Rebels to Set Formal Peace Process Agenda." Associated Press, 21 December 2005. Accessed via LexisNexis Academic on 25 November 2006.

"Colombian Leader Calls on FARC, ELN Rebels to Choose Path of Peace." BBC, 16 July 2008. Accessed via LexisNexis Academic on 19 September 2008.

"Colombian Leader Urges U.S. Mayors to Support Trade Deal." BBC, 14 June 2009. Accessed via LexisNexis Academic on 14 October 2009.

"Colombian Rebels Extend Highway Blocks." United Press International, 6 September 1996. Accessed via LexisNexis Academic on 30 September 2006.

"Colombian Security." *Latin American Weekly Report*, 17 September 1992. Accessed via LexisNexis Academic on 11 October 2006.

"Colombia's Arauca under Siege by Paramilitaries, Rebels—Daily." BBC, 14 October 2008. Accessed via LexisNexis Academic on 18 November 2008.

Colprensa. "Jefe paraco sí ordenó asesinatos: Fiscalía apela fallo que absuelve a Emiro Pereira Rivera—jefe de las AUC sí ordenó asesinato de congresista y ganaderos." Centro de Medios Independientes de Colombia, 31 August 2005. Accessed at http://colombia.indymedia.org/print.php?id=30083&comments=yes on 20 September 2006.

"Combates con el ELN en Arauca: 22 muertos." *El Nuevo Siglo*, 23 August 1997, 8.

"Comité de ganaderos de Arauca se crece." *ASPAVISION* (Magazine of the Araucan Association of Professionals [ASPA]), January 1990, 6.

Comité Permanente por la Defensa de los Derechos Humanos. "Detenido Martín Sandoval y un grupo de 13 dirigentes sociales en Arauca." 4 November 2008. Accessed at www.prensarural.org/spip/spip.php?article1610 on 11 November 2008.

"Comprende escolta y ayuda económica protección a concejales de Cartagena del Chairá." www.eltiempo.com, 10 July 2008. Accessed on 30 December 2008.

Comunidad de Paz de San José de Apartadó. "Breve historia y estado de la Red de Comunidades y la Universidad Campesina de la Resistencia." Agencia Prensa Rural, 28 November 2006. Accessed at www.prensarural.org/spip/spip.php?article149 on 15 December 2006.

"Concejales de Caquetá se salvaron otra vez." www.eltiempo.com, 26 November 2005. Accessed on 30 December 2008.

"Condenas en Arauca por vínculos con ELN." *Boletín de Prensa*, no. 261, 14 September 2005. Accessed at www.fiscalia.gov.co/pag/divulga/Bol2005/sept/bol261.htm on 5 September 2006.

Coronell, Daniel. "El mapa del fracaso: El Plan Colombia hubiera podido funcionar si se hubiera aplicado con la misma severidad en todas las zonas coqueras del país." www.semana.com, 2 September 2006. Accessed on 18 November 2006.

"Corte estudia renuncia por 'Elenopolítica.'" www.eltiempo.com, 22 May 2008. Accessed on 29 November 2008.

Cortés, Carlos. "Capturas masivas: La suerte del lotero del Chairá." www.semana.com, 12 September 2004. Accessed on 15 December 2006.

"Corto paro de Sintrainagro." *Voz,* 29 May 2002, 4.

Council on Hemispheric Affairs. "Colombia: The Betancourt Rescue and Beyond." 9 July 2008. Accessed at www.coha.org/2008/07/colombia-the-betancourt-rescue-and-beyond on 15 July 2008.

County of Palestina, Huila. "Nuestro municipio." Accessed at www.palestina-huila.gov.co/nuestromunicipio.shtml?apc=m-I1--&m=f&s=m#historia on 27 February 2008.

Cuadrado Simanca, Oswaldo. "Comunicado de Sintrainagro." February 2005. Accessed at www.rel-uita.org/ on 20 August 2006.

"Cura para la paz: Al cumplirse 40 años de la muerte de Camilo Torres, la Iglesia de hoy ha renunciado a las armas, pero no a la transformación social. El padre Jacinto encarna ese otro camino." www.semana.com, 11 February 2006. Accessed at www.semana.com/wf_InfoArticulo.aspx?IdArt=90712 on 13 December 2006.

"Daba plata oficial a la guerrilla." *El Tiempo,* 7 November 2005, 1:3.

DCIndymedia. "Human Rights Abuses against Trade Unionists Worsen in Colombia." DC Indymedia, 4 June 2001. Accessed at http://dc.indymedia.org/newswire/display/9595/index.php on 20 December 2006.

"De concejal en Caquetá a obrero raso en Bogotá." www.eltiempo.com, 13 May 2007. Accessed on 30 December 2008.

"De Navidad, llegó la luz a Cartagena del Chairá." www.eltiempo.com, 20 December 2007. Accessed on 30 December 2008.

"Defenderemos la tierra con la vida: U'was." www.eltiempo.com, 19 December 2006. Accessed on 8 December 2008.

"Del Río, a juicio por crimen de 'paras.'" www.eltiempo.com, 27 December 2008. Accessed on 28 December 2008.

"Desmantelamos célula de las Farc: Santos." www.eltiempo.com, 22 December 2006. Accessed on 30 December 2008.

"Details of Uribe's Meeting with ELN Revealed." *Latinnews Daily,* 12 January 2004. Accessed via LexisNexis Academic on 20 October 2006.

"Detenciones masivas en Caquetá." Agencia Prensa Rural, 14 May 2008. Accessed at www.prensarural.org/spip/spip.php?article1243 on 30 December 2008.

"Detenido dirigente agrario en el Caquetá." Agencia Prensa Rural, 10 October 2007. Accessed at www.prensarural.org/spip/spip.php?article 755 on 21 December 2007.

"Detenidos lugarteniente de 'don Mario' y 2 escoltas que iban en vehículo del ministerio del interior." www.eltiempo.com, 29 August 2008. Accessed on 27 December 2008.

"DLN garantiza seguridad a liberales del Caquetá." www.eltiempo.com, 29 January 1988, 7C.

"Doce mujeres colombianas que trabajan en contra de la guerra aspiran al Premio Nobel de Paz." www.eltiempo.com, 30 June 2005. Accessed on 4 December 2006.

Durango, Hernán. "Durante el gobierno Uribe han sido encarcelados tres mil araucanos." Agencia Prensa Rural. Accessed at http://prensarural.org/spip/spip.php?article1632 on 11 November 2008.

"El acoso sigue in S. J. de Apartadó." www.eltiempo.com, 30 March 2008. Accessed on 28 December 2008.

"El Arauca vibrador." *Voz,* 19 November 1997, 14.

"El coco de los díalogos regionales." *El Tiempo,* 24 September 1995, 8A.

"El cura más popular del Caguán." *El Espectador,* 30 July 2008. Accessed at www.dhcolombia.info/spip.php?article605 on 31 December 2008.

"El dossier de Urabá." *Semana,* 3 May 1988, 27–34.

"El narco-agro: Mas de un millón de hectáreas estan en manos de los narcotraficantes." *Semana,* 29 November 1988, 35–38.

"El otro despeje: El ELN quiere el despeje en el sur de Bolívar, pero Carlos Castaño se opone." www.semana.com, 7 February 2000. Accessed on 1 January 2007.

"El Plan Patriota." www.semana.com, 12 February 2006. Accessed on 16 December 2006.

"Elecciones en Urabá serán ilegítimas." *Voz,* 19 February 1997, 7.

Emanuelsson, Dick. "Militares norteamericanos encabezan 20 mil soldados colombianos en operativo militar contra la guerrilla." Agencia Prensa Rural, 14 April 2004. Accessed at www.prensarural.org/emanuelsson20040415/htm on 30 December 2008.

———. "Un viaje al ojo del huracán del Plan Patriota." Agencia Prensa Rural, 21 December 2004. Accessed at www.prensarural.org/emanuelsson2004122/htm on 30 December 2008.

"Embajador de E. U. precisa alcances de veto a comandos de unidades militares." www.ElTiempo.com, 7 November 2009. Accessed on 13 January 2009.

"Emboscada legal a la guerrilla." *El Tiempo,* 11 November 1992, 3A.

"En Arauca rechazan declaraciones sobre alcalde." *El Tiempo,* 14 April 1997, 11A.

"En Arauca, PCC fija posición ante sanción a gobernador." *Voz,* 22 October 1997, 4.

"'Enemies' of Peace Killed Americans." *Newcastle Herald* (Australia), 8 March 1999. Accessed via LexisNexis Academic on 1 March 2008.

"Enemigos íntimos: Las guerrillas están enfrentadas en Arauca. La orden que tienen las FARC es acabar con cualquier vestigio de los elenos." www.semana.com, 15 April 2006. Accessed on 8 September 2006.

"Entrevista con el Secretario General del regional del Partido Comunista de Urabá: Esto es mucho mas que fascismo." *Voz,* 20 November 1996.

"Estado deberá pagar a familiares de víctimas del bombardeo en Santo Domingo." www.semana.com, 23 May 2004. Accessed on 26 September 2006.

"Estreno del documental 'Hasta la última piedra.'" www.eltiempo.com, 16 September 2007. Accessed on 28 December 2008.

"E.U., tras la cabeza del comandante de la Fuerza Aérea Colombiana (FAC), general Héctor Fabio Velasco." www.eltiempo.com, 6 July 2003. Accessed on 26 September 2006.

"Eurodiputados enviarían misión de verificación por judicialización de Luz Perly Córdoba." *Europa Press* (Brussels), 20 October 2004. Accessed at http://prensarural.org/aca/perly20041020.htm on 2 September 2006.

"Exterminio de UP, otro caso en la impunidad que empieza a moverse." www.eltiempo.com, 8 November 2008. Accessed on 16 January 2009.

"Fábrica de chocolates que funciona en Remolino del Caguán, espera vender sus productos en Italia." www.eltiempo.com, 8 March 2007. Accessed on 30 December 2008.

"FARC asesinan al gobernador de Caquetá." *El Tiempo,* 23 June 1996, 3B.

"FARC Comments on Murders of Congressman Turbay and of His Companions." BBC, 8 January 2001. Accessed via LexisNexis Academic on 14 December 2006.

"FARC contra ELN: Las dos principales guerrillas están en una guerra a muerte por todo el país, en la que hay traiciones, fusilamientos y centenares de muertos. ¿Por qué se están matando?" www.semana.com, 2 March 2007. Accessed on 2 January 2008.

"FARC han declarado la guerra al liberalismo." *El Tiempo,* 25 March 1987.

"FARC Invites President-Elect Chávez, Other Venezuelans, to Peace Talks." BBC Summary of World Broadcasts, 31 December 1998. Accessed via LexisNexis Academic on 20 September 2006.

"Farc vuelan lancha en Cartagena del Chairá." *El Tiempo,* 30 May 2007, 1:7.

"Far Right Colombian Group Admits to Killings." *Morning Star* (London), 16 October 2001, 3. Accessed via LexisNexis Academic on 19 October 2006.

Fedepalma. "Distribution of Oil Palm Planted Area According to Zones (In Hectares)." Accessed at www.fedepalma.org/statistics.shtm on 28 December 2008.

———. "The Oil Palm Agroindustry in Colombia." Brochure downloaded from www.fedepalma.org/publicaciones.shtm#otras on 29 December 2008.

Fellowship of Reconciliation. Update on the Massacre in San José de Apartadó, Colombia." 22 April 2005. Accessed at www.forusa.org/documents/Updateon SJAMassacre_001.pdf, 3 September 2006.

Fellowship of Reconciliation Colombia Program. "San José Community Awarded Peace Prize." Accessed at www.forcolombia.org/italypeaceprize on 26 December 2008.

Fensuagro (Federación Nacional Sindical Unitaria Agropecuaria). "¡Alto a las fumigaciones en Arauca!" Press release, 30 September 2003. Accessed at http://colombia.indymedia.org/news/2003/09/6268.php on 26 November 2006.

"Fin del Plan Patriota, llega el Plan Victoria." www.eltiempo.com, 10 December 2006. Accessed on 30 December 2008.

"Fiscalía abre proceso de 'Farcpolítica.'" www.eltiempo.com, 25 May 2008. Accessed on 17 January 2009.

Flamini, Roland. "Analysis: Tide Slowly Turning in Colombia." United Press International, 16 February 2004. Accessed via LexisNexis Academic on 15 August 2007.

"Forced Strike Imposed by Rebels Creates Humanitarian Crisis in Arauca." *Financial Times Information,* 11 June 2003. Accessed via LexisNexis Academic on 1 September 2006.

Forero, Juan. "Colombia's Coca Survives U.S. Plans to Uproot It." *New York Times,* 19 August 2006, A1.

"Former Parliamentarian Murdered in Colombia." Deutsche Press-Agentur, 17 October 2001. Accessed via LexisNexis Academic on 19 October 2006.

Giraldo, Fabio Arias, and Gustavo R. Triana. "Apoyamos la huelga en Banur s.a. y reclamamos pronta solución." Central Unitaria de Trabajadores press release, 12 May 2008. Accessed at www.cut.org.co//index.php?option=com_content&task=view&id=1195&Itemid=456 on 29 December 2008.

"Gobierno rechaza intimidación de bandas criminales en el Urabá." Caracol Radio, 16 October 2008. Accessed at www.caracol.com.co/nota.aspx?id=691187 on 27 December 2008.

Gómez, Carlos Mario. "Acuerdo bananero asegura la paz laboral en Urabá." *El Colombiano,* 25 January 1996, 2B.

"Gracias y desgracias de una region." *Opción,* June 1988, A1.

"Grave crisis humanitaria generada por el Ejército nacional en poblaciones del Bajo Caguán, Caquetá, denunció misión humanitaria." Prensa Reiniciar, 27 October 2008. Accessed at www.reiniciar.org/?Q=node/216 on 16 January 2009.

"Guerrilla Attacks Force Colombia to Import Oil." Inter-Press Service, 7 October 1986. Accessed via LexisNexis Academic on 1 December 2006.

Haven, Paul. "Crews Clean up after the Latest Attack on Oil Pipeline." Associated Press, 10 January 1996. Accessed via LexisNexis Academic database on 30 September 2006.

Hilton, Isabel. "Colombia's Oil Pipeline Is Paid for in Blood and Dollars: Trade Unionists are the Prime Targets of the US-Funded 18th Brigade." *Guardian,* 20 August 2004, 22. Accessed via LexisNexis Academic on 1 September 2006.

"HH dice que 'para' que participó en asesinato de Manuel Cepeda está libre." www.eltiempo.com, 11 June 2008. Accessed on 28 December 2008.

"Hierven las campañas en Arauca." *El Tiempo,* 23 October 2003.

"Howard County Calendar: Community Events." *Washington Post,* 8 September 2005, final edition. Accessed via LexisNexis Academic on 29 December 2008.

Humanidad Vigente Corporación Jurídica (HVCJ). "Masacre de Caño Seco (Arauca): Cuatro años de impunidad." Agencia Prensa Rural, 6 August 2008. Accessed at www.prensarural.org/spip/spip.php?article1427 on 11 November 2008.

"Immediate Resumption of Talks with Colombian ELN Rebels Said Unlikely." BBC, 20 April 2008. Accessed via LexisNexis Academic on 23 November 2008.

"Imprudencia." *El Espectador,* 7 April 1997, 5A.

"Indígenas U'wa dicen que Ecopetrol busca comprar con mercados su apoyo a exploración petrolera." www.eltiempo.com, 11 May 2007. Accessed on 8 December 2008.

"Informe especial: La contra-revolución en Urabá." *Semana,* 17 May 1988, 26–35.

"Internacionales: Parlamentarios europeos apoyan campesinos colombianos." Caracol Radio, 3 July 2000. Accessed at http://www.carocol.com.co/nota .asp?id=127069 on 1 September 2006.

"Interview: Ingrid Betancourt." *Observer* (U. K.), 30 November 2008. Accessed at LexisNexis Academic on 10 January 2009.

Iturralde, Manuel. "Una masacre anunciada." *Semana,* 10 April 2008. Accessed at www.semana.com/noticias-opinion-on-line/masacre-anunciada/110863 .aspx on 26 December 2008.

Jaimes, Arturo. "Acuerdos en Ocaña y Saravena: Terminó paro del nororiente." *El Tiempo,* 14 June 1987, 1A–1D.

"Jesús Abad Colorado, uno de los distinguidos con el 2006 International Press Freedom Award." www.eltiempo.com, 20 November 2006. Accessed on 28 December 2006.

Johnson, Owain. "Analysis: Few Prospects for Colombia Peace." United Press International, 1 June 2002. Accessed via LexisNexis Academic on 8 October 2006.

Johnson, Tim. "Colombian Rebel: Rogue Unit Killed U.S. Activists." *Miami Herald,* 11 March 1999, A14. Accessed via LexisNexis Academic on 1 March 2008.

Kotler, Jared. "Colombia Military Investigating Bomb Deaths following FBI Report." Associated Press, 13 December 2000. Accessed via LexisNexis Academic on 26 September 2006.

———. "Killings Provoke Outrage, but Colombia Peace Efforts Go On." Associated Press, 24 February 2001. Accessed via LexisNexis Academic, 14 December 2006.

Knox, Paul. "Moral Suasion, not Courts, Works for Rights Winner Priest 'Given up on Colombian Justice' in Fight for Political Victims." *Globe and Mail*

(Toronto), 13 December 1997. Accessed via LexisNexis Academic on 29 December 2008.

Kraul, Chris. "Bush Pushes Trade Pact to Aid Colombia and His Legacy." *Los Angeles Times,* 13 November 2008. Accessed at LexisNexis Academic on 13 January 2009.

———. "In Colombia, Paramilitary Groups Still Spreading Terror." *Los Angeles Times,* 3 December 2008. Accessed at LexisNexis Academic on 10 January 2009.

———. "Village's Unarmed Rebellion: On Strategic Land in Colombia's Civil War, a Group of Peasants Stands up against Violence. But a Refusal to Take Sides Offers Little Protection." *Los Angeles Times,* 18 September 2006.

Kushner, Adam. "The Truth about Plan Colombia: The U.S.-Backed War on Drugs Is Failing, as Coca Traffickers Stay One Step Ahead of Uribe." *Newsweek,* 3 January 2009. Accessed at LexisNexis Academic on 5 January 2009.

"La gran encuesta de la parapolítica." www.semana.com, 5 May 2007. Accessed on 17 August 2007.

"La gran redada: La estrategia de capturas masivas del gobierno podría ser un remedio peor que la enfermedad." www.semana.com, 6 October 2003. Accessed on 15 December 2006.

"La guerra de la tierra." www.semana.com, 21 June 2008. Accessed on 26 December 2008.

"La Julia, otro 'santuario' de las Farc que languidece sin la coca." www.eltiempo.com, 28 April 2007. Accessed on 30 December 2008.

"La ley del Caguán: *Semana* revela el documento que ha servido de base a las exigencias de las FARC en la zona del despeje." www.semana.com, 4 December 1999. Accessed on 25 August 2006.

"La Occidental: Un coloso en apuros." *Eco-Impacto* 3, no. 20 (1988).

"La otra Cartagena: Las FARC insisten en el despeje de otro municipio de Caquetá. ¿Intenciones de paz o estrategia de guerra?" www.semana.com, 29 November 1999. Accessed on 13 December 2006.

"La presencia paramilitar." www.semana.com, 5 February 2006. Accessed on 25 November 2006.

"La reconquista de Arauca." www.semana.com, 1 March 2003. Accessed on 25 August 2006.

"La toma de Arauca." www.semana.com, 21 July 2003. Accessed on 10 September 2006.

"Las guerras de los narcos de 'Tercera Generación.'" www.eltiempo.com, 6 April 2008. Accessed on 28 December 2008.

LaTorre, Hector. "Colombia: Renuncia polémico militar." BBCMundo.com, 26 August 2003. Accessed on 10 November 2006.

Leahy, Patrick. "Statement of Senator Patrick Leahy on the Massacre at San José de Apartadó." 17 November 2005. Accessed at http://leahy.senate.gov/press/200511/111705a.html on 3 September 2006.

"Libres Victor Oime y su hijo." *Voz,* 14 February 2007, 10.

"Llaman a Gloria Cuartas y al padre Javier Giraldo para declarar en caso contra el general Del Río." www.eltiempo.com, 16 September 2008. Accessed on 28 December 2008.

Lobe, Jim. "U.S. Oil Firm Occidental Sued for 1998 Colombia Bombing." Inter-Press Service, 25 April 2003. Accessed via LexisNexis Academic on 17 September 2006.

"Los desertores: Este es el relato hecho a semana por tres ex-guerrilleros de las FARC que tomaron parte en el asalto a Las Delicias y en el secuestro de 60 soldados." www.semana.com, 19 May 1997. Accessed on 13 December 2006.

"Los 'esperanzados' en homenaje a Del Río." *El Tiempo,* 29 April 1999, 6A.

Lozano, Pilar. "Cinco años para derrotar a las FARC." *El País,* 28 July 2005. Accessed at www.elpais.es/articulo/elpporint20050728elpepiint_13/Tes on 9 August 2006.

Observatorio para la Protección de los Defensores de Derechos Humanos. "Acción urgente: Asesinato, Colombia." 31 March 2006. Accessed at http://protectionline.org/spip.php?article401 on 2 September 2006.

"Masacre en Arauquita." *Voz,* 25 July 2001, 11.

"Masacre: Invasiones bárbaras—En uno de los actos más sanguinarios del conflicto, las FARC masacraron a 13 adultos y 4 niños. Los civiles son cada vez más los víctimas de las retaliaciones de los grupos armados." www.semana.com, 9 January 2005. Accessed on 18 November 2006.

"Maurel & Prom: History." Accessed at www.maureletprom.com/1_discover/saga_3.php?rub=2 on 25 November 2006.

Mesa por Arauca. "Campaña internacional denuncia explotación petrolera en Arauca." Agencia Prensa Rural, 31 January 2005. Accessed at www.prensarural.org/arauca2005-131.htm on 1 September 2006.

Miller, Andrew, and Bart Beeson. "Colombian Indigenous Travel to New York to Urge Investors Not to Buy Shares of Colombian State Oil Company Ecopetrol." Amazon Watch Press Release, 17 November 2008. Accessed at www.amazonwatch.org/newsroom/view_news.php?id=1685 on 8 December 2008.

Miller, T. Christian. "A Colombian Village Caught in a Cross-Fire: The Bombing of Santo Domingo Shows How Messy U.S. Involvement in the Latin American Drug War Can Be." *Los Angeles Times,* 17 March 2002. Accessed at http://articles.latimes.com/2002/mar/17/news/mn33272 on 26 September 2006.

————. "The Politics of Petroleum: Riding Shotgun on a Pipeline." *Los Angeles Times,* 16 May 2004. Accessed at www.amazonwatch.org/newsroom/view _news.php?id=796 on 20 November 2006.

"Misión de observación al corazón del Plan Patriota." Agencia Prensa Rural, 28 October 2005. Accessed at www.prensarural.org/planpatriota20051028 .htm on 30 December 2008.

"Misioneros de guerra: Pampurí—la historia de un hospital cerrado por el ELN." *El Tiempo,* 10 September 1995, 24A.

"Monumento a la libertad U'wa se presentará el 16 de julio en el parque principal de Güicán." www.eltiempo.com, 9 July 2007. Accessed on 8 December 2008.

"Muerto de la risa." www.semana.com, 3 October 2009. Accessed via LexisNexis Academic on 14 October 2009.

"Muerto en combate hombre de confianza de 'Grannobles, hermano del 'Mono Jojoy.'" www.eltiempo.com, 24 August 2008. Accessed on 22 November 2008.

"Multinational Oil Company Forced to Suspend Production after Attacks." BBC, 22 July 1997. Accessed via LexisNexis Academic on 8 September 2006.

"Municipio de Arauquita quedó sin concejales." *El Colombiano,* 21 February 2003, 8A.

Murillo, María Luisa. "Por fin, alcalde en C. del Chairá." *El Tiempo,* 24 August 1998, 7E.

————. "Yo recibí una orden del grupo de las FARC." *El Tiempo,* 16 August 1997, 6A.

Muse, Toby. "With Landslide Win, Colombia's Uribe Looks to 4 More Years Combating Violence, Boosting Economy." Associated Press, 29 May 2006. Accessed via LexisNexis Academic on 23 June 2006.

"New Oil Deposits Found in Northwest Colombia." BBC, 1 July 2005. Accessed via LexisNexis Academic on 1 September 2006.

"No cede la violencia pre-electoral: Asesinan a dos candidatos en Caquetá." Caracol Radio, 23 October 2007. Accessed at www.caracol.com.co/noticias/497443 .asp on 21 December 2007.

"No descartan que Julio Acosta esté en el exterior." www.eltiempo.com, 26 June 2008. Accessed on 14 November 2008.

"Nominan a Nobel de Paz a 2 comunidades colombianas." *El Tiempo,* 14 February 2007. Accessed at www.eltiempo.com on 28 December 2008.

"Noticias breves de justicia." www.eltiempo.com, 8 July 2008. Accessed on 30 December 2008.

"Nuevos hechos de violencia en el Caquetá." *Voz,* 21 April 1988.

"Ocampo Madrid, Sergio. Por los municipios: Apartadó." *El Tiempo,* 2 July 1989, 12A.

"Ocho Premios Nacionales de Paz continúan y fortalecen sus iniciativas." www.eltiempo.com, 30 October 2006. Accessed on 20 December 2006.

O'Neil, Shannon, and Sebastian Chaskel. "Holding Up Trade Deal Won't Solve Colombia's Woes." *Washington Times,* 27 November 2008. Accessed at Lexis-Nexis Academic on 12 January 2009.

"Operación aérea con linternas y faroles." *El Espectador,* 20 February 1999, 4A.

Organizaciones Sociales de Arauca. "Acción urgente Arauca." 4 March 2002. Accessed at www.nadir.org/nadir/initiativ/agp/free/colombia/txt/2002/0304 on 2 September 2006.

———. "Acompañamiento permanente." 6 August 2006. Accessed at www.organizacionessociales.org/index.php?option=com_content&task=view&id=112&Itemid=47 on 5 December 2008.

———. "Audiencia pública de la comisión de DDHH del senado de la República." 27 September 2007. Accessed at www.organizacionessociales.org on 2 January 2008.

———. "Carta abierta a la opinión pública." 28 April 2006. Accessed at www.organizacionessociales.org/index.php?option=com_content&task=view&id=100&Itemid=28 on 5 December 2008.

———. "Constancia pública del Senado." 3 October 2007. Accessed at www.organizacionessociales.org on 2 January 2008.

———. "Cultivos de uso ilícito: No!" 18 December 2007. Accessed at www.organizacionessociales.org/index.php?option=com_content&task=view&id=170&Itemid=34 on 2 January 2008.

———. "Informe preliminar de la misión de observación sobre ejecuciones extrajudiciales e impunidad en Colombia [1]." 10 October 2007. Accessed at www.organizacionessociales.org on 2 January 2008.

———. "La vida no vale nada." 10 October 2007, accessed at http://www.organizacionessociales.org on 26 December 2007.

———. "Misión de acompañamiento y solidaridad 14/17 Junio 2006 por Oscar Paciencia." Slide show accessed at www.organizacionessociales.org/antigua on 5 December 2008.

———. "Misión de verificación." 25 January 2007. Accessed at www.organizacionessociales.org on 2 January 2008.

———. "Reporte Paro 24 Horas." Accessed at www.organizacionessociales.org/index.php?option=com_content&task=view&id=442&Itemid=28 on 5 December 2008.

"Otorgan premio nantes 2008 a Gloria Cuartas." www.eltiempo.com, 25 June 2008. Accessed on 28 December 2006.

"Otra masacre en Arauca." *El Pais,* 12 July 1997, A3.

"Otra víctima de 'paras' asesinada no alcanzó a denunciar en justicia y paz." www.eltiempo.com, 10 February 2007. Accessed on 27 December 2008.

Occidental Petroleum. "Occidental Receives Contract Extension in Colombia." Press release, 23 April 2004. Accessed at http://phx.corporate-ir.net/phoenix

.zhtml?c=76816&p=irol-newsArticle_Print&ID=518626&highlight= on 16 September 2006.

"Paramilitary Massacres across the Land: FARC Reneges on Pledge to Halt Mass Kidnappings." *Latin American Weekly Report,* 16 October 2001, 486. Accessed via LexisNexis Academic on 14 December 2006.

"Paras posibles autores: Asesinado periodista radial en Arauca." *El Tiempo,* 29 June 2002, 2–6.

"Paro armado llega a Arauca." *El Tiempo,* 13 February 2003, 1–5.

"Paro bananero en la región de Urabá." *El Colombiano,* 11 August 2001, 3B.

"Pass the Pact: U.S. Economic Woes Strengthen the Case for Free Trade in Colombia." *Washington Post,* 12 November 2008. Accessed at LexisNexis Academic on 10 January 2009.

"Peace Recedes." *Economist,* 11 August 2001. Accessed at www.economist.com on 31 December 2006.

Penhaul, Karl. "En Cartagena del Chairá: Experimento electoral orientado por las FARC." *El Colombiano,* 24 August 1998, 3.

Pérez M., José Alejandro, and Adriana M. Hurtado Bernal. "Sin acuerdo el pliego bananero." *El Mundo,* 6 January 1996, 5.

Permanent Peoples' Tribunal Session on Colombia "Accusation against the Transnational Dyncorp." Prepared for the Hearing on Biodiversity, Humanitarian Zone, Cacarica, [Colombia], 24–27 February 2007. Accessed at www .prensarural.org/spip/spip.php?article673 on 2 January 2009.

"Perpetran masacres en Colombia." *La Prensa,* 12 October 2001. Accessed at http://mensual.prensa.com/mensual/contenido/2001/10/12/hoy/mundo on 14 December 2006.

"Plan Patriota: Recuperar el territorio considerado por años la retaguardia profunda de las FARC es el objetivo de la ofensiva de las fuerzas armadas." www.semana.com, 2 October 2005. Accessed on 15 December 2006.

Pombo, Roberto. "Barco rediseñó el proceso de paz." *El Tiempo,* 23 June 1987.

"Por caída del dólar, bananeros han perdido $1,24 billones." www.eltiempo.com, 12 June 2007. Accessed on 27 December 2008.

"Por ella ofrecían un millón de dólares entrega de 'Karina' en Antioquia, otro duro golpe a moral de las Farc." www.eltiempo.com, 19 May 2008. Accessed on 28 December 2008.

"Porque sí a las bases." www.semana.com, 8 August 2009. Accessed on 14 October 2009.

"Por muerte de sindicalistas en Arauca, destituido 20 años un coronel del Ejército." *Semana,* 2 September 2008. Accessed at www.semana.com on 5 December 2008.

Priest, Dana. "U.S. May Boost Military Aid to Colombia's Anti-Drug Effort." *Washington Post,* 28 March 1998, A19.

"Premio Nacional de Paz reconoce esfuerzos e iniciativas en pro del bienestar de las comunidades." www.eltiempo.com, 17 April 2008. Accessed on 30 December 2008.

"President Gaviria on Drug Trafficking, Guerrillas and Latin American Integration." BBC, 3 September 1992. Accessed via LexisNexis Academic on 3 September 2006.

"Primera Asamblea Comunitaria Municipio de Cartagena del Chairá." 5–7 December 2003. Accessed at www.mamacoca.org/FSMT_sept_2003/es/lat/Asamblea%20comunitaria%20cartagena%20del%20chaira.htm on 21 December 2007.

"Procuraduría abre pliego de cargos contra militares por la muerte de los sindicalistas en Arauca." www.semana.com, 18 May 2006. Accessed on 8 September 2006.

"Pura sangre." *Semana,* 19 April 1988, 28–29.

Purdum, Todd S. "U.S., Citing Better Human Rights, Allows Aid to Colombia Military." *New York Times,* 10 September 2002.

Raigozo, Camilo. "Chino, a usted lo matan hoy." *Voz,* 10 August 2005, 10.

Ramírez, Gustavo León. "Bananeros mantienen los diálogos laborales." *El Colombiano,* 14 April 2000, 1B.

———. "Bananeros y trabajadores persiguen un Pacto Social." *El Colombiano,* 20 January 2005, 1B.

———. "El gobierno promete $5.000 millones a los bananeros." *El Colombiano,* 4 December 1996, 2A.

———. "En pliego bananero, el llamado es a concertar." *El Colombiano,* 24 March 2004, 3B.

———. "La huelga, un suicidio para los bananeros." *El Colombiano,* 19 January 1996, 3B.

———. "La mediación de mintrabajo evitó un paro y una huelga." *El Colombiano,* 24 May 2002, 1B.

———. "Obreros bananeros votan la huelga." *La República,* 20 January 1996, 32.

———. "Sintrainagro alerta contra el arancel de la Unión Europea." *El Colombiano,* 4 November 2004, 3B.

———. "Sintrainagro, en paro indefinido desde el jueves." *El Colombiano,* 8 February 2000, 3B.

———. "Sólo San Isidro no salió a votar." *El Colombiano,* 27 October 1997, 9C.

———. "Trabajadores bananeros amenazan con huelga." *El Colombiano,* 4 January 1996, 3A.

"Rebels Blew up Colombia's Main Oil Pipeline 586 Times since 1982." Agence France-Presse, 29 December 1998. Accessed via LexisNexis Academic on 9 October 2006.

"Rebels Dynamite Oil Pipeline." Associated Press, 24 December 1997. Accessed via LexisNexis Academic on 4 October 2006.

"Rebels Sabotage Oil Pipeline." *Calgary Herald,* 8 January 2001, C5. Accessed via LexisNexis Academic on 9 October 2006.

"Re-election: Colombia's Gamble on Uribe." *Latin American Weekly Report,* 1 November 2005. Accessed via LexisNexis Academic on 18 November 2006.

"Renace, Ciénaga, renace: Entrevista con Sintrainagro." *Opción,* May 1991, 24–35.

"Renuncia masiva en Arauquita." *El Tiempo,* 2 November 2002, 1–3.

Restrepo, Olga Luz. "Por qué el pueblo U'wa se niega a la exploración petrolera en su territorio." www.semana.com, 3 December 2007. Accessed on 2 January 2008.

Restrepo, Orlando. "Militares echaron candado a su base." *El Tiempo,* 26 May 1997, 14A.

"Rights Abuses in Colombia Worst in Region—Human Rights Watch." BBC Monitoring Latin America, 19 January 2006. Accessed via LexisNexis Academic on 30 December 2007.

Rivera, Guillermo, Adela Torres, Valerio Maza, Jorge Esteban Gulfo, and Daniel Guerra. "Comunicado público: Apartadó, 31 de julio de 2008." Accessed at www.cut.org.co//index.php?option=com_content&task=view&id=1404&Itemid=450 on 27 December 2008.

Rivera Zapata, Guillermo. "Inminente cese de actividades de trabajadores bananeros." Sintrainagro press release, 15 May 2006. Accessed at www.cut.org.co/noticias/comun1.html on 20 August 2006.

———. "Referencia: Denuncia nacional e internacional. Asunto: Conductas antisindicales de Jaime Ortiz Franco." Sintrainagro press release, 7 June 2007. Accessed at www.colsiba.org/PAGINAS%20NUEVAS%202007/sintrainagro_junio2007.htm on 26 October 2007.

Rivera, Guillermo, and Adela Torres. Letter to John Sweeney et al., AFL-CIO, celebrating the rejection of the Free Trade Agreement between Colombia and the United States. 11 April 2008. Accessed at www.cut.org.co//index.php?option=com_content&task=view&id=1090&Itemid=585 on 27 December 2008.

Rodríguez, Carlos. "La CUT saluda el acuerdo laboral entre Sintrainagro y el sector bananero." CUT press release. 25 May 2006. Accessed at www.cut.org.co/p_presidencia/pres_comun23.html on 20 August 2006.

Rodríguez, Diana. "Remolinos: Un día de narcomercado." *El País,* 22 January 1995, 8A.

Rohter, Larry. "McCain Heads Today to Colombia Where Adviser Has Long Had Ties." *New York Times,* 1 July 2008. Accessed via LexisNexis on 3 May 2010.

Rueda, Camilo. "¡Arauca existe, insiste, y resiste!" Agencia Prensa Rural, 18 September 2004. Accessed at www.prensarural.org/rueda20040918.htm on 2 September 2006.

Ruiz, Marta. "El río de la guerra: Con el Plan Patriota las Fuerzas Armadas se metieron a la madriguera de las FARC." www.semana.com, 26 July 2004. Accessed on 13 December 2006.

———. "Semana en el corazón de la guerra: Marta Ruiz recorrió el Caguán y los Montes de María, regiones donde se pone a prueba el Plan Patriota." *Semana,* 5 February 2006. Accessed at www.semana.com on 16 December 2006.

"¿Saldo en rojo? La seguridad democrática se rajó en Arauca." www.semana.com, 12 February 2006. Accessed 8 September 2006.

Sánchez, Luís Guillermo. "Forum in Defense of Employment Concludes with Great Success." Accessed at www.rel-uita.org/sindicatos/foro-defensa-empleo_eng.htm on 27 December 2008.

Sarmiento, Gilda. "Se madura conflicto en Urabá." *El Espectador,* 9 June 1989.

"Scandals Undermined Support for Colombian President in 2008." BBC Worldwide Monitoring, 31 December 2008. Accessed at LexisNexis Academic on 10 January 2009.

Schemo, Diana Jean. "Colombian Rebels Release 70 Soldiers and Marines." *New York Times,* 16 June 1997, A8.

Schmitt, Eric. "$1.3 Billion Voted to Fight Drug War among Colombians." *New York Times,* 30 June 2000, A1.

"Secuestrados tres agentes por rebeldes de las Farc." *El País,* 11 June 2006, A10.

"Semana de Pasión." *Semana,* 27 September 1988, 54–57.

"Siguen ataques en Arauca." *El Tiempo,* 21 September 2003, 1–10.

"Singulares elecciones en Cartagena del Chairá." *Vanguardia Liberal,* 24 August 1998, 7A.

"Son 69 los militares que deben responder en indagatoria por la masacre de San José de Apartadó." www.semana.com, 22 February 2007. Accessed on 2 January 2008.

"Take Action: U'wa Leaders in San Francisco, DC & Chicago!" 14 October 2005. Accessed at www.amazonwatch.org/view_news.php?id=982 on 8 November 2006.

"Terminó paro en Cartagena del Chairá." *El Tiempo,* 25 August 1997, 15A.

"Tierra para indígenas de Arauca." *El Tiempo,* 14 April 1996, 13A.

"Top Colombian 'Peacemaker' Gunned Down." *Toronto Star,* 30 December 2000. Accessed via LexisNexis Academic on 14 December 2006.

Torchia, Christopher. "Colombia's Rebel Groups Share Leftist Ideology, Simmering Rivalry." Associated Press, 20 August 1997. Accessed via LexisNexis Academic on 30 September 2006.

"Trying to Attract the Foreign Companies: Bidding War Fails, Samper Vows to Abolish 'War Tax.'" Intelligence Research Ltd., 11 August 1994. Accessed via LexisNexis Academic on 11 October 2006.

"Turbay Cote, un año secuestrado." *El Tiempo,* 16 June 1996, 17A.

Twomey, Steve. "An Unnatural Journey for Nature's Cause: Leaders of Colombia's U'wa Tribe See Protests as a Fight for the Simple Life." *Washington Post,* 20 April 2002, B3. Accessed via LexisNexis Academic on 17 September 2006.

"Una semana de cierre completó la frontera." *El Tiempo,* 8 April 1997, 8A.

"Undemobilized Paramilitary Blocs Control Bulk of Drug Crops—Colombian Weekly." BBC, 7 November 2005. Accessed via LexisNexis Academic on 1 September 2006.

UNHCR (United Nations High Commission on Refugees). "UNHCR Briefing Notes: Some 2,000 Colombians Flee Irregular Armed Groups in Arauca." Summary of what was said by UNHCR spokesperson William Spindler at a press briefing, 22 January 2008. Accessed at www.unhcr.org/news/NEWS/4795e66a2.html on 26 November 2008.

"UP amenazada por FARC." *El Tiempo,* 21 November 2002, 1–4.

"Upsurge in Violence Leads to State of Emergency: Chronology." Agence France-Presse, 12 August 2002. Accessed via LexisNexis Academic on 11 August 2006.

"Urabá: ¿Qué te AUGURAn?" *Opción,* February–June 1990, 35.

"Urabá: Página histórica del movimiento sindical." *Colombia Hoy Informa* 78 (April 1990): 28–30.

"Uribe les jala las orejas a militares." www.eltiempo.com, 28 October 2008. Accessed on 14 November 2008.

"U.S. Approves Troop Increase." *Latinnews Daily,* 11 October 2004. Accessed via LexisNexis Academic on 18 November 2006.

"U.S. 'Outsourcing' War on Drugs: Private Militia Firms Hired to Assist Colombian Army Eradicate Jungle Operations." *Hamilton Spectator* (Ont., Canada), 18 June 2001. Accessed via LexisNexis Academic on 26 September 2006.

"Venezuela pide ocupación militar de Arauquita." *El Tiempo,* 5 April 1997, 8A.

Vidal, John. "Colombia's U'wa Have Their Prayers Answered." *Manchester Guardian Weekly,* 29 May 2002, 26. Accessed via LexisNexis Academic on 17 September 2006.

Vieira, Constanza. "Colombia: Indigenous Women Brave War Zone to Express Solidarity." Inter-Press Service, 25 July 2005. Accessed via LexisNexis Academic on 20 November 2006.

———. "El sur del país va a explotar." Inter Press Service, 1 August 2005. Accessed at www.prensarural.org/vieira20050801.htm on 15 December 2006.

"Violencia tiene acorralados a los alcaldes de Caquetá." *El Colombiano,* 12 October 2001. Accessed at www.elcolombiano.com/historicod/20011012/nnh001.htm on 14 December 2006.

Vincent, Isabel. "Liberal Candidate Leads in Colombia Election: Presidential Vote Close in Second Round." *Globe and Mail* (Toronto), 20 June 1994. Accessed via LexisNexis Academic on 11 August 2007.

Ward, Olivia. "Bloodbath in a Peaceful Village." *Toronto Star,* 21 May 2005. Accessed via LexisNexis Academic on 2 September 2006.

"Weekly Assesses Performances of Colombia's Ministries in 2004." BBC, 25 January 2005. Accessed via LexisNexis Academic, 15 August 2007.

"William, dos años metido en las selvas del patriota." *El Tiempo,* 7 May 2006. Accessed at www.eltiempo.com on 30 December 2008.

"World in Brief." *Washington Post,* 2 January 2000, A18.

BOOKS, THESES, PAMPHLETS, REPORTS, AND JOURNAL ARTICLES

"Acta de compromiso entre el gobierno y las comunidades del departamento (de Arauca). Jornada Agraria, abril de 1992." Signed in Saravena, Arauca, 2 May 1992.

Acuerdo del gobierno y los campesinos del Caquetá: Textos documentales de los acuerdos suscritos entre el Gobierno Nacional y Departamental y los representantes de los campesinos en Florencia y Morelia (agosto y octubre de 1987). Pamphlet. Florencia, August 1988.

Aguilar Z., Luis Ignacio. "Sustitución de importaciones y apertura económica." *Análisis Político* 13 (May–August 1991): 79–85.

Alvarez de Gil, Sabina. "Historias de Urabá y AUGURA en su contexto." *AUGURA* 9, no. 2 (1983): 35–52.

Americas Watch. *The Drug War in Colombia: The Neglected Tragedy of Political Violence.* New York: Human Rights Watch, 1990.

Amnesty International. *Blood at the Crossroads: Making the Case for a Global Arms Trade Treaty—Executive Summary.* 17 September 2008. Pdf downloaded from www.amnesty.org/en/news-and-updates/report/arms-trade-treaty-could-fail-without-human-rights-20080917 on 26 November 2008.

———. "Colombia." In *Amnesty International Report 2006: The State of the World's Human Rights.* London: Amnesty International, 2006.

———. *Colombia: Un laboratorio de guerra. Represión y violencia en Arauca* (Colombia, a Laboratory of War: Repression and Violence in Arauca). London: Amnesty International, 2004. Accessed at http://web.amnesty.org/library/Index/ESLAMR230042004 on 11 August 2006.

Andreas, Peter, and Coletta Youngers. "U.S. Drug Policy and the Andean Cocaine Industry." *World Policy Journal* (Summer 1989): 528–61.

Angell, Alan, Pamela Lowden, and Rosemary Thorp. *Decentralizing Development: The Political Economy of Institutional Change in Colombia and Chile.* Oxford: Oxford University Press, 2001.

"Anteproyecto de Desarrollo Agropecuario de Sustitución de Cultivos Ilícitos para el Bajo Caguán: ponencia dirigida al programa de sustitución de cultivos del gobierno nacional" (Proposal for the development of agricultural alternatives to illicit crops in the Lower Caguán: addressed to the national government's crop substitution program). [Authors include activists from the Communal Action Committees of the Lower Caguán, a county council representative from the UP, the county official assigned to the local jurisdiction of Remolino, and representatives of the Remolino branch of INCORA, October 1990.]

Arango Zuluaga, Carlos, ed. *De Cravo Norte a Tlaxcala: Los diálogos por la paz.* n.p: n.p., 1992.

Arenas, Jacobo. *Cese el fuego: Una historia política de las FARC.* Bogotá: Editorial la Oveja Negra, 1985.

Arizala, José. "Las experiencias alternativas de tipo partidistas, independientes del bipartidismo: la Unión Patriótica." In *Entre movimientos y caudillos: 50 años de bipartidismo, izquierda, y alternativas populares en Colombia,* ed. Gustavo Gallón, 159–65. Bogotá: Editorial Presencia, 1989.

Arnson, Cynthia. "Colombia, el Congreso de los Estados Unidos, y el TLC." *Boletín Hechos del Callejón* 27 (July 2007): 12–15. Accessed at http://indh .pnud.org.co/boletin_hechos on 17 August 2007.

——. *Colombia's Peace Processes: Multiple Processes, Multiple Actors.* Washington, DC: Woodrow Wilson International Center for Scholars, 2006.

——. "Editor's Introduction." In *The Peace Process in Colombia with the Autodefensas Unidas de Colombia-AUC,* ed. Cynthia Arnson, 1–12. Washington, DC: Woodrow Wilson International Center for Scholars, 2005.

——. "Summary of Conference Presentation by Alberto Chueca Mora." In *The Social and Economic Dimensions of Conflict and Peace in Colombia,* ed. Cynthia J. Arnson, 2–9. Latin American Program Special Report. Washington, DC: Woodrow Wilson International Center for Scholars, October 2004.

Artunduaga Bermeo, Felix. *Historia general del Caquetá.* Florencia, 1984.

Asociación de Juntas de Cartagena del Chairá. "Militarización e impactos social del Plan Patriota en el sur del país." Brochure distributed by activists from the Caguán at the press conference to protest Plan Patriota, Bogotá, 28 July 2005.

Asojuntas-Saravena. "Declaración Foro Comunal en Saravena." Accessed at www .organizacionessociales.org/index.php?option=com_content&task=view&id= 406&Itemid=47 on 5 December 2008.

AUGURA. *Actividad bananera de Urabá.* Pamphlet. Medellín: AUGURA, 1988.

————. "Coyuntura Bananera Colombiana: Primer semestre de año 2001." August 2001. Accessed at www.augura.com.co/esta_interna.htm# on 19 October 2007.

————. "Coyuntura Bananera Colombiana: [Segundo semestre de año] 2003." April 2004. Accessed at www.augura.com.co/esta_interna.htm# on 19 October 2007.

————. "Coyuntura Bananera Colombiana 2007." April 2008. Pdf downloaded from www.augura.com.co/esta_interna.htm on 27 December 2008.

————. *Informe de Actividades, 1997.* Medellín: AUGURA, 1998.

————. "Urabá: Area sembrada en banano." 2004. Accessed at www.augura.com.co/esta_areasembradaurababanano.htm on19 October 2007.

Autoridades Tradicionales, Cabildo Mayor y Pueblo U'wa, Resguardo Indigena Unido U'wa. "Ecopetrol S. A. reinicia actividades petroleras en territorio U'wa." Press release, 8 November 2006. Accessed at www.etniasdecolombia.org/pdf/Comunicado%20U%B4was.pdf on 6 December 2006.

Aznárez, Juan Jesús. "Votando entre asesinatos, secuestros, y extorsiones." *Página/12,* 24 October 2003. Accessed at www.pagina12.com.ar/imprimir/diario/elmundo/4-27205.html.

Bagley, Bruce. "Drug Trafficking, Political Violence, and U.S. Policy in Colombia under the Clinton Administration." In *Elusive Peace: International, National, and Local Dimensions of Conflict in Colombia,* ed. Cristina Rojas and Judy Meltzer, 21–52. New York: Palgrave Macmillan, 2005.

Banco de la República. "Indices de precios al consumidor y del productor." Accessed at www.banrep.gov.co/series-Estadísticas/see_precios.htm on 20 August 2006.

Beaufort, Elizabeth. "La elección de alcaldes en el Caqueta y su contexto político." Seminar paper, Department of Political Science, Universidad de los Andes, Seminario de Elección Popular de Alcaldes, 1988.

Bedoya Madrid, Claudia. "Paralizada Urabá por huelga bananera." *El Tiempo,* 8 July 1998, 12A.

————. "Los trabajadores bananeros suspenden el paro indefinido." *El Tiempo,* 11 February 2000, 18A.

Bejarano, Ana María. "La Violencia regional y sus protagonistas: el caso de Urabá." *Análisis Político* 4 (May–August 1988): 44.

Bergquist, Charles. *Labor in Latin America: Comparative Essays on Chile, Argentina, Venezuela, and Colombia.* Stanford: Stanford University Press, 1986.

Blanding, Michael. "The Case against Coke." *The Nation,* 14 April 2006. Reprinted at www.iradvocates.org/, accessed on 26 October 2007.

Botero Herrera, Fernando. *Urabá: Colonización, violencia y crisis del Estado.* Medellín: Universidad de Antioquia, 1990.

Botero Herrera, Fernando, and Diego Sierra Botero. *El mercado de fuerza de trabajo en la zona bananera de Urabá.* Medellín: Universidad de Antioquia, Centro de Investigaciones Económicas, and Corporación Regional de Desarrollo de Urabá, 1981.

Brecher, Jeremy, Tim Costell, and Brendan Smith. *Globalization from Below: The Power of Solidarity.* 2nd ed. Cambridge, MA: South End Press, 2002.

Burki, Shahid Javed, Guillermo Perry, and William Dillinger. "Prologue." In *Beyond the Center: Decentralizing the State,* ed. Shahid Javed Burki, Guillermo Perry, and William Dillinger, 1–7. Washington, DC: World Bank, 1999.

CAJSC (Comisión Andina de Juristas, Seccional Colombiana). *Arauca: Serie Informes Regionales de Derechos Humanos.* Bogotá: Gráficas El Quijote, 1994.

———. *Detrás del terrorismo y la guerra al narcotráfico: Los derechos humanos en Colombia al inicio del nuevo gobierno.* Bogotá: Comisión Andina de Juristas, 1990.

———. *Urabá. Informes regionales de derechos humanos.* Bogotá: Editorial Códice, 1994.

Campbell, Tim. *Decentralization and the Rise of Political Participation in Latin American Cities.* Pittsburgh: University of Pittsburgh Press, 2003.

Campbell, Tim, and Harald Fuhr, eds. *Leadership and Innovation in Subnational Government: Case Studies from Latin America.* Washington, DC: World Bank, 2004.

Campos Zornosa, Yezid. *Memoria de los silenciados: El baile rojo—relatos.* Bogotá: Grafiq Editores, 2003.

Carroll, Leah A. "Backlash against Peasant Gains in Rural Democratization: The Experience of Leftist County Executives." *Berkeley Journal of Sociology* 39 (1994–95): 133–88.

———. "Violent Democratization: The Effect of Political Reform on Rural Social Conflict in Colombia." Ph.D. diss, University of California, Berkeley, 2000.

———. "A Window of Opportunity for the Left Despite Trade Liberalization: Palm Workers, Patrons, and Political Violence in Colombia." *Political Power and Social Theory* 13 (1999): 149–200.

Castro, Jaime. *Decentralizar para pacificar.* Bogotá: Planeta Colombiana Editorial, 1998.

———. *Elección popular de alcaldes.* Bogotá: Editorial La Oveja Negra, 1986.

———. *La cuestión territorial.* Bogotá: Editorial La Oveja Negra, 2002.

———. "La reforma política: Un compromiso histórico." In *Reformas políticas: Apertura democrática,* ed. Cristina de la Torre, 15–43. Bogotá: Editorial Nikos, 1985.

———. *Proceso a la violencia y proceso de paz.* Bogotá: Editorial La Oveja Negra, 1986.

————. *Respuesta democrática al desafío guerrillero.* Bogotá: Editorial La Oveja Negra, 1987.

CCMA (Coordinación Colombiana de Medios Alternativos). "El día de ayer, en el marco del Tercer Encuentro Nacional de Víctimas Crímenes de Estado, varias organizaciones defensoras de derechos humanos y diversos colectivos realizaron balances regionales de la situación humanitaria en la mayoría de regiones del país." 10 July 2006. Accessed at http://frentesocialypolitico.org/article.php3?id_article=540 on 4 September 2006.

Chernick, Marc. "Negotiating Peace amid Multiple Forms of Violence: The Protracted Search for a Settlement to the Armed Conflicts in Colombia." In *Comparative Peace Processes in Latin America,* ed. Cynthia J. Arnson, 297–318. Washington, DC: Woodrow Wilson Center Press; Stanford: Stanford University Press, 1999.

Chernick, Marc W., and Michael F. Jiménez. "Popular Liberalism, Radical Democracy, and Marxism: Leftist Politics in Contemporary Colombia, 1974–1991." In *The Latin American Left: From the Fall of Allende to Perestroika,* ed. Barry Carr and Steve Ellner, 61–81. Boulder, CO: Westview Press, 1993.

CIJP (Comisión Intercongregacional de Justicia y Paz). "1981–1994: Trece años en búsqueda de paz." *Justicia y Paz* 7, no. 3 (July–September 1994): 1–23.

Collier, Ruth Berins, and David Collier. *Shaping the Political Arena: Critical Junctures, the Labor Movement, and Regime Dynamics in Latin America.* Princeton, NJ: Princeton University Press, 1991.

Colombian Solidarity Committees of North America. *Death and Torture in Caquetá (Colombia), 1979–1981.* In collaboration with Center for Investigation and Popular Education (CINEP), Permanent Committee for the Defense of Human Rights, and Committee in Solidarity with Political Prisoners, all based in Bogotá. New York, 1982.

Comisión de Verificación de la Ejecución de los Líderes Araucanos Héctor Alirio Martínez, Leonel Goyeneche, y Jorge Prieto. "Crónica de otra muerte anunciada en Arauca." August 2004. Accessed at www.aquiestoypais.org/article.php?sid=406 on 2 September 2006.

Comisión Valenciana de Verificación de Derechos Humanos. "Colombia: Rompiendo el silencio. Valencia (España)." April 2005. Accessed at www.euro-colombia.org/coinco_eur_documentos.asp on 24 August 2006.

Comisión Verificadora. *Informe final sobre Urabá.* Bogotá: CINEP, 1995.

Comité Coordinador del Primer Foro por la Paz y el Desarrollo. *Primer Foro por la Paz y el Desarrollo: Conclusiones.* 23 August 1986. Pamphlet in author's possession.

Comité Negociador, Marcha Campesina a Arauca. *Arauca paró por paz y progreso: Acuerdos logrados por el paro cívico intendiencial de febrero 12 al 25 (1987).* Pamphlet. Arauca, 1987.

Comité Permanente de Derechos Humanos. "Incumplen convenio de paz." *Boletín de Prensa,* 23 March 1984, 2–3.

Concejo Municipal de Apartadó (City Council of Apartadó). "Acuerdo #008 de 23 noviembre 1990, sobre presupuesto de ingresos y egresos para el período fiscal del 1 de enero al 31 de diciembre de 1991." Photocopies in author's possession.

Conklin, Beth A. "Body Paint, Feathers, and VCRs: Aesthetics and Authenticity in Amazonian Activism." *American Ethnologist* 24, no. 4 (1997): 711–37.

Cornelius, Wayne, Todd A. Eisenstadt, and Jane Hindley, eds. *Subnational Politics and Democratization in Mexico.* La Jolla: Center for U.S.-Mexican Studies, University of California, San Diego, 1999.

Coronell, Daniel. "Coca Moves to the Right." *Berkeley Review of Latin American Studies* (Fall 2006): 22–24.

Corpourabá. "Plan de desarrollo económico y social de Urabá." *AUGURA* 9, no. 2, 1983: 11–17.

CSV (Comisión de Superación de la Violencia). *Pacificar la paz: Lo que no se ha negociado en los acuerdos de paz.* Santafé de Bogotá: IEPRI, CINEP, Comisión Andina de Juristas, and CECOIN, 1992.

de Angulo Piñeros, Luis Fernando. "Producción de petróleo y desarrollo regional." In *Petróleo: presente y futuro,* 301–6. Bogotá: Universidad Javeriana, 1991.

de Janvry, Alain. *The Agrarian Question and Reformism in Latin America.* Baltimore: Johns Hopkins University Press, 1981.

de la Calle, Humberto. "Palabras del Ministro del Goberniero Delegatorio de funciones presidenciales Humberto de la Calle Lombana en el Congreso Bananero." *AUGURA* 17, no 1 (1991): 28–29. [Special issue: *Congreso Bananero 1991, Memorias.*]

de Urbina, A. Ortiz, and L. Iglesias Kuntz. "Gloria Cuartas, Colombia's Messenger of Peace." Interview with *UNESCO Courier,* December 1998. Accessed from www.unesco.org/courier/1998_12/uk/dires/intro.htm.

Delgado, Alvaro. *Luchas sociales en el Caquetá.* Bogotá: Ediciones CEIS, Editorial Colombia Nueva, 1987.

———. *Política y movimiento obrero, 1970–1983.* Bogotá: Ediciones Colombia Nueva, 1984.

———. "¿Sindicatos de paramilitares?" 12 June 2006. Accessed at www.voltairnet .org/article141624.html on 20 August 2006.

———. "Una baba espesa." 10 June 2005. Accessed on www.voltairenet.org/ article125811.html#article125811 on 25 August 2007.

Departmento de Arauca. *Plan de Desarrollo Departamental 2004–2007.* Arauca: Departamento de Arauca, 2004.

Dudley, Steven. *Walking Ghosts: Murder and Guerrilla Politics in Colombia.* New York: Routledge, 2004.

Earle, Duncan, and Jeanne Simonelli. "The Zapatistas and Global Civil Society: Renegotiating the Relationship." *European Review of Latin American and Caribbean Studies* 76 (April 2004): 119–26.

Eaton, Kent. "Backlash in Bolivia: Regional Autonomy as a Reaction against Indigenous Mobilization." *Politics and Society* 35, no. 1 (March 2007): 1–32.

———. "The Downside of Decentralization: Armed Clientelism in Colombia." *Security Studies* 15, no. 4 (October–December 2006): 1–30.

———. *Politics beyond the Capital: The Design of Subnational Institutions in South America.* Stanford: Stanford University Press, 2004.

Eaton, Kent, and J. Tyler Dickovick. "The Politics of Recentralization in Argentina and Brazil." *Latin American Research Review* 39, no. 1 (2004): 90–102.

Ecopetrol (Empresa Colombiana de Petróleos). *Informe annual 1986.* Bogotá: Editorial Presencia Ltda., 1986.

Editora Lesi. *Nueva constitución política de Colombia.* Bogotá, 1992.

Endrizzi, Dimitri. "Apéndice." In *Dios y cocaína: De cómo un misionero sobrevivió en el Caguán,* by Giacinto Franzoi. Bogotá: Intermedio Editores, 2009.

Escobar, Cristina. "Clientelism, Mobilization, and Citizenship: Peasant Politics in Sucre, Colombia." Ph.D. diss., University of California, San Diego, 1998.

"Estamos dando resultados positivos para el país: General Mora." Colombian president's Web site. 26 October 2002. Accessed at www.presidencia.gov.co/cne/octubre/07/26102002.htm on 14 December 2006.

Evans, Peter. "Counterhegemonic Globalization: Transnational Social Movements in the Contemporary Global Political Economy." In *The Handbook of Political Sociology: States, Civil Societies, and Globalization,* ed. Thomas Janoski, Robert Alford, Alexander Hicks, and Mildred A. Schwartz, 655–70. Cambridge: Cambridge University Press, 2005.

Fanon, Frantz. *The Wretched of the Earth.* New York: Grove Press, 1963.

FARC-EP. "Propuesta de las FARC-EP a la Audiencia Especial con representación de 21 países." 30 June 2000. Accessed at www.derechos.org/nizkor/colombia/doc/paz/cultivos.html on 9 August 2006.

Fellowship of Reconciliation. "FOR Peace: The Blog of the Fellowship of Reconciliation." Accessed at http://forpeace.net/blog/ on 26 December 2008.

Florini, Ann M. *The Third Force: The Rise of Transnational Civil Society.* Tokyo: Japan Center for International Exchange and Carnegie Endowment for Peace, 2000.

Foro Social Humanitario. *Efectos del Plan Colombia y la seguridad democrática en la región del Arauca y el Oriente: Documento central Saravena: Agosto 3–5, 2005.* Saravena, Arauca: Foro Social Humanitario, 2005. Accessed at www.organizacionessociales.org on 23 August 2006. Printout in author's possession.

Fox, Jonathan. "Editor's Introduction." *Journal of Development Studies* (Special issue: *The Challenge of Rural Democratization: Perspectives from Latin America and the Philippines*) 26, no. 4 (July 1990).

Franzoi, Giacinto [Father Jacinto]. *Dios y cocaína: De cómo un misionero sobrevivió en el Caguán.* Bogotá: Intermedio Editores, 2009.

Gamson, William. *The Strategy of Social Protest.* Belmont, CA: Wadsworth, 1990.

García, Clara Inés. *Urabá: Región, actores y conflicto.* Medellín: INER/CEREC, 1996.

García, Mario Camilo. "Plan Patriota: violencia, desplazamiento, y miseria." *Actualidad Colombiana,* August 2005. Accessed at www.actualidadcolombiana .org on 26 November 2006.

García Durán, Mauricio. "Guerra y paz con la guerrilla: De Turbay a Gaviria." *Análisis 6: Conflicto social y violencia en Colombia.* Documentos ocasionales 65 (February 1992): 55–63.

García V., Martha Cecilia. *Las cifras de las luchas cívicas: Cuatrienio barco, 1986–1990.* Bogotá: CINEP, 1990.

Gaviria Trujillo, César. "Mensaje del Presidente del República, César Gaviria Trujillo, al Congreso Bananero 1991." *AUGURA* 17, no 1 (1991): 28–29. [Special issue: *Congreso Bananero 1991, Memorias.*]

Goldman Environmental Prize. "Berito Kuwar U'wa: Colombia: Oil and Mining." Accessed at www.goldmanprize.org/node/121 on 29 December 2007.

———. "Recipients by Year." Accessed at www.goldmanprize.org/recipients/ year on 8 November 2006.

González, José Jairo, and Roberto Ramírez M. "Aspectos de la violencia en el Caquetá, 1978–1982." In *Memorias, V. Congreso Nacional de Sociología: Poder político y estructura social en Colombia,* 81–101. Bogotá: Universidad de Antioquia (Medellín), 1987.

Hanson, Stephanie. "Backgrounder—FARC, ELN: Colombia's Left-Wing Guerrillas." Council on Foreign Relations, 11 March 2008. Accessed at www.cfr .org/publication/9272/ on 11 November 2008.

Hartlyn, Jonathan. "Colombia: The Politics of Violence and Accommodation." In *Democracy in Developing Countries,* vol. 4, *Latin America,* ed. Larry Diamond, Juan J. Linz, and Seymour Martin Lipset, 290–334. Boulder, CO: Lynne Rienner, 1989.

Hartlyn, Jonathan. *The Politics of Coalition Rule in Colombia.* Cambridge: Cambridge University Press, 1988.

Helmsing, A. H. J. *Firms, Farms, and the State in Colombia.* London: Allen & Unwin, 1986.

Henríquez Gallo, Jaime. "El papel de las empresas nacionales en la comercialización del banano y el caso colombiano." *AUGURA* 16 (1990): 81–85.

———. "Parliamentarians and Banana Production." *AUGURA* 12, no. 2 (1986): 103–13.

"Hocol: About the Company." Accessed at www.hocol.com.co/html_ingles/company/historia.htm on 25 November 2006.

Human Rights Watch. *Breaking the Grip? Obstacles to Justice for Paramilitary Mafias in Colombia.* New York: Human Rights Watch, 2008.

———. "Colombia's Checkbook Impunity—A Briefing Paper." 22 September 2003. Accessed at www.hrw.org/backgrounder/americas/checkbook-impunity.htm on 15 November 2006.

———. *State of War: Political Violence and Counterinsurgency in Colombia.* New York: Human Rights Watch, 1993. Accessed at www.hrw.org/reports/1993/colombia/statetoc.htm on 26 September 2006.

HVCJ (Humanidad Vigente Corporación Jurídica). *Informe de derechos humanos Arauca 2002 José Rusbel Lara.* Bogotá: Humanidad Vigente Corporación Jurídica, 10 April 2003.

Instituto Geográfico Agustín Codazzi. *Atlas de Colombia.* Santafé de Bogotá: Instituto Geográfico Agustín Codazzi, 2002.

Inter-American Commission on Human Rights. "Admissibility: María del Consuelo Ibarguen Rengifo, et al., Colombia." Report No. 55/04, Petition 475/03, 13 October 2004. Accessed at www.cidh.oas.org/annualrep/2004eng/Colombia.475.03eng.htm on 20 August 2006.

International Campaign to Ban Land Mines. "Landmine Monitor 2007: Colombia." Accessed at www.icbl.org/lm/2007/colombia on 23 November 2008.

———. "Landmine Monitor 2008: Colombia." Accessed at www.icbl.org/lm/2008/countries/colombia.php on 23 November 2008.

International Peace Observatory. "What Is IPO?" Accessed at www.peaceobservatory.org/en/15142/what-is-ipo on 5 December 2008.

Inter-Parliamentary Union. "Colombia: Case No. CO/01—Pedro Nel Jiménez Obando; Case No. CO/02—Leonardo Posada Pedraza; Case No. CO/03—Octavio Vargas Cuéllar; Case No. CO/04—Pedro Luís Valencia Giraldo; Case No. CO/06—Bernardo Jaramillo Ossa; Case No. CO/08—Manuel Cepeda Vargas; Case No. CO/139—Octavio Sarmiento Bohórquez." Resolution adopted by consensus by the IPU Governing Council at its 178th session, Nairobi, 12 May 2006. Accessed at www.ipu.org/conf-e/117/117.pdf on 8 August 2006.

Jaramillo, Jaime Eduardo. "Estudio del proceso de colonización en el Bajo y Medio Caguán." In *Memorias, V Congreso Nacional de Sociología: Poder político y estructura social en Colombia,* 41–64. Medellín, 1985.

Jaramillo, Jaime Eduardo, Leonidas Mora, and Fernando Cubides. *Colonización, coca y guerrilla.* 2nd ed. Bogotá: Universidad Nacional de Colombia y Alianza Editorial Colombiana, 1989.

Keck, Margaret E., and Kathryn Sikkink. *Activists beyond Borders: Advocacy Networks in International Politics*. Ithaca, NY: Cornell University Press, 1998.

Lapan, Tovin. "Killer Cola?" *Berkeley Review of Latin American Studies* (Winter–Spring 2006): 35–39. Accessed at www.clas.berkeley.edu:7001/Publications/newsletters/index.html on 3 September 2006.

LAWG (Latin American Working Group). *Informe 2005: Comentarios de las organizaciones de derechos humanos de Colombia sobre el cumplimiento de los acondicionamientos de la asistencia militar estadounidense*. Washington, DC: LAWG, 2005. Accessed at www.lawg.org/countries/colombia/colombian _ngo_report.htm on 25 November 2006.

LAWGEF (Latin American Working Group Education Fund). *The Wrong Road: Colombia's National Security Policy*. Washington, DC: LAWGEF, 2003. Accessed at www.lawg.org/misc/Publications.htm on 1 September 2006.

Leal Buitrago, Francisco, and Andrés Dávila Ladrón de Guevara. *Clientelismo: El sistema político y su expresión regional*. Bogotá: Instituto de Estudios Políticos y Relaciones Internationales, 1990.

LeGrand, Catherine. "The Colombian Crisis in Historical Perspective." *Canadian Journal of Latin American and Caribbean Studies* 28, no. 55/5 (2003): 165–209.

———. *Frontier Expansion and Peasant Protest in Colombia, 1830–1936*. Albuquerque: University of New Mexico Press, 1986.

Lipschutz, Ronnie. "Reconstructing World Politics: The Emergence of Global Civil Society." In *Civil Societies and Social Movements*, ed. Ronnie Lipschutz, 389–420. Hampshire, UK: Ashgate Press, 2006.

Loewenberg, Sam. "Big Guns Back Aid to Colombia: Well-Financed U.S. Lobby Seeks Relief from Drug Wars." *Law News Network*, 23 February 2000.

"Los abusos de Riowa." U'wa Community Web site. Accessed at www.uwa colombia.org/riowa/index.html on 2 October 2006.

Manor, James. *The Political Economy of Democratic Decentralization*. Washington, DC: World Bank, 1999.

Martin, Gerard. "Desarrollo económico, sindicalismo y proceso de paz en Urabá." Senior thesis, Universidad de los Andes, School of Business Administration, 1986.

Marulanda, Elsy. *Colonización y conflicto: Las lecciones del Sumapaz*. Bogotá: Tercer Mundo Editores and Instituto de Estudios Políticos y Relaciones Internacionales, 1991.

Matus Caile, Miguel. *Historia de Arauca 1818–1819: Consagración de Santander en la epopeya de los Llanos*. Bogotá: Tercer Mundo Editores, 1992.

McAdam, Doug. *Political Process and the Development of Black Insurgency, 1930–1970.* Chicago: University of Chicago Press, 1982.

Medina Gallego, Carlos. *Autodefensas, paramilitares y narcotráfico en Colombia.* Bogotá: Editorial Documentos Periodísticos, 1990.

Mendes, Chico. *Fight for the Forest: Chico Mendes in His Own Words.* London: Latin American Bureau, 1990.

Migdal, Joel S. *Strong Societies and Weak States: State-Society Relations and State Capabilities in the Third World.* Princeton, NJ: Princeton University Press, 1988.

Ministerio de Gobierno de Colombia. *Política de paz del Presidente Betancur. PAZ. La paz es un derecho pero también es un deber.* Pamphlet. Bogota: Ministerio de Gobierno de Colombia, April 1985.

Misas Arango, Gabriel. "Apertura económica y apertura política: dos escenarios no siempre coincidentes." *Análisis Político* (January–April 1991): 43–51.

Molano, Alfredo. "Violence and Land Colonization." In *Violence in Colombia: The Contemporary Crisis in Historical Perspective,* ed. Charles Bergquist, Ricardo Peñaranda, and Gonzalo Sánchez, 195–216. Wilmington, DE: Scholarly Resources, 1992.

Moore, Barrington, Jr. *Social Origins of Dictatorship and Democracy: Lord and Peasant in the Making of the New World.* Boston: Beacon Press, 1966.

Municipio de Florián, Santander. "Datos generales." Accessed at www.florian .gov.co/generales.htm on 25 August 2007.

———. "Hidrografia." Accessed at www.florian.gov.co/generales.htm and www .florian.gov.co/hidrogra.htm on 25 August 2007.

Municipio de Leiva, Nariño. "Nuestro municipio." Accessed at http:/leiva-narino .gov.co/nuestromunicipio.shtml?apc+m-I1=&m=F&s=m on 25 August 2007.

Municipio de Sabana de Torres. "Nuestro municipio." Accessed at www.sabana detorres-santander.gov.co/nuestromunicipio.shtml?apc=I=&s=m&m=I on 20 August 2007.

Municipio de Valencia, Córdoba. "Economía." Accessed at http://www.valen-cia.gov.co/economia.html on 25 August 2007.

———. "Geográfica." Accessed at www.valencia.gov.co/geografica.html on 25 August 2007.

———. "Historia." Accessed at www.valencia.gov.co/historia.html on 25 August 2007.

Naciones Unidas. Oficina contra la Droga y el Delito. "Presentan productos del desarrollo alternativo de la zona del Caguán." Comunicado de Prensa 006, 6 March 2007. Accessed at www.unodc.org/pdf/colombia/comunicados2007/ 006-CHOCAGU%C1N.pdf on 31 December 2008.

Observatorio de los Derechos Humanos en Colombia. "Kidnapping and Death of Congressman Rodrigo Turbay Cote." Accessed at www.derechoshumanos

.gov.co/observatorio/04_publicaciones/04_01_boletines/04_boletin_23/ casos23i.htm on 15 December 2006.

Ocampo, José Antonio. "Reforma del estado y desarrollo económico y social en Colombia." *Análisis Político* 17 (September–December 1992): 540.

O'Connors, Bernard. "El Mercado Común Europeo y la regulación del mercado del banano después de 1992." In *Congreso Bananero 1991: Memorias,* 59–64. Medellín: AUGURA, 1991.

O'Donnell, Guillermo. "On the State, Democratization, and Some Conceptual Problems: A Latin American View with Glances at Some Postcommunist Countries." *World Development* 21, no. 8 (1993): 1355–69.

O'Donnell, Guillermo, and Philippe C. Schmitter. *Transitions from Authoritarian Rule: Tentative Conclusions about Uncertain Democracies.* Baltimore: Johns Hopkins University Press, 1986.

Olesen, Thomas. "The Zapatistas and Transnational Framing." In *Latin American Social Movements: Globalization, Democratization, and Transnational Networks,* ed. Hank Johnston and Paul Almeida, 179–96. Lanham, MD: Rowman and Littlefield, 2006.

O'Neill, Kathleen. *Decentralizing the State: Elections, Parties, and Local Power in the Andes.* New York: Cambridge University Press, 2005.

ONIC (Organización Nacional Indígena de Colombia). "La Minga sigue . . . en Arauca y en la Univ. Nacional." Accessed at www.organizacionessociales.org/ index.php?option=com_content&task=view&id=432&Itemid=28 on 5 December 2008.

Organizaciones Sociales del Departamento de Arauca. "Masacres borrascosas: Informe de la Comisión de Verificación de la Masacre de Tame." Agencia Prensa Rural, 2 July 2004. Accessed at www.prensarural.org/arauca20040702 .htm on 2 September 2006.

Oxy (Occidental Oil and Gas Corporation). "Colombia: Technology." Accessed at www.oxy.com/OIL_GAS/world_ops/latin_america/tech_colo.htm on 13 October 2006.

Paige, Jeffrey. *Agrarian Revolution: Social Movements and Export Agriculture in the Underdeveloped World.* New York: Free Press, 1975.

———. *Coffee and Power: Revolution and the Rise of Democracy in Central America.* Cambridge, MA: Harvard University Press, 1997.

Pécaut, Daniel. "Guerrillas and Violence." In *Violence in Colombia: The Contemporary Crisis in Historical Perspective,* ed. Charles Bergquist, Ricardo Peñaranda, and Gonzalo Sánchez, 217–39. Wilmington, DE: Scholarly Resources, 1992.

Pécaut, Daniel. *Política y sindicalismo en Colombia.* Bogotá: Ediciones la Carreta, 1973.

Pedraza Torres, Hilario. "Departamento Nacional de Planeación. El proceso de paz en el Caquetá (caso del Caguán)." Paper presented in Villa de Leyva (Boyacá), July 1986. In author's possession, courtesy of León Zamosc.

Peñate, Andrés. "Arauca: Politics and Oil in a Colombian Province." M.A. thesis, University of Oxford, St. Antony's College, 1991.

Pérez Bareño, Leonel. "Arauca: Colonización y petróleo." In *Memorias del V Congreso Nacional de Sociología.* Serie Memorias de eventos científicos 44. Medellín: Universidad de Antioquia, 1987.

Peterson, George E. *Decentralization in Latin America: Learning through Experience.* Washington, DC: World Bank: 1997.

Pizarro, Eduardo. *Insurgencia sin revolución: La guerrilla en Colombia en una perspectiva comparada.* Bogotá: Tercer Mundo Editores, 1996.

———. "Las terceras fuerzas en Colombia hoy: Entre la fragmentación y la impotencia." In *De las armas a la política,* ed. Ricardo Peñaranda and Javier Guerrero, 297–333. Bogotá: Tercer Mundo Editores, 1999.

———. "Revolutionary Guerrilla Groups in Colombia." In *Violence in Colombia: The Contemporary Crisis in Historical Perspective,* ed. Charles Bergquist, Ricardo Peñaranda, and Gonzalo Sánchez, 169–93. Wilmington, DE: Scholarly Resources, 1992.

PNUD-Colombia (Programa de las Naciones Unidas de Desarrollo), "¿Cómo va el ELN?" *Hechos del Callejón* 5 (July 2005): 12–14. Accessed at www.hechos delcallejon.pnudcolombia.org.co/indexphp?option=com_docman&task=cat _view&gid=49&itemid=4 on 22 May 2010.

Presidencia de la República. *Constitución Política de Colombia.* Bogotá: Presidencia de la República, 1991.

"Programa de Gobierno 2008–2011 de Oswaldo Cuadrado Simanca [Plan de Desarrollo Municipal]." Pdf downloaded from http://apartado-antioquia .gov.co/planeacion.shtml?apc=p1l1--&x=3101235 on 27 December 2008.

Ramírez G., Margarita "Consolidación de la actividad bananera de Urabá." *AUGURA* 9, no. 2 (1983): 77–91.

Ramírez Tobón, William. "Estado y crisis regional: el caso de Urabá." *Análisis Político* 20 (September–December 1993): 30.

Red de Hermandad y Solidaridad. "Llamado europeo a la insurgencia Colombiana." Accessed at www.organizacionessociales.org/index.php?option=com _content&task=view&id=92&Itemid=28 on 5 December 2008.

Redford, Kent H. "The Ecologically Noble Savage." *Cultural Survival Quarterly* 15, no. 1 (31 January 1991): 46–48.

Relief Web. "Colombia: Key Facts on Recent Displacement in Arauca." 30 July 2008. Accessed at www.reliefweb.int/rw/rwb.nsf/db900SID/STRI-7H2QYV? OpenDocument on 26 November 2008.

Restrepo, Luis Alberto. "La difícil recomposición de Colombia." *Nueva Sociedad* 192 (July–August 2004): 46–58.

Rey de Marulanda, Nohra, and Juan Pablo Córdoba Garcés. *El sector bananero de Urabá: Perspectivas económicas actuales y de mediano plazo.* Medellín: Ediciones Gráficas, 1990.

Reyes Posada, Alejandro. Map "Predios decomisados por el INCORA a narcotraficantes." Instituto de Estudios Políticos y Relaciones Internacionales, Universidad Nacional de Colombia, 1990.

Reyes Posada, Alejandro, and Ana María Bejarano. "Conflictos agrarios y luchas armadas en la Colombia contemporánea: Una visión geográfica." *Análisis Político* 5 (September–December 1988) : 6–27.

Richani, Nazih. "Multinational Corporations, Rentier Capitalism, and the War System in Colombia." *Journal of Latin American Politics and Society* 47, no. 3 (Fall 2005): 113–44.

———. *Systems of Violence: The Political Economy of War and Peace in Colombia.* Albany: State University of New York Press, 2002.

Roldán, Mary. *Blood and Fire: La Violencia in Antioquia, Colombia, 1946–1953.* Durham, NC: Duke University Press, 2002.

Romero, Mauricio. *Paramilitares y autodefensas, 1982–2003.* Bogotá: Editorial Planeta, 2003.

Rudel, Thomas K., Diane Bates, and Rafael Machinguiashi. "Ecologically Noble Amerindians? Cattle Ranching and Cash Cropping among Shuar and Colonists in Ecuador." *Latin American Research Review* 37, no. 1 (2002): 144–59.

Rueschemeyer, Dietrich, Evelyn Huber Stephens, and John D. Stephens. *Capitalist Development and Democracy.* Chicago: University of Chicago Press, 1992.

Santamaría, Ricardo, and Gabriel Silva Luján. *Proceso político en Colombia: Del frente nacional a la apertura democrática.* Bogotá: CEREC, 1986.

Sintrainagro Executive Board. [Letter addressed to the participants at the 1991 Banana Congress.] *AUGURA* 17, no 1 (1991): 133–34. [Special issue: *Congreso Bananero 1991, Memorias.*]

Skocpol, Theda. "Bringing the State Back In: Strategies of Analysis in Current Research." In *Bringing the State Back In,* ed. Peter B. Evans, Dietrich Rueschemeyer, and Theda Skocpol. Cambridge: Cambridge University Press, 1985.

Smith, Jackie, Charles Chatfield, and Ron Pagnucco. *Transnational Social Movements and Global Politics: Solidarity beyond the State.* Syracuse, NY: Syracuse University Press, 1997.

Soltani, Atossa, and Kevin Koenig. "U'wa Overcome Oxy: How a Small Ecuadorian Indigenous Group and Global Solidarity Movement Defeated an Oil Giant, and the Struggles Ahead." *Multinational Monitor* (January–February 2004): 9–12.

Tarrow, Sidney. "From Lumping to Splitting: Specifying Globalization and Resistance." In *Globalization and Resistance: Transnational Dimensions of Social Movements,* ed. Jackie Smith and Hank Johnston, 229–50. Lanham, MD: Rowman and Littlefield, 2002.

Tesh, Sylvia. "Resisting the Expansion of the Panama Canal: Why No Environmental Alliances." Paper presented at the Annual Meeting of the Latin American Studies Association, 15–18 March 2006.

Thayer, Millie. "Traveling Feminisms: From Embodied Women to Gendered Citizenship." In *Global Ethnography: Forces, Connections, and Imaginations in a Postmodern World,* ed. Michael Burawoy, Joseph A. Blum, Sheba George, Zsuzsa Gille, Teresa Gowan, Lynne Haney, Maren Klawiter, Steven H. Lopez, Seán O Riain, and Millie Thayer, 203–33. Berkeley: University of California Press, 2000.

Tilly, Charles. *Regimes and Repertoires.* Chicago: University of Chicago Press, 2006.

———. *Social Movements, 1768–2004.* Boulder, CO: Paradigm, 2004.

Tilly, Charles, and Sidney Tarrow. *Contentious Politics.* Boulder, CO: Paradigm, 2007.

United Nations Working Group on Arbitrary Dentention. "Civil and Political Rights, including the Questions of Torture and Detention: Opinions of the Working Group on Arbitrary Detention." UN Doc. E/CN.4/2002/77/Add.1 (11 December 2001).

UNODC (United Nations Office on Drugs and Crime). "Chocaguán: Comité de Cacaoteros de Remolino del Caguán y Suncillas." Ca. 2005. Accessed at www.unodc.org/colombia/es/chocaguan.html on 20 December 2006.

———. "Coca Cultivation in the Andean Region." June 2005. Accessed at www.unodc.org/pdf/andean/Part1_excutive_summary.pdf on 21 June 2006.

———. "Departamento de Meta: Cultivos ilícitos de coca, censo 31 de diciembre de 2004." Accessed at www.unodc.org/pdf/colombia/simci/META.pdf on 18 August 2007.

Uribe de Hincapié, María Teresa. *Urabá ¿Región o territorio? (Un análisis en el contexto de la política, la historia, y la etnicidad).* Medellín: Instituto de Estudios Regionales of the Universidad de Antioquia and CORPOURABA, 1992.

Urueta, Gloria. "Colonización y territorialidad en el Guaviare." In *Identidad democrática y poderes populares,* edited by Jaime Caycedo Turriago and Carmenza Mantilla Santos, 115–25. Bogotá: CEIS/UniAndes Editores, 1993.

U.S. Department of State. "Colombia: Country Reports on Human Rights Practices, 2005." 8 March 2006. Accessed at www.state.gov/g/drl/rls/hrrpt/2005/61721.htm on 15 November 2006.

USLEAP (U.S. Labor Education in the Americas Project). "Colombia Fact Sheet: Murders of Trade Unionists and Impunity under Uribe, February 2008 Update." Accessed at www.usleap.org/press on 30 March 2008.

Valencia Granada, Alberto. "Marco institucional de la colonización reciente en el Caquetá." Report to the program Historia de las Localidades, Colcultura-PNR, Universidad de Amazonía, Florencia, July 1990.

Van Cott, Donna. *From Movements to Parties in Latin America: The Evolution of Ethnic Politics.* New York: Cambridge University Press, 2005.

Visbal Martelo, Jorge. *Intervención del Doctor Jorge Visbal Martelo, presidente de Fedegan (Federación Colombiana de Ganaderos) en el acto de instalación del XXIV Congreso Nacional de Ganaderos, Cartagena de Indias, 24–25 de noviembre de 1994.* Pamphlet. Bogotá: Federación Colombiana de Ganaderos, 1994.

Wickham-Crowley, Timothy. "Winners, Losers, and Also-Rans: Toward a Comparative Sociology of Latin American Guerrilla Movements." In *Power and Popular Protest,* ed. Susan Eckstein, 132–81. Berkeley: University of California Press, 1989.

Willis, Eliza, Christopher da C. B. Garman, and Stephan Haggard. "The Politics of Decentralization in Latin America." *Latin American Research Review* 34, no. 1 (1999): 7–56.

Wilson, Suzanne, and Leah A. Carroll. "The Colombian Contradiction: Lessons Drawn from Guerrilla Experiments in Demobilization and Electoralism." In *From Revolutionary Movements to Political Parties,* ed. Kalowatie Deonandan, David Close, and Gary Prevost, 258–93. New York: Palgrave Macmillan, 2007.

WOLA (Washington Office on Latin America). *Colombia Besieged: Political Violence and State Responsibility.* Washington, DC: Washington Office on Latin American, 1989.

Zamarra, Cthuchi. "San José de Apartadó: Una experiencia de noviolencia en medio de la guerra." 23 October 2004. Accessed at www.nodo50.org/tortuga/article.php3?id_article=832, 2 September 2006.

Zamosc, León. *The Agrarian Question and the Peasant Movement in Colombia.* Cambridge: Cambridge University Press, 1986.

———. "Peasant Struggles of the 1970s in Colombia." In *Power and Popular Protest,* ed. Susan Eckstein, 102–31. Berkeley: University of California Press, 1989.

Zuluaga Nieto, Jaime. "De guerrillas a movimientos políticos (Análisis de la experiencia colombiana: El caso del M-19)." In *De las armas a la política,* edited by Ricardo Peñaranda and Javier Guerrero, 1–74. Bogotá: Tercer Mundo Editores and IEPRI, 1999.

and unity, 281, 304
websites of, 35
See also allies and alliances; labor movement; peasants' and settlers' movements; urban squatters' movement
Soldier for a Day program, 246, 247
South Africa, 294
Sowing of Oil loan program, 205, 362n.62
Spain, 268, 269–70, 272
squatters. *See* rural squatters; urban squatters
Standard Fruit, 61, 335n.20
States of Internal Commotion, 16, 19, 110, 160, 229, 247
Statute of Security, 62
Stephens, Evelyn Huber, 298–99
Stephens, John D., 298–99
Suárez, Jairo, 114
Sumapaz, 23–24

Tame, 197
assassinations in, 119, 248, 265, 372n.119, 375n.148
as "cradle of liberty," 275, 375n.150
paramilitary base in, 245, 248, 257
Patriotic Union in, 190, 217
TANs. *See* transnational advocacy networks
Tarrow, Sidney, 294, 295, 296, 309
Tesh, Sylvia, 312
Thayer, Millie, 313
Tiempo, El, 162, 167, 172
as source, 34, 35, 112
Tilly, Charles, 294, 295, 296, 297, 309, 383n.61
Toronto Star, 112
Torres de Guerrero, Stella, 363n.75
Transfer Committee, 137–38, 140, 141
transnational advocacy networks (TANs), 174, 269–70, 314–17
and Coca-Cola/Chiquita Banana unions, 316
and crop substitution programs, 171–72, 175, 315–16

denounce guerrilla attacks, 269, 379n.215
emphasis on "soft power," 310
and environmental issues, 310–11, 315
favor participatory democracy, 311–12
general principles of, 309–13
and human rights issue, 89, 288, 310
importance of for social movement success, 41, 46, 112, 175, 256–57, 285, 286–87
importance of message-bearer for, 311
and indigenous struggle, 242, 243–44, 256–57
and Luz Perly Córdoba case, 259–60
and murdered trade unionists case, 260, 268
new strategic possibilities for, 297
pacifist slant of, 311, 312
pitfalls of reliance on, 256, 260–61, 312–13, 317
and target vulnerability, 46, 48, 312, 317
See also allies and alliances
Turbay, Hernando, 126, 127, 154
Turbay Ayala, Julio César, 62, 126, 127
Turbay Cote, Diego, 164
Turbay Cote, Rodrigo, 137, 142, 154, 164
kidnapping and murder of, 160, 166
Turbayista Liberals
about, 126
attacks on Patriotic Union by, 144, 146
electoral strength of, 123, 124–25, 133, 138, 140, 144, 152–53, 154–55, 156, 163–64
FARC assassination of, 146
opposition to pacted peace, 138, 140
as representative of cattle ranchers, 122, 126, 156
ties to military of, 122, 126
vote buying by, 153
Turbo, 56, 57, 73–74, 85, 92, 93, 117

LEAH CARROLL
is an independent scholar who works with the Office of Undergraduate Research at University of California, Berkeley.